PLACE MAKING IN THE PRETTY HARBOUR

PLACE MAKING IN THE PRETTY HARBOUR
The Archaeology of Port Joli, Nova Scotia

Edited by Matthew Betts

COLLECTION MERCURE
ARCHÉOLOGIE NUMÉRO 180

MUSÉE CANADIEN DE L'HISTOIRE
ET LES PRESSES DE L'UNIVERSITÉ D'OTTAWA

© 2019 Canadian Museum of History

All rights reserved. No part of this book may be reproduced or transmitted in any form or by any means electronic or mechanical, including photocopying, recording, or any retrieval system, without the written permission of the publisher.

**Co-published by
the Canadian Museum of History
and the University of Ottawa Press**

The University of Ottawa Press gratefully acknowledges the support extended to its publishing list by the Government of Canada, the Canada Council for the Arts, the Ontario Council for the Arts, the Federation for the Humanities and Social Sciences through the Awards to Scholarly Publications Program, and the University of Ottawa.

Copy editing: Alicia Peres
Proofreading: Heather Lang
Typesetting: Édiscript enr.
Cover design: Édiscript enr.

**Library and Archives Canada
Cataloguing in Publication**

Title: Place-making in the Pretty Harbour: the archaeology of Port Joli, Nova Scotia / by Matthew Betts.
Names: Betts, Matthew W., 1974- author. | Canadian Museum of History, publisher.
Series: Mercury series. | Archaeology paper (Canadian Museum of History); 180.
Description: Series statement: Mercury series | Archaeology paper; 180 .| Includes bibliographical references and index.
Identifiers: Canadiana (print) 20190151803 | Canadiana (ebook) 20190151811 | ISBN 9780776627779 (softcover) | ISBN 9780776627786 (PDF)
Subjects: LCSH: E'se'get Archaeology Project. | LCSH: Micmac Indians—Nova Scotia—Port Joli—Antiquities. | LCSH: Port Joli (N.S.)—Antiquities. | LCSH: Excavations (Archaeology)—Nova Scotia—Port Joli. | LCSH: Micmac Indians—Nova Scotia—Port Joli—History. | LCSH: Harbors—Nova Scotia—Port Joli—History.
Classification: LCC E99.M6 B48 2019 | DDC 971.6/24—dc23

The Mercury Series
Strikingly Canadian and highly specialized, the *Mercury Series* presents research from the Canadian Museum of History and benefits from the publishing expertise of the University of Ottawa Press. Created in 1972, the *Mercury Series* is the Canadian Museum of History's primary vehicle for the publication of academic research, and includes numerous landmark contributions in the disciplines of Canadian history, archaeology, culture and ethnology. Books in the series are published in either English or French, and all include a second-language summary.

La Collection Mercure
Remarquablement canadienne et hautement spécialisée, la *Collection Mercure* réunit des ouvrages portant sur des recherches effectuées au Musée canadien de l'histoire, et elle s'appuie sur le savoir-faire des Presses de l'Université d'Ottawa. Mise sur pied en 1972, la *Collection Mercure* est le principal véhicule qu'utilise le Musée canadien de l'histoire pour publier ses recherches scientifiques. Elle comprend plusieurs contributions remarquables à l'histoire, à l'archéologie, à la culture et à l'ethnologie canadiennes. Les ouvrages de la série sont publiés en français ou en anglais, et ils comportent un résumé dans l'autre langue officielle.

How To Order

All trade orders must be directed to the University of Ottawa Press:

Web: www.press.uottawa.ca
Email: puo-uop@uottawa.ca
Phone: 613-562-5246

All other orders may be directed to either the University of Ottawa Press (as above) or to the Canadian Museum of History:

Web: http://www.historymuseum.ca/shop/#publications
Email: publications@historymuseum.ca
Phone: 1-800-5550-5621 (toll-free) or 819-776-8387 (National Capital Region)
Mail: Mail Order Services
Canadian Museum of History
100 Laurier Street
Gatineau, QC K1A 0M8

Pour commander

Les libraires et autres détaillants doivent adresser leurs commandes aux Presses de l'Université d'Ottawa :

Web : www.presses.uottawa.ca
Courriel : puo-uop@uottawa.ca
Téléphone : 613-562-5246

Les particuliers doivent adresser leurs commandes soit aux Presses de l'Université d'Ottawa (voir plus haut), soit au Musée canadien de l'histoire :

Web : http://www.museedelhistoire.ca/magasiner/#publications
Courriel : publications@museedelhistoire.ca
Téléphone : 1-800-5550-5621 (numéro sans frais) – 819-776-8387 (région de la capitale nationale)
Poste : Service des commandes postales
Musée canadien de l'histoire
100, rue Laurier
Gatineau (Québec) K1A 0M8

Abstract

This book describes the work of the E'se'get Archaeology Project, a community-based research endeavor focused on defining the archaeological record of Port Joli Harbour, Nova Scotia. The project was undertaken by the Canadian Museum of History, in close collaboration with Acadia First Nation and the University of New Brunswick. Five seasons (2008-2012) of survey and excavation was undertaken at a remarkable archaeological location. Port Joli Harbour contains the largest concentration of shell midden sites in Nova Scotia. The preservation in these ancient middens provides an unrivaled view into ancient Mi'kmaw life on the South Shore from 1600 years ago until well after the arrival or Europeans. The massive archaeological assemblage recovered includes specimens never before discovered by archaeologists in the region. In addition to unique shell midden sites, the project resulted in the first detailed excavation of wigwam floors in the province, and the discovery of the first archaeological sweat lodge on the Maritime Peninsula. With nearly 22,0000 artifacts, and tens of thousands of animal remains, the recovered assemblage provides the highest resolution dataset relating to ancient Mi'kmaw coastal life in Nova Scotia ever produced.

The volume attempts to revive the tradition of a site monograph, a form of publication which has not occurred in the Mercury Series in over 20 years, but once formed the bulk of the series. Over nine chapters, this volume provides a complete description and synthesis of the archaeological data recovered from Port Joli. Hundreds of artifact plates, technical drawings, profiles, and maps, in addition to a complete artifact description and analyses provide a comprehensive reference to the archaeology of the harbour. It also provides a detailed overview of the physiographic and climatic history of Port Joli. It presents data from previous archaeological work in the area conducted by John Erskine, Thomas Raddall, and others, providing a complete synthesis of one of Nova Scotia's richest indigenous archaeological records. A complete analysis and interpretation of the data results in a thorough interpretation of ancient life in the harbour, as well as an assessment of the record in the context of the regional archaeological record. The volume ends with a grand synthesis, taking the form of a culture history of Port Joli, summarizing how Port Joli, the "pretty harbour", became a central place for Mi'kmaq and their unique way of life.

Résumé

Ce livre décrit les travaux liés au projet archéologique E'se'get, une initiative de recherche communautaire dont l'objectif était de caractériser le patrimoine archéologique de Port Joli, en Nouvelle-Écosse. Entrepris par le Musée canadien de l'histoire, le projet a été mené en étroite collaboration avec la Première Nation Acadia et l'Université du Nouveau-Brunswick. Pendant cinq saisons (de 2008 à 2012), on a effectué des relevés d'observation et des fouilles sur un site archéologique remarquable. Port Joli recèle la plus grande concentration d'amas coquilliers de la Nouvelle-Écosse. La préservation de ces amas offre une perspective incomparable de la vie des Micmacs sur la côte sud il y a 1 600 ans jusqu'à bien après l'arrivée des Européens. L'énorme assemblage d'artefacts recueillis comprend des spécimens que les archéologues n'avaient jamais découverts dans la région. Outre la découverte de sites d'amas coquilliers uniques, le projet a permis d'effectuer la première fouille détaillée de sols de wigwams dans la province et de mettre au jour la première suerie archéologique de la péninsule maritime. Comptant près de 22 000 artefacts et des dizaines de milliers de restes d'animaux, l'assemblage archéologique récupéré fournit l'ensemble de données de la plus haute résolution jamais obtenu concernant la vie côtière des Micmacs en Nouvelle-Écosse au cours de cette période.

L'ouvrage tente de renouer avec la tradition de la monographie archéologique, type d'étude qui n'a pas été publiée dans la collection Mercury depuis plus de 20 ans, mais qui autrefois en composait la majeure partie. Divisé en neuf chapitres, l'ouvrage présente une description et une analyse complètes des données archéologiques recueillies à Port Joli : des centaines d'artefacts, tels que des assiettes, et des dessins techniques, des profils et des cartes, ce qui en fait une référence archéologique exhaustive consacrée au port. On y trouve également un aperçu détaillé de l'histoire physiographique et climatique de Port Joli, de même que les données de travaux archéologiques antérieurs réalisés dans ce secteur par John Erskine, Thomas Raddall et d'autres personnes. Il s'agit de l'un des plus importants inventaires archéologiques autochtones de la Nouvelle-Écosse. L'analyse complète des données donne lieu à une interprétation approfondie de la vie d'autrefois dans le port, de même qu'à une évaluation du registre dans le contexte des registres archéologiques de la région. Sous la forme d'un compte rendu de l'histoire culturelle de Port Joli, la monographie se termine par une grande synthèse qui raconte comment ce « joli port » est devenu un lieu central pour les Micmacs et leur mode de vie unique.

Table of Contents

Abstract v

Résumé vi

List of Tables xv

List of Figures xvii

Acknowledgements xxv

Foreword xxix

Chapter 1
The E'se'get Archaeology Project
Matthew Betts 1
    Introduction 1
    Shell Midden Archaeology 3
    Port Joli's Harbour—A Natural and Archaeological Preserve 5
    The E'se'get Archaeology Project 7
    Previous Shell Midden Archaeology in the Port Joli Region 9
    Survey Methods 10
    Excavation Methods 11
    Community Archaeology 14
    Structure of the Book 18

Chapter 2
Palaeoenvironmental Context
Karen Neil and Konrad Gajewski 21
    Introduction 21
    Site Description 21
    Climate of the Holocene in Southwestern Nova Scotia 22
    Holocene Sea-Level Fluctuations in Southwestern Nova Scotia 23
    History of Southwestern Nova Scotia during the Holocene 24
        Regional Environmental Setting 24
        Local Archaeological Setting 28
    Summary 30

Chapter 3
The Sites

MATTHEW BETTS 33
   Introduction 33
   East Coast of Port Joli's Harbour 35
      AlDf-06 (MacAdam Garden, Port Joli No. 12, AlDf-05) 35
         Description and Excavation Approach 35
         Stratigraphy 38
         Summary 39
      A2009NS27-1 40
         Description and Excavation Approach 40
         Stratigraphy 42
         Summary 42
      AlDf-02 (Robertson Lake Outlet, Port Joli No. 11) 43
         Description and Excavation Approach 43
      AlDf-03 (Post Office, Port Joli No. 8) 44
         Description and Excavation Approach 44
      AlDf-04 (Port Joli No. 10) 45
         Description and Excavation Approach 45
      AlDf-36 (AlDf-01) 46
         Description and Excavation Approach 46
      AlDf-11 (McDonald Shell Heap) 48
         Description and Excavation Approach 48
      AlDf-12 (Vogler) 51
         Description and Excavation Approach 51
      AlDf-13 (Alexander) 53
         Description and Excavation Approach 53
   West Coast of Port Joli's Harbour 53
      AlDf-07 (Upper Path Lake Brook, Port Joli No. 2) 53
         Description and Excavation Approach 53
      AlDf-08 (Lower Path Lake Brook, Port Joli No. 7) 56
         Description and Excavation Approach 56
         Stratigraphy 58
         Summary 62
      AlDf-35 (Maxwell's Brook) 62
         Description and Excavation Approach 62
         Stratigraphy 64
         Summary 65
      AlDf-28 66
         Description and Excavation Approach 66
      AlDf-27 (Bill Brook or AlDf-10) 68
         Description and Excavation Approach 68
      AlDf-26 69
         Description and Excavation Approach 69

AlDf-25 (Scotch Point, Port Joli No. 3, AlDf-09)	70
Description and Excavation Approach	70
Stratigraphy	76
Summary	77
AlDf-24 (Epte'jijg Utju'sn Gta'nogeway, "Warm Breeze by the Ocean")	78
Description and Excavation Approach	78
Site Mapping	80
Area A: Description and Excavation Approach	80
Area A: Stratigraphy	80
Area A: Features	86
The Burial: Features 1 and 3	86
Reburial of Human Remains and Grave Goods	90
Area A: Summary	90
Area C: Description and Excavation Approach	91
Area C: Stratigraphy	92
Area C: Summary	95
AlDf-30 (Jack's Brook, Su'ne'gati, "Cranberry Patch")	95
Description and Excavation Approach	95
Area A: Description and Excavation Approach	98
Area A: Stratigraphy	100
Area B: Description and Excavation Approach	102
Area B: Stratigraphy	104
Black Soil Area: Description and Excavation Approach	105
Black Soil Area: Stratigraphy	105
AlDf-31 (Su'ne'gatij, "Little Cranberry Patch")	109
Description and Excavation Approach	109
Stratigraphy	109
A Typology of Sites around Port Joli's Harbour	112

Chapter 4
Chronology
MATTHEW BETTS 115
    Introduction 115
    Absolute Dating 116
    Relative Dating 122
    The Port Joli Chronological Sequence 126

Chapter 5
Architectural Features
M. GABRIEL HRYNICK AND MATTHEW BETTS 129
    Introduction 129
    Background 129
    Methods 131
        Locating Features 132

    Excavating Features 132
    Partially Excavated Features 133
        AlDf-24 (Epte'jijg Utju'sn Gta'nogeway, "Warm Breeze by the Ocean") 133
            AlDf-24, Area C, Level 2 Activity Area 133
            AlDf-24, Area C, Feature 4, Levels 3a and 3b................................ 134
            AlDf-24, Area C, Partial House Feature, Levels 3f to 3h 139
            AlDf-24, Area A, Feature 2 142
        AlDf-30 (Jack's Brook, Su'ne'gati, "Cranberry Patch") 143
            AlDf-30, Black Soil Area, Feature 1, Levels 3a to 3c....................... 145
            AlDf-30, Black Soil Area, Feature 2, Levels 3d, 3e, and 3f 145
            AlDf-30, Black Soil Area, Feature 3, Level 4 147
            AlDf-30, Area A: Post Moulds and Stakes 152
            AlDf-31 (Su'ne'gatij, "Little Cranberry Patch") 152
            AlDf-25 (Scotch Point, Port Joli No. 3, AlDf-09) 155
            AlDf-08 (Lower Path Lake Brook, Port Joli No. 7) 155
    Discussion 155
    Conclusions.. 159

Chapter 6
The Ceramic Assemblage
JENNETH CURTIS, ERIN INGRAM, AND MATTHEW BETTS 161
    Introduction 161
    History of Ceramic Research on the Maritime Peninsula 162
        The Petersen and Sanger Ceramic Sequence.. 162
        Regional Comparisons to the Petersen and Sanger Sequence 163
    Analytical Methods.. 165
    E'se'get Ceramic Assemblages 166
        Form 167
        Manufacture... 177
        Decoration 183
        Tools 183
        Technique 188
        Configuration 188
        Delimitation.. 189
    Comparison with the Petersen and Sanger Ceramic Sequence 191
        Manufacture... 191
        Form 192
        Decoration 192
    Conclusion... 195
    Appendix A: Ceramic Plates from E'se'get Archaeology Project Contexts 197
    Appendix B: Ceramic Plates from Port Joli legacy Collections........................... 212

Chapter 7
Lithic Technology and Other Artifacts
Matthew Betts and Kenneth R. Holyoke 217
    Introduction 217
    Lithic Analysis Considerations.. 218
    AlDf-06 (AlDf-05) 221
        Unifaces 221
        Debitage and Cores 222
        Ground-Stone Artifacts 222
        Other Artifacts 222
        AlDf-06 Discussion 222
    A2009NS27-1 223
    AlDf-08 223
        Projectile Points and Bifaces 224
        Unifaces 224
        Debitage and Cores 225
        Other Artifacts 225
        AlDf-08 Discussion 225
    AlDf-35 226
    AlDf-24, Area A Midden.. 226
        Projectile Points 227
        Bifaces 227
        Unifaces 227
        Cores, Hammerstones, and Debitage 227
        Other Artifacts 228
        Organic Artifacts 228
        Composite Artifacts 229
        AlDf-24, Area A Midden, Discussion.. 230
    AlDf-24, Area A, Feature 2 230
        Projectile Points 230
        Bifaces 230
        Unifaces 231
        Cores and Debitage 231
        Historic Artifacts 231
        Organic Artifacts 232
        AlDf-24, Area A, Feature 2, Discussion.. 232
    AlDf-24, Area C 233
    AlDf-24, Area C, Protohistoric (levels 1, 2, and 2b) 233
        Projectile Points and Bifaces 233
        Unifaces 236
        Cores, Hammerstones, and Debitage 237
        Other Artifacts 237
        Organic Artifacts 238
        European Historic Artifacts 238

AlDf-24, Area C, Feature 4 (levels 3a and 3b) 238
    Projectile Points and Bifaces 238
    Unifaces 239
    Cores, Hammerstones, and Debitage 239
    Organic Artifacts 240
    Other Artifacts 240
AlDf-24, Area C, Middle (levels 3c to 3e) 240
    Projectile Points and Bifaces 240
    Unifaces 241
    Cores 241
    Organic Artifacts 241
    Other Artifacts 241
AlDf-24, Area C, Lower (levels 3f to 3j) 242
    Bifaces 242
    Unifaces 242
    Cores and Debitage 242
    Other Artifacts 243
    AlDf-24, Area C: Summary 243
AlDf-30 246
AlDf-30, Area A Midden 247
    Bifaces 247
    Unifaces 247
    Hammerstones and Debitage 247
    Other Artifacts 247
AlDf-30, Black Soil Area: Levels 1, 2, and 2b 248
    Bifaces 248
    Unifaces 248
    Cores and Debitage 248
    Other Artifacts 248
AlDf-30: Black Soil Area: Levels 3a to 3f 249
    Projectile Points and Bifaces 249
    Unifaces 250
    Cores, Hammerstones, and Debitage 250
    Other Artifacts 250
    Organic Artifacts 251
AlDf-30, Area B Midden 251
    Debitage and Other Artifacts 251
    AlDf-30: Discussion 251
AlDf-31 256
Discussion and Conclusions 256
Appendix A: Artifact Plates from the E'se'get Archaeology Project 261
Appendix B: Artifact Plates from Port Joli Legacy Collections 306

Chapter 8
Animal and Plant Remains
MATTHEW BETTS 325
    Introduction 325
    Fish 326
    Birds 330
    Mammals 331
    Shellfish 332
    Plant Remains 335
    Data from Legacy Collections 336
    Seasonality Indicators 342
    Procurement and Consumption Strategies around Port Joli's Harbour 344

Chapter 9
An Archaeological History of Port Joli
MATTHEW BETTS 349
    Introduction 349
    Earliest Times 350
    Middle Maritime Woodland Period (2200–1300 Years Ago) 351
    Late Maritime Woodland Period (1300–550 Years Ago) 353
    Protohistoric Period (550–330 Years Ago) 358
    Place-making in the Pretty Harbour 359
    Conclusions: The Future of Archaeological History in Port Joli 362

Bibliography 365

Contributors 379

List of Tables

Table 4.1	Chrono-cultural sequences, compared.	117
Table 4.2	Radiocarbon dates from archaeological contexts around Port Joli's harbour.	118
Table 4.3	Chronological sequence for prehistoric archaeological sites and deposits in Port Joli's harbour.	125
Table 5.1	AlDf-24, Area C: Constituents of materials from column samples taken along the north-south baulk.	137
Table 5.2	AlDf-24, Area C: Material constituents from column samples taken along the east-west baulk.	138
Table 6.1	Major attributes identified in the Petersen and Sanger Ceramic sequence.	164
Table 6.2	Ceramic variables used in analysis of E'se'get assemblages.	167
Table 6.3a	Summary of Port Joli ceramic assemblages.	168
Table 6.3b	Summary of form attributes in Port Joli vessel lots.	169
Table 6.3c	Summary of manufacturing attributes in Port Joli vessel lots.	170
Table 6.3d	Summary of decorative attributes in Port Joli vessel lots.	171
Table 6.3d	Summary of decorative attributes in Port Joli vessel lots (continued).	172
Table 6.3d	Summary of decorative attributes in Port Joli vessel lots (continued).	173
Table 6.3d	Summary of decorative attributes in Port Joli vessel lots (continued).	174
Table 6.3e	Summary of metric attributes in Port Joli vessel lots.	175
Table 6.4	All-sherds table. Summary of selected ceramic attributes on all sherds recovered during the E'se'get Archaeology Project.	179
Table 6.4	All-sherds table. Summary of selected ceramic attributes on all sherds recovered during the E'se'get Archaeology Project (continued).	180
Table 7.3	Distribution of tools by level and material in AlDf-30.	252
Table 7.4	Distribution of lithic materials in relation to axial feature in AlDf-30, Black Soil Area.	255
Table 7.5a	Mean metric attributes by time period for all projectile points in the E'se'get assemblages (x) = sample size.	257
Table 7.5b	Mean metric attributes by time period for all preforms in the E'se'get assemblages (x) = sample size.	258
Table 7.5c	Mean metric attributes by time period for all scrapers in the E'se'get assemblages (x) = sample size.	258
Table 7.6	Percentages of stone tool material type by time period in the E'se'get assemblages.	258
Table 8.1	Port Joli faunal assemblages by taxa: Number of identified specimens (NISP) per species, percentage of overall NISP, minimum number of individuals (MNI), richness, and unidentified counts.	328
Table 8.2	Fort Joli faunal assemblages: Bulk-sample constituents (by percentage of total weight).	333
Table 8.3	Port Joli faunal assemblages: Presence/absence (and qualitative abundance) in shell middens excavated by John Erskine. Large X means present and common, and small x means present but rare.	339

Liste of Figures

Figure 1.1	A springtime view of Port Joli's southwestern harbour shore, facing north.	1
Figure 1.2	Modern map of Port Joli's harbour.	2
Figure 1.3	Articulated domestic dog bones (left rear foot) preserved in a Port Joli shell midden (AlDf-30).	3
Figure 1.4	An extensive Port Joli clam flat at low tide, facing north.	5
Figure 1.5	Drawing a feature plan at AlDf-30 using a vector-based drawing app on an iPad Pro.	13
Figure 1.6	Community members and park visitors at a guided tour of the excavations at AlDf-24.	15
Figure 1.7	The E'se'get Archaeology Project crew for the 2010 field season, including both UNB graduate and undergraduate students, Acadia First Nation high school students, Acadia First Nation Band members, and staff from the Mi'kmaq Rights Initiative.	16
Figure 2.1	Port Joli's harbour: Evolution of the coastline, based on bathymetry data and a reconstructed sea level curve of the region.	24
Figure 2.2	Palaeoenvironmental record from Path Lake, Port Joli, Nova Scotia.	25
Figure 2.3	Port Joli region, Nova Scotia: Palaeoenvironmental summary including Path Lake organic and carbonate content, principal components of the pollen assemblages, pollen and charcoal accumulation rates, palaeoclimate reconstructions, sea level	27
Figure 2.4	The fen surrounding AlDf-30, Port Joli, Nova Scotia: Pollen-percentage diagram	29
Figure 2.5	The fen surrounding AlDf-30, Port Joli, Nova Scotia: Palaeoenvironmental summary, including pollen percentages, pollen and charcoal concentration, organic and carbonate content, and magnetic susceptibility.	31
Figure 3.1	Distribution of prehistoric archaeological sites around Port Joli's harbour.	34
Figure 3.2	AlDf-06: Site map, showing location of the three 2012 test excavation units.	37
Figure 3.3	AlDf-06: Photograph of site, facing southwest.	38
Figure 3.4	AlDf-06: Profile plan of 2012 test excavations.	39
Figure 3.5	A2009NS27-1: Plan view, based on subsurface soil probing and showing location of 2009 test unit.	41
Figure 3.6	A2009NS27-1: Soil profile of the (2009) 25 cm^2 test unit.	43
Figure 3.7	AlDf-03: Site map and stratigraphic profile, redrawn from Erskine (1959), with measures converted to metric.	45
Figure 3.8	AlDf-36 (also known as AlDf-01): Plan view, based on subsurface probing.	47

Figure 3.9	AlDf-11: Plan view, including soil profiles, redrawn to scale from Millard (1966), with metric conversions.	49
Figure 3.10	Eric Millard excavating at AlDf-11, around 1966	50
Figure 3.11	AlDf-12 (Vogler site): Plan view, redrawn from Millard (1966)	52
Figure 3.12	AlDf-07: Photograph of site, facing north. Subject is standing in one of the many large collector trenches.	54
Figure 3.13	AlDf-07: Plan view, based on subsurface probing.	55
Figure 3.14	Photograph by John Erskine detailing his 1957 excavations at AlDf-07	56
Figure 3.15	Top: AlDf-08 (Port Joli No. 7) in 1957, photographed by John Erskine	57
Figure 3.16	AlDf-08: Plan view, based on subsurface soil probing, and showing location of 2012 excavations.	59
Figure 3.17	AlDf-08: Photograph of the site, facing northwest.	60
Figure 3.18	AlDf-08: Profile plan of 2012 excavations.	61
Figure 3.19	AlDf-35: Photograph of site, facing northwest.	63
Figure 3.20	AlDf-35: Site plan.	64
Figure 3.21	AlDf-35: Test Unit 1 profiles.	65
Figure 3.22	AlDf-28: Photograph of site, facing southwest, from northeast edge of site.	66
Figure 3.23	AlDf-28: Plan view, based on subsurface probing.	67
Figure 3.24	AlDf-26: Plan view based on surface observation and test excavation, redrawn from original plans and notes by Powell (1995).	70
Figure 3.25	AlDf-26: East-west profile of Test Unit x-6, redrawn from Powell (1995).	71
Figure 3.26a	AlDf-25: Plan view, based on subsurface probing.	72
Figure 3.26b	AlDf-25: Port Joli No. 3 site map, redrawn from Erskine (1962)	73
Figure 3.27a	AlDf-25: Erskine's original excavation photos from 1962	75
Figure 3.27b	AlDf-25: The same boulder in 2008 as in Erskine's 1962 photo, facing east.	75
Figure 3.28	AlDf-25: Photograph of the site in 2012, facing west.	76
Figure 3.29	AlDf-25: South, west, east, and north soil profiles, Test Unit 1	77
Figure 3.30	AlDf-24: Photograph facing west	79
Figure 3.31	AlDf-24: Plan view, derived from total station surveying, subsurface probing, and excavation.	81
Figure 3.32	AlDf-24: 3D representation facing west	82
Figure 3.33	AlDf-24, Area A: Stratigraphic profiles.	83
Figure 3.34	AlDf-24, Area A: Photograph of view of Level 3g, from Unit N56W50 (Test Unit 1, also called Test Unit A in field notes), 2008	84
Figure 3.35	AlDf-24, Area A: Features 1 and 3, facing south	87
Figure 3.36	AlDf-24, Area A: Plan view of Feature 1 and Feature 3.	89
Figure 3.37	AlDf-24, Area C: Stratigraphic profiles.	93
Figure 3.38	AlDf-30: The first archaeological map drawn of Port Joli's harbour, featuring Thomas Raddall's recollection of the sites at Jack's Brook, redrawn from Raddall's (n.d.) original sketch	96

Figure 3.39	AlDf-30: Photograph of site, facing east, looking at Area A	97
Figure 3.40	AlDf-30: Plan view, based on subsurface probing and excavation.	99
Figure 3.41	AlDf-30, Area A: Stratigraphic profiles	101
Figure 3.42	AlDf-30, Black soil Area and Area B: Stratigraphic profile.	103
Figure 3.43	AlDf-30, Area B shell midden: Photograph of Unit N52W48, Level 6 (subsoil) exposed, facing south	107
Figure 3.44	AlDf-30, Area B: Tomcod and Atlantic cod bones recovered from Unit N52W48, in midden contexts	107
Figure 3.45	AlDf-30: Photograph of Test Units 3 (nearer) and 4 (farther), facing east, showing detail of the levels 2b and 3b rock feature, with Level 4 (subsoil) exposed below it	108
Figure 3.46	AlDf-31: Photograph facing northeast. Midden B is in the foreground, with a soil probe lying in the collector's trench. Midden A is at the apex of the knoll.	108
Figure 3.47	AlDf-31: Plan view, based on subsurface probing and excavation.	110
Figure 3.48	AlDf-31: Profile view of excavations, showing details of features	111
Figure 3.49	Types of shell middens at prehistoric archaeological sites around Port Joli's harbour.	113
Figure 4.1	Calibrated probability distributions from Port Joli samples	120
Figure 4.2	AlDf-24, Area A midden: Correlations between stratigraphic profiles and the location of dated radiocarbon samples.	121
Figure 4.3	AlDf-24, Area C: Correlations between stratigraphic profiles and the location of dated radiocarbon samples.	122
Figure 5.1	Traditional birchbark wigwam built by Mi'kmaw Elder Todd Labrador and Mi'kmaw artist Melissa Labrador in Kejimkujik National Park, Nova Scotia.	130
Figure 5.2	AlDf-24, Area C: Stratigraphic profiles of site, showing the Protohistoric activity surface (Level 2) and Feature 4.	135
Figure 5.3	AlDf-24, Area C: Photograph of Feature 4, facing south.	136
Figure 5.4	AlDf-24, Area C, Feature 4: Plan-view drawing.	139
Figure 5.5a	AlDf-24, Area C, Feature 4: Plan-view drawing, showing the patterned division of projectile points (P), bifaces (B), scrapers (S), and cores (C)	140
Figure 5.5b	AlDf-24, Area C, Feature 4: Plan-view drawing, showing the patterned division of debitage.	141
Figure 5.5c	AlDf-24, Area C, Feature 4: Plan-view drawing, showing the patterned division of ceramics.	142
Figure 5.6	AlDf-24, Area A: Plan-view drawing of the partially excavated Feature 2.	144
Figure 5.7	AlDf-30: Stratigraphic profile showing domestic features 1 and 2, and the sweathouse, Feature 3.	146
Figure 5.8	AlDf-30: Photograph of Feature 1, facing southwest	147
Figure 5.9	AlDf-30: Plan-view drawing of Feature 1, a dwelling feature.	148
Figure 5.10	AlDf-30: Plan-view drawing of Feature 2, a dwelling feature.	149

Figure 5.11	AlDf-30, Black Soil Area: Plan-view drawing of Feature 3, the sweathouse..	150
Figure 5.12	AlDf-30, Black Soil Area: Photograph of Feature 3, facing north.......	151
Figure 5.13	AlDf-31: Plan-view drawing of Feature 1b, an example of a Port Joli post mould..	153
Figure 5.14	AlDf-24: Photograph of post-mould.	157
Figure 6.1	AlDf-24:163,164,165,Vessel Lot 11, Area C, N51W51, Level 3g (early Late Maritime Woodland)...	176
Figure 6.2	AlDf-24: 522,Vessel Lot 27, Area A, N52W50, Level 3m (Middle Maritime Woodland)...	176
Figure 6.3	AlDf-24: 533, 557,Vessel Lot 31, Area A, N53W50, Level 3 and 3b (Middle Maritime Woodland).	176
Figure 6.4	AlDf-24: 7,Vessel Lot 46, Area A, N56W50, Level 3D (Middle Maritime Woodland).	177
Figure 6.5	Examples of round and notched castellations in the E'se'get assemblage. A: AlDf-24:271,Vessel Lot 47, AlDF-24, Area A, Middle Maritime Woodland. B: AlDf-24:19,Vessel Lot 8, AlDf-24, Area C, early Late Maritime Woodland..	178
Figure 6.6	Sherd exhibiting coil breaks. AlDf-24: 403,Vessel Lot 14, AlDf-24 Area C, early Late Maritime Woodland...	181
Figure 6.7	Sherds with combed interiors. A: AlDf-24: 398,Vessel Lot 20, AlDf-24, Area C, early Late Maritime Woodland. B: AlDf-24: 403,Vessel Lot 14, AlDf-24, Area C, early Late Maritime Woodland.	182
Figure 6.8	Sherds with complex multiple exterior bands. A: AlDf-24: 533, 557,Vessel Lot 31, AlDf-24, Area A, Middle Maritime Woodland. B: AlDf-24:7,Vessel Lot 46, AlDf-24, Area A, Middle Maritime Woodland.	184
Figure 6.9	Rim sherd with a plain first exterior band. AlDf-24 C: 207,Vessel Lot 35, AlDf-24 C, early Late Maritime Woodland...	185
Figure 6.10	Rim sherd exhibiting evidence of knotted cord decoration. AlDf-24: 208, 210, 211, 213,Vessel Lot 3, AlDf-24, Area C, early Late Maritime Woodland..	186
Figure 6.11	Sherds with evidence of splint-wrapped-stick decoration. A: AlDf-24:522,526,Vessel Lot 27, AlDf-24, Area A, Middle Maritime Woodland. B: AlDf-24:206,Vessel Lot 10, AlDf-24, Area C, early Late Maritime Woodland..	187
Figure 6.12	Evidence of sherds with very complex design elements, including superimposed (A, C), plaits (B), horizontal differentiation (D)...........	188
Figure 6.13	Sherd with punctates in the second exterior band. AlDf-24: 74, 75, Vessel Lot 49, AlDf-24, Area C, early Late Maritime Woodland.........	189
Figure 6.14	A Middle Maritime Woodland rim with a delimiter. AlDf-24:706, Vessel Lot 38, AlDf-24, Area A..	190
Figure 6.15	Deep punctates used as a delimiter. AlDf-24: 562, 567,Vessel Lot 33, AlDf-14, Area A, Late Maritime Woodland..	191
Figure 6.16	A collared rim sherd. AlDf-24: 39,Vessel Lot 60, AlDf-24, Area A, Middle Maritime Woodland..	193

Figure 6.17	Selected AlDf-24, Area A, Middle Maritime Woodland rims and body sherds	197
Figure 6.18	Selected AlDf-06 rims and body sherds...	198
Figure 6.19	Selected AlDf-08 rims and body sherds...	199
Figure 6.20	Selected Late Maritime Woodland AlDf-24, Area A, Feature 2 rims and body sherds...	200
Figure 6.21	Selected Protohistoric AlDf-24, Area C, levels 1 and 2 body sherds...	201
Figure 6.22	Selected later Late Maritime Woodland AlDf-24, Area C, Feature 4 (levels 3 and 3b) rims and body sherds	202
Figure 6.23	Selected Late Maritime Woodland AlDf-24, Area C, (levels 3c to 3e) rims nd body sherds	203
Figure 6.24	Selected early Late Maritime Woodland AlDf-24, Area C (levels 3f to 3k) rims and body sherds	204
Figure 6.25	Selected Middle Maritime Woodland AlDf-25 rims and body sherds	205
Figure 6.26	Selected later Late Woodland AlDf-30 (levels 1-2c) rims and body sherds...	206
Figure 6.27	Selected Middle Maritime Woodland AlDf-30 (levels 3 to 4) rims and body sherds...	207
Figure 6.28	Selected Middle Maritime Woodland AlDf-30 (Area A Midden) rims and body sherds	208
Figure 6.29	Selected Maritime Woodland AlDf-30 (Area B Midden) rims and body sherds...	209
Figure 6.30	Selected Middle Maritime Woodland AlDf-31 rims and body sherds	210
Figure 6.31	Selected body sherds from AlDf-35...	211
Figure 6.32	Selected Middle Maritime Woodland AlDf-25 rims and body sherds.	212
Figure 6.33	Selected early Late Maritime Woodland AlDf-03 rims and body sherds.	213
Figure 6.34	Selected later Late Maritime Woodland AlDf-07 rims and body sherds...	214
Figure 6.35	Selected later Late Maritime Woodland AlDf-08 rims and body sherds.	215
Figure 6.36	Selected Late Maritime Woodland AlDf-01 rims and body sherds. ...	216
Figure 6.37	Selected Late Maritime Woodland AlDf-11 body sherds.	216
Figure 7.1	Stone tool typology used for the E'se'get Archaeology Project..........	219
Figure 7.2	Projectile points, bifaces, scrapers, and cores from AlDf-06 (all levels)	261
Figure 7.3	Ground stone celt from AlDf-06. AlDf-06:24.	262
Figure 7.4	Projectile points and bifaces from AlDf-08 (all levels)	263
Figure 7.5	Scrapers from AlDf-08 (all levels)	264
Figure 7.6	Cores from AlDf-08 (all levels)...	265
Figure 7.7	Projectile points, bifaces, and unifaces from AlDf-24 Area A (all levels)	266
Figure 7.8	Cores from AlDf-24 Area A (all levels)	267

Figure 7.9	Hammerstone from AlDf-24 Area A (all levels). AlDf-24:614.	268
Figure 7.10	Worked bone and ground ochre from AlDf-24 Area A (all levels)	269
Figure 7.11	Left, rolled iron bead from AlDf-24 Area A (AlDf-24:588). Right, native copper nodule from AlDf-24, Area C (AlDf-24:317).	270
Figure 7.12	A clay-lined clam shell (spark holder) in situ during excavation, AlDf-24, Area A, N56W50, Level 3h (AlDf-24:17)	270
Figure 7.13	Clay-lined clam shells (spark holders) from AlDf-24 Area A (all levels)	271
Figure 7.14	Projectile points, bifaces, and unifaces from AlDf-24, Area A, Feature 2 (all levels)	272
Figure 7.15	Cores from AlDf-24, Area A, Feature 2 (all levels)	273
Figure 7.16	Historic door hardware from AlDf-24, Area A, Feature 2	274
Figure 7.17	Organic artifacts from AlDf-24, Area A, Feature 2 (all levels)	275
Figure 7.18	Projectile points and bifaces from AlDf-24, Area C (levels 1, 2, and 2b)	276
Figure 7.19	Scrapers from AlDf-24, Area C (levels 1, 2, and 2b)	277
Figure 7.20	Cores from AlDf-24, Area C (levels 1, 2, and 2b)	278
Figure 7.21	Hammerstones and ground stone from AlDf-24, Area C (levels 1, 2, and 2b)	279
Figure 7.22	Organic artifacts from AlDf-24, Area C (levels 1, 2, and 2b)	280
Figure 7.23	Projectile points from AlDf-24, Area C, Feature 4 (levels 3 and 3b)	281
Figure 7.24	Bifaces from AlDf-24, Area C, Feature 4 (levels 3 and 3b)	282
Figure 7.25	Scrapers from AlDf-24, Area C, Feature 4 (levels 3 and 3b)	283
Figure 7.26	Cores from AlDf-24, Area C, Feature 4 (levels 3 and 3b)	284
Figure 7.27	Hammerstone from AlDf-24, Area C, Feature 4 (levels 3 and 3b). AlDf 24:187.	285
Figure 7.28	Organic artifacts from AlDf-24, Area C, Feature 4 (levels 3 and 3b)	286
Figure 7.29	Projectile points and bifaces from AlDf-24, Area C (levels 3c, 3d, and 3e)	287
Figure 7.30	Scrapers from AlDf-24, Area C (levels 3c, 3d, and 3e)	288
Figure 7.31	Cores from AlDf-24, Area C (levels 3c, 3d, and 3e)	289
Figure 7.32	Organic artifacts from AlDf-24, Area C (levels 3c, 3d, and 3e)	290
Figure 7.33	Manuports from AlDf-24, Area C (levels 3c, 3d, and 3e)	291
Figure 7.34	Scrapers from AlDf-24, Area C (levels 3f, 3g, 3h, 3i, and 3j)	292
Figure 7.35	Cores from AlDf-24, Area C (levels 3f, 3g, 3h, 3i, and 3j)	293
Figure 7.36	Manuport from AlDf-24, Area C (levels 3f, 3g, 3h, 3i, and 3j). AlDf-24:322.	294
Figure 7.37	Biface and Scraper from AlDf-30, Area A Midden (all levels)	295
Figure 7.38	Hammerstones from AlDf-30, Area A Midden (all levels)	296
Figure 7.39	Projectile points, unifaces, and cores AlDf-30, Black Soil Area (levels 1, 2, and 2b)	297
Figure 7.40	Manuports and ochre from AlDf-30, Black Soil Area (levels 1, 2, and 2b)	298
Figure 7.41	Projectile points and bifaces from AlDf-30, Black Soil Area (levels 3a-3f)	299

Figure 7.42	Scrapers from AlDf-30, Black Soil Area (levels 3a-3f)	300
Figure 7.43	Cores and gravers from AlDf-30, Black Soil Area (levels 3a-3f)	301
Figure 7.44	Hammerstone from AlDf-30, Black Soil Area (levels 3a-3f). AlDf-20:475	302
Figure 7.45	Modified whale bone and shell from AlDf-30, Black Soil Area (levels 3a-3f)	303
Figure 7.46	Artifacts from AlDf-31 (all levels)	304
Figure 7.47	Number of lithic artifacts per kilogram from derived from bulk midden samples from various Port Joli contexts	305
Figure 7.48	AlDf-36/AlDf-01 selected projectile points, bifaces, and uniface	306
Figure 7.49	AlDf-36/AlDf-01 ground stone and hammerstones	306
Figure 7.50	AlDf-03 selected projectile points and bifaces.	307
Figure 7.51	AlDf-03 selected ground stone, cores, and hammerstones.	307
Figure 7.52	AlDf-03 selected worked bone and antler	308
Figure 7.53	AlDf-04 selected projectile points, bifaces, unifaces, and ceramic sherds	308
Figure 7.54a	AlDf-06/AlDf-05 selected projectile points and bifaces.	309
Figure 7.54b	AlDf-06/AlDf-05 selected projectile points and unifaces.	309
Figure 7.55	AlDf-06/AlDf-05 selected unifaces.	310
Figure 7.56	AlDf-07 selected projectile points, bifaces, and unifaces.	311
Figure 7.57	AlDf-07 selected cervid faunal remains and worked bone	312
Figure 7.58a	AlDf-08 selected projectile points and bifaces	313
Figure 7.58b	AlDf-08 selected projectile points and ground stone.	314
Figure 7.59	AlDf-08 selected cervid faunal remains and worked bone	315
Figure 7.60	AlDf-25/AlDf-09 selected projectile points and bifaces.	316
Figure 7.61	AlDf-25/AlDf-09 selected unifaces.	317
Figure 7.62	AlDf-25/AlDf-09 selected quartz cores.	318
Figure 7.63	AlDf-25/AlDf-09 selected ground stone.	319
Figure 7.64	AlDf-25/AlDf-09 selected worked bone and antler.	320
Figure 7.65	AlDf-10 selected projectile points and bifaces	321
Figure 7.66	AlDf-10 selected unifaces and cores.	321
Figure 7.67	AlDf-10 worked left tibia of an American beaver	322
Figure 7.68	AlDf-11 selected projectile points and bifaces	322
Figure 7.69	AlDf-11 selected unifaces.	323
Figure 7.70	AlDf-11 selected ground stone	323
Figure 7.71	AlDf-11 hammerstone.	324
Figure 8.1	Port Joli faunal assemblages: Percentage of number of identified specimens (% NISP) of major taxa	327
Figure 8.2	Port Joli faunal assemblages: Percentage of number of identified specimens (NISP) by taxonomic class (including "unidentifiable" fraction in each class)	327
Figure 8.3	Port Joli faunal assemblages: Shell fraction (soft-shell clam). Percentage of weight (in grams) in relation to the total bulk sample	334
Figure 8.4	Mollusc shell fraction (excluding soft-shell clam): Percentage of weight (in grams) in relation to the total bulk sample	334

Figure 8.5	Photograph of a charred butternut recovered from AlDf-24, Area C, Feature 4, Level 3 (later Late Maritime Woodland Period).	337
Figure 8.6	Photograph of a charred butternut recovered from AlDf-24, Area C, Feature 4, Level 3f (early Late Maritime Woodland Period)	338
Figure 8.7	E'se'get faunal assemblages: Comparison of species richness to sample size across all sites.	342
Figure 8.8	Port Joli faunal assemblages: Abundance indices (AI) for select taxa...	346
Figure 9.1	E'se'get Project bulk-sample assemblages: Percentage of soil fraction (by weight per gram of bulk sample) by site.	354
Figure 9.2	E'se'get Project bulk-sample assemblages: Charcoal percentage (by weight per kilogram of soil) by site	355
Figure 9.3	E'se'et Project bulk-sample assemblages: Number of artifacts (per kilogram) by site)	355
Figure 9.4	E'se'get Project bulk-sample assemblages: Number of lithic artifacts (per kilogram) by site.	356
Figure 9.5	Painting by Mi'kmaw artist Melissa Labrador (Acadia First Nation), 2018.	363

Acknowledgements

The E'se'get Archaeology Project is the result of over ten years of intense, collaborative, community, archaeology. As such, many dozens of people have been involved in the work summarized in this book. The project was financially and logistically supported by the Canadian Museum of History and was shepherded over multiple field seasons by successive directors of research, including David Morrison and Dean Oliver. Without their steadfast support, the project would not have been possible. The administration staff of the Research Division, as well as the many colleagues who provided advice and assistance over the years, deserve special recognition.

The project was, from its inception, primarily a collaboration between the Canadian Museum of History and Acadia First Nation. Chief Deborah Robinson, and the Acadia First Nation Council, deserve singular credit for their support and engagement with the project. Their leadership and care made the project possible. The project was assisted by several cultural officers from Acadia First Nation, including Lisa Francis and Judy Boutlier. Judy, in particular, was a significant force behind the public outreach components of the project; she was instrumental in arranging public tours, lectures, and other events, and was the mainspring behind a recent exhibition on the project in the Sipuke'l Art Gallery in Liverpool, Nova Scotia. Her dedication to the culture and history of her people is inspiring. Donna Whynot consistently supported the project, with her advice and encouragement, especially in the execution of cultural events and meetings.

Melissa Labrador ran the projects at the Mi'kmaw field school in 2010, and her advice and enthusiasm for the project has been critical (please see Chapter 9 for a discussion of her Port Joli-related artwork). Deputy Chief Jeff Purdy has been crucial in the final phases of the project, and his enthusiasm and support for the archaeology of Kespukwitk has been invaluable. Finally, I would like to thank Elders Todd Labrador, Dave Paul, and Edward Benham for performing a smudge on the burial remains discovered in 2010, and for providing advice on how to proceed with excavations following their discovery. The guidance of Elders on the project at times such as this was a source of solace and encouragement. The project was proud to have trained Acadia First Nation high school students in field archaeology. Working with Kaitlyn, Ronny, Kolby, Kaylee, Chelsea, Chole, and Sarah was one of the most rewarding times of the project.

All seasons of the project were undertaken with significant participation of the University of New Brunswick. David Black and Sue Blair were critical to the success of that collaboration. David Black participated in all the seasons of the project, and his hard work, advice, mentorship, and good nature will be fondly remembered. Susan Blair was instrumental in planning the UNB field school in 2010 and assisted with the excavations that year.

As all the major excavations of the project took place in Thomas Raddall Provincial Park, the participation of the Nova Scotia Department of Natural Resources (DNR) was critical. In 2010 and 2012, the Park provided all manner of assistance for running the public archaeology tours, including personnel to escort visitors to the site. Mike Silver, Brian

Kinsman, Peter Colp, Norman Anderson, and Justin Croft deserve special credit for their hard work. Norman Anderson was a constant source of help, inspiration, advice, and equipment loans, and his attention and goodwill were very much appreciated.

Several students and assistants contributed greatly to the project. Dr. Gabe Hrynick pursued his master's, and PhD studies on material from the project, receiving the latter in 2015. Gabe's methodological and logistical contributions to the project cannot be understated, and his contributions to Mi'kmaw archaeology, especially in the area of architecture, have been tremendous (including in this volume). Over the course of the project, I have seen him develop into one of the finest archaeologists working in the Atlantic Northeast today, and he has become a trusted colleague and a valued friend. David Black and Kevin McBride, his graduate supervisors for his master's, and PhD, respectively, contributed substantial intellectual fuel to the project through Gabe's research.

The project was lucky to employ several wonderful graduate and undergraduate students as field assistants and laboratory technicians, including Kenneth Holyoke, Andrea Thompson, Jesse Webb, Cora Woolsey, Veronica Lech, Nathalie Jess, Erin Ingram, Jesslyn Jarvis, and Carolyn Tropea. Nathalie spent the most time in the field, and in addition to being one of the finest field archaeologists with whom I've worked, she took on the role of project photographer for many of the public and community events. Carolyn Tropea diligently cleaned, sorted, and labelled the bulk of the collection prior to the 2012 season. Erin Ingram spent four summers cataloguing, analyzing, photographing, and drawing artifacts for the project. The project simply could not have been completed without her meticulous and dedicated laboratory work, which is on full display in both chapters 6 and 7. The UNB field school participants, Caitlyn Howard, Cheryl Whitton, Ana de Santos, Tricia Jarratt, and Jessica Vanoostwaard, worked under very hot conditions and in the presence of ticks and poison ivy. Their contributions are greatly appreciated.

Many archaeologists and other scholars contributed intellectually and substantively to the project. Michael Deal and his student, Sara Halwas, conducted the first macrobotanical study of shell middens on the South Shore of Nova Scotia. Katherine Patton and Meghan Burchell, seeing the enormous data potential locked in the clam shells, convinced me to collaborate on an isotopic study of the shells from Port Joli. Meghan Burchell has developed new techniques to tease data from these complex hard tissues. Their home institutions, including the Memorial University of Newfoundland and the University of Toronto, respectively, generously supported their work on the project. Heather Macleod-Leslie was supported by the Mi'kmaq Rights Initiative (KMKNO) to work on the project in 2010, and she produced very detailed total station maps of AlDf-24. Stephen Augustine kindly provided a definitive translation of the proposed Mi'kmaw names for the sites we excavated.

Several community members from Liverpool and Port Joli assisted the project in various ways. Danielle Robertson was an invaluable source of knowledge about the history of Port Joli. Her enthusiasm and continuous help, and especially her uncanny ability to find shell midden sites again and again, was crucial to the success of the project. We cannot thank her enough. David Dagley provided important insights about the middens and provided critical data on their locations. Linda Rafuse and Kathleen Stitt, of the Queens County Museum, were very supportive of the project and generously organized public lectures, provided space for meetings, arranged for collections access, and assisted with networking with local collectors. Their assistance was invaluable. Marg Millard provided access to some of her father's photographs of his excavations, and her insights into his research were critical to our interpretation of his work. Kelly Frank allowed us to test deposits on his front lawn, and other local landowners, too numerous to thank, permitted us to survey or walk across their properties as we conducted our work. Laurie Boisvert deserves credit for the gourmet meals that kept the crew in good spirits and full of energy during the long 2010 field season.

The authors of this volume were supported, funded, and inspired in various ways by many people and organizations. Gajewski and Neil would like to thank the Natural Sciences and Engineering Research Council of Canada (NSERC), as well as the University of Ottawa, for supporting their work in the Laboratory for Paleoclimatology and Climatology. Curtis was supported by Parks Canada to study the ceramic materials from the project. The pottery code used in Chapter 6 was developed by David Smith, and he deserves special thanks for sharing the code with us and for inspiring our way of thinking about ceramic analysis. Hynick was supported by a dissertation grant from the National Science Foundation and through various funds from the University of New Brunswick, the University of Connecticut, and Bates College.

The staff of the Nova Scotia Museum deserve singular praise for their backing of the project. Stephen Powell first recommended Port Joli as an important archaeological target prior to the establishment of the project. His insights and assistance in navigating all manner of collections, permitting, and practical aspects of the archaeological work was critical, and very much appreciated. Later, Catherine Cottreau-Robins assisted with access to collections and archives, and the management of collections. Her contributions to the project will not be forgotten. Roger Lewis also provided his deep insights into the culture and archaeology of Nova Scotia.

The project connected with avocational and professional archaeologists throughout the province. Sara Beanlands, Ben Pentz, Darryl Kelman, Bruce Stewart, Mike Sanders, Laird Niven, Rob Ferguson, Jonathan Fowler, and numerous others provided insights, advice, and field support. Their site visits were welcome and always entertaining. The Nature Conservancy of Canada provided access to their properties in Port Joli, and kindly allowed us to test a site on one of them. Their approach to the stewardship of these properties is an inspiration.

Special recognition must go to Dirk van Loon, the director of the Harrison Lewis Coastal Discovery Centre. Dirk is a tireless advocate for the history, culture, and environment of the South Shore, and his knowledge, interest, and passion are infectious. His brainchild, the Harrison Lewis Centre, was and is the perfect facility for archaeology on the South Shore of Nova Scotia, and it takes credit for a great deal of our success. Dirk supported the project in ways too subtle and numerous to list, and we owe him more than we can repay. Some of the fondest memories of the project were his annual end-of-season meals, where he served corn on the cob and his farm-grown meat, while dozens of hummingbirds flitted about in the setting sun.

As the director of the project and editor of the volume, I have the opportunity and privilege to make many personal acknowledgements. My parents, Carl and Nancy Betts, provided meals, lodging, and kindness to many of the personnel on the project as we passed through Halifax on our way to and from Port Joli. They visited the excavations many times, and always brought laughter (and food) with them. Involving them in my work is one of the great highlights of my career. My pugs, Chester and Fergus, once visited Port Joli, and while the sites didn't impress, the smells of the beaches and clam flats were thoroughly appreciated. They deserve credit for their steadfast companionship, at my feet or in my lap, whenever I worked from home over the last ten years. And finally, to my partner Karen: it is not conceivable to describe all you have contributed to my work and life. You make it all possible, all worthwhile.

    Matthew Betts, Ottawa, April 2019

Foreword

It is my pleasure to help present this research that has been conducted on the lives of my ancestors and the heritage of our Mi'kmaw Nation in Nova Scotia. As Chief of Acadia First Nation for over 30 years, I have witnessed increasing change in how archaeologists work with our heritage and our communities. The E'se'get Archaeology Project has been a wonderful step forward in building good relationships between archaeologists and our people, with our ancestors providing the bridge connecting us.

The lands, waters and resources in and around Mi'kma'ki—the traditional territory of the Mi'kmaq since time immemorial—have remained the thread that has connected us to our past, and will provide linkages to our future. As archaeological work is conducted in Mi'kma'ki, the found artefacts provide us with literal touchstones to the stories we have heard from our Elders, the lessons that we have learned on the lands and waters, and the rich history which we are so deeply rooted and connected to.

In this time of reconciliation, opportunities for non-Indigenous people to become important allies in increasing the visibility of our culture, the understanding of our heritage and the use of our language are critical. Research projects like this help us embrace our Mi'kmaw language and culture and celebrate the strengths our collaborations create for all of us—recognition and understanding.

The artefacts, made by our ancestors' hands, are important finds to both us and the archaeologists, just as the use of our language and cultural perspectives in this project are also important finds to us. The sites and artefacts that have brought the archaeologists here to work are an opportunity, in and of themselves, for reconciliation. When archaeologists examine our archaeological heritage, we want them to remember not only that our ancestors made these items, but that they used these places and tools to sustain themselves and raise future generations of Mi'kmaq, which is who we are, and so incredibly proud and humbled by.

Under the direction of Matthew Betts, the E'se'get Archaeology Project respected, from the beginning, the importance of our language in understanding our people and our territory by using <u>our</u> words to mark and identify our places and what they mean to us. It has been a rewarding experience for my community to both teach and learn from Matthew and his team members over the years of work at Emsik. This is a very special place to us and our ancestors, because of the resources and legacy we enjoy here, but it is also a special place for archaeologists because of the rich and abundant stories available from the sensitive and unique features here, many preserved in the shell middens of our ancestors' meals. Matthew's work and that of his colleagues has made careful use of these unique contexts and preservation environments. This project focused on faunal analysis which is much needed research that both improves the understanding and narrative of our Mi'kmaw history and provides important details about our harvests and our management practices, which are thousands of years old. Our rights and title implementation directly benefit from details such as these.

The E'se'get Archaeology project was a valuable experience for Acadia First Nation and our community members. Matthew opened multiple opportunities for us to actively participate in the process of archaeology and to help present the project and our heritage to the broader community; which is an important change necessary in the discipline of archaeology today. I look forward to future collaborations and partnerships with Matthew and archaeologists broadly and am delighted to begin your journey into our story at Emsik.

    Chief Deborah Robinson
    Acadia First Nation

Chapter 1
The E'se'get Archaeology Project

MATTHEW BETTS

Introduction

For as long as the harbour has existed, the Mi'kmaq have lived there.[1] They called it Emsik (or Pemsik or Pems'g) which meant "blown along by the wind" or "pass by, in air" (Brown 1922: 117), possibly a reference to the breeze that constantly blows up and down the harbour. It was an idyllic place to call home, and still is. Its shallow, sun-warmed waters teem with codfish, eels, and herring. Thousands of migrating and moulting waterfowl congregate throughout the year to eat eelgrass in massive flocks at its headwaters. White sand beaches, glistening with fresh water from dozens of streams, are fenestrated with the siphon holes of millions of soft-shell clams. The beaches back onto a verdant forest wall of short spruces and towering pines, which shelter deer and moose. Here and there glittering bedrock headlands stab through the forest and beach to plunge into the sea.

Figure 1.1 A springtime view of Port Joli's southwestern harbour shore, facing north.

---

1. Our spelling of Mi'kmaq and use of the variant, Mi'kmaw, follows the standard outlines in the *Mi'kmaw Resource Guide* (1997).

2 Place-Making in the Pretty Harbour

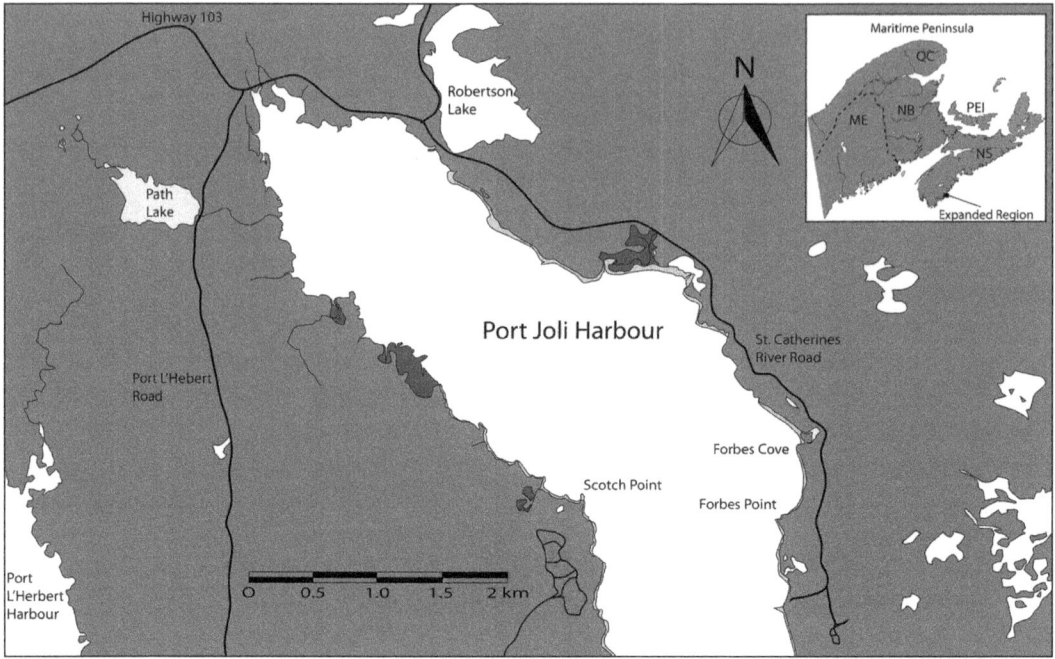

Figure 1.2 Modern map of Port Joli's harbour.

When Pierre Dugua de Mons and Samuel de Champlain sailed down the South Shore of Nova Scotia in May of 1604, they comprehended that the Mi'kmaq had already named all the features of this coastline. Regardless, they lost a sheep overboard at their first stop and promptly commemorated the incident by renaming the anchorage Port Mouton (Dugua de Mons 1939). Using Port Mouton as a base, Champlain scouted southward down the coast on a mapping and survey expedition (Champlain 1907). Emsik was the first harbour he encountered, and its natural beauty inspired Champlain to rename it Port Joli, "Pretty Harbour." The first written record of the harbour, "P Joly," occurs on his exquisite 1607 map. For more than four centuries, through multiple Mi'kmaw, French, and Loyalist occupations (and reoccupations), Champlain's evocative name for the harbour has endured. Its equally evocative Mi'kmaw name is now only recorded in a handful of historical sources and place-name databases.

This book is about the Mi'kmaw history of Emsik, or Port Joli as it is now known, and the excavation and study of the unique archaeological deposits which are found there. Port Joli is a special archaeological and historical place because it contains the densest concentration of shell middens (based on number of sites per linear kilometre of shoreline) of any coastline in Nova Scotia. At their least complex, shell middens are ancient refuse heaps composed of mollusc shells, animal bones, and the artifactual and stratigraphic detritus of everyday life. Archaeologically, they are crucial deposits, especially in Atlantic regions, because they tend to have excellent organic and non-organic preservation. As mollusc shells decompose, they leach calcium carbonate into surrounding soils and substantially reduce acidity levels, creating an environment amenable to the preservation of organic and non-organic remains, especially animal bones, antlers, and teeth. This is a tremendous benefit in

Figure 1.3 Articulated domestic dog bones (left rear foot) preserved in a Port Joli shell midden (AlDf-30).

a region where generally acidic soil chemistry effectively dissolves organic materials in archaeological deposits older than a few hundred years.

The animal remains preserved in shell middens not only provide evidence of human economies, but they contain significant information that can be used to reconstruct ancient climatic conditions, local ecosystems, and animal populations. The organic (bone and antler) tools preserved in these deposits provide insights about the perishable technologies so often missing from non-shell midden sites in Nova Scotia, as well as the functional and social relations involved in their production, use, and discard. In short, shell middens can provide a crucial record of the past—of ancient human behaviours, of palaeoclimate, and of former environments.

Shell Midden Archaeology

Interest in shell midden archaeology has a long history in Nova Scotia, beginning with the first excavations at a large shell midden in Frostfish Cove (in St. Margarets Bay) in 1863 (Ambrose 1867). The importance of these deposits to Nova Scotian archaeology was almost immediately recognized by early European naturalists, as J. P. Gilpin (1874: 227) noted: "These collections of oyster and clam shells mixed with bones of fish, birds, and mammals, have not yet been studied with the care they deserve. They are the collection of ages, and would well reward a thorough investigation."

Unfortunately, although the pioneering excavations of H. I. Smith and W. J. Wintemberg (1929) and, later, John Erskine (1958, 1960, 1961, 1998) have provided a basic framework for shell midden archaeology in the province, Gilpin's appeal for a detailed examination of these intriguing deposits has largely remained unanswered. Significant shell midden research has been conducted in adjacent Atlantic states and provinces for over thirty years (e.g., Black 1992, 2004; Bourque 1995; Davis 1978; Sanger 1987); these studies have provided relatively detailed regional sequences spanning the Late Archaic to Late Maritime Woodland periods. In contrast, no in-depth, diachronic investigation (representing multiple time periods) of a sequence of shell middens sites has been conducted in the province of Nova Scotia for nearly four decades. Recent work on shell middens in the province has typically been limited in scope, reflecting the largely mitigative and exploratory nature of the investigations, although some important work from stratified sites has taken place (e.g., Davis 1987). Regardless, sequences of economic, technological, and settlement change derived from shell midden sites remain largely absent from modern reconstructions of Nova Scotian prehistory (Davis 1997).

Part of the reason for this deficit is that a combination of environmental and cultural processes has resulted in significant destruction of shell midden sites in the province. Coastal subsidence and oceanic sea level rise have intensified erosion on most shorelines in Nova Scotia, with the result that many shell midden sites have either been inundated or, more frequently, destroyed (e.g., Davis 1980, 1983; Davis and Christianson 1981). Furthermore, historic mining of shell midden deposits for use in lime kilns, agricultural activities (e.g., ploughing and gardening), and intensive coastal development have destroyed many shell middens.

Perhaps the most alarming cultural process has been active collecting and "pot hunting" by amateur collectors and treasure hunters. Collecting has been a factor in shell midden preservation since the late nineteenth century but intensified with the activities of a few determined collectors in the mid-twentieth century. Their hobby-level exploration of these resources is partially the result of the knowledge vacuums left by the lack of professional exploration of shell middens. Most collectors have a deep respect for the history of the place they reside, and their willingness to donate and share their collections with community museums reveals this. Unfortunately, their hobby has also been destructive, and some intensively collected sites, including in Port Joli (see Chapter 3) are no longer of practical scientific value.

The unrelenting forces of coastal erosion, development, and collecting continue to assault these irreplaceable resources, and it is essential that we renew and intensify efforts to locate, salvage, and investigate the few remaining undisturbed shell midden sites. The large complexes of shell midden sites that once existed in Merigomish Harbour, Mahone Bay, and St. Margarets Bay (Smith and Wintemberg 1929) have largely been destroyed by erosion, cultivation, collecting, and development such that their archaeological potential is now greatly diminished (Davis and Christianson 1981; D. Keenlyside 2007, pers. comm.; S. Powell 2007, pers. comm.). As described below, Port Joli, with such a density of shell midden sites, provides one of the only remaining locations where it is possible to conduct the type of detailed research necessary to understand these crucial deposits and the cultures and times they represent (Powell 1990, 1995). With such a record, we may be able to build up chronological sequences of cultural change and place these developments within the context of other shell midden–derived sequences from adjacent provinces and states (e.g., Black 1992; Bourque 1995; Davis 1978; Sanger 1987; Spiess and Lewis 2001).

Port Joli's Harbour—A Natural and Archaeological Preserve

The extraordinary concentration of shell middens in Port Joli, while unique today, may not have been unique in the recent past. A constellation of natural and human processes has conspired to preserve the middens in Port Joli and, fortunately, will continue to protect them for the foreseeable future. Perhaps most important among these is the protected nature of its harbour. Port Joli's harbour is long and shallow, with substantial headlands on both sides of its mouth (figure 1.2). These headlands, combined with the length of the harbour, mitigate the intensity of large storm surges and, more importantly, large waves associated with hurricanes and coastal storms. Notably, the harbour also has a bend in it; from its relatively open mouth, it veers suddenly northwest at about the location of Forbes Point (opposite the harbour from Scotch Point). The result is that storm waves are directed from the outer harbour toward the northeast into Forbes Cove and the Bijou Rocks area, which bears the brunt of the assault, and where there is significant coastal erosion today. As a result of the bend, the largest waves from these large storms do not penetrate substantially up the harbour, and when they do, they tend to impact the northeastern coast. The southwestern coast and the western head of the harbour are largely protected from these storms.

The second advantageous natural feature is the expansive beaches, the clam flats, and the bedrock headlands in Port Joli. The foreshore clam flats and extensive beaches (at low tide) dampen wave energy, greatly reducing the impact of storm surges and wave action. The bedrock headlands further deflect wave energy, protecting sites near the beaches.

Figure 1.4 An extensive Port Joli clam flat at low tide, facing north.

Additionally, the beaches often back onto bedrock and boulder outcrops at the margin of the forest. The bedrock armours the coastal edge and forest from erosion, substantially reducing the rate of destruction. Moreover, the location of the high-water mark, which is generally within 5 to 10 m of the modern forest–bedrock transition, leaves few beach locations that were advantageous to place habitation or other sites without risk of inundation. Instead, the shell middens and habitation sites are generally located about 30 m or more into the forest, several metres above the high-tide mark. This has undoubtedly protected many sites from erosion.

The third advantage enjoyed by Port Joli is the early establishment of a migratory bird sanctuary at the head of the harbour. Approximately 40 percent of Atlantic Canada's Canada goose population overwinters in the Port Joli region, and the (generally) year-round open water of the harbour attracts thousands of migrating green-winged teal, mergansers, scaups, eiders, and other waterfowl annually. As stated in the *Migratory Bird Convention Act*, "No person shall, in a migratory bird sanctuary, carry on any activity that is harmful to migratory birds or the eggs, nests or habitat of migratory birds . . . ." (Migratory Bird Sanctuary Regulations, C.R.C., c. 1036, 10[1]). This law has effectively protected the head of Port Joli's harbour from major habitat alteration (i.e., land development), which has further protected archaeological sites in the protected habitat area. In addition to the sanctuary, two parcels of Canadian Wildlife Service (CWS) lands also exist in the harbour, and, though very small, both protect shell middens that occur within their boundaries.

The fourth, and most substantial, advantage of Port Joli was the establishment, in 1994, of Thomas Raddall Provincial Park. Covering over 650 ha, the park is both a nature and heritage preserve. Several historic properties, including historic buildings and an historic cemetery, in addition to four major shell midden sites, are located within its boundaries. The same protections the park affords to the natural ecosystem extend to the archaeological sites within it, which are thus protected from both development and collecting. It is no coincidence that the largest intact shell midden sites in the province are located within the boundaries of a provincial park, or that the bulk of the E'se'get excavations took place within its borders. As will be outlined below, the infrastructure and staff at the park were also critical to the success of the E'se'get Archaeology Project.

The fifth, and most recent, advantage of Port Joli's harbour is that many private properties have been purchased north and south of the Park by the Nature Conservancy of Canada (NCC). Combined with the provincial park, these purchases create an expansive nature preserve which protects the majority of the southwestern shoreline of Port Joli. While the original intent for the establishment of the park, bird sanctuary, and CWS and NCC lands was to protect Port Joli's special ecosystem, these collective properties have also protected an expansive ancient Mi'kmaw cultural landscape, which happens to contain some of the most detailed information on Mi'kmaw lifeways in the entire province. The residents of Port Joli, who worked with the NCC, the Department of Natural Resources, and the CWS to protect these lands, deserve immense credit for their foresight and concern for the natural and historical integrity of this special place.

The E'se'get Archaeology Project

"E'se'get" is a Mi'kmaw word meaning "to dig for clams," and its use as a project name has a double meaning. Not only is the archaeology of the South Shore the result of thousands of years of Mi'kmaq digging for clams, but the excavation of their shell middens involves literally digging through the clam shells they collected. It was the perfect name for a collaborative shell midden archaeology project.

The E'se'get Archaeology Project is an ongoing collaborative research endeavour between the Canadian Museum of History, Acadia First Nation, and the University of New Brunswick. In addition to these institutions, significant partnerships were developed with the Mi'kmaq Rights Initiative and the Department of Natural Resources, on whose land much of the excavations took place. At its most basic level, the E'se'get Project was designed to define the late Holocene prehistory of Nova Scotia's South Shore and, in particular, the relationship between ancient Mi'kmaq and the Port Joli landscape and ecosystem (Betts 2009, 2010). A primary goal of the project is to produce a sequence of radiometrically dated economic, settlement, and technological data to contribute to a nuanced culture history of the region.

Such specific goals are rare in modern archaeological practice in North America, because, frankly, there are few places left where unique culture histories are left to be developed. One of these places is the Maritime Peninsula, a region stretching from Southern Maine, and including New Brunswick, Nova Scotia, Prince Edward Island, and portions of Quebec, where a regional dearth of post-secondary archaeology programs and research has left many regions largely unexplored with modern archaeological techniques.

The E'se'get Project has four main goals:

1. To determine the nature of Maritime Woodland Period exploitation of the intertidal and near-shore ecosystems of the southwestern Nova Scotian shore. A primary component of this research is to develop a concise, radiometrically dated, chronological sequence to provide a framework for analyzing shifts in human economies, settlement patterns, and social relations.
2. To explore and document the animal remains and economic and ecosystem information preserved in these shell middens
3. To locate, relocate, and fully record shell midden sites in Port Joli and adjacent regions and to assess the level of modern cultural (e.g., looting and development) and natural (e.g., erosion and inundation) disturbance to these deposits. Where necessary, this project aims to mitigate further loss through precise excavation and documentation.
4. To actively seek both the approval and participation of Mi'kmaw First Nations at all stages of the research, and to fully share all data recorded with interested groups. A primary goal of this project is to develop positive partnerships between the Canadian Museum of History Corporation and Mi'kmaw First Nations in the exploration of their past.

Two central premises have guided this research: (1) that the pre-contact Mi'kmaq were a central part of coastal ecosystems and had a recursive socio-economic relationship with those ecosystems and (2) that the Mi'kmaq were agents in their own history. Their long-term, repeated engagement with the landscape and resources dynamically and recursively created Mi'kmaw history, and indeed their unique culture. The recurring, cyclical, everyday relationships between place, people, and animals preserved in these middens reveal Mi'kmaw history as certainly as their oral history has done. We have sought to use the archaeological record of Port Joli to assemble a record of Mi'kmaw culture history on the South Shore.

Culture histories are difficult to produce because they require extensive data and its critical assessment (Lyman and O'Brien 2004). They are somewhat of a lost art in archaeology, although a recent resurgence in the importance of history in the discipline has seen archaeologists attempt to re-engage with culture history building and refinement (e.g., Holly 2013, Sassaman 2010). Culture histories document the "who," "what," "when," "where," and "how," and then place these together in a synthesis that tracks the "why." In this case the "why" involves critically assessing how Mi'kmaw social and economic lifeways evolved both in response to, and as structuring agents of, a larger northwestern Atlantic ecosystem. To effectively conduct this sort of research, we must track how pre-contact Mi'kmaw socio-economies developed, were maintained, and were subsequently reproduced during periods of cultural and environmental change.

The E'se'get Project began with a limited field-survey project in 2008, following an initial consultation with Acadia First Nation. The survey was conducted at the head of the harbour at Port Joli and throughout Thomas Raddall Provincial Park, and test excavations were implemented at AlDf-24, AlDf-25, AlDf-30, AlDf-31, AlDf-35, and A2009NS27-1 (see Chapter 3). A community event was also held in Port Joli for Acadia First Nation. In 2009, we returned to Port Joli for intensive survey and site visits along the entire coast of Port Joli, with a specific emphasis on the southern shoreline (only known sites were visited on the north shoreline, due to limited private property access). Community events and site tours were conducted for Acadia First Nation and community residents.

The summer of 2010 represented the most intensive field season for the E'se'get Project. In addition to significant community collaboration and outreach (see below), five weeks of excavations were carried out at AlDf-24 and several days of excavation at AlDf-30. In addition to community events, the project ran a University of New Brunswick archaeological field school, focused on undergraduate training. The final season of excavation in Port Joli took place in 2012 and focused on testing AlDf-06 and AlDf-08 over several days, as well as a four-week excavation of house deposits at AlDf-30.

Four years of intensive laboratory work at the Canadian Museum of History followed the final season of excavation. Facilitated by loans of the material we excavated from the Nova Scotia Museum, the analysis included detailed cataloguing, description, and attribute coding for ceramics, lithics, and other artifacts. Faunal analyses were conducted under contract by professionals at the University of Toronto (reference collections at the Canadian Museum of History and the Canadian Museum of Nature were also used). In 2016, the artifact loan expired and the entire collection, except for the bulk midden samples, was transferred to the Nova Scotia Museum, where it resides in perpetuity.

From its inception, the E'se'get Project has been collaborative in nature. The primary, and most important, collaboration has been between Acadia First Nation and the Canadian Museum of History. The nature of this collaboration, and its results, will be described in detail later in the chapter. The University of New Brunswick (UNB) also collaborated extensively on the project, providing assistance in the form of field labour, equipment, and expert consultation. One graduate student from UNB (Gabriel Hrynick) also trained on the project and completed a master's thesis on data from AlDf-24. Additional training for undergraduates from UNB was provided by the project, and graduate student field assistants were regularly employed. The Mi'kmaq Rights Initiative supported the project from the earliest moments, and in 2010, they contributed substantially by creating digital surveys of AlDf-24. The Nova Scotia Museum, and especially Stephen Powell, assisted with advice, knowledge, and support in terms of loans and loan extensions.

Several other collaborations occurred over the course of the project. The University of Connecticut supported one PhD student (Gabriel Hrynick), who wrote a dissertation on data from AlDf-24 and AlDf-30 (see Chapter 5). The Nature Conservancy of Canada and the Canadian Wildlife Service kindly provided access to their properties for survey and testing purposes. The Harrison Lewis Coastal Discovery Centre was a major contributor to the work life of the project, and their facilities were crucial to its success, especially behind the scenes.

Finally, a special partnership developed between the Canadian Museum of History and the Department of Natural Resources. The professional staff of Thomas Raddall Provincial Park were critical in this regard. In addition to permits and permissions to access sites within the park, staff provided important logistical support for community archaeology events and general fieldwork activities (including the loan of equipment). The E'se'get Project simply would not have been possible without their support, and their enthusiasm for protecting and exploring the archaeological resources in their park was inspiring.

Previous Shell Midden Archaeology in the Port Joli Region

Prior to the E'se'get Archaeology Project, much of what we knew of Port Joli's archaeology came from the work of collectors and avocational archaeologists. The archaeological potential of Port Joli was first noted by Thomas H. Raddall (n.d., 1974), an author, historian, and amateur collector, who conducted some exploratory excavations in the Port Joli middens in the early and mid-twentieth century.

When John Erskine, a naturalist working for the Nova Scotia Museum, visited the region in 1957, Raddall introduced him to these unique deposits. An amateur with little archaeological training, Erskine was so impressed by the deposits at Port Joli that he was prompted to undertake a two-decades-long reconnaissance of shell midden deposits across Nova Scotia (Erskine 1958, 1959, 1960, 1961, 1962, 1986, 1998). At Port Joli, Erskine excavated almost continuously between 1957 and 1964, resulting in the testing or complete excavation of more than a dozen sites on the east and west shores of the harbour. His excavations, while lacking in methodological rigour by professional standards, resulted in a relatively comprehensive collection of artifacts and faunal remains which suggested an intensive occupation spanning the Maritime Woodland Period, around 2500–500 cal BP. The quantity of the material he recovered, and the size of the sites he recorded, suggested an intensive exploitation of the littoral and marine resources in this region over a relatively long period.

Between 1966 and 1968, Eric Millard documented previously unrecorded archaeological sites on the eastern side of the harbour, one of which, AlDf-1, he excavated over the following three summers. This was to be the last archaeology conducted in the region for nearly thirty years. In the early and mid-1990s, Stephen Powell revisited the area, ostensibly to re-evaluate the sites Erskine discovered and to conduct further reconnaissance in preparation for the development of Thomas Raddall Provincial Park. While Powell (1990, 1995) described that many of the coastal sites in the park had been extensively disturbed by collectors (presumably after Erskine's excavations), he also located a new class of relatively undisturbed interior (non-littoral) shell midden sites. This small complex of shell midden sites in Port Joli represents one of the best remaining sequences of shell midden sites in southwestern Nova Scotia, if not the entire province (S. A. Davis 2007, pers. comm.; S. Powell 2007, pers. comm.).

Survey Methods

Our reconnaissance for archaeological sites focused on the coastline of Thomas Raddall Provincial Park, the western and eastern shores of Port Joli's harbour, and the western shore of Port L'Hebert (figure 1.2). Unfortunately, time constraints did not allow for systematic survey in the Port Mouton area, north of Port Joli, along the coast, as was initially planned for the project.

We developed a site model based on the observations of Raddall (n.d., 1974), Erskine (1962), and Powell (1990, 1995), augmented by additional data produced by comparing a plot of known sites against water features, clam beds, and surface topography. We further refined this model with data from field observation and survey, which indicated that areas of intertidal productivity, combined with low-relief terrain and advantageous windbreaks (e.g., knolls and large glacial boulders) were often associated with shell midden sites. In practical application, our shoreline surveys were focused on locating "glistening beaches" (i.e., locations where groundwater percolates through beach sediments) and other areas where the nutrients from freshwater effluent creates an amenable environment for softshell clam beds, such as the mouths of streams and rivers. In those locations, we surveyed along shorelines, including the banks of rivers, streams, creeks, and dry watercourses, to a distance of about 500 m from the water's edge. In 2009, we spent significant resources attempting to falsify our survey model by surveying less-promising locations, particularly along rocky shorelines, or unproductive sandy shores without local clam beds (both with and without local freshwater sources). We found no prehistoric sites in these less-promising locations.

In locations deemed to be of high site potential, we used a 2 cm bore soil probe (70 cm in length) to test for the presence of subsurface shell deposits. However, in many instances high-potential sites were easily distinguished by (a) the low density and unique variety of tree and vegetation, (b) the presence of previous collecting activity (e.g., pits or shell on the surface), or (c) obvious anthropogenic mounds or depressions. Positive soil probes (cores with evidence of shell, bone, charcoal, artifacts, or cultural horizons) or surface evidence of cultural activity (e.g., surface shell, bone, or artifacts) prompted us to set out a cross-shaped transect oriented along the cardinal directions, along which soil probes were taken at metre intervals to determine the extent of cultural deposits. We used these probes to aid in the creation of detailed maps using the plane-table method (bearings and distances were measured with an engineer's compass and 50 m tapes). These maps should be considered preliminary survey data unless more detailed maps were developed from site excavation (see Chapter 3).

The 2008 survey focused on Thomas Raddall Provincial Park and the western shore of Port Joli's harbour. Walking surveys were conducted along 5 km of shoreline between the head of the harbour and the northern boundary of the provincial park, as well as the entire shoreline of Thomas Raddall Provincial Park between Scotch Point and its northern boundary (figure 3.1). We also surveyed a small public allotment on the east shore of Port Joli, just south of the outlet to Robertson Lake. The 2008 survey resulted in the relocation and mapping of six previously known sites and the discovery of two new shell midden sites (one may be a previously known site; see AlDf-36 [AlDf-01], in Chapter 3).

In 2009, we conducted walking surveys along the same 5 km of shoreline as in 2008, between the head of Port Joli's harbour and the northern boundary of the provincial park, but this time focusing on Nature Conservancy of Canada and Canadian Wildlife Service properties. We also surveyed CWS coastal properties east of the head of Port Joli's harbour, between East Port L'Hebert Road and St. Catherine's River Road. In Thomas Raddall Provincial Park, we surveyed the coastline south of Scotch Point to the western boundary of the park, where it intersects Sandy Bay. In Port L'Hebert, we surveyed the coastline west of Granite Village southward for approximately 3 km.

The 2009 survey resulted in the visiting and relocation of two previously known sites and the discovery of one previously unrecorded site. This was not an entirely unexpected result, given the focus on portions of the coast deemed to have a low site potential. The high-energy coast of the southerly sections of Thomas Raddall Provincial Park and the rocky shores of the northwestern harbour of Port L'Hebert are not amenable to soft-shell clam colonies, and their exposed and rugged shores are not suitable for large habitation sites. We did locate one small new midden near the head of Port Joli's harbour (temporarily labelled A2009NS27-1), which was positioned in a location of high intertidal productivity, shelter, and access to fresh water, fitting our site location model very well. In 2010, we conducted a brief final survey to relocate AlDf-08, facilitated by knowledge (and permission) from the landowner, who knew of an archaeological deposit that matched the description of the site.

After three seasons of intensive survey, we developed a relatively comprehensive inventory of shell midden sites on the west side of Port Joli's harbour. More survey is required on the eastern coasts of the harbour and the eastern and southwest coasts of Port L'Hebert, where there is a high site potential. Given the remoteness of the Port L'Hebert coast, the potential for significant undisturbed deposits is likely.

Excavation Methods

The E'se'get Archaeology Project employed a standardized excavation strategy applied to all sites and units. Based on information from previous archaeological work, or survey mapping that often involved transects with soil probes, each "site" was divided into several site areas, labelled alphabetically. Within each "area," a separate 1 × 1 m grid system was imposed, with axes aligned on a north–south (true) bearing; the primary "unit" of excavation was thus a 1 × 1 m square. Each point (peg) in the grid was labelled with a north and west coordinate, typically beginning at North 50 and West 50 (N50W50), with grid numbers changing sequentially as they proceeded north and west. Each peg served as a unit datum for the square to the northwest of it (i.e., each square's unit datum was its southeast peg). While all artifacts' and features' proveniences and the stratigraphy were recorded in relation to a unit datum, unit-grid elevations (the ground elevation of each peg) were taken with reference to an area datum, which in turn was linked to a centrally located site datum. These measurements were taken via digital transit and recorded on large area maps.

Although artifacts, stratigraphy, and features were typically mapped in relation to the unit datum as described above, topography sometimes forced the assignment of a different peg as a unit datum for elevation purposes. Excavation followed natural stratigraphy, with arbitrary, approximately 5 cm, levels assigned in deep strata for additional vertical control. In this system, Level 1 is the sod, Level 2 is the active root-bearing deposit, Level 3 is the "undisturbed" culture-bearing deposit, and Level 4 is the subsoil (B horizon). Within "levels," each natural and arbitrary stratigraphic deposit was given a further alphabetic designation (e.g., 3a, 3b, 3c), with "a" being the uppermost designation within the level.

Specially designed unit-level record forms were used to describe stratigraphic and artifactual information in a standardized format. A field catalogue was kept of all recovered materials on the unit-level record forms. Features were numbered sequentially by site in the order of their discovery (e.g., Feature 4). Sub-features, such as hearths or pits within a larger feature, were given an alphabetic designation in relation to a feature number (e.g., Feature 4a). Features were each recorded on a specially designed feature record form, and new unit-level records were kept for the features, with internal stratigraphy numbered separately from the surrounding stratigraphic matrices. Plan maps were recorded for any features and any anthropogenic remains.

All deposits were excavated by trowel and all formal artifacts were mapped in relation to the unit datum. Undifferentiated midden deposits were screened through 6 mm mesh (e.g., AlDf-24, Area A; AlDf-06, AlDf-30, Area A midden; AlDf-31, AlDf-25), while features and "kitchen middens" associated with dwelling features and black soil middens were screened through 3 mm mesh to enhance the recovery of small artifacts and animal remains (AlDf-24 Area A, Feature 2, AlDf-24 Area C, AlDf-30 Black Soil Area, AlDf-30 Area B Midden, AlDf-06, AlDf-08, AlDf-35). Bulk midden samples were recovered from a representative portion of each stratigraphic layer for later analysis of shell, small faunal remains, and pollen. Any artifacts encountered while taking the sample were kept with it to facilitate weight-based and artifact-per-volume analysis. These consisted of 3L to 5L samples of unscreened matrix, typically taken from the centre of a unit, with a closing and opening depth recorded for each sample. Faunal remains, undecorated pottery, and lithics were collected in level bags representing each natural or arbitrary level from the 1 × 1 m unit. Within features, especially potential dwelling floors, excavation proceeded by quadrant, with all recovered materials mapped and bagged by quadrant.

In 2012, our excavation procedures transitioned to an entirely digital recording environment. Every item of data—including unit-level record forms, notes, and mapping—was collected digitally, using a tablet computer with software allowing us to create digital forms, maps, and notes. As far as we are aware, this is the first time such a comprehensive suite of excavation data has been digitally collected in Nova Scotia. The great advantage of this system was that data was collected in the format it is to be used—digitally—and therefore no conversion was necessary once the field season was completed. This greatly increased the efficiency of our post-fieldwork data processing and safeguarded against the loss of data caused by digitization and transcription errors.

Traditional paper-based forms were replaced with PDF-based fillable forms on iPads, using the application PDF Expert. Tablet computers are increasingly being utilized by archaeologists to record field data (e.g., Fee et al. 2013), including to produce maps. Most of these systems use custom-built databases; however, we developed a new system that used PDF-based digital forms. Our rationale for using PDF forms is sixfold:

- Many archaeologists use paper forms to collect their field data (e.g., Kipfer 2007). Using PDF-based forms mimics their normal paper-based workflows and therefore requires less training and creates less "digital shock."
- The data in PDF forms is digital and can be instantly compiled into a spreadsheet database using Adobe Acrobat Professional software.
- PDF forms are platform–independent: they can be used with iOS, Android, or Windows-based devices.
- The PDF forms incorporate graph paper that can be used to draw detailed plan maps. These maps can be directly exported to standard illustration software in a vector format.

Figure 1.5 Drawing a feature plan at AIDf-30 using a vector-based drawing app on an iPad Pro.

- Archaeological permitting agencies often require original paper versions of data for archival purposes. PDF forms can be printed without additional formatting, in a manner consistent with previously archived documents.
- Digital PDF forms can be backed up to a "digital cloud" daily, minimizing the risk of lost or destroyed paper forms.

While the graph paper incorporated into the PDF forms was used to create highly accurate unit-level maps, we used a vector-based drawing application to produce site and feature maps and profiles. With traditional paper drawings, each sheet must be scanned, and these scans must then be loaded into illustration software to be traced by hand. The traces must then be digitally concatenated and formatted to produce a publication-quality map. This process is time-consuming and can introduce transcription errors during the tracing process. Using the tablet, we produced the maps and profiles in a format in which they would be eventually used—digitally.

Finally, all photographic logs and field notes were created digitally on the iPad, using the spreadsheet and word processing applications, respectively. We found the camera feature on the iPads allowed for traditional field notes to be augmented with candid photographs of the excavations, which greatly increased the detail and effectiveness of the traditional note-taking process.

Community Archaeology

As described above, shell midden deposits represent a crucial heritage resource for the Mi'kmaq. Through careful excavation, documentation, study, and commemoration, shell middens can contribute much to the understanding of traditional Mi'kmaw lifeways and, as such, can provide an important resource to reinforce deep historical connections with past ecosystems and landscapes. Unfortunately, past excavation and study of these deposits was often conducted without community consultation or participation. In response to this deficit, the E'se'get Archaeology Project was designed from the ground up with Indigenous and local community involvement in mind. Four tenets formed part of this commitment:

- Consulting with Acadia First Nation on all aspects of planning, project objectives, data presentation, and dissemination.
- Open data sharing with Acadia First Nation, including submission of copies of all documentation pertaining to the excavations.
- Offering plain-language community presentations and site tours to transfer knowledge and provide a direct access to community members to their archaeological heritage.
- Building archaeological capacity and knowledge among Acadia First Nation youth through training and direct exposure to their archaeological past.

Collaboration with Acadia First Nation started tentatively but grew substantially as trust and capacity increased within the community. The first two seasons of survey, in 2008 and 2009, involved significant consultations, both on site and at band meetings at the Medway office. Here we discussed all aspects of the project and set common goals for excavation and dissemination of knowledge within the community. Public lectures were first held in 2009 at Medway, outlining the data obtained from the 2008 and ongoing 2009 field season. Plans were made at that time for a significant community archaeology project to coincide with fieldwork in 2010.

In consultation with Acadia First Nation, the 2010 season was designed with significant public and student participation as a primary goal. The objectives of the public archaeology portion of the project were: (1) to engage the community in the archaeological process, (2) to educate the public about the region's archaeological resources and (pre)history, (3) to receive community feedback on the project, and (4) to alert the public to the damage caused by unlicensed collecting and development. Highlights of the public archaeology program included:

- *AFN Cultural Day (July 4, 2010):* The project team was invited to participate in Acadia First Nation's cultural day, held at the Queens County Museum. Three project team members attended; artifacts and animal remains from recent excavations at AlDf-30, as well as computer slide shows of previous and current excavations, were displayed. Pamphlets were distributed describing the E'se'get Project and the public archaeology program, which was to begin the following week. Over 250 individuals visited the project booth, including local avocational archaeologists, band members, and residents of Queens County.
- *Public Archaeology Program (Fridays and Saturdays July 9 to July 31, 2010):* Local First Nation members, local residents, and tourists were invited to visit the excavations

Figure 1.6 Community members and park visitors at a guided tour of the excavations at AlDf-24.

at the AlDf-24 site. Groups of up to fifteen visitors were allowed on site during "scheduled" tours. A Department of Natural Resources employee guided visitors to the site and provided natural-history insights; on site, visitors were given an introduction to local archaeology and an in-depth tour of recent excavations, finds, and preliminary interpretations. The Public Archaeology Program was very successful, resulting in 192 total visitors (average 27.5 visitors per day), of which 128 (66.5 percent) were local residents and 64 (33.5 percent) were tourists or campers.

- *University of New Brunswick Archaeological Field School (July 5 to August 7, 2010):* Archaeological training was provided to six undergraduate and three graduate students from the University of New Brunswick. Under the supervision of Dr. Betts and Dr. Black, students were introduced to archaeological excavation methods and basic laboratory and cataloguing skills.
- *Acadia First Nation Student Program (July 18 to 23, 2010):* Seven Mi'kmaw high school students participated in the dig for five days. The students worked side-by-side with university students during the day, learning the process of archaeological investigation. They camped within Thomas Raddall Provincial Park and were introduced to camping skills and traditional activities in the evenings. They were supervised by two chaperones and a camp coordinator, hired from Acadia First Nation by the E'se'get Project.
- *Television and Radio Interviews (July 20 and 22, 2010:* The project was covered in a video interview presented on the Aboriginal People's Television Network (APTN)

Figure 1.7 The E'se'get Archaeology Project crew for the 2010 field season, including both UNB graduate and undergraduate students, Acadia First Nation high school students, Acadia First Nation Band members, and staff from the Mi'kmaq Rights Initiative.

nightly national news broadcast on July 20, and in an interview on CBC Radio Canada One Halifax on July 22.
- *Public Lectures (July 31, 2010, and May 28, 2011:* Public lectures were offered in Thomas Raddall Provincial Park on July 31, 2010, to present preliminary findings; a longer and more detailed interpretation of project findings was presented during a public lecture at the Queens County Museum on May 28, 2011. An overview of the project, including recent interpretations and findings, was also presented privately to members of Acadia First Nation on May 17, 2011—part of ongoing consultations with the band.
- *E'se'get Archaeology Project Blog (June 24 to August 7, 2010):* During the 2010 field season the project investigators and students maintained a blog in which anecdotes and reports of the fieldwork and project were recorded. The blog continued in 2012 and was so successful that it was awarded a national prize (see below). The blog can be accessed at: http://coastalarchaeology.wordpress.com/.
- *Site-Naming Exercise (July 22, 2010):* Many of the sites within Thomas Raddall Provincial Park are not named and are only distinguished by their Borden number. On July 22, 2010, students from the Acadia First Nation field school, accompanied by band members, chose Mi'kmaw names for three of the sites within Thomas Raddall Provincial Park. These names reflect the students' understanding of the prehistory of the sites, their geographic locations, and the students' personal experiences working on the sites. The names, listed below, were recommended to the Department of Tourism, Culture, and Heritage as candidates for official site names (translations kindly provided by Stephen Augustine, who was then Curator, Ethnology of the Eastern Maritimes, Canadian Museum of History):
  – AlDf-24 – Epte'jijg Utju'sn Gta'nogeway (Warm Breeze by the Ocean)
  – AlDf-30 – Su'ne'gati (Cranberry Patch)
  – AlDf-31 – Su'ne'gatij (Little Cranberry Patch)

In 2012, we continued our collaboration with Acadia First Nation and local communities. A public lecture was given at the Queens County Museum and work on the fieldwork blog continued, garnering more than ten thousand unique views in two months. In fact, in May 2013, the E'se'get Archaeology Project blog received the Canadian Archaeological Association's Public Outreach Award. Two Acadia First Nation archaeology days were held; youth and adult members from multiple communities were bused to Thomas Raddall Provincial Park, given a tour of AlDf-30, and provided an opportunity to view artifacts and ask questions. The day ended with a feast and discussion about the project.

Though excavation was completed in 2012, consultation and community outreach has continued and has intensified with the establishment of the Sipuke'l Gallery, Acadia First Nation's public cultural centre. Every year, public lectures arranged by Acadia First Nation have been given at the gallery, and site tours, also arranged by Acadia First Nation, have been conducted within Thomas Raddall Provincial Park. In 2013, project staff were honoured to be invited to a major cultural event hosted on June 21 (National Indigenous Peoples Day) by Acadia First Nation. The event, called Kespukwitk Celebrated: Ancient Mi'kmaw Culture Remerges, was a celebration of Mi'kmaw culture, art, and resilience. We were invited to present the archaeological knowledge we had unearthed together: there could have been no greater endorsement of the project.

Structure of the Book

This book represents our attempt at a type of archeological publishing that was common in the latter half of the twentieth century but which has largely fallen out of use in modern archaeological discourse. "Site monographs," or descriptive compilations of data and interpretations from an archaeological site or sites, were once the mainstay of archaeological publication. Culture historians needed voluminous primary data for seriation and classification, and descriptive reports were critical for placing sites and their assemblages within archaeological sequences, traditions, and "cultures." Unfortunately, the site monograph is a publication format that has largely been abandoned in modern archaeological practices.

With the dawn of "the New Archaeology" (Processual Archaeology) in the late 1960s, archaeologists started to require different types of data. Less interested in culture history, archaeologists stopped publishing complete summaries of sites and assemblages in favour of focusing on subsets of the data for targeted interpretations and reconstructions. The trend has continued as interpretative and theoretical paradigms wax and wane, and with them interest in different types of archaeological data. As a result, many sites have not been fully described, and indeed even subsets of the data are rarely published in full. We believe this practice is problematic and that the first, best, destiny of archaeological publication should be descriptive site reports filled with primary data.

Without detailed presentation and description of excavation methods, contextual data, stratigraphic profiles, radiocarbon dates, artifact descriptions, artifact plates or photos, and catalogues, it is very difficult to assess the validity of the original excavator's interpretations of sites and assemblages. Often, modern interpretations of excavations occur as short, general summaries in targeted methodological and theoretical papers. For some important sites and assemblages, these interpretations can become monolithic truths about the past, which can be perpetuated for generations with little scientific verification or falsification. Moreover, without primary data, conducting nuanced comparative analyses; developing broad databases and compilations; and constructing data-rich regional and extra-regional culture histories are extraordinarily difficult.

Finally, and perhaps most importantly for modern archaeological practice, primary data are also crucial for collaborative and capacity-building archaeology. Indigenous communities and Indigenous scholars and storytellers need to assimilate these data for their own purposes, whether for writing their own archaeological histories or as evidence to assert their rights and title. Providing these data in a format that Indigenous scholars can access and deploy should be a critical part of modern archaeological practice.

With these benefits in mind, this book presents a comprehensive description and interpretation of the results of the E'se'get Archaeology Project. It includes detailed site and contextual summaries; stratigraphic profiles and site photographs; summary artifact catalogues; detailed descriptions and basic analysis of artifact assemblages; and full-colour plates of artifacts. To provide a comprehensive assessment of the archaeology of Port Joli, it also includes a compilation of data from previous excavations by avocational archaeologists, including representative artifact plates from their excavations. Unfortunately, detailed analyses of these legacy collections were not possible for this book, nor would they be entirely appropriate. These sites were often excavated without detailed stratigraphic control or the use of fine-screening protocols, and while the site descriptions are very useful, the artifact assemblages are often difficult to assess given the lack of contextual information.

The analyses presented in this book tend to eschew theoretical and paradigmatic frameworks (other than that provided by the culture-historical paradigm), in favour of descriptive summaries and inductive reasoning. As suggested above, this is intentional; by removing the site monograph from such bias, we hope to create a work that will ultimately be serve as a detailed reference and compendium from which to draw data to make new inferences using whatever theoretical or methodological approach may be appropriate to the insights being sought.

This book includes nine chapters and reflects the collaborative and multidisciplinary nature of the E'se'get Archaeology Project. This first chapter presents an introduction to the E'se'get Archaeology Project. Chapter 2, written by Karen Neil and Konrad Gajewski, presents the environmental and climactic history of Port Joli, and crucially establishes the timing and development of Port Joli's harbour, which, as we shall see, is critical to understanding the timing and nature of the original Mi'kmaw occupation of the harbour.

Chapter 3, written by Matthew Betts, presents a detailed overview of the archaeological sites around the harbour of Port Joli, and presents a history of their exploration. This chapter is highly descriptive and includes site maps, profiles, and photographs of the sites. In short, it presents the critical contextual data necessary to understand Port Joli's archaeological history. Chapter 4, again written by Betts, presents a chronological model for the occupation of Port Joli's harbour and the archaeological deposits in the harbour. Based on radiometric dates obtained by the E'se'get Archaeology Project and those from previous work, as well as a typological consideration of certain artifact types and classes, the chapter builds a framework for understanding temporal shifts in Mi'kmaw lifeways within the harbour.

A major focus of the E'se'get Project was the careful and detailed excavation of dwelling floors and other structures. Chapter 5, written by Gabriel Hrynick and Matthew Betts, presents a detailed review of the architectural deposits unearthed in the harbour and explores how Port Joli's inhabitants organized their domestic lives, from a spatial perspective.

Ceramics represent a very large proportion of the artifacts recovered during the E'se'get Project. Chapter 6, authored by Jenneth Curtis, Erin Ingram, and Matthew Betts, exhaustively documents the ceramic tradition in Port Joli. This attribute-based analysis carefully considers variability over time and compares this ceramic variability to sites in the greater Maritime Peninsula region. Chapter 7 presents a detailed description of lithic and other artifacts recovered during the E'se'get Project, and includes artifact plates from legacy collections excavated by Erskine, Millard, and others. Authored by Matthew Betts and Kenneth Holyoke, the chapter focuses specific attention on describing the lithic artifacts from the E'se'get Project, including metric analyses.

Chapter 8, written by Matthew Betts, presents a detailed analysis of the floral and faunal remains recovered during the project. These data are critical for developing a model of procurement and consumption practices in Port Joli, and indeed are the first time a detailed and comprehensive modern floral and faunal analysis has been conducted on a Nova Scotia shell midden.

The final chapter in the volume, Chapter 9, collates all the data acquired during the E'se'get Project and from earlier researchers, and attempts to construct a culture history of ancient Mi'kmaw lifeways in Port Joli. Honouring a commitment with Acadia First Nation, the chapter is intended as a plain-language summary of the archaeological history of the harbour, which can be shared and used by members of that community to develop their own understandings of the past. At the same time, it attempts to explore the archaeological concept of "place-making," and how, over the course of 1500 years, the Mi'kmaq created a special place they called Emsik, while, in turn, this special place was also creating their unique culture.

Chapter 2
Palaeoenvironmental Context

KAREN NEIL AND KONRAD GAJEWSKI

Introduction

Several factors must be considered when interpreting the environmental history of southwestern Nova Scotia during the mid- to late-Holocene, including sea level changes, climate variability, and changes in vegetation composition. For instance, as a result of a general rise in sea level of roughly 27 m between 7000 cal BP to present, the harbour coastline of Port Joli evolved significantly through time before reaching its current state. This is an important factor to consider when studying maritime cultures that inhabited the Atlantic coast of Nova Scotia, as their dependence on coastal ecosystems would have made them vulnerable to sea level changes. Additionally, shifts in vegetation associated with climate changes (e.g., changes in moisture, temperature, severity of weather conditions), including high-frequency climate variations during the late-Holocene neoglacial cooling (the last around 3000 cal BP), aligned with culturally significant periods of human occupation in Nova Scotia. Vegetation succession and climate in the Holocene is often studied at millennial, century, and decadal time scales by conducting high-resolution palaeoecological studies, which can provide insights into how humans occupying specific regions may have interacted with their environment.

Site Description

The Canadian Appalachian orogen extends from Newfoundland through Nova Scotia to Quebec (Goodwin 2008). The Meguma terrrane, comprised of Cambrian-Ordovician sediments, covers the majority of southwestern Nova Scotia (MacDonald et al. 1992). Port Joli's harbour, however, is located within a small area of younger Devonian-Carboniferous granitoid rocks (MacDonald et al. 1992). Most surficial deposits surrounding Port Joli's harbour are fine- to coarse-grained sediments, and clay- to silt-sized sediments are more highly represented than sand-sized sediments (Miller 2004). These deposits are thought to have been transported from the Scotian Shelf off the Atlantic coast as a result of sea level rise during the Holocene (Miller 2004). Historical records from the region surrounding Port Joli's harbour describe the terrain as rocky and unsuitable for agriculture, conditions which would allow for more tolerant vegetation types such as spruce and berries (Jost 2009). In southwestern Nova Scotia, soils tend to be fairly acidic due to podsolization as they are heavily influenced by moist and humid climates (Wilson 2011). Wetlands and peatlands are therefore abundant along the Atlantic coast and upland regions and also contribute to the formation of acidic soil conditions. Pre-European-era forests in Nova Scotia are not thought to have had frequent disturbances (natural or anthropogenic) and were therefore classified as late successional (Mosseler et al. 2003). Before European settlement, 60 to 85 percent of the forest composition in northeastern North America was represented by old-growth stands (Thurston 2011). Today, the forests of Nova Scotia are principally characterized as early successional, where fewer than 1 to 5 percent of the trees are older than one hundred years (Mosseler et al. 2003).

The Atlantic Maritime provinces are classified in the Acadian Forest Region (AFR; Rowe 1972). The high abundance of red spruce (*Picea rubens*) is one of the most distinguishing features of the AFR, as this shade-tolerant species thrives in moist conditions (Mosseler et al. 2003). Associated species in this forest type include balsam fir (*Abies balsamea*), eastern hemlock (*Tsuga canadensis*), eastern white pine (*Pinus strobus*), yellow birch (*Betula alleghaniensis*), sugar maple (*Acer saccharum*), and American beech (*Fagus grandifolia*) (Mosseler et al. 2003). The AFR is further subdivided into ecoregions, where Port Joli's harbour is characterized as part of the Atlantic Shore Ecoregion, with a forest type described as Acadian-Boreal Coastal. White spruce (*Picea glauca*) is common here, as it is well adapted to survival in coastal regions where salt spray can affect plant growth (Thurston and Barrett 2011). White spruce is also an important successional species in tracts of abandoned farmlands (Mosseler et al. 2003). Eastern white pine is more abundant in areas with sandy outwash soils, and northern white cedar (*Thuja occidentalis*) and red maple (*Acer rubrum*) are commonly found in swampy areas (Mott 1974).

Path Lake (43°87'00" N, 64°92'42" W, 10 m ASL) was chosen as the principal site for a palynological study spanning the past approximately nine thousand years of the Holocene (Neil et al. 2014); the lake is located northwest of Port Joli's harbour, approximately 600 m from the shoreline. The lake (approx. 25 ha) is easily accessible from the east by Port L'Hebert Road, south of Nova Scotia Highway 103. A small spring feeds into the lake from the northwest corner, and an exit channel flows toward the ocean from the eastern side of the lake. A 4.16 m sediment sequence recovered from Path Lake was used to develop a regional-scale reconstruction of vegetation and climate, which showed how the AFR of southwestern Nova Scotia evolved over the course of the Holocene.

Multiple sediment cores were also taken from a local fen (43°84'87" N, 64°89'02" W, 5 m ASL) near Port Joli's harbour, and one core (44 cm recovery) was chosen for further pollen analysis. The core site is located in close proximity to the AlDf-30 archaeological dig site, found in the Thomas Raddall Provincial Park. The centre of the fen at the coring location was densely covered in tall ferns and small shrubs (red maple), and the outer edge was forested (spruce, alder [*Alnus*], maple). The high plant diversity and productivity, as well as the presence of a small stream surrounding the base of a knoll, led to its classification as a fen-type ecosystem. The primary characteristics of a fen include an accumulation of peat; a water table near the vegetation surface; and a diverse vegetation community comprised of a combination of ferns, sedges, mosses, graminoids, and shrubs (Warner and Rubec 1997). At the core site, a decomposed peat accumulation was overlain by a mat of unconsolidated *Sphagnum* moss.

Climate of the Holocene in Southwestern Nova Scotia

Following the maximum of the Pleistocene glaciation and prior to the current interglacial (the Holocene), there was a global transition period during which the climate was generally warming (late glacial; 14,000–10,000 cal BP). Nova Scotia is located near the edge of the former Laurentide Ice Sheet margin, and deglaciation patterns for the region during this period have been closely examined (Mayle and Cwynar 1995; Scott et al. 1995). Separation and subsequent deglaciation of the ice sheet toward local centres (such as South Mountain, southwest Nova Scotia) and away from the coast occurred prior to 12,000 cal BP (Mayle and Cwynar 1995; Mott et al. 2009; Stea and Mott 1989). However, during this period of warming, the well-known Younger Dryas chronozone (12,900–11,600 cal BP) represents a major reversion to cooler conditions that affected many regions across Nova Scotia (Mayle and Cwynar 1995; Mott and Stea 1993). Another notable climate variation of the early Holocene is the so-called "8200 cal BP event," which was recorded in several lakes in Nova Scotia and represents a global cooling of 4°C (Lennox et al. 2010). The "8200 cal BP event" is thought to be related to a large influx of freshwater into the North Atlantic during the collapse of the Laurentide Ice Sheet (Lennox et al. 2010; Spooner et al. 2002).

The period between 8100 and 3500 cal BP is described as the warmest portion of the Holocene (Lennox et al. 2010) in eastern North America. Palaeoclimate reconstructions from freshwater lakes near the Atlantic coast of Nova Scotia at this time show little variance in mean July temperature; for example, Port Joli's harbour averaged 18.5±1.0°C, and Penhorn Lake near Halifax averaged 20±0.5°C (McCarthy et al. 1995). At around 3000 cal BP, palaeo-records show a transition to relatively wet and cool conditions in Nova Scotia (Lennox et al. 2010; Ogden 1986; Railton 1973). Mean July temperatures show a decrease of over 1°C in Nova Scotia and Newfoundland by 1500 cal BP, and this regional cooling is associated with increased precipitation (McCarthy et al. 1995). Superimposed on these broad-scale changes are higher frequency climate variations, the latest of which is a cool period termed the Little Ice Age, which occurred across North America between 600 and 100 cal BP (Wanner et al. 2008).

Holocene Sea-Level Fluctuations in Southwestern Nova Scotia

Relative sea level changes in Nova Scotia during the Holocene are due to a combination of postglacial isostatic adjustments (Edgecombe et al. 1999), regional crustal subsidence, and local sea level rise (Forbes et al. 2009). Using seismic reflection and foraminiferal analysis, Edgecombe et al. (1999) interpreted an emergence of Halifax Harbour from 8400 to 7000 cal BP as sea level dropped, followed by the continuous submergence of the harbour from 7000 cal BP to present. The most recent rate of sea level rise in Nova Scotia is approximately 0.3 cm per year (Scott et al.1995), and future projections for Halifax Harbour estimate a sea level rise of 73 to 130 cm between the years 2000 and 2100 (Forbes et al. 2009).

A locally reconstructed sea level curve for Port Joli's harbour only includes data after 7000 cal BP (figure 2.3); at the earliest point in this curve, sea level was approximately 27 m lower than the present mean sea level. Between 7000 and 3500 cal BP, sea level rose almost 19 m at a relatively rapid rate of 0.54 cm per year. For the second half of the record, from 3500 cal BP to present, sea level only rose by 8 m, at a rate of 0.23 cm per year. Using the reconstructed Holocene sea level curve and the bathymetric map of Port Joli's harbour, the evolution of the coastline can be shown across multiple points in time (figure 2.1). Prior to 3750 cal BP, the coastline was relatively smooth, indicating that the harbour had not yet formed. Only after 3000 cal BP did the coastline begin to show a slight indentation, signalling natural harbour formation. At 1750 cal BP, sea level would have been approximately

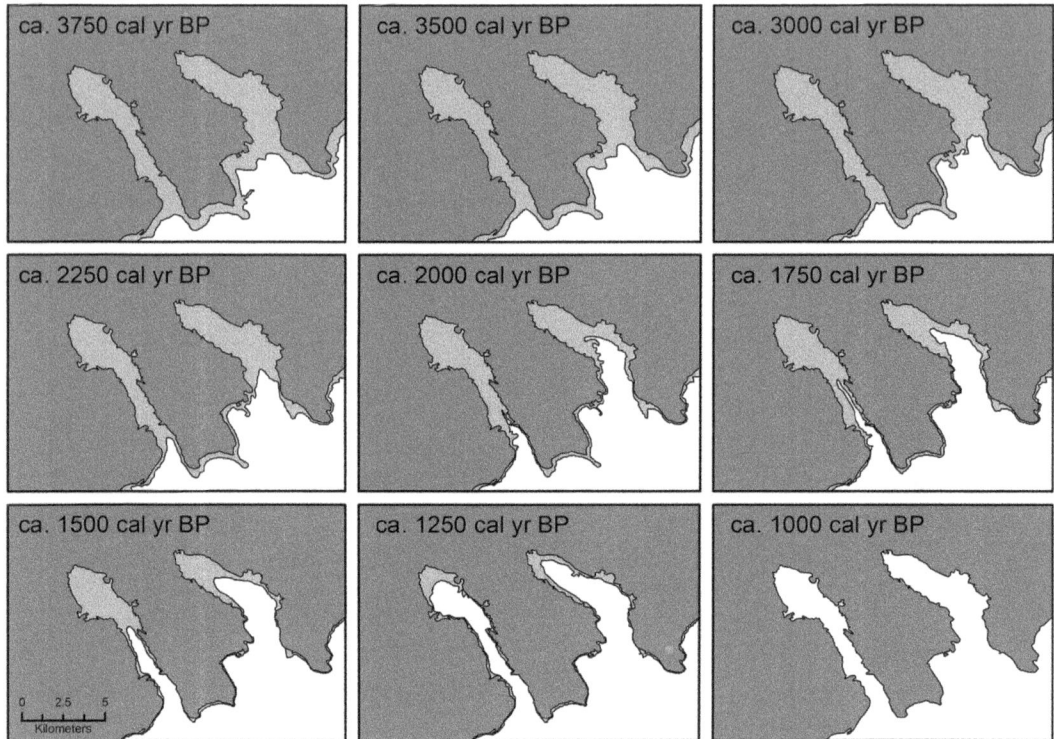

Figure 2.1 Port Joli's harbour: Evolution of the coastline, based on bathymetry data and a reconstructed sea level curve of the region. Data indicates that the present-day coastline was reached around 1000 cal BP.

1.3 m lower than the present mean sea level, at which point the harbour had progressed almost 4 km inland. For the following 750 years it became gradually wider, and by 1000 cal BP Port Joli's harbour had roughly the same shape as present. Currently, the mouth of the harbour is approximately 7 m deep and becomes progressively shallower moving inland.

History of Southwestern Nova Scotia during the Holocene
Regional Environmental Setting

The boundary between forest and tundra was located in the Maritime provinces during the late glacial period; vegetation near this transition zone was highly responsive to climatic conditions, which changed greatly over relatively short distances (Mayle and Cwynar 1995). The abrupt change to a cooler and wetter climate in the Younger Dryas caused the vegetation in Nova Scotia to shift from predominantly boreal forest or woodland (spruce, pine, larch, fir, and birch) to shrub tundra and herbaceous tundra (Levesque et al. 1994; Mott and Stea 1993). Tree species re-colonized at the end of the Younger Dryas when climatic conditions were similar to those of the present, and most of Atlantic Canada was then dominated by a spruce-birch forest (Anderson 1985; Lennox et al. 2010; Mott and Stea 1993; Serreze and Barry 2005). In southwestern Nova Scotia, spruce populations were slowly declining and the abundance of hardwood taxa, such as birch (*Betula*), ironwood (*Ostrya*), hornbean (*Carpinus*), oak (*Quercus*), and elm (*Ulmus*), increased in response to slight improvements in climatic conditions (Miller 2004).

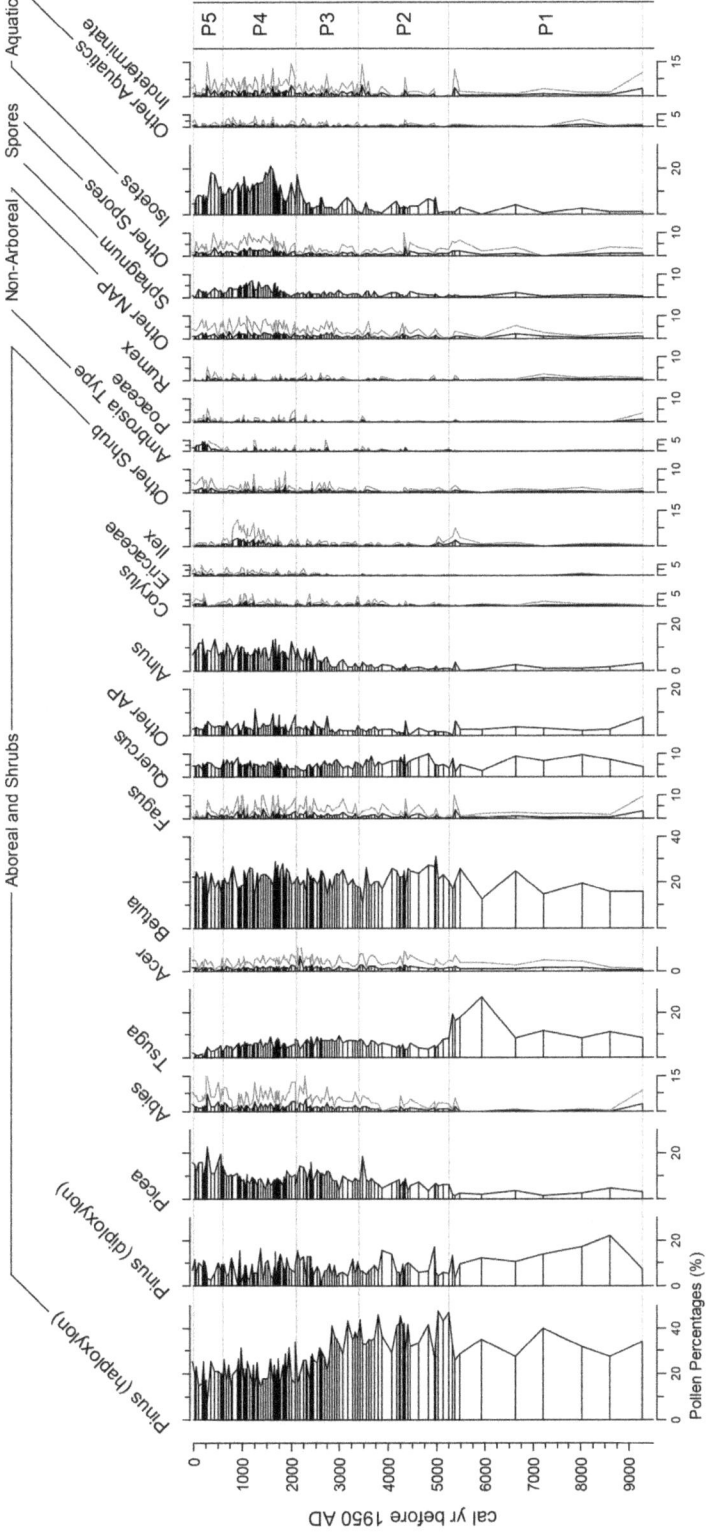

Figure 2.2 Palaeoenvironmental record from Path Lake, Port Joli, Nova Scotia. Pollen percentages of the major taxa are shown, and a 3x exaggeration is applied to taxa representing a smaller portion of the total pollen record.

Based on the interpolated ages of six calibrated carbon-14 dates, the basal date of a sediment core retrieved from Path Lake was determined to be just over 9600 cal BP. The earliest samples from Path Lake analyzed for pollen therefore correspond to post–Younger Dryas climate conditions, when cold-adapted species such as spruce (*Picea*) and fir (*Abies*) were relatively low in abundance (figure 2.2). The region surrounding Port Joli's harbour at this time instead had high amounts of pine (*Pinus*)—including soft pines (*haploxylon*), like white pine, and hard pines (*diploxylon*), like red pine, as well as hemlock (*Tsuga*), birch, and oak (*Quercus*). At around 8800 cal BP in Nova Scotia, white pine (*Pinus strobus*) began to increase in abundance, and by 7500 cal BP it had outcompeted spruce to become the dominant species in Atlantic Canada (Anderson 1985). In the Path Lake record, pine already represented a larger portion of the total pollen sum than spruce near the base of the record (approx. 9500 cal BP), although pine is often overrepresented in fossil assemblages due to the large amounts of pollen produced and the efficient transport of these grains by the wind.

An increase and subsequent decline in hemlock pollen has been comprehensively studied in Nova Scotia (Green 1987; Lennox et al. 2010; Mott 1974; Mott and Stea 1993; Mott et al. 2009; Ogden 1986). In the Path Lake record, hemlock declined between 6000–5000 cal BP, which is consistent with pollen records from other lakes in Nova Scotia. The decline is thought to have been the result of a pathogen attack (Davis 1981), but more recently it has been suggested that drought may have been a contributing factor (Haas and McAndrews 2000). A gradual re-colonization of spruce and fir occurred following the decline of hemlock at Path Lake (at 5250 cal BP), indicating a response to a shift toward moister climatic conditions (Green 1987).

A more prominent transition to a cooler and wetter climate regime began in southwestern Nova Scotia between 3400 and 3000 cal BP (Lennox et al. 2010; Railton 1973). Mid-Holocene climate change and sea level rise have been shown to impact ecological succession by influencing groundwater levels, specifically in southwestern Nova Scotia (Martin et al. 2005). Increased annual precipitation (reconstructed from the Path Lake pollen record) and/or local sea level rise were therefore likely to have resulted in a higher local water table than previously (figure 2.3). The higher local water table favoured an increased abundance of quillwort (*Isoetes*) within Path Lake, as well as species common to wetland development in the area immediately surrounding the lake, such as moss (*Sphagnum*) and alder (*Alnus*). Based on the combined sea level curve and bathymetric data from Port Joli's harbour, it was determined that formation of the harbour only occurred after 3000 cal BP.

The shrub gallberry (*Ilex*) was relatively absent from the Path Lake pollen record before it suddenly appeared around 1700 cal BP, and declined just as suddenly around 900 cal BP. Gallberry is an understorey shrub that responds quickly and prolifically to fire disturbances. During the time when gallberry first appeared, charcoal accumulation rates in the Path Lake record showed small peaks that coincided with culturally significant periods (the Middle Maritime Woodland Period from 1630–1380 cal BP, and the later Late Maritime Woodland Period from 850–660 cal BP). These periods were also reflected as increases in the frequency of cultural radiocarbon dates in coastal Nova Scotia and Port Joli's harbour (figure 2.3), following the assumption that larger populations would have produced more archaeological sites and thus more dated contexts (Rick 1987; Munoz and Gajewski 2010; Peros et al. 2010; Neil et al. 2014).

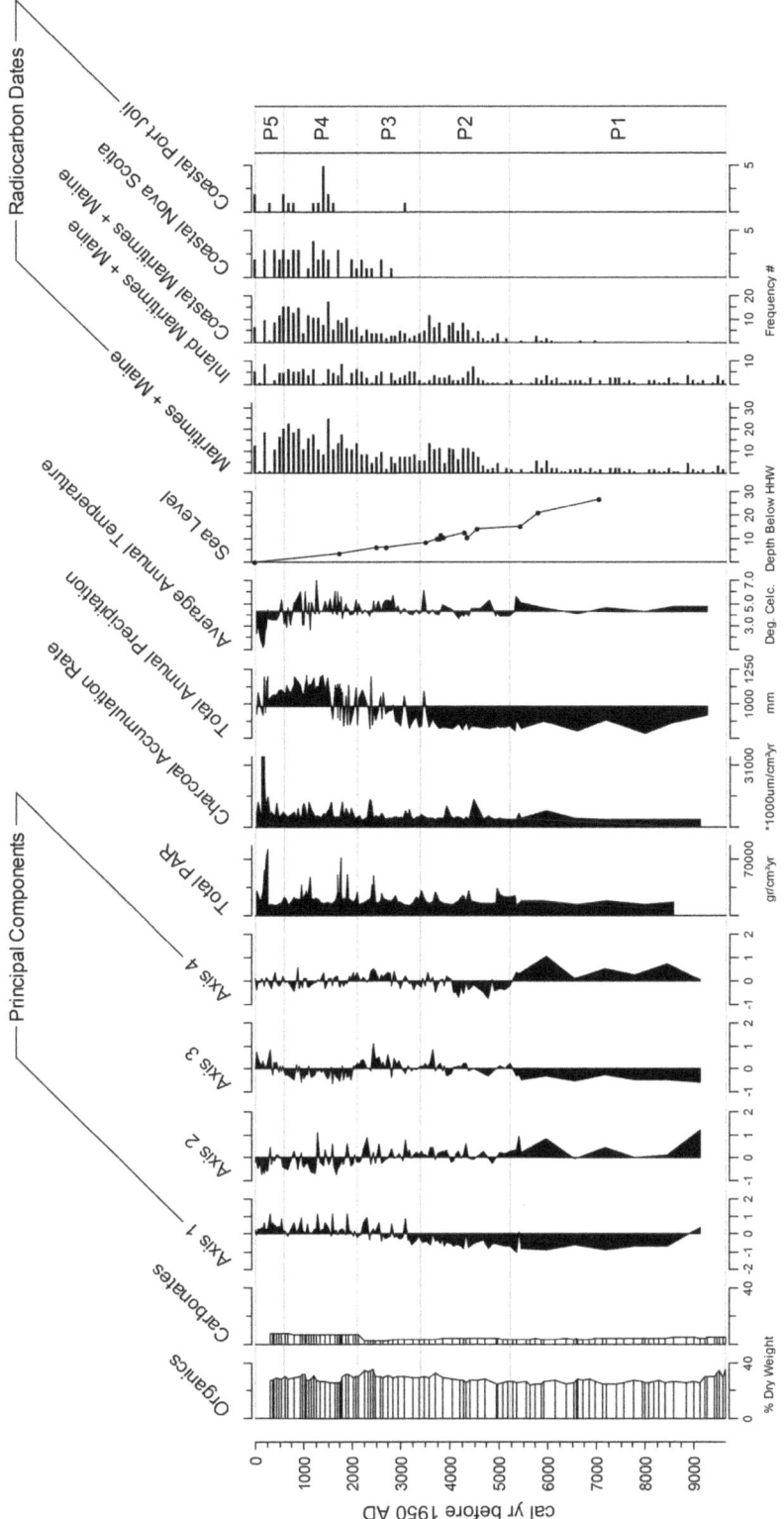

Figure 2.3 Port Joli region, Nova Scotia: Palaeoenvironmental summary including Path Lake organic and carbonate content, principal components of the pollen assemblages, pollen and charcoal accumulation rates, palaeoclimate reconstructions, sea level (Edgecombe et al. 1999; Ogden 1986; Scott et al. 1995), and archaeological radiocarbon dates.
Note: Archaeological frequency distributions of carbon-14 dates are interpreted as representing palaeodemographic levels. The carbon-14 dates were obtained from the Canadian Archaeological Record Database (http://www.canadianarchaeology.ca), to which were added dates from the present study.

During the Little Ice Age (600–100 cal BP; Wanner et al. 2008), cooling intensified, allowing spruce-fir forests (Loucks 1962) to spread from the Atlantic coast landwards toward the upland regions (Miller 2004). The Path Lake record shows this as an increase in spruce and fir, which led to a significant decrease in the average annual temperature reconstruction by almost 4°C (figure 2.3), starting at 600 cal BP. Other well-known climatic shifts during the Holocene, however, such as the Medieval Warm period, are not captured in the reconstructed temperatures before 600 cal BP. Reconstructed total average annual precipitation for Path Lake shows a general trend consistent with other palaeoclimate records from the region (Green 1987; Lennox et al. 2010; Railton 1973; Ogden 1986). As Path Lake is located in close proximity to the Atlantic coast, it is perhaps more reasonable to believe that fossil pollen assemblages from this site are representative of an ecosystem primarily driven by moisture rather than temperature. This could explain why the zonation of the Path Lake stratigraphic sequence (figures 2.2 and 2.3) is more clearly related to the division between dry, transitional, and wet climate regimes.

European settlement of Nova Scotia and subsequent clearance of lands occurred between 350 and 200 cal BP (Levac 2001). This is indicated by an increase in the pollen of asters (Compositae family), grasses (Poaceae family), dock (*Rumex*), and ragweed (*Ambrosia*) (Levac 2001) and decreasing relative abundances of larch (*Larix*), hemlock, and beech (*Fagus*) (Miller 2004). The rise in ragweed, which is one of the most commonly used indicators of European settlement in palaeo-records, is dated at roughly 350 cal BP in Path Lake. This is slightly early when compared with historical records from the region, as we would expect to see a small lag between settlement and associated environmental changes. However, dating in the uppermost sediment of a core is difficult due to compaction, which may introduce a certain degree of error. The amount of micro-charcoal observed on the pollen slides of Path Lake is indicative of the size and frequency of regional fire disturbances in the past. Charcoal influx in the Path Lake record showed a peak that was thirteen times greater than the average for the Holocene between 180–160 cal BP, and could be a strong indication of the use of fire to clear forests following initial European contact.

Local Archaeological Setting

The base of a core retrieved from a fen near Port Joli's harbour consisted of finely grained, light grey, sandy clay, indicating a complete record of sediment accumulation was recovered; however, the uppermost section of the core was not completely intact as the sediment was too unconsolidated to collect. A basal date of roughly 7000 cal BP was obtained for this sedimentary sequence, and samples from the core were analyzed for pollen. The early record from 7000–3000 cal BP shows high pollen percentages of aquatic species (e.g., quillwort), fern, and fern allies (*Osmunda, Dryopteris*), as well as *Sphagnum* mosses (figure 2.4; zone F1), indicative of a shallow pond with abundant macrophytes and wetlands around the shoreline. Vegetation communities comprising mosses, heath (Ericaceae), and sedges (Cyperaceae) are more characteristic of a minerotrophic "poor fen" (Muller et al. 2003), and their high relative abundances in the early record could suggest that this site was in a transitional stage from a pond to a fen or bog environment. This type of hydroseral succession may have been initiated by a cooler and wetter climate as shown in the Path Lake record (figure 2.3), resulting in a gradual infilling of sediments and organic

Palaeoenvironmental Context **29**

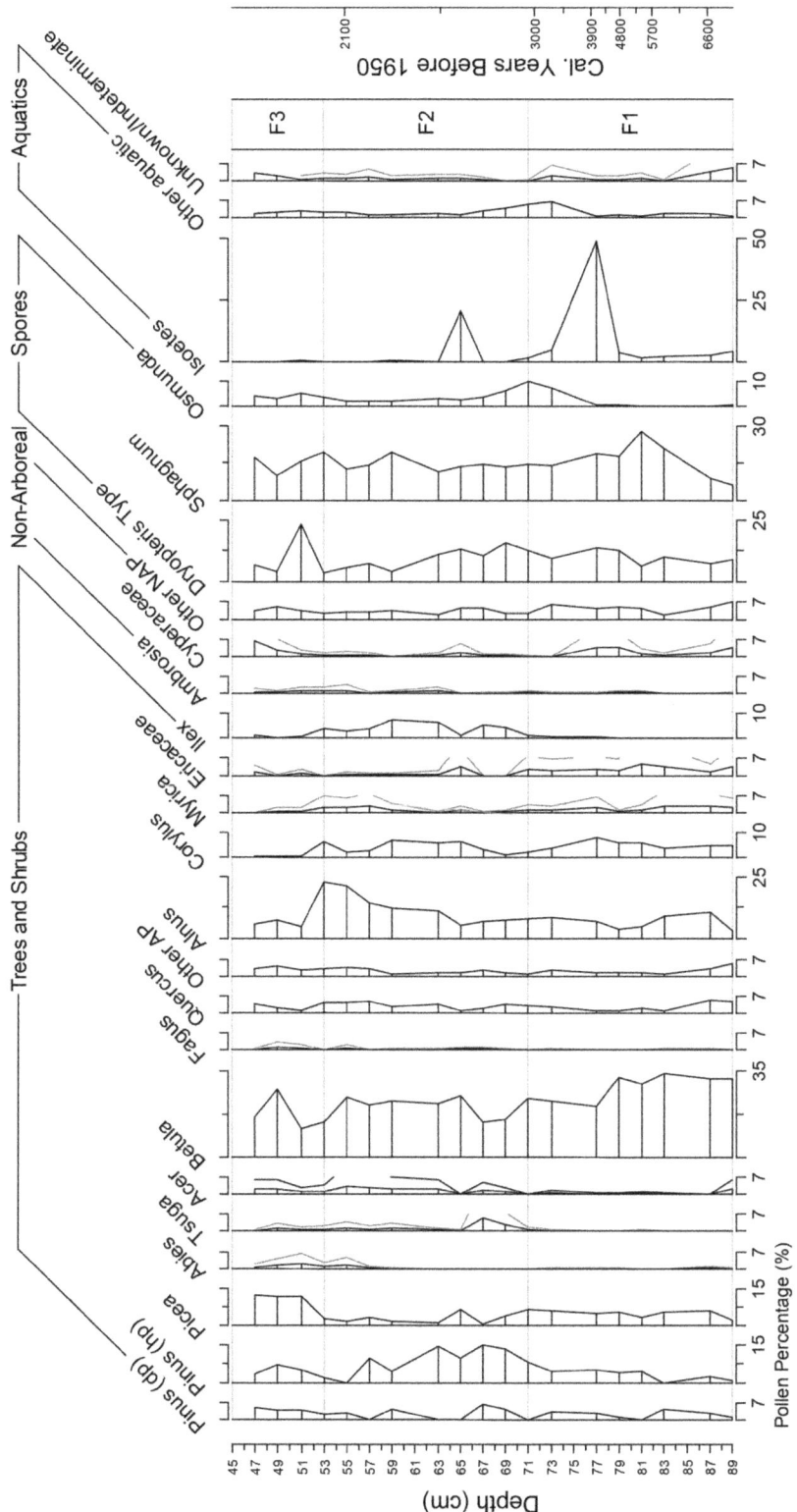

Figure 2.4 The fen surrounding AlDf-30, Port Joli, Nova Scotia: Pollen-percentage diagram. Only major taxa are shown, and a 3× exaggeration is applied to taxa representing a smaller portion of the total pollen record.

matter within the basin until a more mature vegetation community was able to develop (Wetzel 2001).

Organic content of the sediments did increase rapidly in the record after 3000 cal BP (figure 2.5; zone F2), suggesting that this was an important stage in the progression from open water to a fen-type environment. An increase in gallberry (*Ilex*) and relatively high values of fern spores at this time (figure 2.4) reflected vegetation changes typically associated with fen succession as well. In drier fens where the water table is lower than the vegetation surface, shrubs and small trees tend to be more prominent features of the ecosystem (Warner and Rubec 1997). For instance, an increase in the relative abundance of maple (*Acer*) after 3000 cal BP indicated the establishment of red maple stands within and along the periphery of the site. Between 3000 and 2000 cal BP, high abundances of other shrub taxa, such as alder (*Alnus*), hazel (*Corylus*), sweet gale (*Myrica*), and gallberry, as well as pine (*Pinus*), perhaps indicated a more developed vegetation community surrounded by minimal standing water. Some of the pollen, particularly that of pine, may have originated from upland trees; however, increases in organic content, as well as pollen and charcoal concentrations after 3000 cal BP, signalled significant changes in ecosystem productivity that were likely related to hydroseral succession.

After 2000 cal BP, pollen percentages of most arboreal species had increased at the site (figure 2.4; zone F3), such as that of spruce (*Picea*) and birch (*Betula*). Wooded and/or forested fens are generally dominated by a combination of black spruce (*Picea mariana*), larch (*Larix*), birch, and willow (*Salix*) (Fraser and Keddy 2005), which was consistent with the vegetation composition seen in the uppermost zone of the site. Total charcoal concentration in this zone was mainly comprised of larger-sized particles, suggesting a local fire source (Ohlson and Tryterud 2000). Increased abundances of arboreal and shrub species, and the somewhat drier conditions of the site relative to earlier successional stages (e.g., swamps or marshes) could explain an increase in local fire disturbances (Kuhry 1994).

Martin et al. (2005) completed a palaeoenvironmental study of the Pleasant River fen ecosystem in central southwestern Nova Scotia to determine the effects of climate change on wetlands, and their study showed similarities to the Port Joli site described above. The evolution of the Pleasant River fen was characterized by succession from a productive shallow lake before 8600 cal BP to an acidic, wooded fen after 1700 cal BP (Martin et al. 2005). At roughly 3000 cal BP, the regional transition to cooler and moister climatic conditions (Lennox et al. 2010; Railton 1973) was reflected in the Pleasant River fen sediments by increased clastic inputs and changes in the pollen assemblages (Martin et al. 2005). Similarities in the timing and direction of change between both sites ultimately show that environmental responses to wetter mid-Holocene conditions (after 3000 cal BP) were widespread in Nova Scotia and were recorded in both coastal and inland sites.

Summary

Climate and sea level changes affected the vegetation of the Port Joli region over the course of the Holocene. After around 3000 cal BP, increases in effective soil moisture and/or precipitation seemed to have the greatest influence on the environment at both regional and local scales, presumably driven in part by Holocene sea level rise. Alder (*Alnus*), mosses (*Sphagnum*), and quillwort (*Isoetes*) are commonly associated with wetland-type

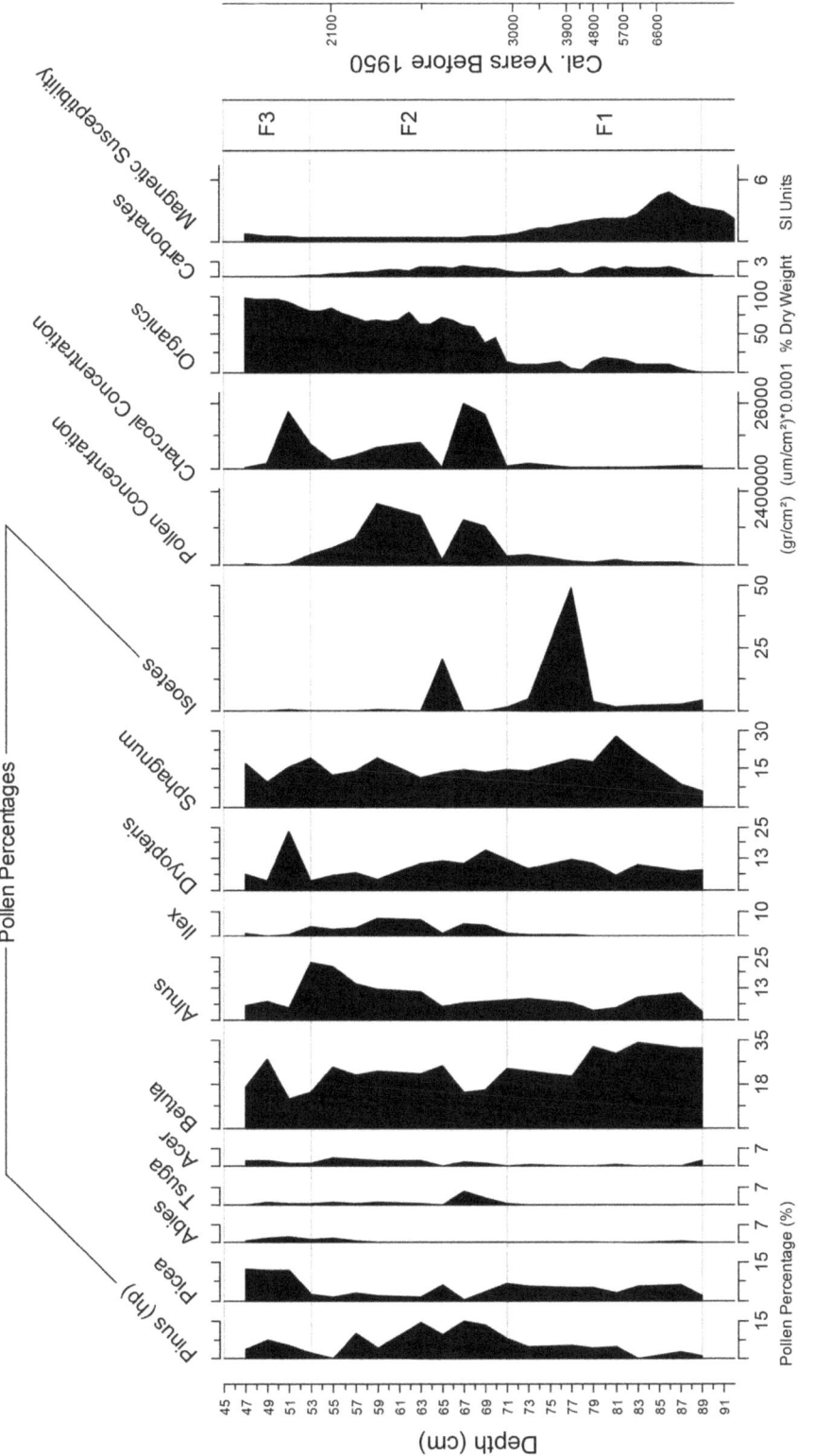

Figure 2.5 The fen surrounding AlDf-30, Port Joli, Nova Scotia: Palaeoenvironmental summary, including pollen percentages, pollen and charcoal concentration, organic and carbonate content, and magnetic susceptibility.

environments; changes in the abundances of these taxa at Path Lake and the more localized fen site tracked the initial transition toward wetter conditions after around 3000 cal BP, the timing of which is consistent with results from other multi-proxy records in the region (Lennox et al. 2010; Railton 1973).

Reconstructed total annual precipitation was consistently above average for the Holocene after 2000 cal BP, and coincided with culturally significant periods in coastal Nova Scotia. Prior to European contact at around 350 cal BP, as indicated by a rise in ragweed (*Ambrosia*) pollen, there was little evidence to suggest that human activity significantly altered the forests near Port Joli's harbour. However, after initial European settlement had occurred, a large influx of micro-charcoal in the Path Lake record suggests the use of fire to clear forests for agriculture.

Chapter 3
The Sites

MATTHEW BETTS

Introduction

Eighteen ancient Mi'kmaw archaeological sites have been discovered in more than sixty years of avocational and professional archaeology around Port Joli's harbour.[1] Such a remarkable number of prehistoric sites, spanning a coastline that stretches only 11 linear km (and representing an area less than 20 km^2), is unique in the province of Nova Scotia. This chapter presents a description and overview of the prehistoric sites in the harbour, including a history of their archaeological scrutiny. The review only documents prehistoric and early historic Mi'kmaw deposits and excludes the abundant Euro-Canadian deposit around the harbour.

The Mi'kmaw archaeological sites in Port Joli have been subjected to wildly different levels of scrutiny, with vastly different methodologies, over the past half century. In all cases we attempt to describe the nature of the deposit, including stratigraphic information whenever possible. We attempt to summarize spatial (vertical and horizontal) patterning at the sites, and we provide a brief interpretation of the behaviours that may have resulted in the deposit. This review proceeds geographically, beginning with a site at the head of the harbour, and moving in sequence southward along the eastern harbour shore of Port Joli. We then return to the head of the harbour and again proceed in sequence, site by site, southward along the western harbour shore of Port Joli.

More archaeological sites are known, and have been excavated, from the western shore of the harbour than the eastern shore (figure 3.1). Both sides of the harbour have relatively equally productive clam flats and topographic features, as well as access to streams and small lakes or ponds. Therefore, the distribution is likely more a result of taphonomic processes and related site accessibility than due to a real settlement bias. The eastern shore of the harbour has experienced substantially more private development than the western shore, which has likely obscured or destroyed archaeological sites. Furthermore, limited access to these private properties has resulted in fewer surveys of the eastern coastline. Erosion is also much more prevalent on the wave-exposed eastern shore, and, as will be documented below, this has substantially destroyed evidence of archaeological sites. Finally, large portions of the western shore have been protected by provincial parks, Nature

---

1. Currently, twenty-five Borden numbers have been registered for Port Joli's harbour. As will be described below, multiple Borden numbers have been assigned to the same sites over the course of many years of research by multiple archaeologists. Early archaeologists often did not keep detailed maps or descriptions of site locations, and, prudently, new Borden numbers were assigned in cases where potential ambiguity existed in identifying a formerly discovered site. The present monograph conflates many of these sites for the first time.

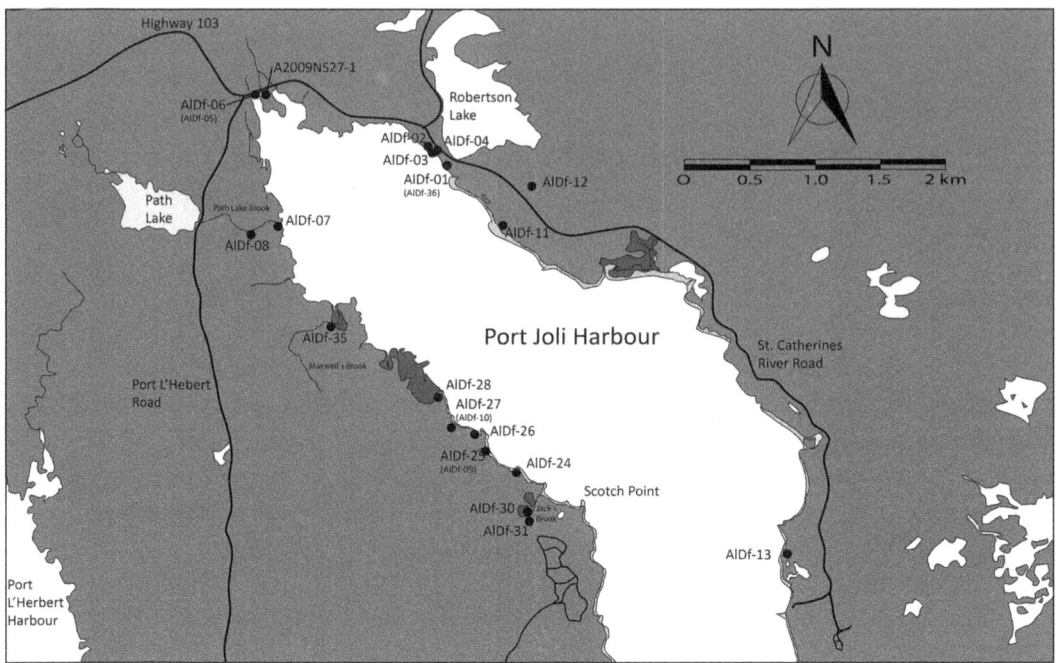

Figure 3.1 Distribution of prehistoric archaeological sites around Port Joli's harbour.

Conservancy of Canada lands, and Canadian Wildlife Service properties. While these organizations protect sites from development, they also permit greater access to researchers, hence increasing site visibility.

Terminology is critical to the description of these sites, and we utilize the nomenclature formalized by Black (2002) throughout this volume. We differentiate between deposits that are shell-bearing, wherein soil matrix is greater than 50 percent of the deposit matrix by volume, and shell middens, where shell matrix is greater than 50 percent of the deposit matrix by volume. In Port Joli, shell-bearing deposits can often be characterized as "black soil" middens (e.g., Black 2002), or highly organic deposits, which often contain high quantities of highly comminuted charcoal and broken or crushed shell admixtures. These deposits are often associated with dwelling surfaces and other defined features, typically hearths or processing structures. Because of this, they tend to contain high frequencies of lithic and ceramic artifacts, though this is not always the case, especially in late pre-contact or early contact deposits. Bone preservation in black soil middens can be excellent if shell is present or very poor if shell is absent or present in low quantities. The presence of high quantities of shell above or below black soil deposits can also contribute to good organic preservation in black soil middens. Just as in Passamaquoddy Bay, black soil middens around Port Joli's harbour can appear to have little internal stratification (e.g., Black 2002: 312), though strata can be defined by careful observation of changes in the density and completeness of shell valves, the frequency and nature of artifacts, the texture of soil, the frequency and presence of comminuted charcoal, and the presence of interdigitated house floors and/or shell middens.

Shell midden deposits, in contrast, are commonly characterized by very high proportions of shell when compared to soil (by volume). The soil matrix in shell middens is often the same as it is in black soil middens and is typically a highly organic dark black or very dark brown-grey loam. However, the quantity of comminuted charcoal is often diminished in shell middens when compared to black soil middens, and charcoal fragments tend to be larger and spatially localized in shell middens. Artifact frequencies are comparatively lower in shell middens when compared to shell-bearing deposits, and often ceramic fragments tend to be the dominant artifact type. Lithics are present but are relatively rare and are generally restricted to formal tools and large utilized flakes, as compared to high concentrations of formal lithic tools and debitage in shell-bearing black soil deposits. Because of the high quantity of shell, shell middens tend to have excellent organic preservation. Like the black soil middens, stratification is often difficult to discern in true shell middens. However, distinct strata can be ascertained through scrutiny of the frequency of artifacts or artifact types, the preservation of shell valves (e.g., complete, coarsely broken, or crushed), and especially the proportion of associated soil matrix. In Port Joli, we have observed that shell midden deposits often do not have internal or interdigitated features or house floors within them, a trait that stands in contrast to Passamaquoddy Bay (e.g., Black 2002: 308).

Shell midden deposits also appear to occur in two distinct types. The first is a classic "kitchen midden," (*køkkenmødding*), which tends to be thin, less than 50 cm deep, and often quite small, less than 150 m^2 in area. These smaller middens often contain broken shell and higher proportions of soil matrix and are often contiguous with, and sometimes interdigitated within, black soil middens. They may appear in multiple spatially discrete locations contiguous with habitation-derived black soil middens, in effect ringing the black soil deposits with discontinuous mounds of shell. The second type of shell midden was theorized by David Sanger (1996: 523) as "a shell midden composed of nearly 100 per cent shell [which] could reflect a location specifically designed to dry shellfish for storage." Such a deposit would have limited soil development and would necessarily be spatially discrete, the result of focused processing activity. It would also have the potential to be quite large, as shellfish storage would require significant collecting and processing of shells to accumulate any stockpile. Such a site was never encountered by Sanger (or others) in Maine. As we shall see below, they have now been identified, for the first time, in Port Joli.

Note: In the following review, the official Borden Number comes first, followed by (when applicable) the descriptive name, Erskine's numbered names, and earlier or double Borden numbers—in that order—in parentheses.

East Coast of Port Joli's Harbour
AlDf-06 (MacAdam Garden, Port Joli No. 12, AlDf-05)
Description and Excavation Approach
AlDf-06 was first excavated by John Erskine in 1957 after locals informed him that "a grave had been unearthed [there] in search for treasure" (Erskine 1986: 87). Though the grave appears to have been apocryphal, the site was nevertheless well known to collectors in the area due to its proximity to the highway and its repeated use as a family garden (the "MacAdam Garden"). Every spring when the garden was ploughed, and after heavy rains, numerous artifacts would emerge from the dark, rich soil. Hunting for them was somewhat of a local pastime that persisted until recent years, when the site was converted to a family lawn and boat landing/dock.

AlDf-06 sits on a triangular peninsula of land that protrudes into the head of Port Joli's harbour. The site is flanked on the east and west by two streams, which bifurcate some 500 m inland from a larger single watercourse known as Douglas Brook. The landform is very flat, consistent with its intensive use as a garden, with a slight swale in the northern portion of the site near the highway. It is bordered on the east, south, and west sides by a steep (approx. 2 m) embankment which abruptly terminates in a tangle of boulders before it meets the harbour. The harbour itself is very shallow in this area, and extensive mud flats, filled with clams, are exposed at every low tide. North of the small peninsula and the former Highway 103 is a cleared area with abundant large boulders and several modern outbuildings. Because of their artificial separation due to the road construction, we consider AlDf-06 and AlDf-05 to be the same site; throughout this volume, we use AlDf-06, the area of the site we and Erskine tested, to refer to both site areas.

The largest site around the harbour, covering several thousand square metres, AlDf-06 has been, apparently, destroyed by development, cultivation, and collecting. The most extensive damage occurred with the construction of Highway 103, which bisects the site from west to east. North of the highway, the landowner indicates that large, but relatively shallow, shell midden deposits once characterized much of the area where the family home, outbuildings, and turnaround driveway are located. If so, the site is roughly twice the size of that shown on the map shown in figure 3.2, though we did not have the opportunity to ground-truth the observations of the landowner. He reported that he was aware of no distinct shell deposits south of the highway. Our excavations and probes confirmed his account, and we could discern no areas south of the highway where shell predominates over soil.

Erskine's exploration at the site appears to have taken place along its extreme southern edge, at both the west and east "sides." Similar to our observations below, he found that the almost entire thickness of the deposit had been ploughed. Projectile points and scrapers were abundant; however, in stark contrast to our observations, on the "west side" of the site Erskine (1986: 87) "unearthed a hearth" which was found intact below the plough zone. He described that shell was limited throughout the deposit, again confirmed by our observations, and that bone preservation was excellent, a characteristic we did not observe.

To determine the boundaries of the site, we probe-tested at every metre along a cross-shaped transect which roughly divided the peninsula into four quadrants. The probes revealed that the entire peninsula (figures 3.2 and 3.3) was once a dense "black soil midden" (e.g., Black 2002), characterized by sparse and highly fragmented shell in a richly organic cultural matrix. The site is now almost completely devoid of any vegetation except for lawn grass (figure 3.3), but previous observation of the site in 2008 and Erskine's photographs from 1957 indicate that its margins were once heavily vegetated with thick bushes and low scrub trees, suggesting that the margins next to the embankments were possibly less disturbed by repeated ploughing.

Our objectives for the test excavation of the site were: (1) to locate any area of the site that had not been disturbed by ploughing activity, (2) to obtain formal artifacts or datable materials that we could use to place the site in an archaeological sequence, and (3) to obtain a faunal sample. We placed a 1 × 3 m grid oriented north-south (true) along the eastern margin of the site, in an area that we suspected had been formerly covered in heavy

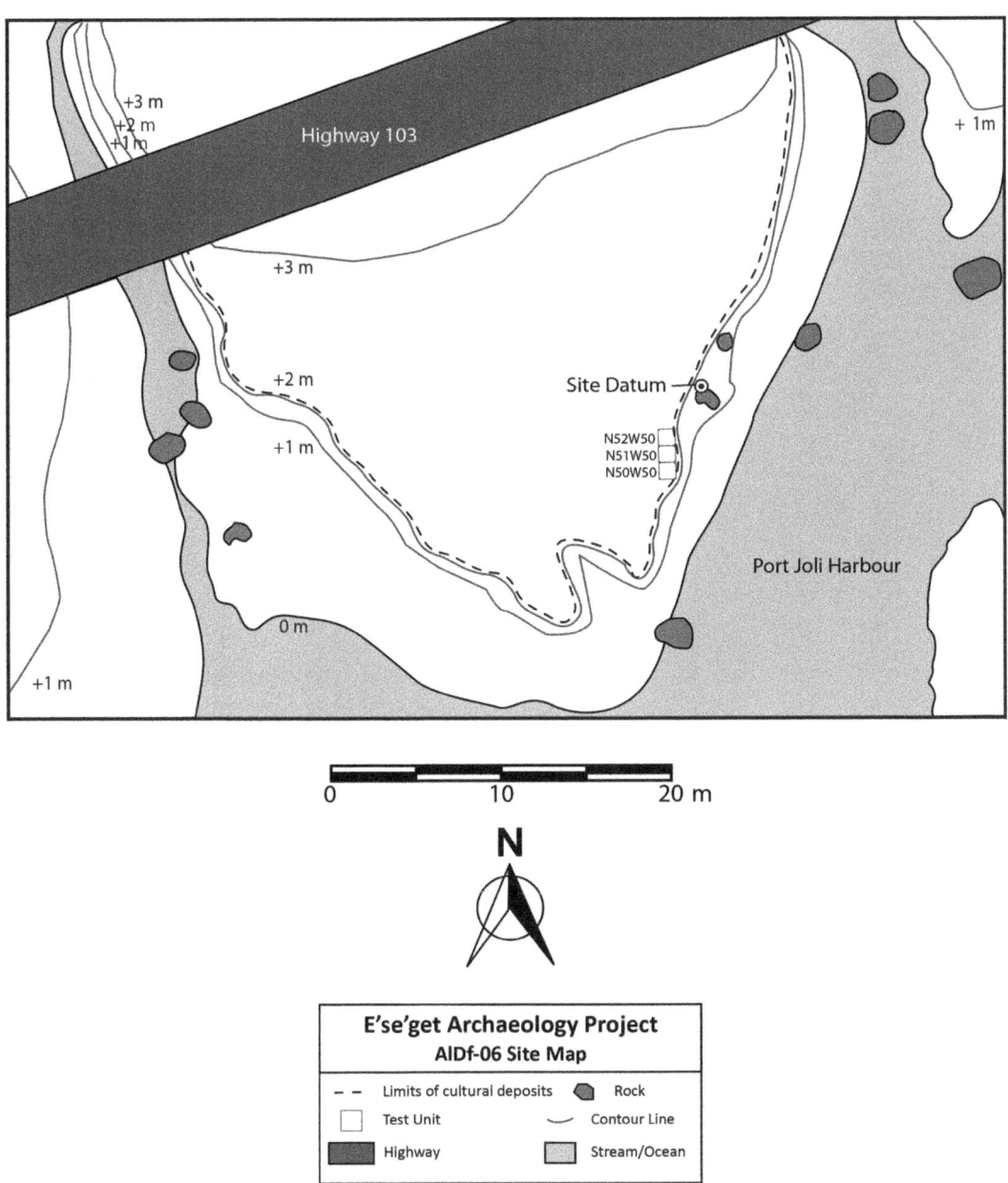

Figure 3.2 AlDf-06: Site map, showing location of the three 2012 test excavation units.

vegetation. Excavation proceeded by trowel and the recovered soil matrix was screened through 3 mm (1/8 inch) mesh. Our probe transects and excavations indicate the deposit ranged between around 15 cm to around 35 cm in depth, although the latter extreme is likely a result of intensive ploughing into the subsoil in some areas of the site.

Figure 3.3 AlDf-06: Photograph of site, facing southwest.

Stratigraphy

The stratigraphic sequence can be described as follows (see figure 3.4 for profile depths corresponding with figure 3.2):

- Level 1 consisted of a sod layer in dark brown-black organic sandy loam with limited root development. Highly fragmented cultural material (e.g., small Indigenous and European pottery fragments, glass, and lithic material) was present in the sod layer, which appeared to be sitting directly on a highly disturbed cultural deposit.
- Level 2a was a dark brown sandy loam with abundant rocks, small cobbles, and significant amounts of fragmented cultural material, including fire-cracked rock. Both historic ceramics and glass and prehistoric ceramics and flakes were present in this level, but few faunal remains or charcoal specimens were present. The highly fragmented nature of the artifacts and the soft texture of the soil matrix are likely related to the repeated ploughing it has experienced over the last half-century.
- Level 2b represented a distinct textural transition from the level above, occurring as a much firmer sandy loam deposit, which retained the same colour characteristics as the level above. Artifact frequencies were similar to Level 2a, with a mix of historic ceramics and glass as well as prehistoric ceramics and lithics. A few highly fragmented faunal remains were recovered from the deposit, along with a few clam shells, though these were also small and highly fragmented. No charcoal was encountered. The mixed nature of the deposit and the fragmented artifacts (even

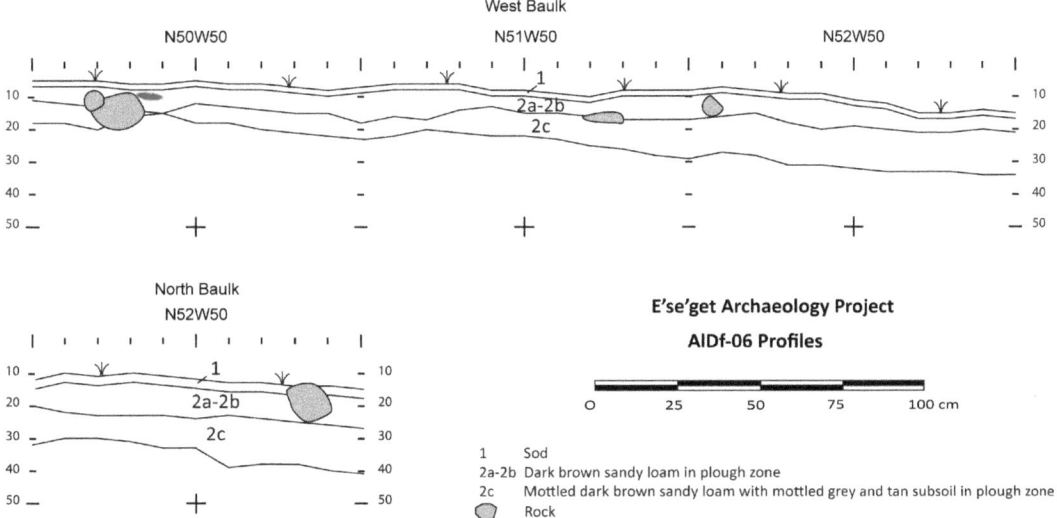

Figure 3.4 AlDf-06: Profile plan of 2012 test excavations.

formal lithic tools were fragmented) suggest this layer also experienced repeated ploughing and tilling, though its firmness suggests that this disturbance was not as recent (or perhaps as frequent) as in the layer above it.
- Level 2c was a mottled dark brown sandy loam with grey/tan sandy mottling, likely due to mixture with the subsoil below it. This layer was very artifact-rich, containing abundant prehistoric ceramics and lithic materials, although still mixed with occasional historic ceramics and glass.
- Level 3 was not designated in this deposit; in our methodology Level 3 should always represent an undisturbed cultural layer (see Chapter 1).
- Level 4 was the natural subsoil layer, which can be described as an undulating mottled light grey to yellow/orange/brown sand, with abundant cobbles and rocks. It is entirely consistent with the B horizon in other areas of Port Joli.

Summary

In summary, the AlDf-06 deposit is best described as a large "black soil midden" (e.g., Black 2002) characterized by an abundant cultural and organic component, but with little shell admixture. The entire deposit, from its upper levels to the subsoil, was apparently disturbed and mixed by ploughing. While some artifacts were recovered, the deposits exhibit thorough stratigraphic mixing, removing any hope of an intact prehistoric cultural layer. Moreover, because of the extensive historic use of the area surrounding AlDf-06, the entire landscape has been extensively altered and disturbed. The low levels of animal bones and intact Indigenous pottery undoubtedly relate to significant mechanical attrition caused by ploughing and gardening.

The site was evidently very large when occupied, and the horizontal distribution of the site is conspicuously inverted from sites further south toward the head of the harbour, which have large shoreside shell middens backed by landside black soil middens. Evidently, at AlDf-06, activity areas, and likely wigwam floors, were placed on the flat area closest to the clam flats, while shell processing activities occurred behind this area on the landward margin of the site. Why this might have been so is intriguing, but close access to the water, and perhaps the view of the harbour, was clearly a preoccupation of those who lived at the site. Alternatively, shoreside middens may have been present at AlDf-06, but have since eroded. In this case, midden areas may have been distributed around a central black soil area where wigwams were placed and other activities took place.

Erskine excavated at AlDf-06, which he labelled "Port Joli XII," in 1957, and records (Erskine 1986: 87) finding a much higher density of artifacts, including ceramics and animal remains from the deposit. Similar to the E'se'get excavations, he excavated at the margins of the deposit, on both the east and west sides of the peninsula. He records high densities of lithic artifacts, and "the remains of smelts" (Erskine 1986: 87) but no evidence of house features, hearths, or "ash"—Erskine's (1958: 2) descriptor for black, charcoal-rich soil—and noted that shell density was very low. The artifact densities notwithstanding (and not unexpected given the amount of collecting that has since occurred here), his observations are very similar to our own. This was evidently a very large and intensely occupied habitation site with large associated shell middens, the result of domestic discard. So large and deep is this site that it only could have been produced by repeated occupation by multiple families (e.g., multiple wigwams and associated activities) over a considerable period of time. Given its size, it appears to have represented a sort of central place in the harbour, for the duration of its occupation.

A2009NS27-1
Description and Excavation Approach

This is a small and unique shell midden site at the head of the harbour in Port Joli, just east of a small bridge covering the western fork of Douglas Brook. Approximately 30 m south of Highway 103, the site sits on a small wooded knoll, and can be easily accessed by crossing the ditch from the highway. It is located on Canadian Wildlife Service property, the western edge of which is practically contiguous with the western margin of the site. Like all sites in the region, it is situated in a treeless area among a mass of small- to medium-sized boulders, which frame the site and provide shelter. One very large glacial erratic blocks southwesterly winds, which blow up through the harbour. The knoll slopes from a high point of about 3 m above sea level (ASL) in the northwest to a low point of about 2 m ASL in the southeast, where it meets the high-water mark. Subsurface probing revealed an irregularly shaped shell-bearing deposit (figure 3.5), covering approximately 45 m^2.

Probing revealed that the depth of the shell-bearing deposit varied between around 45 cm in the north, to around 5 cm in the south and east portions of the site. A similar stratigraphy characterized all areas that we probed. The uppermost cultural layer was a relatively thick, highly organic, shell-bearing black soil layer with very low densities of crushed and broken shell fragments. Below this was a relatively homogenous shell midden layer composed of alternating areas of highly fragmented and coarsely broken valves. The valves tended to be more complete and relatively larger in size as the deposit descended to the subsoil horizon, and, furthermore, the proportion of soil increased just above the subsoil. To the southeast of the site, an open area appeared to carry black soil deposits, but we could not discern the edges or the size due to the very dark nature of the humus characteristic

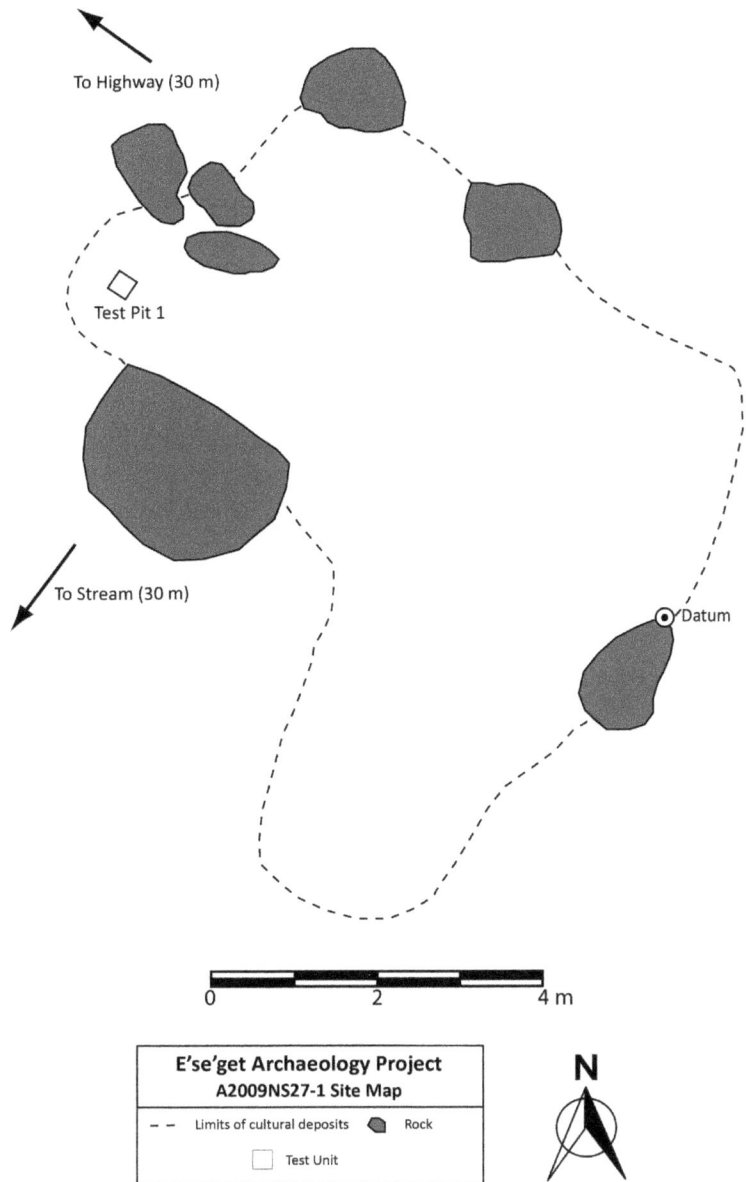

Figure 3.5 A2009NS27-1: Plan view, based on subsurface soil probing and showing location of 2009 test unit.

of Port Joli forest soils. No evidence of disturbance was discerned on the surface of the site, though a later test pit proved that some turbation has occurred (see description of layer 2, below).

Consistent with our testing protocol, a small (25 × 25 cm) test unit was excavated in the northwestern margin of the midden at A2009NS27-1 (figure 3.5), where subsurface probing suggested a relatively deep deposit.

Stratigraphy

As described below, the midden we encountered here was quite unlike anything else excavated in the region previously (figure 3.6):

- Level 1 was a thin sod layer, composed of shoreside grasses with a loosely consolidated root mat, less than 1 cm thick.
- Level 2 was a sub-sod layer composed of dark brown organic sandy loam with abundant broken clam shell. Of immediate note was the very small size of clam shell in this layer, approximately one quarter to one half the average size of clam shells from other middens in the area. This was unexpected and suggests something unique about the clam colonies that were exploited in the area. A plastic Hostess Munchies chip bag was encountered in this deposit, suggesting that the layer was disturbed at some point in the recent past (around the last ten to twenty years, based on the style of the bag).
- Level 3 was a midden layer composed of unbroken clam shell in a grey-black sandy loam. While the clam valves were still much smaller than those recovered from other sites in the area, they increased slightly in size as the level was excavated. While the top of the layer included primarily broken and coarsely broken fragments, near the bottom of the layer, the shells became more complete, and soil fraction appeared to increase. The deposit was relatively loose, and broken clam shells were abundant; it is uncertain if this represents a disturbed layer of some sort. A flake, as well as a small fragment of fire-cracked rock, was encountered in this layer, suggesting a prehistoric deposit.
- Level 4 was a typical subsoil layer, composed of a mottled grey/brown sandy clay with abundant pebbles and cobbles.

Summary

With such a limited spatial test, interpreting this small site is difficult. However, it appears to exhibit qualities of both a shell midden (Level 3) and black soil midden (Level 2). We interpret the lower levels as a small "kitchen" midden (a midden resulting from immediate domestic discard, often near a house structure), with an associated black soil midden to the southeast, which was likely once a series of living-floors. The upper level of the site appears to have been entirely a black soil deposit, though a relatively sterile one. Again, there are analogues for such a deposit (see AlDf-24 C, Level 2), and this may represent a series of living or working surfaces, from the more recent occupation of the site. Where the associated shell midden may be located is unknown, though it is important to note that the site has seen relatively little archaeological exploration. Though limited, the available data indicate that this was a small site where wigwam structures were repeatedly placed, resulting in the build-up of deposits from small domestic-refuse middens. The patterning in the clam-valve sizes is intriguing and needs further study. A tentative hypothesis is that exploitation pressure (perhaps from the nearby AlDf-06) is responsible for the variability in the valve sizes, especially when compared to other sites with substantially large clam shells.

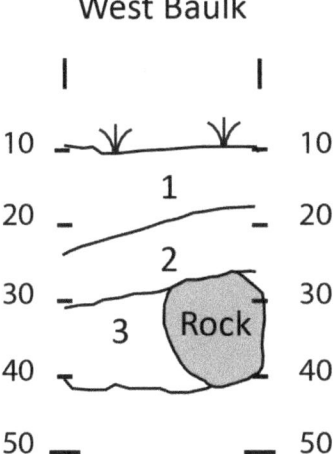

E'se'get Archaeology Project
A2009NS27 Profile

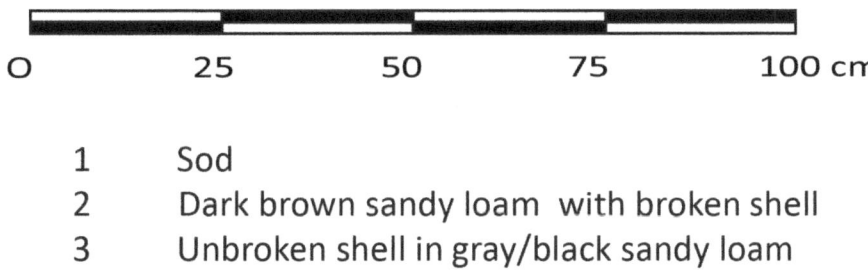

1 Sod
2 Dark brown sandy loam with broken shell
3 Unbroken shell in gray/black sandy loam

Figure 3.6 A2009NS27-1: Soil profile of the (2009) 25 cm² test unit.

AlDf-02 (Robertson Lake Outlet, Port Joli No. 11)
Description and Excavation Approach

Very little information is available on the work conducted by John Erskine at this location in 1957. His total written account of this work is just one isolated paragraph, which we shall quote verbatim (Erskine 1958: 12):

> On the Northern side of the outlet from Robertson Lake is a stretch of fairly flat pasture studded with boulders and clumps of native hawthorn. At the edge of the tide, a deposit of shell fifteen inches [38.1 cm] deep was being eroded. A test-hole of one square yard [0.83 m²] turned up shell and bones and a few chips and was evidently in a marginal area. Random testings showed ash widely distributed, and it seems likely that a large amount of campsite remains. Such a scanty testing gives too little information to allow one to date it with any conscience, but the position and type of site corresponds with PJ#8 [Port Joli No. 8].

The site appears to have been primarily a black soil midden—Erskine (1958: 2) often described black charcoal-rich soil as "ash"—and the density of artifacts recovered (see Chapter 7) indicates that it was likely a rich living-floor deposit. Near the seaward edge of the site was a relatively deep but actively eroding shell midden deposit. It is unknown how large the shell midden deposit was, but the comparison to AlDf-03 ("PJ#8") suggests quite a large and complex site.

AlDf-03 (Post Office , Port Joli No. 8)
Description and Excavation Approach

AlDf-03 was named the Post Office site because it was directly across the road from the village's former post office. It was the subject of extensive excavation between 1957 and 1959 by John Erskine, who claimed to have excavated the entire site within that time. This midden site was actively eroding when he encountered it and he suggested that "most had been taken by the sea" at that time (Erskine 1959: 345). Little if anything is left of the site today, but it once sat around 30 m south of the Robertson Lake Outlet site. The seaward edge of the site was characterized by a line of very large boulders (which are extant), the spaces around which much of the deposit appears to have accumulated, up to a depth of about 75 cm. Erskine observed that this deposit appeared to diminish in depth as it stretched into the ocean. On the landward edge of the site, beyond the boulders, the deposit diminished to about 30 to 45 cm deep.

The site was quite large, covering more than 20 × 20 m, even in its eroding state. Erskine kept a relatively detailed account (and profile) of the site's stratigraphy (1959; figure 3.7). The upper layer was an "ashy loam" 15 cm deep, but without shell admixture. "Ash" appears to have been the term Erskine used to describe a black soil deposit with highly comminuted charcoal (e.g., Erskine 1958: 2). He interpreted that an historic occupation, likely a "fish-house," had disturbed this layer of the site and that historic artifacts, such as wrought nails and bottle glass, "had penetrated the site quite deeply" (Erskine 1958: 3). Erskine believed that the layer was the remains of an early- to late-Historic wigwam campsite.

Below this layer was another "ashy" black soil deposit with highly fragmented shell, abundant animal remains, and artifacts. Erskine (1959: 345) interpreted this layer as another palimpsest of dwelling, or wigwam, floors "at the extreme landward limit of the site." As he noted, "the bottom 2 inches [5 cm] of this layer was unusually black" and contained an abundance of formal tools. The bottom cultural layer was about 15 cm thick and composed of crushed and trampled shell, with abundant animal remains and very limited soil development. Erskine considered this deposit to be the margin of a much larger shell midden which had been "destroyed by the sea." The subsoil horizon at the site was described as "discolored" (Erskine 1959: 345), which could be the typical mottled grey/orange horizon characteristic of Port Joli.

Erskine theorized that the site developed in relation to the boulders; initially thin shell middens developed on the seaward side of the boulders, with black soil middens forming on the landward side. After the deposition of the midden, wigwam floors were placed on top of it, with the boulders forming the eastern edge of the wigwam walls. Once the area west of the boulders had filled in to the top of their height, the wigwam floors progressively moved east over the boulders and toward the landward edge of the site. In general

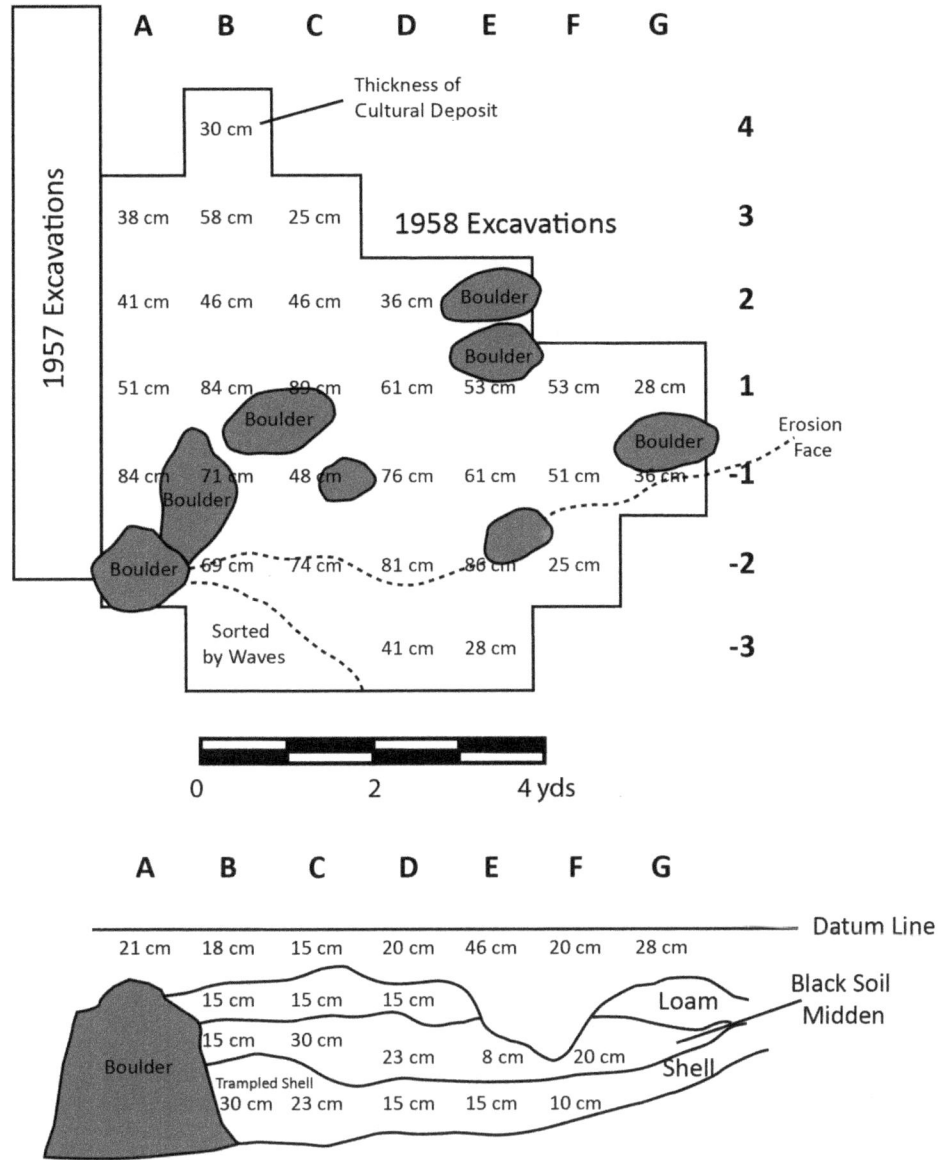

Figure 3.7 AlDf-03: Site map and stratigraphic profile, redrawn from Erskine (1959), with measures converted to metric.

composition, this appears to have been primarily a very large black soil midden, with a small seaside shell midden being the first component to develop.

AlDf-04 (Port Joli No. 10)
Description and Excavation Approach
Like some of John Erskine's other excavations, very little is known about AlDf-04, or Port Joli No. 10. Erskine (1959: 348) described that only a small portion of the site, a "strip about one yard [0.91 m] wide" remained intact when he excavated it in 1959, the remainder having been destroyed by the nearby road construction. His published records indicate that

it was a shell midden, and that it was "40 yards [36 m] inland" east of AlDf-03 and located just to the west of the modern road. Erskine claimed a small knoll of boulders separated it from AlDf-03 (Erskine 1959: 12).

Erskine's test excavations revealed the western margin of a dwelling floor, or rather a deposit containing a series of dwelling floors, which was approximately 4.5 × 0.9 m wide and about 35 cm deep across its entire surface (Erskine 1959: 12). The precise nature of the matrix was not described, though Erskine places it in his shell midden group, indicating significant shell admixture. Given his identification of the deposit as a dwelling surface, it was most likely a black soil midden with comminuted charcoal and broken-shell fragments. The presence of stone projectile points and a bone needle indicated to Erskine a potentially domestic deposit. Given its proximity to AlDf-03, the two sites appear to represent a deposit very similar in general layout to AlDf-08 (see below), a very large black soil midden covering an expansive area, with spatially discrete pockets of shell midden at the margins of the deposit.

AlDf-36 (AlDf-01)
Description and Excavation Approach
This small site is located approximately 150 m south of the small bridge crossing the Robertson Lake Outlet, on the east coast of Port Joli's harbour. Composed of a large single black soil midden, the site is positioned on a small beach terrace just south of a small headland. It is flanked on the east by a large boulder ridge, or low cliff, and on the west by a cobble beach. An ancient brook, now dry, is located approximately 50 m north of the site. In 2008, the site was heavily vegetated with apple trees and no evidence of erosion was present at the site. However, its low position near the water may leave it vulnerable to inundation by storms.

The archaeological potential of the site was first recognized in the 1960s by Eric Millard (an engineer, though untrained in archaeology) and he dug there repeatedly between 1967 and 1969. Unfortunately, no record of his excavation exists, and the small quantity of written material he donated to the Nova Scotia museum indicates the site was not particularly productive. Evidence of his work, and likely others, was evident when we visited the site, and fragmented shell could be seen on the surface through low vegetation. The site was characterized by a large number of protruding boulders and large cobbles; their somewhat jumbled nature suggests the smaller ones had been moved during the collector's activities.

Probing at metre intervals along cardinal transects revealed a semi-lunar shell midden approximately 13 × 8 m, abutting a large, steep-sided boulder ridge or low cliff (figure 3.8). The midden itself is shallow (less than 30 cm in depth), and composed of a dominating proportion of coarsely broken shell in a dark black organic loam. The disturbed areas appear as a series of haphazard depressions and associated backdirt, suggesting collecting, rather than excavation, is responsible for the disturbance. Probing revealed extensive "black soil" horizons with abundant crushed shell adjacent to and surrounding the midden. In total the evidence indicates the deposit was a rather small habitation site with an associated "kitchen midden."

If the site had habitation-derived living surfaces, this may be at odds with the small amount of material Millard recovered, as such deposits tend to be artifact-rich. A possible

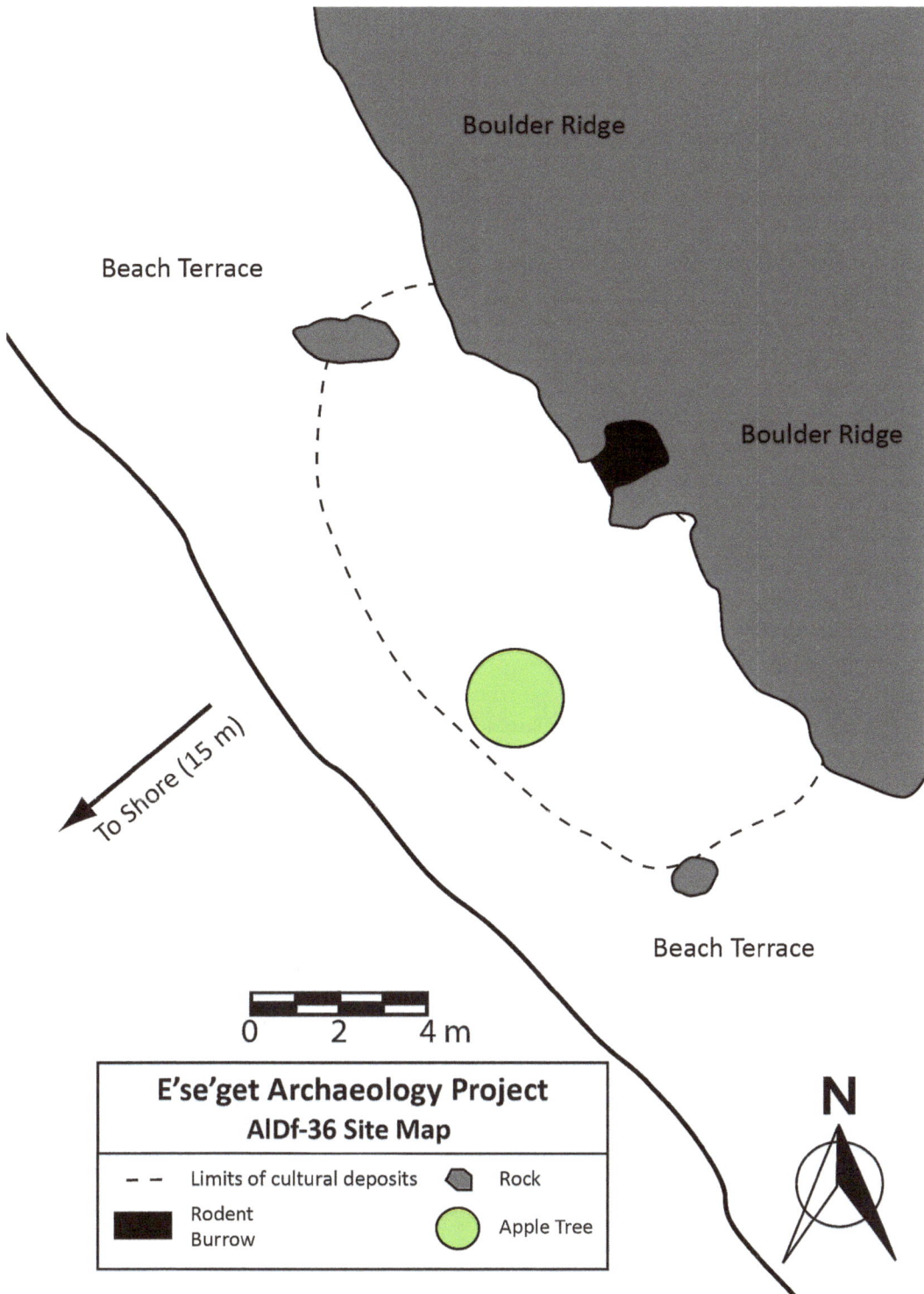

Figure 3.8 AlDf-36 (also known as AlDf-01): Plan view, based on subsurface probing.

explanation may be that this easily accessible site had been the subject of local collecting for many years, and Millard was just one of many avocational collectors to have dug in the site. If that is the case, the site is likely of little future archaeological value.

AlDf-11 (McDonald Shell Heap)
Description and Excavation Approach

AlDf-11 was described as an eroding shell midden when Eric Millard first excavated there in the fall of 1966 and the summer of 1967. The site sits adjacent to a large clam flat on the eastern side of Port Joli's harbour, approximately 270 m directly southwest of St. Catherine's River Road. The site is on a gently sloping but boulder-strewn hill that ascends from the beach. At the time it was excavated by Millard, it was treeless and sparsely vegetated save for short grasses, a trait characteristic of many undisturbed shell-bearing sites in the harbour.

Though formally untrained in archaeological techniques, Millard was an engineer, and applied his scientific rigour to the excavations. He was a meticulous excavator, and kept detailed profile drawings, site plans, artifact plots, and profiles of the excavation (Millard 1966). He even screened the deposits through window mesh, indicating that the fauna he recovered was very representative of the deposit he excavated (see Chapter 8). The following account is paraphrased from Millard's (1966) handwritten report, with metric conversions inserted in place of the imperial measurements he used.

Millard (1966) excavated the site vertically in four phases. The first two phases cut a 0.6 m × 4.2 m trench northward through the deposit, while phase 3 extended westward approximately 1.2 m to create a U-shaped trench that skirted large boulders concentrated in the southeast corner of the site. Phase 4 expanded the excavation northward by about 1.2 m, then extended southward and eastward to excavate the eastern margin of the site to its eroding face. According to Millard's detailed site plan (figure 3.9), he excavated approximately 50 percent of the site, and used the backdirt to protect the remaining portion of the site.

Millard (figure 3.10) kept detailed profiles and stratigraphic notes. The root-bearing sod layer was unusually thick, around 15 cm, and overlaid a thin (about 1 cm) black sooty stratum of the same matrix "literally covered" (Millard 1966: 3) with quartz flakes. It seems apparent that the sod layer was in fact a cultural layer with a black sooty matrix and abundant quartz flakes. This shell-free layer descended onto shell-bearing deposits over 40 cm deep, containing a high proportion of broken and complete clam shells ranging in size from 4 cm to over 10 cm in length. This layer was also artifact-rich, containing many retouched flakes and, near the bottom, a hearth, labelled "Hearth 1" by Millard. The hearth area, like others found below it, was unusually formal and robust, approximately 60 cm in diameter and ringed with stones about 7 cm to 15 cm in diameter. It also contained a cut nail, a fragment of a kaolin pipe bowl, and a brass button, all discovered in situ, suggesting this upper layer was an Historic or Protohistoric deposit.

Near the bottom of this layer, around the same layer as Hearth 1, many fragments of broken mammal bones were found, just at the transition to a "sooty black greasy soil" with decreasing quantities of shell fragments but considerable amounts of fragmented bone. This new fourth layer was deepest next to the boulders in the north of the site, where it was an

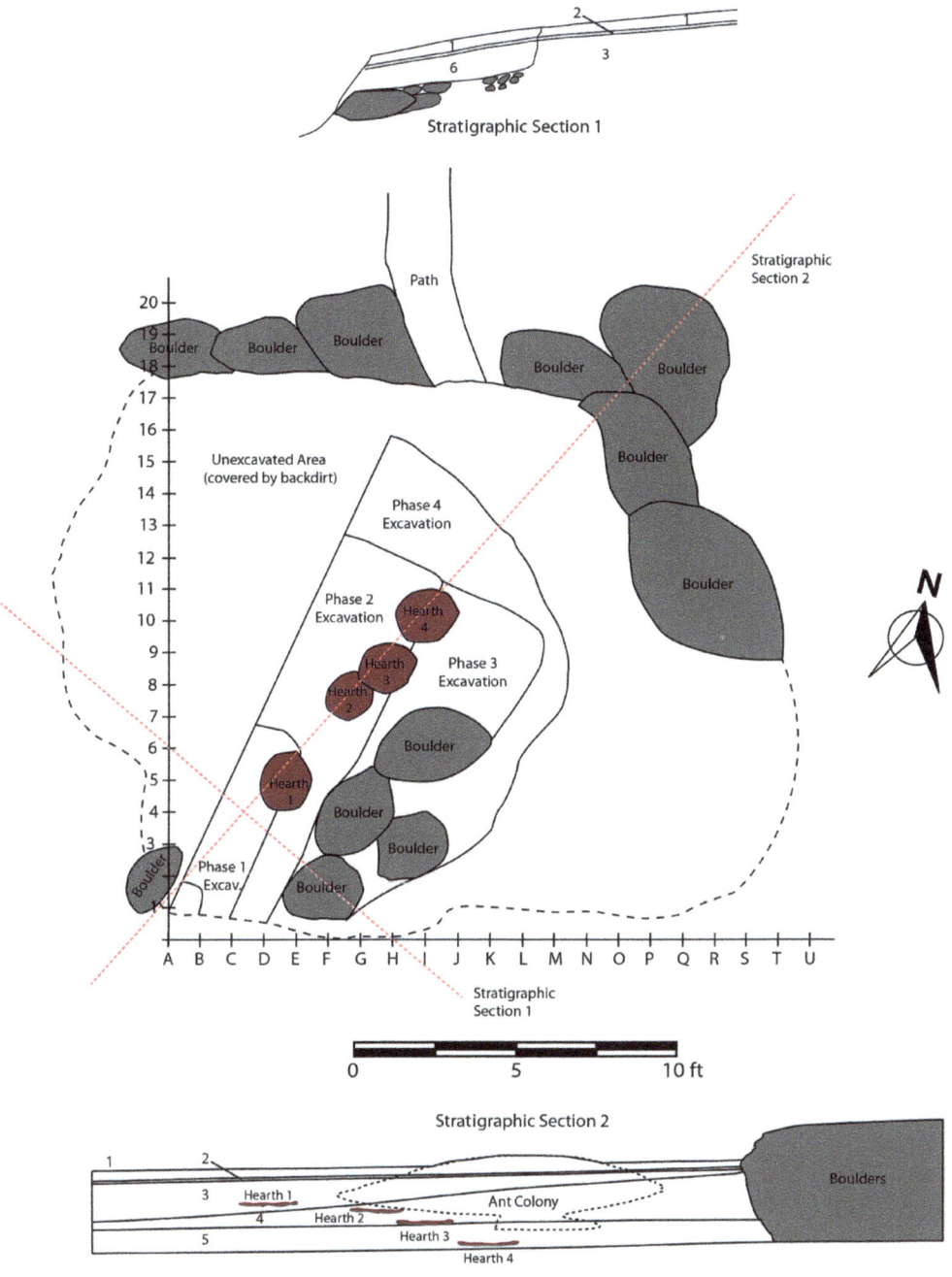

1 Sod
2 Dark black sandy loam with abundant quartz flakes
3 Broken and unbroken clam shells in dark black sandy loam
4 Dark black greasy sandy loam with limited shell and abundant bone
5 Dark black greasy sandly loam with limited shell and abundant flakes
6 Fine broken clam shells in a dark black greasy sandy loam

Figure 3.9 AlDf-11: Plan view, including soil profiles, redrawn to scale from Millard (1966), with metric conversions.

Figure 3.10 Eric Millard excavating at AlDf-11, around 1966. Used with permission of Marg Millard.

impressive 68 cm in depth. It became progressively shallower toward the southern margin of the site, where it was only around 30 cm in depth. The deposit contained at least three hearths, a significant quantity of bone, and many large flakes.

The four hearths in the deposit were horizontally contiguous, moving northward and eastward in an arc as the layers descended (and the deposit moved back in time). In his notes, Millard related the hearths to a sequence of changes in the midden stratigraphy that he did not record in his profile, and his observations are relevant for interpreting the site. The first hearth was associated with abundant broken mammal bone, clam shell fragments, charcoal fragments, historic artifacts, and several beaver tooth chisels, and likely marked a distinct new layer from that above it. Hearth 2 was approximately 7 cm below Hearth 1, near the lower limit of the clam shell fragments, which by this time had decreased in proportion substantially. This layer was associated with abundant lithic material and large amounts of broken animal bone. Only twenty ceramic fragments were found in this layer and all were found in the same layer as Hearth 2. Hearth 3 was associated with a sooty black soil with no clam shell discernable in the matrix. Millard noticed a significant increase in bone fragments in this layer, implying that the "place . . . [of the shell had] been taken by bone fragments," which had "been broken into small pieces" (Millard 1966: 4). It appears that, going back in time, shellfish gathering and processing was replaced with mammal butchery and processing, perhaps for bone grease and marrow, in this occupation layer.

All the layers associated with hearths had large quantities of projectile points, "choppers," and scrapers. Hearth 3 had been "very heavily burned" and had a much larger and heavier stone ring, composed of 15 cm- to 20 cm-diameter stones, creating a ring 92 cm in diameter. Hearth 4, near the bottom of the deposit, contained "burned bone" (Millard 1996: figure 1) and large unbroken animal bones, including an intact ungulate scapula. The layer associated with Hearth 4 contained fire-cracked and heat-altered rock that had been so exposed to heat that it became friable when moved.

Millard did not formally interpret the deposit he encountered, but comparing it to other sites and deposits in Port Joli, it appears highly unusual. Structurally, it compares best with AlDf-24, Area C, which contains a series of overlapping dwelling surfaces and a significant quantity of fragmented mammal bone. Like AlDf-11, these deposits included a hearth which remained roughly in the same place as the deposit developed stratigraphically. However, the sizes and positions of the overlapping hearths at AlDf-11 are in stark contrast with AlDf-24, Area C. First, the AlDf-11 hearths are placed nearby, and sometimes between, large boulders, precluding the construction of a wigwam or house structure over them. Furthermore, no other hearths that we encountered in Port Joli were encircled by a formal ring of rocks or cobbles such as those at AlDf-11.

The size of these hearths, which ranged from 60 cm up to 92 cm in diameter, with evidence of "heavy burning" (Millard 1966: 4) and large fire-cracked cobbles, would not have been suitable within a wigwam-like structure. Furthermore, such relatively shell-free deposit was not encountered in any other stratum in the entire harbour. The large size of the lithics from the site (see Chapter 7) is also abnormal in comparison to the other living floor surfaces encountered in Port Joli, which contain a higher proportion of small finishing and retouching flakes. As with AlDf-11, large quantities of fragmented bone were recovered from other sites in Port Joli, but (as will be described in Chapter 8), the species richness of AlDF-11 is comparatively low.

Indeed, the unique nature of the site and the material recovered from it suggest a special-purpose occupation. The quantity of bone material recovered, its fragmentation, and its identification (see Chapter 8), in conjunction with the large wind-protected hearths, the general dearth of ceramics, the large lithic flakes, and the lack of traditional dwelling surfaces, all combine to indicate a site focused on the processing of large terrestrial mammals, likely caribou and deer, rather than a habitation site. This hypothesis will be explored further in Chapter 9, but the location of the site—near a large, linear beach and near (just south of) the narrow strip of land that is sandwiched between the beach and Robertson Lake—might be pertinent to its interpretation. The site sat at the end of a choke point, through which travelling ungulates had to pass to avoid a long detour (around Robertson Lake) when moving from the inner to outer harbour. This large and continually used site was thus placed at an ideal intercept point and may have been a location where multiple families came together in the fall to intercept, kill, and process caribou or deer.

AlDf-12 (Vogler)
Description and Excavation Approach

The Vogler site is named for Fred Vogler, who discovered it. Like other observant local residents (see AlDf-30, below), Vogler saw some shells in the roots of a tree blown down during a storm. He informed Eric Millard, who decided to recreationally excavate the site in the summer of 1966. Millard took detailed notes of his excavations, including horizontal plans of the site (Millard 1966).

Like some other sites in the harbour, AlDf-12 is located far inland, approximately 450 m from the high-water mark at a major beach and clam flat on the eastern side of Port Joli's harbour. The area is currently dry, and no brooks or streams are known to be present, though the site is located about 300 m south of the southeastern tip of Robertson Lake. At the time the site was excavated, it was described as a "low sloping clearing" (Millard 1966: 5), which was relatively devoid of vegetation, a characteristic that seems associated with many shell middens in the harbour.

Millard's explorations revealed an oval-shaped shell midden deposit approximately 6 × 4.5 m in area, with the longer axis oriented east to west (figure 3.11). The flat top of the midden sloped gently to the southwest, following the natural terrain of the clearing. He tested the southern portion of the midden via a trench, approximately 2 m (long) ×

1.5 m (wide). Broken shell was encountered directly beneath the sod, as well as "fine" (Millard 1966: 5) projectile points in situ. The depth of the deposit was approximately 25 to 30 cm at the southern end. He observed "discontinuous" (Millard 1966: 5) shell in this area, indicating perhaps a denser shell deposit that abutted a black soil midden. At 1 m north of the trench, he tested the deposit via eight small (25 × 25 cm) test units (see figure 3.11). Only one of these exhibited evidence of shell, which was described as "finely broken" in a deposit about 4 cm thick.

Stratigraphically, he described the deposit thusly (Millard 1966: 5): "Turf and roots 3" to 4" [8 cm to 15 cm] deep, then shell and black soil 4" to 6" [10 cm to 15 cm] deep on [overlaying] fine sand, some of which appears to be beach sand. Then Granit boulders, up to 12" [30 cm] diameter with smaller stones in between (on TOP of clam shell)." The latter feature was interpreted by Millard as an attempt to level the sloping shell midden below to accommodate the entrance to a "wigwam or shelter." (Millard 1966: 6) The soil

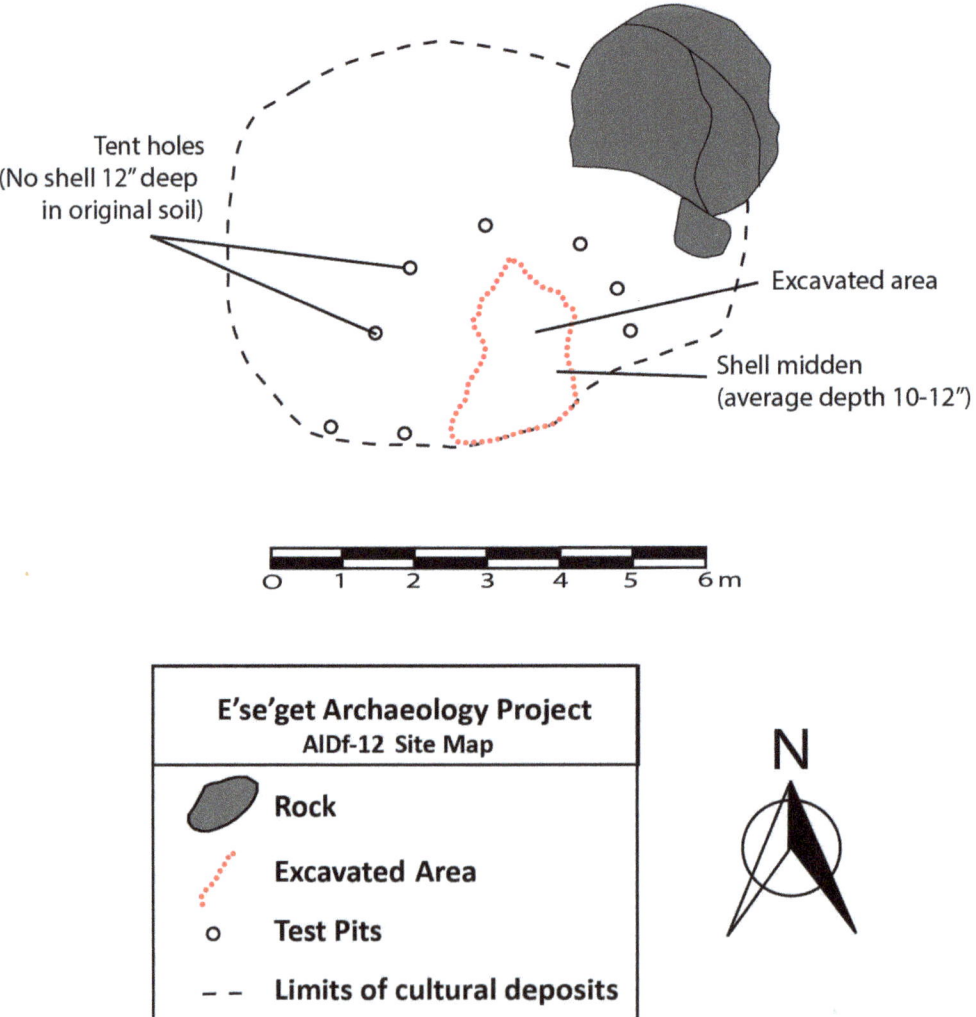

Figure 3.11 AlDf-12 (Vogler site): Plan view, redrawn from Millard (1966).

matrix throughout the deposit was described as black, but not of a "sooty nature." (Millard 1966: 6)

Millard interpreted the deposit as a shelter, or wigwam, but found no charcoal— which he attributed to only having tested its southerly margin and entrance. The nature of the deposit—which was primarily a black soil midden with a spatially discrete but contiguous shell midden—is consistent with a dwelling floor and an associated "kitchen" midden. This is also consistent with the large quantity of material recovered from the small excavations, which included decorated pottery, abundant animal bones, and lithics.

AlDf-13 (Alexander)
Description and Excavation Approach

The Alexander site has never been investigated by professional archaeologists. A shell midden was reported by Eric Millard (1968) as being located in the garden northwest of the house of a local resident, Peter Alexander. Other sites in the harbour (e.g., AlDf-06) often had gardens placed on black soil deposits, because the high organic content created excellent growing conditions. Therefore, it is suspected that this site had a black soil component, likely with a shell admixture (hence the report of a shell midden by Millard). Beyond this, nothing further is known of the site, and it appears to never have been tested.

West Coast of Port Joli's Harbour
AlDf-07 (Upper Path Lake Brook, Port Joli No. 2)
Description and Excavation Approach

AlDf-07, known as Upper Path Lake Brook, was excavated by John Erskine during his 1957 and 1959 field seasons (Erskine 1958, 1959). It is a difficult site to locate, even with general GPS coordinates, and we found it only after more than an hour of hard survey through dense stands of mixed and boggy forest. It is located approximately 50 m south of London Brook (now dry) and about 85 m east of Sandy Hollow Road. Erskine (1986: 90) indicated the site was far inland, but no site could be found in that location. We found what is likely AlDf-07 far to the east of Erskine's map, within 50 m of the high-water mark, where massive flats of eelgrass extend out into the ocean. The tree line ends roughly 20 m east of the site, where a line of boulders marks the transition from forest to foreshore eelgrass beds. The site itself is typical of shell midden sites in the region—largely treeless and nestled in a boulder field ringed by large birch trees and conifers (figure 3.12). It is oriented roughly north-south, parallel to the shore, and measures about 24 m (north-south axis) × 16 m (west-east axis) (figure 3.13).

There is obvious evidence of collecting activity at the site. In fact, it is literally cratered by collector's pits. After an hour of transect and spot probing the site, we encountered no intact deposits of any kind. The site seems to have been a black soil midden with broken shell admixture, which occurred in two oval-shaped concentrations, both apparently disturbed. No evidence of exposed shell is now visible, suggesting relatively limited recent disturbance. No evidence of distinct shell middens was encountered, though it is possible shell midden deposits were mixed into black soil deposits (the site was the most disturbed midden encountered around Port Joli's harbour). Determining the depth of the deposit was difficult due to the hummocky and secondary nature of

Figure 3.12 AlDf-07: Photograph of site, facing north. Subject is standing in one of the many large collector trenches.

the deposit, but around 15 to 30 cm is likely a good estimate. While the site is effectively lost to further archaeology, the work of Erskine (1958, 1959) provides a record of the deposit.

AlDf-07, or "Port Joli Number II," as he called it, was the first site Erskine claimed to have found in his early archaeological explorations of the province. Erskine undertook to excavate the site over two seasons. He laid out a grid system of square yards, determining that a central boulder at the site was used as a "fire-back," based on the greater depth of "ash" (which Erskine [1958: 2] repeatedly used to describe very black, organic soil containing highly comminuted charcoal) encountered on one side of it. On the other side of the boulder, he found a substantial quantity of "chips and points," which he interpreted as indicating a wigwam floor. Nearby, he noted the stub of a burned wigwam pole still in situ, which he took as evidence of late historic Mi'kmaq use of the site. A photograph of the site taken by Erskine (figure 3.14) confirms the black nature of the soil and the limited proportion of broken shell.

Erskine (1959: 11) described encountering a "chipping floor" or wigwam floor which he believed faced south, based on the distribution of projectile points and debitage (cf. Hrynick et al. 2012). While his documentation of stratigraphy at the site is limited, he did note vertical variability in the distribution of lithic materials as follows: "At the bottom the chips were chiefly of slate.... Above them were masses of transparent quartz ... but in the uppermost level there were some chips of jasper." In regard to faunal remains, he indicated "the usual game but no vertebrae of sea fish"(Erskine 1986: 90). In summary, the site appears to have been a rather large black soil midden, containing the remains of several

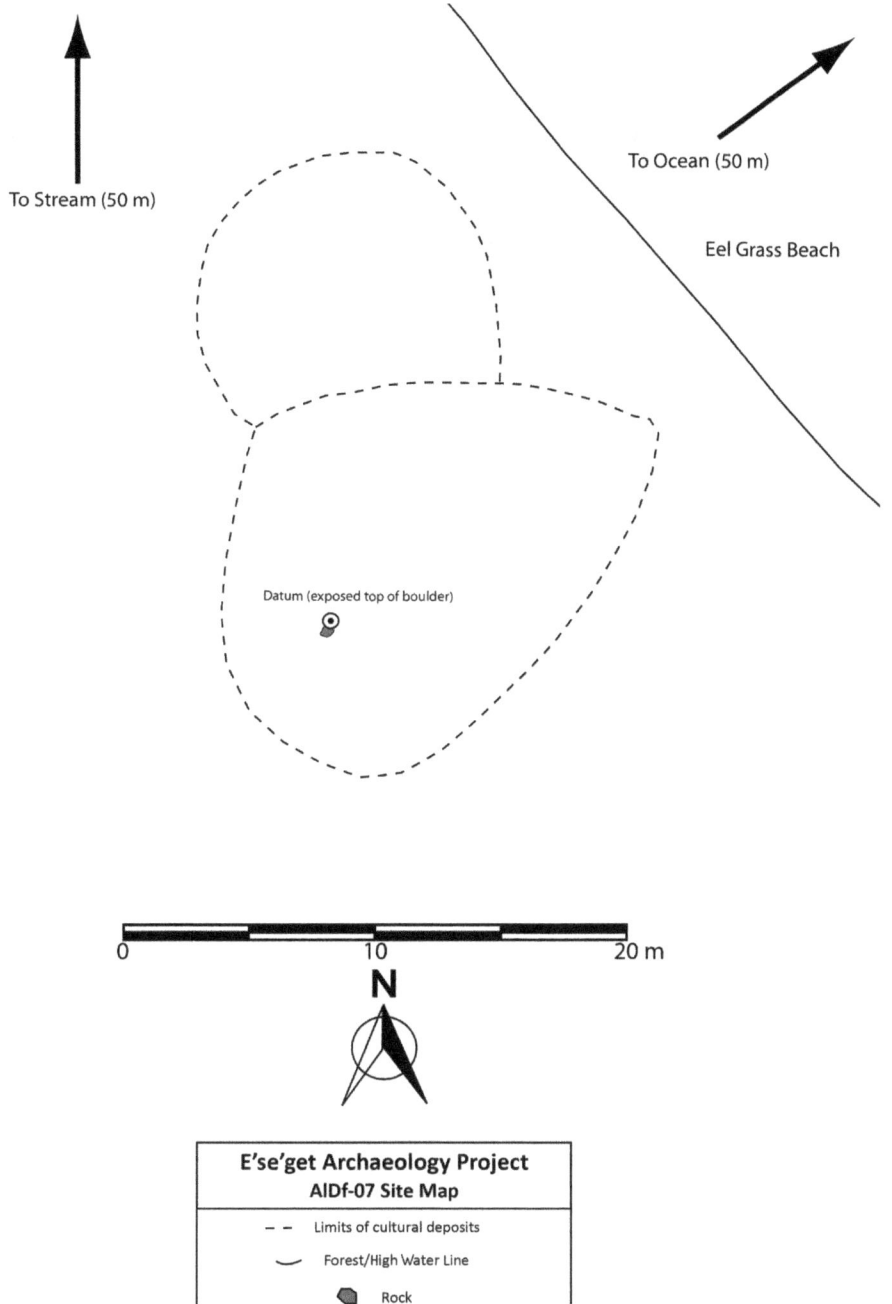

Figure 3.13 AlDf-07: Plan view, based on subsurface probing.

concatenated house floors. The lack of associated shell midden deposits is unusual, but as described above, the highly disturbed nature of the site may be obscuring the presence of such distinct deposits.

Figure 3.14 Photograph by John Erskine detailing his 1957 excavations at AlDf-07. Note the very black nature of the soil and the proportion of broken clam shell. © Michael Deal, used with permission.

AlDf-08 (Lower Path Lake Brook, Port Joli No. 7)
Description and Excavation Approach

In 1957, John Erskine discovered his seventh site in Port Joli ("Port Joli VII"), which he described as located "on the slope south of Lower Path Lake Brook, about three hundred yards from the harbour" (Erskine 1986: 91). He plotted this location on a map in his 1962 report on the Port Joli Excavations (Erskine 1962: 3), which was used as the basis of the site's Maritime Archaeological Resource Inventory (MARI) form coordinates. However, we failed to relocate the site despite intensive surveys in 2008 and 2009. Fortunately, in 2012, a knowledgeable local informant and local historian, Danielle Robertson, who had just transferred her property to the Nature Conservancy of Canada, took us to a site that matched Erskine's description. We noticed surface disturbance consistent with previous excavation, but we could find no evidence of recent looting—a rarity in this area of Nova Scotia. We tested the site in 2012 but were still uncertain if it was AlDf-08.

Upon our return to the lab, we compared our photographs of this new site to Erskine's original 1957 photographs of Port Joli No. 7 and discovered that a large boulder to the north of the site matched perfectly in both sets of photographs (figure 3.15). This conclusively establishes that the position of AlDf-08, or Port Joli No. 7, was incorrectly described by Erskine in his 1962 map (and provides support for the fact that he incorrectly positioned the nearby AlDf-07 on his map). In fact, it is located approximately 500 m to the southeast of his originally marked location. Part of the confusion in the location of the site may stem from the fact that the course of Path Lake Brook seems to have been altered by the paving of the modern road to the west. The brook's course is now several hundred metres north, and AlDf-08 now sits nearby a dry watercourse, the former course of Path Lake Brook.

Erskine (1986: 91) focused his excavations at the site on the large glacial erratic boulder at its northern edge, the same boulder that led to the confirmation of the site's identity. His units are today nothing but a diffuse triangular depression, the result of time and perhaps visits by collectors. Near the boulder he found two hearths encircled by small stones, one superimposed above the other, in what may have been the remains of a wigwam that had been repeatedly erected in the spot. The deposit contained many roots and he had difficulty digging, but he described that stratigraphy was intact and more than 9 inches (23 cm) deep, containing abundant lithics. Erskine (1986: 91) called the location a "campsite" with

Figure 3.15 Top: AlDf-08 (Port Joli No. 7) in 1957, photographed by John Erskine. © Michael Deal, used with permission. Bottom: AlDf-08 in 2012, facing north. Note that the boulder is the same in both photographs.

evidence of multiple dwellings (wigwam floors). He recorded that "clams were unusually scanty" and that it contained "more than fifty times as much ash [black soil] than PJ #3 [AlDf-25]" (Erskine 1986: 91), a large shell midden site (see below). This clearly indicates that the deposit was primarily a black soil midden, rather than a typical shell midden. Erskine noted that the distribution of this black soil was extensive, but relatively thin compared to other sites he had visited.

Our recent probing and testing of AlDf-08 reveals in fact that the site is a large mixed-deposit site, much larger than Erskine may have originally suspected. As he recorded, the site contains extensive black soil middens with shell admixtures, which manifest as rich organic soil deposits containing some broken shell and abundant artifacts and animal remains. However, the site also contains areas of more classic shell midden deposits composed of layers of broken and crushed shell in a thin, dark black soil matrix. The majority of the site is a highly organic black soil deposit with shell occurring only in quantities great enough to preserve organic remains. In fact, shell was present in proportions far smaller than more typical shell midden sites at AlDf-24, Area A; AlDf-25; and AlDf-30, Area A, where shell was typically greater than 50 percent of the volume of excavated matrix. The most comparable deposit we encountered was AlDf-06—although there, the quantity of shell is somewhat higher in AlDf-08, likely a consequence of having escaped plough damage subjected to the former.

The boundaries of the site were determined using a hand-held soil probe employed on a transect-offset mapping system (figure 3.16). Approximately 30 m (long) × 20 m (wide), with the long axis oriented along true north, the site is located in the lee of two large boulders on the northern and western margins of the site. The site slopes downhill to the south and east, with distinct shell middens present in the east and west margins of the black soil midden. A disturbed area, approximately 5 m (wide) × 7 m (long), occurred directly adjacent to the large northern boulder, with a backdirt pile occurring directly south of this. This disturbance corresponds well with Erskine's (1986: 91) description of his excavation of the site in 1957, 1959, and 1962.

We established a 1 × 1 m grid over a flat and apparently undisturbed area of the site, near Erskine's units and within 5 m of the northern boulder. Excavation revealed a deep and rich black soil midden approximately 45 cm deep. The midden was excavated by trowel and screened through 3 mm (1/8 inch) mesh.

Stratigraphy

The stratigraphic composition of the midden was as follows (figure 3.18):

- Level 1, the sod, consisted of dark brown-black organic sandy loam with abundant root matter, which was extremely difficult to remove and was as much as 10 cm thick in places. Cultural material was limited to two flakes, with no faunal preservation indicated.
- Level 2 was an ashy dark black-grey organic sandy loam with abundant roots. The sand appeared to have been heat-altered, and was sometimes tinged with orange and red hues. The level did not extend across the unit, and disappeared in the east, perhaps indicating a hearth feature. Shell was generally absent in this level, though

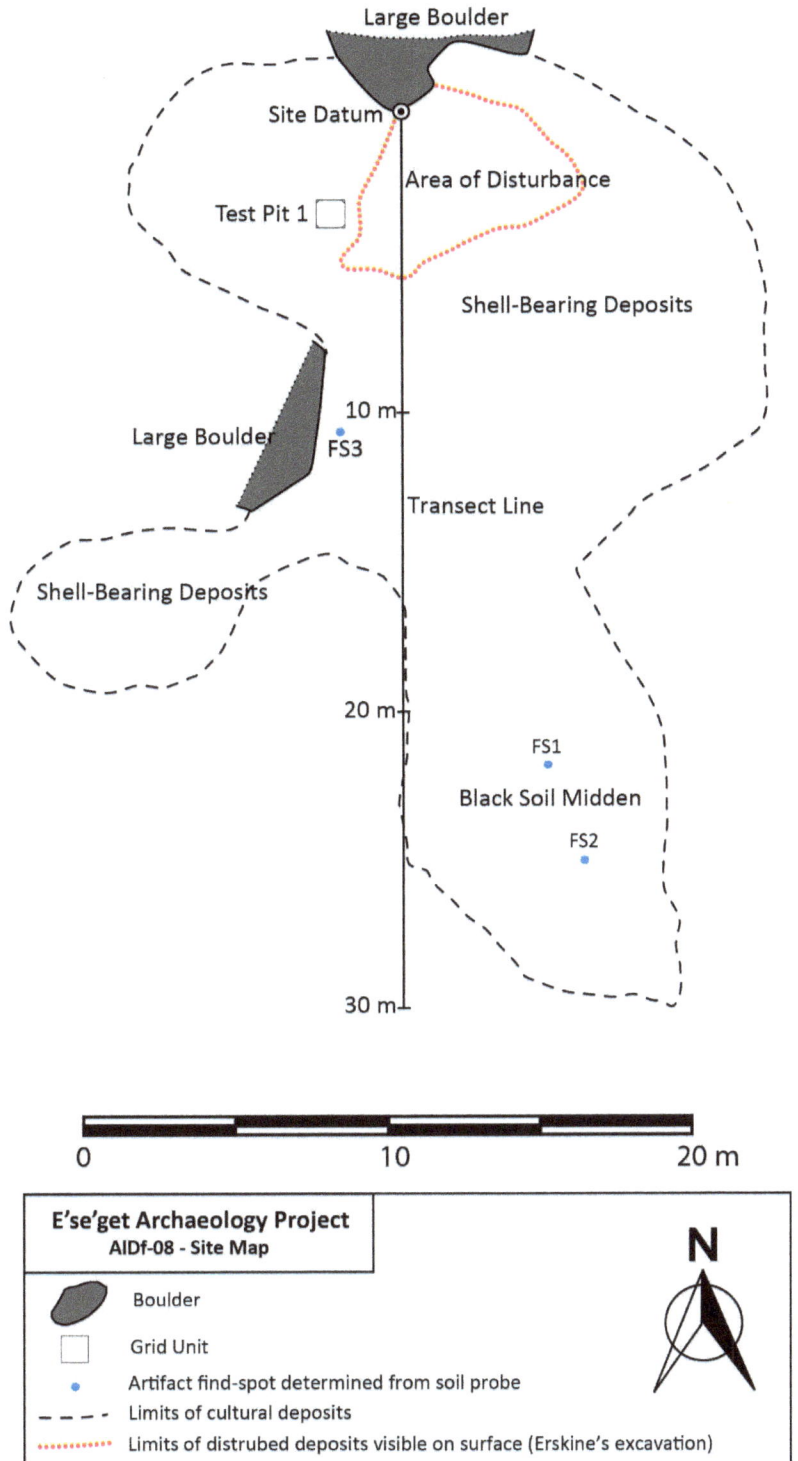

Figure 3.16 AlDf-08: Plan view, based on subsurface soil probing, and showing location of 2012 excavations.

Figure 3.17 AlDf-08: Photograph of the site, facing northwest. Subject is standing next to test unit.

finely broken flecks of shell could be discerned throughout. Faunal preservation was excellent in this layer, perhaps due to the presence of shell below. Highly comminuted charcoal occurred throughout the level and was so abundant that it sometimes clogged the screen. Artifacts, specifically primary debitage, were abundant, and one thumbnail scraper was recovered. This level was roughly contiguous with upper stratigraphic unit 3 in the profile.

- Level 3a was a dark black-grey sandy loam distinguished from Level 2 by the presence of fragmented clam shell and a red/brown sandy loam mottling. Burnt bone and shell were present in the level, and faunal preservation and artifact recovery were excellent. The presence of a red-brown-grey lens of sandy loam, together with the presence of burnt bone and shells, suggested the presence of a small hearth, which may be associated with a living surface. This level was roughly contiguous with lower stratigraphic Level 3, including levels 4, 5, and 6 in the profile.
- Levels 3b to 3d were distinguished by a change in colour to a dark black sandy loam, firm in texture, and containing large amounts of burnt shell and bone and fire-cracked rock. The layer was extremely rich in lithic debitage, including both primary and secondary flakes. In the northwest quadrant of the unit, a distinct lens of burnt shell suggests the extension of a hearth area to the north (as the deposit increased in depth, this deposit covered an increasingly large portion of the unit, eventually covering the entire northern part of the unit). Clam shell was abundant, with both highly fragmented and occasional whole valves occurring throughout the deposit. Large fragments of charcoal were abundant in the lower portions of

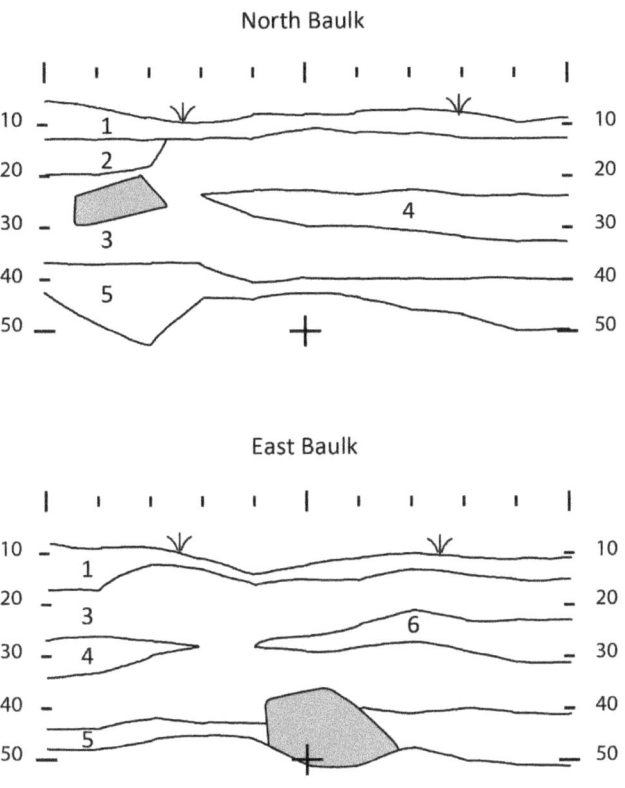

1 Sod
2 Grey ash and heat-altered sandy loam
3 Black-grey sandy loam with finely broken shell
4 Bown-grey loamy sand (heat-altered?)
5 Mottled redish-brown sandy loam at interface with subsoil
6 Unbroken and coarsely broken clam shells in a dark black-brown sandy loam
   Rock

Figure 3.18 AlDf-08: Profile plan of 2012 excavations.

the level. Formal artifacts included unifacial scrapers, corner-notched projectile points, and abundant lithic debitage.

- Levels 3e to 3f appeared to represent a natural transition to a compact dark black sandy loam deposit distinguished from layers above by its compactness and a radical decrease in the frequency of shell. Unlike levels above, ceramic sherds, including

dentate-stamped and cord-wrapped-stick decorated pieces, were abundant in this layer. Lithic frequencies were again high, although they appeared to increase in proportion from levels above. The compactness of this level, as well as the absence of shell and abundance of lithics, suggests that it could have been a living-surface of some kind.
- Level 3g was a dark reddish brown sandy loam with brown/orange sandy mottling, which represented a transition to the B horizon below it. No artifacts were recovered, and the deposit directly overlaid Level 4 (subsoil).
- Level 4 was the natural subsoil layer which can be described as an undulating mottled light grey/yellow/orange/brown sand, with abundant cobbles and rocks. It was entirely consistent with the B horizon in other areas of Port Joli.

Summary

In summary, the high density of lithic debitage, compact nature of the deposit, dark black soil with abundant charcoal, burnt bone, fire-cracked rock, and limited nature of the shell deposits strongly suggest a series of superimposed living floors in this unit—essentially like the deposit excavated at AlDf-24, Area C (see below). The site would appear to be a very large black soil site, the result of relatively extensive and recurrent occupation by dwelling structures, with at least two associated kitchen middens. This interpretation corresponds very well with the observations of Erskine, who interpreted the site as the remains of a "campsite" (Erskine 1986: 91). However, unlike in the deposits we excavated, Erskine described an early historic component in the uppermost level, consisting of "chinaware, the point of a stake, and two charred bits of . . . wooden arrowpoints" (Erskine 1986: 91). We found no evidence of historic material at the site.

AlDf-35 (Maxwell's Brook)
Description and Excavation Approach

We discovered this previously undocumented site during our survey of the west shoreline of the harbour in Port Joli in 2008. It is located on Canadian Wildlife Service property 80-33A, about 350 m inland from the coast, and about 20 m south of Sandy Hollow Road (now a hiking path). Composed of single shell midden and associated black soil deposits, the site abuts a large boulder located on the south bank of Maxwell's Brook. It can be reached from the harbour's shore by following Maxwell's Brook from its mouth through a dry salt marsh to the location of a boulder field, through which the stream runs. The site is in the southern lee of the largest boulder in the boulder field (figure 3.19), and is relatively unvegetated, though several small-sized conifers have taken hold in the midden (perhaps related to disturbance).

It is relevant to note that this site is near the presumed location of AlDf-19, a single Borden number given to two shell middens presumably discovered and sketched in the 1930s by T. H. Raddall. Prior to the E'se'get Project, archaeologists were unable to relocate these sites, so a Borden number was assigned with general coordinates. As described below, comparison of modern maps with Raddall's (n.d.) original plans has revealed that the sites Raddall discovered do not occur on Maxwell's Brook, but rather approximately 2 km south,

Figure 3.19 AlDf-35: Photograph of site, facing northwest.

on Jack's Brook (officially unnamed on maps) in what is now Thomas Raddall Provincial Park (see AlDf-30 and AlDf-31).

The site is adjacent to and abutting a very large boulder, which protects it from northerly winds. In 2008 we mapped the site, and then we briefly tested it in 2009 to assess the stratigraphy and to obtain radiocarbon faunal samples. The site is relatively small and oval-shaped, roughly 12 m (long) × 8 m (wide), just slightly larger than its adjacent boulder in horizontal extent. Transect-based probing revealed that the site was composed of two areas, a shell midden abutting the large boulder and a black soil midden with abundant broken shell south of the trench. The black soil midden had a significant shell admixture in comparison to other black soil middens we encountered around Port Joli. Importantly, probing revealed that the proportion of shell appeared to diminish gradually from the shell midden into the black soil midden (i.e., there was no distinct line of demarcation) and continued to diminish toward the southerly margins of the site, petering out entirely after several metres.

Beyond the edges of the collector's trench the stratigraphy of the site appears to be well preserved, and, as described below, preservation in the midden was excellent. The collector's trench is contiguous with the large boulder that dominates the site. The trench extends for about 8 m in an east-west orientation, and abundant coarsely broken and unbroken shell has been strewn around the boulders on the site, revealing the density of shell in the deposit. On the east margin of the trench, under dense leaf letter and understorey, we encountered a slumped cut bank, which exhibited a dense shell-dominant midden with protruding mammal, fish, and bird bone. Thus, this site appears to have significant intact shell midden deposits.

In 2009 we excavated a 25 × 25 cm test pit by trowel in a presumably undisturbed portion of the AlDf-35 black soil midden, about 6 m to the southeast of the large boulder that dominates the site (figure 3.20).

Stratigraphy

The stratigraphy encountered in AlDf-35, Test Unit 1, was as follows (see also figure 3.21):

- Level 1 was characterized by a dense root mat in dark brown–black organic humus, with occasional broken shell (possibly caused by the large collector's trench to the

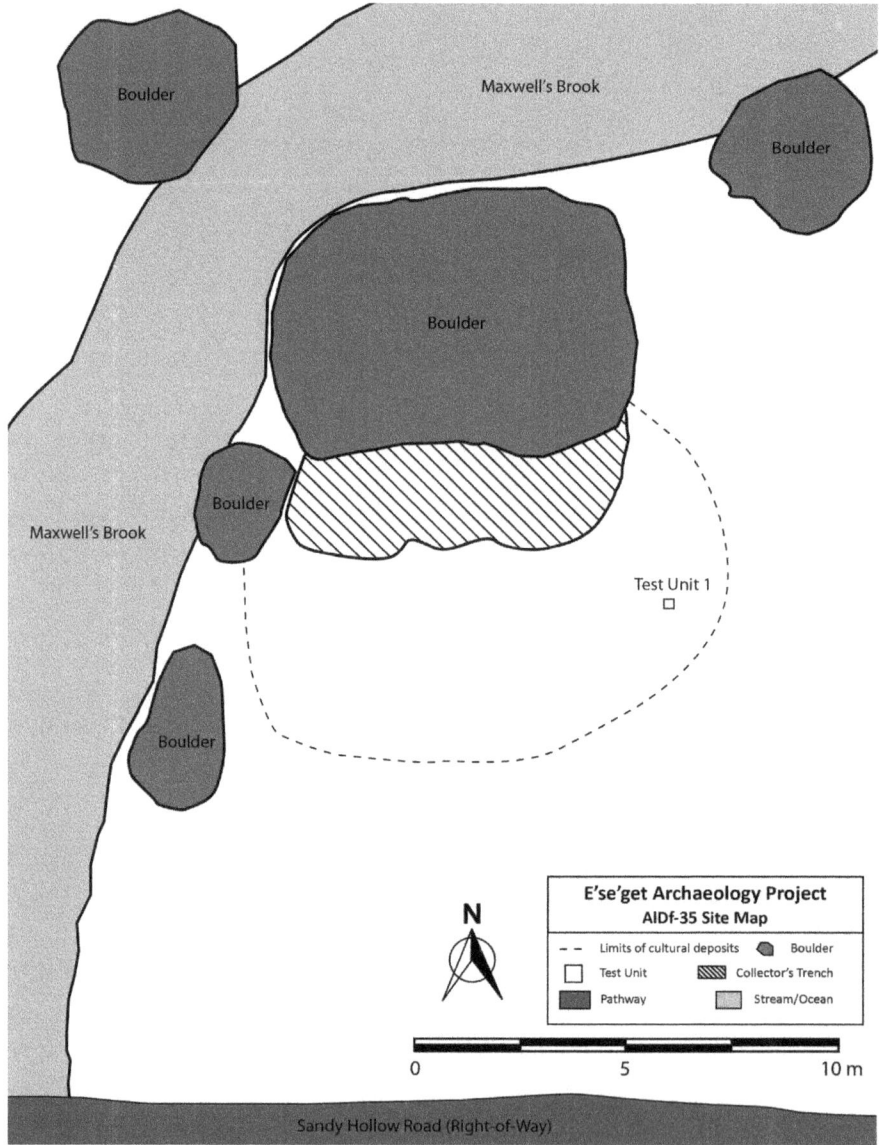

Figure 3.20 AlDf-35: Site plan.

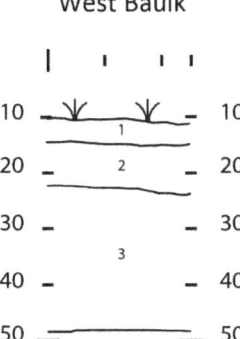

West Baulk

1 Sod
2 Dark brown humus
3 Unbroken and coarsely broken clam shells in a dark black humus

E'se'get Archaeology Project
AlDf-35, Test Unit 1, West Profile

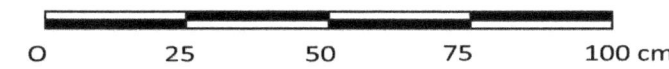

Figure 3.21 AlDf-35: Test Unit 1 profiles.

north east). No artifacts or faunal remains (besides shell) were recovered in this layer.
- Level 2 was a typical sub-sod layer, characterized by dark brown organic humus with abundant roots. No shell occurred in this layer, confirming the possible secondary nature of the shell in Level 1 above it. No artifacts or faunal remains were recovered in this layer.
- Level 3 was a compacted dark black humus with abundant broken and unbroken soft-shell clam valves. Other midden materials included bones of large mammals, as well as grit-tempered and shell-tempered pottery and lithics. Uncharacteristic of other midden deposits in Port Joli, bones of large terrestrial mammals are very abundant in this midden—so much so, that it appears to be a defining characteristic of the site.
- Level 4 was a typical subsoil layer characteristic of the region; it was composed of a mottled orange/tan gravelly sand with abundant small cobbles and pebbles.

Summary
The test unit was placed in a black soil midden, which is probably the remains of recurrent living surfaces, as indicated by the relatively high proportion of lithic debitage recovered.

The fauna from AlDf-35 included a large quantity of cervid remains, in significant quantity for a small test pit. It appears to have been a small habitation site with an associated shell midden, the result of discard from the domestic habitation.

AlDf-28
Description and Excavation Approach

AlDf-28 is a relatively small site first discovered by Stephen Powell (1990) on a shoreline survey conducted prior to the establishment of Thomas Raddall Provincial Park. At the time, Powell observed exposed shell at the site, but little shell was observed during our visit in 2009. AlDf-28 is difficult to see from the shore as it is separated from the rocky beach by a large knoll to the north and by a bog and alder thicket to the north and east. To access the site, one must approach from the west, skirting the southerly base of the large knoll. The site is currently on Nature Conservancy of Canada property, which we accessed with permission. Similar to other shell midden sites in the region, AlDf-28 sits among large boulders which ring the site to the west and north. Along with the large northerly knoll, these provide significant shelter from coastal winds.

The midden deposit itself is largely treeless, and the surface topography is best described as cratered, presumably a consequence of recent collecting activity (figure 3.22). As figure 3.23 indicates, exploring with soil probes revealed a semi-lunar black soil midden which extends for about 12 m on the north-south axis and about 10 m on the west-east axis (though it is likely that the eastern portion of the site has been covered by an actively developing bog). The midden is characterized by finely and coarsely broken clam shells in

Figure 3.22 AlDf-28: Photograph of site, facing southwest, from northeast edge of site.

The Sites   67

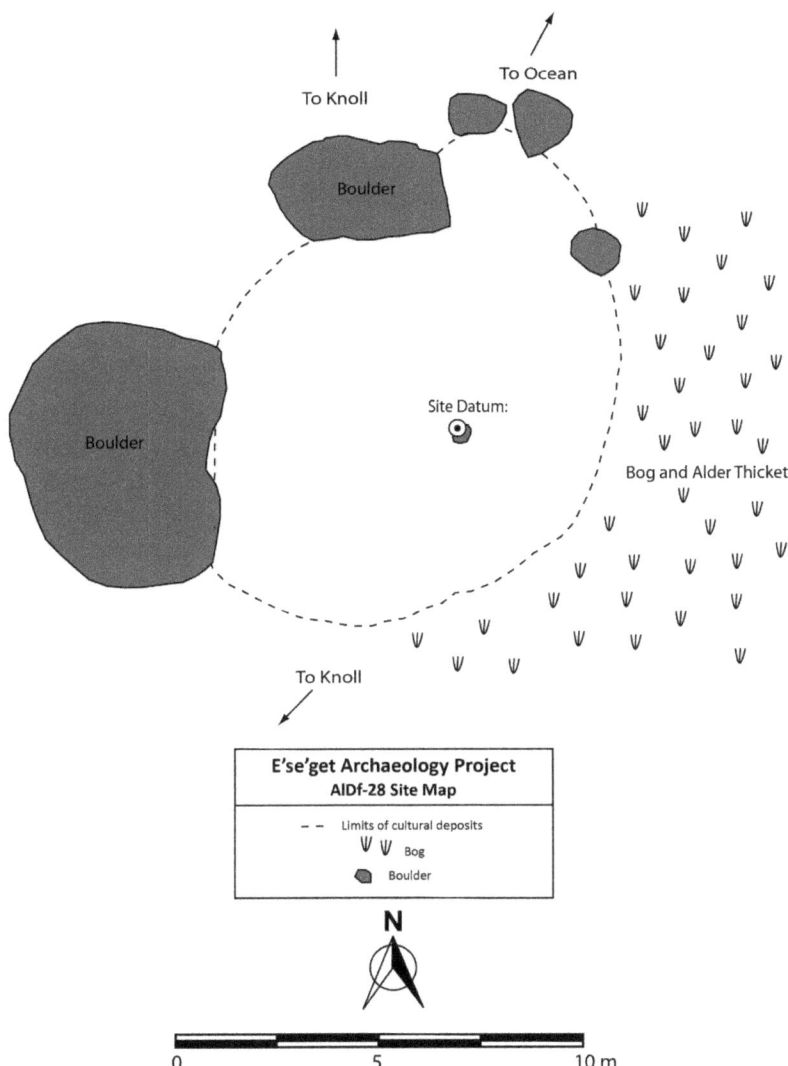

Figure 3.23 AlDf-28: Plan view, based on subsurface probing.

a dark brown–black sandy loam, loose in texture. Significant disturbance has been caused by collecting, particularly at the base of the large boulders in the west and north of the site. No indications of areas where shell predominated over soil were encountered, but, similar to AlDf-07, significant digging may have resulted in mixing with adjacent black soil deposits. Our probing suggests that no undisturbed deposits remain at the site, though it is possible that some unmolested portions of the midden are covered by the bog. Unfortunately, a dense alder thicket is also growing in the bog, suggesting any cultural deposits in this area would be disturbed by root action.

AlDf-27 (Bill Brook or AlDf-10)
Description and Excavation Approach
Very little is known about this small site, though it was completely excavated by John Erskine between 1962 and 1964 (Erskine 1964). Located on the south side of a small stream, Bill Brook, where it crosses Sandy Hollow Road, the site is approximately 30 m inland east from the harbour shoreline. It was rediscovered by Stephen Powell in 1990 during a survey for the nearby Thomas Raddall Provincial Park. Powell (1990) described the site as small and shallow, about 8 × 8 m in area, and oval in outline. Unlike many middens in the area, it was heavily wooded, suggesting it was disturbed in the past, likely by Erskine.

We could not locate the site in our surveys between 2008 and 2010, and no evidence of shell or artifacts could be discerned in the area (despite intensive probing), though Powell collected several quartz flakes from the site in 1990. The glacial boulders associated with the site also appear to be missing. Unfortunately, a small wooden bridge was built in the presumed location of this site by a property owner and it appears that the construction either covered or more likely (if the missing boulders are any indication) destroyed this site. If so, it must have been a very small site indeed, as the bridge's footprint is not much larger than the dimensions described by Powell in 1990. Erskine (1964) records that when he excavated the site, it was even smaller than when Powell encountered it: "the camping spot [was] limited by boulders to a circle three yards [2.7 m] in diameter" (Erskine 1964: 9). Erskine did not refill excavation units with backdirt and this practice may account for the discrepancy in size noted by Powell some twenty-six years later.

Erskine describes the deposit as a black soil midden with a limited amount of fragmentary shell. As a result, animal bones were "poorly preserved," but dominated by cervids (Erskine 1964: 10). Erskine's (1964: 10) excavations revealed two "outdoor hearths," presumably inside the small boulder ring, as the hearths were described as "under" them or with the boulder "projecting" into them (Erskine 1964: 10). One hearth had been repeatedly placed in the same location to a depth of 43 cm. Lithics were common in the deposit, though flakes were large and roughly made, and a Levanna point was recovered. Ceramics were common in about 55 percent of the units, and they predominately had a shell temper.

Stratigraphically, "the uppermost seven inches, including the turf was ash-black sand, probably blown in from the beach and mixed by roots and animals" (Erskine 1964: 9). A small historic bead was encountered, along with a "rotted point of a wigwam pole," (Erskine 1964: 10), which Erskine indicated was the result of an early historic occupation in the extreme upper levels of the deposit. Interestingly, he noted that if there was such an occupation, especially after the decline of flint knapping and the adoption of metal tools, "campers might leave very little to mark their passing."

Erskine (1964: 10) described the small site as "a small summer fishing camp of a time when the sea was much lower," presumably because he found occasional cod bones in the poorly preserved deposit. Based on Erskine's description, we can interpret the site as a black soil midden with limited shell admixture. However, no kitchen midden was described by Erskine, despite the complete excavation of the site. The area was too small (less than 3 m in diameter) to support even the smallest dwelling floor we encountered in Port Joli, and the evidence of large robust "outdoor" hearths repeatedly placed in the same footprint suggests, instead, a special-use site, similar in nature to AlDf-11. While the faunal preservation is poor, the preponderance of cervid remains is similar to AlDf-11. Furthermore, the site is located at a choke point between a large marshy upland to the west and a portion of coastline where the beach narrows (figure 3.1). The easily navigable forest in this region in this area is only about 150 m wide, indicating that this site too may have been ideally placed to intercept caribou, moose, or deer moving from the inner to the outer harbour.

AlDf-26
Description and Excavation Approach

AlDf-26 was discovered and tested by Stephen Powell during his seminal 1990 survey. We were unable to visit the site during the E'se'get Project as it was located on a private parcel of land, which we did not have permission to access. Fortunately, the property on which the site sits was subsequently purchased by the Nature Conservancy of Canada after the E'se'get Project had ended, effectively protecting the site from development and destruction. As described by Powell (1990), the site is very large and, in many respects, conforms to a class of sites typified by AlDf-24 and AlDf-25 (described below). Unfortunately, the site is heavily disturbed, and surface shell suggests much of the site's surface has been impacted by previous collecting.

Like other shell middens in Port Joli, Powell (1990: 4) observed that AlDf-26 was located in a treeless grassy clearing. On top of the knoll, Powell discovered the remains of a cellar depression, likely Loyalist in age. Powell originally believed that the site was the location of Erskine's famous Port Joli No. 3 (Erskine 1962), and it bears many similarities (its large size and kidney shape being the most striking), but our subsequent analysis strongly suggests Port Joli No. 3 is actually present-day AlDf-25 (see below).

As described in Powell's map, visible shell on the site covered a very large kidney-shaped mound some 35 × 15 m, with the long axis oriented roughly east-west (figure 3.24). The site sits at the base, and extends up the side, of a very high knoll that ends in a jagged boulder cliff at the shore. A small sandy beach abuts the base of the cliff and though the intertidal in this area is very rocky, very large clam flats occur just south of a small point about 50 m south of the site (adjacent to AlDf-25). Large piles of boulders and cobbles dot the landscape around the site, which Powell (1995: 1) believed were the result of early historic land-clearing activities.

Powell (1995) conducted test excavations at the site in 1995, including three shovel tests in areas outside of the midden. Two test units in the main midden area revealed the structure of the midden. The first, x-5, was 1 × 0.5 m and was placed in the main midden area. Though thoroughly disturbed, it revealed "a 50 cm thick layer of shell (most of which were crushed), with black organic soil" (Powell 1995: 3), indicating a thick shell midden deposit. This layer sat directly on the A horizon, or the buried soil surface before the midden was deposited. The second test unit, x-6, was a profile trench positioned to ascertain the structure of the midden at its southeastern margin. The profile Powell recorded (figure 3.25) shows an undisturbed deposit covered in black soil and shells (backdirt) from previous explorations in the midden. Below this was a buried sod layer without shell, which Powell interpreted as the original mound surface prior to recent collecting activity. Below the layer was the margin of the midden (Level 3), "an undisturbed shell deposit with black organic soil and artifacts . . . from 20 to 12 cm in thickness" (Powell 1995: 3). Just as Powell expected,

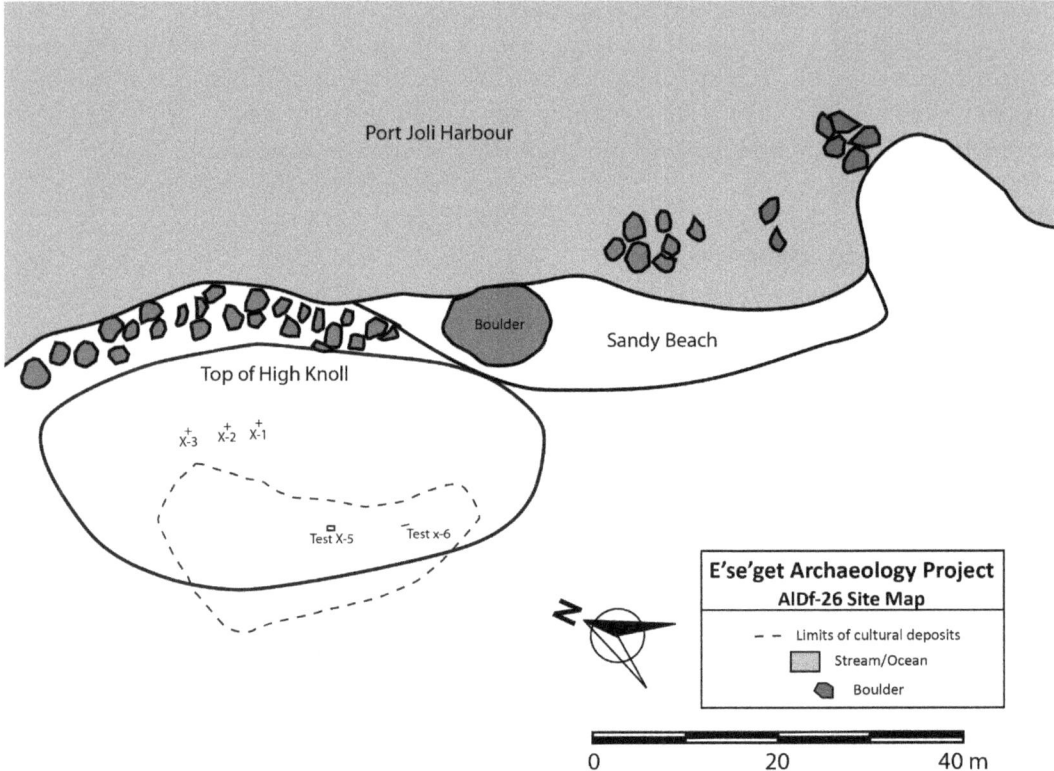

Figure 3.24 AlDf-26: Plan view based on surface observation and test excavation, redrawn from original plans and notes by Powell (1995).

the midden diminished in thickness at its margins, indicating a true shell mound. Underneath this was another buried sod horizon, the original surface before the midden was deposited, and below that, the B horizon subsoil characteristic of Port Joli.

The disturbance and limited testing make it difficult to interpret this site, but it seems to be quite unusual compared to sites previously described in this chapter. The most striking characteristic is the extremely large size of the shell midden deposit, which covers at least 500 m², and which is much more extensive than anything previously reviewed here. Like many sites in the harbour, the midden is adjacent to expansive black soil deposits with some shell admixture, which may be the remains of a habitation area or an activity area associated with the main midden. In many respects the site is similar in structure to both AlDf-24 and AlDf-25, and we believe the descriptions of these sites, below, provide an excellent analogue for AlDf-26.

AlDf-25 (Scotch Point, Port Joli No. 3, AlDf-09)
Description and Excavation Approach

AlDf-25 is another very large shell midden site located at the northern part of the third beach north from Scotch Point. It sits practically on the edge of the northern boundary of Thomas Raddall Provincial Park, and is directly adjacent to a large glistening beach, or clam flat, which continues to be used by local clam diggers. The site is approximately 35 m from

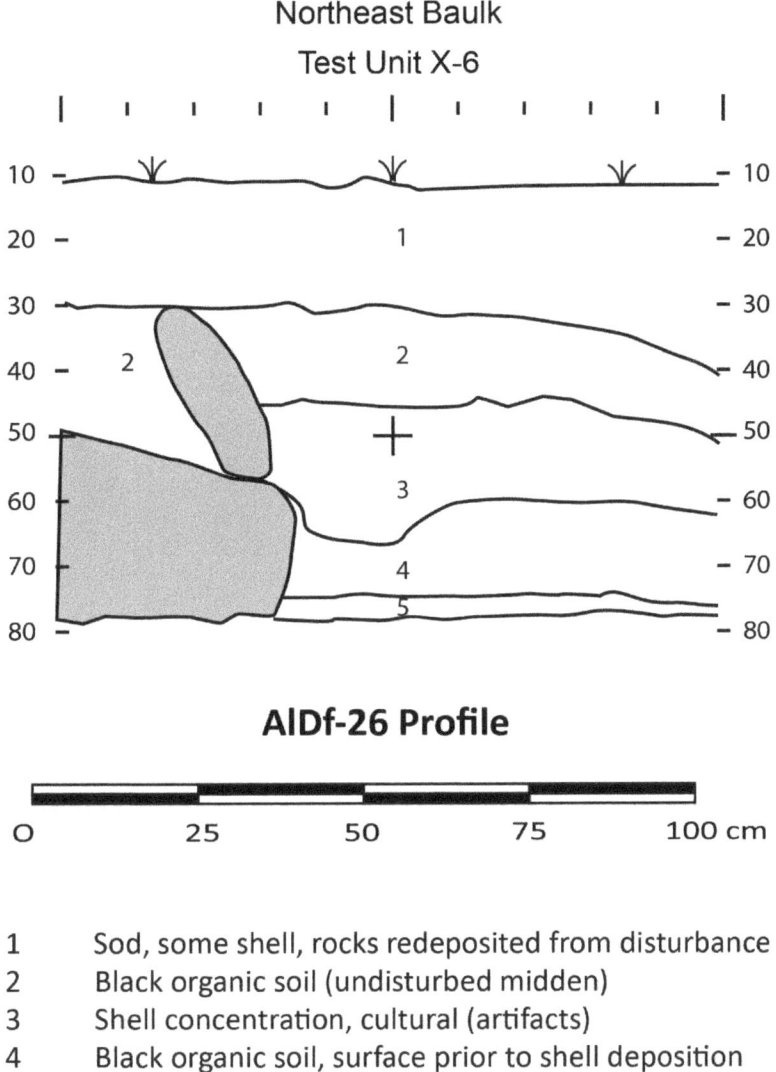

1. Sod, some shell, rocks redeposited from disturbance
2. Black organic soil (undisturbed midden)
3. Shell concentration, cultural (artifacts)
4. Black organic soil, surface prior to shell deposition
5. Subsoil
   Rock

Figure 3.25 AlDf-26: East-west profile of Test Unit x-6, redrawn from Powell (1995).

the shore, on a small flat area dominated by beach grasses. The midden is a large kidney-shaped mound, rising about 1.5 to 2 m above the surrounding surface, oriented north–south on its long axis (figure 3.26a). Unlike most other middens in Port Joli, AlDf-25 is extensively overgrown by willow, alder, and very large pine, fir, and spruce trees, such that it is virtually invisible from the beach. On the western and northern margin of the site is a small boulder-lined brook in a low-lying area, which is dry during the summer months.

A short distance from the southeast corner of the midden is a low knoll with a large glacial erratic at its apex. Several anthropogenic piles of boulders and cobbles sit around and against the erratic. The piles vary in size and shape, from neatly stacked linear mounds

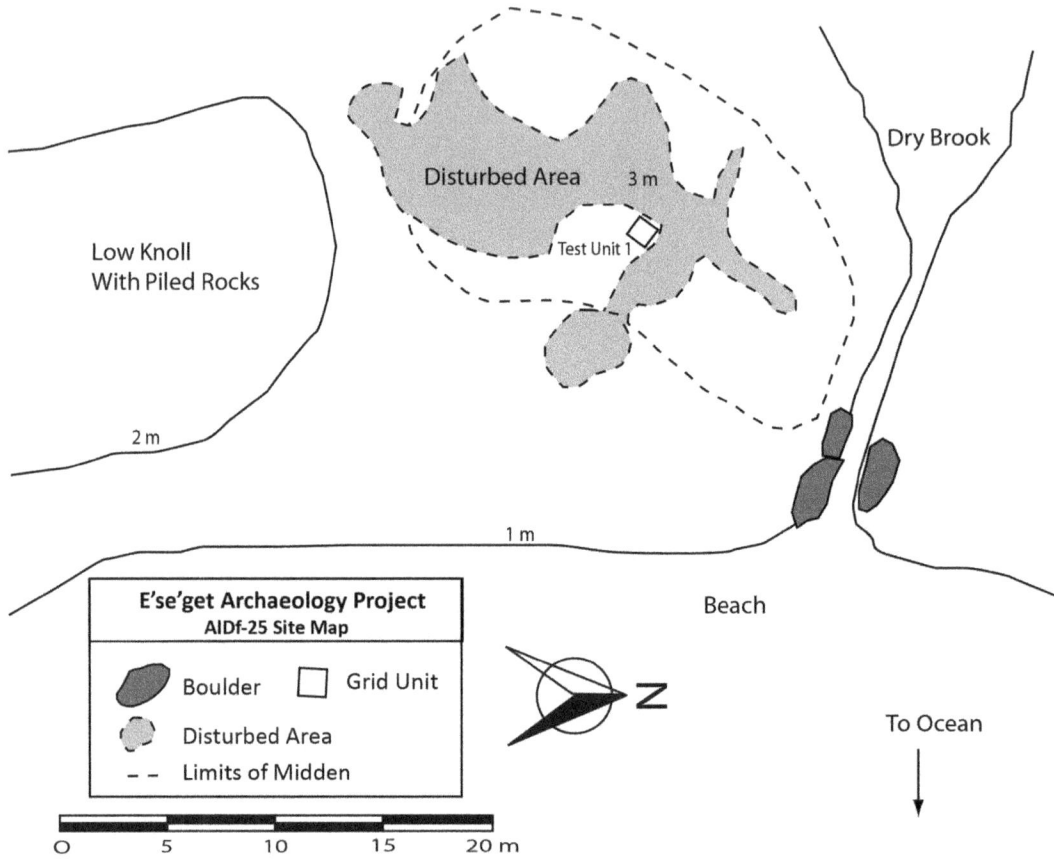

Figure 3.26a AlDf-25: Plan view, based on subsurface probing.

to jumbled, cone-shaped, cairns. Their function remains a mystery, although the extent of lichen and vegetative cover suggests a more recent deposit than the adjacent midden and glacial erratic. The land surrounding this knoll and the midden is particularly flat; reconnoitering the adjacent flatland to the south of these deposits indicated the presence of very few boulders or cobbles. This suggests the area may have been cleared for farming, which may be the source of the mysterious stone cairns (e.g., Erskine 1962: 4).

The midden mound itself is heavily disturbed. The northern margin, though dominated by alder and willow growth, shows no obvious signs (pits, etc.) of subsurface digging, but the presence of tree growth argues against this. The west, south, and particularly the east sides of the midden are cratered by pits and backdirt deposits. One particularly prominent feature is a shallow linear trench running roughly north-south, which extends into various large "lobes" on the east and west slopes of the midden. The flat area between the shell midden and the low knoll to the south exhibits similar evidence of disturbance. The outlines of a roughly rectangular pit can be discerned around the trunk of the large fir tree that now grows in the middle of this depression.

This pattern of subsurface disturbance at AlDf-25 is remarkably similar in outline to the excavation trenches in John Erskine's (1962) map of the Port Joli No. 3 excavations (figure 3.26b). In fact, the map created in 2008 compares very favourably to Erskine's sketch

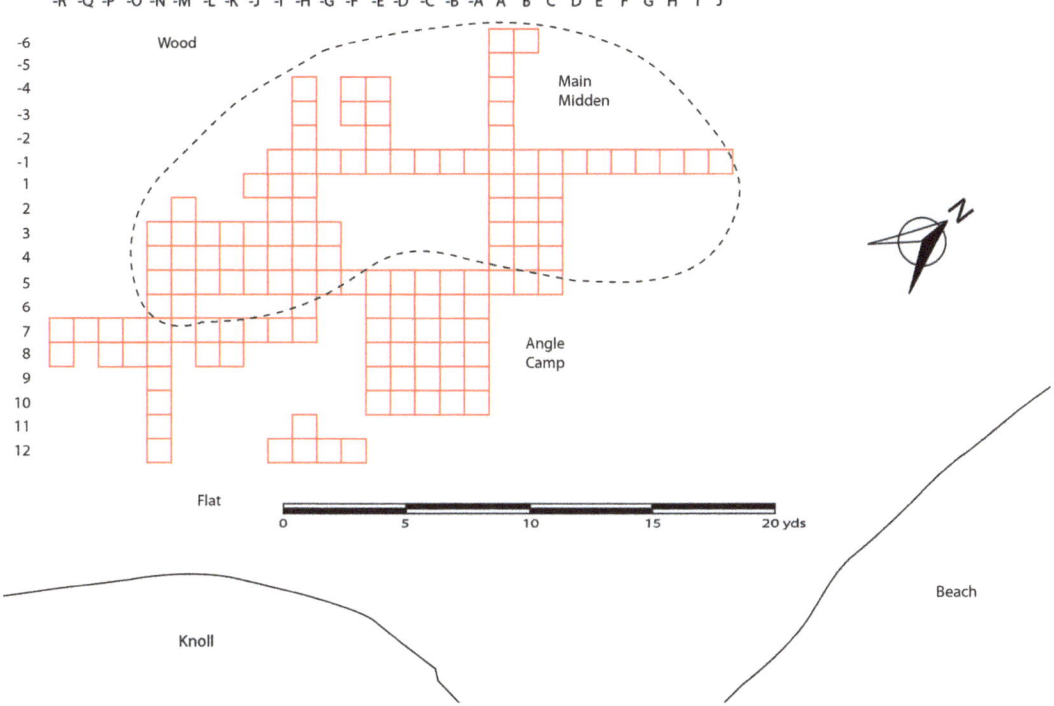

Figure 3.26b AlDf-25: Port Joli No. 3 site map, redrawn from Erskine (1962).

map and to his description of the local topography of the site, which is worth noting verbatim (Erskine 1962: 4):

> In July 1957 I walked the shore from Sand Cove to Scotch Point, searching both sides of every brook that flowed to Port Joli Harbour. I found nothing. Continuing past Scotch Point I found a cove, sheltered from the surf, where the beach glistened with fresh water flowing through it from a brook. This looked so good I spent an hour searching inland, passing a great ruined beaver-dam. I was returning to the shore on the north side of the brook when I saw a treeless area to my left and found this very large site beside a much smaller brook, now summer-dry. . . . The obvious part was a kidney-shaped mound covering about 270 square yards [225 m²] and set from twenty to forty yards [18 to 36 m] back from the beach. Between the southern end and the beach was a knoll about 12 feet [3.6 m] high, and between knoll and mound a flattish strip about 10 yards [9 m] wide extended some forty yards [36 m] from the shore until it was lost in the rocky woods. The mound rose some six feet [1.8 m] above this flat strip and seven feet [2 m] above the woodland on its western edge. The knoll showed no signs of occupation although someone had packed loose stone around the boulders to clear the land for the scythe.

Both Erskine's map and his description of the local topography are consistent with the site data recorded in 2008 at AlDf-25. Moreover, a unique boulder in photographs Erskine labelled "PJ3" precisely matches the boulder in photos we took in 2008 (figures 3.27a and 3.27b). The significant level of vegetation growth on AlDf-25 is obviously a product of the considerable post-depositional disturbance of the deposit. In fact, the vegetation on this mound was noticeably denser and more diverse than on any other shell midden site encountered. The root action from these plants has undoubtedly caused significantly more subsurface disturbance of the site. Despite this grim prognosis, test excavations in 2008 in a seemingly undisturbed portion of the site did reveal intact deposits (see description below).

Erskine dug at the site on three separate occasions between 1957 and 1962, and his extensive excavations are worth summarizing in detail. He noted the special character of the site, writing (Erskine 1962: 4) that "it was ... unlike any I should ever find again and was probably the largest undisturbed site in Nova Scotia." When he first discovered it, the mound and adjacent flat area were treeless. His excavation of the mound covered more than 80 m^2, including a transect that ran practically the entire length of the mound (figure 3.26b). The mound was revealed as a dense shell midden with "untrampled clamshells of unusual size" (Erskine 1962: 4) pottery and bone, but very few stone tools or debitage and limited soil matrix. Localized charcoal was present in the deposit, but he did not encounter "trampled," or highly fragmented, shell, suggesting no living surfaces or house floors were in the deposit. Erskine observed that the mound was six feet (1.8 m) higher than the flat area adjacent to it. However, the depth of the deposit only ranged between 30 cm to 90 cm, a trait we confirmed in our test excavations of the site (see below). This indicates that the mound was at least partially natural. Erskine (1959: 9) stated "the regular curved mound overlay a very irregular base of knolls and boulders." The bottom layer of the midden was described as "a shallow layer of ash [black soil] with many potsherds" (Erskine 1962: 5), suggesting the area was first used as a habitation site or activity area before the midden developed on top of it.

Excavation in the flat area adjacent to the shell mound, which Erskine (1962) called the "angle camp," revealed a very different type of deposit. The deposit was approximately 50 cm deep, and contained much less shell and abundant amounts of "ash" (which Erskine often used to describe black organic soil with large proportions of comminuted charcoal). Erskine (1959: 9) described three house-floor deposits, or "wigwam sites" in this location, which were relatively shallow and contained a low density of artifacts. (More details of this deposit can be found in Chapter 5.)

To ground-truth Erskine's work at AlDf-25, and to obtain a datable sample, we dug a 1 × 1 m test unit on the midden mound of the site. Test Unit 1 was carefully positioned in one of the very few locations on the shell mound that appeared to be undisturbed. It was placed in an area of the site that was between three intersecting trenches, in what seems to have been a habitually used path, both for wildlife (as the deer droppings indicated) and for tourists who have visited the site recently. The unit slopes from the west to the east at a steep angle and would have formed the southern edge of the midden.

Figure 3.27a AlDf-25: Erskine's original excavation photos from 1962 (note boulder in background, to east). © Michael Deal, used with permission.

Figure 3.27b AlDf-25: The same boulder in 2008 as in Erskine's 1962 photo, facing east.

Figure 3.28 AlDf-25: Photograph of the site in 2012, facing west.

Stratigraphy

A description of the stratigraphy of the unit follows (figure 3.29):

- Level 1 was the surface stratum, composed of a thin vegetative root mat with abundant willow and alder roots. The soil matrix was best described as very compact dark brown organic humus, with abundant decayed leaf litter. The compact nature of this layer was likely a result of recent trampling by collectors and pot hunters, as was evidenced by the nearby collection pits.
- Level 2 consisted of abundant broken shell in a dark brown-black sandy loam. This could suggest previous disturbance but may also be consistent with extensive trampling in this heavily used portion of the site. Abundant roots also suggest heavy disturbance of this layer, which may have also led to the jumbled nature of the deposit. If so, the previous collecting activity, and the subsequent tree growth related to it, may be impacting the little remaining intact deposits in the site. While the deposit was relatively sterile, some small fragments of pottery and bone were recovered from basal levels.
- Level 3a marked the beginning of a layer of unbroken soft-shell clam valves (though still mixed with abundant fragmented shells), suggesting a relatively undisturbed deposit. Decorated pottery and abundant bone were mixed with small amounts of blue mussel shell throughout a dark grey/brown/black humic matrix. An interesting characteristic of the layer was the very small size of the soft-shell clam valves, which are markedly smaller than those encountered at sites further south, such as AlDf-24 and AlDf-30.

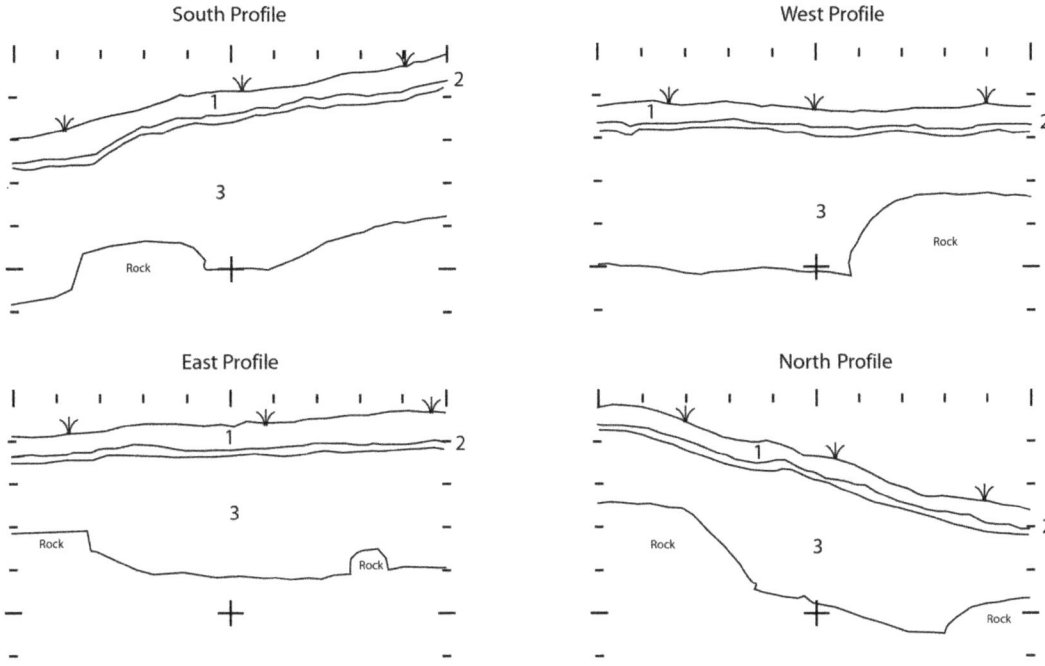

1 Sod
2 Coarsely broken shell in dark brown/black sandy loam
4 Unbroken and coarsely broken clam shells in a dark brown/black sandy loam

Figure 3.29 AlDf-25: South, west, east, and north soil profiles, Test Unit 1.

- Level 3b marked the beginning of layer composed primarily of unbroken clam shells. Though relatively sterile of artifacts and faunal remains, we collected a large bulk midden sample from the northwest corner of the unit. The shells in this layer were markedly larger than those in the layer above.
- Level 3c marked an arbitrary subdivision which appears in all respects to represent the same deposit as levels 3a and 3b (i.e., levels 3a to 3c should be aggregated for analytical purposes). It was composed of relatively abundant unbroken shell, though broken shell becomes more abundant at the base of the level. The soil matrix was the same grey/brown/black humus that characterizes all the shell midden deposits in the area. Several large cobbles were encountered in this unit, including one very large rock in the north wall. At a depth of 42 cm to 50 cm, we encountered a mottled, pebbly sand (light grey/orange), indicating a subsoil horizon. The slope of this horizon suggests a significant subsurface mound in this area, which obviously contributes to the midden's large appearance (e.g., see Erskine 1962: 7). A subsurface soil probe in this bottom layer revealed a sterile B Horizon extending for at least 20 cm below the bottom of the test pit (70 cm below the corner datum).

Summary

Our excavations confirm that Erskine's notes accurately capture the salient details of the midden. It is quite deep and largely devoid of lithics but contained abundant animal bones and pottery. There was no evidence of living-floors in our test pit; instead it appears to have been a primary refuse midden with some evidence of cooking or smoking activity (due to the abundant charcoal). Occasional cobbles recovered in the matrix, as well as layers of trampled shell, suggest some sort of additional cultural activity occurred on the midden, perhaps associated with processing clams and/or animal remains. While no evidence of living or working surfaces occurred on the main midden area, Erskine's (1962) "angle camp" provided abundant evidence of dwelling features and their associated domestic activity, and the area appears to have been repeatedly reoccupied over many centuries. The proximity of this living area and the main midden area may suggest contemporary occupation.

AlDf-24 (Epte'jijg Utju'sn Gta'nogeway, "Warm Breeze by the Ocean")
Description and Excavation Approach

AlDf-24 is another large shell midden site located adjacent to the second beach north (approximately 1 km) from Scotch Point (figure 3.1). It sits on a low terrace system and small headland, which is eroding at its western margin to expose bedrock and large boulders. Discovered by Stephen Powel (1990) during a survey for Thomas Raddall Provincial Park, it may be the largest intact shell midden site known in Nova Scotia (e.g., Erskine 1962: 3). The site is between two large, clam-rich "glistening beaches" separated by the rocky headland on which it sits. Like many shell midden sites on Nova Scotia's South Shore, the main portion of the site is situated in the southeastern lee of a very large glacial erratic. Topographically, the site sits approximately 50 m from the shore, on a small terrace system, likely a small boulder-fringed esker, that extends to the south. The main portion of the site, on the lowest "terrace," is bordered on both the eastern and western margins by two small marshes. Portions of the largest shell midden are subsequently waterlogged, at least seasonally. Subsurface probing on a 1 m grid system imposed over the site revealed at least four significant midden concentrations and peripheral shell-bearing black soil midden deposits which extend southward from the main midden.

AlDf-24 is dominated by a large, flat-topped shell mound, Area A, which rises at least 1 m above the level of the surrounding natural forest surface (figure 3.30). Powell's (1990) initial survey of the midden indicated that the entire surface of the site was littered with visible clam shell, which he interpreted as the detritus from recent collecting activity. No surface shell was visible in 2008, except for broken shell at two active anthills, suggesting that collecting had not occurred here in many years. Regardless, Area A bears the craters caused by significant collecting in the past. Much of this disturbance is concentrated on the western half of the midden, with the most significant damage adjacent to the large glacial erratic. The northern and eastern portions of the midden appeared to not have been disturbed by recent collecting.

To the south of Area A, on the landward side of the site, several other activity areas were located via the subsurface soil probe. Area B is an extensive, shallow, shell-bearing black soil deposit with significant quantities of dark, organic, charcoal-rich soil mixed with finely crushed shell. Area B is comparatively undisturbed, although here, too, pits have been excavated by collectors next to small boulders. Probing reveals that this deposit is very thin—about 15 cm average depth—and it likely represents a living area, perhaps composed of

Figure 3.30 AlDf-24: Photograph facing west. The subject is standing on the natural forest surface at the base of the midden mound. The midden is the flat grassy area rising behind the subject. Note the large glacial erratic in the background.

multiple interdigitated living floors. A possible analogue for this deposit is the "angle camp" area from the nearby AlDf-25, which was also adjacent to a very large shell midden.

Area C, located south of a boulder ridge on a small, level terrace, consists of a small, shallow, shell-bearing, black soil deposit abutted by a small "kitchen" midden on its eastern margin. The surface of the deposit was very flat, though it was clearly an anthropogenic mound, as evidenced by the steepness by which it terminated in the east. The boulders on the north and western sides of the space created a natural barrier to activity, and these effectively contained the deposit to an area not larger than 6 × 6 m, the perfect size for the placement of a wigwam-like dwelling structure (especially in a boulder-strewn forest where flat-level ground was at a premium). Like other shell-bearing deposits in Port Joli, Area C's surface had little vegetation except for forest grasses. The adjacent midden was approximately 5 m (long) × 3 m (wide) and was roughly crescent-shaped, as it hugged the edge of the terrace deposit. The easternmost face of the kitchen midden was extensively disturbed by collectors' activities, but the majority of the deposit appears to have been undisturbed.

A very thin (about 5 cm) shell-bearing black soil deposit extends southward from Area C uphill to the last terrace. The Area D deposit is in a tiny flat area, only about 3 × 3 m, surrounded by boulders on the west side and a boulder slope on the east. This midden was only located by subsurface probing, as no other physical surface indications, save for the lack of vegetation, pointed to a cultural deposit in this area. The deposit was very thin, less than 10 cm deep, and appeared to be a shell-bearing black soil deposit, with highly comminuted shell. As there is no visible evidence of collecting in Area D and given that this deposit was not included in Powell's MARI map, it seems this deposit was unaffected by the collecting that seems to have affected other areas of the site. No indications of a shell midden were encountered in Area D.

Vegetation cover on all the cultural areas of AlDf-24 is generally sparse, consisting of large birches and poplar on the margins of the middens and forest grasses on the surfaces of the deposits. The western and southern margins of Area A and much of the surface of Area B contain extensive growth of poison ivy, which can reach knee-height in summer. Willows, alder, spruce, and pine trees have begun to grow in the disturbed areas of the site, particularly on the western portion of Area A.

Site Mapping

A primary goal of the 2010 work at AlDf-24 was to precisely map the site using a total station transit system. This work was undertaken by Heather Macleod-Leslie, of Kwilmu'kw Maw-klusuaqn (the Mi'kmaq Rights Initiative), assisted by a co-worker. Figure 3.31 displays the map produced for AlDf-24, while figure 3.32 displays a three-dimensional representation of the site. The terraced nature of the site can be seen clearly in this latter figure. As will be discussed below, both Area A and Area C represent substantially culturally modified surfaces; by inference we can expect that the terrains of Areas B and D are also substantially modified by similar cultural processes.

Area A: Description and Excavation Approach

The dominating feature of AlDf-24 is the large oval-shaped shell midden mound, Area A, which is approximately 20×15 m in area, covering more than 300 m^2 (figure 3.31). To assess the overall chronological and spatial variability of the midden, a vertical excavation strategy was required, consisting of a transect cutting across the deepest intact deposits. The western half of the midden had been substantially impacted by previous collecting activities, requiring excavation of the undisturbed eastern portion of the midden. A 6×1 m trench aligned north-south (true) was imposed over the midden, cutting through the apex of the mound. To explore variability near the centre of the mound, we extended the trench westward by several units at both of its ends, thereby creating a U-shaped excavation area.

Given the vertical excavation strategy in this very deep midden, the excavation became a highly technical procedure. Most units extended over 1 m deep, and the matrix was composed almost entirely of complete and coarsely broken soft-shell clam valves. The relatively low proportion of soil created a highly unstable matrix where wall collapses were likely; therefore, midden walls were sloped toward the centre of each unit to avoid collapses, a fact that is recorded in the profile drawings (figure 3.33). This strategy worked very effectively (no collapses occurred), though it reduced the amount of excavated volume at lower levels considerably.

Area A: Stratigraphy

As the stratigraphic profiles (figure 3.33) indicate, the midden did not develop on a uniform surface, but instead was deposited on a small knoll strewn with numerous large boulders, some greater than 3 m^3 in volume. As the midden accumulated, it filled in the spaces between the boulders, eventually creating a large flat-topped mound. Very little evidence

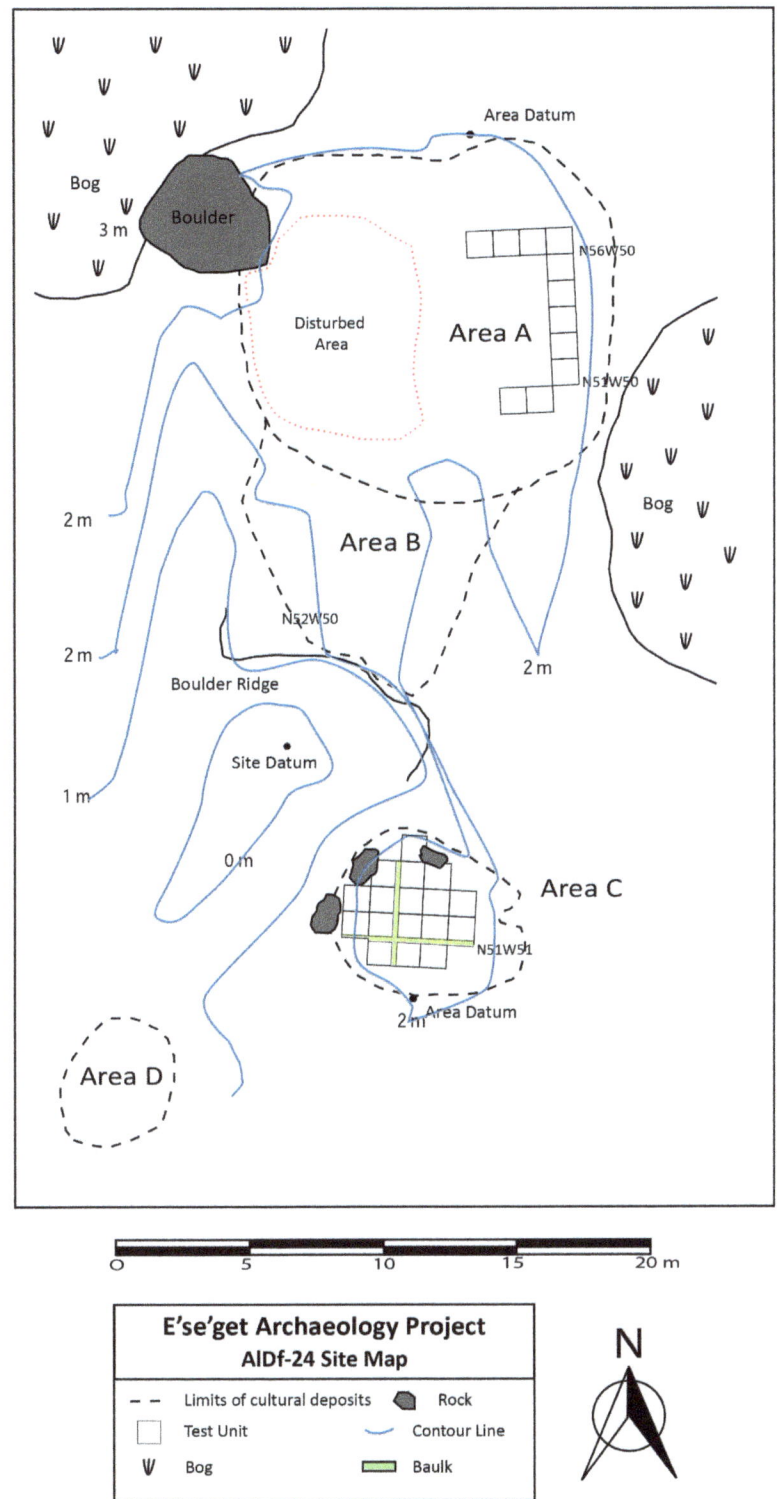

Figure 3.31 AlDf-24: Plan view, derived from total station surveying, subsurface probing, and excavation.

Figure 3.32 AlDf-24: 3D representation facing west. Purple dots represent spatial data, while tan dots represent the location and elevation of the margins of excavation trenches.

of activity areas or features, in the form of significant artifact-rich soil lenses, hearths, or rock alignments, occurred within the midden. In fact, much of the midden is composed of large unbroken clam shells so numerous that in some layers there was very little soil matrix between the shells (figure 3.34). It appears that only after most of the boulders had been completely covered in shells and the midden surface levelled out, formal features were constructed on the midden mound itself (e.g., see features 1, 2, and 3, figure 3.33). These three features occur immediately below the sod layer, indicating that they formed after the bulk of the midden deposits had been created.

The midden is clearly stratified, exhibiting a continuous profile across 7 m on the north–south axis (figure 3.33). Alternating strata manifested primarily as shifts in the degree of shell fragmentation and the presence of unbroken shells and the portion of soil matrix; the presence of minute amounts of mollusc shell other than soft-shell clam (such as urchin or mussel); and the density of artifacts, particularly pottery. Typically, layers transitioned from strata with abundant but highly fragmented shell, increased numbers of artifacts and faunal remains, and increased soil fraction to relatively sterile layers with few artifact and faunal remains, and predominately unbroken shells with little soil matrix. Nevertheless, in no instances other than the immediate pre-subsoil layer did any strata manifest as a shell-bearing black soil deposit (see Black 2002).

The stratigraphy encountered at AlDf-24, Area A, was as follows (based on data from units N56W50 and N56W51, also known as Test Unit 1 (Test Unit A) and Test Unit 2 (Test Unit B), respectively):

- Level 1 was composed of a thin, but dense, vegetative root mat in a dark black humic matrix. A few broken shells were encountered in this level, but no artifacts or faunal remains were recovered.
- Level 2 can be described as the first shell layer below the sod, composed of abundant, trampled soft-shell clam valves in a dark grey/brown/black humus. Unlike in Unit 1, bone and artifacts were sparse in Test Unit 2, with only one chert flake encountered. Though loose in texture, the deposit appeared to be undisturbed by recent anthropogenic activity.
- Level 3a consisted of a layer of large unbroken clam shells in a very sparse dark brown-black humic matrix. Loose in texture, this layer yielded larger amounts of bone and ceramic sherds at increasing depth. Many of the pottery sherds were found in clusters, and many of the individual pieces in these clusters mended. Cod, mammal, bird, and hare bones were abundant in this layer. In Test Unit 2, we

The Sites 83

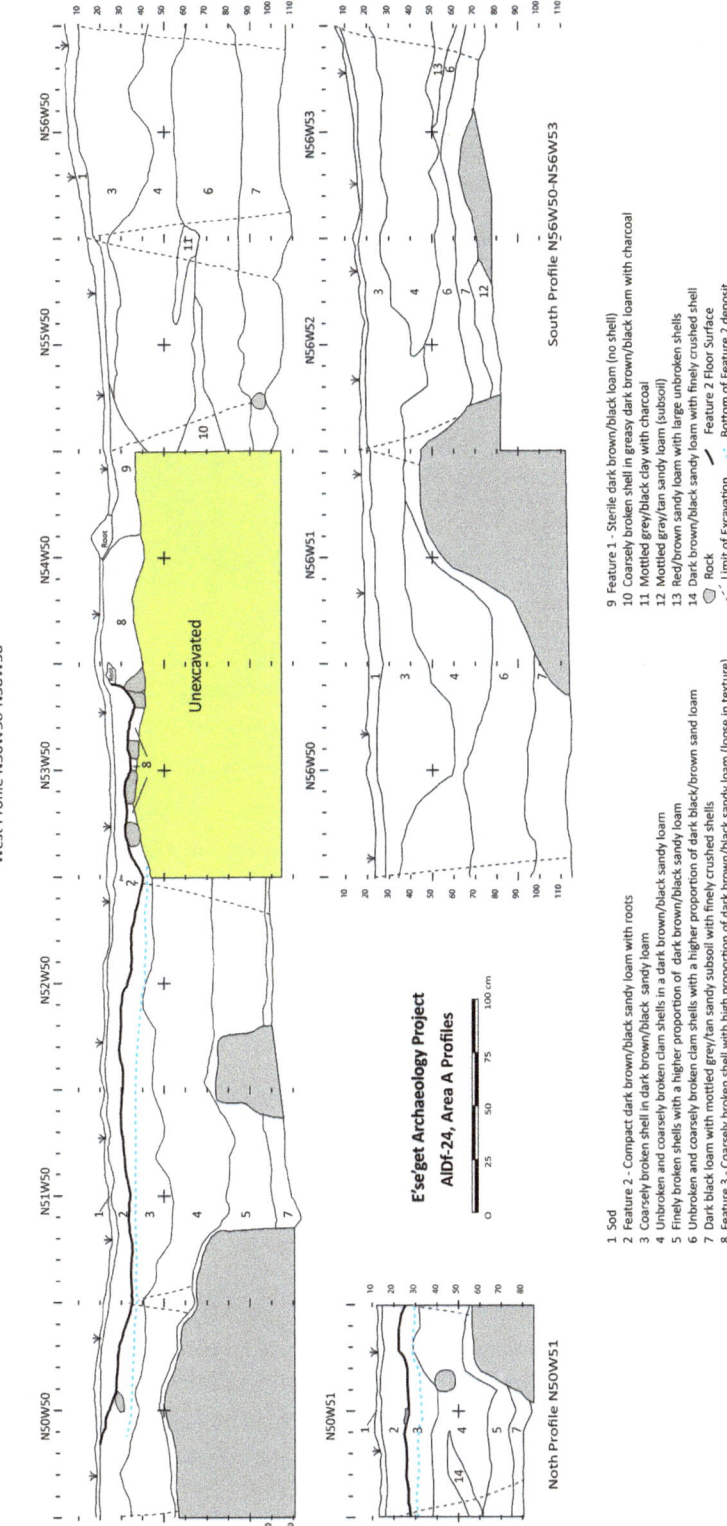

Figure 3.33 AIDf-24, Area A: Stratigraphic profiles.

Figure 3.34 AlDf-24, Area A: Photograph of view of Level 3g, from Unit N56W50 (Test Unit 1, also called Test Unit A in field notes), 2008.

encountered a raw nodule of red ochre, which appeared to be unmodified. The amount of bone and pottery in this layer was so abundant it is possible that this was a buried surface or activity area, although the large amount of unbroken shell and the minuscule frequency of lithic artifacts would tend to contradict this (see chapters 7 and 8).

- Level 3b was an arbitrary subdivision of Level 3, composed of large unbroken clam shells in a loose dark grey/brown/black humus. Unlike Level 3a, Level 3b was relatively sterile, with few artifacts and low densities of faunal remains. However, some calcined bones and charcoal flecks were discovered clustered in the western portion of Test Unit 1 and the eastern portion of Test Unit 2. This deposit was associated with surf clam (*Spisula solida*) and blue mussel (*Mytilus edulis*), large mammal bone, and fish bone (see Chapter 8). It does not appear to have been a formal feature, but might represent some sort of single dumping episode from housecleaning or other domestic activities.
- Level 3c was another arbitrary subdivision of Level 3, composed of large unbroken soft-shell clam valves in a dark grey/brown/black humus matrix. Increasing amounts of charcoal and bone were encountered near the base of the level, but no other evidence suggested a hearth area or other feature. This material originally was limited to the northern end of test units 1 and 2, but soon extended to the east, following the natural grade of the slope. In Test Unit 2, we encountered a semi-circular feature which extended into the west wall of Unit 2. Approximately 50

cm in diameter, and extending about 22 cm into the unit, the feature was composed of a thin (2.5 cm) lens of compacted dark grey-brown sandy loam with abundant charcoal. It did not appear to be a hearth and may instead represent a single dumping episode from housecleaning or domestic activity. An interesting phenomenon encountered in this level was the presence of tiers of stacked whole clam valves, pressed dorsal side down onto the surface of the midden. These could sometimes be stacked as much as five to eight valves deep.

- Level 3d was another sub-level of the relatively homogenous Level 3, differentiated by the increased density of bone and pottery. Level 3d contained even less of the dark grey/brown/black humus and increasing amounts of unbroken soft-shell clam valves. Many of the large unbroken clam shells which were oriented ventral side up were stained a dark brown, likely a result of annual flooding from the nearby bog. The increased amount of charcoal and pottery in this layer suggest a multi-use deposit, but perhaps not a living-surface, as lithic materials were largely absent. Screening revealed large pieces of nacreous and prismatic blue mussel shells.

  Note: Level 3e was skipped in error in 2008. In both 2008 and 2009, 3f stratigraphically follows 3d.

- Levels 3f to 3h appeared in contrast to Level 3d, with increased amounts of broken shell, pottery, and charcoal covering N56W51 and, moving west to east, the first three quarters of N56W50 (the eastern quarter of the unit continued to be composed of large unbroken shell in a sparse soil matrix). In N56W51, a large boulder appeared in the western wall, at a depth of 36.5 cm. The layer was probably some sort of activity surface, although its exact nature is uncertain. Well-preserved fish bone was very abundant in this level; while soft-shell clam was still ubiquitous, small amounts of blue mussel were also present. Unbroken shells became more common in the lower levels of 3f, appearing first at the east and west walls, and finally forming a continuous layer across the unit (marking the beginning of Level 3h). Levels 3f and 3g appear to have been deposited into a shallow hollow, and eventually extended over the unbroken shell layer of Level 3h.

- Level 3i, though similar to the levels above it, was a distinct layer of very broken and trampled clam shell in a dark grey-black organic humus. Charcoal was common, and the level contained abundant pottery as well as an excellently preserved bone awl, made from a caribou metapodial. Virtually no lithic materials were recovered. Blue mussel was present in this level and the dominant clam shells appeared to be smaller in size than in layers above it. Some of the soft-shell clam valves were found with clean sand deposits in them, creating a striking contrast against the dark organic soil matrix of the level. It seems clear that the sand was placed in these shells deliberately before they were placed in the midden. At this level, the boulder in the west wall of N56W51 extended about 50 cm into the midden.

- Level 3j was an arbitrary sub-level of 3i, essentially the same deposit. Again, bone, charcoal, and pottery were abundant, and even some complete blue mussel valves were encountered.

- Level 3k began at a natural juncture where bone and artifacts became less frequent, the proportion of organic soil increased, and broken shell predominated. In nature it was similar to 3i and 3j, though with far fewer bones and artifacts. Charcoal was slightly less abundant than in the layer above it. Small amounts of sea urchin occurred in this layer, representing the first evidence of this species in the entire midden. At this level, the boulder in the west wall of N56W51 covered between 70 and 90 percent of the unit.

- Level 3l occurred only in Test Unit 2, due the presence of a possible feature in N56W50 (see below). Large unbroken clam shells predominated in this layer, which consisted of a black/grey/brown organic matrix. The stratum appeared to be limited to a small (10 cm) margin skirting the edge of the boulder, and was only about 5 cm in thickness.
- Level 3m represented a distinct transition from levels 3k and 3l, with very fragmented shell in a greasy black/brown/grey organic humus. A large ungulate distal phalanx and several articulated fish vertebrae were encountered, but bone was otherwise uncommon. Pottery was also uncommon, save for two decorated sherds, and no lithics were encountered. Level 3m exhibited an arrangement of small- to medium-sized cobbles, in a roughly linear alignment, which extended from the margin of the boulder in a line toward the southeast corner of N56W50.
- Level 3n was the lowest cultural layer found in the deposit. It occurred as a lens of greasy, compacted dark grey-black organic humus, overlain by the trampled shell of 3m. Shell fragments were present in the layer (all are fragmented and trampled) but in diminished quantities relative to the level above it. The matrix was very rocky, with numerous stone pebbles and small cobbles encountered. Artifactual materials included the only formal lithic tool found in the midden deposit: a stemmed quartz point (see Chapter 7), as well as several large utilized chert flakes. No pottery and relatively few animal remains were encountered. It is important to note that Level 3n may not have been cultural in nature. Virtually no material culture was recovered from this layer, save for several large black rhyolite flakes and a stemmed quartz projectile point (recovered in 2009). It is possible that midden matrix was turbated by root action, resulting in the penetration of artifacts into this stratum.
- Level 4 represented the subsoil layer of the midden, signalling the termination of the cultural deposit. Like all other subsoil deposits in the area, this level was characterized by a mottled grey/brown/tan sandy loam, firm in texture with abundant pebbles (gravels) and small cobbles. The surface of this layer was hummocky, a condition likely caused by the large roots that penetrated the deposit. The level rose to a maximum height in the centre of Test Unit 1, where it was intersected by a large taproot from an adjacent tree. The boulder, which had now penetrated about 25 cm into N56W50, appeared to extend further under this level, suggesting it may actually be part of a bedrock outcrop.

Area A: Features
The Burial: Features 1 and 3

The only domestic feature encountered in Area A was a possible house floor (Feature 2), which will be described fully in Chapter 5. The northern end of the house feature overlaid a single human interment, which was placed directly on top of the midden itself. As such, it resulted in the trampling and crushing of the burial feature (see figure 3.33), but the house floor did not appear to have been excavated into the burial feature itself.

Feature 1, the first component of the burial feature, is best described as a shallow trench filled with sterile dark brown sandy loam almost completely devoid of shell (figure 3.35). Located in units N54W50 and N55W50, it was approximately 35 cm deep, 60 cm wide, and over 1 m long, with a long axis oriented almost exactly west-east (true). It is apparent that shell was removed from this feature and placed elsewhere, and it later filled with a sterile sandy loam. It was originally assumed that Feature 1 was caused by recent looting activity, although this assumption was disproved with the discovery of Feature 3.

Contiguous with the south margin of Feature 1 was a low, circular mound of shell rising to an apex in the centre of unit N54W50 (figure 3.36). This feature, called Feature 3, extended from N54W50 to N53W50 and was approximately 150 cm in width on its north-south axis. It reached a height of about 15 cm above the surrounding sod surface. The southern margin of this feature appears to have been trampled by the activities that created Feature 2; there is no evidence that the burial deposit was otherwise disturbed during the dwelling feature construction and occupation. The matrix of the northern portion of the feature was a loose coarsely broken shell in a brown-black sandy loam, with abundant flakes and pottery fragments. These were almost certainly deposited by the activities associated with the Feature 2 house use/construction but may have been related to the trench located to the north.

Figure 3.35 AlDf-24, Area A: Features 1 and 3, facing south. Unit N54W50 is in the mid background (N53W50 is in the far background) and N55W50 is in the foreground. Note the sterile nature of the Feature 1 deposit and the small mound of shell matrix directly adjacent on its south margin (Feature 3). The apex of a grave marker stone can be seen near the centre of N54W50; this marker stone was visible on the surface of the mound prior to excavation.

The burial deposit likely spanned at least 2 m in diameter, suggesting a non-flexed burial. Again, the southern half of the deposit was truncated by Feature 2, which compressed it unnaturally (see figure 3.33). At a depth of approximately 15 to 20 cm below the surface of the Feature 3 apex, an ovoid alignment of small- to medium-sized cobbles was encountered. This was approximately 1.8 m in diameter on its north-south axis and featured a large triangular stone at its north end, which was placed standing upright on its long axis (this rock protruded above the surface of the sod prior to excavation (see figure 3.36, "Grave Maker Stone?"). A few centimetres north of the angular stone, near the margin of the Feature 1 trench, two flat cobbles were also placed on edge. No other stones encountered in the Area A excavations were placed upright in this manner, suggesting these were intentionally placed to mark the location of the feature. If so, the upright stones and the accompanying ovoid rock feature appear to have been intentionally buried along with the human remains.

Despite the odd placement of these stones, the triangular stone resembled an "anvil stone" (see Chapter 5) from house features in Area C, and the remaining arrangement of rocks was consistent with those found in other house features encountered at AlDf-24. Therefore, given its close association with Feature 2, it was initially believed that Feature 3 was part of another house floor. With this assumption, the stones were carefully mapped and then removed, and excavation proceeded without knowledge that a burial had been disturbed.

Following the mapping and removal of the Feature 3 stones, two artifacts were encountered. The first was a great white shark (*Carcharodon carcharias*) tooth (figure 3.36), located to the northeast of the ovoid rock feature, at the southerly margin of Feature 1. The second was a worked piece of antler placed near the centre of the rock feature. Slightly to the west of the angular marker stone, four loose human incisors and a small fragment of a (left) human mandible were discovered. Only the lower incisors and a fragment of mandible were disturbed during excavation; the majority of the mandible remained partially buried and undisturbed in the midden deposit. No other human remains were observed or exposed from the deposit (see below for explanation). Analysis of detailed photographs of the mandible, of which the entire tooth row from C_1 to M_3 (from the first incisor to the last molar) was exposed, indicate the individual was aged 35 to 45 years at time of death, based on dental wear patterns (J. Young 2011, pers. comm.).

No further evidence of burials or human remains was encountered, suggesting that the burial was an isolated feature and that the midden was not used as a multi-interment cemetery. This is potentially corroborated by the fact that the Feature 2 house floor was placed on top of and intruding into the burial (it is assumed that the house would not have been consciously constructed over a known burial location).

The nature of Feature 1 may reveal much about the timing of the Feature 3 burial and the use of the Feature 2 dwelling in relation to the development of the Area A midden. Feature 1 was filled with sterile sediment, indicating that it formed sometime after the midden had stopped developing. As is clearly displayed in the profiles (figure 3.33), Feature 3, the burial, was deposited before the Feature 2 house occupation. The burial "markers," rock alignment, human remains, and burial objects were located in the Level 2b/3a interface (the transition between the shell-free house floor and the underlying shell layer), meaning the burial was placed on top of the midden (i.e., no pit was dug for the burial itself). Thus,

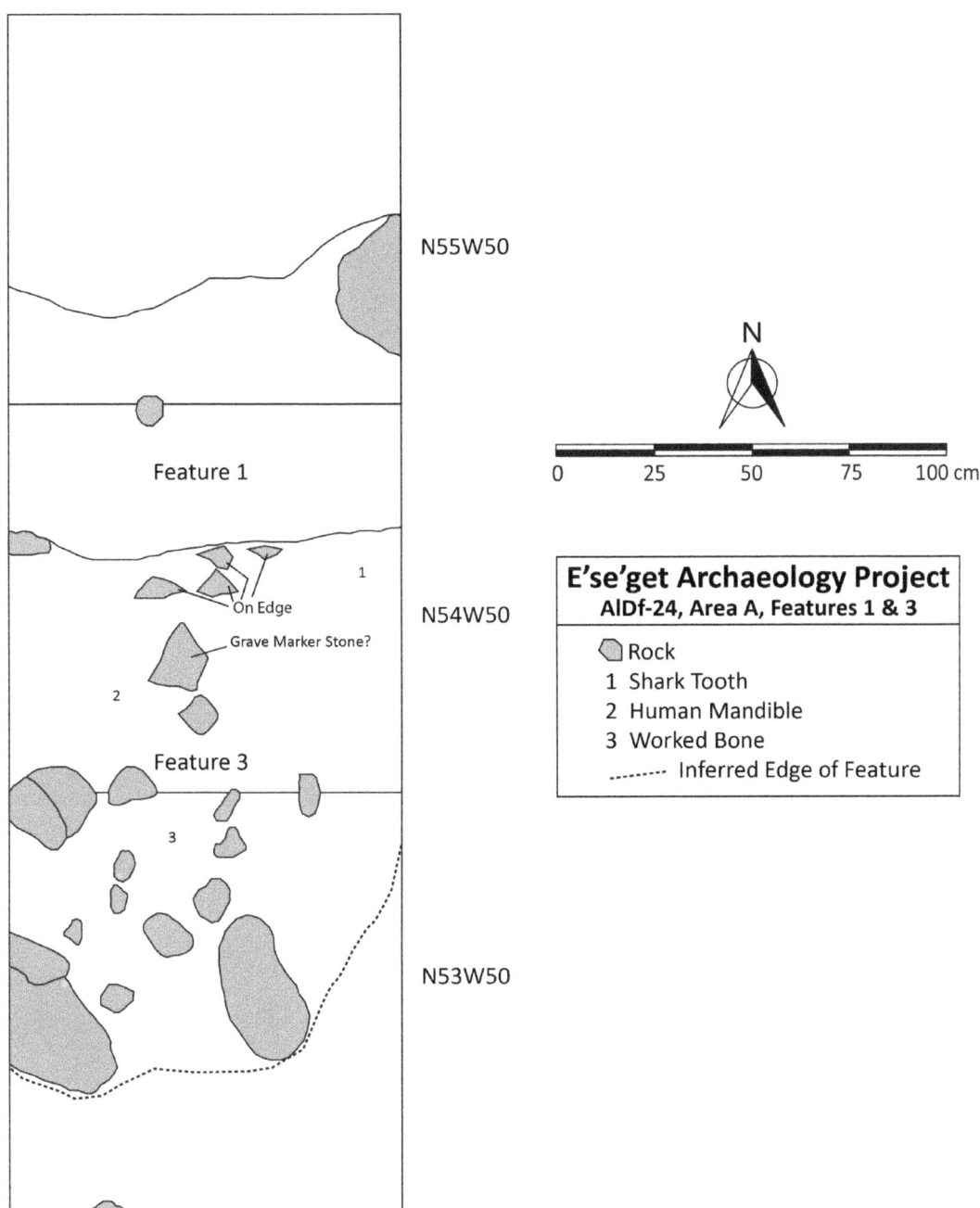

Figure 3.36 AlDf-24, Area A: Plan view of Feature 1 and Feature 3.

the small mound of shell matrix covering the burial was likely derived from Feature 1. If so, Feature 1 might be termed a borrow pit, created during the construction of the Feature 3 burial. The burial has clearly been disturbed, a situation that may have been caused both by the construction and use of the Feature 2 house floor above it and, more recently, by the roots of a large willow bush that was growing on top of the burial. However, if this proposed sequence of events is accurate, it suggests the midden had stopped developing substantially by the time the burial was placed on it (or else the borrow pit would have filled with shell matrix rather than shell-free sediment). Subsequently, Feature 1 appears to have been already filled when the Feature 2 dwelling was occupied, as a small sample of lithic debitage was found in uppermost levels (1 to 3) of the relatively sterile fill, but not below it. Thus, the burial was placed on top of the midden and the entire deposit was not culturally active for some time before the Feature 2 dwelling was placed on top of it.

Reburial of Human Remains and Grave Goods

Upon discovery of the human remains, excavation ceased immediately in the two units containing the remains and what was now understood as a burial feature. The units were covered with a tarp, and a human-remains protocol, which had been created several months earlier by agreement with Acadia First Nation (AFN), the Department of Natural Resources (DNR), and the Nova Scotia Museum, was implemented. Members of the AFN council, the Nova Scotia Museum, and the Nova Scotia Medical Examiner Service were contacted, and a forensic team from the Royal Canadian Mounted Police (RCMP) was dispatched to assess the burial. Staff members at the DNR and the Mi'kmaq Rights Initiative were also contacted. Forensic anthropologists from the Nova Scotia Medical Examiner Service inspected the remains and deemed that the site was not a crime scene.

Following that determination, the human remains and surrounding units were thoroughly documented (maps, profiles, photographs), without further disturbing the feature. Elders from Acadia First Nation, accompanied by representatives from the DNR and the RCMP, visited the site and performed a smudging ceremony. Following the ceremony, the human remains and artifacts were reburied using backfill materials from Area A. The feature rocks and artifacts were returned as closely as possible to their original positions (with the aid of photographs and maps). In keeping with the wishes of the Elders, no modern markers or covering materials were used to define the excavation limits. The sod from the unit was replaced, and the two units involved were not disturbed for the remainder of the season. After this incident, special care was taken during the excavation of rock alignments or features within Area A, but no further burials were encountered.

Area A: Summary

How did this unique shell midden develop, and what human actions were responsible? Analysis of the bulk samples from each of the midden levels is revealing (see chapter 8) in this regard. AlDf-24 Area A contained only 0.425 artifacts per kilogram, in stark contrast to 1.85 artifacts per kilogram in the Area C kitchen midden (see below). The Area A midden did contain a high percentage of charcoal by weight—0.33 percent compared to only 0.111 percent of charcoal by weight in the AlDf-24 Area C kitchen midden. The amount of soil fraction is also significantly different in the Area A midden. Only 20 percent of the midden (all levels combined) was composed of soil fraction in Area A, compared to 34 percent in the Area C midden (the lowest soil fraction in other excavated sites was AlDf-30, at 38 percent). In fact, three individual strata in Area A—levels 3c, 3f, and 3h—had soil fractions so small that they did not register on our digital scale.

David Sanger (1996: 523) proposed that, in a deposit such as this, "A shell midden composed of nearly 100 percent shell could reflect a location specifically designed to dry shellfish for storage." If the abundant charcoal in a midden without house features is any indication, this activity likely included active smoking as well and evidently included the processing and cooking of mammals, birds, and fish (either for storage or for immediate consumption). In the 1990s Sanger (1996: 523) noted that such unique shell middens were entirely hypothetical: "Our survey and testing found no sites of this type, and none have been reported by other investigators." However, nearly fifty years ago, John Erskine (1986: 110) proposed that Port Joli No. 3 (AlDf-25) was "a clam drying site." As Erskine noted (1962: 4), such sites are rare, "unlike any" known from the Maritime Peninsula. AlDf-26 almost certainly belongs to this class of sites as well. If AlDf-24, AlDf-25, and AlDf-26 represent a class of unique sites, they appear to have only occurred in one special place: the western shore of Port Joli's harbour.

The presence of numerous large boulders on the original ground surface may have limited the attractiveness of the location for domestic activities (e.g., hearths, dwellings), although other sites in Port Joli have similar subsurface boulders variously associated with shells, hearths, dwelling floors, lithic scatters, etc. (e.g., see Area C description below; Erksine 1962, 1986). As described above and in Chapter 5, the only features encountered in the Area A midden occurred immediately below the sod surface. The lack of features within the midden, combined with its general deficit of artifacts and even soil, suggests that it accumulated as a special-purpose area of activity—something that precluded other activities from occurring on it. The size of the midden suggests that this activity was very intensive; however, the magnitude of that intensity can only be determined by assessing the amount of time it took for the midden to accumulate (see the discussion of radiocarbon dates, Chapter 4).

Area C: Description and Excavation Approach

In 2009, a small (50 × 50 cm) test pit (Test Unit 3) was excavated in AlDf-24, Area C, which revealed compact, highly organic, deep black artifact-rich layers, suggesting the possibility of several dwelling features. Based on the observations of John Erskine, and our test excavations, we believed it likely contained a series of dwelling surfaces. A major goal of the 2010 field season was to horizontally expose one of these features using methods that would provide a high-resolution record of both the dwelling and horizontal artifact patterning within it. Before this time, dwelling-feature excavation in the Maritime Peninsula had not focused on fine-grained recovery and detailed positional control of materials such as debitage and fauna (e.g., Hrynick 2011). A 6 × 5 m grid was imposed on the surface of Area C (figure 3.31); given the horizontal nature of these excavations, a cross-shaped baulk system was utilized, allowing for the exposure of large areas while still maintaining a stratigraphic cross-section of the entire deposit.

Following the exposure of a house floor (Feature 4; see Chapter 5), the horizontal excavation strategy transitioned to a vertical excavation strategy, in order to determine the overall stratigraphic variability and chronological range of the Area C deposit. Five 1 × 1 m units, contiguous with the eastern and northern sides of the baulks, were excavated to the B horizon, effectively creating an L-shaped trench. This strategy worked extremely well and had the advantage of maintaining large portions of the deposit for later archaeological investigations.

Excavation revealed that Area C contained two primary archaeological deposits: a black soil deposit between 20 cm and about 50 cm deep, composed of a complex stratigraphic palimpsest of multiple house floors, and a relatively deep shell midden, located on the eastern margin of Area C. Figure 3.37 documents the stratigraphy encountered in the Area C excavations.

Area C: Stratigraphy

A summary of the stratigraphy at AlDf-24, Area C, follows, derived from Unit N52W53, which penetrated to the bottom of the cultural deposits:

- Level 1 was a dark brown, nearly black sandy loam with abundant root matter. Debitage, shell, and lithics were found in the sod layer.
- Level 2 was the immediate post-sod layer characterized as a dark brown–black sandy loam with abundant roots. Loose in texture (likely from root action), the deposit was nevertheless artifact-rich, with abundant flakes and lithic tools. Shell was limited, but crushed and broken fragments were flecked throughout the matrix. Bone and charcoal were common in this level. Level 2 varied in thickness, from about 6 cm to more than 10 cm in places.
- Level 3a was a natural transition from the dry, root-laden stratum above to a very dark black, compact, greasy stratum. This layer had highly comminuted charcoal in high proportion throughout and an increased proportion of highly crushed shell than the layer above. Lithics, especially debitage, was extremely abundant in this layer. Bone, especially fragment mammal bone, was common in this layer. Ceramics were present in significant quantities. This layer ended in an arbitrary subdivision. As described above and in Chapter 5, this likely was the remains of a dwelling surface, which we labelled Feature 4.
- Level 3b was an arbitrary subdivision of the dwelling floor stratum, based on depth. Its soil characteristics are identical to the stratum above it (Level 3), but had somewhat smaller amounts of lithic debitage than the layer above it. Highly fragmented shell increased in frequency near the bottom of the level. Charred animal bone was common in this layer, as were ceramic fragments. The entire dwelling floor stratum (Feature 4) averaged between about 5 and 10 cm in depth.
- Level 3c represents a natural transition from Level 3b, to a compact black/brown/grey sandy loam, slightly lighter and more mottled than the layer above it. Shell increased in this unit, and some areas of the site, particularly on the southern edge, show evidence that the nearby kitchen midden was articulated with the level. Lithic debitage was greatly decreased from the house floor above, but was still common in comparison to other shell-bearing sites in Port Joli. Burned mammal bone and ceramics were present, but in far smaller quantities than the stratum above. Near the bottom of the level the colour began to darken, indicating an imminent level change.
- Level 3d, in contrast to the level above, saw the return of a compact, greasy, charcoal rich, black sandy loam, without evidence of brown/grey mottling/podsolation.

The Sites 93

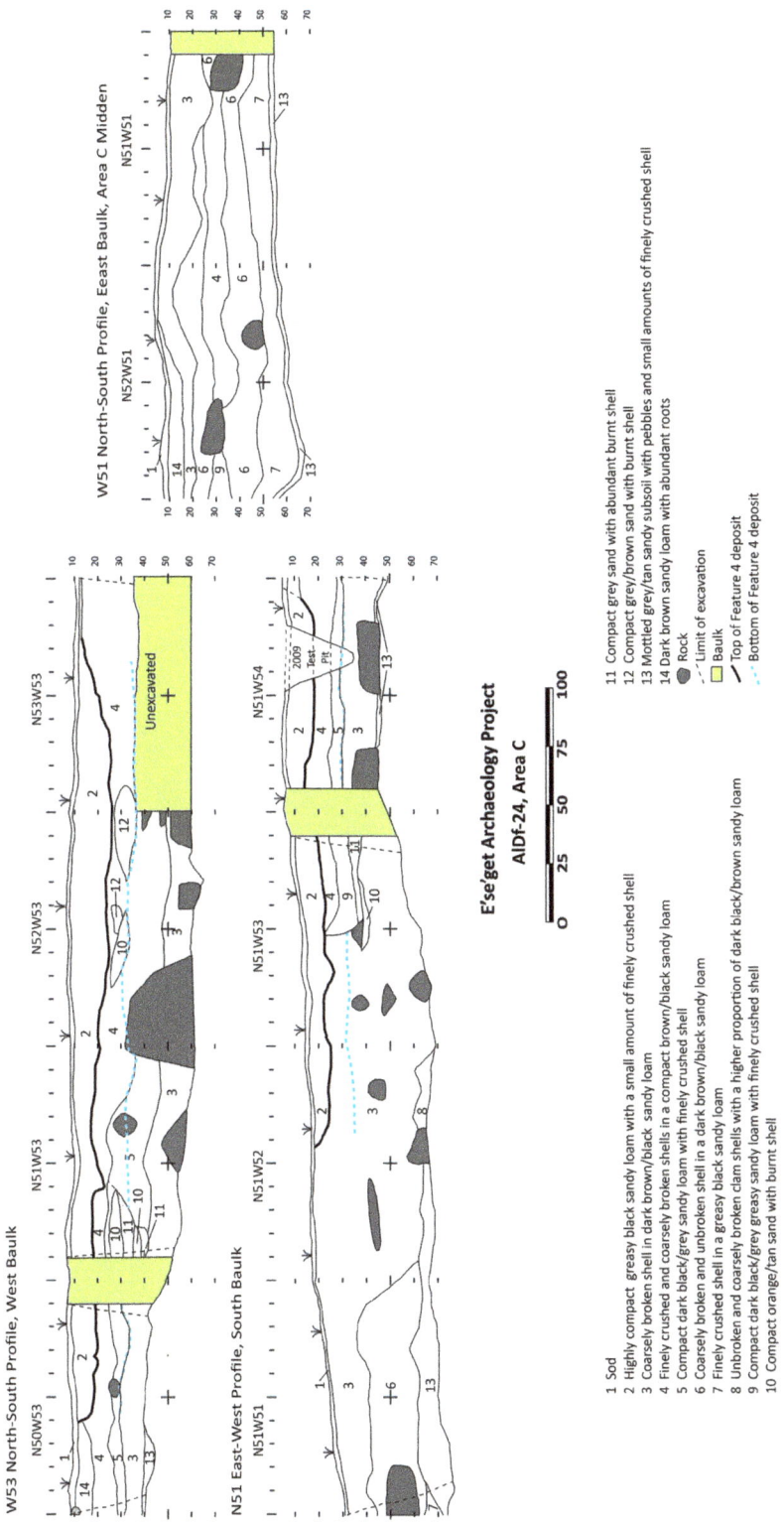

Figure 3.37 AlDf-24, Area C: Stratigraphic profiles.

Highly fragmented clam shell occurred throughout the unit, and evidence of burned shell occurred in the eastern portion of the unit. Debitage frequencies were lower than in strata above 3d, although burned bone persisted throughout the unit. The layer was about 2 to 5 cm in depth.

- Level 3e appeared as a black-grey sandy loam with some brown mottling, fairly compact, with finely broken shell throughout. This layer was thin, less than 1 cm in places, and no more than 5 cm at its maximum depth in the southwest corner of the unit. Ceramic fragments increased dramatically in this level. Some evidence of a hearth occurred in the east with grey ashy soil and burnt shell.
- Level 3f was a transition to a very artifact-rich layer, characterized by a very black sandy loam with highly comminuted charcoal and with finely crushed shell. Ceramics, in particular, increased dramatically in this layer. The transition to this dark black compacted layer with abundant comminuted charcoal and artifacts almost certainly suggests the start of a living-surface. The layer was deep and ended arbitrarily after 5 cm.
- Levels 3g and 3h were arbitrary subdivisions of Level 3f above them and had precisely the same characteristics, except that shell fragments became larger and more intact than the layer above. Ceramic density was similarly high as the layer above, though more lithics began to appear in Level 3g. Artifacts began to decrease substantially in frequency at the bottom of 3h, to be replaced by abundant small rocks and pebbles. Combined, the two levels ranged between 7.5 and 15 cm thick.
- Levels 3i to 3k were considered a natural level, with a greasy, dark black compact sandy-loam matrix, but with much less shell than layers above. Artifact frequencies decreased substantially in this level, and rocks became increasingly common. The level was very thin and appeared to overlay the subsoil. Given the nature of the matrix, and the gradual transition in layers above, we interpret 3i as the same deposit as levels 3f to 3h, above.
- Level 4 was the typical subsoil horizon around Port Joli's harbour, characterized as a grey/orange/tan mottled loamy sand with abundant rocks, cobbles, and gravel.
- To the east of Feature 4, a relatively deep and complexly stratified midden was deposited to a depth of about 55 cm below the surface. It appears from the stratigraphic profile that Feature 4 and earlier house floors developed on top of the midden surfaces and were occupied as the midden developed around them. As described above, the midden contained a much denser proportion of artifacts and faunal remains than was recovered from the Area A midden, by an order of magnitude. While unbroken and coarsely broken shell did occur in the midden, their density was also less than in the Area A midden, and in general the Area C midden was characterized by higher proportions of grey/brown sandy loam and more coarsely broken and finely crushed shell. One enigmatic stone feature, labelled Feature 5, was discovered in the northern part of the midden. The feature is best described as a rock alignment/cairn of unknown function, perhaps a rock pile created from the repeated dismantling/reconstruction of a house structure.

Area C: Summary

The rich, complex, Area C deposit contrasted significantly with the relatively sterile and homogenous midden in Area A. The upper stratum of the black soil deposit (Level 2) was quite thin, and appeared to represent an ephemeral house floor, or perhaps an activity area. The compact nature of the soil and the abundance of quartz and chert debitage and formal lithic artifacts recovered from Level 2 clearly suggest it was a culturally active surface—perhaps a location used for making or repairing stone tools, or a sporadically used dwelling surface.

Levels 3 to 3b were an apparent house-floor deposit, labelled Feature 4 (see Chapter 5). These strata appeared to be the floor of a wigwam-style tent structure, approximately 3 m long and 2.75 m wide. This house-floor deposit contained significant amounts of comminuted cultural charcoal, lithic debitage, and artifacts, and quantifiably less shell than surrounding deposits. Feature 4's floor deposit was trampled into the surfaces that existed below it, creating a mixed deposit that could not always be defined in profile (figure 3.37), particularly where it overlay midden deposits with large amounts of shell. However, the limits of the floor deposit could be determined during excavation based on soil compactness and presence of comminuted charcoal, as well as artifact densities (see Chapter 5).

Underneath the Feature 4 floor deposit were alternating lenses of dark black compacted soil, distinguished by variable amounts of shell, which extended to a maximum of about 55 cm below the surface (levels 3c to 3k). These appear to be alternating lenses of a complex palimpsest of shell-bearing deposits, shell middens, and cultural surfaces, likely representing concatenated dwelling floors. A stratum of compact, greasy, charcoal- and artifact-rich soil (levels 3d, 3e, and 3f) may be another defined house floor, though it was not easily discernable in profile or in all units (this potentially suggests it was not occupied repeatedly or as intensely as Feature 4). The stratigraphy can be interpreted as a series of dwelling surfaces superimposed one on top of another, in essentially the same footprint, generation after generation. It speaks to the permanence of this place in the yearly, generational, and multigenerational cycles of this Indigenous population.

A complex articulation occurred between the house floors in the black soil midden and the more homogeneous shell midden; in fact, it was often difficult to discern the exterior margins of the house floor levels, which could only be located by scrutiny of the matrix for increased charcoal or lithic debitage and decreased quantities of shell. Because the house floors developed on top of and beside the midden, the floor layers often appeared to gradually transition to higher densities of the more coarsely broken shell that characterizes the midden. Regardless, the midden was clearly the discard zone of the domestic activities that took place in and around the house floors to its west, and was practically contiguous with the external wall of the house structures placed there repeatedly over the occupation of the area. Much of the midden likely accumulated from debris tossed, dumped, or swept out the door of the wigwam, suggesting a rather consistent easterly opening in the dwelling (no defined shell midden deposits occurred in the western portion of Area C).

AlDf-30 (Jack's Brook, Su'ne'gati, "Cranberry Patch")
Description and Excavation Approach

AlDf-30 and AlDf-31 (see below) were first discovered by Thomas Head Raddall, a writer and local historian living in Liverpool, Nova Scotia. In 1935, Reverend George Beck was walking along an old ox-track (Sandy Hollow Road) and noticed shell and artifacts spilling from the roots of a tree that had been overturned in a recent storm (Raddall n.d.). He alerted Raddall, who became interested in the deposits. Between 1935 and 1938, Raddall regularly visited the Scotch Point beach on family outings, and, with his son and other family members, recreationally excavated portions of nearby AlDf-30 and AlDf-31 (T.H. Raddall II 2012, pers. comm.; Raddall n.d.). In an essay Raddall (n.d.) described a pair of sites he encountered in the area; an included map shows two midden sites flanking a small brook, which he labelled "Jack's Brook," separated from the shore by a large swamp.

The Nova Scotia Museum assigned AlDf-19 as the Borden number to the sites described by Raddall, and the associated MARI forms provide estimated locations. The AlDf-19 MARI form indicates that John Erskine could not locate the sites described in Raddall's essay, and provincial archaeologists were not able to relocate them in subsequent surveys. However, comparison of Raddall's map (figure 3.38) with modern maps (e.g., figure 3.1)

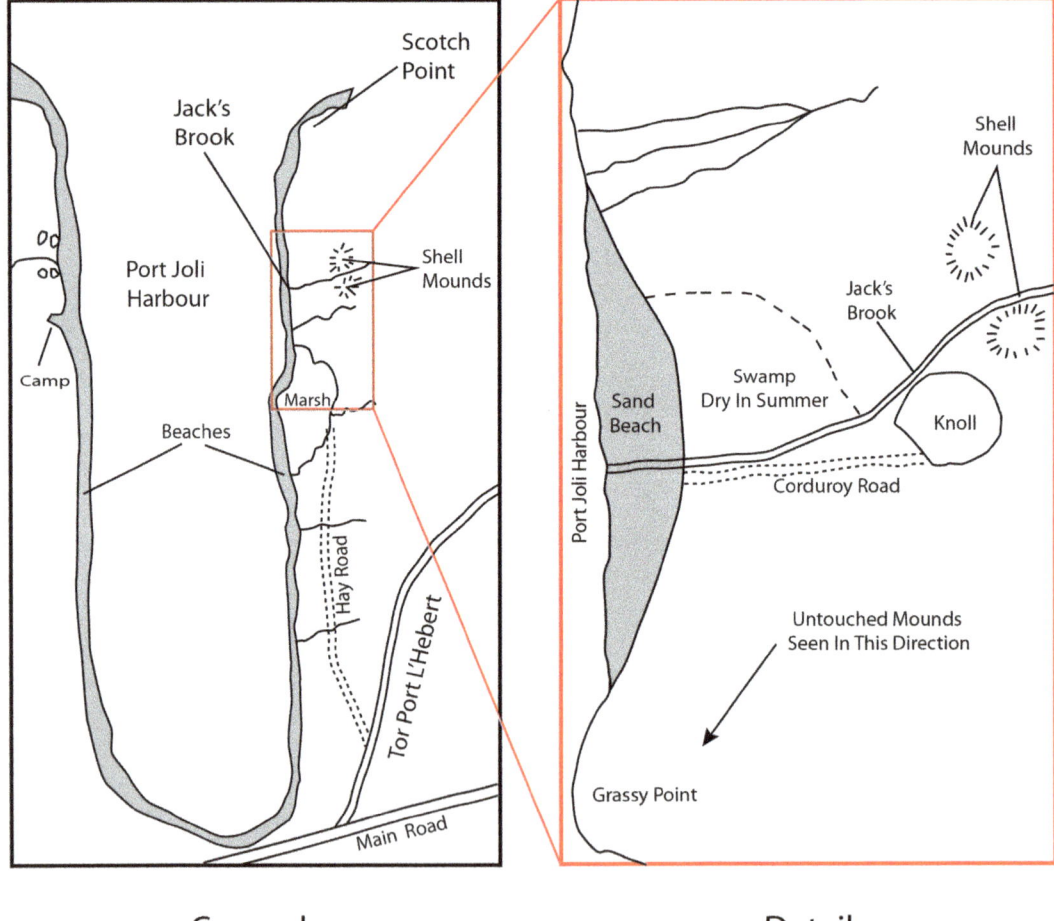

Figure 3.38 AlDf-30: The first archaeological map drawn of Port Joli's harbour, featuring Thomas Raddall's recollection of the sites at Jack's Brook, redrawn from Raddall's (n.d.) original sketch. Note the orientation of Raddall's map is the opposite of that in figure 3.1.

makes it clear that AlDf-30 and AlDf-31 are the sites first encountered by him in 1935. Furthermore, both sites exhibit ancient overgrown collector's pits, consistent with Raddall's activities at the sites.

These sites therefore hold a special place in the archaeology of the region—and the province. They are the deposits which first attracted Raddall to archaeology and which therefore incited Raddall to convince Erskine to work in the area (though Erskine could not locate these deposits). Furthermore, the sites appear to have been the inspiration for a specific scene in one of Raddall's novels, *His Majesty's Yankees* (1942). Raddall could not have known at the time he visited them that he was exploring some of the most unique shell middens in Nova Scotia.

AlDf-30's location, about 300 m inland from the high-tide mark and surrounded by a freshwater fen, is unique in Port Joli's harbour, and indeed all of Nova Scotia. As such, it is unlikely that it would have been found on a typical archaeological survey, and without the observant eye of the Reverend Beck, it may never have been discovered. The first professional archaeologist to visit the site was Stephen Powell (1990), who was conducting surveys for the proposed provincial park. He was informed of the site by a local collector, and though he suspected they were Raddall's sites (S. Powell 2009, pers. comm.), he did not have access to Raddall's early essay to satisfy his suspicions.

AlDf-30 sits on a small treeless knoll in what is otherwise a dense, mixed forest. To the immediate east of the site is Jack's Brook, a very small, shallow stream that flows into Port Joli's harbour near Scotch Point. The brook is fed by a fen that surrounds the knoll on the east, west, and south sides. Similar to the AlDf-24 middens, the site is sparsely vegetated and

Figure 3.39 AlDf-30: Photograph of site, facing east, looking at Area A. The Black Soil Area is in the background.

is now covered primarily in sarsaparilla (*Aralia nudicaulis*); the site is ringed by birch and spruce trees, which are denser to the north end of the site.

Surface observation, excavation, and probing indicated the presence of three small midden mounds on the northwest, southwest, and northeast edges of the site, connected by a black soil deposit that extends between them (figure 3.40). Area A, the most northerly shell mound, is small and dominated by a relatively recent (within about ten years) and invasive collector's pit. Probing revealed that this deposit is at least 30 cm deep in its thickest region. Area B, the most easterly midden, is also the largest and roughly the same thickness (about 30 cm) as Area A. Area B is marked by several deep trenches and pits, out of which grow several small spruce trees and low bushes. Given the obvious age of these pits (no surface shell could be discerned), these appear to be the result of Raddall's explorations over eighty years ago. Area C is the most southerly and most shallow of the middens and appears simply to be a shell-rich continuation of the black soil deposit that connects all the middens. Subsurface probing revealed possible black soil deposits to the west of the Area C midden, but their full extent could not be determined due to extensive forest growth.

Area A: Description and Excavation Approach

The Area A midden was excavated in stages in each of three field seasons: 2008, 2009, and 2010. Excavation proceeded from the southwestern margin of the midden, to its apex in 2009, and toward its easterly margin in 2010. These units were positioned to access the apex of the Area A midden mound, to assess the damage caused by looting in that area, and to ascertain the location of the southern margin of the midden. Excavations revealed a well-preserved shell midden, approximately 30 cm in depth at its apex, with abundant complete and coarsely broken soft-shell clam valves. The stratigraphy and materials recovered indicate little stratigraphic differentiation in the midden, other than the disturbance caused by looting and an enigmatic feature, labelled Feature 2. (Feature 1 refers to a potential dwelling floor, described in Chapter 5.)

As displayed in the profile from the excavation (figure 3.41), while collecting activity has caused extensive damage to the north side of Area A, the collector's trench did not penetrate into the subsoil of the Area A midden, instead leaving about 10 cm of undisturbed midden at the base of the trench. Nevertheless, excavation reveals that collecting occurred at the thickest portion of the midden deposit, resulting in significant damage to the deepest part of the midden.

Near the modern-day collector's trench, a small semi-lunar region of grey-brown sandy loam, without evidence of shell, extended into the eastern baulk and through the midden to the underlying subsoil (figure 3.41). This deposit, labelled Feature 2, was internally stratified, with a compact grey-brown sandy loam overlaid by a loose grey sandy silt. Several dark brown-black stains in the second layer of the feature may have been caused by a decayed root mass. Given the lack of shell or any other cultural material in the deposit, this feature may be best explained as the remains of a small tree around which the midden originally formed. If a tree was located here, the greyish sand at the top of the pit may indicate a previous forest fire which destroyed the tree, over which levels 1 and 2 of the surrounding deposit developed. An alternative explanation may be that Feature 2 was a previous collector's pit (this may account for its sterile nature); however, the surface

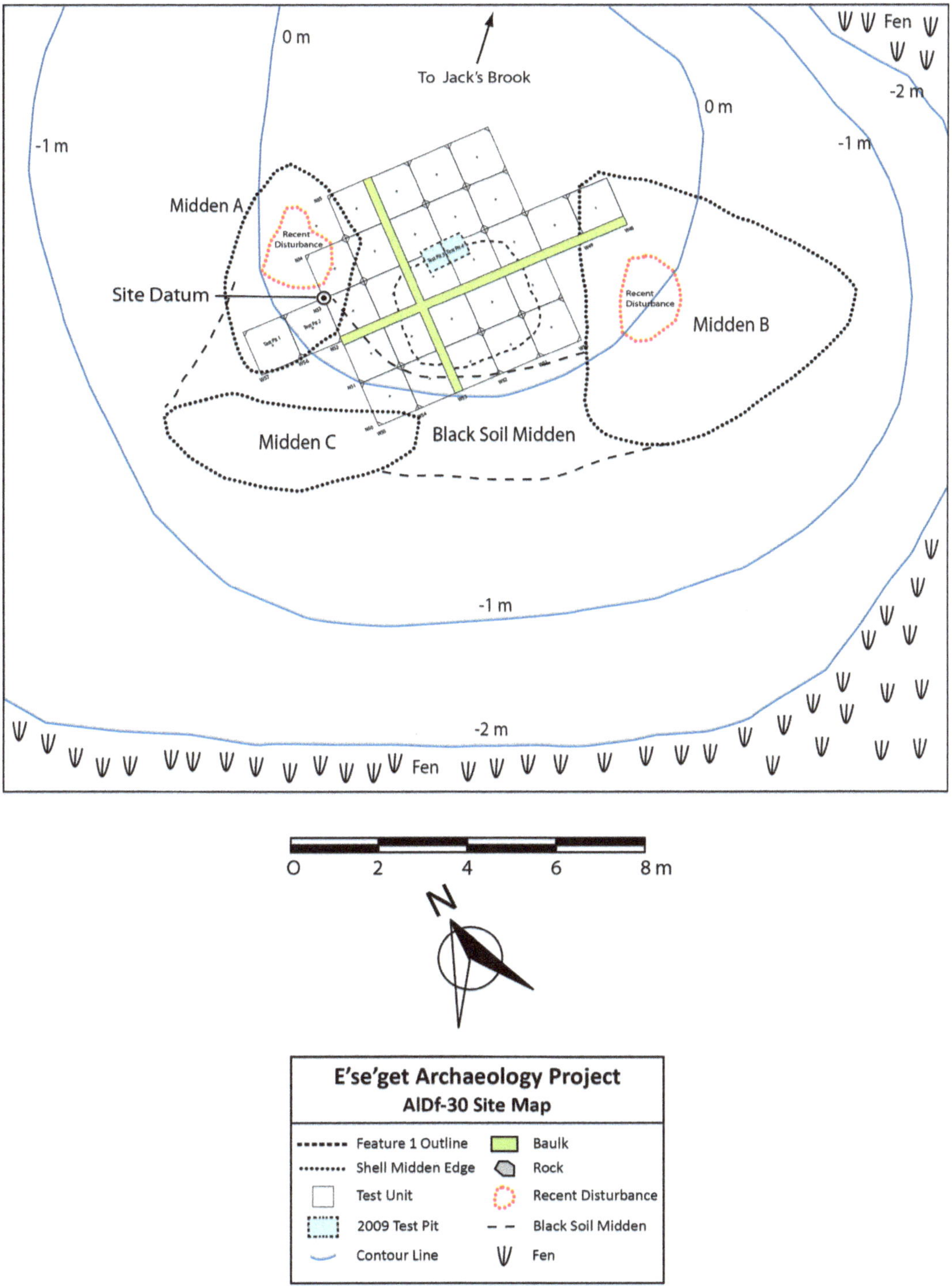

The Sites **99**

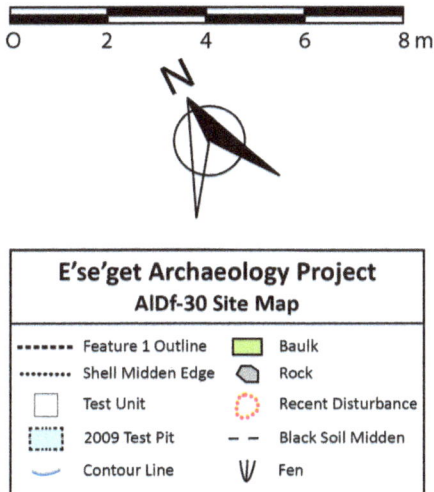

Figure 3.40 AlDf-30: Plan view, based on subsurface probing and excavation.

topography indicated no evidence of a surface depression (or associated backdirt), which is inconsistent with the visible surface depressions and spoil heaps of other twentieth-century collectors' pits on the site.

On the southern edge of the excavations (N51W55), the location of the southern margin of the Area A midden was discovered. As shown in the profile (figure 3.41), the Area A midden is relatively uniform in depth (approx. 15 to 20 cm thick), but increases slightly in thickness as it moves north toward the apex of the midden. At its southeastern margin the midden abruptly ends in a "step" of about 10 cm, transitioning to a very thin (approx. 1 cm) scatter of shells. This deposit abuts a large granitic cobble, beyond which no evidence of shell could be discerned (although several artifacts were recovered).

The stepped nature of the midden's southerly termination, as well as its distribution in relation to the rock, suggests that the deposition of shells occurred in an intentionally constricted area. This corresponds well with the subsurface probing of the site conducted in 2008 and 2009, which revealed that three relatively small and sharply defined midden areas characterized the site (rather than one uniform midden). This has obvious implications for site-use and site-formation processes, suggesting that the deposition of midden deposits occurred in a spatially patterned manner rather than as a broad midden over the entire site's surface.

Area A: Stratigraphy

A description of the stratigraphy of the Area A midden follows:

- Level 1, the sod, consisted of a brown-black organic sand with abundant root matter and vegetation. A few broken shells and some pottery fragments were encountered in the root mat, but no other artifacts or animal bones were recovered.
- Level 2 can be described as the first shell layer consisting of a dark brown-black sandy humus with abundant broken shell. Presumably, the broken shell was caused by root action and trampling of the Level 1 surface. Bone and pottery were present and in good condition, though root matter was still dense in this level.
- Level 3a was distinguished from Level 2 by the presence of large unbroken clam shells in a dark grey-black sand and humus matrix. Animal remains tended to be concentrated in the northern portions of the excavation. Abundant articulated cod vertebrae occurred throughout this layer. Very small pebbles (1 to 2 cm in diameter) occurred throughout Level 2. Near the bottom of this level the density of faunal material (and in particular, bird bone) increased.
- Level 3b was an arbitrary sub-level of Level 3 and was composed of large unbroken shells in a dark grey-black sand and humus matrix. The matrix and characteristics were indistinguishable from the layer above.
- Level 3c was the lowest midden layer, associated with the top of a sterile subsurface layer (Level 4). Large unbroken soft-shell clam shells appeared to lie flat over this subsurface layer, although a few appeared to have been impressed into its surface (see description below). Pottery is abundant in this layer, but less abundant than in upper levels. Incorporated into the lower portion of Level 3c is a grey beach sand, which was difficult to distinguish as a unique deposit. It may represent a fine layer

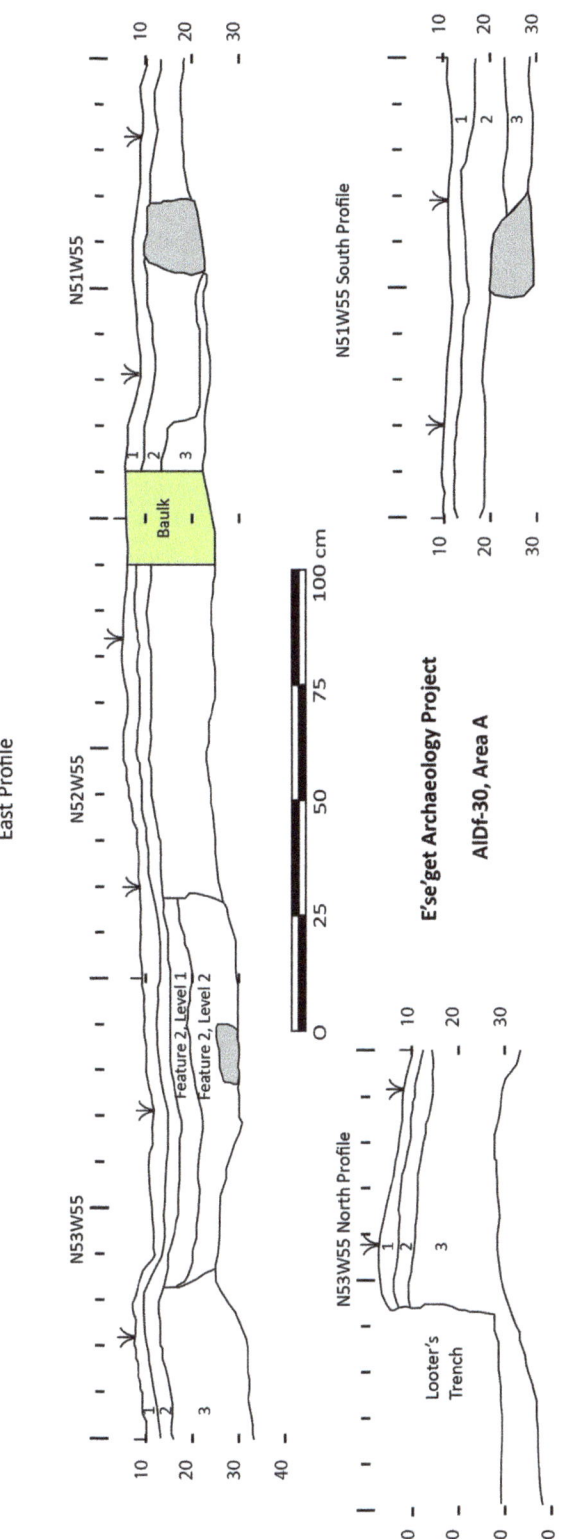

Figure 3.41 AIDf-30, Area A: Stratigraphic profiles.

of sand that either blew (or was placed) over the shells impressed into Level 4 and which subsequently settled between them over time. Small rocks (approx. 3 to 6 cm in diameter) are common in this layer. In the northwest corner of the unit, the stratum appeared to dip into a depression, part of which was lined with fire-cracked rock and cobbles on its southern margin. It seems unlikely that this was a feature, however.

- Level 4 can be described as an undisturbed subsoil B horizon, composed of a mottled light grey to yellow-brown sand. Several clam shells were pressed vertically into the subsoil stratum. The surface of this layer was undulating and "hummocky" and we originally suspected this was the result of rodent activity. However, the lack of burrowing rodents in the area (i.e., the resident snowshoe hares do not burrow) implies a different agent. The mottled and undulating appearance may in fact have been caused by root action or frost action, and several large decayed root stains were encountered at the surface of this unit. Tree roots appear to avoid undisturbed shell midden deposits in this area of Nova Scotia, and the evidence from this unit suggests they tend to burrow under the primary shell deposit, perhaps leading to the undulating nature of the surface of Level 4. This is also what may have caused the appearance of shells being pressed "on edge" into the surface of Level 4 when in fact they were likely originally deposited flat onto its surface.

Area B: Description and Excavation Approach

A single 1 × 1 m unit, N52W48, was excavated in an undisturbed portion of the Area B shell midden in 2012. Immediately to the east of the unit, undulating topography may indicate past excavation in the Area B midden. If so, this disturbance was presumably the result of Thomas Raddall's explorations in the late 1930s. The midden was primarily composed of broken and unbroken soft-shell clam shells with abundant faunal remains and ceramic sherds. Approximately 25 cm in depth, it was a relatively homogenous deposit, although the proportion of crushed to unbroken shell sometimes varied with depth. Like the Area A midden, however, whole shells tended to be laying horizontally, a trend that increased at greater depths.

A significant quantity of small fish remains were recovered from the midden, in contrast with faunal remains recovered from the Area A midden, which was dominated by very large cod bones. It is possible that this apparent difference is a recovery issue, given that the Area A midden was screened with 6 mm mesh while the Area B midden was screened through 3 mm mesh. However, as described in Chapter 8, the faunal remains do not support this conclusion, with large cod vertebrae occurring in much smaller frequencies in Area B than in Area A. Furthermore, virtually no cervids were encountered in the Area B context, in comparison to Area A. Thus, the faunal evidence suggests a different procurement and consumption strategy resulted in the archaeofaunas in Area B.

As is visible in the profile drawing (figure 3.42), a lens of mottled grey-brown-orange subsoil was identified in the shell midden. This soil may have been deposited in the midden when one of the features was excavated in the adjacent black soil midden, and, given the stratigraphy of that area, it was presumably Feature 3, which necessarily disturbed the subsoil. In the field records, this lens was referred to as levels 4 and 5, reflecting initial confusion

The Sites **103**

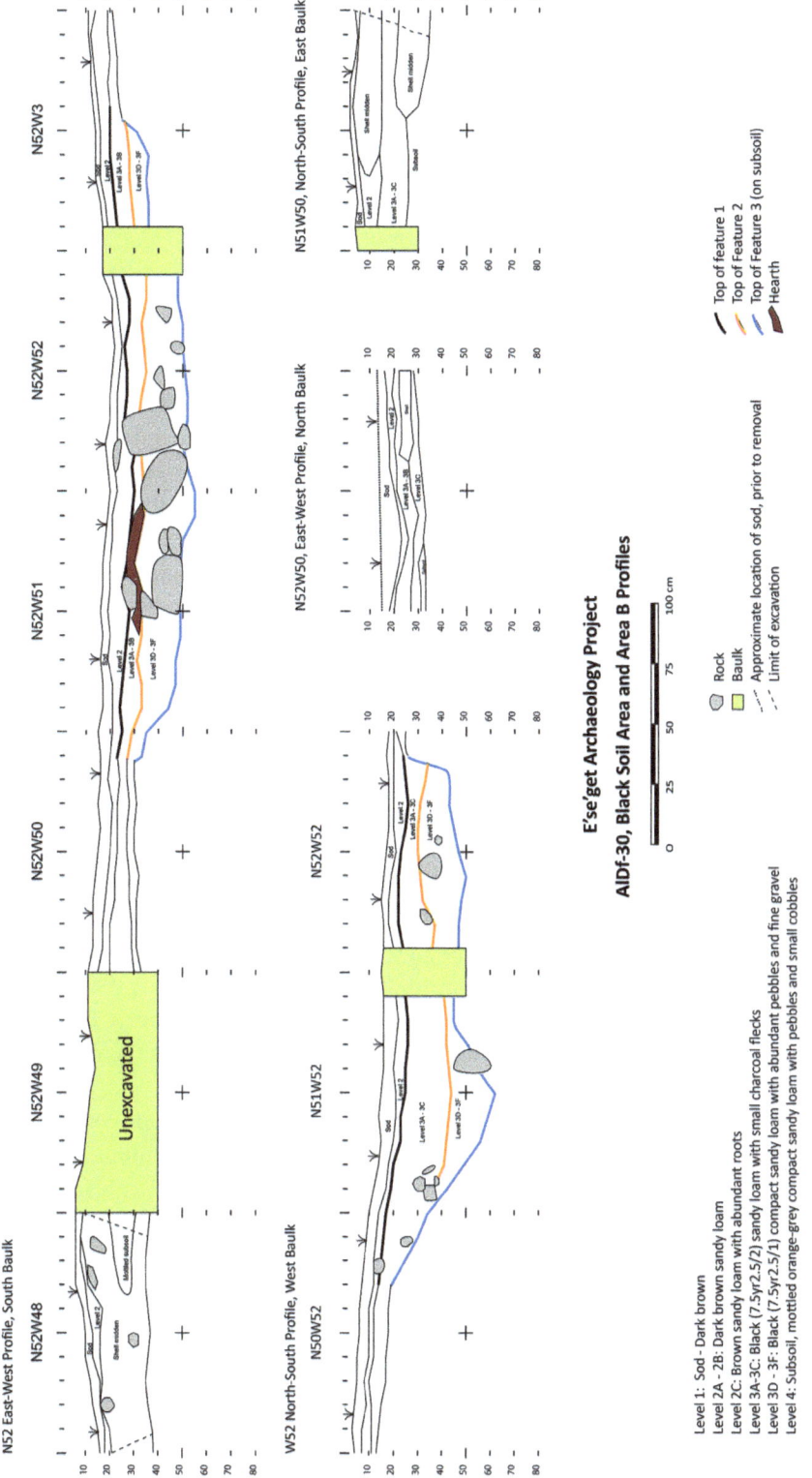

Figure 3.42 AlDf-30, Black soil Area and Area B: Stratigraphic profile.

about the presence of an apparent subsoil lens. In this unit, contrary to other areas of the site, the subsoil was designated Level 6.

Area B: Stratigraphy
A description of the stratigraphy of the Area B midden follows:

- Level 1 consisted of a dark brown-black organic sandy loam supporting some native vegetation and a thick root mat.
- Levels 2a to 2c consisted of a dark brown-black sandy loam with abundant broken shell. Abundant animal bones were recovered in this layer along with some lithic debitage (in contrast to the Area A midden). One small piece of grit-tempered pottery was recovered. In the northwest corner, a sterile deposit was recovered that descended onto a small layer or cobbles, which may have been related to the nearby dwelling floors.
- Level 3a consisted of a somewhat diffuse midden consisting of broken soft-shell clam valves in a black sandy loam. This stratum sloped downward toward the northeast portion of the unit. Sand is absent in the northeast corner, which appears to be a lens of subsoil. The shell consisted of coarsely broken valves with a few whole shells and abundant small-fish bone. Whole valves were more common near the upper surface of 3a. Artifacts, including ceramics and lithics, were extremely common in this level. The abundance of lithics, in particular, is in stark contrast to the Area A midden, where few lithics were recovered, and may relate to the presumed entrance of the nearby dwelling and other features (see Chapter 5).
- Level 3b was differentiated from Level 3a by the presence of large whole clam valves throughout the level. The matrix was a dark organic sandy loam. Large-mammal bones were recovered with increasing frequency as this level descended. Small-fish bone, likely tomcod, were very common throughout the level.
- Level 3c was an arbitrary subdivision from Level 3b above it, though it could be characterized by an increased frequency of large-cod vertebrae and mammal bone, particularly in the southwest quadrant. Level 3c was deeper in the western half of the unit, and descended on the natural subsoil in the eastern half of the unit. Ceramic and lithic artifacts were still abundant in this level, but the density decreased as the unit was excavated.
- Level 3d was an arbitrary subdivision from Level 3c above. Confined to the western half of the unit, it followed the natural subsoil, which was higher in the eastern portion of the unit. Artifacts were noticeably less frequent in this level.
- Levels 4 and 5 reflected an intrusive layer into the deposit. Appearing as a semi-lunar arch of sediment in the north and northeastern portions of the unit, levels 4 and 5 are sandwiched between Level 3a above it, and Level 3b, found immediately below it. Level 4 consists of a small pile of cobble stones, sitting on Level 5, which was a lens of grey-black sediment, which appears consistent with the mottled matrix subsoil in the Port Joli area. Some artifacts and animal remains are associated with these levels in the unit-level record forms, but it seems clear that these come from the transition layers between Level 3a above and Level 3b below.

- Level 6 was the undisturbed subsoil horizon, composed of a mottled light grey to yellow-brown sand. This layer sloped sharply from a high point on the eastern half of the unit to a low point in the western half of the unit.

Black Soil Area: Description and Excavation Approach

In 2009 we briefly tested an area between the Area A midden and Area B midden, near the northern margin of the site (see figure 3.40). Our subsurface probing in this area revealed thick "black earth" deposits, similar in description to the soil deposits found in the "angle camp" area of John Erskine's Port Joli #3 (Erskine 1962: 9). We placed two 50 × 50 cm test pits, labelled Test Unit 3 and Test Unit 4, approximately 3.5 m east of Test Unit 2 (figure 3.40). The units were positioned at the apex of a small knoll, near the edge of what appeared to be a slight depression, suggesting the presence of a subsurface feature (e.g., Matthew 1884; Sanger 1987). Both units sloped from a high point in the southeast to a low point in the northwest, consistent with their placement on the edge of a slight depression.

Below the sod, two distinct layers of dark brown-black sandy loam was exposed, both rich in debitage and burnt animal bone. This suggested a living surface of some sort, or perhaps a dwelling surface. As excavation of this level continued, it became clear that the dark brown-black matrix was limited to the southern approximately 35 cm of the unit. Mottled sandy subsoil (Level 4) began to appear at a depth of about 20 cm in the north, while the compacted artifact-rich deposit (levels 2b and 3) continued to a depth of around 30 cm in the south. Within the artifact-rich deposit, abundant cobbles were encountered that were arranged along a graded slope, clearly the margin of an anthropogenic "pit" of some sort (see figure 3.45). The cobbles exhibited no evidence of burning or charring, and were not associated with abnormal frequencies of charcoal, though their spatial arrangement suggests some sort of feature. Unfortunately, we were unable to completely test the feature in 2009 and committed to return to it at a later date.

In 2012, we returned to AlDf-30 and devoted over four weeks to the evaluation of the features identified in 2009, with the expectation that we would be digging a palimpsest of living floors similar to AlDf-24, Area C. As will be described in Chapter 5, we were correct in our expectation of dwelling floors, but we also encountered an unexpected feature that was totally unique in the Maritime Peninsula, and indeed exceedingly rare (archaeologically) in North America: a sweathouse (see Chapter 5) The Black Soil Area excavations revealed the presence of three deposits: two buried dwelling floors, labelled Features 1 and 2, and a possible ritual feature, labelled Feature 3 (figure 3.42). Unlike AlDf-24, Area C, the features appear to correspond very well to the stratigraphic transitions in the site; the description of stratigraphy below reveals these correlations (see Chapter 5 also).

Black Soil Area: Stratigraphy

Level 1 consisted of dark brown sandy loam with abundant vegetation or root matter. No artifacts or animal bones were recovered from this layer.

Levels 2a to 2c were characterized by a dark brown sandy loam with abundant roots, which extended across the entire surface of the excavation. Shell was virtually non-existent in this layer, although artifact densities were relatively significant. The levels did not appear to have horizontal boundaries and did not exhibit characteristics typical of a dwelling surface (i.e., compactness, with abundant comminuted charcoal). However, the significant quantity of artifacts, especially lithic debitage, suggests it was an area of substantial activity, perhaps even an ephemeral dwelling surface. These upper levels may represent one end of a continuum of archaeological manifestations relating to dwellings. It is possible that a variety of short-use structures, both domestic and special purpose, were utilized by the ancient Mi'kmaq who lived around Port Joli's harbour, and that wigwam-style dwellings were the most intensively used and thus were most visible, archaeologically. A variety of artifact concentrations could have been contained within short-term structures, and analysis of the spatial patterning of the artifacts in this layer may provide more clues about its use.

Levels 3a to 3c varied significantly in relationship to a probable dwelling feature, labelled Feature 1 (figure 3.42). Outside of Feature 1, levels 3a and 3b appeared as a brown sandy loam with abundant pebbles, sometimes mottled with tan/grey subsoil. Calcined bone, lithics, and ceramic materials were relatively abundant, but not in the high frequencies characteristic of Feature 1. Charcoal flecks were encountered, but not in significant proportion, and the soil was not characterized by comminuted charcoal. Shell occurred only in trace amounts. Inside the feature, levels 3a to 3c appeared as a compact black sandy loam with moderately abundant comminuted charcoal and corresponded with Feature 1. As described in chapter 5, the margins of the feature were relatively distinct, marked by a slight colour change to a browner-coloured soil with less comminuted charcoal. Feature 1, like many Middle Maritime Woodland dwelling features (e.g., Black 2004), was less artifact-dense than many Late Maritime Woodland dwelling features (e.g., Hrynick et al. 2012), including Feature 4 at AlDf-24, Area C. However, it did contain significant quantities of lithic debitage and ceramics, as well as calcined charcoal. Again, shell density was extremely low, occurring only in trace amounts.

Levels 3d to 3f, together, represent another domestic occupation or living surface, labelled Feature 2. It was distinguished from the Feature 1 surface above it primarily by changes in soil colour. The deposit can be characterized as a very compact and firm dark black sandy loam with abundant pebbles and higher concentrations of comminuted charcoal than the Feature 1 layers above it. In the bottom-most levels of the feature, the soil became mottled with orange subsoil and pebbles, emphasizing the trampled nature of the feature and its contiguous contact with the subsoil surface. Similar to Feature 1, large boulders and cobbles intruded into this unit from deeper stratigraphic levels, producing a rather undulating and rough floor surface. The remaining characteristics of the feature will be described in Chapter 5.

Level 4, which is the same deposit as Feature 3, appears to have been dug into the Area A subsoil and is not represented by a distinct fill deposit that could be distinguished stratigraphically from the layers above. The subsoil is typical for Port Joli's harbour, a mottled loamy sand with abundant small pebbles and cobbles. Interestingly, as clearly displayed in the photographs (figures 3.43 and 3.45; see also Chapter 5), much of the subsoil in the area of Feature 3 was a buff-orange to reddish brown in colour, which contrasts with the light tan/grey subsoil that is more typical for the area. This may indicate that the entire area was exposed to heat (see Chapter 5).

Cultural deposits related to this feature were difficult to identify. It is possible that portions of levels 3e and 3f may be related to the use of the feature, though they are

Figure 3.43 AlDf-30, Area B shell midden: Photograph of Unit N52W48, Level 6 (subsoil) exposed, facing south. Note the stratigraphic mixing evident in the south baulk.

Figure 3.44 AlDf-30, Area B: Tomcod (left) and Atlantic cod (right) bones recovered from Unit N52W48, in midden contexts. Note the abundance of small-fish (tomcod) bone.

Figure 3.45 AlDf-30: Photograph of Test Units 3 (nearer) and 4 (farther), facing east, showing detail of the levels 2b and 3b rock feature, with Level 4 (subsoil) exposed below it. Note depression contour and stratigraphy visible in east (far) profile.

Figure 3.46 AlDf-31: Photograph facing northeast. Midden B is in the foreground, with a soil probe lying in the collector's trench. Midden A is at the apex of the knoll.

indistinguishable from the house-floor levels (Feature 2) above Feature 3, and hence are likely better associated with the more recent feature. We carefully attempted to discern any materials in direct association with the excavated subsoil transition at the bottom of Level 4, which were in direct contact with the subsoil surface. Charcoal was found in direct association with the subsoil, though in limited quantities and only in N51W52 (it was one of the largest charcoal fragments in the entire deposit). A thorough interpretation of Feature 3 can be found in Chapter 5.

AlDf-31 (Su'ne'gatij, "Little Cranberry Patch")
Description and Excavation Approach
This small site is located on the southeast side of Jack's Brook, opposite AlDf-30. As discussed above, the site was first explored, recreationally, by Thomas Head Raddall in 1935, and the southern portion of the site still bears the scars of his excavations. In many respects, AlDf-31 is very similar to its neighbour. Like AlDf-30, it is also situated on a small knoll, which forms part of a complex ridge system that skirts the nearby fen on the south and west sides. Well hidden, the site is separated from the brook by dense stands of alders and willows. Approximately 300 m from the coast, it is surrounded by very large deciduous trees, and some are encroaching in the southerly portion of the site, though the site itself is sparsely vegetated. It is composed of two shell concentrations oriented roughly northeast to southeast on the long axis (note: a magnetic anomaly in this area makes compass bearings inaccurate), with black earth deposits separating the two refuse features.

Area A, the larger midden, is located approximately 5 m northeast of the somewhat smaller midden in Area B (figure 3.47). Area A is a noticeable shell heap, located directly on top of the knoll. It is quite large, and covers approximately 30 m^2, though the northern boundary of the midden could not be determined due to the presence of dense undergrowth. Probing revealed a depth of about 40 cm for some areas of this deposit. The southerly midden was shallower (approx. 20 cm) and is located at the base of the low knoll. Area B has been disturbed by a very large collector's pit, around 1 × 2 m, and several large trees from the surrounding forest have begun to encroach on this area of the site. Black soil deposits were encountered between both middens and around the margins of the site, and it seems clear that much of this cultural deposit was impacted by the growth of the nearby trees. However, the majority of the midden deposits appear to be intact.

We established two 1 × 1m test units on the surface of the AlDf-31 site, in an area just west of the apex of the Area A midden. The surface of these units sloped gently from the northeast to the southwest, but was in general quite flat, without indication of any underlying depression. As is described below, the deposits we encountered were inconsistent with other "on midden" units excavated at sites in the region:

Stratigraphy
Level 1, the surface sod, was relatively thick in these test units—notable because it stood in contrast to the thin sod covering other middens in the region. The matrix was a dark brown-black organic humus, loose in texture with abundant decaying organic matter and roots.

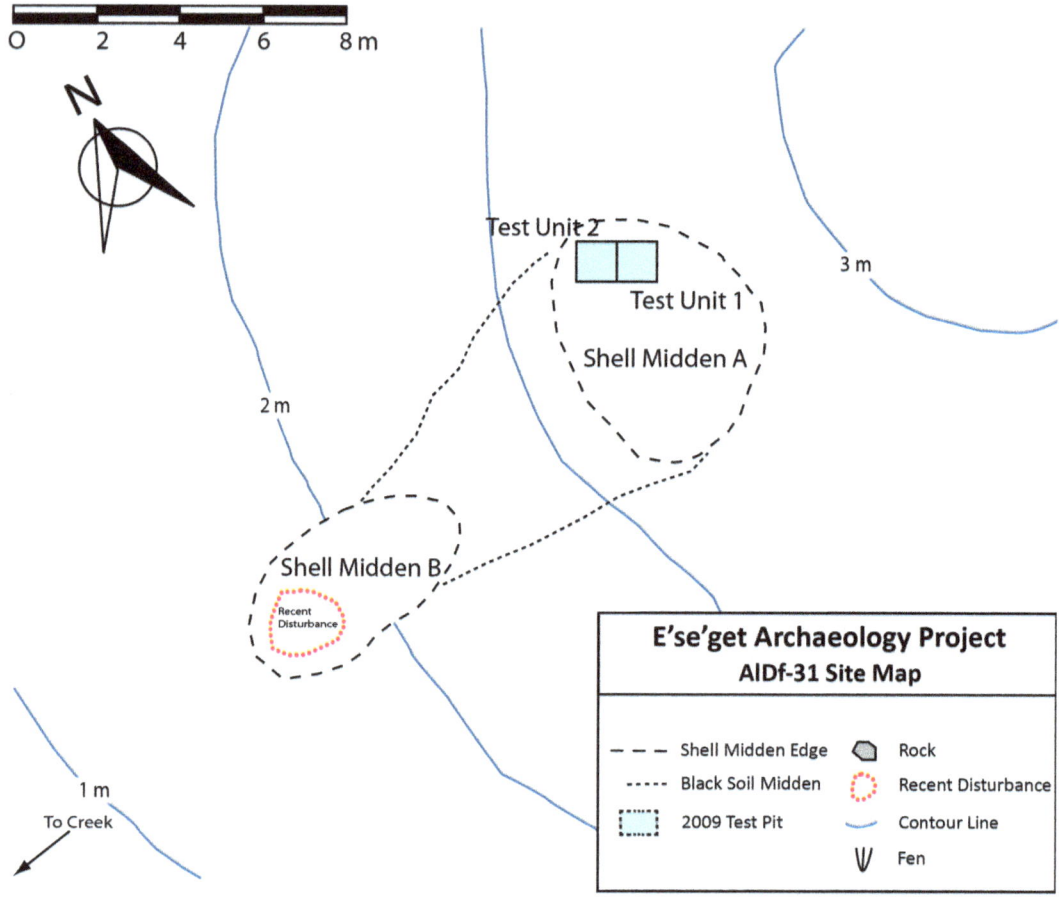

Figure 3.47 AlDf-31: Plan view, based on subsurface probing and excavation.

Level 2, the first sub-sod layer, exhibited abundant roots and organic material in a dark brown/grey sandy loam. The texture of this layer was relatively loose, with occasional shell and bone. Abundant charcoal and a quartz flake further betrayed the cultural nature of this level.

Levels 3a and 3b can be described as a dark grey/brown-black sandy loam, typical of the black soil deposits in the region. The texture was loose, though it became more compacted in the lower levels of the units. Broken shell was very abundant, as were extremely large cod vertebrae, charcoal, and burnt bone. Ceramics were also recovered. Level 3b did not extend across both pits, and a layer of mottled grey/brown sandy loam, typical of subsurface deposits in the region, began to appear approximately 19.5 cm below datum in the northeast portion of Test Unit 1.

Level 3c was in many ways identical to those above it, composed of a dark grey-brown-black sandy loam with abundant broken clam shell; it is set off here primarily because the texture of the soil changed to a more compacted deposit. Additionally, bone and charcoal were present in this deposit, but rarer than in levels above. Similar to levels 3a and 3b, Level 3c was restricted to the southwest of Test Unit 1, and subsoil deposits were encountered across much of the northeastern portions of Test Unit 1 at approximately 22 cm below

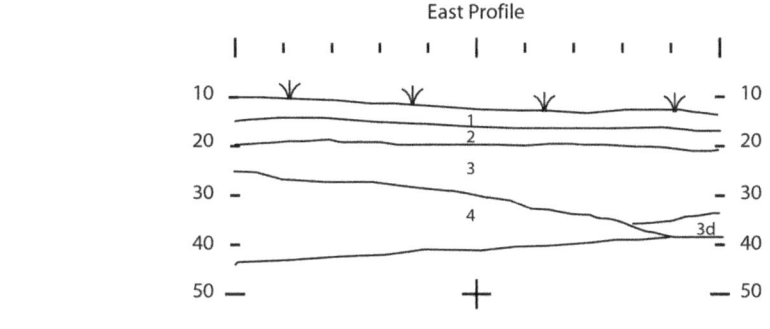

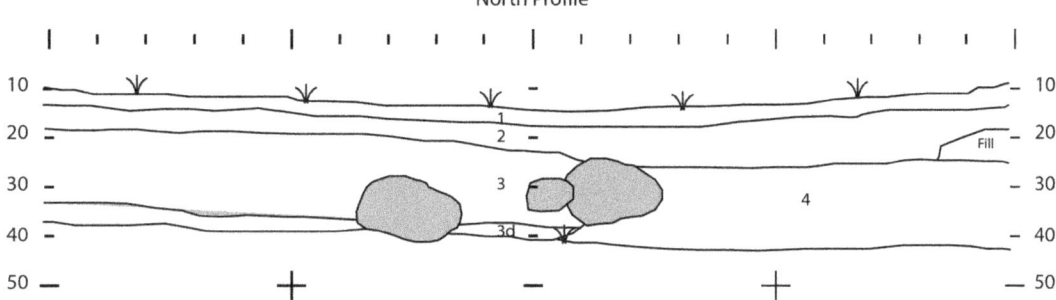

Level 1 - Sod; dark brown organic humus with roots and vegetation
Level 2 - Active Layer - Dark bown sandy loam with roots, some shell, and cultural materials
Level 3 -3c - Dark brown/black sandy loam with coarsely broken clam valves, artifacts, and faunal remains
Level 3d - Dark grey/black sandy loam, compact in texture with achitectural stone.
Level 4 - Subsoil - Mottled gray/brown sandly loam with gravel and cobbles.
 Rock

Figure 3.48 AlDf-31: Profile view of excavations, showing details of features

datum. This obviously suggests that levels 3b and 3c (and 3d) accumulated in a depression of some sort (see Chapter 5, as well as description, below).

Level 3d represented a marked transition from the shell-bearing layer above it, appearing as a compacted dark grey-black sandy loam, about 5 cm thick. This surface exhibited a line of small cobbles skirting the margin of the shallow pit dug into the subsurface layer (Level 4) to a depth of approximately 15 cm. Level 3d appeared to only occur within the interior of the line of stones, representing a deposit which filled the depression. Though the stones were not recognized as a feature during excavation, we have subsequently been able to provide a possible interpretation based on comparisons to other deposits in Port Joli. A full description appears in Chapter 5.

Level 4, which was not excavated, was like all other sub-soil horizons excavated in Port Joli. It was composed of mottled grey-brown sandy loam with abundant gravel and small cobbles (not associated with the feature). If levels 3c and 3d together represented some sort of living-surface, then it would have been deposited in a depression which had been excavated at least 15 cm into the Level 4 sub-soil deposit. As described in Chapter 5, given the nature of the sub-soil–midden transition, it is possible this surface was dug through an already existing (though likely thin) midden deposit. .

A Typology of Sites around Port Joli's Harbour

The review of sites presented above compiles information from more than eighty-three years of avocational and professional archaeological scrutiny around Port Joli's harbour. Such scrutiny has created the most detailed account of prehistoric settlement patterns and site structure in the province of Nova Scotia. Erskine (1959: 344) divided the sites around the harbour into three "types," including: "*a*, shore-camps, such as PJ No.8 [AlDf-03]; *b*, camps withdrawn into the woods, such as PJ No.2 [AlDf-07], No.7 [AlDf-08], and No.10 [AlDf-04]; and clamming camps, such as PJ No.3 [AlDf-25]." Erskine's keen observations, made over sixty years ago, are still relevant today, but the E'se'get Project provides further data that can be used to expand the range of variability and refine the definition of site types. Based on the total data recovered by all researchers and avocational archaeologists, Port Joli shell-bearing sites can be classified into five primary types (figure 3.49).

The first are large shell midden mounds, located within 30 m of the high-water mark and greater than 300 m^2 in area. As discussed above, such shell middens are rare in the Maritime Peninsula and may be unique to Port Joli. They have limited artifact densities (especially lithics), large portions of unbroken clam shells, very limited soil development, and large amounts of charcoal. These middens can have depths up to 1 m and universally have large shell-bearing "black soil" (Black 2002) deposits located at the landward edge of the sites. Beyond occasional hearth areas or charcoal scatters, they tend to be feature-free, and contain no interdigitated living surfaces, pits, or other features within the body of the midden (though some dwelling floors have been encountered on top of the midden deposits). However, they do often contain alternating lenses of broken, whole, and crushed shell, often with varying proportions of soil associated with each strata type. Regardless, shell always predominates over soil to a significant degree in these middens (see Chapter 8).

Such sites were likely the result of intensive clam processing, as first theorized by Erskine (1986: 110) and then Sanger (1996: 523). Only three of these sites are known, including (from north to south) AlDf-26, AlDf-25 (AlDf-09), and AlDf-24. These large sites are all located at mid-harbour, opposite the most extensive clam flats on the west side of the bay, north of Scotch Point (figure 3.49). It is possible that other, similar sites on the eastern side of the harbour may have been associated with the extensive clam flats there. However, erosion has impacted most, if not all, these coastal sites, and it is possible that evidence of such middens has been destroyed by wave action.

The second type of site is composed of large shell-bearing black soil deposits, greater than 300 m^2, with a high proportion of organic matrix and limited proportions of shell. These black soil middens are often characterized by high quantities of lithic debitage, comminuted charcoal, and fragmented faunal remains. Often, shell is present, but finely broken or crushed, and in some strata, shell may be absent entirely. These deposits appear to be palimpsests of recurring dwelling floors placed in the same area, often directly on the footprint of the house floor below it. Peripheral shell midden deposits are present at the margins of most of these sites but tend to be relatively small (less than 25 m^2). It is important to note that one site, AlDf-07, did not appear to have shell midden deposits, but this site is

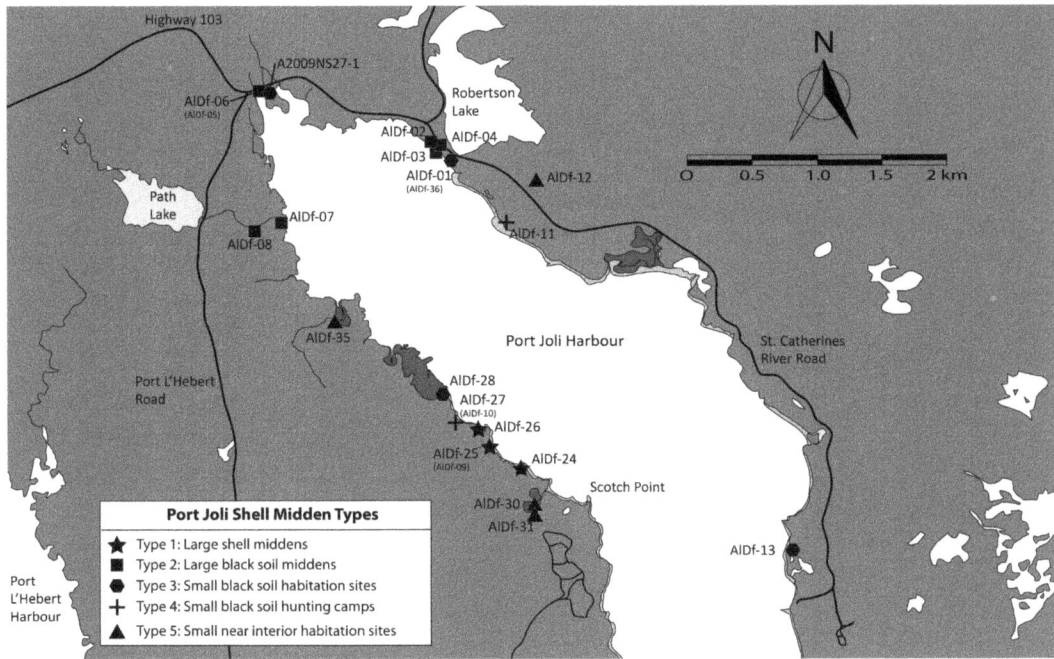

Figure 3.49 Types of shell middens at prehistoric archaeological sites around Port Joli's harbour.

completely disturbed by collecting, and hence shell midden may have been mixed with black soil midden here. These large sites have the greatest locational variability and can occur adjacent to the coastline or as much as 350 m inland. However, all the sites are located closer to the head of the harbour, and all are adjacent to streams or rivers (or relict stream beds). AlDf-03, AlDf-04, AlDf-06 (AlDf-05), AlDf-07, AlDf-08, and likely AlDf-02 can be classified as large black soil middens.

The third type of site consists of small shell-bearing black soil middens with small peripheral shell middens located close to the coast. These are often less than about 150 m^2 and less than 50 cm in depth and situated within 30 m of the shoreline. The associated shell middens are always positioned on the seaward edge of the site, and are often eroding when encountered. The deposits are associated with high quantities of lithic debitage and comminuted charcoal. Like the large black soil middens, most of these sites appear to be palimpsest of living floors which were repeatedly placed in the footprint of a previous lower floor, resulting in the aggregation of highly organic, charcoal-rich shell-bearing soil deposits. If so, the sites are noted for being somewhat ephemeral, and, while repeatedly used, appear to have been less frequently occupied, and likely by smaller corporate groups, than the larger sites. The adjacent middens represent the patterned discard of domestic life, but the trampling and tracking of the shell from this midden into the house floors resulted in superb organic preservation. This type of site includes AlDf-28, A2009NS27-1, AlDf-13, and AlDf-01 (AlDf-36).

The fourth type of site is made up of very small shell-bearing black soil middens that appear to be the remains of shoreside ungulate hunting and processing camps. Such camps are often located close to choke points on the landscape, where ungulates moving from the inner to outer harbour were forced to take a route squeezed between the high-water mark and a difficult-to-traverse feature, such as a lake or upland bog. Like most shell-bearing deposits around Port Joli, such sites are often placed contiguously with large boulders and glacial erratics, but in spaces too small to support a normally sized structure (approx. 3 m in diameter). The sites contain deposits similar to dwelling floors, including compact black soil, rich in artifacts, especially lithics. They may also contain alternating lenses of dense shell. However, the hearths they exhibit are often larger than those associated with dwelling floors and are more formal, with cobbles and stones around their margins. These data, combined with the large amount of ungulate bones found at these sites, suggest they were locations where ungulates were processed after being hunted nearby, perhaps by cooperating family groups. These sites include AlDf-11 and AlDf-27 (AlDf-10).

The fifth type of site is similar in some respects to the third type, except that the fifth types are all located between 140 and 400 m inland from the coast, what Erskine (1959: 344) would call "camps withdrawn into the woods." These "near-interior" sites are all located in forested locations at higher elevations and are often associated with freshwater streams, lakes, and—in three cases—fens or marshes. They tend to be rather small sites, about 150 m^2 or less, and include small shell midden deposits containing broken and unbroken shells, typically less than 50 cm in depth. The middens occur in multiple distinct loci near the edges of the sites and are often associated with extensive shell-bearing black soil deposits. As will be described in Chapter 5, they contain evidence of dwelling surfaces in the black soil deposits, and some contain evidence of ritual structures. Sites exhibiting these characteristics include AlDf-12, AlDf-35, AlDf-30, and AlDf-31.

Chapter 4
Chronology

MATTHEW BETTS

Introduction

Grappling with the chronological sequence of the sites, deposits, and assemblages is central to the development of a culture-history for Port Joli's harbour. It is important to recognize that the chronology presented in this volume is not static and will never be complete. Future research will inevitably expand, refine, modify, or even nullify the sequence. In this chapter, multiple competing lines of absolute and relative dating evidence are used to develop a chronological model. Such a process is incremental and reflexive; as one connection is made, new patterns and hypotheses are generated, and the sequence must be reorganized. We will attempt to avoid any potential circularity of reasoning, which is inherent in such reflexivity. Indeed, the process will sometimes even be at odds with the structure of the monograph itself; for example, the following analysis refers to artifactual data not yet presented (please refer to chapters 6 and 7 for full descriptions and tabulations). Regardless, presenting the chronology early in the monograph is essential for the culture-history analysis that follows. The Port Joli chronology must necessarily refer to the culture-history frameworks proposed for the region by previous researchers, which relies on its own terminology and sequencing. In fact, comparing Port Joli's cultural development with these other sequences is a critical outcome of the project.

This volume adopts the "Maritime Woodland" terminology first proposed by Keenlyside (1983) and most recently refined and developed by Black (1992: 10; 2002: 304). While we recognize the value of Petersen and Sanger's (1991) "Ceramic sequence" for relatively dating sites and assemblages on the Maritime Peninsula, like Black (1992: 10) we view the adoption of "Ceramic" terminology to be redundant with "Woodland" terminology. As first outlined by Black (1992: 10), both sequences use precisely the same temporal divisions, and both are explicitly based on the appearance and widespread use of a broadly homogenous ceramic technology in the region.

The use of shared stone tool types through the Northeast (e.g., Braun 1980: 98; Holyoke 2012; Justice 1987; Leonard 1995; Ritchie 1971), and other artifact types (such as harpoons, leister points, and ground-stone technology), argues for a geographically broad "Woodland" cultural manifestation in the North American Northeast. As discussed by Turnbull and Allen (1988: 251), "Maritime Woodland" terminology accepts this cultural connection while recognizing fundamentally unique economic strategies in the Maritime Peninsula. Specifically, the horticulture and agriculture that defines much of the Woodland Period in the interior Northeast and southern Atlantic states is supplanted by an intensive maritime subsistence orientation (without evidence of agriculture) on the Maritime Peninsula. Why agriculture was not adopted on the Maritime Peninsula is one of the fundamental questions of Northeastern prehistory.

Table 4.1 outlines the chrono-cultural model adopted for this volume. As described above, it follows the Maritime Woodland sequence most recently elucidated by Black (1992, 2002), but for the sake of clarity (and comparison), Petersen and Sanger's (1991) Ceramic Period sequence is also included. To further increase its utility, Erskine's (1962) local Cultural sequence for Nova Scotia is also included, though it is not discussed further in the volume.

Absolute Dating

A significant goal of the E'se'get Archaeological Project was to develop a radiometrically dated sequence of archaeological deposits for Port Joli. Charcoal and terrestrial mammal bone samples were carefully collected from all strata/features throughout the 2008 to 2012 excavations in Port Joli. In practice, the radiocarbon samples were treated like artifacts, with three-dimensional coordinates taken for all samples (in addition to the typical unit-level data recorded for faunal remains). By April 2013, nineteen Accelerator Mass Spectrometer (AMS) radiocarbon dates were obtained from thirteen charcoal samples and seven bone or tooth samples from the Port Joli excavations (table 4.2). All the bone assays were run on a terrestrial ungulate—caribou (*Rangifer tarandus*) or white-tailed deer (Odocoileus virginianus)—to avoid issues with ancient marine carbon contamination. We could discern no appreciable difference between the charcoal and bone dates. One standard radiocarbon date from wood charcoal had previously been obtained for AlDf-03 by John Erskine (who called it Port Joli No. 8), resulting in a total of twenty radiocarbon dates amassed for the Port Joli sequence.

The accumulated radiocarbon dates span a period of approximately 3150 radiocarbon years BP to approximately 0 radiocarbon years BP (table 4.2). Two dates returned modern ages that are not consistent with the prehistoric artifact assemblages from the deposits in which they were derived. Additionally, the early date of 3150 BP hints at an Early Maritime Woodland Period (Black 1992) occupation at AlDf-25, but unfortunately it is not consistent with its associated artifact assemblage (see Chapter 6), nor could clam flats have existed in Port Joli when this shell midden was deposited (see Chapter 2). Therefore, it is reasonable to conclude that it is not related to the shell midden, and if it is cultural, it represents a limited occupation in the harbour. With these three incongruous dates removed from the analysis, the sequence consists of seventeen dates which span approximately 1630 to 380 radiocarbon years BP. Calibrated, the dates span 1610 BP to 510 BP (2σ).

The calibrated probability distributions (2σ) for the seventeen non-modern dates are displayed in figure 4.1. All assays, except for the one conducted by Erskine, were AMS dates run at Beta Analytic Carbon Dating Service with standard pre-treatments (see table 4.2 for details). A large suite of dates associated with AlDf-24, Area A; AlDf-30, Area A midden and Black Soil Area; and AlDf-25 cluster between about 350 to 650 cal AD (ca. 1600–1300 cal BP), suggesting significant occupation of multiple sites during the last centuries of the Middle Maritime Woodland Period (Black 1992) or Ceramic Period 3 (Petersen and Sanger 1993). All dates overlap at 2, suggesting the possibility that the sites were occupied relatively contemporaneously.

Perhaps most intriguing about these data is the range of dates obtained from the AlDf-24, Area A midden (figures 4.1 and 4.2). These samples were collected from strata spanning

Table 4.1 Chrono–cultural sequences, compared

Maritime Woodland Sequence (after Black 1992:92)	Range BC/AD	Range BP	Ceramic Period Sequence (after Petersen and Sanger 1991:126)	Date Range BC/AD	Range BP	Local Cultural Sequence (Erskine 1962:2)	Range BC/AD
Early Maritime Woodland	1250–250 BC	3200–2200 BP	CP1 Early Ceramic	1100–200 BC	3050–2150 BP		
Middle Maritime Woodland	250 BC–AD 650	2200–1300 BP	CP2 early Middle Ceramic	200 BC–AD 300	2150–1650 BP		
Middle Maritime Woodland	250 BC–AD 650	2200–1300 BP	CP3 Middle Middle Ceramic	AD 300–600	1650–1350 BP		
earlier Late Maritime Woodland	AD 650–1000	1300–950 BP	CP4 late Middle Ceramic	AD 600–1000	1350–950 BP	Lower Bear River	AD 600–900
						Upper Bear River	AD 900–1000
later Late Maritime Woodland	AD 1000–1400	950–550 BP	CP5 early Late Ceramic	AD 1000–1300	950–650 BP	Port Joli	AD 1100–1200
						Indian Gardens	AD 1200–1500
Protohistoric	AD 1400–1600	550–350 BP	CP6 late Late Ceramic	AD 1300–1550	650–400 BP	Contact	AD 1550–1700
Historic	AD 1600–Present	350 BP–Present	CP7 Contact (Early Historic)	AD 1550–1750	400–200 BP	Contact	AD 1550–1701

Table 4.2 Radiocarbon dates from archaeological contexts around Port Joli's harbour

Borden	CMC #	Lab # 1	Measured Age BP	13C/12C (o/oo)	Conventional Age BP	2 Sigma Cal BC/AD	2 Sigma Calibration BP
AlDf-25	1744	255229	3180 ± 40	−27.1	3150 ± 40	1500–1380 BC	3450–3330
AlDf-30	1746	255231	1600 ± 40	−22.9	1630 ± 40	340–540 AD	1610–1410
AlDf-24	1745	255230	1520 ± 40	−23.8	1540 +/− 40	420–610 AD	1530–1340
AlDf-25	1747	256563	1520 ± 40	−25.0	1520 ± 40	430–620 AD	1520–1330
AlDf-30	1752	273516	1480 ± 40	−25.3	1470 ± 40	540–650 AD	1410–1300
AlDf-24	1749	273513	1450 ± 40	−23.9	1470 ± 40	540–650 AD	1410–1300
AlDf-24	1748	256564	1410 ± 40	−23.5	1430 ± 40	560–660 AD	1390–1290
AlDf-30	1791	365482	1410 ± 30	−24.6	1420 ± 30	600–660 AD	1360–1290
AlDf-24	1769	297241	1400 ± 30	−23.8	1420 ± 30	590–660 AD	1360–1290
AlDf-30	1781	341499	1330 ± 30	−20.3	1410 ± 30	600–660 AD	1350–1290
AlDf-30	1780	341498	1390 ± 30	−25.8	1380 ± 30	620–670 AD	1330–1280
AlDf-24	1758	288733	1190 ± 40	−20.8	1260 ± 40	660–880 AD	1280–1070
AlDf-03	N/A	S–155	1220 ± 100	−25.00	1220 ± 100	648–1011 AD	1302–939
AlDf-08	1785	343224	800 ± 30	−21.8	850 ± 30	1160–1260 AD	800–690
AlDf-30	1779	341497	730 ± 30	−21.9	780 ± 30	1220–1280 AD	740–670
AlDf-06	1783	341501	610 ± 30	−21.6	670 ± 30	1280–1390 AD	670–560
AlDf-24	1756	286106	610 ± 40	−21.7	660 ± 40	1270–1400 AD	680–550
AlDf-24	1757	288732	340 ± 40	−22.6	380 ± 40 BP	1440–1640 AD	510–310
AlDf-31	1750	273514	40 ± 40	−25.5	30 ± 40 BP	1700 AD	250
AlDf-24	1751	273515	0	−25.3	0 BP	1950 AD	0

Chronology

Area	Feature	Unit	Level	North	West	Depth	Material	Type
A		A (N56W50)	3c - Dates basal level	-	-	BMS	Charcoal	AMS
A	Area A	A (N52W57)	3b	90	23	28	Charcoal	AMS
A		N56W50	3g	25	90	51	Charcoal	AMS
A		A (N56W50)	3c - Dates uppermost level	-	-	Level Bag	Charcoal	AMS
Depr.	Feature 2/3	Test Unit 3	2b/3	21	32	19	Charcoal	AMS
A		N56W50	3m	67	53.5	88	Charcoal	AMS
A		N56W50	3b	-	-	Level Bag	Charcoal	AMS
A		N51W52	3f	0	21	41	Charcoal	AMS
A		N55W50	3N/0, Dates basal level	83.5	18.5	89	Charcoal	AMS
A	Feature 2	N52W51	3d	53	47	25	Terrestrial mammal bone	AMS
A	Feature 1	N51W51	3a	73	46	14.5	Terrestrial mammal bone	AMS
C		N52W53	3i - Dates level 3f-3k in Area C	NE Quad	NE Quad	Level Bag: 50-73 Cm	Caribou bone	AMS
-	N/A	-	-	-	-	-	Charcoal	Stan.
A		Test Unit 1	3E	Level Bag	Level Bag	Level Bag	Terrestrial mammal bone	AMS
A	Upper Level	N53W53	2b	59	41	11	Caribou bone	AMS
East		N50W50	2a	Screen	Screen	Screen	Charcoal	AMS
C	4a	N51W52	1 - Dates levels 3 and 3b in Feature 4	68	79	16.5	Caribou bone	AMS
C	Level 2 Activity Area	N52W53	2	SE Quad	SE Quad	Level Bag: 8-14 cm	Caibou tooth	AMS
A		Test Unit 1	3b	13	57	23.5	Charcoal	AMS
C		3 (N56W54)	3i	17	57	49	Charcoal	AMS

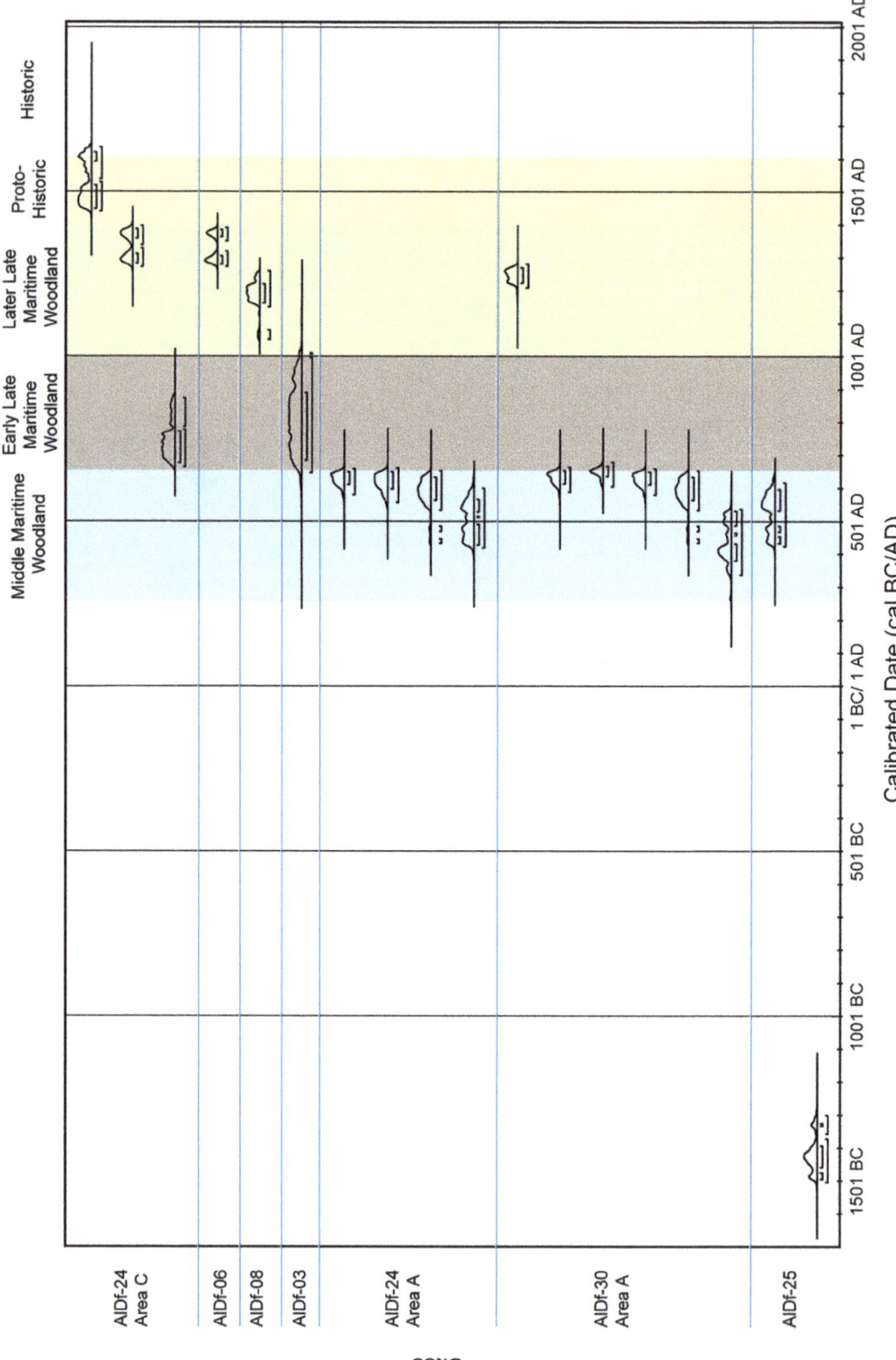

Figure 4.1 Calibrated probability distributions from Port Joli samples. Calibration follows IntCal09, after Heaton et al. 2009; Oeschger et al. 1975; Reimer et al. 2009; Stuiver et al. 1993.

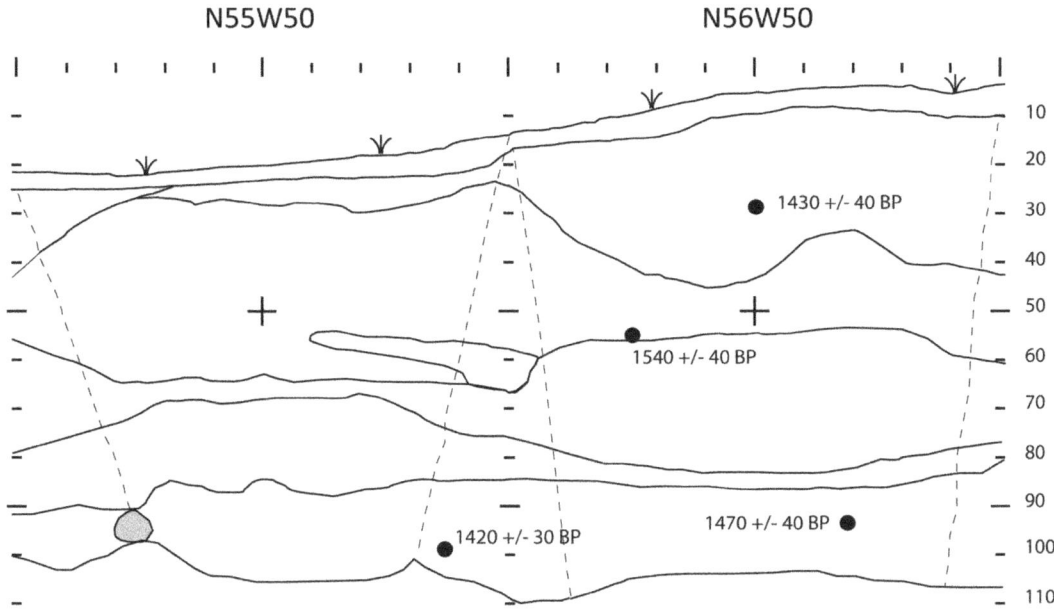

Figure 4.2 AlDf-24, Area A midden: Correlations between stratigraphic profiles (see Chapter 3 for details) and the location of dated radiocarbon samples.

basal to surface levels and clearly indicate the near-contemporary nature of the stratigraphic deposit, suggesting a rapid accumulation of over 1 m of shell sometime in the decades around the late sixth century AD. This deposition was so rapid, in fact, that it cannot be measured within the standards of current radiocarbon-dating precision. This rapid development is consistent with the proposition (see chapters 3 and 6) that the Area A midden was a location where clams were intensively processed for storage by an aggregated group of people.

The three dates from the AlDf-30, Area A midden and Black Soil Area correlate precisely with the stratigraphic sequence from which they derive, indicating that features 1 and 2 are Middle Maritime Woodland in age, contemporary with the latest date on both the adjacent Area A midden and the large midden at AlDf-24, Area A (see below). Feature 3, the lowest and older feature, therefore would have been occupied at some time before about 1400 cal BP.

Unlike the deposits at AlDf-24, Area A, the AlDf-24, Area C, deposits span a much larger time range—from the Early Late Maritime Woodland Period to the early Protohistoric Period. The earliest date, 660 to 880 cal AD (1280–1070 cal BP), is derived from caribou bone found in basal cultural strata, while the latest date, 1440 to 1640 cal AD (510–310 cal

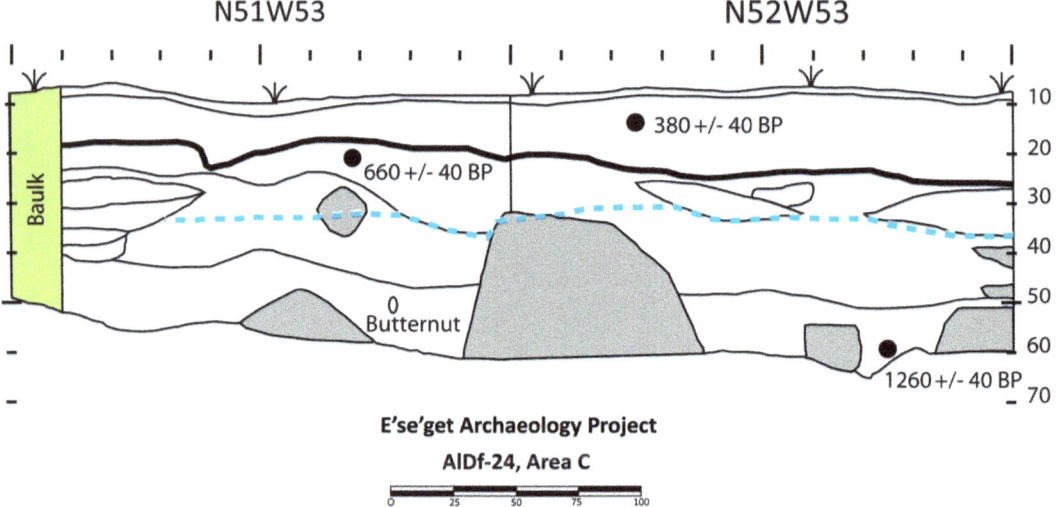

Figure 4.3 AlDf-24, Area C: Correlations between stratigraphic profiles (see Chapter 3 for details) and the location of dated radiocarbon samples.

BP), is derived from caribou bone recovered from the cultural layer immediately below the sod. A radiocarbon date on a caribou bone found in the Feature 4 hearth (Feature 4a) dates the dwelling floor to about 1270 to 1400 cal AD (ca. 680–550 cal BP), or the later Late Maritime Woodland Period. It should be noted that the apparent hiatus displayed by figure 4.1 in the Area C deposits represents a gap in sampling (samples from intervening layers have not yet been assayed; see figure 4.3) and probably not a gap in occupation of Area C. Thus, the layers between these two dated layers likely date to between 880 and 1270 cal AD (ca. 1070–680 cal BP). As such, the radiocarbon dates and the stratigraphic gap indicate that AlDf-24, Area C, was occupied throughout the entire Late Woodland Period, just prior to European contact in the region.

The Level 2 deposit at AlDf-30 unexpectedly returned a Later Late Maritime Woodland date, roughly contemporary with the Feature 4 house deposit at AlDf-24, Area C. Both AlDf-08 and AlDf-06 are similarly dated, though AlDf-06 appears to be the slightly younger deposit of the three. In fact, AlDf-06 is almost precisely contemporary with the Feature 4 deposit at AlDf-24, Area C. The AlDf-03 sample was the only one to be assayed using standard techniques, and consequently the associated error is very broad. Nevertheless, the 2σ probability distribution falls almost entirely with the Early Late Maritime Woodland Period, making it roughly contemporary with the lowest deposits from AlDf-24, Area C.

Relative Dating

The radiocarbon data above are associated with only five of the nineteen shell midden sites in the harbour. Developing a moderately comprehensive sequence therefore necessitates the uses of relative-dating techniques. Here we attempt to employ the use of artifactual and structural (i.e., depositional) horizon markers, or "index fossils" (e.g., Beck 1998) used throughout the region and the greater Northeast to attempt to augment the radiometrically dated sequence. This occurs in three steps. First, we define known artifactual and depositional horizon markers. Second, we correlate known horizon markers associated with Port

Joli contexts which have been radiocarbon-dated, to determine their local applicability as horizon markers. Third, we use these data to extrapolate relative ages using both horizon markers and radiocarbon dates.

As discussed in Chapter 5, the Petersen and Sanger (1991) Ceramic sequence fundamentally altered the way chronological associations were determined on the Maritime Peninsula. In fact, since 1991, it has become the de facto standard for relative dating in the region, such that it is rare to see the more traditional lithic types employed in such relative-dating exercises. Black (2002) has provided an extremely useful summary of the relevant shifts in ceramic technology correlated with his Maritime Woodland chrono-cultural sequence, focusing on the appearance of shell temper and cord-wrapped stick decoration. However, as we will see in Chapter 6, our careful attribute analysis of the Port Joli ceramic sequence draws into question the applicability of shifts in ceramic technology for relative dating in Port Joli, at least on the time scale covering the period of occupation in the harbour.

As such, defining other horizon markers is necessary. Few recent studies have attempted to use changes in lithic technology styles to relatively date sites on the Maritime Peninsula, and thus far, no regional lithic typological sequence has been developed. However, archaeologists often refer to chronological associations between lithic styles and the dated deposits they excavate. For example, side-notched and corner-notched (expanding stem) projectile points are often associated with Late Maritime Woodland deposits (e.g., Holyoke 2012: 43). At some Late Maritime Woodland sites, such as Melanson (BgDb-4), a progression from side-notched to corner-notched points has been identified stratigraphically (Nash and Stewart 1990: 48). Holyoke (2012: 43), based on a regional analysis, has suggested that this transition occurred at the early Late Maritime Woodland to the later Late Maritime Woodland transition (ca. 950 cal BP).

As described in Chapter 7, such a transition from side-notched to predominately corner-notched projectile points does occur in AlDf-24, Area C, and the stratigraphic and radiometric information suggests it occurred almost precisely at the early to later Late Maritime Woodland transition. However, at AlDf-24, Area C, corner-notched points *co-occur* with side-notched projectile points found in the same stratum. Furthermore, at AlDf-30, side-notched points occur in contexts dating to the Middle Maritime Woodland Period. Thus, the appearance of corner-notched points would denote a Later Late Maritime Woodland occupation, but side-notched points appear not to be a reliable horizon marker, at least on the time scales associated with the sites in Port Joli.

Fortunately, other tool types present throughout the Northeast may provide opportunities for greater chronological resolution. The "Levanna" point type (Ritchie 1971), has been recognized in archaeological deposits throughout the Northeast, and has a relatively distinct chronological range, spanning the period from about 600 to 1300 AD (e.g., Fox 2015; Justice 1987; Kinsey 1972; Ritchie 1971; Steponaitis 1980). This range is almost precisely consistent with the Late Maritime Woodland Period. As such, any context with a Levanna point is relatively confidently dated to this time. A similar common point type in the Northeast, known as "Madison" (Ritchie 1971), may provide a similarly useful horizon marker. Like the Levanna points, Madison points are unstemmed and triangular in outline, but are often smaller than Levanna specimens and tend to have straight to slightly convex bases, while Levanna points have a distinct concave base, often with strong "ears." Madison points have a smaller chronological range than Levanna, particularly on the Atlantic seaboard, and date from about 1250 to 1600 AD (Fox 2015; Jirikowic 1999; Ritchie 1971; Steponaitis 1980). This would place them firmly in the Later Late Maritime Woodland Period, extending into the Protohistoric Period.

No Levanna or Madison projectile points have been recovered from a radiocarbon-dated Middle Maritime Woodland context in Port Joli. In fact, they only occur in Later Late

Table 4.3 Chronological sequence for prehistoric archaeological sites and deposits in Port Joli's harbour. The contexts are colour-coded as follows: blue, Middle Maritime Woodland Period; grey, general Late Maritime Woodland association; brown, Early Late Maritime Woodland green, Later Late Maritime Woodland; yellow, protohistoric; white, general Maritime Woodland association. Abbreviations: RC, radiocarbon CN, corner-notched protectible point; LP, Levanna projectile point; MP, Madison projectile point

Context	Features	Units/Levels
AlDf-25	All	All
AlDf-30 Area A Midden	All	N 50-53, W54-57
AlDf-30 Black Soil Midden Lower	1,2,3	N50-55, W 50-53, Test Pit 3, Test Pit 4
AlDf-24 Area A Midden	All	All Units, Area A
AlDf-26 Midden	Midden	All
AlDf-01/AlDf-36	All	All
AlDf-02	All	All
AlDf-27/AlDf-10	All	All
AlDf-11	All	All
AlDf-24 Area C Lower	All	All
AlDf-03/AlDf-04	All	All
AlDf-24 Area C Middle	All	All
AlDf-24 Area C Upper	4	All
AlDf-08	All	All
AlDf-30 Black Soil Midden Upper	N/A	N50-55, W 50-53, Test Pit 3, Test Pit 4
AlDf-06/AlDf-05	All	All
AlDf-07	All	All
AlDf-24 Area A Feature 2	2	N50W50, N50W51, N51W50, N52W50, N53W50
AlDf-24 Area C Proto	All	All
AlDf-12	All	All
AlDf-31	All	All
AlDf-13	All	All
AlDf-28	All	All
AlDf-35	All	All
AlDf-30 Area B Midden	All	N52W48

Maritime Woodland contexts in the Harbour. It should be noted that Madison points are present at AlDf-03 and AlDf-04, associated with an early Late Maritime Woodland radiocarbon date, but Erskine's excavations here did not have precise stratigraphic control. This suggests AlDf-03 and AlDf-04, like AlDf-24, Area C, span the entire Late Maritime Woodland Period. Madison projectile points are also present in the very large assemblage from AlDf-07,

Levels	Period	Absolute/Relative Date Indicator
All levels	MMW	RC Date, CN, Extensive Shell Midden
All Levels	MMW	RC Date
3 and Lower	MMW	RC Date
3 and lower	MMW	RC Date, Extensive Shell Midden
All	MMW	Extensive Shell Midden
All	LMW	LP, Extensive Black Soil Midden
All	LMW	LP, Extensive Black Soil Midden
All	LMW	CN, LP
All	LMW	CN, LP
3f and lower	Early LMW	RC Date and Stratigraphy
All	Early LMW/Later LMW	RC Date, CN, LP, MP
3c, 3d, 3e	Early LMW /Later LMW Transition	Stratigraphy
3, 3b	Later LMW	RC Date, MP, Stratigraphy
All levels	Later LMW	RC Date, CN, LP, MP, Extensive Black Soil Midden
1, 2, 2b, 2c, Portions of 3A	Later LMW	RC Date, LP
All levels	Later LMW	RC Date, LP, MP, Extensive Black Soil Midden
All	Later LMW	CN, MP, Extensive Black Soil Midden
2, 2b, Portions of 3	Later LMW/ Protohistoric/ Historic	Stratigraphic Position, CN, Historic Artifacts
1, 2, 2b, 2c	Protohistoric	RC Date, MP, Historic Artifacts
All	Maritime Woodland	Ceramic Artifacts
All	Maritime Woodland	Ceramic Artifacts
All	Maritime Woodland	Ceramic Artifacts
All	Maritime Woodland	Ceramic Artifacts
Unknown	Maritime Woodland	Ceramic Artifacts
All	Maritime Woodland	Unknown

and the lack of Levanna points in this assemblage may suggest this site dates primarily to the Later Late Maritime Woodland.

Historic artifacts have been recovered from two undisturbed contexts in Port Joli, including AlDf-24 Area A, Feature 2, and the Protohistoric layer from AlDf-24, Area C. The array of artifacts is not particularly diagnostic and include wrought nails and several pieces of red earthenware (see Chapter 7). Nevertheless, the assemblages support the early historic radiocarbon date from AlDf-24, Area C, and suggest a significant time range for the house-floor deposit on the top of AlDf-24, Area A.

Black (2002) has defined a unique horizon marker for the transition from the Middle Maritime Woodland to the Early Late Maritime Woodland periods, which is particularly informative here. In an extensive analysis of archaeological sites, site formation processes, and depositional components, Black determined a structural shift occurred between the Middle Maritime Woodland Period to the Late Maritime Woodland Period. Middle Maritime Woodland deposits in the Quoddy region of New Brunswick tend to be associated with large, spatially distinct shell middens. While these middens are often quantitatively different from the very large and relatively sterile shell middens in Port Joli (e.g., they often contain interdigitated living floors and hearths in the Quoddy region), their size and focus on large quantities of shellfish is comparable. Later Late Maritime Woodland sites in the Quoddy region are drastically different, appearing as large black soil middens, often with shell admixtures, with interdigitated living floors.

Radiocarbon-dated contexts in Port Joli appear to correspond well with this trend. The largest shell midden deposits in the harbour, AlDf-25 and AlDf-24, Area A, date to the Middle Maritime Woodland, and even smaller sites dating to this time tend to have spatially distinct and relatively deep shell midden deposits (e.g., AlDf-30, Area A midden). In contrast, all large dated sites with extensive black soil middens in Port Joli date to the Late Maritime Woodland Period. The radiocarbon evidence from Port Joli therefore indicates that such shifts in site structure can be used as a horizon marker. If so, then AlDf-26 is almost certainly a Middle Maritime Woodland shell midden, and by corollary, AlDf-36 (AlDf-01), AlDf-02, and AlDf-07 are likely all Late Maritime Woodland in age. Of course, the implications for this correspondence with the Quoddy region are profound and will be discussed in full in subsequent chapters.

The Port Joli Chronological Sequence

Table 4.3 outlines the chronological sequence defined for the prehistoric sites around Port Joli's harbour using both radiometric and relative-dating indicators. Unfortunately, six sites or contexts could not be assigned to a period more specific than the Maritime Woodland, based largely on the presence of ceramics. Given the development of the shoreline in Port Joli, and the fact that they all contain shell admixtures of shell middens, then all six almost certainly date after around 1500 cal BP, when the harbour first developed (see Chapter 2). As such, the Port Joli sequence represents a high-resolution record of a seemingly intensive occupation spanning the period between around 1600 cal BP to around 500 cal BP (ca. 400–1500 cal AD), or roughly 1,100 years of in-place history.

There are some clear patterns that develop when scrutinizing this chronology, especially the association of very large shell middens in the Middle Woodland Period near mid-harbour, and the very large black soil middens located near the head of the harbour during the Late Maritime Woodland Period. Also clear is the overwhelming evidence of Late Maritime Woodland occupation, both at new site locations and on top of sites first occupied in the Middle Maritime Woodland Period. This proposed chronological sequence will inform all subsequent analysis, and the patterns suggested here will be explored in full in the chapters that follow.

Chapter 5
Architectural Features

M. Gabriel Hrynick and Matthew Betts

Introduction

Shell middens remain the primary focus of coastal archaeology on the Maritime Peninsula, despite the tendency for artifactual remains to be more abundant off-midden, where people lived much of their lives and conducted daily activities. In this chapter, we review the contributions of the E'se'get Archaeology Project to the understanding of prehistoric Wabanaki architecture and the use and creation of domestic and ritual spaces. Identifying, excavating, and analyzing architecture was a primary focus of the E'se'get Project from its inception, and a central contribution of it has been to situate architectural remains not as epiphenomenal reflections of environmental realities and the necessities of mobility, but primarily as socially significant arenas (e.g., Hrynick et al. 2012; Hrynick and Betts 2017).

We have explored some of the Port Joli features previously in a series of papers about domestic and ritual architecture on the Maritime Peninsula (Hrynick et al. 2012; Hrynick and Betts 2014, 2017). In this chapter we review those features as well as previously unpublished features from Port Joli encountered during the E'se'get Projector by earlier researchers. This large assemblage facilitates comparisons within and outside the Maritime Peninsula, toward our goal of offering both a local architectural history of Port Joli and a comprehensive comparative data set of hunter-gatherer architecture in the greater Northeast.

Background

Prior to the E'se'get Archaeology Project, ancient Wabanaki dwelling features had not been extensively studied outside of New Brunswick's Quoddy region and coastal Maine[1] (Hrynick and Black 2016; Sanger 2010 for reviews). Wabanaki dwelling features throughout the coastal Maritime Peninsula are generally characterized by artifact-rich oval "floor" deposits, about 2.5 to 4 m in diameter, corresponding to conical, bark- or hide-covered wigwams described in the ethnographic record (figure 5.1) (Bock 1978; Butler and Hadlock 1957; Le Clercq 1910: 100–101; Speck 1997: 27–29; Thwaites 1898: 40–41; Wallis and Wallis 1955: 57–59). Compared to surrounding cultural soil matrix in coastal sites, they tend to be characterized by compact, black, charcoal-rich soil, and contain less shell (less than 15 percent of the total feature matrix) (Belcher 1989: 179; Hrynick and Robinson 2012: 34–35; Sanger 2010).

---

1. Maritime Woodland Period dwelling features are essentially unknown from the interior of the Maritime Peninsula, likely due to a variety of factors (see Sanger 2010). Dwelling features may be less visible on the region's interior, where they would not contrast with the surrounding shell matrix. Testing regimes have also been more limited on the interior, and primarily in the context of cultural resource management. A notable exception is reported from the Shubenacadie River by Preston (1974).

Figure 5.1 Traditional birchbark wigwam built by Mi'kmaw Elder Todd Labrador and Mi'kmaw artist Melissa Labrador in Kejimkujik National Park, Nova Scotia.

The Maritime Peninsula has produced a suite of non-midden features from the Maritime Woodland Period. These include pits, hearths, possible clam-steaming features, and living or work surfaces (e.g., Black 2004; Davis 1978; Sanger 1987). Because some of these features have been identified in vertically focused excavations covering small horizontal extents, it is likely that many were portions of larger dwelling features. Sometimes, dwelling features may be visible as surface depressions (e.g., Belcher 1988 Matthew 1884; Moorehead 1922: 171). In profile, they are classically described as "saucer shaped" (Belcher 1988; Sanger 1987, 2010), indicating that their centres are lower than their sides. Some archaeologists interpret this to represent semi-subterranean construction of dwelling features and excavation of the floors into pits by their inhabitants (Sanger 1996, 2010), but this shape may more likely represent a suite of surface-preparation practices and subsequent trampling, rather than intentional excavation (Hrynick 2018).

Throughout the Maritime Peninsula, dwelling features tend to be located to the landward portion of sites, with shell middens separating them from the water (see Chapter 3; Sanger 1996: 521, 2010). Although erosion has eliminated portions of some sites, there are good reasons to believe that this intra-site patterning is not an illusion. The first is that this positioning makes environmental sense, with dwelling features typically placed in the most sheltered positions sites offer. Second, "chronological shingling" (sensu Young et al. 1992) has sometimes left remnants of earlier sites located to the shoreward side of newer ones. In the apparently intact more recent sites, the spatial pattern often holds.

Previously, Sanger (e.g., 1987, 2010: 25–26) and Davis (1978: 13) outlined methods for identifying dwelling features at coastal sites on the Maritime Peninsula. Their approach at Passamaquoddy and Penobscot Bays was to trench landward from shell middens, until encountering the artifact-rich gravel layers that typify Maritime Woodland Period dwelling features. Studies of dwelling features in those regions also tended to take whole dwelling features as a minimum unit of provenience and generally did not regard them as internally stratified. Another thread of research emphasized coastal site stratigraphy but did not expose features to substantial horizontal extents.

David W. Black (e.g., 2004; Bishop and Black 1988; Hrynick and Black 2016), on the Bliss Islands in Passamaquoddy Bay, identified a variety of gravel-covered living-surfaces, arguing that they were part of a stratigraphically complex but interpretable midden stratigraphy (Black 1993). In general, fully excavating dwelling features is rare, due to the wide-area excavation, and therefore time and resources, that doing so would require (Sanger 2010: 36). In relation to previous archaeological work, our approach was informed by the ethnographic literature, which indicates that Protohistoric and Historic Period Wabanaki dwellings were organized according to gender, age, and status, in ways that were rooted in Wabanaki cosmology. In effect, the ways wigwams were built, and the way space was arranged inside of them, indicated more broadly the way that society was socially organized.

Within Algonquian cosmology, which is relational, as are many other hunter-gatherer ontologies, the way places were organized and the gendering of places and activities were ways in which people actively practised their cosmology. As others have noted (e.g., Hoffman 1955: 489–504), there were profound similarities in Cree and Wabanaki cosmology, suggesting a shared Algonquian hunter-gatherer cosmology, in which a game-keeper system was central (Martin 1978; Tanner 1979). For the Wabanaki, there were some variations, but ethnographic accounts of them repeatedly indicate that they had separate male and female spaces (Denys 1968: 408; Le Clercq 1910: 102; Speck 1997: 29; Wallis and Wallis 1955: 226–30). Failure to maintain these appropriate patterns could result in prey refusing to surrender itself to hunters or in animals attacking or imperilling hunters. Accordingly, there is a vast realm of relationships among humans and animals in hunter-gatherer societies beyond the immediate killing and disposing of animals (Hornborg 2013; Tanner 1979). Accessing the majority of these actions archaeologically is challenging because the bones and stone tools from the interaction between hunters and prey are often the best preserved archaeologically and the most easily recovered. Shifting focus to domestic features offers a way to expand that focus.

Methods

From the inception of the E'se'get Archaeology Project, we devoted considerable time and resources to dwelling features themselves, building on the structural elements others had identified and on refinements to coastal-site stratigraphy. We also sought to employ methods that could reveal intra-dwelling spatial patterning. However, a final major influence on our approach was the regional ethnographic record and direct historical analogy for recognizing features. Beginning at least with G. F. Matthew's (1884) seminal account of dwelling features at Bocabec/Phil's Beach near St. Andrews, New Brunswick (see Hrynick and Black 2012), prehistoric dwelling features have been understood by direct historical analogy to wigwams described in the ethnographic literature, which portray continuity in architectural form persisting, in some areas, past the mid-nineteenth century. This record was essential to us in part because at the onset it was not entirely clear what a dwelling feature would look like on Nova Scotia's South Shore. Previous work in the Wabanaki homeland had focused on portions of Maine and New Brunswick where dwelling features are often lined with beach gravel (Hrynick and Robinson 2012), which is generally not available on South Shore beaches. However, the ethnographic record suggested that the wigwam was the standard dwelling form throughout the region. Such structures probably held a nuclear family and tended to be about 3 m wide.

Accordingly, our methods were designed to (1) efficiently identify likely living-surfaces as stratigraphic anomalies when compared to the surrounding site, (2) expose entire dwelling features, and (3) permit the identification of intra-feature spatial patterning and subfeatures. These methods were fully deployed at AlDf-24, Area C, and AlDf-30.

Locating Features

Based on work described above, we anticipated finding architectural features to the landward side of shell-bearing sites, appearing as shell-free, artifact-rich deposits. The glacial landscape of the South Shore has ample large glacial erratic boulders, which can provide further shelter, and Erskine (1962, 1986) often described dwelling floors contiguous with large boulders. Moreover, the boulder-strewn and rocky coasts of Nova Scotia leave little level ground, and many of the sites we examined had few areas large and flat enough to reasonably have contained an approximately 3 m wide dwelling feature. With the exception of AlDf-30 (see below), surface depressions did not betray the locations of the architectural features we excavated.

To locate architectural features, we employed a 2 cm bore, hand-held soil probe at 1 m intervals across probable dwelling areas. This technique—which we also used to delineate shell midden sites—permits a quick preliminary examination of site structure, while minimizing disturbance. For instance, at AlDf-24, Area C, the probe indicated a dwelling feature as a greasy black lens with little shell, and brought up a small piece of lithic debitage. Following positive probe tests, we then explored the location with small 25 × 25 cm and 50 × 50 cm hand-excavated test units. Similarly, at AlDf-30 the probe revealed a deposit of dark black sandy loam, inconsistent with other shell midden deposits at the site. Test pitting in this area then revealed the edge of a dwelling floor deposit.

Excavating Features

Building upon probes and tests, we opened large horizontal excavations by trowel, working out from the initial test unit to expose entire strata. All units were excavated simultaneously, and natural stratigraphic surfaces were "chased" and exposed across the entire grid surface. This was repeated for every natural stratigraphic transition across the entire excavated area. We retained 20 cm wide cross-shaped baulks over these areas, to preserve stratigraphic profiles and for the collection of column samples. We piece-plotted formal tools and decorated ceramics, and passed all excavated sediments through 3 mm hardware mesh to enhance recovery of lithic debitage, charcoal, and small animal remains. Minimally, all non-formal artifacts, samples, and fauna were recorded and collected by 50 cm² unit quadrants of natural stratigraphic levels. In the case of thick stratigraphic levels, we divided natural levels arbitrarily at about 5 cm intervals. The result of these methods, as we illustrate below, were near-fully excavated dwelling features with precise stratigraphic profiles. This high-resolution excavation permitted us, in cases with sufficient sample size, to identify divisions of space within dwellings based on artifact patterning.

Partially Excavated Features

Although the methods described just above are ideal for examining the remains of dwelling features, they are also time-consuming. As a result, some architectural features were identified around Port Joli's harbour and only partially excavated rather than fully exposed. In these cases, we also excavated stratigraphically using the same methods for provenience and recovery. However, the information derived from these excavations will be necessarily limited.

Many other features were excavated by researchers prior to the E'se'get Project. Details from these excavations are highly variable, but we attempt to present what is known about each, below. Together, the high-resolution excavations from the E'se'get Project, combined with mid-century excavations by prior researchers, provide a large data set from which to consider the Wabanaki architectural tradition in Port Joli specifically and the South Shore of Nova Scotia more generally.

AlDf-24 (Epte'jijg Utju'sn Gta'nogeway, "Warm Breeze by the Ocean")
AlDf-24, Area C, Level 2 Activity Area

Area C, located to the landward side of AlDf-24 and in the lee of multiple glacial erratics, contained a series of stratified features. Immediately below the sod layer in AlDf-24, Area C, our excavations encountered compact dark brown soil with abundant lithic debitage and formal lithic tools. Shell was limited in this level, and highly fragmentary when it was encountered. This surface does not appear to constitute a clearly defined feature; or, if it was a dwelling surface, it was not as intensively (or repeatedly) occupied as the features discovered stratigraphically below it. However, this clearly was a surface on which people made or repaired lithic tools and used pottery. Given that this activity occurred in the only area on the landscape where a dwelling surface could have been placed, it remains possible that it was an ephemeral structure. The margins of the surface could not be defined and covered the entire exposed surface of the deposit, though the eastern edge of the surface did contain more shell where it neared the margins of the midden. No evidence of a hearth could be discerned.

As outlined in Chapter 4, this stratum is associated with a Protohistoric date, and very few Protohistoric dwellings have been encountered or excavated on the Maritime Peninsula. Perhaps this sort of ephemeral deposit is typical of Protohistoric dwellings, and if so, it would represent a significant change in the way space and the landscape was utilized at Port Joli.

AlDf-24, Area C, Feature 4, Levels 3a and 3b

Levels 3a and 3b of AlDf-24, Area C, are a later Late Maritime Woodland (see table 4.3) dwelling feature that was identified in a soil probe which yielded two strata of black sandy loam soil and a piece of lithic debitage. Subsequently, the probe was expanded into a 50 × 50 cm test excavation, which confirmed the presence of a black, greasy, sandy, artifact-rich stratum. In the subsequent season, we expanded excavations into a roughly 4 × 3.5 m horizontal area, and exposed Feature 4 in its entirety (see figure 5.2 for stratigraphy and figure 5.3 for photograph of Feature 4). This was the first feature we fully excavated at Port Joli. It therefore served as something of a model for our subsequent work on architectural features in the harbour.

The feature itself was encountered in levels 3a and 3b in Area C, and was characterized by compact, greasy, black sandy loam, permeated with crushed charcoal. Highlighting the care with which dwelling features must be excavated, the edges of the feature could only be discerned by feel and by close visual inspection. The texture of the soil as it was trowelled changed from hard, compact dwelling deposits to looser, more crumbly midden deposits, and, visually, abrupt changes in the charcoal content inside and outside the feature were evident (usually this could only be discerned by inspection of a soil sample in the palm of the hand). Within the feature, shell quantities were low when contrasted with the underlying shell-bearing black soil midden (less than 7 percent of the matrix within the feature, compared to nearly 50 percent in the underlying midden; tables 5.1 and 5.2). The shallow saucer shape of this feature and its makeup are quantified and schematically displayed in tables 5.1 and 5.2, which describe the column samples from the edges of the feature and schematically display the constituents of the edge of a saucer-shaped floor.

Feature 4 was about 3 m at its maximum diameter, roughly oval in shape, and with the long axis oriented northeast-southwest (figure 5.4). Excavation suggests the feature was a shallow depression no more than 15 cm deeper than the surrounding surface when it was occupied. The feature is defined by two ephemeral semi-circles of stones, one associated with the eastern exterior of the feature and the other with some type of interior alignment. The exterior ring was composed of five "rock stops"—clusters of rocks to support wigwam posts. (On the west, there were several large glacial erratics against which posts could be positioned.)

Three possible post moulds were encountered on the southeast of the dwelling, in line with the arrangements of stones that probably functioned as rock stops on the eastern margin of the house. A large angular stone which likely functioned as an anvil stone was placed near the centre of the floor deposit (figure 5.5) and was surrounded by abundant amounts of spirally fractured, long bone fragments from terrestrial ungulates—caribou (*Rangifer tarandus*), moose (*Alces alces*), and white-tailed deer (*Odocoileus virginianus*). The floor deposits appeared to extend to a small ridge of boulders in the western edge of Area C and these likely formed the western wall of the structure. On the east, the feature abutted a relatively deep (approx. 50 cm) shell midden composed of coarsely fragmented clam shells.

There were two protrusions of the feature to the north and to the northeast, characterized by depressions and coarsely broken shell trampled into the feature. The most northerly depression was more pronounced. These likely correspond to entrances; in a point we return

Architectural Features | 135

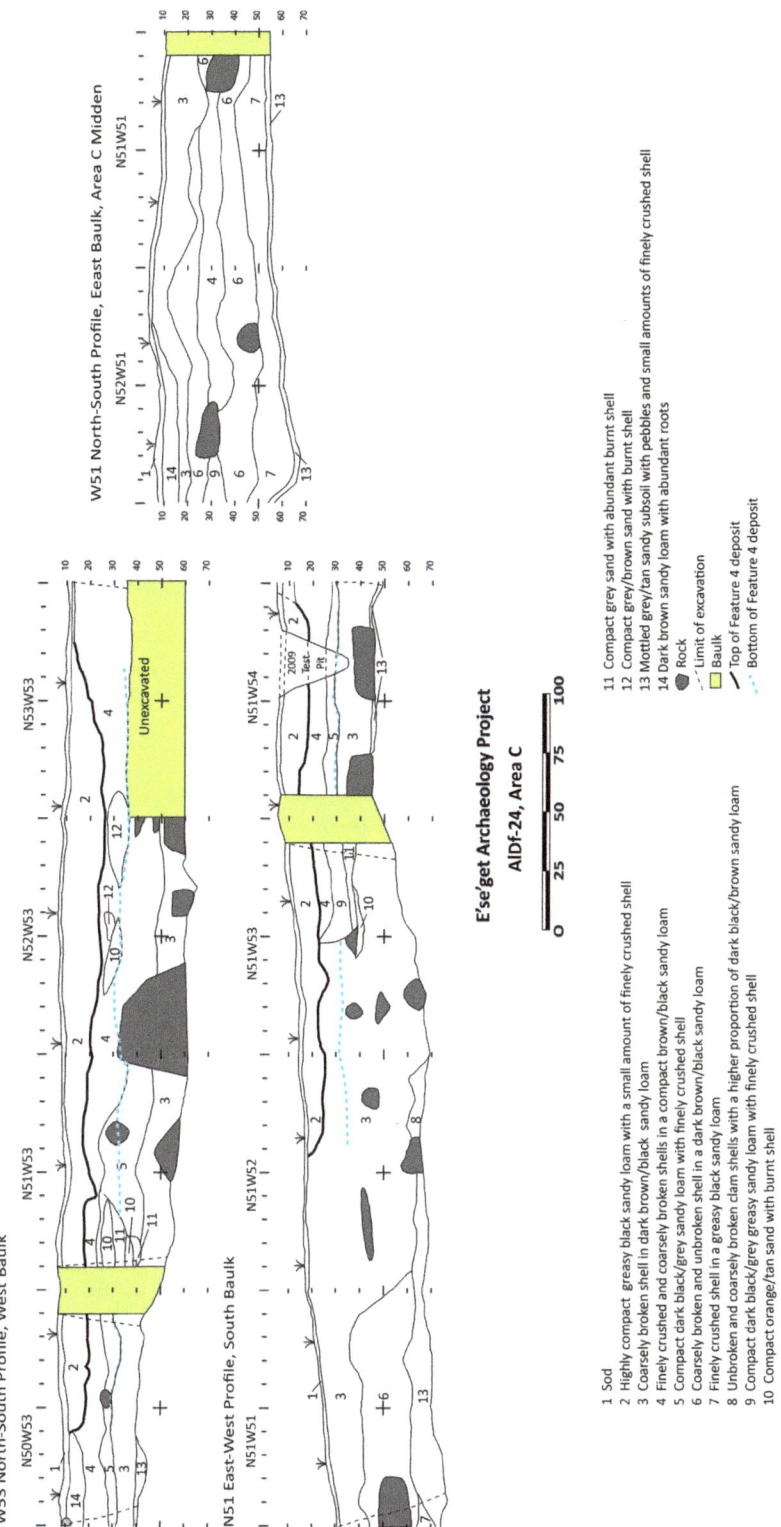

Figure 5.2 AlDf-24, Area C: Stratigraphic profiles of site, showing the Protohistoric activity surface (Level 2) and Feature 4.

Figure 5.3 AlDf-24, Area C: Photograph of Feature 4, facing south.

to later, they were unlikely to have been used at the same time and, like the large extended hearth (discussed below), suggest re-occupation with slight variation in sub-feature placement or dwelling orientation. In profile (figure 5.2), the feature was saucer-shaped at its top, representing the last time it was occupied; its bottom was less clearly defined and in profile was entirely invisible. We defined it by feel and observation as we excavated, noting the compactness of the soil, the presence of comminuted charcoal and the density of artifacts, particularly debitage. We do not interpret the feature as being dug into the soil. Rather, the shallowly depressed centre may result from floor preparation and clearing and subsequent trampling into the relatively soft shell-bearing black soil stratum below it.

Within Feature 4 we identified two amorphous hearth features (figure 5.4). Feature 4a was a large hearth feature characterized by a large area of orange/tan mottled or grey soil with abundant burnt shell, bone, and charcoal. The hearth extended from the eastern edge of the dwelling toward its centre and to a depth of at least 10 cm below the original level of the Feature 4 floor. It is likely that this entire feature was not in use when the dwelling was occupied, and it therefore probably represents a palimpsest of many fires built in the same general location over many occupations (Hrynick 2011; Hrynick et al. 2012).

Feature 4b was an enigmatic deposit that appears to have been a pit or perhaps a pit hearth. Approximately square and about 75 cm wide, it penetrated from the surface of Feature 4 (Level 3) to about 20 cm below it. It was filled with alternating lenses of heat-altered orange/tan loamy sand and grey loamy sand with burnt shell. It was similar in composition and size to "pit hearths" encountered in house features elsewhere in Nova Scotia (Preston 1974). It is possible that the feature was originally used as a storage pit and

Table 5.1 AlDf-24, Area C: Constituents of materials from column samples taken along the north-south baulk.

Column Level	Material	Coordinates				
		N45-55	N55-65	N65-75	N75-85	N85-95
Level I	BONE %	0	0	0	0	0
	BONE COUNT	0	0	0	0	0
	DEBITAGE %	0	0	0	0	0
	DEBITAGE COUNT	0	0	0	0	0
	SHELL %	0	0.072	0.436	0.000	0.000
	SHELL CRUSH	NA	NA	0.778	NA	NA
	SAMPLE WEIGHT (g)	190.2	276.4	367.4	229.0	315.3
Level II	BONE %	**0.013**	**0.438**	**0.247**	0.221	0.023
	BONE COUNT	**3**	**12**	**4**	4	1
	DEBITAGE %	**0.033**	**0.038**	**0.000**	0.138	0.094
	DEBITAGE COUNT	**4**	**3**	**1**	5	5
	SHELL %	**0.067**	**1.620**	**8.232**	4.368	3.865
	SHELL CRUSH	**0.667**	**0.083**	**0.134**	0.179	0.313
	SAMPLE WEIGHT (g)	**1517.8**	**1049.2**	**728.9**	361.7	426.9
Level III	BONE%	**0.194**	0.039	0.142	0.229	0.698
	BONE COUNT	**9**	9	8	19	12
	DEBITAGE%	**1.199**	0.117	0.370	6.217	0.085
	DEBITAGE COUNT	**10**	12	15	7	9
	SHELL%	**1.287**	30.857	32.715	24.558	34.961
	CRUSH SHELL	**0.337**	0.149	0.205	0.210	0.145
	SAMPLE WEIGHT (g)	**567.0**	1281.7	1406.1	743.1	1060.6
Level IV	BONE%	0.362				
	BONE COUNT	16				
	DEBITAGE%	0.233		NOT EXCAVATED		
	SHELL COUNT	15				
	SHELL%	29.137				
	CRUSH SHELL	0.275				
	SAMPLE WEIGHT (g)	1078.0				

NOTES: Materials from Feature 4 or likely containing trampled materials from Feature 4 are bolded and enclosed in a triple-line border. Consult Hrynick and Robinson (2012: 34–35) for comparative data from a dwelling surface in Machias Bay, Maine.

then was subsequently used as a hearth or a location to dump material from cleaning the nearby Feature 4a hearth.

Perhaps the most notable attribute of Feature 4 is that it exhibited a binary division of space divided along the northeast-southwest axis of the feature, extending from the area of what is likely the entrance to the southwest portion of the dwelling. Ceramics were more prevalent on the southeast half of the dwelling and lithic debitage was concentrated on the northwest. Scrapers and bone tools were mostly in the southeast. Bifaces were not as clearly

Table 5.2 AlDf-24, Area C: Material constituents from column samples taken along the east-west baulk.

Column Level	Material	Coordinates				
		W37-47	W47-57	W57-67	W67-77	W77-87
Level I	BONE %	0	0	**0**	0	0
	BONE COUNT	0	0	**0**	0	0
	DEBITAGE %	0	0	**0.027**	0.069	0
	DEBITAGE COUNT	0	0	**1**	2	0
	SHELL %	1.712	0.611	**0.267**	3.356	0.577
	SHELL CRUSH	0.190	0.400	**1.000**	2.464	0.063
	SAMPLE WEIGHT (g)	146.0	343.6	**374.9**	289.0	294.7
Level II	BONE %	0.059	0.305	**0.799**	0.091	0.137
	BONE COUNT	8	12	**3**	7	10
	DEBITAGE %	0.184	0.044	**0.141**	0.216	0.808
	DEBITAGE COUNT	10	4	**6**	11	13
	SHELL %	21.528	11.450	**6.651**	4.137	0.534
	SHELL CRUSH	0.127	0.196	**0.258**	0.317	1.150
	SAMPLE WEIGHT (g)	1684.2	688.2	**425.5**	1206.2	804.6
Level III	BONE%	0.146	0.337	**0.238**	0.101	0.040
	BONE COUNT	18	13	**21**	13	4
	DEBITAGE%	0.457	0.357	**0.153**	0.367	0.182
	DEBITAGE COUNT	48	24	**15**	20	9
	SHELL%	60.606	59.274	**55.454**	48.358	29.919
	CRUSH SHELL	0.124	0.154	**0.145**	0.131	0.191
	SAMPLE WEIGHT (g)	1576.4	980.2	**1305.4**	1285.4	495.0
Level IV	BONE %		NOT EXCAVATED		0.625	0
	BONE COUNT				85	0
	DEBITAGE %				0.105	5.305
	DEBITAGE COUNT				8	10
	SHELL %				54.666	39.782
	CRUSH SHELL				0.119	0.216
	SAMPLE WEIGHT (g)				1520.7	522.1

NOTES: Materials from Feature 4 are bolded and enclosed in a triple-line border. The high percentages of shell in Level 3 represent, stratigraphically, the midden immediately underlying Feature 4, and are enclosed in a double-line border. These levels may contain artifacts trampled into loose midden matrix from Feature 4. Consult Hrynick and Robinson (2012: 34–35) for comparative data from a dwelling surface in Machias Bay, Maine.

patterned but appeared to form clusters around the entrance and anvil stone (figure 5.5a). Our analysis of this patterning (Hrynick et al. 2012; Hrynick and Betts 2014) indicated a bilateral division of space which may relate to a gender division of space inside the dwelling. Such an organization of domestic space is noted in the ethnographic record of the region (e.g., Denys 1968: 408; Le Clercq 1910: 102; Speck 1997: 29).

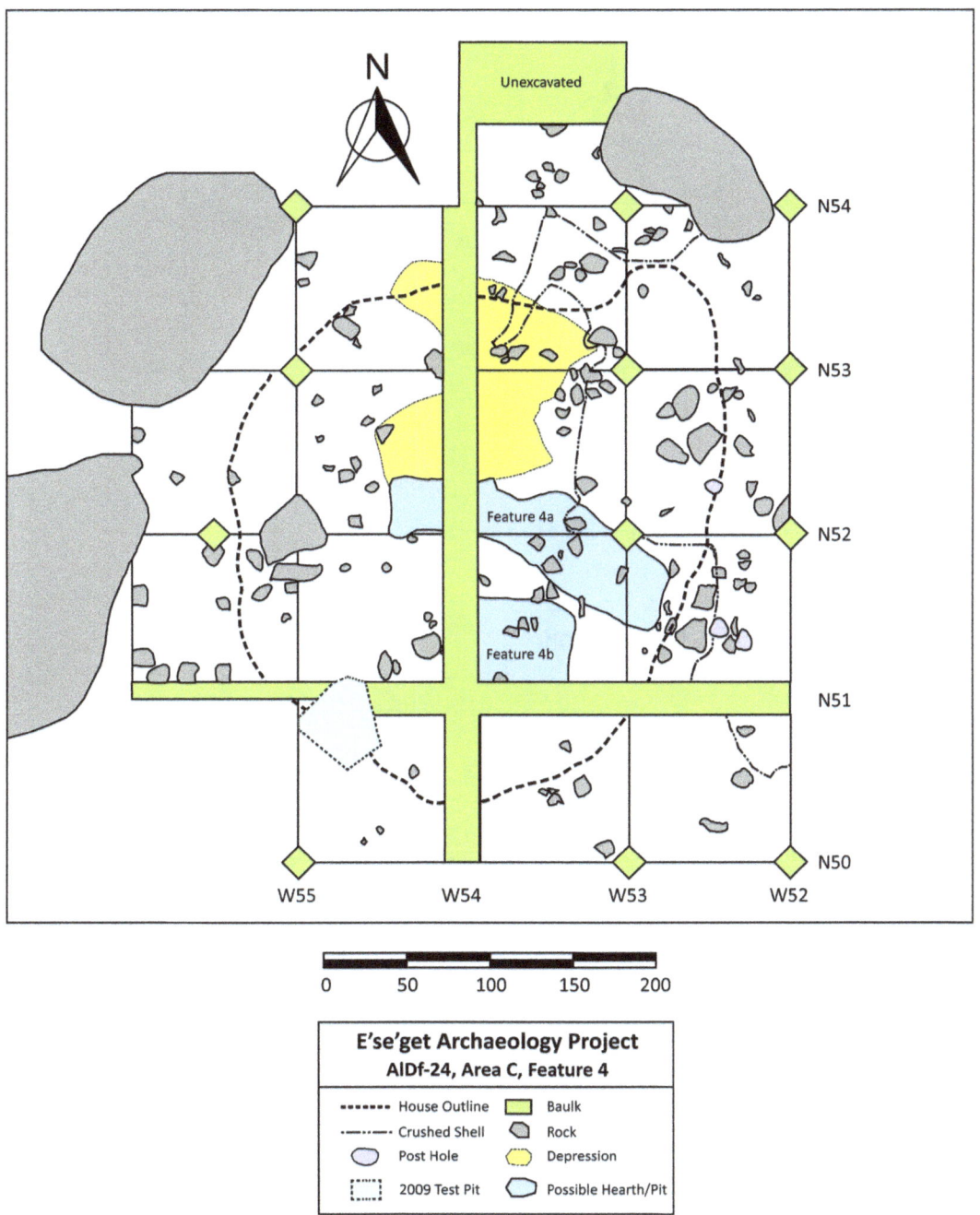

Figure 5.4 AlDf-24, Area C, Feature 4: Plan-view drawing.

AlDf-24, Area C, Partial House Feature, Levels 3f to 3h

Following the excavation of AlDf-24, Area C, we excavated five 1 × 1 m units on the east and north of Area C down to the B Horizon. As described in Chapter 3, there were alternating lenses of dark-black compacted soil with variable amounts of shell below the Feature 4

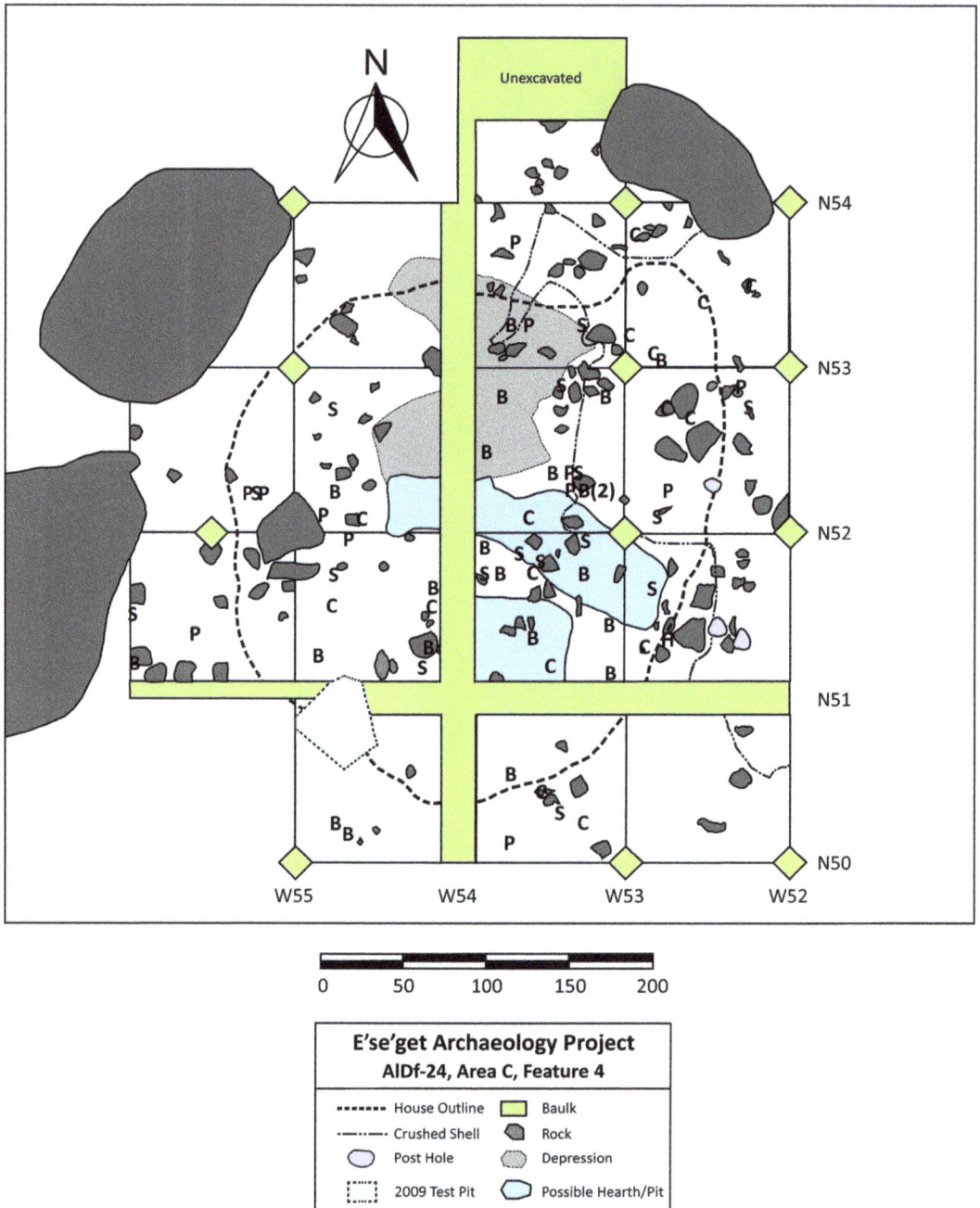

Figure 5.5a AlDf-24, Area C, Feature 4: Plan-view drawing, showing the patterned division of projectile points (P), bifaces (B), scrapers (S), and cores (C).

deposit. One stratum, designated Levels 3f, 3g, and 3h (the latter two being arbitrary subdivisions of the former), was not clearly defined in the profile (figure 5.2), but was evident during excavation as a dark black, compact, greasy layer, containing little shell, abundant

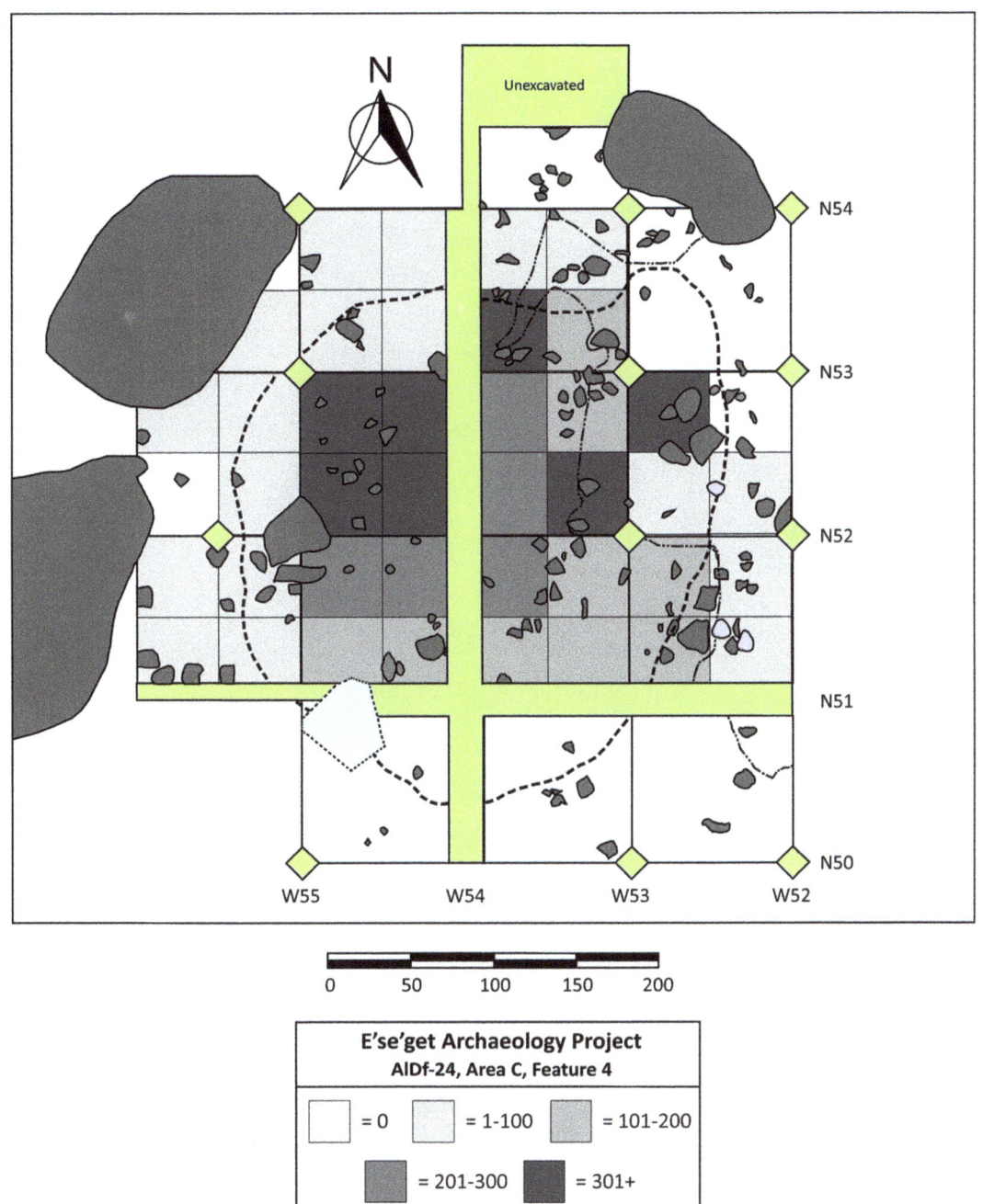

Figure 5.5b AlDf-24, Area C, Feature 4: Plan-view drawing, showing the patterned division of debitage.

artifacts, and abundant debitage. Likely, this is another dwelling feature. Unfortunately, little further can be said about the feature, as only several square metres of it were exposed; however, given the topography of the site, we suspect it was similar in size to Feature 4.

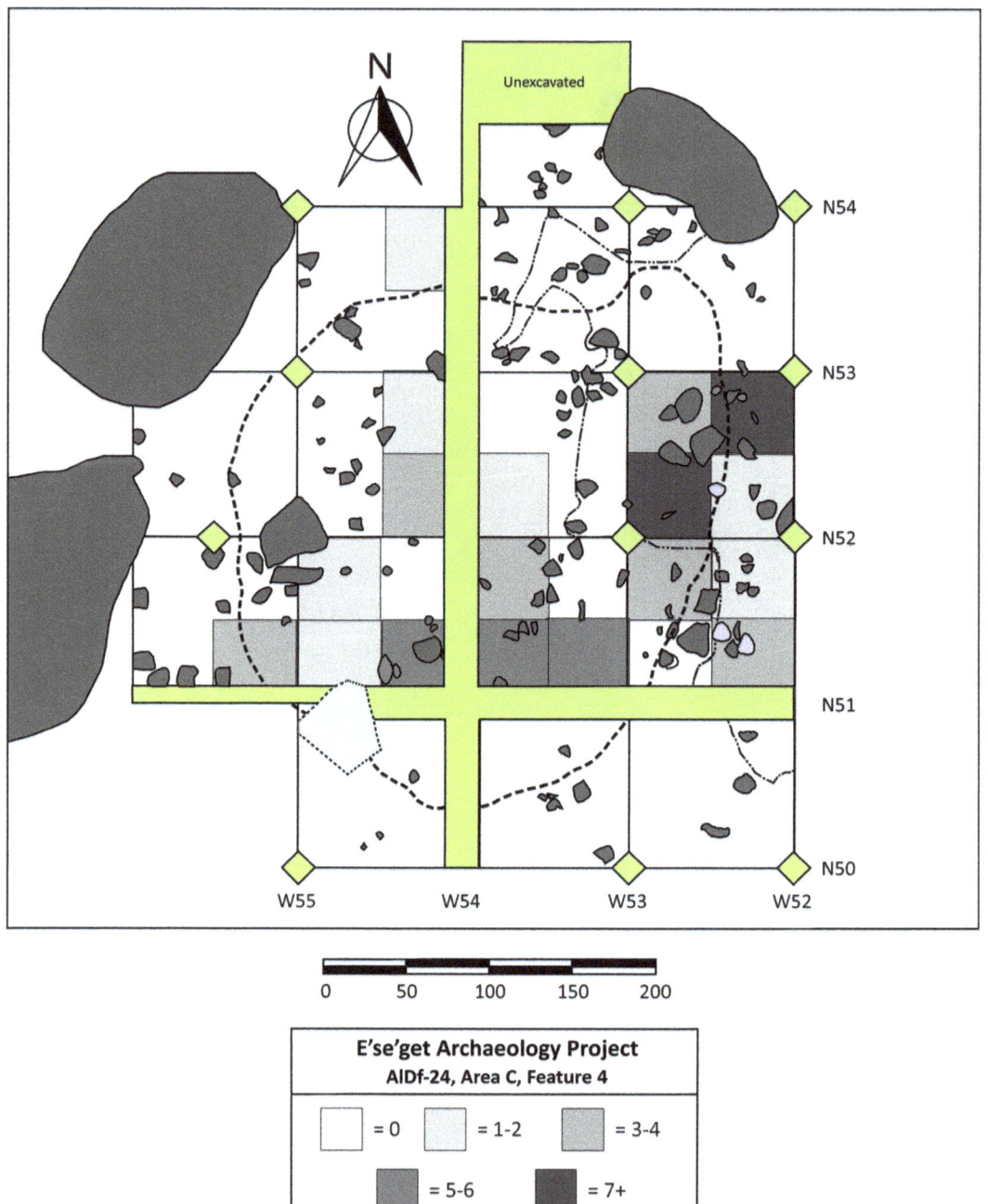

Figure 5.5c AlDf-24, Area C, Feature 4: Plan-view drawing, showing the patterned division of ceramics.

AlDf-24, Area A, Feature 2

The only domestic feature encountered in Area A was a possible house floor (Feature 2), which appeared as a shallow lens of compact dark brown–black organic soil with little shell and abundant lithic remains, including thumbnail scrapers and corner-notched projectile points. In contrast, most of the Area A shell midden was practically devoid of lithic materials (see Chapter 7). In horizontal plan, the edge of the dwelling was amorphous but tended to manifest as a transition from a matrix with large proportions of coarsely broken clam shells outside the dwelling to small amounts of finely crushed shell with increased proportions of dark black soil and an increased amount of lithic debitage inside the dwelling. The soil matrix inside the dwelling also contained large amounts of comminuted charcoal and fragmented pottery, in comparison to adjacent strata. No sub-features were observed in the dwelling, although an arrangement of three small cobbles in the northeast corner of the feature (figure 5.6) may have been used as "rock stops" to support superstructure poles. While only the eastern portion of the dwelling was excavated, it appears to have been oval and approximately 3 m in diameter, which is consistent with the size of wigwam-type features excavated on the Maritime Peninsula (e.g., Hrynick and Black 2016; Sanger 2010).

Feature 2 appeared immediately below the sod, and is represented as Level 2, and portions of 3a and 3b in some units. The dwelling was shallow and slightly basin-shaped, extending about 8 to 12 cm below the original surface of the midden when it was occupied. However, it does not appear to have been intentionally excavated into the midden, as it had no heaped shell berms surrounding it. Rather, the feature appears to be a floor interface created by repeated trampling of the shell matrix that formed the surface of the midden (Level 3a). The floor clearly was depressed by trampling, into the top of the Level 3a midden surface, and Level 2 appears to be the result of repeated occupations of the dwelling, likely over multiple years. Further evidence of trampling on the floor surface is found in the frequencies of lithic debitage, charcoal, and formal lithic tools occurring in levels 3a and 3b deposits below the Level 2 feature deposits (deposits beyond the feature margins rarely contained lithic material). Chapter 7 describes this assemblage in detail.

The northern end of Feature 2 was constructed over a human interment (Feature 3), and the original floor surface rested directly on several rocks which formed part of the mortuary feature (see Chapter 3). As such, it appears to have resulted in the trampling of the shell mound and the burial feature itself. Regardless, the dwelling feature appears to have been occupied after most of the eastern part of the midden developed (and after the burial was deposited). If so, the house was constructed on the level midden surface that had itself been deposited over the underlying natural boulder surface that characterizes the B Horizon.

AlDf-30 (Jack's Brook, Su'ne'gati, "Cranberry Patch")

The black soil area between the Area A and Area B shell midden at AlDf-30 contained a series of three superimposed architectural features: two dwelling floors and a sweathouse. We previously presented detailed information about these features elsewhere (Hrynick and Betts 2014, 2017), focusing primarily on their cosmological implications and on architecture as an historical and agential cosmological practice at Port Joli.

The unique geographic location of AlDf-30 has already been reviewed in Chapter 3. The architectural features were located on top of a small, treeless knoll, without evidence of the typical boulders or hummocky topography that characterizes much of the Port Joli region. Perhaps because of this, and unlike other Port Joli sites, the surface of the site overlaying the features was visible as a slight surface depression. Testing the edge of this depression

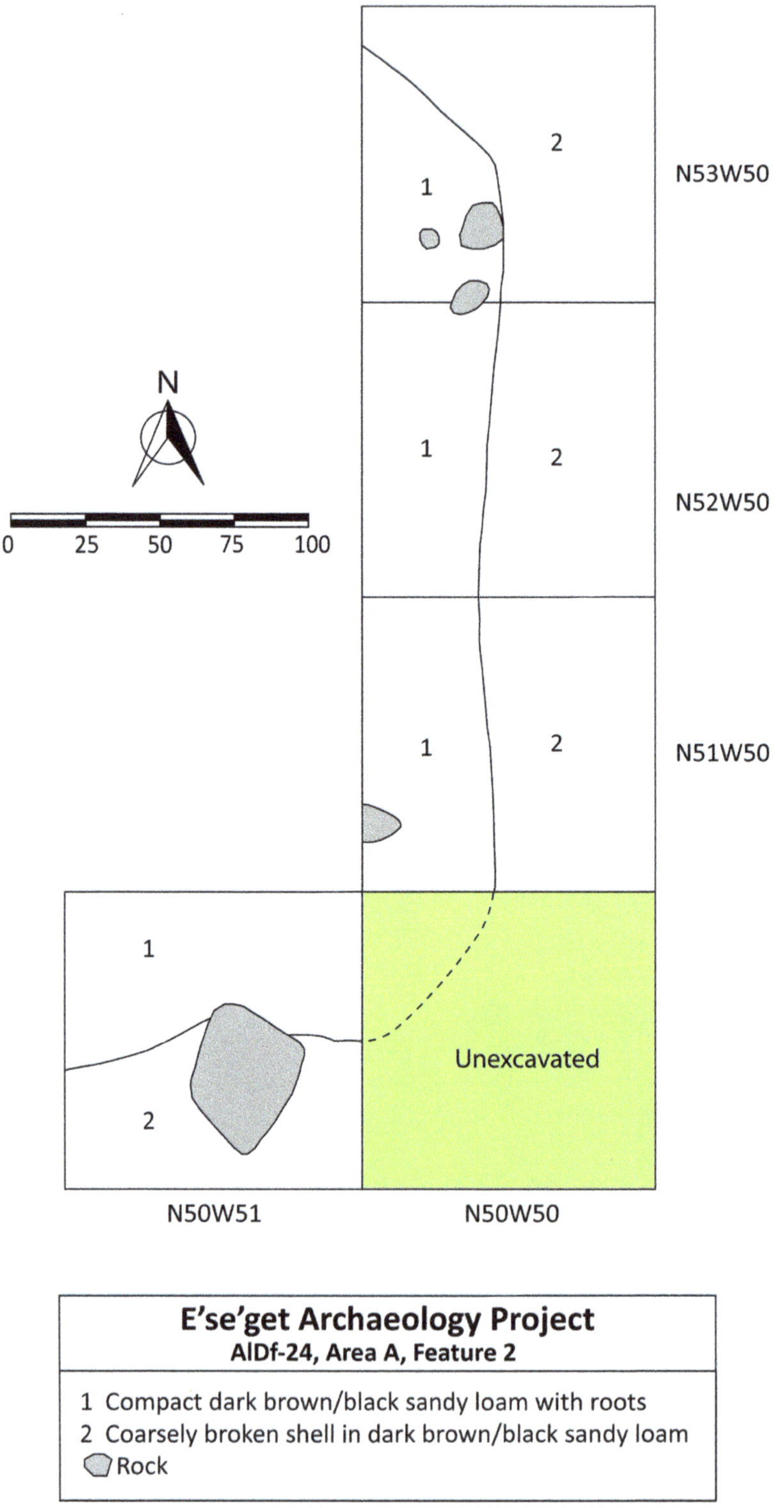

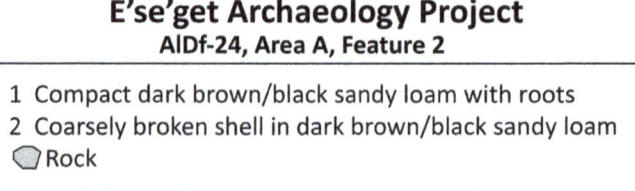

Figure 5.6 AlDf-24, Area A: Plan-view drawing of the partially excavated Feature 2.

indicated the margin of a greasy black stratum, which we later exposed, revealing the three features described below.

AlDf-30, Black Soil Area, Feature 1, Levels 3a to 3c

Feature 1 (figure 5.9) was a roughly oval dwelling feature comprising compact black sandy loam (see figure 5.7 for stratigraphy and figure 5.8 for a photograph). Shell was present but in very low quantity and was highly fragmentary. The feature was approximately 3 m × 2.5 m. It was shallow and saucer-shaped, but without evidence of built-up berms or an excavated floor surface. It is more likely that the floor was cleared of debris and any depression of the surface was caused by repeated trampling or use of the structure. The margins of the feature were relatively distinct, marked by a slight colour change to a browner-coloured soil with less comminuted charcoal outside of the dwelling. At many Maritime Woodland Period sites, the margins of dwelling features contain dense artifact concentrations, which become more diffuse beyond the margins of the feature (Hrynick et al. 2012; Sanger 2010). This was clear here, but Feature 1, like many Middle Maritime Woodland dwelling features (e.g., Black 2004), was less artifact-dense than many Late Maritime Woodland dwelling features (e.g., Hrynick et al. 2012), including Feature 4 at AlDf-24, Area C. This may reflect a comparatively shorter period of occupation.

Near the northern margin of the feature, in unit N52W51, a roughly oval, approximately 30 × 40 cm hearth feature was encountered (Feature 1a; figure 5.9). Characterized by the presence of fire-reddened sandy loam, the precise size and shape of the hearth was impossible to discern as it extended into Area A's unexcavated east-west baulk. The feature was recognized at the top of Level 3a and continued throughout the Feature 1 dwelling to Level 3c. The hearth contained small amounts of calcined bone, lithics, and ceramics, and a small collection of fire-cracked rocks near its centre.

Large rocks and cobbles protruded into this layer from levels that were stratigraphically deeper. These appear to have formed a kind of axial, or midline, feature dividing the floor roughly into a western and eastern half. This bilateral separation of the dwelling may represent a physical architectural manifestation of a similar division of space we identified from artifact patterning in the Late Maritime Woodland dwelling surface (Feature 4) at AlDf-24, Area C (Hrynick et al. 2012). We speculated that the bilateral patterning in AlDf-24, Area C, Feature 4 may correlate with the gendered division of domestic space known in the region's ethnohistorical record (Hrynick et al. 2012). However, within the feature there was no statistically significant patterning of artifacts, although our statistical tests suffered from the relatively low artifact counts within the feature (see Hrynick and Betts 2014).

AlDf-30, Black Soil Area, Feature 2, Levels 3d, 3e, and 3f

Feature 2 was stratigraphically directly below Feature 1. The feature was characterized by a very compact, sandy loam, distinguishable from Feature 1 by its darker black colour, presumably the result of a higher charcoal content. In the lowest levels of the feature, the black soil was mixed with orange subsoil and pebbles, likely resulting from the floor being trampled into the natural subsoil. Shell was rare in this deposit, and the faunal preservation was subsequently limited to calcined remains.

146 Place-Making in the Pretty Harbour

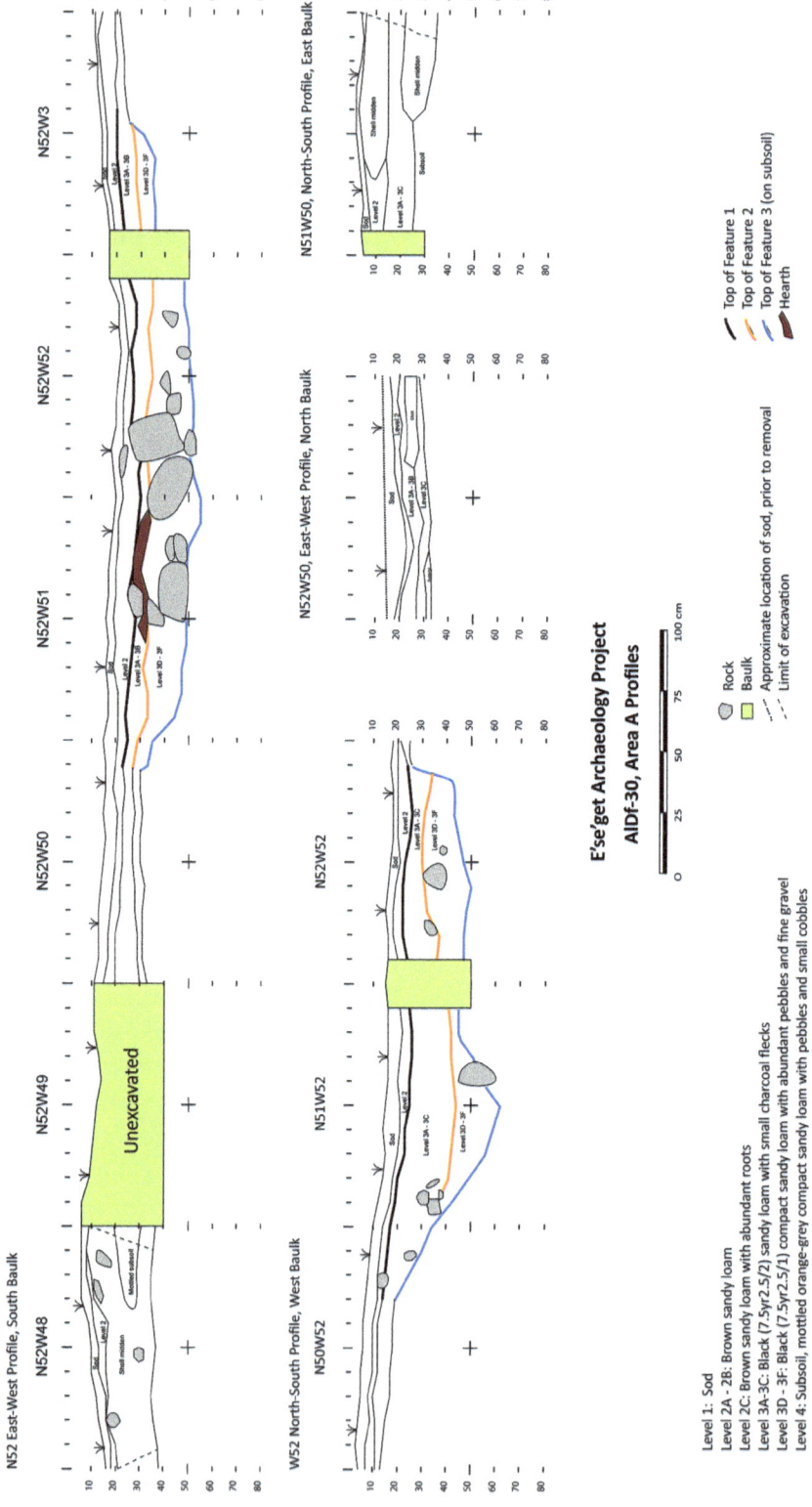

Figure 5.7 AIDf-30: Stratigraphic profile showing domestic features 1 and 2, and the sweathouse, Feature 3.

Figure 5.8 AlDf-30: Photograph of Feature 1, facing southwest.

Feature 2 (figure 5.10) was oval in shape, about 3 m in diameter, and roughly the same size and orientation as Feature 1 above it, which essentially sat in Feature 2's footprint. In profile (figure 5.7, it displayed the classic "saucer-shaped" appearance associated with dwelling features on the Maritime Peninsula (Sanger 2010). As in Feature 1, large boulders and cobbles intruded into this unit from deeper stratigraphic levels, producing a rather undulating and rough floor surface. Again, the rocks clearly suggest a bilateral division of space, which would have been architecturally significant given the increasing size and number of the cobbles incorporated into the dwelling surface. No evidence of a distinct hearth feature was encountered, although the Level 3d deposit in unit N52W51 contained an oval rock alignment which was roughly contiguous with the location of the Feature 1 hearth, exhibited increased amounts of charcoal, and overlaid subsoil that was a deep orange in colour rather than the typical mottled light tan and grey subsoil, suggesting it was possibly heat-altered.

AlDf-30, Black Soil Area, Feature 3, Level 4

Feature 3 (figure 5.11) was very small, roughly 2.5 × 2 m, and its margins, especially on the north, south, and west sides, were very steep, creating a near bowl-like depression (figure 5.7), in some instances excavated more than 40 cm into the subsoil. The primary element of the feature was a large central boulder propped by another large stone at a slight angle (figures 5.7 and 5.11). This central stone feature is the same architectural element that penetrated features 1 and 2, and which formed their axial sub-features. Twenty-three other large stones were piled around this central alignment. In the southwest of the feature, a

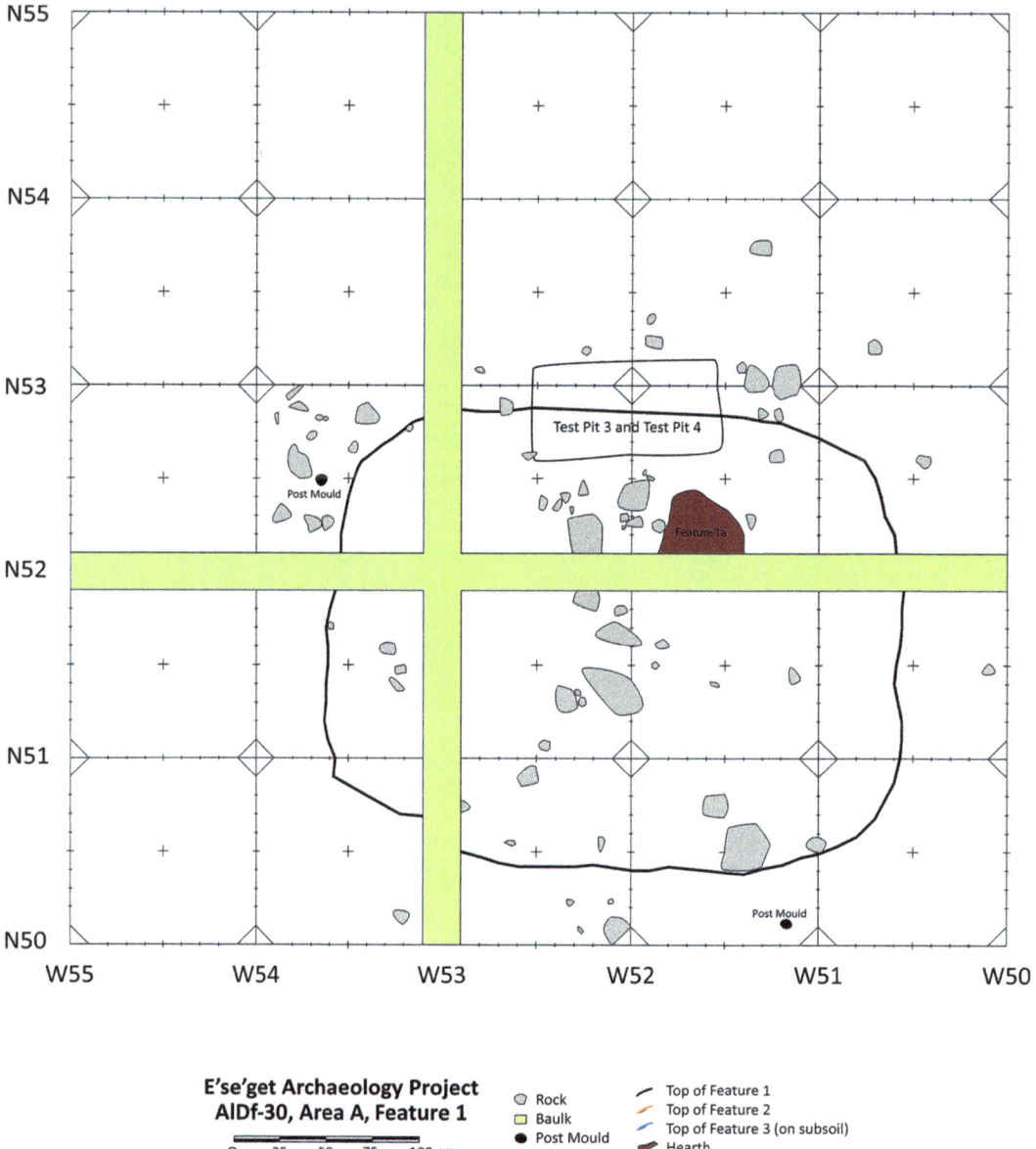

Figure 5.9 AlDf-30: Plan-view drawing of Feature 1, a dwelling feature.

small, flat-bottomed pit was lined with a series of smaller cobbles. Immediately northwest of the central stone, a small bench or step may have been shaped into the subsoil, forming the northern margin of the cobble-lined pit feature (figure 5.12).

The edges of the feature were less steep on the eastern margin, leading us to believe the entrance may have been on that side of the structure. We note, however, that the subsoil in this area of the feature was disturbed and apparently mixed, suggesting that some of the material excavated from the feature was deposited along the eastern margin forming a shallow berm (located primarily in N51W50). Further evidence of excavation

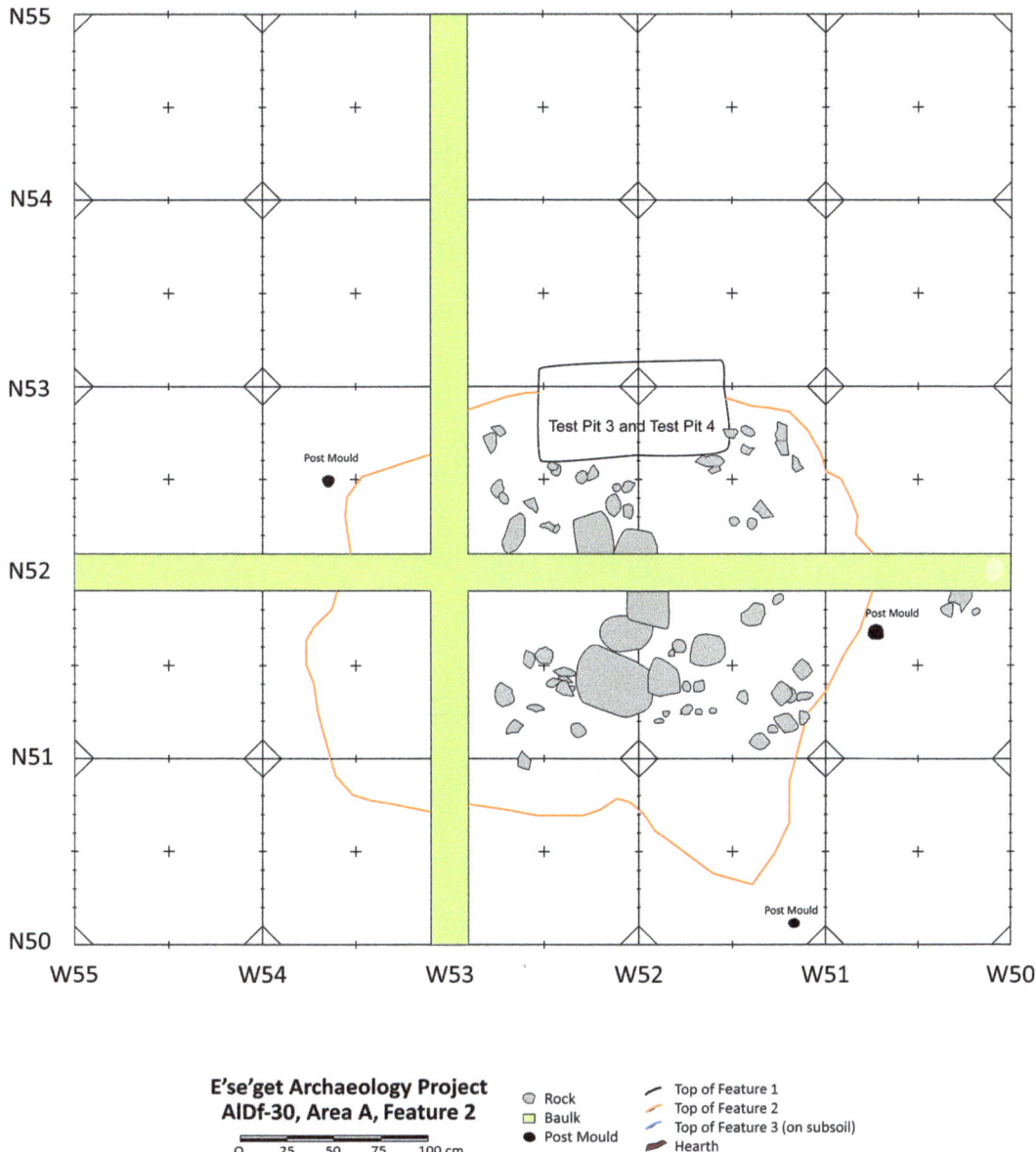

Figure 5.10 AlDf-30: Plan-view drawing of Feature 2, a dwelling feature.

comes in the form of a lens of re-deposited mottled subsoil in the Area B midden (see Chapter 3).

A fragment of fire-cracked rock was discovered in association with the subsoil in N51W51, and two fragments of the same large fire-cracked cobble, reddened, and heat-altered, were recovered from opposite sides of N51W52. While these cobble fragments were identified in upper levels, both were resting on stones that formed part of the large central boulder feature that extended into upper levels of all units. We believe they were deposited when the feature was first used.

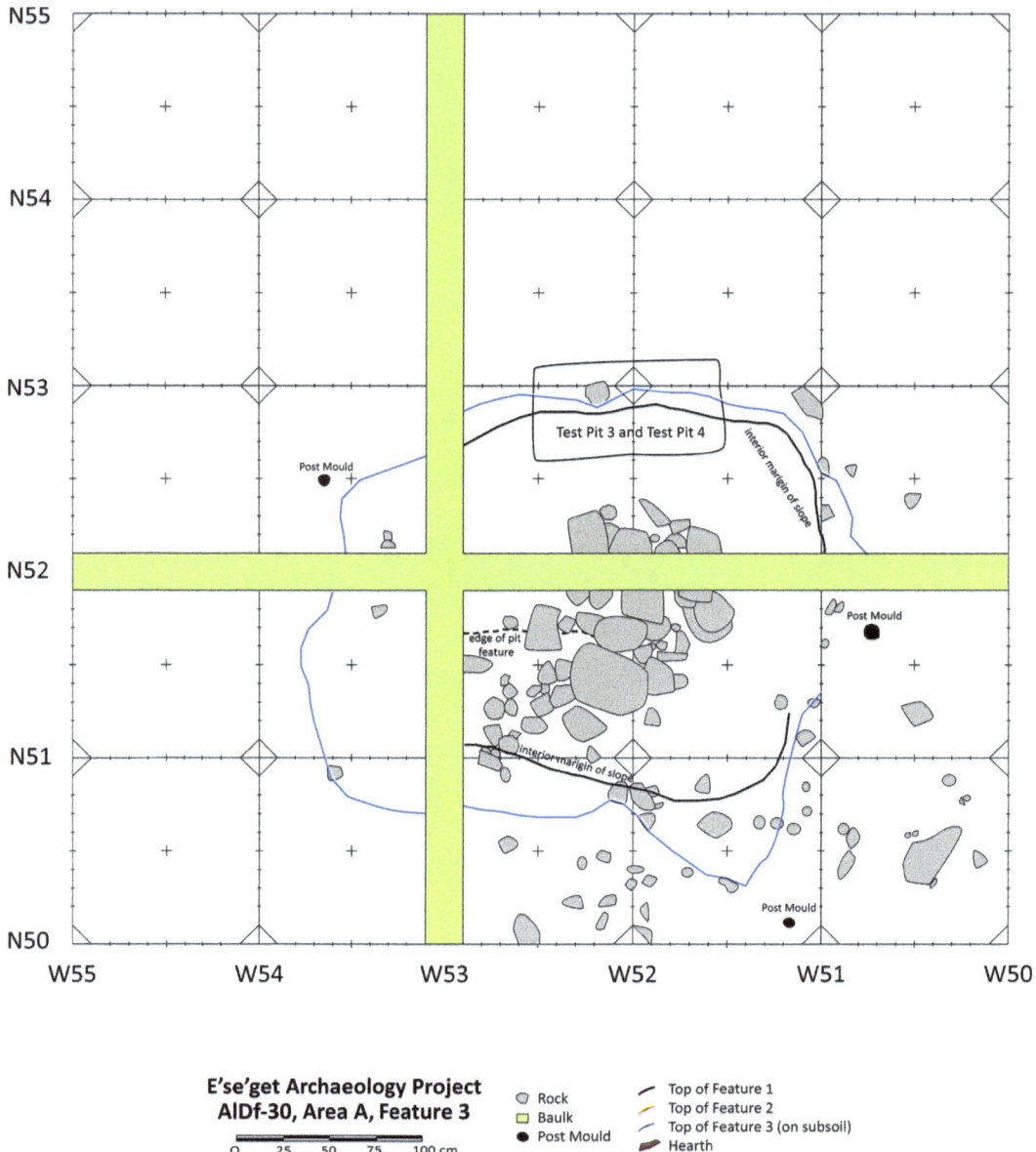

Figure 5.11 AlDf-30, Black Soil Area: Plan-view drawing of Feature 3, the sweathouse.

The first step in interpreting this feature was assessing the possibility that it was an unusual dwelling feature. However, it was devoid of artifacts, excluding the limited fire-cracked rock and a single piece of charcoal. Second, the feature was small, nearly 1 m smaller in diameter than a typical dwelling feature. In fact, coupled with its central stone architecture, it was impossible even to recline in. Thirdly, its unique sub-features (i.e., bench or step, large central stone, and partial cobble paving) were not consistent with other dwelling features in the archaeological or ethnographic record. Finally, it lacked an interior hearth, which is inconsistent with currently known Maritime Peninsula dwelling features (Hrynick and

Figure 5.12 AlDf-30, Black Soil Area: Photograph of Feature 3, facing north.

Black 2016; Sanger 2010). Other possible features—such as storage or cooking features—were unlikely candidates based on the absence of artifacts, charcoal, and abundant fire-cracked rock, and the presence of the large central stone feature.

However, the ethnohistoric literature from the Maritime Peninsula describes that a variety of sweathouse-type structures existed shortly after sustained European contact in the region, and that the purposes for such structures were myriad, ranging from treating physical ailments to increasing the success of a hunt (e.g., Denys 1968 [1672]: 416; Lescarbot 1914 [1618]: 185–86; Prins and McBride 2007: 18; Speck 1917: 312, 1997: 48; Wallis and Wallis 1955). While some sweathouse-type structures described in the ethnohistoric literature would have left ephemeral archaeological signatures, several may have left unique archaeological signatures consistent with Feature 3.

Much of the ethnohistoric literature indicates that although sometimes sweats were conducted in repurposed wigwams, purpose-built sweathouses were, like Feature 3, smaller than typical wigwams. However, sweathouse structures often included interior hearths to heat stones, which were then doused in water to produce steam, suggesting that charcoal, hearth features, and fire-cracked or otherwise heat-altered rock (caused by the thermal shock of being doused with cool water) would be prominent in any archaeological manifestation of a sweathouse. As stated above, Feature 3 did not exhibit significant amounts of fire-cracked rock or charcoal; however, Denys (1968 [1675]: 416) describes how many sweathouses did not contain fires and that rocks were heated outside the structure and brought to the participants inside by wives or children. Furthermore, some sweathouses did not employ water directly applied to stones, instead simply using heat produced by hot stones, over which hemlock boughs were placed (Wallis and Wallis 1955: 124).

Wallis and Wallis (1955: 124) document a kind of therapeutic sweathouse that may have produced an archaeological signature very similar to the one encountered in Feature 3. Utilized in the spring, these sweathouses were small wigwam-like structures with poles held in place by interwoven spruce bark covered with blankets or skins to make them airtight. Within the structure, a large stone was placed in the centre with three smaller stones around it. A small fire was built on top of the stones until they were hot. The participants then poured a syrup, made from "black cherry, choke cherry, juniper, white maple, fir, pine, and a second growth of ash" (Wallis and Wallis 1995: 124) boiled together, over the large stone. The heat from the stone vaporized the syrup, and the vapour produced was inhaled as a medicinal treatment. Neil and Gajewski (Chapter 2 in this volume; see also Neil et al. 2014) have shown that AlDf-30 would have yielded a wide variety of plant resources, including those which could have been used medicinally and as inhalants (see Speck 1917: 312). Additionally, the nearby stream could have been used to provide water for creating steam within the sweathouse and by participants to submerse themselves after sweat.

As described by Wallis and Wallis (1955: 124), the structure was used only by men, who sat nude within it, inhaling the vapour and rubbing each other's backs with a hide. We believe such a sweathouse could be expected to produce a similar archaeological signature to Feature 3, especially if the heated stones were brought into the structure rather than being heated inside it (though any fire used within such structures was apparently quite small).

AlDf-30, Area A: Post Moulds and Stakes
Three post moulds were identified at AlDf-30, Area A (features 1b, 1c, and 1d). These were all outside of the series of concatenated features, and probably represent posts for wigwam-style structures placed over the features. Each post mould was shallow, like other post moulds observed at AlDf-24, Area C (Betts 2011; Hrynick et al. 2012). Rocks now scattered around the outside of the margin of the features may have been used as rock stops (e.g., Hrynick et al. 2012) to support poles of a superstructure, and one of the post-moulds (Feature 1d) was surrounded by medium-sized cobbles which suggest this. Such rock stops could have become disarticulated when they were dismantled or during subsequent reuses of the black soil area. However, we believe the post moulds are most likely associated with Feature 1 because that is the most recent occupation, and if they were associated with an older occupation, such ephemeral features would likely have been obscured by surface deposition and by trampling.

Finally, a large broken piece of whale bone, grooved and split, and tapered at one end, was discovered lying horizontally in Level 3b of unit N50W50, near the margin of the dwelling features. According to Black (2004: 108), stake-like whale bone artifacts were also occasionally found near domestic features in Maritime Woodland sites in the New Brunswick Quoddy region, and are likely structural features. This tenuous association suggests to us that whale bones may sometimes have served an architectural purpose.

AlDf-31 (Su'ne'gatij, "Little Cranberry Patch")
As described in Chapter 3, at AlDf-31 an enigmatic pit feature was encountered in Level 3d of the Area A midden, near the apex of the knoll on which the site sat (see figure 3.47 for

a plan-view drawing of the site). This nearly straight-walled pit extended about 15 cm into the subsoil layer (Level 4), though its horizontal dimensions are uncertain. The pit was filled with a relatively sterile deposit (Level 3d), which was devoid of any shell, artifacts, faunal remains, or charcoal, which occurred only in the subsoil feature and not outside the rock ring which encircled it.

A possible post mould, about 15 cm in diameter, was encountered in the northeast quadrant of Test Unit 1 and appears to have extended some 10 cm into the subsoil, outside the ring of stones in Level 3d (figure 5.13). Another post mould, about 12 cm in diameter, was encountered in the southwest corner of Test Unit 2. These post moulds extended to a depth of 14 cm below the upper horizon of the subsoil layer in Test Unit 1 and approximately 5 cm into the depression surface (the boundary between levels 3d and 4) in Test Unit 2 (figure 5.13; see also figure 3.48 for soil profiles).

Outside of the depression, a line of rocks was encountered, sitting on a compacted deposit (approx. 5 to 10 cm in depth) of broken shells pressed on their edges into the subsoil margin surrounding the edge of the depression feature (see figure 5.13). During excavation, this was initially considered to be a disturbed deposit, but on closer examination it appears to represent fill composed of a small amount of midden and subsoil that were mixed together during the construction of the depression feature. Thus, this might have been a backfill

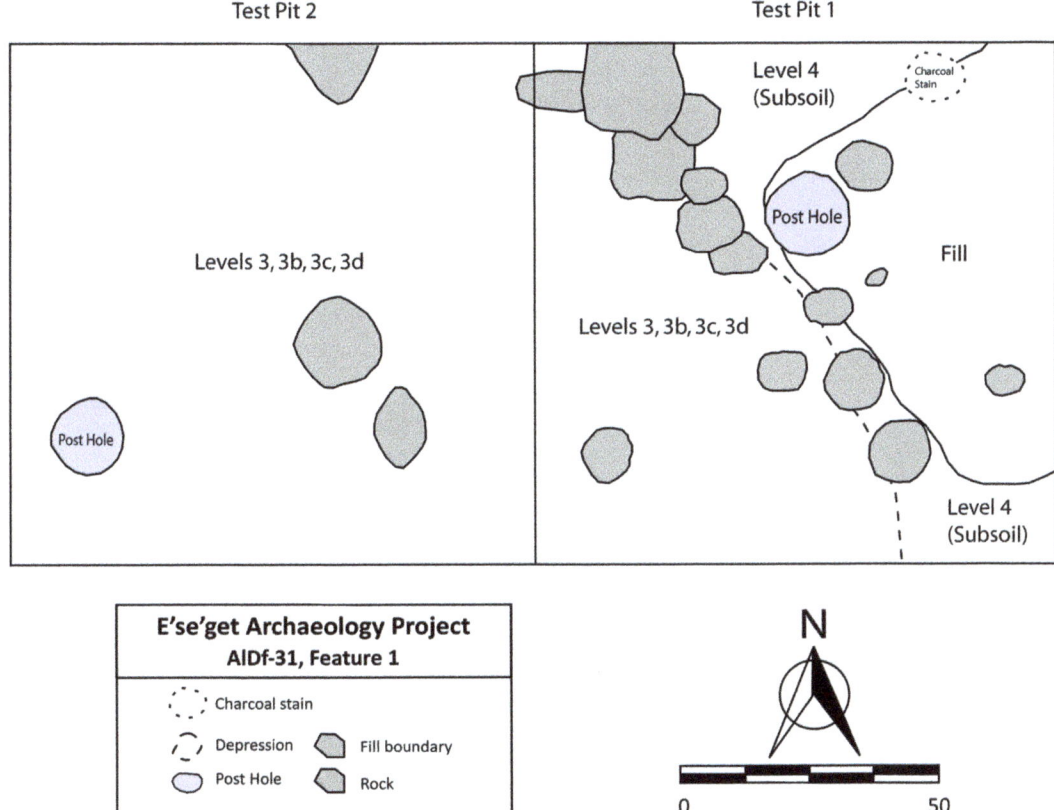

Figure 5.13 AlDf-31: Plan-view drawing of Feature 1b, an example of a Port Joli post mould.

deposit created during the construction of the depression feature or might have formed some sort of berm surrounding the feature. Some of this fill was found inside the post mould in Test Unit 1.

In summary, the deposit at AlDf-31 is relatively complex in comparison to others encountered at Port Joli. A depression was excavated into the original surface of AlDf-31, through a thin shell midden that had already formed over the site. The depression appears to have had a superstructure built over it, as evidence by the two post-mould features. The excavated material was placed as backdirt around the edge of the depression, forming a berm and thereby increasing its effective depth. The boundary was further reinforced by a partial "ring" of small stones, which may have been used to hold down a covering over the structure. If we are correct that the ring is an indication of size, the structure may have been about 3 m in diameter and roughly oval, like nearly all other structures encountered in the harbour. A sterile, though likely cultural, compact organic surface was deposited into the depression, followed by a black soil midden which subsequently filled in the depression and spread over the entire surface.

At the time we excavated AlDf-31, we had little understanding of the diversity of archaeological deposits and features from around Port Joli's harbour, and no analogue for understanding the patterning observed in test units excavated at this site, so its function remained a mystery. However, the excavation of AlDf-30 in 2012 revealed a likely analogue. The only other true subsurface feature encountered around Port Joli's harbour is the potential sweathouse at AlDf-30. Like the feature at AlDf-31, it too was a sterile deposit without evidence of artifacts and shell, and contained only a trace amount of charcoal. It may have also been associated with post-moulds, and was subsequently filled in by a black soil midden, in the case of AlDf-30, dwelling floors.

Though the AlDf-31 feature appears far shallower than the AlDf-30 feature (note that the initial discovery of the AlDf-30 features indicated a shallow feature approx. 15 to 20 cm in depth), only a small fraction of AlDf-31 was excavated, and it therefore may have been deeper. Even if it was not deeper than it appears, the added berm of backdirt made it a considerably depressed surface. The ring of stone surrounding the feature, which has no analogue in Port Joli, may have been used to create a more airtight structure by holding down skins or furs which covered the structure.

Thus, the proximity of AlDf-31 to AlDf-30 and their similarity in terms of structure, access to a fen and brook, and relative seclusion from habitation sites, suggests that AlDf-31 may also have been the location of a ritual structure, perhaps a sweathouse. If this is the case, unlike at AlDf-30, the AlDf-31 sweathouse was constructed only after the site had been occupied, resulting in the shell-laden backdirt. It is conceivable that, if both sites developed contemporaneously, they may have functioned in tandem, with domestic activities taking place at one, while the other was used as a ritual space. If so, these activities apparently did not alternate within sites (i.e., there are no alternating lenses of sterile/non-sterile deposits in either). In both sites the sweathouse was used, and then the site was used as a domestic one for all future occupations. This may imply that once a sweathouse site turned to a domestic site it could no longer be used as a ritual space.

AlDf-25 (Scotch Point, Port Joli No. 3, AlDf-09)

AlDf-25 was excavated by John Erskine in 1959. In addition to the large kidney-shaped mound (see Chapter 3), Erskine excavated an area he called the "angle camp," at AlDf-25, located in the concavity to the south of the U-shaped midden mound. Here he excavated a deposit between 31 and 51 cm in depth, where "ash" (his term for black soil) predominated over shell, and where animal bones, ceramics, and especially lithics were very abundant. The deposit appears to have been composed of at least three sequential strata consistent with dwelling surfaces, which he termed "wigwam sites" (Erskine 1959: 9).

The house floors were nestled in a flat area about 3 to 4 m wide, the only place large enough to put a wigwam due to the numerous boulders surrounding the large shell midden. Lithic artifacts, and especially projectile points and scrapers, were very abundant in this deposit, which Erskine described as showing stratigraphic "evidence of repeated occupation." (Erskine 1962: 4). Interestingly, Erskine (1962: 4) also "found that the wigwam had had its own midden outside its southward-facing door, well trampled shell with rabbit [presumably hare] bones," indicating a classic kitchen midden. Erskine (1962: 5) described that he discovered a pattern in the distribution of projectile points which suggested the entrance moved from the south to the east over time.

AlDf-08 (Lower Path Lake Brook, Port Joli No. 7)

The large shell-bearing black soil deposits encountered at AlDf-08, as we have already suggested, likely represent repeated and intensive, dwelling occupations (Erskine 1959; Chapter 3). Erskine (1959: 347) claims to have excavated a "wigwam" deposit some distance from the large boulder that dominated the site. Unfortunately, he did not describe the deposit in detail. Our test excavations encountered intact portions of likely the same or a similar feature as that excavated by Erskine, providing a more nuanced look at the site's occupation. Test Unit 1 revealed a series of superimposed living surfaces, manifested as alternating lenses of dark black, greasy, sandy loam with small amounts of crushed shell and large amounts of highly comminuted charcoal. The deposit was 45 cm thick, similar in depth to the deposits encountered at the "angle camp" at AlDf-25 and Area C at AlDf-24. In our limited vertical excavation, the precise nature of these floors is impossible to discern. However, the stratigraphy and artifact contents suggest that Level 3, a black sandy loam layer with highly comminuted clam shell and abundant artifacts, likely represented a dwelling surface.

Level 3 also contained a red brown sandy loam lens with burnt animal bone and shells, which may represent an associated hearth. The upper layers likely represent dwelling surfaces as well, particularly Level 2 which had almost no shell, but these were obviously more ephemeral and less artifact-dense than the deposit below it. What seems clear from this evidence was that AlDf-08 was repeatedly and intensively occupied, and like other sites, dwelling surfaces were clearly placed one on top of the other repeatedly during the period the site was in use.

Discussion

Structurally, Port Joli dwelling features are notably consistent at each site where they have been recognized, indicating a stable architectural tradition from at least the Middle Maritime

Woodland to the later Late Maritime Woodland periods. Considering ethnographic accounts for Nova Scotia and the Maritime Peninsula more broadly, this tradition can likely be extended to more recent times (Hrynick and Black 2016; Lelièvre 2017: 106–32). Regionally, the Port Joli dwellings are largely consistent with contemporaneous birch-bark dwelling features identified elsewhere on the Maritime Peninsula (Hrynick and Black 2016; Sanger 2010).

The architectural tradition can be characterized as follows: dwelling features were generally oval, between 2.5 and 3.5 m in diameter, and often associated with large boulders which form one or more sides of the dwelling structure. Dwelling floor deposits can be identified by a confluence of traits. First, floor strata are dark brown to black and highly organic (usually a sandy loam), with abundant, highly comminuted charcoal. Lithic artifacts, especially debitage, are very abundant, and pottery is usually present in high quantities. When shell is abundant, animal bones (typically highly fragmented) are frequent. Evidence of spatial segregation in the houses is evident in both Middle and Late Maritime Woodland contexts, either through spatial patterns in artifacts or the imposition of a formal axial features.

On the coasts of Maine and New Brunswick, dwelling features tended to be lined with manuport water-rolled gravel from nearby beaches for reasons that remain unclear but may have been to make a reusable surface for wigwams (Hrynick 2018). Port Joli dwelling surfaces were not paved with manuport gravel, likely reflecting the South Shore's sandy, rather than gravelly, beach deposits. The already-sandy soils at Port Joli make it difficult to determine if beach sand had been added to any of the deposits, but this is a possibility. At Port Joli, as elsewhere on the Maritime Peninsula, dwelling features have much less shell than surrounding middens—consistently less than the threshold offered by Belcher (1989: 179) and Sanger (2010) of 15 percent of shell (by weight) per unit of soil matrix—often occurring in negligible quantities.

When entire Port Joli features are excavated, they typically exhibit a range of sub-features. Again, these are regionally and diachronically consistent with other known dwellings. Dwelling deposits tend to include at least one hearth and peripheral rock stops to support posts. Post-moulds are rare on the Maritime Peninsula (Sanger 1996: 522), as they are at Port Joli. At AlDf-24, where three were identified, the post-moulds (figure 5.14) were shallow—about 10 cm to 15 cm in diameter and about 10 cm deep—compact, and shell-free in all but one instance, rendering them difficult to identify. Their ephemeral nature also suggests that wigwam poles were not placed deeply into the ground; rather, the posts were probably held in place with rock stops, at least at Port Joli. A pit hearth or pit feature is also present in one of the Port Joli features (AlDf-24, Area C, Feature 4). Anvil stones surrounded by spirally cracked mammal bone were present in Feature 4 at AlDf-24, Area C. Erskine (1986: 88) identified similar features at AlDf-07, where he thought they were associated with wigwams (though he had trouble defining their functions adequately).

Port Joli architecture offers insight into patterns of abandonment and reuse of architectural surfaces. One of the most remarkable traits of the dwelling features around Port Joli's harbour is that, at most sites, dwellings occupied the same footprint for centuries, and in one case (AlDf-24, Area C), over a millennium. At other multi-dwelling feature sites on the Maritime Peninsula, such as Minister's Island (Sanger 1987) or at Teacher's Cove (Davis 1978), both in the New Brunswick Quoddy region, dwelling features overlap, but often

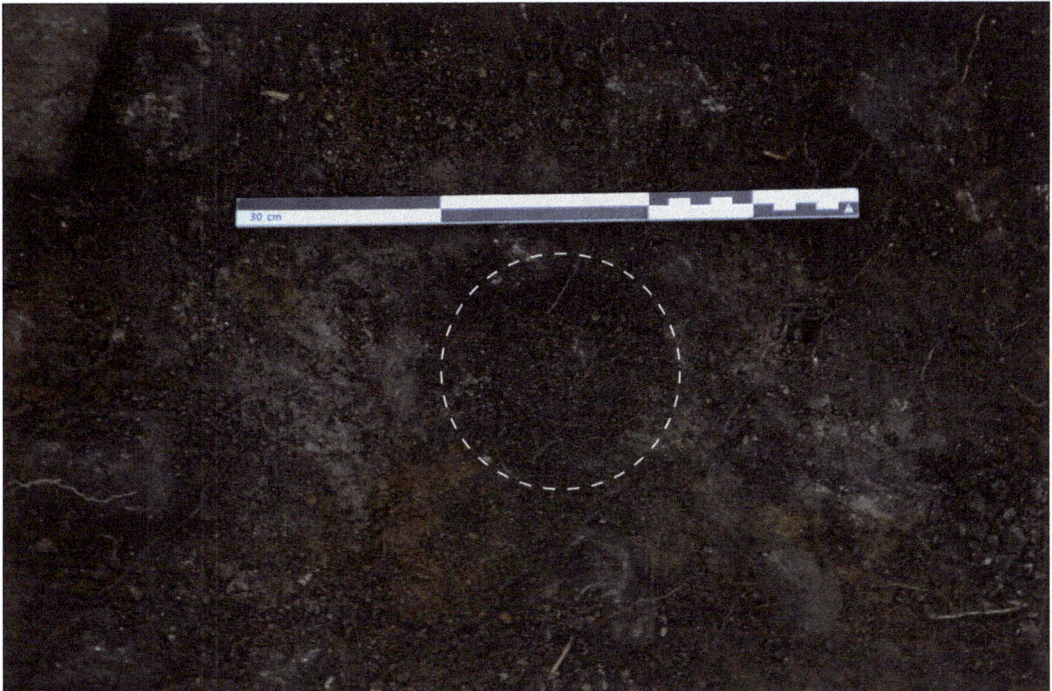

Figure 5.14 AlDf-24: Photograph of post-mould.

not as precisely as they tend to at Port Joli. Similarly, house floors are rarely found in shell middens in Port Joli. At other sites, such as Devil's Head in the Maine Quoddy region, dwelling features apparently shifted somewhat through time (Hrynick and Betts 2017). It is possible that this reflects more dramatic changes in prehistoric site structure in the Quoddy region due to more substantial prehistoric sea-level rise changing the physiography there (see Black 2000). Perhaps a more likely proximal cause is that more sedentism at Port Joli, compared to elsewhere on the Maritime Peninsula (Betts et al. 2017), drove comparatively increased investment in sites (following Binford 1990).

Part of the remarkable consistency in dwelling placement at Port Joli may be due in part to the natural topography of the coastline, which is characterized by hummocky terrain littered with countless large boulders, making level ground large enough for a wigwam-structure rare. Moreover, there appears to have been a preference for such areas where large glacial erratics afforded natural shelter. Even at sites with a fair amount of level ground, Port Joli sites do appear to be more spatially segregated than others on the Maritime Peninsula, and those spatial patterns are maintained more precisely through time than at other sites in the region. Perhaps the best evidence of this was with the structures identified at AlDf-30: despite boulder-free level ground in all directions around the site, three distinct dwelling strata (probably representing dozens of repeated constructions) were placed in the precise footprint of the preceding structure. That the large central rock feature of the first structure, a sweathouse, was incorporated as an axial dividing feature in the subsequent wigwam structures indicates purposeful reuse of structural footprints and, in this case, perhaps with a symbolic importance. Regardless of the reason, the permanence of dwelling sites on the landscape is remarkable, and the resulting routines that developed around these effectively permanent habitations must have been critical to the development of Mi'kmaw history on the South Shore.

The consistency in size, placement, door orientation, and general location of the hearths does not mean that diachronic changes are not evident in the architectural data set at Port Joli, consistent with different lengths of occupation. For instance, AlDf-24, Area A, Feature 4, dating to the later Late Maritime Woodland Period, is far more artifact-rich than its Middle Maritime Woodland counterparts at AlDf-30. Furthermore, the floor deposits tend to be thicker and darker (with more comminuted charcoal) during the Late Maritime Woodland Period. Hearths are also more prominent in the later Late Maritime Woodland features. The possible appearance of a pit in Feature 4 may also reflect a shift in the domestic use of space. Finally, not all dwelling features were constructed on previous architectural features. At AlDf-24, Area A, an undulating, boulder-strewn surface was filled in with shell to form a flat mound, after which it was used as a living surface (Feature 2). House floors on top of midden surfaces would seem to be a Late Maritime Woodland trait, if only because the local topography required generations of midden development to create a readily habitable landscape and provide a readily useable surface for dwelling features

Hearth features in dwellings tend to seem elongated as they shifted positions gradually as the deposits were excavated. It is unlikely—maybe impossible—that the hearths could have been this large as they likely would have made the living surface uninhabitable or burned the superstructure. Rather, a structure was probably repeatedly placed over the same surface over many years, perhaps centuries, with a slight shift in position or orientation resulting in elongated features over time. The apparent slight shifts in doorway orientation and post-mould orientation at some sites may be similarly explained.

Perhaps the most unique architectural trait of Port Joli are its sweathouses. That sweathouses like those at AlDf-30 and AlDf-31 have been so rarely identified in the archaeological record of the Maritime Peninsula is puzzling. Since identifying the Port Joli sweathouses, one possible Late Maritime Woodland sweathouse at Melanson, Nova Scotia, was brought to our attention (Nash and Stewart 1990; K. Leonard 2015, pers. comm.), though it was never fully recognized as such at the time of its excavation. Still, this makes only three sweathouse features identified on the Maritime Peninsula. Archaeologically, sweathouses, like house floors, are difficult to excavate and interpret, and the preferred vertical excavation technique in the region is not suited to their identification. Furthermore, sweathouses were not always stand-alone structures but were often expediently employed wigwams (Wallis and Wallis 1955: 124). Others may have been ephemeral, short-term structures, such as that at AlDf-31. Additionally, in many cases, sweathouses were likely separated from dwellings, serving as distinctly segregated and, likely, male spaces (see Hrynick and Betts 2014). The Port Joli sweathouses certainly imply that testing away from large habitation sites and in locations not typically associated with traditional coastal-site models is warranted (e.g., Black 2004; Kellogg 1994).

There are other differences between Port Joli's prehistoric architecture and that found elsewhere on the Maritime Peninsula. The axial feature reused repeatedly at AlDf-30 is unique in the regional inventory, as is the pronounced division of space evident in the artifact distributions at AlDf-24, Area C, Feature 4. However, we stress that the ethnographic record speaks to similar gendered patterning throughout the region and among other Algonquian hunter-gatherers, such as the Cree (e.g., Tanner 1979), and Erskine (1986) had noted spatial patterning suggestive of segregated spaces in house deposits previously.

The relative lack of feature diversity at Port Joli sites is interesting, especially in light of probable year-round occupation at AlDf-24 (see Chapter 7). Elsewhere, such as southern New England (e.g., McBride 1984), year-round occupation is often associated with villages, which would be evidenced by larger sites and a wider range of feature types. Some archaeologists (e.g., Leveillee et al. 2006) have suggested that, staying with the southern New England example, these features could be dispersed over the landscape rather than within a single locale or "site," narrowly conceived. As Port Joli has shown, conventional site models may not account for the full array of past features; speculatively, this leaves possible the presence of dispersed, diverse sites associated with the same people and political organization. As a caveat, E'se'get Archaeology Project excavations targeted middens and architectural features, and thus may have encountered fewer non-architectural and non-midden features.

Conclusions

The Port Joli architectural data set spans the Middle and Late Maritime Woodland periods, and numbers three fully excavated dwelling features, the first confidently identified and fully excavated sweathouse on the Maritime Peninsula, a series of partially excavated probable dwelling features, and another possible sweathouse. Structurally, these features suggest an architectural tradition that is contiguous with surrounding areas of the Wabanaki homeland and continuous from the Middle Maritime Woodland Period into the contact period, expanding this pattern from elsewhere in the Maritime Peninsula (Hrynick and Black 2016). Future work on the Maritime Peninsula may serve to expand this pattern deeper into the past.

The E'se'get Archaeology Project emphasizes the interpretation of the use of domestic space, drawing on ethnographic accounts that highlighted the role of spatial patterning in maintaining, modifying, or reifying "sacred ecology," the patterned series of lifeways essential to maintaining the correct order of the world in the Wabanaki relational cosmological system (Hornborg 2013; see Hrynick and Betts 2017). Importantly, this shifts cosmological focus away from hunting—a male activity in the ethnohistoric record—to an area that was dominated by women in the ethnohistoric record: the dwelling. Conversely, the AlDf-30 sweathouse expands upon archaeologists' understanding of prehistoric, sequestered, male ritual activity. We expand on these topics in a series of publications related to architecture as gendered spaces within Wabanaki cosmology (Hrynick et al. 2012; Hrynick and Betts 2014, 2017).

Ultimately, the architectural features around Port Joli's harbour record essential economic, social, and ritual spaces and the activities that took place in them. None of this is to neglect the cultural-ecological (sensu Sanger 1996) basis of much of how people on the Maritime peninsula confronted the realities of Port Joli and constructed appropriate housing. Rather, the Port Joli architecture expands the range of historical practices surrounding ancient Wabanaki architecture—and the range of architectural forms. The result is a richer understanding of the ways people dwelled in and built their world around Port Joli's harbour.

Chapter 6
The Ceramic Assemblage

JENNETH CURTIS, ERIN INGRAM, AND MATTHEW BETTS

Introduction

In the Atlantic Northeast, the largest artifact assemblages on many Maritime Woodland archaeological sites are composed of ceramic sherds. Archaeologists have therefore spent more resources describing, classifying, and documenting ceramic assemblages than practically any other artifact class. Several key studies have documented ceramic variability on a regional and pan-regional level (e.g., Bourgeois 1999; Godfrey-Smith et al. 1997; Kristmanson 1992; Petersen and Sanger 1991). This pioneering research participated in a greater tradition of Northeastern pottery analysis that had an attribute-based culture-history focus. A significant concern of these studies was the definition and application of a chronologically based sequence composed of general attributes of decoration, temper, and surface finish (e.g., Kristmanson 1992: 14; Petersen and Sanger 1991: 122).

Such research has tracked chronological, regional, and intra-regional variability in ceramic manufacture and decoration, leading to important insights into population movements, technological innovation, and technological diffusion. With this foundation, it is now possible to extend such analysis toward finer levels of inquiry regarding ceramic variability. Detailed scrutiny of tool types and application techniques, linked to specific locations or zones on vessels, can only lead to a greater understanding of the ceramic tradition on the Maritime Peninsula, from both chronological and spatial perspectives.

In this chapter, we describe the ceramic assemblages recovered from around Port Joli's harbour during the E'se'get Archaeology Project (EAP) and apply a comprehensive ceramic-attribute analysis to the assemblage, using the chronology developed in Chapter 4 as an organizational and comparative tool. Our goal with this analysis is threefold: (1) to measure ceramic design and decoration using higher-resolution attribute analysis than previously employed, (2) to describe and report the total variability in the Port Joli ceramic assemblages and how that changed over time, and (3) to compare and contrast our findings with existing regional studies, most notably the classic Petersen and Sanger (1991) Ceramic sequence. We employ a highly detailed attribute analysis using the Northeast Woodland Pottery Analytic Code developed by David Smith (1983, 1987, 2011) at the University of Toronto. To our knowledge, such high-resolution attribute analysis has never been published on ceramic assemblages from the Atlantic Northeast.

Our comprehensive, data-rich analysis has allowed us to confirm key aspects of the Petersen and Sanger (1991) sequence as well as providing new insights on the timing and patterning of changes in ceramics both locally and regionally. We support our discussion with detailed data tables, drawings, and photographs to facilitate and encourage comparisons, thereby aiming to foster a deeper understanding of temporal and spatial patterning on the Maritime Peninsula.

History of Ceramic Research on the Maritime Peninsula

Description and interpretation of ceramic variation has been key to archaeological research on the Maritime Peninsula since the earliest professional archaeological efforts. While work during the nineteenth century recognized the importance of ceramics (see discussion in Kristmanson 1992: 7), the first in-depth consideration of ceramic decoration and attributes occurred in H. I. Smith and W. J. Wintemberg's (1929) seminal report on excavations in Merigomish and Mahone Bay, Nova Scotia. Smith, in particular, was very interested in accurately describing the decorative attributes he observed on the pottery from Merigomish, and especially the tools and techniques used to make the impressions on the vessels. In some of the earliest experimental archaeology in Canada, he re-created tools and implements and tested various application techniques on clay test pieces. Wintemberg, in contrast, was concerned with the culture-historical implications of vessel morphology, temper, and spatial distribution.

In the mid-1950s and 1960s, John Erskine (1986) collected voluminous ceramic assemblages from dozens of sites across Nova Scotia. Like previous scholars, his pioneering work was largely culture-historical in aim, and his description of the ceramic decoration he found focused primarily on changes in general attributes (colour, decoration, and surface finish) over time and space. While his descriptive techniques and periodization were generally impressionistic rather than quantitative, his recognition of variability through space and time was critically influential in the development of subsequent ceramic attribute studies.

Research published in the 1970s and 1980s by Sanger (1987) and others (e.g., Allen 1981, 1984; Bourque 1971; Connolly 1977; Davis 1971, 1978; Myers 1972) added a groundbreaking feature to ceramic analysis—the application of descriptive terminology rooted in the Northeastern pottery attribute–analysis tradition (e.g., Hurley and Wagner 1972). Some of the first vessel-lot analysis was conducted during this period (e.g., Allen 1981). This approach was easily transferred to describe ceramic variability on the Maritime Peninsula, as the same suite of attributes was discovered to be present in assemblages here. Bourque (1971) was one of the first archaeologists to develop a formal (i.e., testable) pottery sequence based on changing attribute frequencies.

The Petersen and Sanger Ceramic Sequence

In the late 1980s, James Petersen and David Sanger (1991) conducted a seminal ceramics study for Maine and the Maritime Peninsula. Working with assemblages from dozens of sites, they tracked "general attribute modes of temper, surface finish, and decoration" and "vessel morphology attributes" (Petersen and Sanger 1991: 122). Given its broad scope, the study focused on general attributes and was not designed as a highly detailed attribute analysis. Its primary aim was to develop a sequence of pottery attributes which could be used as "markers of spatial and temporal variation" (Petersen and Sanger 1991: 122). Petersen and Sanger's sequence was "meant simply to serve as an heuristic model to be used in testing different data sets and to be tested itself as additional data accumulate" (Petersen and Sanger 1991: 124). Importantly, the authors recognized that new information could lead to modifications and the identification of local heterogeneity. The sequence that resulted from their study has been the primary analytical tool for Indigenous ceramics and, one could argue, for chronological typology on the Maritime Peninsula for the last twenty-five years.

Subsequent regional analyses conducted in New Brunswick and Nova Scotia were designed to compare local assemblages to the sequence, often using it as a recursive means to position undated assemblages temporally (e.g., Bourgeois 1999; Kristmanson 1992), while pointing out critical discrepancies and temporal anomalies. Numerous monographs and reports documenting site variability throughout the region have repeatedly used the sequence as a classificatory aid, often directly associating assemblages with the date ranges defined by Petersen and Sanger (for an overview, see Deal 2016: 26–27). Not surprisingly, these studies have indicated significant correspondence between the Petersen and Sanger sequence and regional ceramic assemblages, at least on a very general attribute level.

Table 6.1 outlines the attributes defined by the Petersen and Sanger sequence. The table is useful because it will permit more direct comparison of the Port Joli ceramic assemblages to identified trends in the greater Northeast. We will present our analysis in considerably higher resolution than that described by Petersen and Sanger. This contrast is purposeful and is meant to reveal how much variability is masked by studies that adopt a more generalized attribute analysis following Petersen and Sanger. Regardless, our data-rich analysis will permit critical comparison to their sequence because our attributes can be combined or collapsed into more general categories for comparative purposes.

Regional Comparisons to the Petersen and Sanger Sequence

Several important regional studies have supported the general chronology proposed by the Petersen and Sanger sequence, while exposing important local variations in the expression of attributes. In New Brunswick, Bourgeois (1999) developed a ceramic sequence for the Saint John River Valley. He documented that variability in pottery decoration evident in some regions for CP 1 (Ceramic Period 1; see Chapter 4) is not present on the Saint John River. In particular, the occurrence of stamped decoration simultaneously with undecorated and cord-paddled ceramics was not observed. In CP 2, he was able to document that castellations were characteristic in the Saint John River Valley, but often uncommon elsewhere (though we note that Petersen and Sanger did mention the presence of castellated vessels in CP 2). The presence of interior channelling, interior stamping, additive collared rims, and exterior bossing was also unique to the Saint John River Valley, in contrast, Bourgeois states, to coastal New Brunswick and Nova Scotia during CP 2 (Bourgeois 1999: 67).

Like the rest of the Maritime Peninsula, the CP 3 was marked by the increase in dentate-stamped decoration, but in the Saint John River Valley, Bourgeois identified that cord-wrapped-stick-decorated pottery was also represented, at least in the coastal portion of the river valley. In CP 4, vessel thickness increased substantially in the Saint John River Valley, as did the use of organic tempering, in contrast to other regions. CP 5 ceramics from the river valley were largely consistent with those in the Petersen and Sanger sequence, but Bourgeois observed that in CP 6 vessels with extrusive collars and geometric motifs, consistent with an Owasco-Iroquoian influence, were also present. In the Saint John River Valley there is no evidence of post-Contact (CP 7) ceramics.

The most relevant research relating to the Port Joli assemblage is Helen Kristmanson's (1992) examination of ceramic variability in southwestern Nova Scotia. While limited by the coarse contextual data available for the collections she studied, she was nevertheless able

Table 6.1 Major attributes identified in the Petersen and Sanger Ceramic sequence.

Ceramic Period	Temporal Range	Temper	Surface Finish	Decoration	Morphology
CP1	3050–2150 BP	grit	– fabric impressed interior/exterior often smoothed over	– undecorated	– simple rims with rounded lips – conoidal form
CP2	2150–1650 BP	grit	– smoothing on interior and exterior – channelling (with toothed implement) occasionally on interiors	– elaborate decoration – pseudo scallop shell, dentate, simple linear tool (stamped, rocked, and dragged) – incision and non-standardized punctates typically secondary	– castellations (rare) – thin lips and walls – conoidal form
CP3	1650–1350 BP	grit, shell temper possible	– smoothed exteriors and interiors – fabric impressed exterior appears on some vessels	– increase size of dentate – simple linear tool (rocked) – pseudo scallop shell disappears – variety of punctates used to fill decorative field	– thicker rims and vessel walls – thickened rims or low collars appear – conoidal form
CP4	1350–950 BP	grit, shell increases	– fabric impressed exterior increases – smoothed exterior decreases	– cord wrapped stick dominant – dentate disappears – rocker stamping disappears – discrete circular punctates – incision and trailing associated with circular punctates	– straight to excurvate rims with rounded lips – some low collared/thickened rims – conoidal form
CP5	950–650 BP	shell dominant especially on coast, grit also	– combination of: – smoothed exterior: – fabric impressed exterior – smoothed over fabric impressed exterior	– cord wrapped stick stamps often applied vertically – smaller circular punctates (often secondary, rarely applied alone)	– simple straight to excurvate rims without collars – globular form appears toward end of period
CP6	650–400 BP	shell, grit increases	– possible increase in fabric impressed exteriors	– cord wrapped stick (stamped) – circular punctates disappear – rarely incised – vessel bodies often undecorated	– very thin walls – rarely thick collared rims and globular forms
CP7	400–200 BP	grit dominant	– fabric impressed exteriors	– incision – cord wrapped stick – undecorated	– thin walls – collared and collarless rims

to discern some possible regional differences from the Petersen and Sanger sequence. Importantly, Kristmanson was able for the first time to demonstrate that fabric-impressed vessels were present in Nova Scotia in CP 1, something not identified by Petersen and Sanger (1991). She noted that drag-stamping was not present in any assemblage in southwestern Nova Scotia, as predicted by the Petersen and Sanger model. Unfortunately, Kristmanson's study was hampered by a lack of deposits firmly dated to between CP 4 and CP 7. She noted that Z-twist dominated in cord-wrapped-stick decoration on the coast, and that S-twist seemed to dominate in the interior, except for the Eel Weir site (Kristmanson 1992: 69). She also observed that Z-twist is not always associated with shell-tempered vessels (as it had been predicted by Petersen and Sanger) and that vessels impressed with S-twist cordage were found in conjunction with shell temper at both interior and coastal sites. Regarding temper, Kristmanson (1992: 74) states:

> The data seem to suggest a slight increase in the use of shell as tempering material at some point during CP 4/5/6, approaching equal proportions with grit tempered vessels, which seems to demonstrate a slight decline. However the data further suggests that as time progressed, somewhere in the latter range of CP 5–7, the predominant choice for tempering material returned to grit.

Like Petersen and Sanger's, Kristmanson's analysis revealed that vessel thickness decreased over time, but perhaps not as dramatically as they might have suggested. On Nova Scotia's South Shore, interior channelling only occurred on cord-wrapped-stick-decorated vessels dating from CP 4 to CP 7 and not on dentate-stamped vessels dating to CP 3, as predicted by the Petersen and Sanger sequence.

As part of her study, Kristmanson conducted extensive experimental work on defining finishing and decorating tools (Kristmanson and Deal 1993). This study revealed that finger- and stone-smoothing were preferred interior treatments, while cord-wrapped-stick-smoothing was prevalent on vessels with cord-wrapped-stick decoration. Other rarely occurring finishes included smoothing with leather and twigs or grasses.

Kora Stapelfeldt's 2009 thesis focused on the form and function of pottery in the Atlantic provinces, and as such it is not directly comparable to an attribute-based analysis. Nevertheless, the study resulted in several important revelations. She noted distinct similarities in size and decorative motifs across the Maritime provinces (Stapelfeldt 2009: 136), which could only be explained by direct and close contact between pottery makers. Vessel form was relatively stable over the entire Maritime Woodland Period, though "spherical or more globular forms" (Stapelfeldt 2009: 136) were preferred in later periods.

Analytical Methods

Using the chronological model from Chapter 4 (see table 4.3), we grouped the EAP-collected ceramic assemblage by dated context for analysis. The unit of analysis for this study is the individual ceramic vessel; thus, analysis began by grouping together ceramic sherds from the same context into "vessel lots," or lots where attributes indicate that sherds come from the same pot. Ceramic sherds were compared based on decoration, surface treatment, colour, temper, and wall thickness. Because of the fragmentary and friable nature of the collection, a primary goal was to look for mends which would serve as a more concrete basis for the vessel lots. Once a satisfactory number of mends had been established, more sherds were added to the vessel lots based on comparable attributes.

Tables 6.3a to 6.3e describe the Port Joli ceramic vessel assemblage, organized by dated context. Many sherds, including several small rim fragments, could not be assigned to individual vessels because their decoration was either plain or indeterminate, or they were simply too small or too poorly preserved to be confidently placed with any single vessel. These sherds were included in the overall summary of ceramic attributes from each site, in which each individual sherd was analyzed and are presented in table 6.4. We refer to this throughout the chapter as the "all-sherds" analysis or the "all-sherds" table.

A diameter board with concentric rings of graduated sizes was used to measure the inside orifice diameters of the rim sherds. This measurement assumes that the vessel orifice was circular. However, Staplefeldt (2009) found that most vessels in the region were ellipsoidal in form; thus, the circular measurement provides an estimate of the orifice size rather than an exact measurement. Additionally, we observed on very large sherds that orifices were often irregular in shape, rather than symmetrical, adding an additional source of deviation from our estimated size and shape. Digital calipers were used to measure thickness of both the top of the rim, the sherd body, and a standardized 2 mm distance from the top of the rim (to account for flaring rims).

As with most of ceramic studies in the Maritime Peninsula region (see above), we chose to use an attribute-analysis approach but have applied it on a more detailed and comprehensive scale. An attribute is the smallest unit of analysis applicable to ceramics (Clarke 1978: 157; Smith 1983: 22). Variables such as vessel wall thickness or decorative technique each contain multiple attributes which form the basic analytical units. Attributes are mutually exclusive and can be recorded without having to make value judgments about which are most important. This level of detail allows for a comprehensive analysis of the E'se'get ceramic assemblage so that inter-site patterns as well as intra-site patterns can be discerned between strata and contexts.

Attributes for each vessel were recorded using the Northeast Woodland Pottery Analytic Code developed by David Smith (2011). This code was initially developed for the study of Iroquoian ceramics in the mid-1980s (Smith 1983; 1987) and was subsequently expanded by Smith for use with ceramic assemblages from additional periods and regions across northeastern North America (see Bekerman 1995; Curtis 2004a; Watts 1997, 2008). A very large number of attributes can be recorded with this code, although those available for analysis represent a smaller subset depending on the fragmentary nature of the artifacts. While all possible attributes were recorded for the E'se'get assemblages, variables for analysis and presentation here were selected based on their relevance to the research objectives: to describe and report the total variability in the Port Joli ceramic assemblages, and to compare our findings with existing regional studies, most notably the classic Petersen and Sanger Ceramic sequence. The variables addressed in the analysis are listed below (table 6.2).

E'se'get Ceramic Assemblages

The E'se'get ceramic database consists of thirteen assemblages from seven archaeological sites (tables 6.3a to 6.3e). These contexts conform to the chronology developed in Chapter 4

Table 6.2 Ceramic variables used in analysis of E'se'get assemblages.

Manufacture	• temper type • coil breaks • exterior surface treatment • interior surface treatment
Form	• lip form • lip thickness • rim form • rim thickness • orifice diameter • exterior rim profile • castellation form
Decoration	• first exterior decorative band—tool, technique, configuration • second exterior decorative band—tool, technique, configuration • lip decorative band—tool, technique, configuration

(table 4.3), and thus the contextual and chronological details are not repeated here. Three of these assemblages are attributed to the Late Middle Maritime Woodland Period based on radiocarbon dates and stratigraphic contexts. These three assemblages provide a total of seventy-seven late Middle Maritime Woodland vessels, including thirty-eight with rims. Six assemblages are attributed to the Late Maritime Woodland Period and together yielded forty-eight vessels, among which seventeen included rim sherds. Two of these assemblages are believed to date to the earlier Late Maritime Woodland Period, while four are dated to the later Late Maritime Woodland Period. A final assemblage, with two vessel lots but no rims, dates to the Protohistoric Period. An additional three vessels come from undated contexts.

In this section, we describe assemblage attributes from each context. As the assemblages are often quite small, we also group them into single regional assemblages for the two time periods represented: late Middle Maritime Woodland (Ceramic Period 3) and Late Maritime Woodland (Ceramic periods 4 to 5). This facilitates comparisons between the two periods at the regional level as well as our subsequent comparison with the Petersen and Sanger sequence.

Form

On average, the E'se'get ceramic assemblage represents a collection of collarless vessels with straight to out-flaring rims and straight to rounded lips (table 6.3b; figures 6.1 to 6.4). These rim fragments are most likely derived from conoidal vessels, as is typical of the Atlantic region throughout the Maritime Woodland Period (see Stapelfeldt 2009). Indeed, these form attributes are consistent across the thousand-year span of the E'se'get assemblage, with no significant change evident through the Middle to Late Maritime Woodland transition. A single basal sherd is also present in the assemblage from AlDf-24, Area A Midden. This sherd has the form of a rounded point that is consistent with the typical conoidal vessel form.

Castellations are present on several rims (13 percent; see table 6.3a) in both the Middle and Late Maritime Woodland Period assemblages (figure 6.5). Castellations are raised

Table 6.3a Summary of Port Joli ceramic assemblages.

Context/Assemblage	Period (after Black)	Period (after Petersen and Sanger)	# Vessels with rims	# Vessels without rims	# Sherds not associated with vessel
AlDf-25	MMW	CP3	2	1	2
AlDf-30 Area A Midden and Black Soil Midden Lower	MMW	CP3	17	18	997
AlDf-24 Area A Midden	MMW	CP3	19	20	642
AlDf-24 Area C Lower	Early LMW	CP4	10	6	109
AlDf-24 Area C Middle	Early LMW / Later LMW Transition	CP4/CP5	4	8	47
AlDf-24 Area C Upper	Later LMW	CP5	0	3	192
AlDf-08	Later LMW	CP5	1	9	81
AlDf-30 Black Soil Midden Upper	Later LMW	CP5	2	2	138
AlDf-06/AlDf-05	Later LMW	CP5	0	4	34
AlDf-24 Area C Proto	Protohistoric	CP7	0	2	42
AlDf-31	Maritime Woodland	Ceramic Period	1	2	0
AlDf-35	Maritime Woodland	Ceramic Period	0	2	9
AlDf-30 Area B Midden	Maritime Woodland	Ceramic Period	1	1	89

The Ceramic Assemblage 169

Table 6.3b Summary of form attributes in Port Joli vessel lots.

Attribute	AlDf-30 Midden & Features		AlDf-24 Area A		AlDf-25		CP 3 Total		AlDf-24 Early Context		AlDf 24 Middle Context		AlDf-30 Late Context		AlDf-08		CP 4-5 Total	
	n	%	n	%	n	%	n	%	n	%	n	%	n	%	n	%	n	%
Rim Form																		
Collarless	16	100	17	94	2	100	35	97	10	100	4	100	2	100			16	100
Collared			1	6			1	3										
Total	16	100	18	100	2	100	36	100	10	100	4	100	2	100			16	100
Upper Rim Orientation																		
vertical	4	27	6	35			10	29	2	20	1	25					3	18
outflaring	11	73	11	65	2	100	24	71	8	80	3	75	2	100	1	100	14	82
Total	15	100	17	100	2	100	34	100	10	100	4	100	2	100	1	100	17	100
Exterior Rim Profile																		
straight	4	27	1	6	1	50	6	18	3	33							3	21
concave	6	40	3	19			9	27	2	22	2	50	1	100			5	36
convex	5	33	12	75	1	50	18	55	4	44	2	50					6	43
Total	15	100	16	100	2	100	33	100	9	99	4	100	1	100			14	100
Lip Form																		
straight (flat)	7	54	6	32			13	38	4	40	1	25	1	50			6	35
round (convex)	6	46	10	52	2	100	18	53	6	60	3	75	1	50	1	100	11	65
complex			3	16			3	9										
Total	13	100	19	100	2	100	34	100	10	100	4	100	2	100	1	100	17	100
Castellation																		
Absent	16	94	15	79			31	89	6	75	4	100	2	100			12	80
Round			4	21			4	11	2	25					1	100	3	20
Total	16	100	19	100			35	100	8	100	4	100	2	100	1	100	15	100

Table 6.3c Summary of manufacturing attributes in Port Joli vessel lots.

Attribute	AlDf-30 Midden & Features		AlDf-24 Area A		AlDf-25		CP 3 Total		AlDf-24 Early Context		AlDf 24 Middle Context		AlDf-30 Late Context		AlDf-08		CP 4-5 Total	
Temper Type	n	%	n	%	n	%	n	%	n	%	n	%	n	%	n	%	n	%
Grit	17	100	19	100	2	100	38	100	7	70	2	50	2	100	1	100	12	71
Shell									2	20	0						2	12
Grit & shell									1	10	2	50					3	18
Total	17	100	19	100	2	100	38	100	10	100	4	100	2	100	1	100	17	101
Coil Breaks																		
Present	1	6	1	5			2	5	1	10	0		1	50			2	12
Absent	16	94	18	95			34	95	9	90	4	100	1	50	1	100	15	88
Total	17	100	19	100			36	100	10	100	4	100	2	100	1	100	17	100
Surface Modification - Interior																		
Smoothed	14	100	18	100	1	50	33	97	7	70	2	50	1	50	1	100	11	65
Combed-horizontal									1	10							1	6
Combed - hor over oblique right									1	10							1	6
Combed - oblique right over oblique left											1	25					2	12
Combed - oblique left over horiz											1	25					1	6
Smoothed over fabric imp					1	50	1	3					1	50			1	6
Fabric imp over smoothed																		
Total	14	100	18	100	2	100	34	100	10	100	4	100	2	100	1	100	17	101
Surface Modification - Exterior																		
Smoothed	16	94	18	95	1	100	35	95	9	90	3	75	2	100	1	100	15	88
Fabric impressed			1	5			1	3										
Smoothed over fabric imp									1	10	1	25					1	6
Fabric imp over smoothed	1	6					1	3									1	6
Total	17	100	19	100	1	100	37	101	10	100	4	100	2	100	1	100	17	100

Table 6.3d Summary of decorative attributes in Port Joli vessel lots.

Attribute	AlDf-30 Midden & Features		AlDf-24 Area A		AlDf-25		CP 3 Total		AlDf-24 Early Context		AlDf 24 Middle Context		AlDf-30 Late Context		AlDf-08		CP 4-5 Total	
	n	%	n	%	n	%	n	%	n	%	n	%	n	%	n	%	n	%
First Interior Decorative Band																		
Tool																		
Plain	12	92	17	100	2	100	31	97	9	100	4	100	2	100	1	100	16	100
Dentate	1	8					1	3										
Total	13	100	17	100	2	100	32	100	9	100	4	100	2	100	1	100	16	100
Technique																		
Plain	12	92	17	100	2	100	31	97	9	100	4	100	2	100	1	100	16	100
Stamped	1	8					1	3										
Total	13	100	17	100	2	100	32	100	9	100	4	100	2	100	1	100	16	100
Configuration																		
Plain	12	92	17	100	2	100	31	97	9	100	4	100	2	100	1	100	16	100
Oblique left	1	8					1	3										
Total	13	100	17	100	2	100	32	100	9	100	4	100	2	100	1	100	16	100
Lip Decorative Band																		
Tool																		
Plain	4	33	3	19			7	25	4	40	3	75	1	50			8	47
Square end			1	6			1	4										
Blunt end			1	6			1	4										
Linear	3	25	3	19			6	21	3	30					1	100	4	24
Dentate	3	25	6	38	2	100	9	32	1	10							1	6
Cord-wrapped-stick	2	17	1	6			3	11	2	20	1	25	1	50			4	24
Splint-wrapped stick			1	6			1	4										
Total	12	100	16	100	2	100	28	101	10	100	4	100	2	100	1	100	17	101
Technique																		
Plain	4	24	3	16			7	18	4	40	3	75	1	50			8	47
Stamped	12	71	14	74	2	100	28	74	6	60	1	25	1	50			8	47

Table 6.3d Summary of decorative attributes in Port Joli vessel lots (continued).

Attribute	AlDf-30 Midden & Features		AlDf-24 Area A		AlDf-25		CP 3 Total		AlDf-24 Early Context		AlDf 24 Middle Context		AlDf-30 Late Context		AlDf-08		CP 4-5 Total	
	n	%	n	%	n	%	n	%	n	%	n	%	n	%	n	%	n	%
Incised	1	6	2	11			3	8									1	6
Total	17	101	19	101	2	100	38	100	10	100	4	100	2	100	1	100	17	100
Configuration																		
Plain	4	29	3	16			7	19	4	40	3	75	1	50			8	47
Vertical	4	24	5	26	2	100	11	30	2	20			1	50	1	100	4	24
Oblique right	7	41	6	32			13	35	2	20	1	25					3	18
Oblique left	1	6	3	16			4	11	2	20							2	12
Vertical punctate string			2	11			2	5										
Total	16	100	19	101	2	100	37	100	10	100	4	100	2	100	1	100	17	100
First Exterior Decorative Band																		
Tool																		
Plain			4	27			4	15	4	44	2	50					6	43
Elliptical			1	7			1	4										
Linear	1	11	1	7			2	8										
Linear and Squared			1	7			1	4										
Dentate	3	33	7	47	2	100	12	46	1	11			1	100			2	14
Cord-wrapped stick	4	44	1	7			5	19	4	44	2	50					6	43
Splint-wrapped stick	1	11					1	4										
Total	9	99	15	102	2	100	26	100	9	99	4	100	1	100			14	100
Technique																		
Plain			4	25			4	13	3	33	2	50					5	33
Stamped	10	77	9	50	1	100	20	65	6	67	2	50	1	50			9	60
Stamped and Incised			1	6			1	3										
Incised	1	8	2	13			3	10										
Rocker-stamped	2	15	1	6			3	10										
Drag-stamped													1	50			1	7
Total	13	100	17	100	1	100	31	101	9	100	4	100	2	100			15	100

Table 6.3d Summary of decorative attributes in Port Joli vessel lots (continued).

Attribute	AlDf-30 Midden & Features		AlDf-24 Area A		AlDf-25		CP 3 Total		AlDf-24 Early Context		AlDf-24 Middle Context		AlDf-30 Late Context		AlDf-08		CP 4-5 Total	
	n	%	n	%	n	%	n	%	n	%	n	%	n	%	n	%	n	%
Configuration																		
Plain			4	27			4	14	3	33	2	50					5	30
Vertical	2	17	3	20			5	21	1	11	1	25					2	13
Oblique right	4	33	5	30			9	32	3	33	1	25					4	27
Oblique left							2	7	1	11							1	7
Horizontal	2	17	1	7			3	11					2	100			2	13
Plaits	2	17					2	7										
Superimposed			2	14			2	7										
Horizontal difference	2	17					2	7	1	11							1	7
Second Exterior Decorative Band																		
Tool																		
Plain							1	9										
Semi-annular			1	11														14
Linear			1	11			1	9			1	50					1	14
Dentate	2	100	5	55			7	64	1	20	1	50					2	29
Cord-wrapped stick			1	11			1	9	3	60							3	43
Splint-wrapped stick			1	11			1	9										
Total	2	100	9	99			11	100	5	100	2	100					7	100
Technique																		
Plain			1	10			1	8										
Stamped	2	100	6	60			8	67	4	80	1	50					5	71
Stamped and Incised									1	20							1	14
Incised			1	10			1	8										
Rocker-stamped			2	20			2	17			1	50					1	14
Total	2	100	10	100			12	100	5	100	2	100					7	99
Configuration																		
Vertical	1	50	1	11			2	18										
Oblique right			4	44			4	36										

The Ceramic Assemblage   **173**

Table 6.3d Summary of decorative attributes in Port Joli vessel lots (continued).

Attribute	AIDf-30 Midden & Features		AIDf-24 Area A		AIDf-25		CP 3 Total		AIDf-24 Early Context		AIDf 24 Middle Context		AIDf-30 Late Context		AIDf-08		CP 4-5 Total	
	n	%	n	%	n	%	n	%	n	%	n	%	n	%	n	%	n	%
Oblique left			1	11					2	40							2	29
Horizontal	1	50					1	9	1	20							1	14
Horizontal punctate strings																	1	14
Plaits			2	22			2	18			1	50						
Superimposed			1	11			1	9	1	20							1	14
Horizontal Difference									1	20	1	50					2	29
Total	2	100	9	99			11	99	5	100	2	100					7	100
Third Exterior Decorative Band																		
Tool																		
Dentate			2	100			2	100										
Total			2	100			2	100										
Technique																		
Stamped			2	100			2	100										
Total			2	100			2	100										
Configuration																		
Vertical			1	50			1	50										
Oblique right			1	50			1	50										
Total			2	100			2	100										
Delimitation																		
Absent	16	100	14	78	1	100	31	89	4	44	2	50	2	100			8	53
Horizontal Line			2	11			2	6										
Surface punctates			2	12			2	6	1	12							1	7
Deep punctates									4	44	2	50					6	40
Total	16	100	18	101	1	100	35	101	9	100	4	100	2	100			15	100

Table 6.3e Summary of metric attributes in Port Joli vessel lots.

Attribute	AIDf-30 Midden & Features		AIDf-24 Area A		AIDf-25		CP 3 Total		AIDf-24 Early Context		AIDf 24 Middle Context		AIDf-30 Late Context		AIDf-8		CP 4-5 Total	
	range	average	range	average	range	average	range	average	range	average	range	average	range	average	range	average	range	average
Lip Thickness	3.9-8.8	5.8	2.2-7.4	5.0	2.7-3.5	3.1	2.2-8.8	5.3	3.3-9.6	6.0	2.1-7.7	4.3	6.2-8.0	7.1	6.3	6.3	2.1-9.6	5.7
Rim Thickness	5.5-10.7	8.0	5.1-10.1	7.7	5.9	5.9	5.1-10.7	7.8	5.1-10.5	7.9	5.0-8.8	6.9	8.5-11.4	10.0			5.0-11.4	7.4
Orifice Diametre	90.0-190.0	132.5	100.0-350.0	157.1	100.0-110.0	105.0	90.0-350.0	144.2	80.0-270.0	154.4	110.0-160.0	137.5	130.0-180.0	155.0			80.0-270.0	150
Dentate Width	1.4-2.2	1.7	1.0-2.9	2	1.3-2.2	1.75	1.0-2.9	1.9	1.7	1.7			2.1	2.1			1.7-2.1	1.9

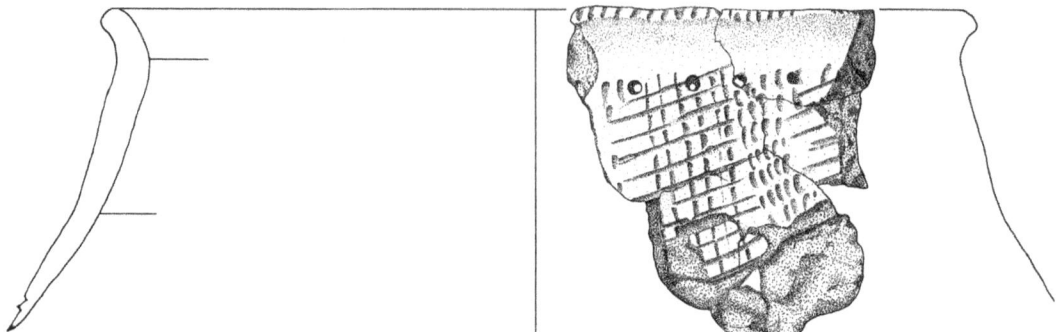

Figure 6.1 AlDf-24:163,164,165, Vessel Lot 11, Area C, N51W51, Level 3g (early Late Maritime Woodland).

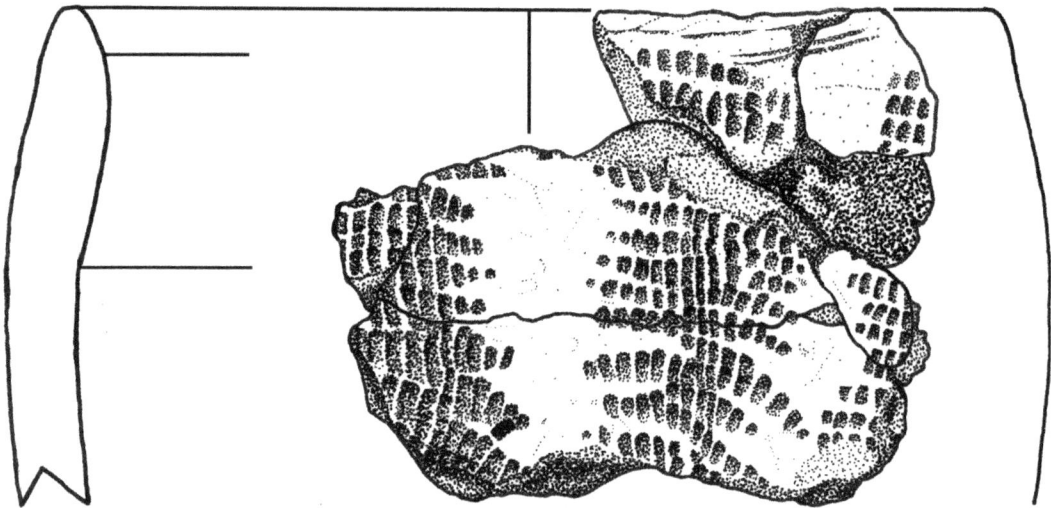

Figure 6.2 AlDf-24: 522, Vessel Lot 27, Area A, N52W50, Level 3m (Middle Maritime Woodland).

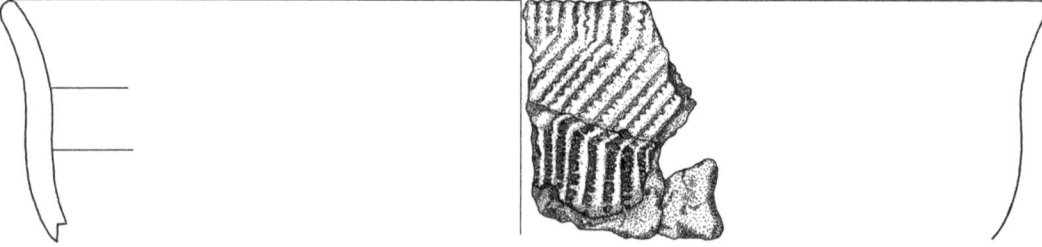

Figure 6.3 AlDf-24: 533, 557, Vessel Lot 31, Area A, N53W50, Level 3 and 3b (Middle Maritime Woodland).

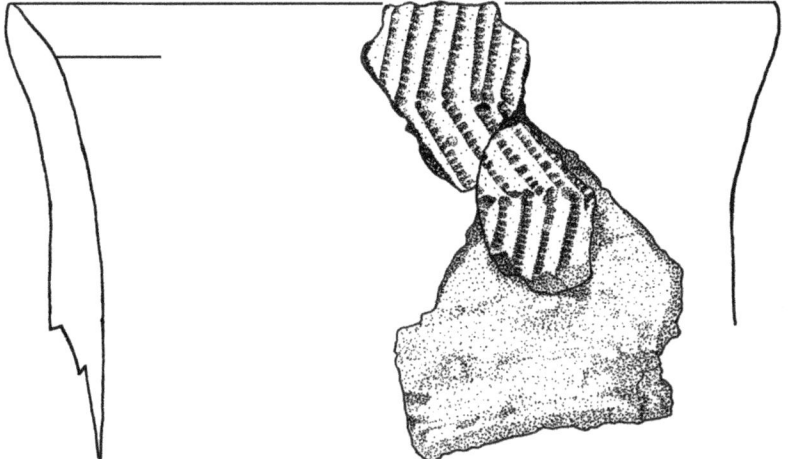

AlDf-24:7, VL. 46
Diam. = 14cm
August 22, 2013
E.I.

Figure 6.4 AlDf-24: 7, Vessel Lot 46, Area A, N56W50, Level 3D (Middle Maritime Woodland).

projections from the vessel rim and have been observed in several shapes among ceramic assemblages in the Northeast (see, for example, Curtis 2004b). All of the castellations in the E'se'get ceramic assemblage are round, without significant angularity or points. In addition, one of the vessels from AlDf-30, Area A Midden, exhibits a scalloped (crenellated) lip.

The E'se'get vessel rims exhibit a wide range in thickness, from just 2 mm to over 10 mm at the lip, and from 5 mm to over 11 mm when measured at 2 mm below the lip (table 6.3e). This variation is evident in both the Middle and Late Maritime Woodland assemblages, with no significant changes in size detected between the periods. Due to the fragmentary nature of the assemblages, it is not possible to determine the volume of each individual vessel, however, an estimate of the orifice diameter of each vessel provides some indication of size. The assemblage would appear to consist primarily of small vessels with orifice diameters ranging from 90 mm to 200 mm (table 6.3c). A couple of larger vessels are present—one from AlDf-24, Area A Midden, with a diameter of 350 mm, and one from AlDf-24, Area C (lower), with a diameter of 270 mm. It is possible that these larger-diameter vessels are from oval-mouthed pots, though we saw no indication of this in our analysis, and, to our knowledge, they have not been reported from the region.

Manufacture

The E'se'get ceramic vessels are overwhelmingly grit-tempered, including all vessels with rims in the Middle Maritime Woodland assemblages (table 6.3c). Shell temper appears in low frequencies in the Late Maritime Woodland; only three vessels from AlDf-24, Area C, had both grit and shell temper and only two vessels had exclusively shell temper. This pattern is confirmed by the all-sherds analysis (table 6.4). Grit temper was used exclusively in the Middle Maritime Woodland assemblages from AlDf-30 and AlDf-25. Shell temper is present in a very small number of sherds (less than 1 percent) in the AlDf-24, Area A, Middle Maritime Woodland assemblage, then increases in frequency in the Late Maritime Woodland assemblages in Area C. The frequency of shell temper is highest (76 percent) in the protohistoric level at AlDf-24; however, this may be skewed by the small sample size as all shell-tempered sherds may have come from the same vessel.

Figure 6.5 Examples of round and notched castellations in the E'se'get assemblage. A: AlDf-24:271, Vessel Lot 47, AlDF-24, Area A, Middle Maritime Woodland. B: AlDf-24:19, Vessel Lot 8, AlDf-24, Area C, early Late Maritime Woodland.

Table 6.4 All-sherds table. Summary of selected ceramic attributes on all sherds recovered during the E'se'get Archaeology Project.

		30: Area A Midden		25		30: House/Sweat		24A: Midden		24C: Lower		24C: Middle		24C: Upper (Feature 4)		8		30: Black Soil Midden		6		24C: Proto		24A: Feature 2		30: Area B Midden		35		31	
		#	%	#	%	#	%	#	%	#	%	#	%	#	%	#	%	#	%	#	%	#	%	#	%	#	%	#	%	#	%
Temper	Grit	471	100	33	100	1042	100	1315	99.47	117	56.8	71	74	28	29.2	147	91.3	157	100	43	100	9	18	53	35.9	147	100	10	52.6	27	100
	Shell	—	—	—	—	—	—	5	0.38	67	32.5	15	15.6	38	39.6	4	2.5	—	—	—	—	38	76	11	17.2	—	—	9	47.4	—	—
	Grit & shell	—	—	—	—	—	—	2	0.15	22	10.7	10	10.4	30	31.3	10	6.2	—	—	—	—	3	6	—	—	—	—	—	—	—	—
Interior Surface Modification	Smoothed	20	4.24	10	30.3	76	7.29	155	11.73	46	22.4	21	21.9	21	21.9	23	14.3	21	13.4	7	16.3	25	50	24	37.5	11	7.5	1	5.3	12	44.4
	Smoothed & fabric impressed	—	—	1	3	—	—	—	—	—	—	—	—	—	—	—	—	2	1.3	—	—	—	—	—	—	—	—	—	—	—	—
	Combed	—	—	—	—	—	—	—	—	33	16	16	16.7	3	3.1	1	0.6	—	—	—	—	2	4	—	—	—	—	—	—	—	—
	Indeterminate	291	61.78	11	33.3	609	58.45	826	62.48	81	39.3	33	34.4	41	42.7	78	48.4	85	54.1	14	32.6	11	22	35	54.7	92	62.6	14	73.7	13	48.1
Exterior Surface Modification	Smoothed	147	31.21	19	57.6	240	23.03	353	26.7	92	44.7	48	50	30	31.3	44	27.3	38	24.2	5	11.6	26	52	23	35.9	27	18.4	1	5.3	11	40.7
	Smoothed & fabric impressed	—	—	—	—	1	0.1	—	—	2	1	—	—	—	—	—	—	—	—	—	—	—	—	—	—	—	—	—	—	—	—
	Fabric impressed	—	—	—	—	—	—	2	0.15	—	—	—	—	—	—	—	—	—	—	—	—	—	—	—	—	—	—	—	—	—	—
	Indeterminate	164	34.82	3	9.1	444	42.61	626	47.35	66	32	21	21.9	35	36.5	58	36	70	44.6	16	37.2	12	24	36	56.3	76	51.7	14	73.7	14	51.9
Exterior Decorative Tool	Cord wrapped (total)	1	1.6	1	5.6	44	27.3	15	5.8	55	57.3	29	43.3	19	86.3	21	40.6	15	46.9	4	80	15	100	9	81.8	2	11.1	1	50	—	—
	Cord (total)	34	53.1	—	—	10	6.2	10	3.9	14	14.6	10	14.9	—	—	6	18.8	2	6.2	—	—	—	—	—	—	2	11.1	—	—	9	75
	Splint wrapped (total)	—	—	—	—	7	4.3	14	5.4	—	—	4	6	—	—	—	—	—	—	1	20	—	—	—	—	—	—	—	—	—	—
	Dentate (total)	29	45.3	17	94.4	75	46.6	193	75.1	—	—	7	10.4	1	4.5	4	12.5	8	25	—	—	—	—	2	18.2	14	77.8	1	50	3	25
	Incised lines (pointed tool?)	—	—	—	—	3	1.9	11	4.3	15	15.6	7	10.4	2	9.1	1	3.1	2	6.2	—	—	—	—	—	—	—	—	—	—	—	—
	Stamped lines (linear tool?)	—	—	—	—	19	11.8	—	—	—	—	—	—	—	—	—	—	3	9.4	—	—	—	—	—	—	—	—	—	—	—	—
	Punctates (pointed tool various shapes?)	—	—	—	—	3	1.9	14	5.4	12	12.5	10	14.9	—	—	6	18.8	2	6.2	1	20	—	—	—	—	—	—	—	—	—	—
	Total	64	100	18	100	161	100	257	99.9	96	100	67	99.9	22	99.9	32	75	32	99.9	5	100	15	100	11	100	18	100	2	100	12	100
Exterior Decorative Technique	Stamped	23	15.2	18	100	169	81.3	238	72.1	83	76.1	53	74.6	20	83.3	22	71	35	71.4	6	100	11	100	12	70.6	19	95	2	66.7	12	100
	Rocker-stamped	128	84.8	—	—	28	13.5	81	24.5	11	10.1	5	7	2	8.3	8	25.8	12	24.5	—	—	—	—	5	29.4	—	5	1	33.3	—	—

Table 6.4 All-sherds table. Summary of selected ceramic attributes on all sherds recovered during the E'se'get Archaeology Project (continued).

	30: Area A Midden		25		30: House/ Sweat		24A: Midden		24C: Lower		24C: Middle		24C: Upper (Feature 4)		8		30: Black Soil Midden		6		24C: Proto		24A: Feature 2		30: Area B Midden		35		31	
Push-pull					8	3.8					6	8.5																		
Incised					3	1.4	11	3.3	15	13.8	7	9.9	2	8.3	1	3.2	2	4.1												
Total	151	100	18	100	208	100	330	99.9	109	100	71	100	24	99.9	31	100	49	100	6	100	11	100	17	100	20	100	3	100	12	100
Total Number of Sherds	471		33		1042		1322		206		96		96		161		157		43		50		64		147		19		27	

An indication of the manufacturing method is found in the presence of coil breaks. Vessels that were built up by coiling ropes of clay may break at the coil joints. Shepard (1965: 183) notes that vessels only break along coils when they are poorly made, thus coil breaks may be evident on only a few vessels even if the technique of coiling was commonly used. A few vessels spread across the E'se'get assemblages do exhibit coil breaks indicating that coiling was used as a manufacturing method during both the Middle and Late Maritime Woodland periods (table 6.3; figure 6.6).

A variety of techniques were used to finish the surface of the vessel before firing. Most vessel interiors in the E'se'get assemblage are smoothed (table 6.3c). Indeed, this technique is used almost exclusively in the Middle Maritime Woodland assemblages. In the Late Maritime Woodland assemblages from both AlDf-24, Area C, and AlDf-30, Black Soil Midden, several vessels exhibit combing on the interior. This technique involves drawing a toothed implement across the surface to produce a pattern of parallel lines. These could be in a simple horizontal pattern or a more complex pattern with lines of different direction superimposed on one another (figure 6.7). The all-sherds analysis confirms these observations (table 6.3). All but one sherd from the Middle Maritime Woodland assemblages have smoothed interior surfaces. Smoothing continues to be the primary technique in the Late Maritime Woodland, but sherds with interior combing are well represented at AlDf-24, Area C. Likewise, for vessel exteriors, the majority in all assemblages are smoothed. A few vessels exhibit texturing by fabric impressions (table 6.3c, table 6.4).

Figure 6.6 Sherd exhibiting coil breaks. AlDf-24: 403, Vessel Lot 14, AlDf-24 Area C, early Late Maritime Woodland.

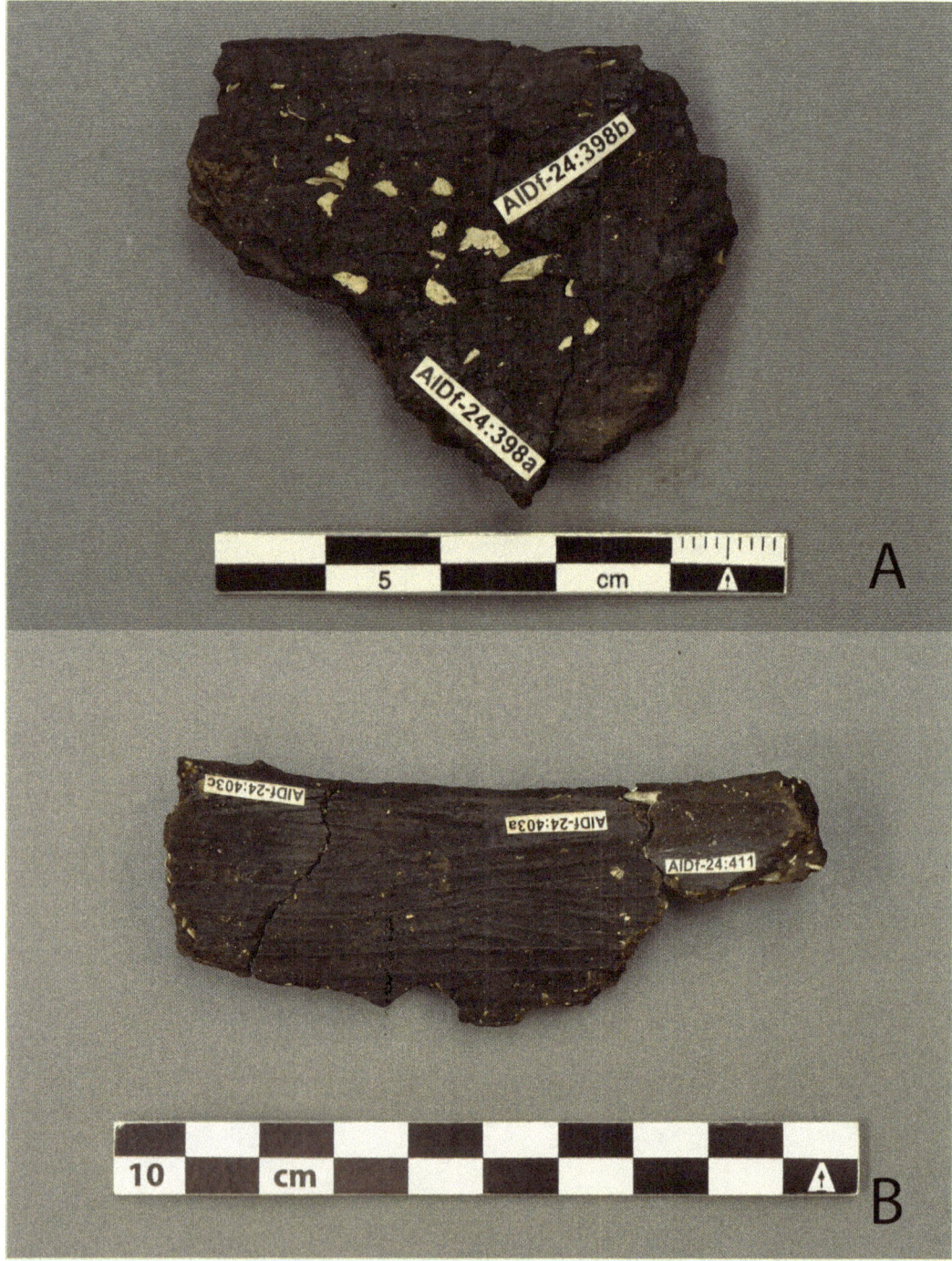

Figure 6.7 Sherds with combed interiors. A: AlDf-24: 398, Vessel Lot 20, AlDf-24, Area C, early Late Maritime Woodland. B: AlDf-24: 403, Vessel Lot 14, AlDf-24, Area C, early Late Maritime Woodland.

Decoration

The E'se'get vessels are decorated with horizontal bands of geometric-line decoration applied to the pot surface before firing. Bands are discrete areas of decoration that encircle the pot horizontally and here are numbered in sequence from the rim to the base of the pot (i.e., the uppermost band is the first band). Only one vessel has decoration on the interior. This vessel was found in the Middle Maritime Woodland Area A midden at AlDf-30, and the interior decoration consists of dentate-stamped left oblique lines (lines slanting upward toward the left). Most vessels have lip decoration, but the incidence is higher in the Middle Maritime Woodland assemblages, at 75 percent, than in the Late Maritime Woodland assemblages, where just over half (53 percent) of the vessels have lip decoration (table 6.3d).

Most of the vessels also have one or more bands of decoration on the exterior. Among more complete vessels, up to three bands of decoration have been observed (AlDf-24 vessels 31 and 46, for example; figures 6.3, 6.1, and 6.8). While nine vessels have plain first exterior bands (figure 6.9), subsequent bands may be decorated, as is the case for seven of these vessels. The remaining two vessels are broken at the upper rim and may well also have been decorated on the portions that are missing. Thus, the presence of plain vessels in the assemblages is uncertain due to the fragmentary nature of the rims that often break near the bottom of the first decorative band. Interestingly, all of the vessels with plain first exterior bands are from AlDf-24 with examples in both Middle Maritime Woodland and Late Maritime Woodland contexts.

Tools

A variety of tools were used to create the decoration on the E'se'get assemblage vessels (tables 6.3d and 6.4). Unfortunately, the tools could not be confidently identified in all instances, and where they could not, they were excluded from the analysis. Nevertheless, the variety of tools is well illustrated by the Middle Maritime Woodland assemblage from AlDf-24, Area A, which includes examples of all the tools present in the entire E'se'get assemblage (table 6.3). Among vessels with rims, the dentate tool is the most common in the Middle Maritime Woodland assemblages—46 percent of vessels exhibit use of the dentate tool in the first exterior band, and 64 percent of those with the second exterior band preserved exhibit the use of this tool (figure 6.8a). The cord-wrapped-stick is the second-most common tool used in the first exterior band at 19 percent overall among Middle Maritime Woodland assemblages (figure 6.5a); it is highest in the AlDf-30 Middle Maritime Woodland assemblage, at 44 percent (table 6.3d). Cord-wrapped-stick becomes the most common tool in the Late Middle Woodland assemblages where 43 percent of vessels exhibit the use of this tool in the first exterior band (figure 6.6).

These patterns are confirmed by an examination of all sherds as presented in table 6.3. This table records the tool used on each individual decorated sherd, including those not associated with a rim sherd. Here it is evident that the dentate tool is again the most common choice in each of the Middle Maritime Woodland assemblages and cord-wrapped-stick is present in all Middle Maritime Woodland assemblages in small amounts. The cord-wrapped-stick tool dominates in the Late Maritime Woodland assemblages, while the dentate tool is present in some, but not all the assemblages.

Figure 6.8 Sherds with complex multiple exterior bands. A: AlDf-24: 533, 557, Vessel Lot 31, AlDf-24, Area A, Middle Maritime Woodland. B: AlDf-24:7, Vessel Lot 46, AlDf-24, Area A, Middle Maritime Woodland.

Figure 6.9 Rim sherd with a plain first exterior band. AlDf-24 C: 207, Vessel Lot 35, AlDf-24 C, early Late Maritime Woodland.

The all-sherds table also indicates the presence of knotted cordage used as a decorative tool in several of the sherds (table 6.4, "Cord"). In these cases, the cord appears to have been knotted along its length, with large, closely spaced knots. The cord was impressed in repeating horizontal or vertical orientations on the body of the vessel (figure 6.10) by hand, without the aid of a stylus or stick, likely by holding the cord tight between the thumb and fore-finger of both hands.

The E'se'get assemblages also include several examples of vessels decorated with a rare tool, the splint-wrapped-stick (figure 6.11). This tool was first identified by Smith and Wintemberg (1929) in assemblages from Merigomish, Nova Scotia. Smith recreated the tool, which is a simple stick wound with squarely cut splint (in this case bark), and then demonstrated the decoration it produced on a small tablet of clay (Smith and Wintemberg 1929: 45, plate IX, figures 12 and 15). Despite its identification by the earliest professional archaeologists in the province, this tool has not subsequently been reported in Nova Scotia. Given its presence at Port Joli as well as Merigomish, it is likely that this tool is present in other Maritime assemblages but has been lumped in with the cord-wrapped-stick tool that produces very similar impressions. These tools may be distinguished by the smooth and square-edged impression of the splint, which lacks the internal texturing and rounded edges created by the fibres and twist of cordage.

Figure 6.10 Rim sherd exhibiting evidence of knotted cord decoration. AlDf-24: 208, 210, 211, 213, Vessel Lot 3, AlDf-24, Area C, early Late Maritime Woodland.

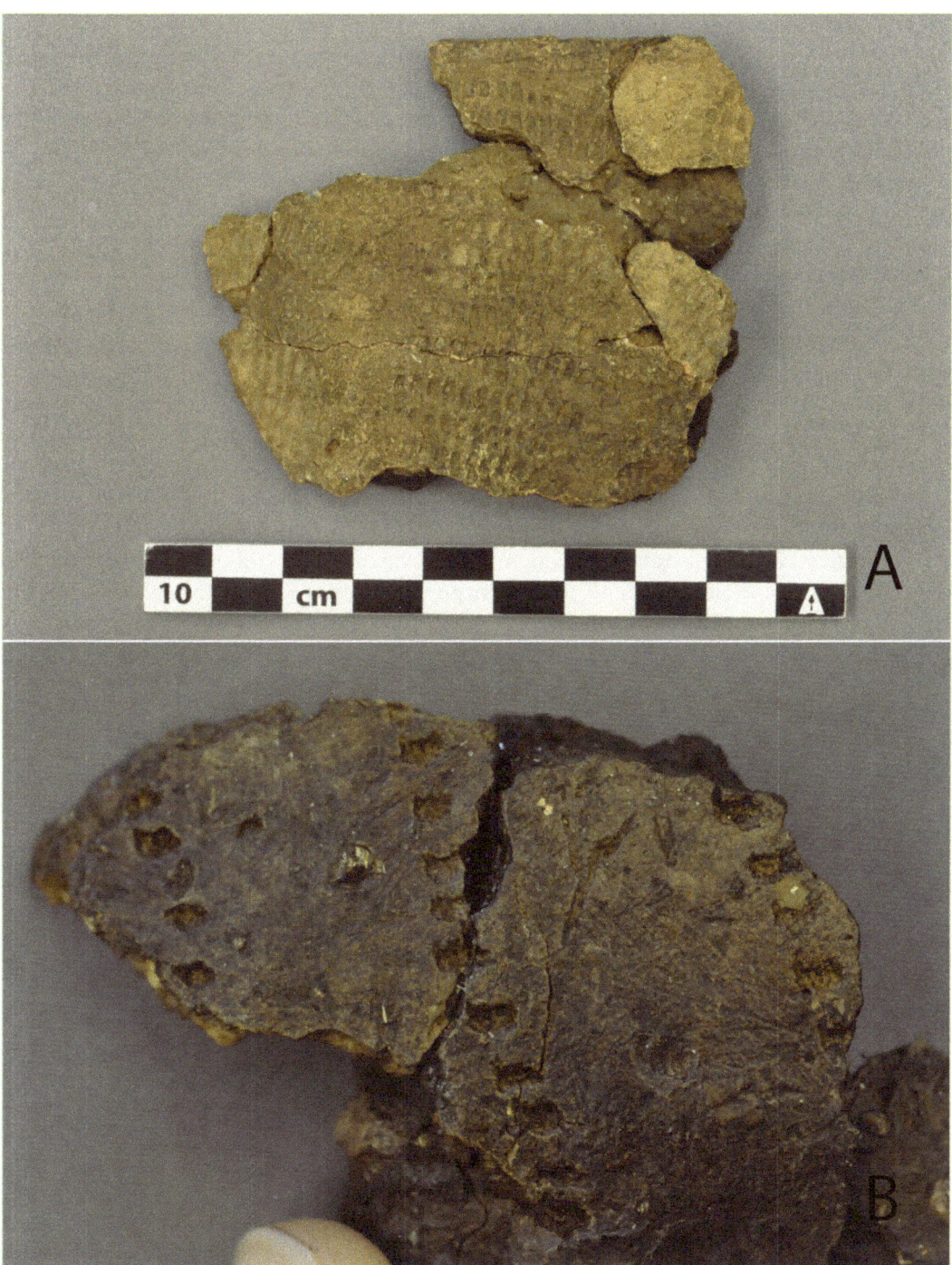

Figure 6.11 Sherds with evidence of splint-wrapped-stick decoration. A: AlDf-24:522,526, Vessel Lot 27, AlDf-24, Area A, Middle Maritime Woodland. B: AlDf-24:206, Vessel Lot 10, AlDf-24, Area C, early Late Maritime Woodland.

Technique

Most of the tools were applied with a simple stamping technique throughout the Middle and Late Maritime Woodland periods while rocker-stamping and incising were employed occasionally (table 6.3d). The all-sherds table (table 6.4) confirms this pattern as well as indicating the occasional use of the push-pull technique. In the all-sherds table, the Area A shell midden assemblage from AlDf-30 shows a high incidence of rocker-stamping in contrast to the vessel rims, but this may be due to the presence of numerous sherds from one or two individual vessels.

Configuration

The tools and techniques presented above were used to produce lines and punctates that were arranged in geometric configurations within bands encircling a vessel. Bands of oblique lines slanting upward toward the right ("right obliques") and bands of vertical lines are the most common configurations in both the Middle and Late Maritime Woodland assemblages (table 6.3d). The Late Maritime Woodland assemblages differ in that they show a higher incidence of plain lips and plain first exterior bands. More complex designs such as plaits, superimposed lines, and horizontal difference (where the configuration of the lines changes along the band) are present in small amounts (table 6.3d, figures 6.1, 6.2, and 6.12).

Punctates are discrete, non-linear impressions, created by the end of a tool stamped into the clay. Most commonly, we think of circular punctates, created by a pointed tool, but the end of the tool could vary in shape to produce punctates of different shapes, such as polygonal or semi-annular. Punctates were used in two different ways by potters in the

Figure 6.12 Evidence of sherds with very complex design elements, including superimposed (A, C), plaits (B), horizontal differentiation (D). AlDf-24: 163, 164, 165, 276, Vessel Lot 11, AlDf-24, Area C, early Late Maritime Woodland, B: AlDf-24:387, Vessel Lot 34, AlDf-24, Area A, Middle Maritime Woodland, C: AlDf-24:572, Vessel Lot 32, AlDf-24, Area A, Middle Maritime Woodland. D: AlDf-24: 208, 210, 211, 213, Vessel Lot 3, AlDf-24, Area C, early Late Maritime Woodland.

Northeast: in decorative strings and as delimiters (Smith 2011). For decorative strings, punctates were arranged to create vertical, oblique and horizontal rows that were in turn used to fill a decorative band in a similar way to the linear tools. Punctates were also used as delimiters (see next section).

In the E'se'get assemblage, punctates were occasionally used as strings to fill a decorative band in a similar way to the linear tools. At AlDf-24, two vessels have lips decorated with vertical punctate strings, one vessel has horizontal punctate strings in the second exterior band (figure 6.13), and another vessel exhibits a complex decorative motif in the second exterior band that combines horizontal punctate strings with incised lines (figures 6.4 and 6.12). The all-sherds table presents additional sherds decorated with punctate strings (table 6.3, "Punctates"). While most of the punctate-decorated sherds appear to come from AlDf-24, this is likely simply a reflection of the relatively large size of the assemblage.

Delimitation

Delimiters are decorative elements that were used to mark boundaries between different contours of the vessel or different decorated areas (Curtis 2004a; Latta 1980: 161; Smith 2011). Delimiters are distinguished from bands on the basis of relative width; they are distinctly narrow with respect to the wider decorated bands on the vessel. Delimiters were produced using a variety of elements such as horizontal lines, punctates of various forms, and bosses.

While a few vessels from the Middle Maritime Woodland assemblages at Port Joli exhibit delimitation (12 percent), the incidence of delimiters increases substantially among the Late Maritime Woodland assemblages (47 percent). The kind of delimiters that were

Figure 6.13 Sherd with punctates in the second exterior band. AlDf-24: 74, 75, Vessel Lot 49, AlDf-24, Area C, early Late Maritime Woodland.

used also changes over time. In the AlDf-24, Area A (Middle Maritime Woodland) assemblage, two vessels are delimited with single horizontal lines and two with rows of shallow punctates (figure 6.14). One vessel in the Late Maritime Woodland assemblage at AlDf-24 also has shallow punctates, but the rest of the delimited Late Maritime Woodland vessels each have a row of deep punctates that produce bosses on the interior of the vessel rim (figure 6.15).

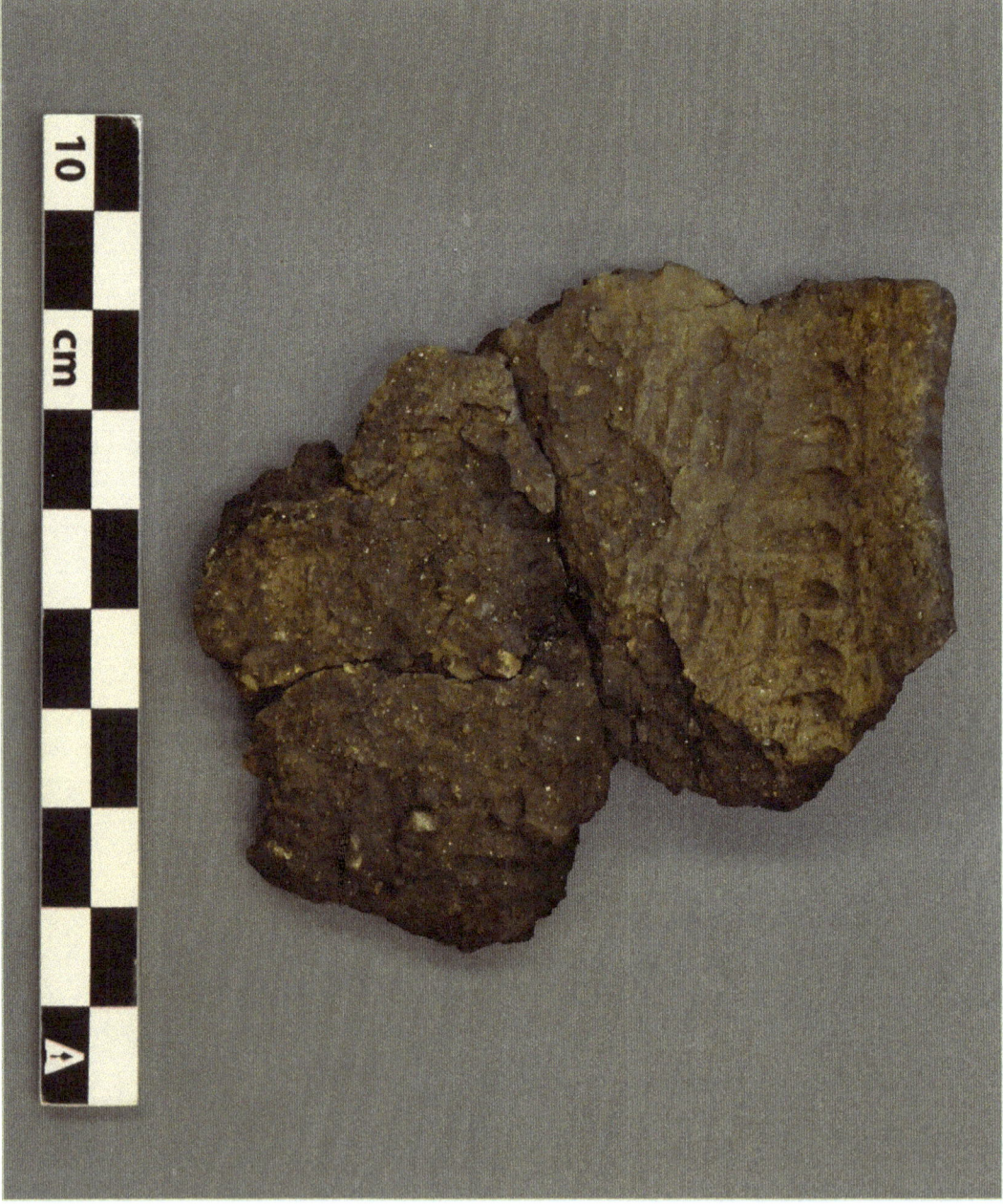

Figure 6.14 A Middle Maritime Woodland rim with a delimiter. AlDf-24:706, Vessel Lot 38, AlDf-24, Area A.

Figure 6.15 Deep punctates used as a delimiter. AlDf-24: 562, 567, Vessel Lot 33, AlDf-14, Area A, Late Maritime Woodland.

Comparison with the Petersen and Sanger Ceramic Sequence

Our analysis of the E'se'get ceramic assemblages indicates support for James Petersen and David Sanger's (1991) observations for many attributes (see table 6.1 above for a summary of their observations), but also some differences. Given the well-dated contexts of the assemblages, these provide new key insights into chronological and spatial variation in ceramic attributes on the Maritime Peninsula.

Manufacture

Petersen and Sanger (1991: 137) note that grit temper is characteristic of CP 3, and this is certainly reflected in the E'se'get assemblages where the vast majority of vessels are grit-tempered (tables 6.3c and 6.4). They identify the possible appearance of shell-tempered ceramics during CP 3 (Petersen and Sanger 191: 137); this is supported by the very small number of shell-tempered sherds at AlDf-24, Area A. While shell temper does increase in CPs 4 and 5 as described by Petersen and Sanger (1991: 142, 144), it does not become the dominant form in the E'se'get assemblages despite the coastal setting of the Port Joli sites. Kristmanson (1992) also noted this regional variation in the use of shell temper, finding that there was only a slight increase in southwestern Nova Scotia before a return to predominately grit-tempered vessels.

In terms of exterior-surface modification, Petersen and Sanger (1991: 139, 143) describe the reappearance of "fabric-paddled" vessels in CP 3, with increasing use of this technique through CPs 4 and 5. The use of exterior fabric-impression occurs very rarely in the E'se'get assemblages for CP 3, with one example in each of the AlDf-24 and AlDf-30 Middle

Maritime Woodland assemblages, but it continues to be rare through CPs 4 and 5 (tables 6.3c and 6.4).

Of note regarding interior surface treatments is the use of combing (or channelling with a toothed implement) in a CP 4 context at AlDf-24, Area C (tables 6.3c and 6.4). As Petersen and Sanger (1991: 133) describe, this technique is normally associated with CP 2. Its occurrence at AlDf-24 may thus represent a regional resurgence of this distinctive technique. This seems particularly unusual as the toothed implement typically used for combing is a dentate tool, and the decorative tool commonly used in CP4 is the cord-wrapped-stick. In fact, the AlDf-24, Area C, vessels with interior combing are all decorated with the cord-wrapped-stick tool. Kristmanson (1992) noted a similar occurrence of interior combing (channelling) on cord-wrapped-stick-decorated vessels in CPs 4 to 7.

Overall, the E'se'get assemblages exhibit a greater continuity in the production of smooth-surfaced, grit-tempered vessels compared to the shift toward textured surfaces and shell-tempered vessels described by Petersen and Sanger for Maine and the Maritime provinces overall.

Form

The common vessel form across the Petersen and Sanger (1991) sequence is the conoidal vessel with collarless, out-flaring rim and rounded lip. This form is certainly represented by the majority of the ceramics in the E'se'get assemblages. The changes noted by Petersen and Sanger in CPs 3 and 4 include a trend toward thicker rims and vessel walls, with the appearance of pots with thickened rims or low collars starting in CP 3 and continuing into later periods. As with the manufacturing attributes, the E'se'get assemblages exhibit greater continuity across CP 3 to CPs 4 and 5 than is observed within the Petersen and Sanger sequence. The lip- and rim-thickness ranges and averages are very similar in the CPs 4 and 5 assemblage compared to CP 3 (table 6.3e). Although the rim-thickness range is slightly greater in CPs 4 and 5, the average is slightly less than in CP 3.

Collared vessels are very rare at the sites around the harbour at Port Joli, with one example in the CP 3 assemblage from AlDf-24, Area A, and one from the undated Area B midden at AlDf-30 (table 6.3a, figure 6.16). Petersen and Sanger (1991: 133) note the presence of castellations in CP 2 and CP 3 assemblages in Maine and the Maritime provinces, but do not indicate whether or not castellations were observed in CP 4 and CP 5 assemblages. At Port Joli, castellations are present in both CP 3 and CPs 4 and 5 (table 6.3a).

Decoration

Petersen and Sanger identify several significant trends with respect to the use of decorative tools and techniques across the ceramic sequence for Maine and the Maritime provinces that may be further investigated with the well-dated E'se'get ceramic assemblages. They note that dentate tools became the dominant type of tool in CP 3 with the decrease or disappearance of the pseudo-scallop-shell tool that was common in CP 2 (Petersen and Sanger 1991: 137). This trend is clear in the E'se'get assemblages, where the earliest assemblage dates to CP 3, and the pseudo-scallop-shell tool is absent from all the assemblages (tables 6.3d and 6.4). The dentate tool is indeed the most common tool used on the CP 3 vessels.

Figure 6.16 A collared rim sherd. AlDf-24: 39, Vessel Lot 60, AlDf-24, Area A, Middle Maritime Woodland.

Petersen and Sanger (1991: 137) also observe "a notable increase in tooth size on dentate stamping tools" in CP 3 compared to CP 2. The Northeast Woodland Pottery Analytic Code (Smith 2011) provides a method for quantifying this change. The width of the tooth impression is measured for up to ten individual impressions and used to calculate the mean width for dentate teeth in the decorative band. While no CP 2 contexts are present in Port Joli, table 6.3b presents the metric data on the size of dentate teeth used in the first exterior decorative band in the E'se'get assemblages, in the hopes that future ceramic studies will also measure this attribute so that quantitative comparisons may be made between CP 2 and CP 3 assemblages.

With respect to decorative techniques, Petersen and Sanger (1991: 137) state that rocker-stamping was the favoured technique of application during CP 3, yet this is not evident at Port Joli. Here, simple stamping remains the dominant form. Rocker-stamping is present in low frequencies in both the AlDf-24 and AlDf-30 assemblages, as represented by vessels with rims (table 6.3d). The all-sherds table (table 6.4) represents a similarly low frequency of use of this technique, with the exception of the CP 3 assemblage from AlDf-30 where 85 percent of the sherds are rocker-stamped. This may simply be due, as indicated above, to the presence of many sherds from one or two rocker-stamped vessels.

Alternatively, the contrast between vessels with rims (table 6.2) and the body sherds (table 6.3) may indicate that rocker-stamping was a decorative or texturing technique applied more often to the bodies of vessels while simple stamping was used to create a clear motif around the rim of the vessel. This pattern is in fact evident in several of the vessels illustrated by Petersen and Sanger for CPs 2 and 3. In their figure 7.7 (Petersen and Sanger

1991: 129), for example, they show a CP 2 vessel from the Eddington Bend site in Maine on which the upper rim is decorated with a double horizontal row of punctates, while the remainder of the vessel is covered with dentate-rocker-stamping. The rocker-stamping lacks distinct patterning and thus has the effect of texturing the exterior surface rather than creating a distinct decorative motif. A similar effect is evident in Petersen and Sanger's (1991: 140) figure 7.9 showing a CP 3 vessel from the Great Diamond Island site in Maine, where dentate-rocker-stamping covers the body of the vessel in general form.

Similar examples are found in the E'se'get assemblages, as illustrated in figure 6.19. In these cases, dentate-rocker-stamping may be more appropriately considered a surface modification used to create a textured surface comparable to that of the fabric-impressed vessels found in later periods. These observations also indicate the value of using a fine-grained attribute-analysis approach, such as Smith's Northeast Woodland Pottery Analytic Code, that distinguishes individual decorative tools and techniques and links them to particular locations on the vessel. This approach facilitates the recognition of more complex patterns in ceramic decoration as opposed to classifying a vessel overall as simply "dentate-rocker-stamped."

Changes in decoration continue into CP 4, as Petersen and Sanger (1991: 143) describe: use of the dentate tool decreases and the cord-wrapped-stick becomes the dominant tool. This trend is clear in the E'se'get assemblages (table 6.3d), following Petersen and Sanger's (1991: 139) observation: "The possible appearance of cord-wrapped-stick decoration during CP 3 is noted at some Maine-Maritime sites . . . but this circumstance remains uncertain given the indirect associations in each of these exceptional cases." The use of cord-wrapped-stick in CP 3 is confirmed by the well-dated and stratigraphically controlled E'se'get ceramic assemblages: several vessels decorated with this tool are present in securely dated contexts at both AlDf-24, Area A, and AlDf-30, Area A Midden. Bourgeois (1999) also identified the use of the cord-wrapped-stick tool during CP 3 in the coastal portion of the Saint John River Valley.

Petersen and Sanger (1991: 142) recognize the use of punctates as delimiters in combination with cord-wrapped-stick-stamped decoration in CP 4: "systematically placed, and more or less discrete punctuations of a uniform cylindrical form, became a hallmark attribute along with cord-wrapped-stick decoration . . . these punctuations . . . represent a broad scale ceramic horizon style across a large portion of northeastern North America when associated with cord-wrapped-stick decoration."

Interestingly, at Port Joli we can see the elements of this horizon style already present in CP 3—the cord-wrapped-stick tool was in use and delimiters were present in the form of incised horizontal lines or shallow punctates. Subsequently we see in CP 4 that these elements are consistently combined and refined (deeper, more discrete, circular punctates) to form the observed horizon style (figures 6.13 and 6.15). These observations indicate continuity in the ceramic sequence around Port Joli's harbour along with participation in widespread interaction networks leading to the emergence of this ceramic style over such a broad area.

Conclusion

Four seasons of archaeological fieldwork on seven archaeological sites around the harbour at Port Joli yielded a series of well-dated assemblages representing the late Middle Maritime Woodland to the Protohistoric periods. Six years of detailed attribute analyses of fifty-five vessels with rims and thousands of individual sherds revealed a clear local homogeneity in vessel form and manufacture that produced conoidal, collarless vessels with straight to out-flaring rims, tempered predominantly with grit, and finished with smooth surfaces. Comparisons with the Petersen and Sanger sequence confirm this local homogeneity as shifts to shell temper, changes in wall thickness, and the use of complex decorative techniques (e.g., rocker- and drag-stamping) seen elsewhere in Maine and the Maritime Peninsula are not well represented.

Regardless, the E'se'get assemblages confirm some aspects of the Petersen and Sanger sequence, such as the shift from dentate to cord-wrapped-stick tool use in the Late Maritime Woodland Period. At the same time the cord-wrapped-stick tool was clearly present in the late Middle Maritime Woodland assemblages around Port Joli's harbour, limiting its use as a horizon marker (see Chapter 4). Use of this tool simply increased during the subsequent Late Maritime Woodland Period and was combined with the development of delimitation using deep exterior punctates. This indicates that, while extremely conservative in their approach to ceramic manufacture, the E'se'get potters were also participating in the development of ceramic styles across the broader Northeast.

A previously under-recognized decoration technique, splint-wrapped-stick was detailed in this analysis. First identified by Smith (in Smith and Wintemberg 1929: 45, plate XI, figure 14) in assemblages from Merigomish, its appearance in Port Joli may indicate a broadly regional tool form not common in other regions of the Maritime Peninsula. It is important to point out that because of its similarity to cord-wrapped-stick implements, the splint-wrapped-stick impression may be present in other assemblages but has simply been conflated with cord-wrapped-stick decoration. More research is necessary to explore the variability in the distribution of this tool type, but it is important to note that despite its identification nearly ninety years ago, to our knowledge it has so far only been identified in Nova Scotia.

Furthermore, the presence of knotted cord (used without a stylus or stick) as a decorative technique is extremely rare on the Maritime Peninsula (figure 6.10). In fact, we know of only one other instance that a "manipulated single cord design" appears on a pottery sherd from the region; one sherd from the Eel Weir site in central Nova Scotia exhibited this form of decoration (Kristmanson and Deal 1993: 76). Given the proximity of the Eel Weir site to Port Joli (it is almost directly inland from the site and easily reachable by known traditional water routes (e.g., Pentz 2008), it is tantalizing to speculate on the relationships between interior versus coastal occupations/populations. A variety of knotted-cord decoration is known from the Atlantic seaboard (e.g., Egloff and Potter 1982; Herbert 2009), so its presence in Nova Scotia is not entirely singular, though it is highly unusual on the Maritime Peninsula. One possible explanation for the rarity of this attribute is that many analyses may have included sherds decorated with this tool in a general category of fabric-impressed or cord-wrapped-stick sherds. Regardless, the clear identification of this attribute at Port Joli provides impetus for renewed scrutiny of collections for this rare (or perhaps overlooked) trait.

In conclusion, our results indicate a clear stability and continuity in the form and manufacture of ceramic vessels across the Middle to Late Maritime Woodland transition at Port Joli. However, greater variability is evident in the decoration of ceramic vessels. While a variety of decorative tools are represented throughout the assemblages, a shift in popularity from dentate in the late Middle Maritime Woodland to cord-wrapped-stick in the Late Maritime Woodland is evident following trends in the broader Northeast. Comparison with James Petersen and David Sanger's observations confirms the homogeneity in form and manufacture within the local ceramic sequence around Port Joli's harbour, as well as participation in broader-interaction networks through which information and trends in ceramic style circulated.

Appendix A: Ceramic Plates from E'se'get Archaeology Project Contexts

Figure 6.17 Selected AlDf-24, Area A, Middle Maritime Woodland rims and body sherds. From top left to bottom right: AlDf-24:566 (V.L. 30); 553,557a,b (V.L. 31); 522,526 (V.L. 27); 706 (V.L. 38); 7,11 (V.L. 46); 3,5 (V.L. 45); 387a (V.L. 34); 19 (V.L. 47); 562,567 (V.L. 33); 572a,b (V.L. 32); 699 (V.L. 34); 693a (V.L. 34); 709 (V.L. 53); 700a,d (V.L. 43); 42 (V.L. 61); 521b,1pc (V.L. 39); 22a (V.L. 34); 23 (V.L. 27); 599b (V.L. 51); 605a,b (V.L. 37); 39 (V.L. 60); 690a (V.L. 72); 39a (V.L. 24); 527a (V.L. 71); 387e (V.L. 34); 521 (V.L. 39); 690d (V.L. 72); 493; 45b (V.L. 70); 583; 1192; 41; 45 (V.L. 70); 625c,d (V.L. 65); 498a; 568b (V.L. 41); 711 (V.L. 57).

Figure 6.18 Selected AlDf-06 rims and body sherds. From top left to bottom: AlDf-6:45a (V.L. 4); 35 (V.L. 3); 27; 31 (V.L. 2).

Figure 6.19 Selected AlDf-08 rims and body sherds. From top left to bottom right: AlDf-8:69 (V.L. 8); 72a (V.L. 5); 22 (V.L. 2); 68 (V.L. 4); 67a (V.L. 4); 74a (V.L. 6); 94a (V.L. 10); 61c (V.L. 3); 80 (V.L. 7); 55 (V.L. 1); 61b (V.L. 9); 59a (V.L. 7).

Figure 6.20 Selected Late Maritime Woodland AlDf-24, Area A, Feature 2 rims and body sherds. From top left to bottom right: AlDf-24: 538 (rim, V.L. 68); 551 (V.L. 68); 536; 549.

Figure 6.21 Selected Protohistoric AlDf-24, Area C, levels 1 and 2 body sherds. From top left to bottom right: AlDf-24:1159; 400,434 (V.L. 17); 241 (V.L. 12); 329 (V.L. 7); 290a; 140b.

Figure 6.22 Selected later Late Maritime Woodland AlDf-24, Area C, Feature 4 (levels 3 and 3b) rims and body sherds. From top left to bottom right: AlDf-24: 305 (V.L. 1); 194 (V.L. 6); 98 (V.L. 4); 181 (V.L. 1); 122; 360a; 147a; 96b; 100a.

The Ceramic Assemblage **203**

Figure 6.23 Selected Late Maritime Woodland AlDf-24, Area C, (levels 3c to 3e) rims and body sherds. From top left to bottom right: AlDf-24: 910a; 460; 459; 472; 388; 346; 391; 1077a; 385a,b; 1076a; 1083a; 1075a; 1078b; 345; 465; 1077b; 1077c; 386; 467; 269; 1078a; 1080a.

Figure 6.24 Selected early Late Maritime Woodland AlDf-24, Area C (levels 3f to 3k) rims and body sherds. From top left to bottom right: 163, 164, 165 (V.L. 11); 403, 411 (V.L. 14); 75c (V.L. 49); 398 (V.L. 20); 396 (V.L. 23); 414 (V.L. 14); 276a (V.L. 8); 74 (V.L. 49); 281 (V.L. 13); 280 (V.L. 13); 274c; 278a (V.L. 54); 166 (V.L. 9); 273 (V.L. 14); 399 (V.L. 59); 64b.

The Ceramic Assemblage **205**

Figure 6.25 Selected Middle Maritime Woodland AlDf-25 rims and body sherds. From top left to bottom right: AlDf-25:10 (V.L. 3); 8c (V.L. 1); 7/8 (V.L. 1); 5 (V.L. 2); 8a (V.L. 1); 8b (V.L. 1); 5b (V.L. 2); 4 (V.L. 1); 3.

Figure 6.26 Selected later Late Woodland AlDf-30 (levels 1-2c) rims and body sherds. From top left to bottom right: AlDf-30:200a (V.L. 21); 66,341 (V.L. 6); 1000 (V.L. 31); 860 (V.L. 37); 854 (V.L. 36); 1009; 272 (V.L. 7); 678a (V.L. 3); 208 (V.L. 22); 970 (V.L. 12); 755; 760 (V.L. 41); 686 (V.L. 39); 967; 680.

Figure 6.27 Selected Middle Maritime Woodland AlDf-30 (levels 3 to 4) rims and body sherds. From top left to bottom right: AlDf-30: 838 (V.L. 6); 110,126c (V.L. 3); 416a (V.L. 5); 500 (V.L. 34); 802 (V.L. 7); 377 (V.L. 25); 547a,b (V.L. 26); 567a (V.L. 11); 292 (V.L. 24); 398 (V.L. 6); 526 (V.L. 9); 567a (V.L. 11); 292 (V.L. 24); 398 (V.L. 6); 526 (V.L. 9); 268 (V.L. 23); 319 (V.L. 32); 317; 495f (V.L. 33); 307; 526 (V.L. 9); 167 (V.L. 5); 526a (V.L. 7); 936 (V.L. 38); 179 (V.L. 20); 282a (V.L. 39a); 498; 422; 314 (V.L. 42); 47a; 47b; 378.

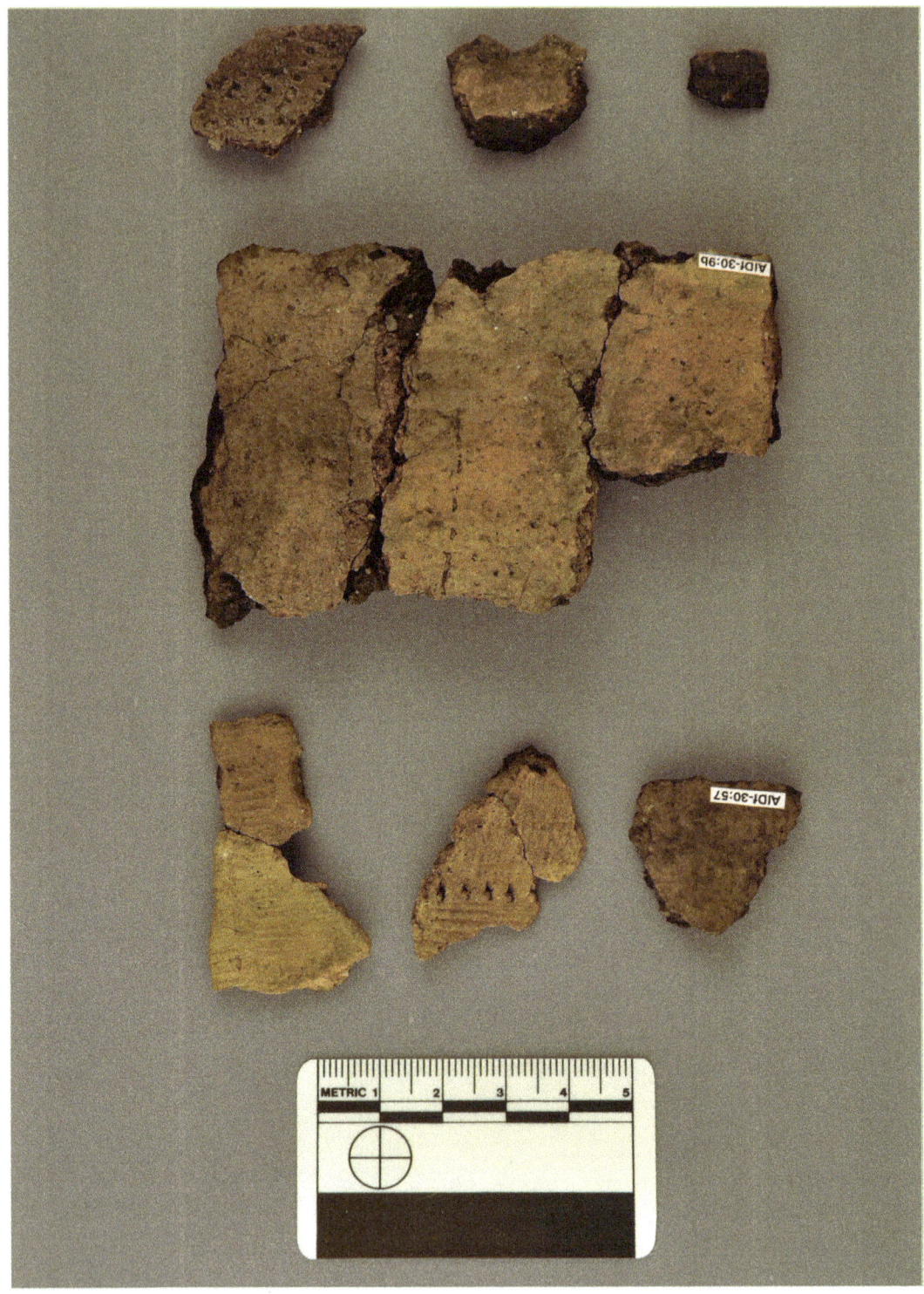

Figure 6.28 Selected Middle Maritime Woodland AlDf-30 (Area A Midden) rims and body sherds. From top left to bottom right: AlDf-30:5 (V.L. 18); AlDf-30:64 (V.L. 1); 7; 9,9a,9b,12 (V.L. 2); 73,76 (V.L. 1); 73f,77 (V.L. 1); 57.

Figure 6.29 Selected Maritime Woodland AlDf-30 (Area B Midden) rims and body sherds. From top left to bottom right: AlDf-30: 674a (V.L. 35); 673 (V.L. 35); 661 (V.L. 35); 666a; :661 (V.L. 35); 661 (V.L. 35); 660 (V.L. 40); 644 (V.L. 27); 619; 622a.

Figure 6.30 Selected Middle Maritime Woodland AlDf-31 rims and body sherds. From top left to bottom right: AlDf-31:1a-d,5a-b (V.L. 1); 7a (V.L. 2); 8b (V.L. 3).

Figure 6.31 Selected body sherds from AlDf-35. From top left to bottom right: AlDf-35: 4 (V.L. 2); 1a (V.L. 1); 1d (V.L. 1).

Appendix B: Ceramic Plates from Port Joli legacy Collections

Figure 6.32 Selected Middle Maritime Woodland AlDf-25 rims and body sherds.

Figure 6.33 Selected early Late Maritime Woodland AlDf-03 rims and body sherds.

Figure 6.34 Selected later Late Maritime Woodland AlDf-07 rims and body sherds.

The Ceramic Assemblage 215

Figure 6.35 Selected later Late Maritime Woodland AlDf-08 rims and body sherds.

Figure 6.36 Selected Late Maritime Woodland AlDf-01 rims and body sherds.

Figure 6.37 Selected Late Maritime Woodland AlDf-11 body sherds.

Chapter 7
Lithic Technology and Other Artifacts

MATTHEW BETTS AND KENNETH R. HOLYOKE

Introduction

Compared to the extent (and duration) of previous avocational excavations by John Erskine and Eric Millard at Port Joli, the E'se'get Archaeology Project excavations were relatively modest in scope. However, because of our rigorous excavation methods and strict screening protocols, the material recovered during the E'se'get Project was almost overwhelming in quantity and diversity, resulting in 22,271 artifacts (including debitage and ceramics). Our goal with the E'se'get Project was to define a detailed culture history for Port Joli, and careful documentation of the local material-culture tradition is a critical component of this goal. Therefore, the analysis that follows focuses less on pattern recognition (though patterns are elucidated when possible) and instead prioritizes description and illustration. As such, the chapter is accompanied by dozens of artifact plates (see Appendix A, figures 7.2 to 7.46). Due to the sheer number of tools and artifacts recovered during this project, it was not feasible to describe each item in-text, however, for the purposes of reference—and to address what we see as a problematic omission in some monographs—all of these tools are depicted graphically. The decision to include in-text references to specific catalogue numbers/artifacts was to highlight classes or specific artifacts that were unique due to material, technology, or context, or because they were particularly illustrative for the discussion of their particular site or context.

The analysis of the artifact assemblage was conducted at the Canadian Museum of History in Gatineau, Quebec, facilitated by an artifact loan from the Nova Scotia Museum between 2008 and 2016. Detailed information pertaining to formal (e.g., projectile points, bifaces, unifaces, cores) and informal (e.g., retouched and utilized flakes) categories of tools, including lithic material type and colour, morphometrics, and detailed descriptions, were completed. Unfortunately, detailed debitage classification (e.g., material type and colour, morphometrics, stage of manufacture) could not be completed for all sites before the loan was required to be returned. As a result, information that can normally be gleaned from detailed debitage analyses (e.g., technological organization, mobility, and lithic economies) is not available. Descriptions of lithic material types and concentrations are largely based on tools; thus, what follows is a largely observational account of the lithic tool industries employed in Port Joli and should be considered preliminary.

The relatively large legacy artifact collection created by Erskine's and Millard's work in Port Joli could not be analyzed in the same detail as the E'se'get collection, due to time constraints. However, the Nova Scotia Museum permitted photography of the legacy material, and the assemblages are presented here as artifact plates for comparative purposes (Appendix B: figures 7.48 to 7.71).

Lithic Analysis Considerations

No standardized and universally adopted lithic typology exists for the Maritime provinces, and researchers have tended to use unique schema and attribute-based typologies (e.g., Allen 1981; Davis 1978; Foulkes 1981; Holyoke 2012; Sheldon 1988; cf. the reduction sequence approach in Burke 1993, 2000), combined with aspects of Ritchie's (1971) seminal Northeastern stone-tool typology. It is generally accepted that many of the projectile points used in the Maritime Woodland Period on the Maritime Peninsula are related to types prevalent throughout the Northeast, but few researchers have attempted to truly assess the variability in the region against these large typologies (cf. Robinson 1996). For example, while it is clear that "Madison"- and "Levanna"-style (Ritchie 1971) projectile points penetrate the Maritime Peninsula in the Late Maritime Woodland Period, they are infrequent; yet unstemmed triangular bifaces—occasionally interpreted as preforms (Burke 2000, 2007; Holyoke 2012)—are common and fit within what might be an expected shape range for Madison- or Levanna-style points (cf. Fox 2015). It is less clear what the relationships are between stemmed and notched points used in the greater Northeast and those from the Maritime Peninsula (and Port Joli). The corner-notched (and possibly side-notched) projectile points from Jack's Reef, New York, (Ritchie 1971; Snow 1980) are characteristic of Middle and early Late Woodland sites in much of New England, found in contexts dating to between as early as 1700 years ago and as recent as 1000 years ago (e.g., Goodby 2013; Rieth 2013). A substantial number of corner- and side-notched points were recovered in contemporaneous Middle and Late Maritime Woodland deposits during the E'se'get Project work and are described in this chapter; however, none of these conform to the Jack's Reef "type." Furthermore, despite evidence that corner- and side-notched projectile points may be sorted chronologically elsewhere in the Maritime Peninsula (with side-notched predating corner-notched points—e.g., Blair 1997; Leonard 1996; Nash and Stewart 1990—or, depending on the site, in the opposite order—e.g., Burke 2000), points from the E'se'get Project do not appear to sort chronologically (see discussion below). Thus, without regional-level analysis of these trends, it is difficult to adopt a standardized chrono-typological approach, or even to adopt other schema.

Simply put, more research is needed, and at the risk of obfuscating the situation further, we have of necessity developed our own attribute-focused lithic typology to conduct our analysis. Like many other classificatory typologies (e.g., Banning 2000), this taxonomic approach to typology is progressive and mutually exclusive to avoid multiple classifications, which can complicate quantification of the material. The E'se'get stone-tool typology can be seen in figure 7.1. Worthy of note is that for a selection of sites, debitage stage of manufacture was completed; this is reported in this chapter as categories of "primary" (larger flakes over 5 mm exhibiting cortical remnants, weathering, or large flat platforms), "secondary" (flakes over 5 mm), and "tertiary" (flakes under 5 mm). While staged classification of this nature can be imprecise, it does offer the ability to further interpret certain lithic material trajectories and general production strategies at sites.

A note is necessary about the "uniface" or "scraper" classification (figure 7.1: Stage A, 1.a.iii) used in this chapter. Many of the unifacial scrapers recovered from Port Joli are of a type commonly known as "thumbnail" scrapers (e.g., Bourque 1971; Foulkes 1981) due to their extremely small size and oval or circular shape. Generally, these may be classed as

Stage A: Tool

Stage B: Debitage

Stage A, Classification Levels 1-2
1) Uniface
    a. Flake Tool
        i. Projectile Point *
        ii. Drill
        iii. Scraper
        iv. Retouched Flake
        v. Utilized Flake
    b. Core Tool
        i. Unidirectional
        ii. Multidirectional

* Unused in E'se'get Analysis

2) Biface
    a. Hafted
        i. Projectile Point
        ii. Drill
        iii. Scraper
        iv. Knife
    b. Other
        i. Drill (hand)
        ii. Scraper (spall)
        iii. Preform
            (Bifacial, thin, possible retouch, just final to prior shaping)
        iv. Blank
            (Bifacial, thick, no retouch, requires thinning to make a tool)

Stage A, Attribute Classification
Hafting Element:
    1) Flake Platform
    2) Flaked Straight
        a. Side-Notched
        b. Corner-Notched
        c. Stemmed
        d. Plain
    3) Flaked Convex
        a. Side-Notched
        b. Corner-Notched
        c. Stemmed
        d. Plain
    4) Flaked Concave

Retouch:
    1) Unimarginal (one surface only)
    2) Bimarginal (both surfaces)

Scraper Shape:
    1) Circular
    2) Semicircle (lunar)
    3) Oval
    4) Rectangular
    5) Triangular
    6) Irregular
    7) Indeterminate

Stage B, Classification
Debitage

    1) Flake
        a. Proximal Flake
        b. Flake Shatter
    2) Non-Flake
        a. Angular shatter

Debitage Stage
    1) Primary Flake
        a. Cortex present
        b. Cortex not present
    2) Secondary Flake
    3) Tertiary Flake

Figure 7.1 Stone tool typology used for the E'se'get Archaeology Project.

end scrapers (or endscrapers) but it is unclear in the literature if thumbnail scrapers must include a striking platform *and* be oval or circular in shape. We have observed that breakage patterns, especially transverse breaks, appear to create the oval shape of a small number of these thumbnail scrapers, and some seem to have started life as large triangular or rectangular unifacial tools. For this reason, we do not classify any of the scrapers as "thumbnails," preferring instead to simply describe their shape and attributes. The function of thumbnail scrapers has been debated in the literature, but they were likely a general-purpose tool used for a variety of hide, wood, reed, bone, and antler shaping and finishing tasks. Some almost absurdly small scrapers were recovered in Port Joli, which are difficult to envision being used for anything but fine woodworking or basketry.

Lithic material was difficult to classify in our lithic analysis. Four basic varieties dominated the assemblages: quartz, quartzite, rhyolite, and multicoloured chert. Without access to a comprehensive comparative collection of regional lithic materials, we developed a comprehensive colour-coding typology, which we applied to all material types. This typology is designed to split colour varieties rather than lumping them together in broad categories; the rationale here was that they may be aggregated at a later date if necessary. The types and colour varieties can be seen in Supplementary Table 1a, along with the typological analysis (available for download from the Canadian Museum of History's online catalogue, under this book's title). For example, the cherts with pink, tan, and stippled grey/white groundmass are likely all the same material, or are the same material with different weathering, and we suspect they likely all come from the same source: Mesozoic-aged cherts originating in the Minas Basin area on the Bay of Fundy coast of Nova Scotia (hereafter referred to as "Minas Basin Multicoloured Cherts" [Black 2004] or, more simply, "Minas Basin cherts" [e.g., Gilbert et al. 2005]). However, without comparable artifacts, petrographic descriptions, or geochemical analyses to verify this, it is better to base our material classification on direct observations rather than hypotheses.

Quartz was ubiquitous and abundant in all sites and, as documented below, most cores were made from this material. It is clear from our survey of Port Joli's harbour and adjacent harbours that quartz cobbles are available in every river, stream, and beach, and thin veins of quartz are common in the bedrock outcrops and glacial erratics that dot the landscape. It is therefore likely that most, if not all, of the quartz in the assemblages was obtained locally. Blackish grey rhyolite, which often weathers to a green-grey cortex, was observed (though rarely) along cobble beaches and rocky river banks, and, therefore, some of the rhyolite material in the archaeological sites may also have been obtained locally.

We observed no chert sources in our landscape surveys and we are aware of none that have been identified in the Queens or Shelburne counties of Nova Scotia, nor are any reported on bedrock maps for the area (White 2012a, 2012b, 2012c). The bulk of the chert material is therefore likely derived from the Bay of Fundy shore sources, especially those near Minas Basin, including the Scots Bay and Blomidon quarries. However, with the assistance of reference artifacts, we were able to identify two possible "exotic" New Brunswick–chert material types in the assemblage and one potential exotic material from the northeastern Cape Breton coast. The chert described as "red with light grey bands and mottling" (see Supplementary Table 1a) is likely Partridge Island (Nova Scotia) chalcedony. A variety of chert described as "bluish grey with grey mottling, and bands" may be

Washademoak Multi-coloured Chert originating in New Brunswick (Black and Wilson 1999), though the identification here is somewhat more tentative. The Partridge Island material is more abundant and is found in contexts spanning the early Late Maritime Woodland to Protohistoric contexts, while the Washademoak material was only identified in one specimen, from a later Late Maritime Woodland context. Material described as chert that is "brown with black flecks," "dark brown with black-and-white mottling," and "dark brown with black mottling" appears to be consistent with variants of Ingonish Rhyolite, originating from Ingonish Island, off the northeast coast of Cape Breton Island. This material is ubiquitous in assemblages from the central portion of Nova Scotia and Cape Breton, and is found throughout Prince Edward Island (e.g., Keenlyside and Kristmanson 2016). A final lumped category of material called "chert/rhyolite" was created for materials that were of indeterminate lithic type, and therefore possibly chert or rhyolite. As a result, it includes multiple distinctive lithic types, all of which are dark grey. Chert/rhyolite is represented by only small quantities of artifacts but is present in all sites described herein, with the exception of A2009NS27-1 and AlDf-35.

Finally, metric attributes were obtained on the 547 tools identified in the E'se'get assemblages (see Supplementary Table 1b, available for download from the Canadian Museum of History's online catalogue, under this book's title). These were derived from standardized attribute lists promoted by Whittaker (1994), and are meant to provide *general* information on the size, shape, and characteristics of the tools. Detailed metric attributes (such as edge angles) were not obtained, as defining specific production and maintenance strategies was not a goal of this chapter.

AlDf-06 (AlDf-05)

As described in Chapter 3, artifact recovery was very limited from the test units excavated at AlDf-06, a result of the long period of cultivation and the resulting fragmentation and collecting that has occurred at the MacAdam Garden site. Nevertheless, enough lithic material was recovered to provide some indication of the lithic technology used and maintained at the site.

One complete projectile point was recovered from the site, made on an opaque, thinly banded quartz, which is common in Port Joli. The point has a convex base, shallow corner notches, and slightly convex blade edges. Deep retouch, creating an almost serrated appearance, is present (see Appendix A, figure 7.2). Like most projectile points recovered on the E'se'get Project, this point was quite small (see Appendix B).

Three biface tip fragments were recovered; one with relatively straight edges was made from an olive tan quartzite, while the other two were made of blackish grey rhyolite, a type of material that commonly occurs in Port Joli sites.

Unifaces

Four formed unifaces (see Appendix A, figure 7.2, third and fourth row down, left and right), often labelled "scrapers" (or, more formally end scrapers/endscrapers) in the region (e.g., Leonard 1996: 64) were recovered from AlDf-06—a relatively high number given the limited nature of the testing conducted. All were lenticular to oval in shape and were generally unimarginal (unilateral) with steep retouch on one distinctly convex edge. One specimen, AlDf-06:36, has bimarginal (bilateral) retouch along two contiguous convex margins. All four scrapers are relatively small, with the largest specimen having a maximum length of 34.85 mm and the smallest having a maximum length of only 15.39 mm. The scrapers are all made from multicoloured fine-grained chert, none of which is immediately identifiable, but which are consistent with the variety of multicoloured cherts available along the Bay of Fundy shore and, in particular, the Minas Basin area.

A large number of retouched and utilized flakes were recovered. Six of eight retouched flakes were made from multicoloured fine-grained chert, while the remaining two were made on the local opaque banded quartz. The thirty-seven utilized flakes represent a much larger range of materials, including fine- and coarse-grained cherts, rhyolite, and quartzite. Interestingly, no utilized flakes were made from quartz.

Debitage and Cores

A significant quantity of debitage was recovered from the meagre excavations at AlDf-06 (see Chapter 3), representing 591 artifacts. An array of materials similar to the unifaces was recovered, but with a distinct emphasis on quartz; detailed lithic material categorization for debitage was not completed for AlDf-06. One very small (maximum length of 28.95 mm), completely spent, multidirectional quartz core was also recovered (see Appendix A, figure 7.2).

Ground-Stone Artifacts

A unique lithic tool recovered from AlDf-06 (see Appendix A, figure 7.3) is a small ground-stone adze or celt, made on a basalt beach or river cobble. This represents the only relatively complete ground-stone specimen recovered during the entire E'se'get Archaeology Project. It appears to have been prepared with minimal effort and was roughly flaked on a distal working edge and then ground. Despite the extreme rarity of celts in the E'se'get assemblages, John Erskine (1962: plate II, plate IV; 1986: 91) described similar adzes from AlDf-25 (Port Joli No. 3), AlDf-14 (Timber Island Brook; not discussed in this book), and AlDf-08 (Port Joli No. 7).

Other Artifacts

Consistent with the historical use of the site as a family garden and, later, a recreational area, some recent and historical material was recovered from this mixed deposit. These included eleven fragments of window glass, probably twentieth-century in origin. A small fragment of historic red earthenware that was recovered could have been deposited at any point throughout the nineteenth or twentieth century. In addition to some unidentifiable iron fragments, a wire nail was also recovered, suggesting a deposition sometime in the twentieth century. In general, the impression was that the site did not have a visible historic component until the nineteenth century, and possibly not until its use as a family garden during that period.

AlDf-06 Discussion

Chert, rhyolite, quartz, and quartzite were recovered from AlDf-06, representing a remarkable array of materials. Unfortunately, while debitage was abundant, the quantity of formalized tools recovered (e.g., bifaces and scrapers) was low, a result of repeated disturbance and collecting in the deposit. However, some observations are possible. For example, it is notable that there are a remarkably high number of retouched and utilized flakes at AlDf-06 for such a small assemblage of tools (14.8 percent retouched flakes and 68.5 percent utilized flakes and accounting for 83.3 percent of the assemblage). Also worthy of note is the lack of quartz scrapers and utilized flakes despite the preponderance of quartz debitage. In fact, only four out of the fifty-four tools (7.4 percent) recovered were composed of quartz, suggesting a surprising emphasis on higher-quality lithic materials (e.g., cherts and rhyolites).

The contrast between the number of tools and the debitage may be related to three factors. First, quartz is highly visible in the black soil of the deposit (see Chapter 3), and may have been easier to spot by collectors who picked up tools after each ploughing of the field, resulting in fewer formal quartz tools recovered during our excavation. Second, the ploughing itself may have resulted in greater breakage of the more friable quartz material than the more durable cherts and rhyolites represented at the site. The lack of organic tools is almost certainly a result of this mechanical attrition over many generations of gardening. Finally, and perhaps most likely, the preponderance of quartz debitage may be related to the poor quality of the raw material, which has many fracture and cleavage planes. Significant reduction may have been required to produce a single useable flake, let alone a specimen large and stable enough for bifacial flaking, which might have resulted in an overabundance of quartz debitage relative to the number of tools. This latter observation can be tracked in less disturbed deposits, as will be demonstrated below.

Despite these observations, it is worth noting that parallels that can be drawn between the high proportion of informal scraping tools (utilized and retouched flakes) in this site assemblage and in other E'se'get sites (below). The high numbers of these tool categories may be reflective of the types of activities at the site (e.g., scraping hides, making baskets, woodworking); however, they could also hint at the "organization of prehistoric social labor" along gender roles (Gero 1991: 164).

A2009NS27-1

Only three artifacts were recovered from the small 25 × 25 cm unit at A2009NS27-1 (not shown). Two small secondary flakes (no retouch or use-wear was present) made on a grey/white mottled chert were recovered. Additionally, a fragment of a Hostess Munchies (ketchup flavour) chip bag was recovered from a depth of 14 cm from the root mat just above the cultural layer. The bag dates to the late twentieth century and indicates some disturbance of the uppermost sod and active layers of the site. The flakes were recovered from levels 1 and 3, respectively; only Level 3 showed no signs of prior disturbance.

AlDf-08

The very limited test excavations (a single 1 × 1 m test unit) at AlDf-08 resulted in an extremely large lithic assemblage. Thirty-eight lithic tools were recovered from the test unit, including many retouched or utilized flakes, in addition to a significant quantity of debitage.

Projectile Points and Bifaces

Four bifaces were recovered from the unit, primarily from the lower levels of the deposit. One of these is the base of a relatively large triangular projectile point with a deeply concave base (see Appendix A, figure 7.4, top right), conforming to the Levanna-style projectile points described by Ritchie (1971). Unusually, it is made on a bright white "bull" quartz (MacDonald 1994), one of the better varieties found locally. Though broken and missing approximately two-thirds of the tip, it was clearly a large point, with a maximum width at the base of 30.31 mm, but relatively thin, with a maximum thickness of 5.94 mm.

The second projectile point from the deposit is a nearly complete corner-notched (or corner removed) specimen with a convex base and relatively straight blade edges, made from blackish grey rhyolite (see Appendix A, figure 7.4, top left). At 40.78 mm, its maximum length is unusually long for a projectile point in Port Joli. Its crudeness is also relatively unusual, though there does appear to be a correlation between cruder points and the black rhyolite material, perhaps a function of its flaking qualities.

The remaining two bifaces are broken tips made from opaque white quartz. The two bifaces appear to have been reworked into scrapers, with the most unusual (see Appendix A, figure 7.5, top left) being a fragment of a reworked Levanna-style point base—possibly the tip fragment from the Levanna-style base described above. One corner, or "ear" of the base of this former projectile point was preserved, as well as part of the concave hafting portion. The retouched scraper edge was flaked from approximately the midline of the former Levanna point, presumably where it broke. This tool is made on a relatively fine-grained multicoloured brown chert, similar to other scrapers described below. The second tool (see Appendix A, figure 7.5, top right) was reworked from the base of a seemingly small, leaf-shaped biface (likely a former projectile point) made from opaque white quartz.

Unifaces

A total of twelve unifacial scrapers were distributed throughout the deposit (fourteen scrapers in total were found, including the two reworked bifaces). Seven of these (see Appendix A, figure 7.5) could be classified as small distal-end (or thumbnail) scrapers, while the remainder, including the reworked bifaces, are larger distal-end scrapers. The larger distal-end scrapers are variously triangular, rectangular, or circular/oval in shape. All have convex working edges, and most have unimarginal retouch, but one triangular scraper made from quartz and the reworked Levanna point base (figure 7.5, top left) have bimarginal retouch. Only two of the distal-end scrapers are made from quartz, while the remainder are made on high-quality brown, pink/red, or tan multicoloured cherts.

Curiously, three of the seven smaller scrapers are broken transversely, at right angles to the long axis of the flake, possibly during use. One of these artifacts, made from a green chert (figure 7.5, bottom row, right), has substantial cortex showing and, given its features, was created from a very small water-rolled pebble of chert. Materials include pink/red multicoloured cherts probably from the Minas Basin Area, as well as brown, tan, and grey/white fine-grained cherts. Only three of the scrapers were made from quartz, and all were an opaque, bright white variety without banding.

Unlike in AlDf-06, only one retouched flake was recovered from the unit, in addition to twelve utilized flakes. These were made from a range of rhyolites in addition to the quartz and chert, including the standard (presumably local) blackish grey rhyolite.

Debitage and Cores

A very large quantity of lithic debitage (748 artifacts) was recovered using a 3 mm mesh screening protocol (used on all shell-bearing black soil midden deposits). As in most deposits from Port Joli, quartz dominated the materials recovered, but multicoloured chert and dark rhyolites were very common. This is a remarkable quantity of debitage for such a small unit, which speaks to the possible amount of lithic reduction taking place at the site, especially for quartz. The quartz debitage indicates a relatively even distribution of primary, secondary, and tertiary flakes, indicating that all forms of raw material reduction, tool production, and likely maintenance occurred at the site. We observed few primary flakes in the rhyolite and chert debitage, suggesting material largely came to the site as blanks, preforms, or finished pieces before being reworked.

Consistent with the quartz-dominant debitage, six small and completely exhausted quartz cores were recovered. Three of the cores were multidirectional while the other three were unidirectional (see Appendix A, figure 7.6). Shapes were variable, suggesting that core preparation and flake removal was not standard, as flakes of various sizes were opportunistically removed. The presence of cortex on two of these small cores indicates that sources were likely small nodules and cobbles found throughout the region—either removed from various small quartz seams in bedrock and glacial erratics, or small cobbles from beaches or riverbanks.

Other Artifacts

No ground-stone artifacts were recovered from the test unit, and despite excellent organic preservation, no worked bone, tooth, or antler implements were encountered.

AlDf-08 Discussion

The artifacts recovered from AlDf-08 indicate an impressive array of stone tools and debitage for such a small excavation, indicating an intensive occupation focused on the manufacture and/or maintenance of lithic tools. The large number of lithic tools recovered from the 1 × 1 m test unit permits an inspection of spatial patterning. The densest concentration of tools occurs in levels 3d (26 percent) and 3e (33 percent), and is also associated with the most formal tools (i.e., all bifaces come from these levels, and over half of the scrapers (eight) come from this level). All cores (exclusively composed of quartz) are associated with levels 3d (one core), 3e (four cores), and 3f (eleven cores). As discussed in Chapter 3, these levels are likely associated with a house floor; those same levels demonstrate the densest concentration of lithic debitage from the deposit. House floor deposits in Port Joli tend to be characterized by high-density concentrations of stone tools, pottery, and lithicdebitage.

Lithic materials indicate a similar array of types as found at other sites in Port Joli, including (for tools only) fifteen artifacts made of chert, six made of rhyolite, and fourteen made of quartz. Worthy of note were two scrapers recovered from the unit that exhibited bifacial flaking: one a reworked chert Levanna-style projectile point base and the other a reworked quartz biface, which was likely a former projectile point as well. This may point to a conservation of workable lithic material, which is intriguing given that one of the artifacts is made on locally available quartz (see discussion below). A blackish grey rhyolite is only found in levels 3b and below, and is used almost exclusively for utilized flakes and for one corner-notched projectile point. It is possible that the point was manufactured on site, and the debitage may have been kept to use for tools as part of an effort to conserve non-local materials. It is notable that chert is present in all levels *except* for 3f (with only one tool) and is relatively evenly distributed. Quartz is absent in the uppermost level (Level 2) and most common in levels 3d and 3e, which are also associated with the only cores collected on site.

Mirroring patterning observed at AlDf-06, there are a large number of utilized flakes (14, or 36 percent) and scrapers (14, or 36 percent) in the AlDf-08 assemblage, representing nearly 75 percent of the entire tool assemblage for all levels. This suggests that cutting and scraping activities—likely associated with butchery, hide preparation, or perhaps birchbark work or basketry production—were critical activities at the site. As stated for AlDf-06, it is possible these industries are tied to social behaviours (e.g., gender roles) associated with domestic activities, something that has been explored with higher-resolution components from the E'se'get Archaeology Project (e.g., Hrynick et al. 2012; AlDf-24, Area C, discussion below).

AlDf-35

As with A2009NS27-1, the small test unit (about 25 × 25 cm) excavated at this site did not result in significant quantities of artifacts (not shown). However, given the small nature of the excavation, the recovery of two flakes, one a primary reduction flake and the other a secondary thinning flake (both made from a grey and white chert), and seven pieces of debitage (for which no material categorization was completed) is notable. No ground-stone or organic artifacts were recovered from the site.

AlDf-24, Area A Midden

For analysis purposes, the AlDf-24, Area A, midden is divided into two contexts. The first is the largest portion of the deposit, a large, approximately 1 m deep Middle Maritime Woodland shell midden, which is largely undifferentiated and composed of alternating layers of complete and coarsely crushed soft-shell clam valves with limited soil development. The other context (AlDf-24, Area A, Feature 2) appears to be a Late Maritime Woodland house floor, which was slightly disturbed by later historic activity.

The two deposits were subjected to different screening protocols, which may have affected lithic recovery. The Area A midden was screened through 6 mm mesh while the living-floor was subjected to 3 mm screening protocols. The latter would obviously enhance the recovery of debitage, though likely not the recovery of lithic tools which tend to be somewhat larger. It should be noted, however, that bulk-sample analysis of the midden deposits, which represents 100 percent recovery, suggest that very few cultural lithics were represented in the Area A midden (see below), indicating that the patterns discussed here are largely comparable.

Projectile Points

One projectile point was recovered from AlDf-24, Area A (see Appendix A, figure 7.7, top left, AlDf-24:28) from the basal layer in the main portion of the midden (N56W50). The point, made from opaque white quartz, was unlike any other projectile point recovered during the Port Joli excavations. It was missing its tip, but the point was small and narrow, with slightly flaring shoulders (the lateral edges were almost parallel) and a slightly contracting stem that terminated on a small striking platform with potential cortex. In many respects, it is like Terminal Archaic (prior to ca. 3500 cal BP) projectile points from elsewhere in the Maritime Peninsula, but the radiocarbon dates from this deposit (see chapter 3) do not support this interpretation. It would appear, then, to be a somewhat atypical Middle Maritime Woodland stemmed point, although it is tempting to consider it an item, possibly even a curated one, from an earlier period.

Bifaces

Three tip fragments were recovered from the AlDf-24, Area A, excavations, all from relatively small bifaces. Only one of the tips (see Appendix A, figure 7.7) was made from chert, a pinkish multicoloured variety, while the other two were made from the ubiquitous blackish grey rhyolite and opaque white quartz, respectively. Six biface base fragments were also recovered, three manufactured from white opaque quartz and three from a more translucent, banded quartz. All are fragmentary, so the shapes of the bifaces are difficult to determine, but one (AlDf-24:560) had a relatively straight base, with nearly straight lateral edges. The remainder appear to have convex or slightly convex bases, and all were likely projectile point preforms or, given their relative thinness, potentially unstemmed bifaces characteristic of the Late Maritime Woodland elsewhere (e.g., Holyoke 2012).

Unifaces

A unique unifacial artifact, a graver—a flake "with a small, sharp projection that has been created by unifacial retouch" (Gramly 2000: 31)—made from a black chert with brown flecks, was recovered from the midden (see Appendix A, figure 7.7, bottom right). The distinct distal spur had been retouched to a hard, sharp point. Opposite the obvious spur is another smaller spur in the location of the presumed base of the tool. The retouch here could represent some sort of preparation for hafting, but if so, the base would be particularly uneven. In any case, the remnant of the flake platform can also be seen in this area of the artifact.

The remaining unifacial artifacts include eleven utilized flakes, two of which are made on multicoloured cherts, two on white quartz, and seven on blackish grey rhyolite. Only one retouched quartz flake was recovered from the main Area A midden.

Cores, Hammerstones, and Debitage

Four relatively large cores were recovered from the Area A midden (see Appendix A, figure 7.8). All were large and exhibited fewer flake removals than cores from the adjacent Area C. Three were manufactured from an opaque white quartz and were unidirectionally flaked, and all exhibited evidence of cortex. One large core, made from a greyish green chert with abundant iron-stained cortex, was unidirectionally flaked (figure 7.8, top left).

The wear on the cortex of this core suggests it was water-worn and may have been collected from the rivers and streams that feed Port Joli's harbour, or from a nearby cobble beach. The size and condition of these cores (ranging in maximum length from 36.3 mm to 64.2 mm) are strikingly different from the very small, spent cores recovered from subsequent Late Maritime Woodland contexts, such as AlDf-24, Area C, and AlDf-08.

One oval-shaped hammerstone (see Appendix A, figure 7.9) was recovered, made from a basalt river or beach cobble. Its proximal and distal ends were significantly battered, and its size suggests it likely would have been used for primary reduction or raw material testing.

For such a large excavation, very little debitage was recovered, totaling only 182 flakes and pieces of shatter. Quartz was the primary material represented, but blackish grey rhyolite and several pieces of multicoloured chert were also present.

Other Artifacts

Four fragments of ochre were recovered, three of which were tiny fragments or nodules. One of these artifacts stands out because it appears to show evidence of grinding. The specimen (see Appendix A, figure 7.10, bottom) is relatively large, about 10 × 10 mm, about 2 mm thick, and rectangular in shape. One flat surface exhibits marks from a natural cleavage plane, presumably when the mineral was removed from a larger parent specimen, but the reverse side and one edge exhibit wear consistent with grinding or polishing. This specimen may have been rubbed against a palette to create ochre powder or may have been rubbed directly on the surface intended for decoration.

A highly corroded rolled metal bead (see Appendix A, figure 7.11, left) was recovered from a depth of 92.5 cm. Originally believed to be copper, the bead was constructed from a thin sheet of hammered iron rolled into a tight tube. The artifact is very similar to "short tube" copper beads recovered from archaeological sites in New Brunswick, including Ministers Island (BgDs-10), the McKinley site, and Augustine Mound (CfDl-2) (see discussion in Leonard 1996: 82). Iron beads are completely unique on the Maritime Peninsula, and in fact are very rare in North America. However, a number of meteoritic beads have been recovered from a network of Middle Woodland (ca. 2200–1550 cal BP) sites in Ohio and Illinois, including Moundville (Ohio), Seip (Ohio), Turner (Ohio), and Havana (Illinois) (Carr and Sears 1985). We were unable to test if the AlDf-24, Area A midden, bead was meteoritic, but the potential connection to these other sites is tantalizing. Long-distance trade is known for sites throughout the Maritime Peninsula, especially for the Early Woodland Period, and it possible that these trade networks persisted into the Middle Woodland Period. What is perhaps most intriguing is the question of how this potentially very rare (and presumably valuable) bead ended up in a large processing and clam-drying midden in Port Joli.

Organic Artifacts

Two bone awls were recovered from the processing midden. The first was constructed from the second metatarsal of a caribou (see Appendix A, figure 7.10, top) and was preserved in excellent condition. The second awl was constructed on a terrestrial mammal long-bone splinter (species unknown, but likely ungulate), and was heavily worn at the distal end (figure 7.10, second from top). A bird tibiotarsus (species unknown) had a small hole cut or chipped into the lateral margin near the midpoint of the diaphysis (figure 7.10, third from top); its function remains a mystery. One beaver incisor was recovered from the midden (figure 7.10, fourth from top). It was broken at approximately midpoint along its length (presumably where it entered the alveolus of the beaver skull), and is a typical modified chisel implement, ground to a very sharp working edge.

Composite Artifacts

In 2008, we encountered a clay deposit associated with a soft-shell clam valve while excavating in the Area A midden, at a depth of about 34 cm. The light brown clay was raw and had no discernable inclusions except for large flecks of charcoal. The shell was a left valve (with chondrophore) and had been deposited on end, unusual for this stratigraphic layer. The clay had spilled out of the valve and had mingled with larger chunks of charcoal and soil matrix at its edges, but a clear line of demarcation between clay and soil was visible (Appendix A, figure 7.12).

We collected the clay sample and its associated shell valve (AlDf-24 A:17), believing at the time that it was the possible remains of pot-making activity. Our initial hypothesis was that ceramic vessels had been made on site, and this specimen represented discarded clay that had become contaminated with charcoal during pottery manufacture. In this scenario, the clamshell would have been used to scoop out and discard the clay without contaminating the rest of the raw material.

In 2010, we recovered an additional clay-lined clam shell valve (see Appendix A, figure 7.13, AlDf-24A:617) from a depth of 39 cm. This time the clay had been placed in the right clam valve, which had also been deposited on end into the midden. The clay, which was also raw, had spilled out from the valve and was associated with much more charcoal than the previous specimen. On the very same day, we encountered a very large deposit of clay, also mixed with abundant charcoal. However, this deposit appeared to have spilled from three contiguously placed left soft-shell clam valves (AlDf-24A:1176a, b, and c). These valves did not appear to have been deposited on end, and the clay appeared to have been smeared over the valves (perhaps by digging activity). Because the bulk of the clay could not be associated with any specific valve, we collected all three valves and the clay as one deposit. In the lab, we discovered that the clay volume was similar to that of the other two artifacts, when evenly distributed among the valves.

We scoured the literature hoping to find analogues for this phenomenon, which was now represented by five unique artifacts. Finally, a review of the ethnohistorical literature revealed that Wabanaki women sometimes used clay-lined clam shells as spark holders to preserve a spark of burning tree fungus for transport (Nicolar 1883: 142; see discussion in Bourque 2001: 281). Nicolar (1883: 142) describes how they may have functioned:

> [S]ome parts of the green hard wood tree produced a dry, rotten wood now called punk, which substance would burn very slowly. . . . It burnt so slow that a very small piece . . . emitted scarcely any smoke, so that it could be carried in a pouch made for the purpose. Then came the question how to prepare it so it will not burn the pouch. Clam shells were found [to be] just what was needed after having been lined with the blue clay and a small aperture having been left open between the two shells through which, what smoke there was might escape; these shells were put together and tied

tightly and put into the pouch made of a whole skin of the "Mo-nim-queh-so"—woodchuck, which can be carried on one's belt outside of all the garments.

The ethnohistoric record suggests that the artifacts would have used both left and right valves of the clam, but we were unable to discern paired valves for any of the artifacts we recovered. This is most likely a result of our excavation method; even careful trowelling in a midden composed of large quantities of unbroken clam valves would have naturally resulted in the removal of the uppermost valve, prior to exposing the clay deposit and its corresponding paired valve.

AlDf-24, Area A Midden, Discussion
The artifacts recovered from the Area A midden must be interpreted from the perspective of the development of the deposit, which is almost certainly the result of communal clam and fish processing and drying activity. The heavily used awl tools may have been used to open clams and remove the flesh inside. Thus, while clams were processed and dried on the midden, the lack of flake tools indicates that fish may have been split and prepared elsewhere and then brought to the site for drying. Concomitantly, the lack of stone tools also suggests animals were rarely butchered (or their hides prepared) in this deposit, though their meat may have been dried or smoked here.

The amount of charcoal recovered, in addition to the remarkable number of spark holders, does indicate that fires were started on or around the midden, likely to assist in the drying and smoking of fish and clams. However, the nature of the spark holders has intriguing ramifications for seasonality, mobility, and perhaps communal ritual activity at the site, something that will be fully explored in Chapter 9.

AlDf-24, Area A, Feature 2
The Late Maritime Woodland Feature 2 house in Area A provides an intriguing contrast to the relatively homogenous and artifact-poor processing midden from the preceding Middle Maritime Woodland Period.

Projectile Points
Two broken projectile points were recovered from the feature. The most complete of the two was side-notched with a convex base and straight blade edges and was missing the tip and a portion of the base (see Appendix A, figure 7.14, top row, left). It was relatively thick (maximum thickness of 6.72 mm), and was constructed from translucent quartz, presumably a local variety. The second projectile point was represented by a broken base and a portion of the neck, which indicated corner-notching (or removed corners) and a straight base (figure 7.14, top row, middle). This point was composed of a multicoloured pink-and-red chert, which in many respects resembles Minas Basin chert varieties. The width of the base (17.92 mm) suggests a very small projectile point.

Bifaces
Seven biface fragments were recovered, all manufactured on translucent white quartz. One specimen, likely a preform or blank (AlDf-24 A:1129b), was roughly rectangular with a

convex base and convex, tapering edges. The six remaining bifaces (see Appendix A, figure 7.14, second and third rows down) were tip fragments, all with convex edges. The variable quality of the points suggests a range of broken projectile points and broken preforms or blanks.

Unifaces

Four scrapers were recovered from the floor deposits. Three were roughly triangular in shape and were made from translucent white quartz and green chert; two of these had unimarginal retouch (see Appendix A, figure 7.14, fourth row down, left and middle), while a third had bimarginal retouch (figure 7.14, fourth row down, middle). A flake platform was present on two of these artifacts. One circular "thumbnail" scraper with unimarginal retouch was recovered (figure 7.14, bottom row, left), created from pink/yellow/red multicoloured chert.

An unusual possible graver, made from brown-and-black multicoloured chert was also recovered (figure 7.14, bottom row, right). The two small spurs are both retouched, but occur on the same retouched edge of the piece. It is uncertain how the graver functioned—if it were even used as such a tool.

Cores and Debitage

Five relatively large cores were recovered from the Feature 2 floor. Three can be categorized as multidirectional cores, while two exhibit only unidirectional flake removal. All were made from opaque white quartz, and three of the artifacts exhibit cortex, suggesting that they were small local cobbles recovered locally from stream beds or cobble beaches.

The feature produced an exceptionally high concentration of lithic debitage, totaling 979 pieces. Like other Late Maritime Woodland deposits in Port Joli, the assemblage was dominated by quartz, with rhyolite and chert common, but in much reduced frequency. Technologically, both primary and secondary flakes were common in the assemblage, with primary reduction notably dominated by quartz. Unfortunately, detailed breakdowns of the debitage stage of manufacture and material are unavailable.

Historic Artifacts

As described in Chapter 3, an Historic Period component was intrusive into Feature 2, and a relatively large assemblage of Historic Period artifacts was recovered. The largest component of this consisted of iron artifacts, which appear to have been associated with a shed or barn door. Wrought iron nails were recovered from N50W51, in association with wrought iron door hardware. The fifty-one wrought iron nail or nail fragments exhibited rose heads, when heads were preserved, and square bodies. Many were clinched, and most were found arranged in two parallel rows, spaced approximately 30 cm apart, running north to south, and parallel with the orientation of a door hinge. This patterning suggests that the nails were used to attached cross-timbers to the door, and one of these cross-timbers also supported the hinge. A large wrought iron staple, U-shaped, was also recovered from the same area. Two cut nails with square heads were recovered from the same unit, also associated with the decayed door. Cut nails with square heads were introduced around 1810 and remained popular into the 1900s.

A large wrought iron door hinge, with a pintle spike inserted, was recovered from the north end of the unit (see Appendix A, figure 7.16, right). The hinge has a slight decorative bulge at the distal end and three round nail holes. Two of these were penetrated by two clinched wrought iron nails. The clinched end of the nail indicates the door planks were roughly 4.5 cm thick. The pintle spike would have been driven into the frame and would have supported the door on its hinge. The spike was slightly clinched on one end, indicating that the door frame was about 15.5 cm wide. A second, smaller wrought iron pintle spike was also recovered nearby (figure 7.16, left).

A large number of sheet-iron fragments, fifty-one in total, were recovered from the area of the door. Their former function is impossible to determine. A small, copper percussion cap was also recovered. Percussion caps were popular for a relatively brief period, between about 1820 and 1860, but continued to be used for some time afterward.

Finally, four small fragments of white Historic Period earthenware, likely china, with flow blue decoration was recovered. The fragments were too small to discern the pattern or the vessel type, though a plate or saucer is likely. Flow blue decoration was introduced in the 1820s and remained popular for many decades after.

Organic Artifacts

Three beaver incisor chisels were recovered from the deposit (see Appendix A, figure 7.17). Both had been ground and reshaped at the distal end, and both were broken at along the length of the tooth, likely during use.

AlDf-24, Area A, Feature 2, Discussion

A remarkable trait of the AlDf-24, Area A, Feature 2 lithic assemblage is the large number of utilized flakes (124 of 167 total tools, or 74.2 percent [table 7.1a–d, pages 234–35]). The utilized flakes at AlDf-24, Area A, are represented by relatively even numbers of cherts and rhyolites, with quartz as a minor component (table 7.1a–d, pages 234–35)—this patterning is also consistent with AlDf-30 (below). However, as reported above, AlDf-08 and AlDf-24, Area C, appear not to conform with this pattern, with quartz appearing in more equal numbers for utilized flakes and AlDf-06 producing no utilized quartz flakes at all. Quartz is ubiquitous among the Port Joli assemblages, and the relative lack of quartz for this tool class is notable and described in more detail toward the end of this chapter. The variants of quartz at AlDf-24, Area A, Feature 2 are also different than in other assemblages. In particular, the large number of "translucent white" quartz artifacts (27 translucent quartz artifacts out of 65 quartz artifacts in total, or 42.1 percent [table 7.1a–d, pages 234–35]) stands in contrast to other sites where it occurs in significantly smaller frequencies (AlDf-24, Area C: 24.0 percent; AlDf-30: 36.5 percent; AlDf-08: 13.3 percent).

Out of all sites, AlDf-24, Area A, had the most heat-altered artifacts (62 total; over double any other site or site component) and heat-alteration is most common for utilized flakes. Of the 62 heat-altered artifacts in the deposit, 56 (90.3 percent) are utilized flakes (also representing 41.5 percent of the total utilized flakes). In Level 2b, 34 of 90 (37.8 percent) tools and 32 of 70 (45.7 percent) utilized flakes are heat-altered. The clear majority of heat-altered artifacts (51 of 62, or 82.3 percent) are made of blackish grey rhyolite—in fact, rhyolite is the most common tool material in all three levels. It is unclear what this correlation means: no other site with heat-altered artifacts appears to have this kind of single material preference, nor is it clear whether heat-alteration of these artifacts was intentional (e.g., to improve the "knappability" or durability of the stone [Domanski and Webb 2007]) or merely the result of artifacts being discarded and subsequently exposed to heating.

With a total of sixteen artifacts, bifaces represent the second-most common tool category, and of those, thirteen (81.3 percent) are composed of quartz. Seven bifaces come from Level 2b alone, the primary house floor level. Finally, compared to other house floor deposits, there is a comparably low number of scrapers in this assemblage, with only four in total.

Based on the nature of the historic artifacts, it is possible to suggest a date for this intrusive assemblage. The preponderance of wrought iron nails, combined with the limited number of cut nails, suggests that the door was built before or just around the time that cut nails had been introduced (perhaps the older door was repaired with cut nails). Furthermore, the percussion cap and flow blue china were both introduced at roughly the same period, around the 1820s. Given this information, it is likely the assemblage dates to the early part of the nineteenth century, probably around 1820. It appears to be associated with a structure that was built on top of the midden—perhaps a fishing shack or barn used by the Loyalist inhabitants of Port Joli.

AlDf-24, Area C

AlDf-24, Area C, was one of the most complex deposits excavated as part of the E'se'get Project. It also resulted in the largest assemblage of lithic and non-lithic artifacts recovered during the project. This stratified deposit represents one of the best means to track change in artifacts over the early Late Maritime Woodland through the Protohistoric periods. Here we present the data both stratigraphically and chronologically and follow it with a brief discussion of change over the depth of the deposit.

AlDf-24, Area C, Protohistoric (levels 1, 2, and 2b)
Projectile Points and Bifaces

The Protohistoric assemblage contains four projectile points, two of which are complete. The first, and largest, point (AlDf-24:177) is made from a brownish black multicoloured chert. The edges are distinctly convex, creating a leaf-shaped outline. The hafting element is a very large stem with a straight base. It is missing a shoulder on one side, although this is not the result of a break, and is possibly intentionally unfinished as it mimics a similarly large biface from the Middle Woodland house floors at AlDf-30 (see Appendix A, figure 7.41; AlDf-30:116), also missing a shoulder. The remaining three projectile points are small, and side- or corner-notched, with straight bases and straight lateral edges. All are made on white quartz (AlDf-24:84; AlDf-24:171; and AlDf-24:350).

Eleven preforms were recovered, which had been thinned and essentially only required the imposition of a hafting element. Five preforms were made from white quartz; four were made from blackish grey rhyolite, and two on a tan grey chert (one of these was heat-altered). Seven of these preforms had distinct convex bases and four had straight or slightly convex bases. The former all had convex lateral margins, while the latter had straight lateral margins. Three indeterminate bifacial tools, all possible preform bases made on opaque quartz, were also recovered.

Table 7.1 Distribution of tools by level and material in AlDf-24 Area A.

A. CHERT

Level	Projectile Points	Bifaces (incl. preforms/ blanks/ind.)	Scrapers	Cores	Retouched/ Utilized*	Total
1	0	0	0	0	0	0
2	0	0	1	1	6	8
2b	0	1	1	0	21	23
3	1	0	0	0	4	5
3b	0	0	0	0	0	0
3c	0	0	0	0	0	0
3d	0	0	0	0	1	1
3f	0	0	0	1	0	1
3m	0	0	0	0	0	0
3n	0	0	0	0	1	1
	1	1	2	2	33	39

* Note: Level 2 includes one graver

B. QUARTZ

Level	Projectile Points	Bifaces (incl. preforms/ blanks/ind.)	Scrapers	Cores	Retouched/ Utilized	Total
1	0	1	0	0	0	1
2	0	1	1	2	14	18
2b	1	5	1	4	19	30
3	0	2	0	1	2	5
3b	0	4	0	1	2	7
3c	0	0	0	0	0	0
3d	0	0	0	0	2	2
3f	0	0	0	0	0	0
3m	0	0	0	0	0	0
3n	1	0	0	0	0	1
	2	13	2	8	39	64

C. RHYOLITE

Level	Projectile Points	Bifaces (incl. preforms/ blanks/ind.)	Scrapers	Cores	Retouched/ Utilized*	Total
1	0	0	0	0	0	0
2	0	0	0	0	15	15
2b	0	1	0	0	34	35
3	0	0	0	0	11	11
3b	0	0	0	0	2	2
3c	0	0	0	0	4	4
3d	0	0	0	0	1	1
3f	0	0	0	0	0	0
3m	0	0	0	0	1	1
3n	0	0	0	0	2	2
	0	1	0	0	70	71

* Note: Level 3: includes one graver

D. CHERT/RHYOLITE AND QUARTZITE*

Level	Projectile Points	Bifaces (incl. preforms/ blanks/ind.)	Scrapers	Cores	Retouched/ Utilized	Total
1	0	0	0	0	0	0
2	0	0	0	0	1	1
2b	0	0	0	0	2	2
3	0	0	0	0	0	0
3b	0	0	0	0	1	1
3c	0	0	0	0	0	0
3d	0	0	0	0	0	0
3f	0	0	0	0	0	0
3m	0	1	0	0	0	1
3n	0	0	0	0	0	0
	0	1	0	0	4	5
TOTALS	3	16	4	10	146	179

* Note: Level 3m artifact is made of quartzite

Four blanks were identified in the assemblage, which are thicker, less refined, and have rough or uneven bases and lateral margins (see Appendix A, figure 7.19, fourth row down). Three were made from white quartz, and the smallest specimen was made from blackish grey rhyolite. The five biface tips in the assemblage are all thin and developed enough to be preforms or projectile points (see Appendix A, figure 7.19, fifth row down). Three of the artifacts are made on white quartz; all have slightly convex blade edges. One piece is made from a pink-red multicoloured chert, with convex lateral margins, and the final specimen is a small tip fragment made from blackish grey rhyolite.

Two small bifacial quartz tools (AlDf-24:218, 819) have been reworked to serve as scrapers. Both appear to have been made from the bases of preforms or blanks. One (218) has unimarginal retouch and is triangular in shape, likely from breakage during use. The other (819) was intentionally flaked into a circular shape. One edge may have simply had relatively steep flaking on one side of the base edge, and was then pressed into service as a scraper. The opposite edge is worked, but is not suitable for use as a scraper, resulting from step fractures.

Unifaces

Twenty-four unifacial scrapers were recovered from the protohistoric deposits in Area C, which outnumbers the unifaces recovered from each of the previous occupations at the site area and represents over 40 percent of the unifaces recovered in all of Area C (figure 7.19). While many had indeterminate shapes or were incomplete, of the complete artifacts, three were oval or circular, five were triangular, and four rectangular. One extremely large specimen (AlDf-24:369) is best described as a large basaltic spall scraper (see Appendix A, figure 7.19). Probably made from a river cobble, the spall was not intentionally retouched. Spall scrapers are common expedient tools (sensu Binford 1977) in the Northeast and were often used for rough-scraping hides or bark removal. Another expedient scraper appears to have been made by introducing relatively haphazard but steep retouch around the margins of a large flake of quartz (AlDf-24:284). It was likely used in a similar fashion as the spall scraper.

The remaining twenty-four scrapers are quite small, and though variously shaped, are best described as "thumbnail scrapers." Included are oval, circular, rectangular, and triangular flake tools. Interestingly twenty-four only four of the twenty-four scrapers are made from quartz, with the rest represented by eight different varieties of multicoloured chert, including varieties described as pink or light pink with multicoloured mottle (eight artifacts), pinkish grey (three artifacts), green (one artifact), dark grey (one artifact), whitish grey (one artifact), bluish grey (one artifact), tan with grey (two artifacts), and red with light grey bands and mottling (three artifacts). These materials are likely all associated with Mesozoic-aged chert formations originating in the Minas Basin area; however, the red with light grey bands and mottling variant is almost certainly "Partridge Island agate," which is found on Partridge Island, a small isthmus on the north shore of the Minas Basin at Parrsboro, Nova Scotia. Notably, of twelve heat-altered artifacts recovered from this component, four of these chert scrapers were heat-altered.

Three retouched flakes were recovered. Two were made from quartz and the other from the ubiquitous blackish grey rhyolite. These are complemented by nine utilized flakes, of which none were composed of chert, with quartz (four utilized flakes) and blackish grey rhyolite (five utilized flakes) nearly evenly represented.

Cores, Hammerstones, and Debitage
Nine cores were excavated from the deposit. Six were made on the local white opaque quartz, and all nine exhibited cobble cortex. The cores were haphazardly flaked, and all but one were multidirectional. One small spent core (see Appendix A, figure 7.20; AlDf-24:477) was roughly conoidal in form, a result of more regular and (very roughly) parallel flake removal.

A mottled blue-grey multicoloured chert core was also roughly conoidal in shape (figure 7.20, AlDf-24:956a), though flake removal was anything but patterned or parallel. Two rough blackish grey rhyolite cores (both multidirectional) were also present in the assemblage.

Two very small hammerstones were recovered. The largest is a quartz cobble, with battering at one end, and was likely destined for use as a core before it was lost or discarded. The second is a fine-grained smooth river pebble, tan and pink in colour, with evidence of extensive battering at one end. A natural notch in the side of pebble made it perfectly ergonomic for use as a small hammerstone for retouch of thinning work.

Debitage, which totaled 5,259 pieces in this deposit, comprising abundant flakes and shatter. Like many sites in Port Joli, most of the material was quartz, but substantial quantities of chert and rhyolite were recovered. Excavators did note that debitage appeared very small and fragmented in this layer. Debitage in this kind of concentration—inside a circumscribed area suspected of being a domestic space—would lend itself well to a detailed analysis through a reduction-sequence study (cf. Burke 1993, 2000) and may reveal further patterns about the ways that tools were being prepared or reused on the site. The persistent use of stone in this component, to the exclusion of potentially available European goods (e.g., glass or metal; see below), is interesting and deserves further explication.

Other Artifacts
One fragment of a chipped and ground celt (see Appendix A, figure 7.21; AlDf-24:87), made from a fine-grained brown-grey material, was recovered from the Protohistoric deposit. Very little can be said about the small fragment other than the observation of a faceted dorsal surface caused by the removal of large flakes, which had been ground and smoothed. Its lateral margins were rounded and smoothed, and its ventral surface was very flat.

A second ground tool (figure 7.21, AlDf-24:473) seems to have been an expedient piece. Made from the same fine-grained material as the celt, this appears to have been a flake that was subsequently ground on nearly all surfaces. The distal tip shows evidence of flakes caused by use, some of which have been obscured by subsequent grinding. The object is so small that it is difficult to imagine its function, but it may best be described as an expedient, or informal, woodworking tool. It is notable that these two atypical tools were made of the same material; however, without technological analysis, these interpretations must remain necessarily broad.

Organic Artifacts

Two beaver teeth (AlDf-24C:15, 22) were recovered from the uppermost levels of AlDf-24, Area C (see Appendix A, figure 7.22). One shows evidence of a modified (ground and sharpened) occlusal surface, while the other is fragmentary. Two pieces of worked antler or bone were recovered; the first was a large fragment from the pedicle of an antler, which had been grooved and snapped, and the other a small fragment of mammal cortical bone with similar evidence of grooving. These are best described as debitage from some sort of organic tool industry.

A final piece of worked antler, fashioned into a wedge, was recovered from Level 2. The flat proximal edge on this relatively large piece showed evidence of battering, suggesting that the tool had been used for heavy woodworking purposes or, alternatively, to assist in the reduction of larger bone or antler pieces.

European Historic Artifacts

Two small fragments of wrought nails (not shown) were recovered from the uppermost levels of AlDf-24, Area C. Though incomplete, they appear to have had rose heads. The very limited amount of Historic Period European material recovered from the otherwise very rich Protohistoric deposit at AlDf-24 is very instructive, and some discussion here is warranted. If we did not have a radiocarbon date placing this deposit in the late sixteenth/early seventeenth century (Chapter 4), this deposit would present essentially as a relatively undisturbed later Late Maritime Woodland deposit, replete with lithics and ceramics. The only hint of European artifacts are fragments of wrought nails, which could easily be dismissed as a later intrusive element. However, given the date, and in the absence of clear stratigraphic disturbance, it is likely the nails are the result of early contact or trade. It is important to acknowledge that this is not an ephemeral deposit, though it is somewhat less intensively occupied than the later Late Maritime Woodland house floor below it. The implications of this will be discussed fully in chapter 9.

AlDf-24, Area C, Feature 4 (levels 3a and 3b)
Projectile Points and Bifaces

Twelve complete and fragmentary projectile points were collected during the excavation of the Feature 4 floor deposits. Eight of the points were side-notched, three were corner-notched, and one had an indeterminate hafting type. Remarkably, only one of the points was made on chert, a multicoloured tan variety. Four points were made on blackish grey rhyolite. The remaining seven points were made on opaque or translucent quartz. Base shapes tended to be straight to slightly convex, while blade edges were predominately straight with only two points indicating convex blade shapes. Two artifacts (see Appendix A, figure 7.23; AlDf-24:120, 357) show significant edge-length asymmetry, presenting scalene triangle outline shapes indicating significant re-sharpening of one preferential edge. In some respects, they are reminiscent of Jack's Reef pentagonal points (e.g., Ritchie 1971), but this relationship requires more systematic scrutiny. In any case, these points may have been reworked as knives (as evidenced by asymmetric lateral edges from constant reworking on the cutting edge) or were used primarily as knives, rather than projectile points. A third point (figure 7.23, AlDf-24:456) may also have been used as a knife. Finally, five of the projectile points (figure 7.23, AlDf-24:332, 456, 378, 455, 436) display deep retouch along both blade edges, creating a serrated-like edge.

Levels 3 and 3b (see Appendix A, figure 7.24) contained twenty-seven bifaces or biface fragments, some of which were undoubtedly former finished projectile points. We have classified two of these bifaces as rough blanks, due to their thickness, while nine of the bifaces were likely preforms awaiting the insertion of hafting elements to transform them into projectile points. Among the preforms, two have distinctly straight bases, while the remainder are convex. Most of the bifaces are roughly triangular, while one small specimen has a distinct leaf-shape. As with the projectile points, chert is underrepresented among the bifaces, with only four artifacts made on chert (including two made of a pink multicoloured mottled and banded variety, one made of reddish brown chert, and one observed as grey from heat-alteration). The remaining twenty-three bifaces were made from the ubiquitous blackish grey rhyolite (seven artifacts) and white quartz (sixteen artifacts). One fragment was composed of an olive quartzite, but only the tip of the specimen remains.

One final bifacial tool appears to have been worked into a scraping implement with retouch around its entire circumference. Roughly oval in shape, the specimen is made on the common pink multicoloured mottled and banded chert popular in Port Joli.

Unifaces

In addition to the bifacial scraper mentioned above, fifteen small unifacial scrapers were recovered from the Feature 4 deposit. Shapes ranged from distinctly triangular to oval/circular, and rhomboidal/rectangular. Only one of the scrapers was bimarginal, the rest exhibiting unimarginal retouch on the dorsal side; all were made on flakes. Unlike the bifaces and projectile points from the deposit, most of the ten scrapers were made of chert—five of which exhibit heat-alteration—with pink and red-dominated multicoloured varieties most common, and grey, tan, and reddish brown multicoloured varieties also represented. One unique triangular uniface (see Appendix A, figure 7.25; AlDf-24:452) was made on a whitish grey siltstone and has two prominent parallel dorsal flake scars.

Twenty-two utilized flakes form part of the flake tool assemblage (not shown in figures). Rhyolite dominates this assemblage with twelve artifacts, followed by quartz with five artifacts, and then chert with five artifacts. Only three retouched flakes were identified, made from quartz, chert, and rhyolite, respectively.

Cores, Hammerstones, and Debitage

Fourteen cores were identified in the assemblage (see Appendix A, figure 7.26), including eleven made from quartz, two from rhyolite, and one from chert/rhyolite. Most of the ten artifacts were crude multidirectional objects, often with cortex, clearly sourced from local river cobbles or quartz seams; four were unidirectional.

One hammerstone (see Appendix A, figure 7.27; AlDf-24:187) made from a beautiful, banded grey fined-grained beach or river cobble was recovered. It has light battering at the proximal end, which is flatter, and extensive battering on the distal margin, which presents a more pointed surface.

A massive quantity of lithic debitage, numbering 7,080 pieces, was recovered from the floor deposits. All stages of reduction were present, including primary, secondary, and tertiary flakes. The vast majority of the assemblage was quartz, the result of working cobbles with numerous fracture planes in an attempt to obtain a sizeable flake for use. Rhyolite was the next most significant material used, followed far behind by chert, which tended to be represented only by tertiary flakes. Unfortunately, these are observational descriptions only, as detailed debitage material and stage of manufacture classification was not completed for this component.

Organic Artifacts
Organic tools are represented by five fragmentary beaver-tooth chisels, three of which preserve the ground distal working edge. A very fine bone awl (see Appendix A, figure 7.28; AlDf-24:99), made into a completely round rod from a large mammal long bone, is broken, likely at about mid-shaft, but has retained a very sharp point. A small fragment of worked ungulate bone (figure 7.28, AlDf-24:306), probably a metapodial, was grooved and snapped and then two flat facets were carved along about two-thirds of its length. Its function is a distinct mystery.

Other Artifacts
A mica nodule (AlDf-24:445) was identified in the floor deposits. This specimen does not appear to have been worked; however, mica occurs locally in quartz seams, thus it may have been brought to the site as a curiosity, or as an incidental discovery in the sourcing or reduction of quartz for tool stone.

AlDf-24, Area C, Middle (levels 3c to 3e)
Projectile Points and Bifaces
Seven projectile points were found in the possible floor deposits sandwiched between Feature 4 and the basal levels of the Area C deposit, three of which, interestingly, appear to be heat-altered—the only projectile points in all of the E'se'get sites to exhibit this characteristic. One rather unusual specimen (see Appendix A, figure 7.29; AlDf-24:910a) is a large point made from blackish grey rhyolite with steep corner notches resulting in a very large expanding stem, and a slightly convex base that was damaged, possibly during use. This specimen would have been too large for an arrow and likely represents a thrusting weapon or knife. A similarly large projectile point (figure 7.29, AlDf-24: 460) is made from quartz, with deep side-notches, and straight blade edges. Retouch along these edges has created a gently serrated appearance.

Two very similar projectile points have straight bases, straight blade edges, and wide side- or corner-notches. One (AlDf-24:388) is made on a dark greenish grey quartzite and the other on a blackish grey rhyolite (AlDf-24:472). The only chert projectile point (AlDf-24:391), made from a bluish grey multicoloured variety (likely heat-treated), occurs as a tiny fragment of a base with a side-notch.

Fifteen bifaces and biface fragments were recovered, with the majority (nine) being made from quartz, and the remainder made of grey or greyish black rhyolites five, a greenish grey quartzite (one), and a dark grey mottled chert (one). Two of these fifteen bifacial artifacts appear to be rough blanks (AlDf-24:465, 1077b). Seven of the fifteen bifacial tools are preforms or preform fragments; the majority are leaf-shaped, with slightly convex edges.

One specimen, made from blackish grey rhyolite (AlDf-24:1076a), seems to have a straight base and straight blade edges, and may be a broken Madison-style projectile point.

Unifaces

Sixteen unifacial scrapers are included in the assemblage (see Appendix A, figure 7.30). In addition, one small scraper (AlDf-24:989a) appears to have been reworked from a translucent quartz biface fragment. It has unimarginal retouch and is semi-lunar in shape. Unlike other levels, roughly even numbers of artifacts are made from quartz (seven) and chert (six), followed in quantity by two rhyolite scrapers and one quartzite scraper. Two artifacts are crude spall scrapers, each made from a quartz flake with abundant cobble cortex on the dorsal surface and heavy-use wear around their circumference. The remaining scrapers are very small, exhibiting a variety of forms (rectangular, oval/circular, and triangular). Only one of the artifacts has bimarginal retouch, and nine exhibit a flake platform. Chert varieties include pink and red-dominated multicoloured as well as reddish brown dominated materials. The rhyolite artifacts are represented by one each of the familiar blackish grey and greyish black material, and the one quartzite tool by the common greenish grey variety.

Three retouched flakes were recovered, made from greyish black rhyolite, pink multicoloured chert, and quartz. Unusually, no utilized flakes were encountered in the deposit.

Cores

Four cores are included in the assemblage; three crude quartz cores and one multidirectional core made from the common pink dominated multicoloured chert. The quartz cores all exhibit cortex and are likely derived from local riverine or beach sources. The chert core (see Appendix A, figure 7.31; AlDf-24:271) is also very rough and exhibits multiple fracture planes; the multidirectional flaking is clearly patterned to avoid these natural flaws. One edge of the core contains multiple parallel flake scars, suggesting exploitation of the core was attempted where the material allowed it, however limited.

Organic Artifacts

One of the organic artifacts recovered from this deposit (see Appendix A, figure 7.32; AlDf-24:1177) is unique to the E'se'get Project. The object is a grooved and snapped ungulate metatarsal (metapodial), with heavy damage to the edges of the bone. Wear in these areas suggests it may have been used as a beamer or bone scraper for working hides. If so, it is the only bone hide-working implement known from Port Joli.

A large, complete beaver incisor chisel (figure 7.32, AlDf-24:203) has been heavily worked and represents only about half the length of the original tooth. The heavily worn working edge is blunted from much use, and polish and use-wear are evident on this distal edge.

Other Artifacts

A large fragment of mica and quartz crystal (see Appendix A, figure 7.33; AlDf-24:1194), with multiple distinct bedding layers, was recovered from the deposit. This beautiful piece shows no sign of use-wear and was likely brought to the site as a curiosity—although, as with the later occupation in Feature 4, mica is likely derived from local quartz and its discovery may be coincidental with lithic sourcing or preparation. The repeated presence of a conspicuous fragment of mica in both house floors is interesting. Mica has been recovered from Archaic burial contexts in the Atlantic Northeast, and in mortuary and ceremonial contexts in Illinois and Missouri (Carr and Sears 1985). While we are not aware of mica being recovered from Maritime Woodland contexts, there is a possibility that it had social or spiritual significance (see below).

A small, very smooth quartz stone (figure 7.33, AlDf-24:60) was unusual for the matrix in which it was found and may have been used as a gaming piece (Leonard 1996). If not, it was undoubtedly brought to the site as a curiosity.

One fragment of copper (see Appendix A, figure 7.11; AlDf-24:317) was recovered from the screen during excavation. The small nodule appears to have been flattened, folded, and pounded along its length multiple times, creating a complex nodule with many folds and voids. After the raw nodule was apparently first flattened, there is evidence that smaller pieces may have been chiseled from the parent fragment. The flat, used blank then appears to have been hammered and folded again in an attempt to create a new flat copper blank. We have found no similarly prepared copper artifacts mentioned in the regional literature.

A small fragment of ochre (AlDf-24:199, not pictured) represents the last artifact of note from this assemblage. There is no evidence that it was ground or worked in any way; however, it was undoubtedly brought to the site.

AlDf-24, Area C, Lower (levels 3f to 3j)
Bifaces
There is a conspicuous lack of bifacial tools for this component of AlDf-24, Area C; however, the deposit as a whole represents a relatively low concentration of lithic tools in general, despite the significant quantity of debitage (see below).

Unifaces
Four unimarginal scrapers (see Appendix A, figure 7.34) form the entire formal stone tool collection from the lowest levels of AlDf-24, Area C. Two of the scrapers are triangular and exhibit flake platforms (AlDf-24:65, 914a), while the other two (AlDf-24: 881a, 1006a) are fragmentary but were likely oval or circular in shape. Two scrapers were made from quartz (AlDf-24:65, 881a), one from greyish black rhyolite (AlDf-24:1006a), and one from a dark grey chert (AlDf-24:914a).

One blackish grey rhyolite utilized flake was recovered (AlDf-24:1184, not pictured), and no retouched flakes were encountered.

Cores and Debitage
Three rough quartz cores are part of the assemblage (see Appendix A, figure 7.35; AlDf-24:420, 321, 67). One is multidirectional, while the other two are unidirectional. All exhibit cobble cortex and are certainly derived locally.

Despite the dearth of formal tools, 151 pieces of debitage were recovered from the relatively limited excavations conducted in these deposits. Like the deposits above, observational accounts suggest the majority of the artifacts were quartz, but rhyolite and chert were both present.

Other Artifacts

A small mica and quartz crystal nodule was recovered from near the bottom of the deposit (see Appendix A, figure 7.36; AlDf-24:322). Like the specimen found directly above it, the mica has multiple bedding planes, and the unusual specimen is not worked. Given the lack of such material in the local soil, it seems likely to be a manuport.

AlDf-24, Area C: Summary

Tables 7.2a to 7.2d (pages 244–45) describe the distribution of lithic tools in the AlDf-24, Area C, deposit. As can be seen in the tables, the seventy-three tools in Level 2 is a significant number, and comparable to the combined number of tools) in the Feature 4 floor deposits (levels 3 and 3b) below it, which total ninety-three. While Level 2 did not have the same characteristics of Feature 4, the abundant number of tools and debitage highly suggest that it was a floor surface. If so, the nature of the occupation must have changed significantly, specifically the activities resulting in the greasy, compact, charcoal-rich nature of the Feature 4 deposit below it. This will be discussed further in Chapter 9.

Level 2 is unique because it contains two blackish grey rhyolite cores as well as five biface preforms/blanks alongside three utilized flakes and one retouched flake of that material. This suggests some *in situ* reduction of material from rhyolite cores with the intention of producing bifaces. Regardless, there is an overall reliance on quartz for bifaces (including projectile points) and cores throughout all levels in the AlDf-24, Area C, deposit.

With regard to tool types, scrapers predominate in all levels in the deposit, again indicating that significant hide preparation, woodworking, or basket-making was conducted in AlDf-24, Area C. However, Level 2 had a ratio of scrapers to projectile points (24:4) that far exceeds all others when compared to other levels (Feature 4, levels 3 and 3b, 10:9; levels 3c to 3e, 15:7; levels 3d to 3f, 14:5). In fact, Feature 4 had an almost even ratio of scrapers to projectiles, suggesting more balance between activities in the deposit. Regardless, in all deposits, scrapers predominated over projectile points, a characteristic seemingly common in Port Joli black soil middens as well as similar sites, such as Teacher's Cove, in New Brunswick (e.g., Davis 1978: table 1).

A consideration of lithic patterning in the stratigraphy of AlDf-24, Area C, exposes the deposit as a "complex palimpsest" of repeated floor occupation (e.g., Hrynick et al. 2012). For example, in Level 3, there are twenty-one bifaces that are preforms/blanks/indeterminate and nine projectile points (46.9 percent of the tools), while in 3b, there are only six preforms/indeterminate and three projectile points (31 percent of the tools). This could suggest that there may have been different strategies being practised, with Level 3 representing the whole suite of biface production—including "gearing up" (Binford 1979) by the production of early-stage bifaces and bifacial tools, and the completion of bifacial tools as projectile points. If the site was occupied in the fall, such gearing up would be necessary to ensure the tools necessary to intercept ungulates at locations away from the campsite.

Throughout the deposit, chert appears to have been favoured for scrapers and scraping tools. Scrapers and utilized flakes represent forty-three of fifty-six (76.8 percent) of the total chert tools, and chert scrapers represent thirty-seven of fifty-nine (62.7 percent) of all scrapers in all periods at Area C. However, quartz is the primary material being reduced from cores in the deposit, again reinforcing the interpretation that it was obtained locally

Table 7.2 Distribution of tools by level and material in AlDf-24, Area C.

A. CHERT

Level	Projectile Points	Bifaces (incl. preforms/blanks/ind.)	Scrapers	Cores	Retouched/Utilized	Total
1	0	0	2	0	0	2
2	1	3	18	1	1	24
3	1	4	8	0	3	16
3b	0	0	3	0	1	4
3c	0	1	0	0	1	2
3d	1	0	3	0	0	4
3e	0	0	3	1		4
3f	0	0	0	0	0	0
3g	0	0	0	0	0	0
3i	0	0	0	0	0	0
	3	8	37	2	6	56

B. QUARTZ

Level	Projectile Points	Bifaces (incl. preforms/blanks/ind.)	Scrapers	Cores	Retouched/Utilized*	Total
1	0	0	0	0	0	0
2	3	15	4	6	7	35
3	6	11	1	7	3	28
3b	1	4	2	4	3	14
3c	0	4	4	2	0	10
3d	1	4	1	1	1	8
3e	0	2	1	0	0	3
3f	0	0	2	1	1	4
3g	0	0	0	2	0	2
3i	0	0	0	0	0	0
	11	40	15	23	15	104

* Note: Level 3f includes one manuport

C. RHYOLITE

Level	Projectile Points	Bifaces (incl. preforms/blanks/ind.)*	Scrapers	Cores	Retouched/Utilized	Total
1	0	0	0	0	0	0
2	0	6	0	2	5	13
3	2	5	0	1	8	16
3b	2	2	0	1	5	10
3c	1	0	0	0	1	2
3d	1	2	2	0	0	5
3e	2	2	0	0	0	4
3f	0	0	0	0	0	0
3g	0	0	1	0	0	1
3i	0	0	0	0	1	1
	8	17	3	4	20	52

* Note: Level 3d includes one possible blank or scraper counted as a biface; Level 3e includes one possible blank or scraper counted as a biface

D. OTHER*

Level	Projectile Points	Bifaces (incl. preforms/blanks/ind.)	Scrapers	Cores	Retouched/Utilized	Total
1	0	0	0	0	0	0
2	0	0	1	0	0	1
3	0	1	1	1	1	4
3b	0	0	0	0	1	1
3c	1	0	0	0	0	1
3d	0	1	0	0	0	1
3e	0	0	1	0	1	2
3f	0	0	1	0	0	1
3g	0	0	0	0	0	0
3i	0	0	0	0	0	0
	1	2	4	1	3	11
TOTALS	23	67	59	30	44	223

* Note: Level 2 includes one schist artifact; Level 3 includes two chert/rhyolite, one coarse-grained siltstone, and one quartzite artifact; Level 3b includes one chert/rhyolite artifact; levels 3c, 3d, and 3e include one quartzite artifact each; Level 3e includes one mica and quartz crystal artifact; Level 3f includes one chert/rhyolite artifact

as (apparently rather poor) lithic raw material. In the absence of detailed debitage counts, it appears that chert was likely being brought to the site as formal tools or minimally, as preforms. This might suggest that initial preparation of the material was being conducted nearer to the source, and much of the material was not obtained locally—the presence of macroscopically distinctive varieties of chert consistent with material originating in the Minas Basin (approximately 140 km, measured in a straight line, northeast of Port Joli's harbour) throughout all levels supports this inference. Interestingly, none of the side-notched projectile points from the deposit were made from chert. This means that *only* quartz/rhyolite and quartzite—presumably locally ubiquitous materials—were used for notched points and could suggest that conservation of chert material was so critical that notching may have been viewed as a potentially risky behaviour that might result in the waste of high-quality tool stone. It may also indicate that perhaps completed, notched chert projectile points were taken from the site when it was abandoned, and only earlier stages of those artifacts remain.

This is consistent with the interpretation of the site as being associated with a late fall or winter encampment (see Chapter 8). If, as the technology suggests, groups at Port Joli were obtaining cherts only from a very distant source, the use of chert for only small scraping tools may be representative of dwindling supplies of materials like chert. This chert might have only been available for trade during gatherings, or from procurement forays directly to the Minas Basin at other times of the year. The lack of chert may suggest that groups at Port Joli had limited access to larger trade networks within the Maritime Peninsula during the Middle and Late Maritime Woodland periods. Alternatively, it may suggest a simple preference for one material class over another for certain tools or tasks.

Hrynick et al. (2012) explored the horizontal spatial patterning of the artifacts in the Feature 4 deposit (see Chapter 5). The resulting analysis revealed a significant bilateral division of space within the house feature, with several technologies (e.g., ceramics, scrapers, projectile points) distributed in clusters that reflected discrete areas of work or tool use. This has been interpreted as possibly representing a gendered division of space and correlates with ethnographic accounts of how historic Wabanaki arranged their domestic spaces.

Finally, although noted above as possibly arriving on site as "curiosities" or the results of co-occurrence with local quartz beds, the repeated and conspicuous inclusion of large fragments of mica is interesting. Mica is present in successive occupations at AlDf-24, Area C, and, most interestingly, the co-occurrence of mica and copper in the Feature 4 deposit evokes some parallels with Hopewell sites where "cultural rules" relating to colour may have been expressed through these raw materials (e.g., Greber 2010). While not in and of itself a revelatory find, these "curiosities" alongside the number of unique artifacts and a human interment at the nearby Area A suggest the AlDf-24 location may have had broader connections, influences, and importance to the people who lived there.

AlDf-30

AlDf-30 is a complex site with multiple activity areas and features, and the only Middle Maritime Woodland deposit with such features excavated as part of the E'se'get Archaeology Project. Radiocarbon dates suggest that the uppermost layers of the site (levels 1, 2a, and 2b) likely date to the Late Maritime Woodland Period. As such, it is prudent to separate contexts for analysis, along the lines previously described in chapters 3, 6, and 7.

AlDf-30, Area A Midden
Bifaces
One biface (see Appendix A, figure 7.37; AlDf-30:59) was recovered from the Area A midden. This was a rather large tip fragment created from the blackish grey rhyolite common in these sites. It is likely that this was a large blank or preform, which has a large hinge fracture, likely introduced while shaping the blank. The edges are sharply convex and the point is very blunt, further indicating an early stage of reduction.

Unifaces
A possible scraper is represented by a rather crude specimen (see Appendix A, figure 7.37; AlDf-30:68), oval in general shape and manufactured on a light tan-and-grey quartz. The specimen is unimarginally retouched on its dorsal margin. However, its other edges show signs of use-wear, suggesting the entire implement may have been used as a rather large spall-like scraper. A flake platform is present, though worn, which is consistent with other small unifacial scrapers in Port Joli.

Two large utilized chert flakes (AlDf-30:11, 67) on brown and black multicoloured material were recovered. Despite being classified as chert, this material was similar in colour to the blackish grey rhyolite reported for the large bifacial tip, described above, and it is possible they are from a finer-grained portion of the core or blank. If so, they are likely to have been created during the reduction of the biface, though we were unable to refit them. Another quartz utilized flake (AlDf-30:58) was also recovered.

Hammerstones and Debitage
Three rather large hammerstones were recovered (see Appendix A, figure 7.38). The largest, measuring over 10 cm long, was an oblong basalt cobble with signs of battering at each end. The other two artifacts were small water-rolled quartz cobbles, with evidence of battering at the most angular margin of the cobble. If the battering had not been present they each might have been identified as raw material for a core, as they are both the same white opaque quartz so commonly used as tool stone in Port Joli. In fact, they may be the best representatives of the type of raw material collected and used, and they may have been intended for such use after being used as expedient hammerstones.

Debitage did not occur in significant quantities in this deposit. This may be partially related to the large (6 mm) mesh size used for the excavation of the deposit. However, it is important to point out that two of the six units excavated in this area were screened through 3 mm mesh (in 2010), and all the debitage recovered came from the units that were screened through the larger mesh size, which indicates that screen size was not responsible for the frequency of debitage. Only twelve pieces of debitage were recovered, including eleven fragments of the greyish black rhyolite and one quartz specimen.

Other Artifacts
A small fragment of red ochre (AlDf-30:658) was recovered from deep in the midden (Level 3b).

AlDf-30, Black Soil Area: Levels 1, 2, and 2b
Bifaces
One very large biface made from brown rhyolite was recovered from the uppermost levels of the site (see Appendix A, figure 7.39). The artifact was broken during the prehistoric occupation, with the tip recovered in Level 2b and the base recovered at the uppermost portion of Level 3a. The point is large, triangular, and thin with a deeply concave base and straight to slightly concave lateral edges. One small quartz biface fragment (AlDf-30:33, not pictured) was also recovered from the upper levels of the site. Broken at the midpoint of the biface, it is missing both its tip and base. It is relatively thin (maximum thickness of 5.36 mm), and hence may have been a fragment of a preform or large projectile point.

Unifaces
Five relatively small scrapers were recovered from the upper layers of the black soil midden. All had unimarginal retouch on the dorsal side of the flake, and only one (see Appendix A, figure 7.39; AlDf-30:1074) showed evidence of a flake platform. Three of the scrapers were triangular (or once were), and two were circular in shape. A range of cherts were used to make the scrapers, including varieties of pink and red, black and grey, brown and black, and red and brown multicoloured varieties.

One quite large graver was recovered, made from a translucent white quartz. The spur, which coincided with a dense crystal inclusion in the opaque quartz, was heavily retouched and showed extensive signs of use-wear. Significant numbers of retouched flakes were recovered from the deposit, numbering ten in total. So invasive was the retouch that two artifacts (not pictured) may have been used as a graver or scraper, respectively, though their unusual shape indicates that they were expedient if used as such.

Significant quantities of utilized flakes (104 artifacts) were identified, representing a range of multicoloured cherts, blackish grey rhyolite, with quartz present, but in the minority.

Cores and Debitage
Cores are represented by three opaque white quartz artifacts (one not pictured). All are unidirectional cores, and all are very small, completely spent, with no signs of cortex. Again, they are likely to have been from local sources.

Debitage was numerous (542 artifacts in total) in the deposit and was again dominated by quartz, with lesser quantities of rhyolite and chert.

Other Artifacts
A large quartz manuport (see Appendix A, figure 7.40; AlDf-30:856), was deposited in this level. The piece is a large water-rolled rectangular cobble of white opaque quartz and was likely brought to the site as raw material for lithic reduction. A small white quartz spall, with cortex adhering, was unusual for its distinct whiteness, smoothness, and crystal inclusions; it was possibly used as a gaming piece or curiosity.

Two fragments of ochre were found in the upper levels of the site. The first was simply a small fragment of raw material, angular in shape and with jagged edges. The second (figure 7.40, AlDf-30:330) was small, but tabular, and ground flat on both sides and on two lateral margins. This specimen was likely used to create ochre powder or was potentially rubbed directly on the surface being decorated.

Finally, two small ferromagnetic stones (not pictured) were recovered from these levels. The stones were heavy, and their rust-coloured hue suggested an iron pyrite of some kind. They repelled a magnet when it was pressed to the surface. While the magnetic properties of the stones were likely unknown to the site's inhabitants, the strange heavy artifacts were likely brought to the site as curiosities or, alternatively, to use as a mineral in producing ochre-coloured powder.

One small fragment of fire-cracked rock (not shown) was collected from the upper layers; it was significantly heat-altered and was granitic in origin.

AlDf-30: Black Soil Area: Levels 3a to 3f

The limited number of artifacts from the two sequential house floors in this area necessitates that both be treated as one unit. Chronologically, this is valid as both contexts date to the latter part of the Middle Maritime Woodland Period. However, combining the assemblage could mask some variability. This potential variability will be addressed later in the chapter.

Projectile Points and Bifaces

Three projectile points are present in the house floor assemblages. The first, and most unique (see Appendix A, figure 7.41; AlDf-30:381), appears to have been a triangular point with a deep basal cavity, consistent with a Levanna-style projectile point, but which has been heavily reworked to become a knife or drill. The former is most likely, as the tip of the point shows little evidence of rotational use-wear. The specimen is made from a blackish grey rhyolite, typical of large projectile points in Port Joli. It is important to note that this artifact is practically identical to a specimen recovered from AlDf-11 (see Appendix B, figure 7.70), which also appears to be a reworked Levanna (or similar triangular) projectile point. The appearance of a Levanna point at a house floor otherwise dated to the Middle Maritime Woodland Period suggests that the deposit was either disturbed in some unknown fashion or that it dates to the transition period between the Middle and Late Maritime Woodland periods.

The second projectile point (figure 7.41, AlDf-30:116) is also relatively unusual for Port Joli contexts. Made from a brownish grey quartzite, this large unfinished point has one large corner-notch removed, a relatively straight base, and one straight finished blade edge. The point is broken at about two-thirds of its length, probably as it was being created. Interestingly, the base is ground, suggesting some preparation for hafting.

The final projectile point is also quite large and very unique. Roughly flaked from a blackish grey rhyolite, it is either a crude leaf-shaped blank or a large projectile point with a crude contracting stem. The blade edges are strongly convex, and various fracture planes and step fractures have created a stepped profile.

None of the nine bifaces recovered from the deposit were complete. Eight are tip fragments from a variety of materials, including pink-dominated multicoloured chert, dark grey chert/rhyolite, brown rhyolite, quartz, and white quartzite. One of the artifacts (figure 7.41, AlDf-30:33), made from opaque white quartz, is missing both its tip and base. It should be noted that this artifact was found in Test Unit 3, Level 2a, and was subsequently determined to be part of the first house flour (Level 3b).

Unifaces

Three gravers were recovered from the deposit, characterized by a distinct distal spur created by reworking of the distal end (one specimen also had unimarginal retouch). Two of the artifacts were made from translucent white quartz, while the third was made from a yellow with red and white multicoloured chert.

Twelve unimarginally retouched scrapers were encountered while excavating the house floors. When it could be determined, all were retouched dorsally, though they exhibited a variety of shapes, from rectangular to triangular to circular. Nine scrapers were made from the local quartz. One of the largest artifacts (see Appendix A, figure 7.42; AlDf-30:812a) was made from a heat-treated grey rhyolite. One chert specimen (figure 7.42, AlDf-30:98) was made from a unique blue-grey multicoloured material, while another (figure 7.42, AlDf-30:719) was made from the same yellow with red and white multicoloured chert as one of the gravers.

Sixteen retouched flakes, made from a wide variety of multicoloured cherts and a minor number of quartz and rhyolite, were recovered. Almost all of the retouched flakes had unimarginal retouch, but two could be classified as bimarginal. A large quantity (176 artifacts) of utilized flakes (not shown) were recovered from the deposit. Unlike in other deposits, although quartz was present, chert was the dominant tool material, followed by rhyolite.

Cores, Hammerstones, and Debitage

Cores are represented by four small quartz artifacts. None of these artifacts exhibit cortex; two are unidirectional, while one is multidirectional. One of the unidirectional cores (see Appendix A, figure 7.43; AlDf-30:830) is made from a very fine translucent crystal and is perhaps the most "formal" core identified in the Port Joli assemblage. This specimen is distinctly diamond-shaped, with evidence of long flakes being removed from both the distal and proximal ends, each eventually forming a distinct point when the core was spent. Many of the flakes produced from this core would have been quite long and thin, perhaps the nearest evidence of blade-manufacture in Port Joli (although we did not find any distinct "blade" tools in Port Joli).

One rather large hammerstone (see Appendix A, figure 7.44; AlDf-20:475) was collected from the Black Soil Area. Like other hammerstones in Port Joli, it was made from a basalt beach or river cobble and was lightly battered along its margin.

Debitage was numerous, with 953 artifacts, including flakes and shatter, recovered from these levels. Unlike the utilized flakes (discussed above), a large percentage of this assemblage was quartz, followed very closely by chert and rhyolite.

Other Artifacts

Like other deposits at AlDf-30, a round, heavy ferromagnetic rock (not pictured), which repelled a magnet when it was pressed to the surface, was found in the uppermost house feature floor deposit. As described in Chapter 3, a magnetic anomaly exists at the site, and perhaps the stone was found while excavating the sweathouse feature or was recovered from the nearby bog. Regardless, this strange stone was almost certainly a manuport, picked up and curated as a curiosity.

Two very small fragments of raw copper nodules (not pictured) were recovered from Level 3b. Both appear to have been unworked, with no evidence of cutting or hammering. They were obviously brought to the site from elsewhere but were perhaps lost before they could be transformed.

Organic Artifacts

Several large fragments of worked bone were found in close proximity to one another (see Appendix A, figure 7.45; AlDf-30:113) near the southeast margin of the uppermost house floor. The bone was identified as cetacean in origin (whale bone) and was likely a modified section of rib. The rib had been split along the long axis, revealing the inner cancellous material, and then the cortical margins had been shaped to create a long rectangular rod. Though all the pieces do not neatly refit, it is obvious the fragments are from the same specimen. One possible interpretation for the specimen, given its location, is that it was a stake used to hold down either floor coverings or hide wigwam coverings. Alternatively, it may have been used to hold down skins for drying.

The only specimen of worked shell recovered in the E'se'get Archaeology Project came from this deposit (AlDf-30:97). The soft-shell valve fragment has been heavily polished or ground around the entire edge, though it is difficult to determine if the shell was intentionally reworked or if the modification happened through repeated wear on an unmodified valve. Whatever the case, it appears to have been used as a scraper or abrader of some kind, perhaps for preparing skin or working bark.

AlDf-30, Area B Midden
Debitage and Other Artifacts

The small, 1 × 1 m excavation in the Area B midden returned few artifacts. A small ferromagnetic cobble (AlDf-30:652, not shown), was recovered, composed of a granitic stone stained red from abundant iron oxide. Like the ferromagnetic stones in the Black Soil Area, it repelled a magnet when applied to the surface. Its heavy weight and unusual colour probably attracted ancient Mi'kmaq to bring it to the site as a curiosity. A small piece of red ochre (AlDf-30:624) was also recovered in the midden (not shown).

Despite screening the deposit through 3 mm mesh, little debitage was recovered, representing only twenty-six flakes or shatter fragments. Again, quartz dominated the assemblage, followed by blackish grey rhyolite, and varieties of multicoloured fine-grained cherts.

AlDf-30: Discussion

Tables 7.3a to 7.3d (pages 252–54) track the distribution of materials and tool types by stratigraphic level at AlDf-30. Worthy of specific note in the AlDf-30 assemblage is the diversity of materials used in the lithic assemblage. Twenty different colour categories were assigned to the material, more than at any other deposit excavated in Port Joli. At AlDf-24, Area C, which had the next highest diversity of material (fifteen colour categories), cherts are predominantly lighter-coloured pinks and reds, whereas at AlDf-30, in

Table 7.3 Distribution of tools by level and material in AlDf-30.

A. CHERT

Level	Projectile Points	Bifaces (incl. preforms/blanks/ind.)	Scrapers	Cores	Retouched/Gravers/Manuports*	Utilized	Total
1	0	0	0	0	0	0	0
2	0	0	0	0	0	8	8
2a	0	0	0	0	0	1	1
2b	0	0	4	0	2	12	18
2b/3a	0	0	0	0	0	0	0
2c	0	1	0	0	3	18	22
3	0	0	0	0	0	2	2
3a	0	0	1	0	5	22	28
3b	0	0	2	0	3	13	18
3c	0	1	0	0	0	8	9
3d	0	0	0	0	0	8	8
3e	0	0	0	0	0	1	1
3f	0	0	0	0	0	0	0
	0	2	7	0	13	93	115

* Note: Level 2b: 2 retouched flakes; Level 2c: 2 retouched flakes, 1 graver/retouched; Level 3a: 5 retouched flakes; Level 3b: 3 retouched flakes

B. QUARTZ

Level	Projectile Points	Bifaces (incl. preforms/blanks/ind.)	Scrapers	Cores	Retouched/Gravers/Manuports*	Utilized	Total
1	0	0	0	2	0	0	2
2	0	1	1	0	1	1	4
2a	0	0	0	0	0	0	0
2b	0	0	0	0	3	5	8
2b/3a	0	0	0	0	0	0	0
2c	0	0	0	2	0	7	9
3	0	0	3	1	0	3	7
3a	0	0	1	0	1	7	9
3b	0	0	1	0	0	5	6
3c	0	0	1	0	0	2	3
3d	0	0	1	1	0	0	2

Level	Projectile Points	Bifaces (incl. preforms/blanks/ ind.)	Scrapers	Cores	Retouched/ Gravers/ Manuports*	Utilized	Total
3e	0	0	1	0	0	0	1
3f	0	0	0	0	1	0	1
	0	1	9	6	6	30	52

* Note: Level 2: 1 graver; Level 2b: 1 retouched flake, 1 graver, 1 manuport; Level 3a: 1 retouched flake; Level 3f: 1 possible graver

C. RHYOLITE

Level	Projectile Points	Bifaces (incl. preforms/blanks/ ind.)	Scrapers	Cores	Retouched/ Gravers/ Manuports*	Utilized	Total
1	0	0	1	0	0	0	1
2	0	1	0	0	1	2	4
2a	0	0	0	0	0	2	2
2b	0	0	0	0	1	13	14
2b/3a	1	0	0	0	0	0	1
2c	0	0	0	0	1	14	15
3	0	0	0	0	0	3	3
3a	0	0	0	0	1	21	22
3b	1	2	0	0	1	4	8
3c	0	1	1	0	0	4	6
3d	0	0	0	0	0	4	4
3e	0	0	0	0	0	3	3
3f	0	0	0	0	0	0	0
	2	4	2	0	5	70	83

* Note: Level 2: 1 retouched flake; Level 2b: 1 retouched flake; Level 2c: 1 retouched flake; Level 3a: 1 retouched flake; Level 3b: 1 retouched flake

D. CHERT/RHYOLITE AND QUARTZITE* (QTE)

Level	Projectile Points	Bifaces (incl. preforms/blanks/ ind.)	Scrapers	Cores	Retouched/ Gravers/ Manuports*	Utilized	Total
1	0	0	0	0	0	1	1
2	0	0	0	0	0	2	2
2a	0	0	0	0	0	0	0
2b	0	0	0	0	0	6	6
2b/3a	0	0	0	0	0	0	0
2c	0	0	0	0	0	3	3

Level	Projectile Points	Bifaces (incl. preforms/blanks/ind.)	Scrapers	Cores	Retouched/ Gravers/ Manuports	Utilized	Total
3	0	0	0	0	0	2	2
3a	0	2	0	0	0	5	7
3b	1	0	0	0	0	5	6
3c	0	1	0	0	0	5	6
3d	0	0	0	0	0	1	1
3e	0	0	0	0	0	2	2
3f	0	0	0	0	0	0	0
unk.	0	0	0	0	0	1	1
	1	3	0	0	0	33	37
TOTALS	3	10	18	6	24	226	287

* Note: Level 1: 1 qte; Level 2: 1 qte; Level 2b: 3 qte; Level 2c: 3 qte; Level 3: 1 qte; Level 3a: 5 qte (including both bifaces); Level 3b: 3 qte (including projectiel point); Level 3d: 1 qte

addition to the pink-dominated groundmass varieties, four types of brown groundmass were encountered, as well as dark grey, greenish grey, and red-dominated groundmasses (although, as indicated before, these materials could all originate in the same formation or even outcrop location). Furthermore, AlDf-30 is the only site where quartzite is present in any concentration, with brown and olive rhyolites represented. This diversity of raw material is reflective of other sub-regions of the Maritime Peninsula, such as on the Lower Saint John River and the Quoddy region in New Brunswick (Blair 2010; Holyoke 2012), where the availability of diverse lithic materials is evidenced in a high diversity of observably different lithic types in assemblages—reflective of local geology and glacial history, which lends itself to fine-grained materials being readily available in both primary and secondary sources.

Did the Middle Maritime Woodland inhabitants of Port Joli have access to a greater diversity of raw material than Port Joli's Late Maritime Woodland inhabitants? There is precedent for such change through time in the Maritime Peninsula; for example, as discussed by Blair (2010: 39) there is a peak in material diversity in the Lower Saint John River Valley during the late Early Woodland, around 2280 to 2020 radiocarbon BP, and a drop-off in diversity by the late Middle Woodland, around 1760 to 1540 radiocarbon BP. It is not clear what mechanisms resulted in this patterning, but in Port Joli it is possibly the result of exhausting local sources of brown chert and quartzite (e.g., river or beach cobbles) upon the initial occupation of the harbour.

Like other deposits (e.g., AlDf-24, Area A, Feature 2 and AlDf-06), utilized flakes form the overwhelming majority of tools at the site and would suggest a technological orientation toward this type of flake production. The relative lack of bifacial tools would indicate that there is less emphasis on biface production, especially in comparison to the Late Woodland deposits at AlDf-24, Area C.

The high incidence of utilized and retouched flakes, paired with the presence of gravers in both levels 2b (one artifact) and 2c (one artifact), and a conspicuously high concentration of scraping tools overall, could indicate basket making or weaving was taking place and would account for the lack of bifacial tools. Additionally, the utilized and retouch flakes and scrapers could be used in butchery and hide preparation, which is consistent with a fall/winter site with more access to large game (see chapter 8). As with other deposits exhibiting large amounts of informal flaking tools, this patterning does suggest an interesting avenue of research into the larger implications for the social aspects (e.g., gender roles) of tool making and tool use among ancestral Mi'kmaq in this area.

The axial feature present in all levels of the Black Soil Area deposit, which protruded from the sweathouse feature into all subsequent house floors, presents an effective division of space which may have resulted in differential artifact patterning. Hrynick and Betts (2017: 7–11) explored spatial patterning in these deposits, but small sample sizes reduced the ability to discern significant patterning. However, table 7.4 displays the distribution of all lithic tools, regardless of level, in relation to the axial feature, using the 50 cm mark in the centre of the W52 grid squares as a rough dividing line (this assumes all material east of W52 was of course also east of the feature, and all material west of W53 was of course also west of the feature.

The table clearly indicates that there is a much higher number of lithic artifacts in the east half (183, adding columns 3 and 5) of the deposit than the west (85, adding columns 2 and 4). This pattern is consistent for most tool types, with projectile points, bifaces, scrapers, retouched flakes, and utilized flakes all occurring in much higher proportion on the east side of the axial feature. Additionally, utilized flakes are present in almost identical proportions to the total number of artifacts in each half of the deposit (144 of 183, or 78.7 percent,

Table 7.4 Distribution of lithic materials in relation to axial feature in AlDf-30, Black Soil Area.

Tool	«West» of Axial Feature (incl. all material W53 west)	«East» of Axial Feature (incl. all units W51 and east)	«West» Half of W52 Units	«East» Half of W52 Units	Unk. Location in W52 units	**Totals**	Total «West» of Axial Ft.	Total «East» of Axial Ft.	Total Unk.
Projectile Points	0	2	1	0	0	**3**	1	2	0
Bifaces	2	4	1	2	1	**10**	3	6	0
Scrapers	3	12	2	1	0	**18**	5	13	0
Cores	2	1	1	2	0	**6**	3	3	0
Gravers	1	1	0	1	1	**4**	1	2	1
Retouched Flakes	1	11	2	2	1	**17**	3	13	1
Manuports	0	0	1	0	0	**1**	1	0	0
Utilized Flakes	30	108	38	36	16	**228**	68	144	16
Sub-total	39	139	46	44	19	**287**	85	183	18

in the east and 68 of 85, or 80 percent, in the west), as do bifaces (4.4 percent in the east and 4.7 percent in the west). This consistent use of space suggests significant continuity in activity in the features over time, but it is unclear if this relates to gendered use of space or some other patterned activity.

AlDf-31

Though several square metres of deposit were excavated at AlDf-31, only three artifacts were recovered (see Appendix A, figure 4.76; two shown), which may be a result of the possible function of the feature that dominated the excavated area. Two lithic artifacts were recovered, both made from opaque white quartz and included a small piece of quartz shatter (clearly the result of cultural activity, not shown), and the second a small smooth unmodified pebble. The latter was certainly brought to the site, as the deposit did not contain gravel or other pebbles. It may have been a gaming piece, or, more likely, it may have been one of the many small pebbles and cobbles that the inhabitants of Port Joli seem to have used as raw material sources for flaked stone tools. Given the depth of the location of the quartz pebble, which was recovered at 20.5 cm below datum in what may have been a sweathouse feature, a gaming piece or manuport may be the better interpretation.

The final artifact was the distal fragment of a worked antler awl, recovered from Level 3b. The awl was relatively small (40.5 mm in length) and somewhat flat, measuring 5.23 mm in thickness and 8.19 mm in width. The awl tapered to a sharp, but relatively worn, point, following the natural curve of the antler tine. It had been broken in antiquity but continued to be used, as the distal end exhibited slight wear and polish.

Discussion and Conclusions

The material-culture tradition in Port Joli is consistent with artifact frequencies and types reported from other Maritime Woodland archaeological deposits throughout the Maritime Peninsula, with some caveats. For example, the abundance of quartz material stands out, especially in comparison to sites closer to chert sources in Minas Basin. Even when compared to Passamaquoddy Bay sites, which themselves are relatively distant from local chert sources, the quantity of quartz material still stands out. It is clear from the nature of chert artifacts described above that Port Joli likely existed at nearly the extreme edge of chert trade/transport networks, and the material present in these assemblages reflects relatively extreme conservation of high-quality chert material. The abundance of quartz suggests that workable, if not ideal, material was abundantly available.

The extreme amount of quartz debitage and the large number of informal quartz cores indicate that significant experimentation and reduction was required to produce tools from the local quartz material; however, the number of formal quartz tools indicates it was a viable alternative to chert. With nearly inexhaustible quantities of local quartz, its friability and propensity to fracture during manufacture was something that could be accepted, with the understanding that a point, flake, or tool would eventually be produced. In this respect, conservation of chert material should not be equated with tool stone stress. Far from it; though more effort was likely required to produce a tool, the abundance of local material ensured it could be produced. Regardless, this tends to suggest that high-quality raw material was rare in Port Joli, a hypothesis supported by the general lack of chert and rhyolite cores in the overall assemblage.

A remarkable trait of the assemblages is the overwhelming number of utilized flakes at AlDf-24, Area A, Feature 2 (124 of 167 total tools, or 74.2 percent), AlDf-06 (37 of 54, or 68.5 percent), and AlDf-30 (226 of 287, 78.7 percent). Though they are less frequent in the AlDf-24, Area C, assemblages, they are still very common. Perhaps the importance of these tools relates to the lack of high-quality raw material. These flakes may represent an attempt to conserve the edges of formal chert tools by utilizing debitage that normally would be discarded. This strategy may have been especially important at AlDf-30, which has the highest proportion of utilized flakes, but where the conservation of chert material was especially important, as indicated by the proportion of chert-utilized flake tools. This may possibly suggest that it took the inhabitants of Port Joli some time to become accustomed to the friable and poor-quality quartz of the harbour. Utilized and retouched flakes—informal, or "expedient tools"—have also been attributed to gendered roles in the production of stone tools (e.g., Gero 1991). With the high resolution of patterned—and possibly gendered—distributions of flaked tools and ceramic vessels from both AlDf-24 and AlDf-30, future research that considers both the functional and social roles of this tool class could be profitable.

The metrics obtained during the stone tool analysis provides an opportunity to assess change through time. To increase sample sizes, we combined assemblages based on the chronology outlined in table 4.3, in Chapter 4. Tables 7.5a to 7.5c document the change in various stone tool metrics by chronological period, with sample sizes indicated (sample sizes varied due to differences in breakage or damage to the tools). While sample sizes are an issue, in general tool sizes appear to be smaller in the Middle Maritime Woodland Period, increase slightly during the early Late Maritime Woodland period, then decline again in the Late Maritime Woodland Period. The size of tools, especially the scrapers, increases again during the Protohistoric Period.

Table 7.5a Mean metric attributes by time period for all projectile points in the E'se'get assemblages (x) = sample size.

Time Period	Max Length	Max Width	Blade Width	Max Thickness	Haft Length	Base Width	Neck Width	Neck Height
Middle Maritime Woodland	27.2 (1)	17.01 (1)	13.9 (2)	7.76 (1)	19.8 (2)	9.62 (1)	16.0 (2)	13.6 (2)
Early Late Maritime Woodland	33.58 (1)	19.02 (1)	18.2 (1)	5.8 (7)	9.6 (6)	18.7 (5)	13.7 (6)	8.7 (6)
Later Late Maritime Woodland	32.3 (6)	17.63 (5)	17.8 (5)	5.7 (16)	7.8 (11)	16.25 (9)	10.8 (13)	7.2 (12)
Protohistoric	31.8 (1)	19.2 (1)	18.71 (1)	7.3 (4)	9.6 (4)	13.9 (1)	11.2 (3)	8.5 (4)

Table 7.5b Mean metric attributes by time period for all preforms in the E'se'get assemblages (x) = sample size.

Time Period	Max Length	Max Width	Max Thickness
Early Late Maritime Woodland	40.3 (1)	20.18 (1)	5.7 (1)
Later Late Maritime Woodland	37.5 (2)	19.8 (2)	6.6 (4)
Protohistoric	35.0 (5)	17.8 (5)	8.5 (5)

Table 7.5c Mean metric attributes by time period for all scrapers in the E'se'get assemblages (x) = sample size.

Time Period	Max Length	Max Width	Max Thickness
Middle Maritime Woodland	21.9 (11)	18.9 (11)	5.36 (11)
Early Late Maritime Woodland	22.5 (14)	21.5 (14)	6.1 (14)
Later Late Maritime Woodland	20.4 (34)	20.8 (34)	5.9 (34)
Protohistoric	20.7 (13)	21.3 (13)	5.2 (13)

The frequencies of raw materials used to make tools also changes over time; table 7.6 displays the percentages of different material types changing over time (using the high sample sizes from AlDf-30 and AlDf-24, Area C). As the table shows, chert artifacts account for nearly 40 percent of the stone tools recovered from the Middle Maritime Woodland deposits at AlDf-30, but this amount declines substantially in the early Late Maritime Woodland and later Late Maritime Woodland periods. A substantial increase in chert artifacts occurs in the Protohistoric Period. While quartz artifacts are relatively infrequent in the Middle Maritime Woodland Period, they tend to account for around 50 percent (45 to 52 percent) of the formal artifacts thereafter. Rhyolite decreases in frequency substantially in the Protohistoric Period.

Table 7.6 Percentages of stone tool material type by time period in the E'se'get assemblages.

Percentages	Chert	Quartz	Rhyolite	Other	Total
MMW AlDf-30	0.400	0.175758	0.278788	0.15758	1
ELMW Aldf-24 C	0.196078	0.529412	0.254902	0.098039	1
LLMW AlDf-24 C	0.215054	0.451613	0.27957	0.053763	1
Proto AlDf-24 C	0.346667	0.466667	0.173333	0.013333	1

It is difficult to account for these changes in material frequency but they may reflect changing relationships within and among Mi'kmaw groups, and prehistoric Wabanaki groups more generally, in the years between around 1800 BP and the arrival of Europeans in the region. Perhaps groups in the area of Port Joli's harbour area were participants in widespread trade in the Middle Maritime Woodland throughout the Maritime Peninsula and, upon integrating Port Joli into their seasonal activities, progressively had less opportunity for participating in seasonal gatherings (e.g., in the spring), where they would "stock up" on supplies not locally available, like chert. In this scenario, groups occupying areas around Port Joli's harbour in the Late Maritime Woodland relied increasingly on abundant local materials (quartz and rhyolite) and obtained chert only opportunistically. Two scenarios may have resulted in less exotics: either Port Joli was too far away from regional trade centres and gatherings, or trade was less intensive and less widespread during the Late Maritime Woodland Period.

During the Protohistoric Period, early European contact changed the ways that Indigenous peoples interacted with one another (e.g., Bourque and Whitehead 1985). The arrival of extremely valuable European trade goods increased the desire for trade exchanges, and as a result trade throughout the Wabanaki world may have intensified once again—or at the very least, it drew those in Port Joli back into greater opportunities for exchange. Thus, the inhabitants in Port Joli may have participated in a much wider network of exchange, resulting in greater amounts of "exotic" materials, like cherts from the Minas Basin area. Alternatively, changes in lithic material concentrations may also be reflective of changing settlement and mobility strategies, or simply a function of the time of year when sites were occupied—if chert was being traded at large gatherings during certain times of the year (e.g., spring or summer gatherings at the Goddard site in Maine or Melanson in Nova Scotia), cold season occupations in Port Joli may have a higher incidence of local material (i.e., reflective of dwindling lithic supplies).

While debitage analysis was not able to be fully conducted on the Port Joli assemblages, bulk-sample analysis can provide some insights into change over time and between deposits. As shown in figure 7.47 (see Appendix A), the quantity of cultural lithics per kilogram of soil increases over time in the Port Joli deposits, with a substantial peak in the earliest deposits at AlDf-24, Area C (the early Late Maritime Woodland). This could be the result of two factors.

Stone tool manufacture and maintenance may have increased in importance over time, which may be related to the increase in cervid procurement in the Late Maritime Woodland (see Chapter 8). The increase in cultural lithics may relate to "gearing up" (Binford 1979) and maintaining projectile points and processing tools related to the hunt and the effective utilization of the carcass. Another possibility is that the deposits represent more intensive activity—an increase in the duration and recurrence of occupation at the Late Maritime Woodland and Protohistoric sites. These two possibilities may not be mutually exclusive: as cervid hunting became more important, sites such as AlDf-24, Area C, which were advantageously positioned to intercept caribou and deer (see Chapter 3), may have become more important.

Beyond stone tools, the remainder of the assemblage exhibits unique attributes. Despite ample access to bone and antler material, organic tool frequencies are extremely low in Port Joli. For example, harpoon heads and leister points are completely absent in the E'se'get collection (though several were found by Erskine, see Appendix B, figures 7.61 and 7.66).

In some respects, this lack of barbed organic hunting implements is reflected in the fauna, where sturgeon and seal are very rare. It is also possible that seals were taken by stalking them at their haul-out locations, which occur on the shores at the mouth of the harbour, negating the need for open-water harpoon technology.

Perhaps the most incredible aspect of the artifact assemblage is the identification of a new class of composite artifact, the spark holder, which has never been identified on the Maritime Peninsula. It is difficult to know how common these artifacts may have been in Maritime Peninsula shell middens. It is possible, given their nature, that archaeologists may have missed them during excavation, as they can appear simply as unusual clay deposits. We only encountered these artifacts in a shell midden type that has, thus far, only been encountered around the harbour at Port Joli. Were these artifacts specifically related to the communal activities at the site? This possibility will be explored further in Chapter 9.

Lithic Technology and Other Artifacts **261**

Appendix A: Artifact Plates from the E'se'get Archaeology Project

Figure 7.2 Projectile points, bifaces, scrapers, and cores from AlDf-06 (all levels). From top left to bottom right: AlDf-6:44; 1; 34; 13; 18; 36; 43; 19.

Figure 7.3 Ground stone celt from AlDf-06. AlDf-06:24.

Figure 7.4 Projectile points and bifaces from AlDf-08 (all levels). From top left to bottom right: AlDf-8:40; 56; 62; 41.

Figure 7.5 Scrapers from AlDf-08 (all levels). From top left to bottom right: AlD-8:42; 36; 58; 54; 8; 39; 47b; 11; 49; 13a; 13b; 89a; 89b; 65.

Figure 7.6 Cores from AlDf-08 (all levels). From top left to bottom right: AlDf-8:71a; 91; 52; 75; 76; 78.

Figure 7.7 Projectile points, bifaces, and unifaces from AlDf-24 Area A (all levels). From top left to bottom right: AlDf-24:28; 564; 627; 1153; 560; 1151e; 487; 1140c; 1140e; 1140; 1165b.

Figure 7.8 Cores from AlDf-24 Area A (all levels). From top left to bottom right: AlDf-24:615; 571; 565; 1117.

Figure 7.9 Hammerstone from AlDf-24 Area A (all levels). AlDf-24:614.

Figure 7.10 Worked bone and ground ochre from AlDf-24 Area A (all levels). From top to bottom: AlDf-24:46; 208; 579; 593; 582.

Figure 7.11 Left, rolled iron bead from AlDf-24 Area A (AlDf-24:588). Right, native copper nodule from AlDf-24, Area C (AlDf-24:317).

Figure 7.12 A clay-lined clam shell (spark holder) in situ during excavation, AlDf-24, Area A, N56W50, Level 3h (AlDf-24:17).

Lithic Technology and Other Artifacts **271**

Figure 7.13 Clay-lined clam shells (spark holders) from AlDf-24 Area A (all levels). From top left to bottom right: AlDf-24:17; 1176a; 1176b; 617; 1176c.

Figure 7.14 Projectile points, bifaces, and unifaces from AlDf-24, Area A, Feature 2 (all levels). From top left to bottom right: AlDf-24:545; 552; 1129b; 546; 502; 1137f; 1107; 1112e; 1110; 668; 1111b; 669; 1145h; 1134b.

Figure 7.15 Cores from AlDf-24, Area A, Feature 2 (all levels). From top left to bottom right: AlDf-24:674; 500; 485; 499; 543.

Figure 7.16 Historic door hardware from AlDf-24, Area A, Feature 2. From left to right: AlDf-24:77; 78.

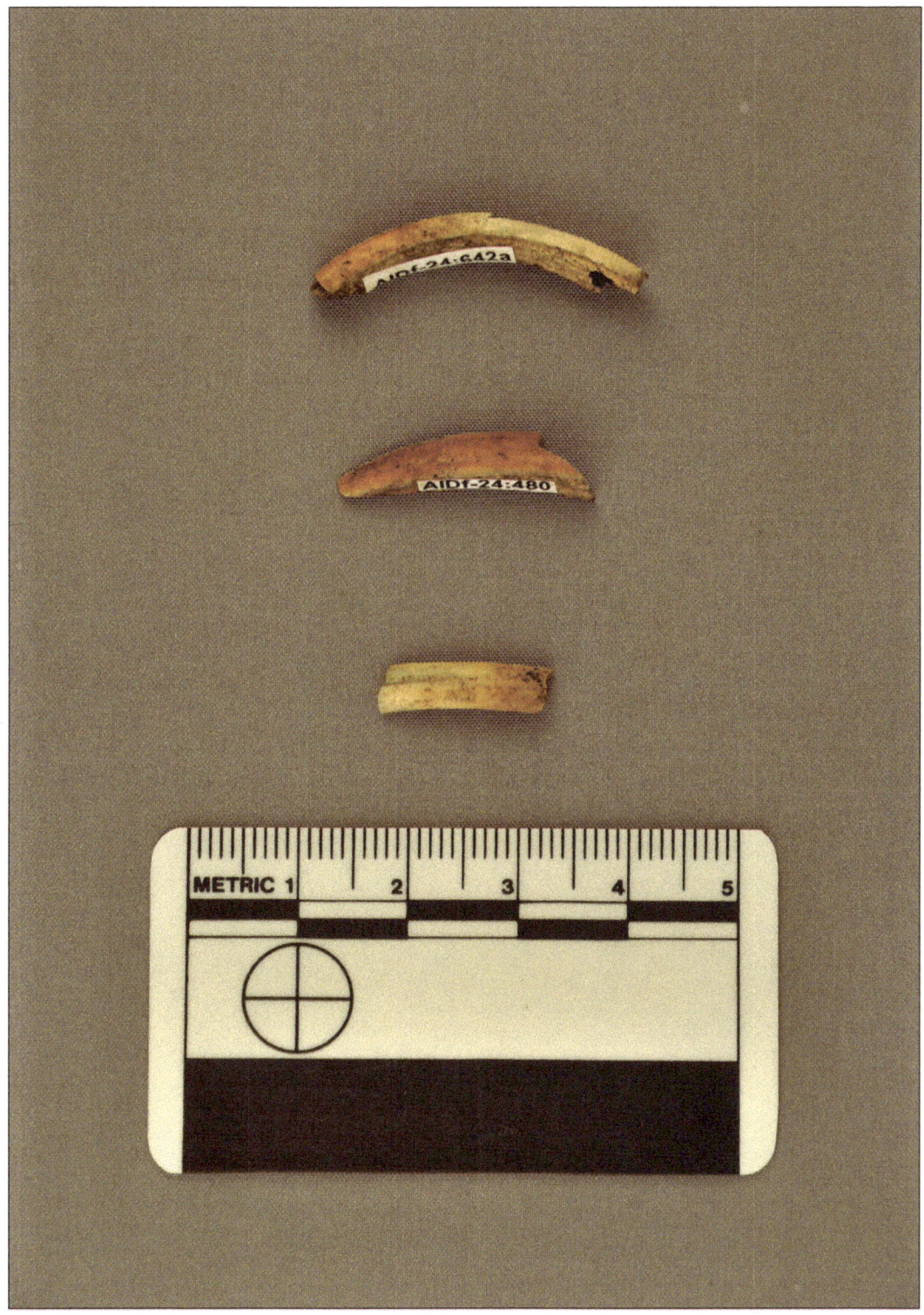

Figure 7.17 Organic artifacts from AlDf-24, Area A, Feature 2 (all levels). From top to bottom: AlDf-24:642a; 480; 642b.

Figure 7.18 Projectile points and bifaces from AlDf-24, Area C (levels 1, 2, and 2b). From top left to bottom right: AlDf-24:177; 84; 171; 350; 157; 451; 240; 50; 85; 151; 156; 368; 80; 339; 155; 367; 327; 176; 225; 326; 854a; 149; 174; 108; 234; 286; 172; 231; 232.

Lithic Technology and Other Artifacts **277**

Figure 7.19 Scrapers from AlDf-24, Area C (levels 1, 2, and 2b). From top left to bottom right: AlDf-24:369; 221; 656; 102; 338; 110; 109; 1051a; 173; 426; 973b; 1018a; 957a; 930a; 81; 1167; 139; 1062a; 972a; 973a; 821a; 889a; 1060a; 284; 218; 819.

Figure 7.20 Cores from AlDf-24, Area C (levels 1, 2, and 2b). From top left to bottom right: AlDf-24:150; 220; 226; 956a; 366; 477; 86; 858a; 228.

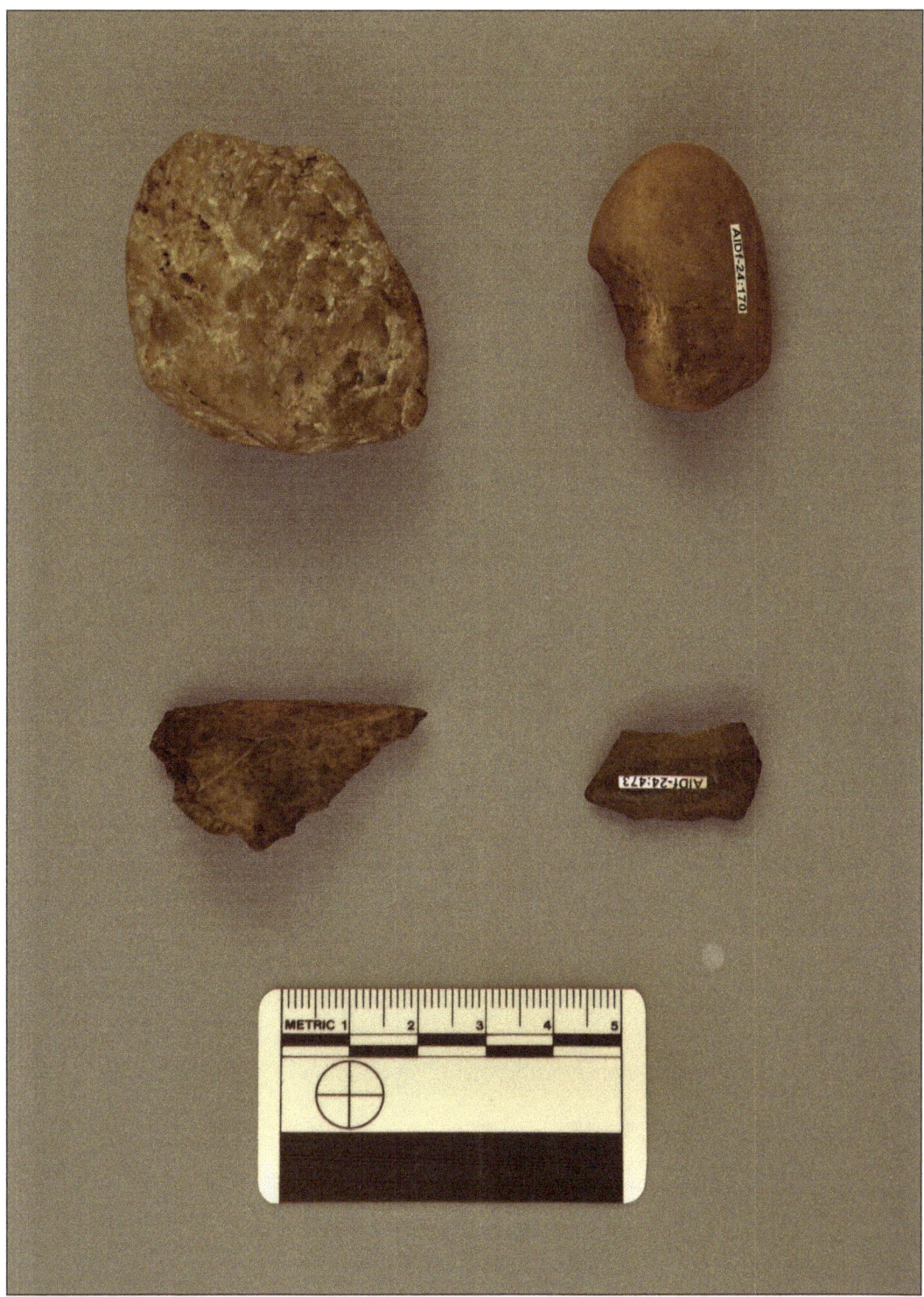

Figure 7.21 Hammerstones and ground stone from AlDf-24, Area C (levels 1, 2, and 2b). From top left to bottom right: AlDf-24:233; 170; 87; 473.

Figure 7.22 Organic artifacts from AlDf-24, Area C (levels 1, 2, and 2b). From top left to bottom right: AlDf-24:340; 449; 154; 224; 136.

Figure 7.23 Projectile points from AlDf-24, Area C, Feature 4 (levels 3 and 3b). From top left to bottom right: AlDf-24:332; 456; 300; 120; 378; 438; 373; 455; 427; 436; 354; 357.

Figure 7.24 Bifaces from AlDf-24, Area C, Feature 4 (levels 3 and 3b). From top left to bottom right: AlDf-24:295; 333; 454; 430; 116; 82; 442; 331; 143; 158l; 380; 189; 145; 372; 371; 343; 249; 376; 248; 257; 379; 254; 428; 242; 292; 302.

Lithic Technology and Other Artifacts **283**

Figure 7.25 Scrapers from AlDf-24, Area C, Feature 4 (levels 3 and 3b). From top left to bottom right: AlDf-24:381; 334; 121; 374; 452; 259; 262; 294; 1174; 353; 358; 53b; 437; 431; 1028a.

Figure 7.26 Cores from AlDf-24, Area C, Feature 4 (levels 3 and 3b). From top left to bottom right: AlDf-24:303; 383; 299; 444; 443; 440; 356; 193; 161; 361; 195; 119; 246; 114.

Lithic Technology and Other Artifacts **285**

Figure 7.27 Hammerstone from AlDf-24, Area C, Feature 4 (levels 3 and 3b). AlDf-24:187.

Figure 7.28 Organic artifacts from AlDf-24, Area C, Feature 4 (levels 3 and 3b). From top to bottom: AlDf-24:306; 99; 188; 182; 307a; 307b; 307c.

Lithic Technology and Other Artifacts **287**

Figure 7.29 Projectile points and bifaces from AlDf-24, Area C (levels 3c, 3d, and 3e). From top left to bottom right: AlDf-24:910a; 460; 459; 472; 388; 346; 391; 1077a; 385a, b; 1076a; 1083a; 1075a; 1078b; 345; 465; 1077b; 1077c; 386; 467; 269; 1078a; 1080a.

Figure 7.30 Scrapers from AlDf-24, Area C (levels 3c, 3d, and 3e). From top left to bottom right: AlDf-24:266; 842; 129; 462; 316; 270; 464; 469; 1084; 907; 463; 1080b; 989a; 870; 1073; 990.

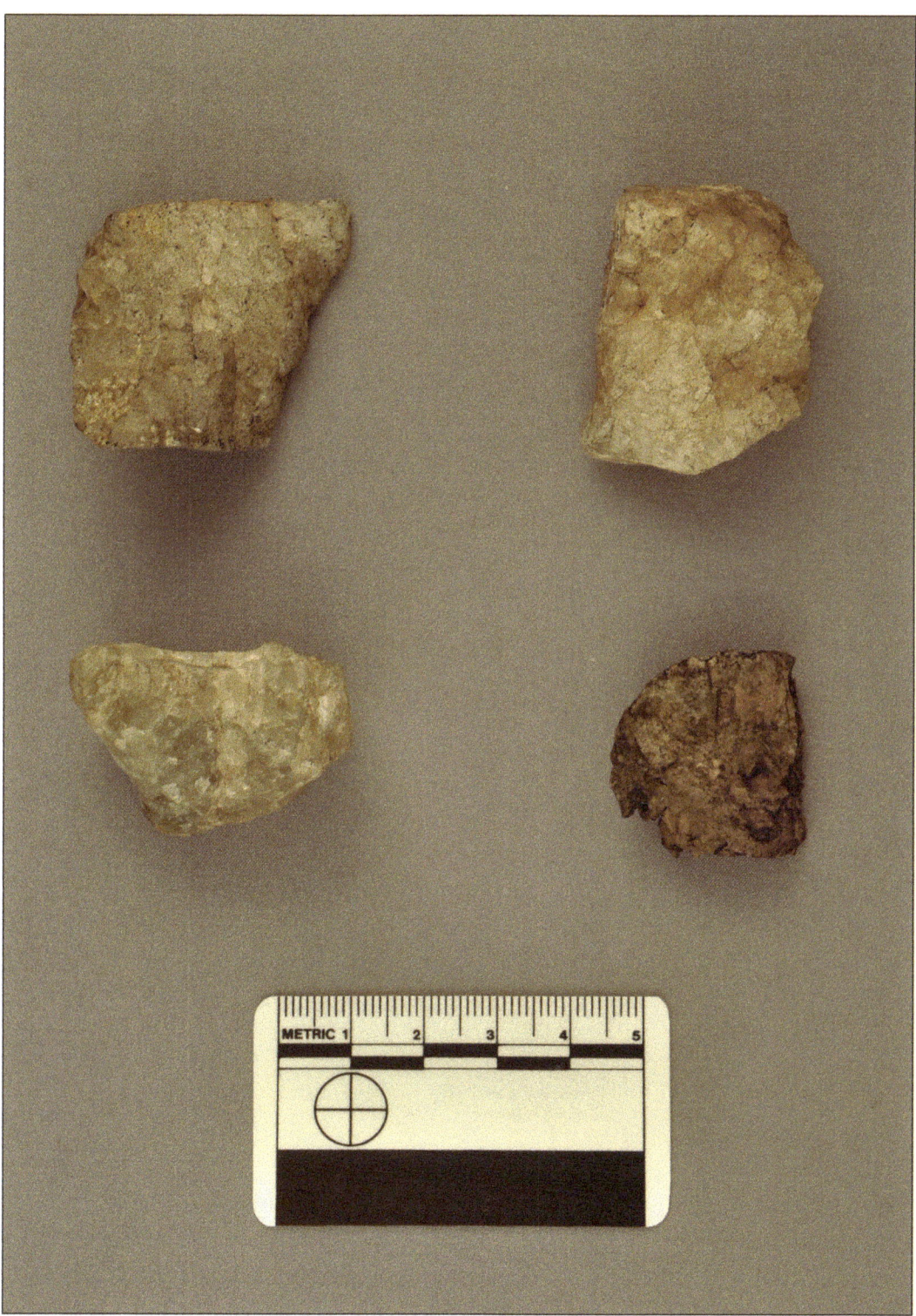

Figure 7.31 Cores from AlDf-24, Area C (levels 3c, 3d, and 3e). From top left to bottom right: AlDf-24:1072a; 458; 58; 271.

Figure 7.32 Organic artifacts from AlDf-24, Area C (levels 3c, 3d, and 3e). From top to bottom: AlDf-24:1177; 203.

Figure 7.33 Manuports from AlDf-24, Area C (levels 3c, 3d, and 3e). From top left to bottom right: AlDf-24:1194; 60.

Figure 7.34 Scrapers from AlDf-24, Area C (levels 3f, 3g, 3h, 3i, and 3j). From top left to bottom right: AlDf-24:914a; 1006a; 65; 881a.

Figure 7.35 Cores from AlDf-24, Area C (levels 3f, 3g, 3h, 3i, and 3j). From top left to bottom right: AlDf-24:321; 420; 67.

Figure 7.36 Manuport from AlDf-24, Area C (levels 3f, 3g, 3h, 3i, and 3j). AlDf-24:322.

Figure 7.37 Biface and Scraper from AlDf-30, Area A Midden (all levels). From top to bottom: AlDf-30:59; 68.

Figure 7.38 Hammerstones from AlDf-30, Area A Midden (all levels). From top left to bottom right: AlDf-30:3; 69; 2.

Figure 7.39 Projectile points, unifaces, and cores AlDf-30, Black Soil Area (levels 1, 2, and 2b). From top left to bottom right: AlDf-30:135,482; 1074; 753a; 1004b; 742c; 463c; 1011a; 1060; 1062.

Figure 7.40 Manuports and ochre from AlDf-30, Black Soil Area (levels 1, 2, and 2b). From top left to bottom right: AlDf-30:856; 476; 330.

Figure 7.41 Projectile points and bifaces from AlDf-30, Black Soil Area (levels 3a-3f). From top left to bottom right: AlDf-30:381; 116; 191; 844; 186; 408; 33; 152; 171a; 293b; 891.

Figure 7.42 Scrapers from AlDf-30, Black Soil Area (levels 3a-3f). From top left to bottom right: AlDf-30:812a; 1066; 98; 942; 48d; 295; 719; 980; 262b; 880; 718; 411.

Figure 7.43 Cores and gravers from AlDf-30, Black Soil Area (levels 3a-3f). From top left to bottom right: AlDf-30:250c; 36d; 568c; 260; 830; 852; 583.

Figure 7.44 Hammerstone from AlDf-30, Black Soil Area (levels 3a-3f). AlDf-20:475.

Figure 7.45 Modified whale bone and shell from AlDf-30, Black Soil Area (levels 3a-3f). From top to bottom: AlDf-30:113a; 113b; 113c; 97.

Figure 7.46 Artifacts from AlDf-31 (all levels). From top to bottom: AlDf-31:2; 3.

Lithic Technology and Other Artifacts 305

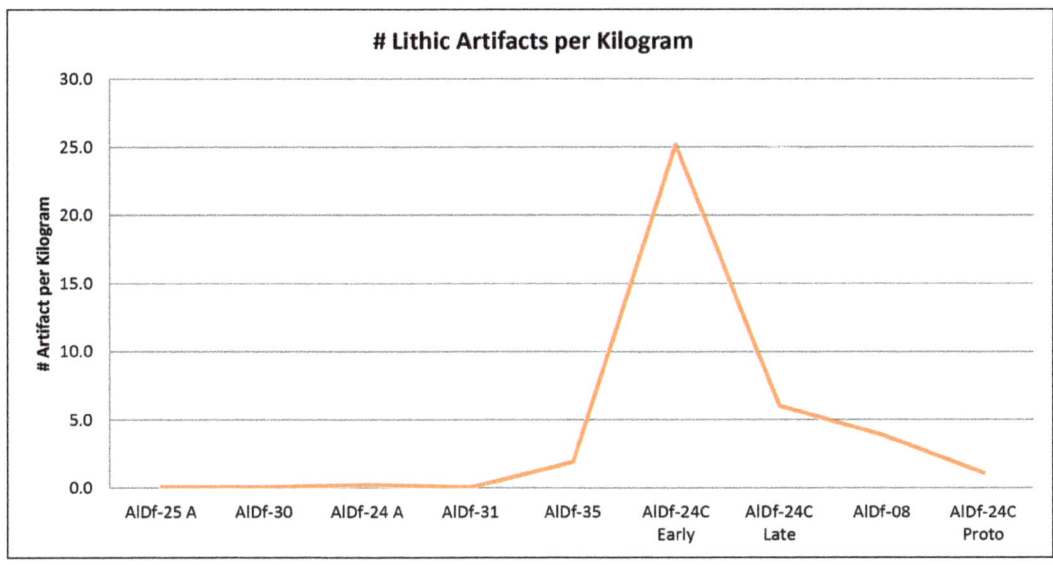

Figure 7.47 Number of lithic artifacts per kilogram from derived from bulk midden samples from various Port Joli contexts.

Appendix B: Artifact Plates from Port Joli Legacy Collections

Figure 7.48 AlDf-36/AlDf-01 selected projectile points, bifaces, and uniface.

Figure 7.49 AlDf-36/AlDf-01 ground stone and hammerstones.

Lithic Technology and Other Artifacts **307**

Figure 7.50 AlDf-03 selected projectile points and bifaces.

Figure 7.51 AlDf-03 selected ground stone, cores, and hammerstones.

308 Place-Making in the Pretty Harbour

Figure 7.52 AlDf-03 selected worked bone and antler.

Figure 7.53 AlDf-04 selected projectile points, bifaces, unifaces, and ceramic sherds.

Lithic Technology and Other Artifacts **309**

Figure 7.54a AlDf-06/AlDf-05 selected projectile points and bifaces.

Figure 7.54b AlDf-06/AlDf-05 selected projectile points and unifaces.

Figure 7.55 AlDf-06/AlDf-05 selected unifaces.

Lithic Technology and Other Artifacts **311**

Figure 7.56 AlDf-07 selected projectile points, bifaces, and unifaces.

Figure 7.57 AlDf-07 selected cervid faunal remains and worked bone. Note spirally fractured long bone fragments.

Figure 7.58a AlDf-08 selected projectile points and bifaces.

Figure 7.58b AlDf-08 selected projectile points and ground stone.

Lithic Technology and Other Artifacts **315**

Figure 7.59 AlDf-08 selected cervid faunal remains and worked bone.

Figure 7.60 AlDf-25/AlDf-09 selected projectile points and bifaces.

Figure 7.61 AlDf-25/AlDf-09 selected unifaces.

Figure 7.62 AlDf-25/AlDf-09 selected quartz cores.

Figure 7.63 AlDf-25/AlDf-09 selected ground stone.

Figure 7.64 AlDf-25/AlDf-09 selected worked bone and antler.

Lithic Technology and Other Artifacts **321**

Figure 7.65 AlDf-10 selected projectile points and bifaces.

Figure 7.66 AlDf-10 selected unifaces and cores.

Figure 7.67 AlDf-10 worked left tibia of an American beaver. Note nine incised lines.

Figure 7.68 AlDf-11 selected projectile points and bifaces.

Figure 7.69 AlDf-11 selected unifaces.

Figure 7.70 AlDf-11 selected ground stone. Note incised lines on bottom specimen.

Figure 7.71 AlDf-11 hammerstone.

Chapter 8
Animal and Plant Remains

MATTHEW BETTS

Introduction

A primary goal of the E'se'get Archaeology Project was to define a high-resolution sequence of human-animal relationships through the analysis of animal remains from shell-bearing deposits. Nova Scotia's normally acidic soils wreak havoc on organic remains, and animal bones often do not survive in such conditions. However, the low-acidity conditions in shell-bearing deposits, due to the leaching of calcium carbonate as bivalve shells decompose, create conditions leading to excellent bone preservation. In most Port Joli deposits with even a trace amount of highly comminuted shell, bone preservation was excellent, with small-fish and bird bone preserved in generally excellent condition.

The tradition of archaeological faunal analyses from Nova Scotia prehistoric archaeological sites is not as developed as it is in other areas of the country—a consequence both of the poor organic preservation and the lack of recent archaeological study of shell midden deposits (e.g., Murphy and Black 1996). As a result, few studies have been able to provide a quantitative diachronic assessment of changes in human-animal relationships from ancient Mi'kmaw sites. Recently, we published preliminary data relating to the Port Joli faunas (Betts et al. 2017). This chapter presents those data in greater detail, augmented by the previously unreported faunas from the E'se'get Project, as well as additional faunal data from the works of Eric Millard and John Erskine.

Faunal remains from the E'se'get Project were analyzed at the Howard Savage Faunal/Osteology Laboratory at the University of Toronto, with additional analyses carried out using collections at the Royal Ontario Museum (Toronto), the Canadian Museum of History (Gatineau), and the Canadian Museum of Nature (Gatineau Facitility). Erskine often provided detailed lists of presence or absence of species, quantified by unit. Much of the fauna was identified by him (he was a trained naturalist), but he often sent unidentified specimens to experts for proper analysis. There is little indication that his identifications were erroneous, and our analysis of faunal assemblages from sites previously tested by him has often confirmed his identifications (on a presence/absence basis), with the exception of great auk, which we were unable to identify in any of the assemblages we analyzed.

Millard's excavations are important because he was careful to screen deposits through window mesh, resulting in recovery that exceeded even our own excavations, which primarily used 3 mm mesh. This permitted the opportunity to analyze a faunal assemblage from his excavations (AlDf-11) in detail, which was accomplished at the Nova Scotia Museum using virtual 2-D and 3-D reference material (Betts et al. 2011; Gilbert 1990; Gilbert et al. 1985; Olsen 1964, 1968). Unfortunately, it was not possible to borrow the AlDf-11 assemblage for comparison to a traditional faunal reference collection from another museum.

Fish

In general, recovery methods employed on the E'se'get Project were designed to maximize the collection of fish remains. Domestic shell-bearing deposits were ubiquitously screened through 3 mm mesh. However, as described in Chapter 1, shell midden deposits, specifically those at AlDf-24, AlDf-25, AlDf-30, and AlDf-31, were screened through 6 mm (1/4 inch) mesh. The large amount of coarsely broken clam shell in these deposits would not pass through 3 mm mesh, and it severely obscured our ability to see and, therefore, collect fauna, while also substantially increasing mechanical attrition (breakage caused by objects colliding and grinding on each other while screening), resulting in broken bone fragments. Fortunately, this collection strategy seems not to have resulted in a biased faunal sample, at least not for the identifiable organic fraction. As described in Betts et al. (2017: 24), to test the effect of screen size on faunal recovery and analysis, we screened three 5 L bulk midden samples (AlDf-24, Area C) through 6 mm mesh, followed by 3 mm mesh. The remains were then each identified at the Canadian Museum of History, using photographic, digital, and physical reference collections. There were no differences in the identifiable assemblages between the samples, the specimens in the fraction screened by 3 mm mesh being too fragmentary for positive identification and entirely fish bones. It should be noted that no small-fish taxa were present in the sample (e.g., herring or tomcod), which may account for this pattern (though such small-fish taxa were identified in the AlDf-24, Area A, sample screened through 6 mm mesh). The proportion of unidentified mammal and bird fraction was not altered by the use of 3 mm mesh, but approximately 5 percent of the total fish bones were recovered by the 3 mm mesh.

As shown in table 8.1, fish bones from species in the family Gadidae, including Atlantic cod (*Gadus morhua*), cod/pollock (Gadidae), and tomcod (*Microgadus tomcod*), dominate in nearly all assemblages (see also figure 8.1). This is not unexpected as one of the world's greatest cod fisheries, Georges Bank, lies just offshore. Georges Bank cod stocks constantly frequent the South Shore coast, moving off- and onshore seasonally, and resident cod stocks are believed to inhabit South Shore waters year-round. Tomcod have only been identified in four contexts, AlDf-24, Area A; AlDf-30, Black Soil Area; AlDf-30, Area B; and AlDf-31. All of these contexts are believed to date to the Middle Maritime Woodland Period.

Of note was the extremely large size of many of the Atlantic cod remains from sites around Port Joli's harbour. While fragmentary lateral margins (likely caused by mechanical action in very shell-dominant middens) prevented precise estimates, many thoracic centra measured greater than 18 mm in diameter, denoting individual cod of more than 1 m in length (e.g., Betts et al. 2014). This large-size phenomenon has been noticed for prehistoric and early historic archaeological contexts throughout the Maritime Peninsula (e.g. Betts et al. 2011, 2017; Jackson et al. 2001, Rojo 1986, 1987, 1990, 2002).

Number of identified specimens (NISP) values reveal that cod and pollock (Gadidae), and indeed fish in general, tend to be more prevalent in the Middle Maritime Woodland contexts, especially at those large shell midden sites closer to the mouth of the harbour (table 8.1, figure 8.1; see also figure 3.1). At some sites, they represent more than 50 percent of the faunal remains by NISP, but through time decrease to a miniscule percentage in assemblages (figure 8.2). Tomcod are very common in some kitchen midden contexts at sites nearer to the mouth of the harbour but, again, tend to be present only in Middle

Animal and Plant Remains **327**

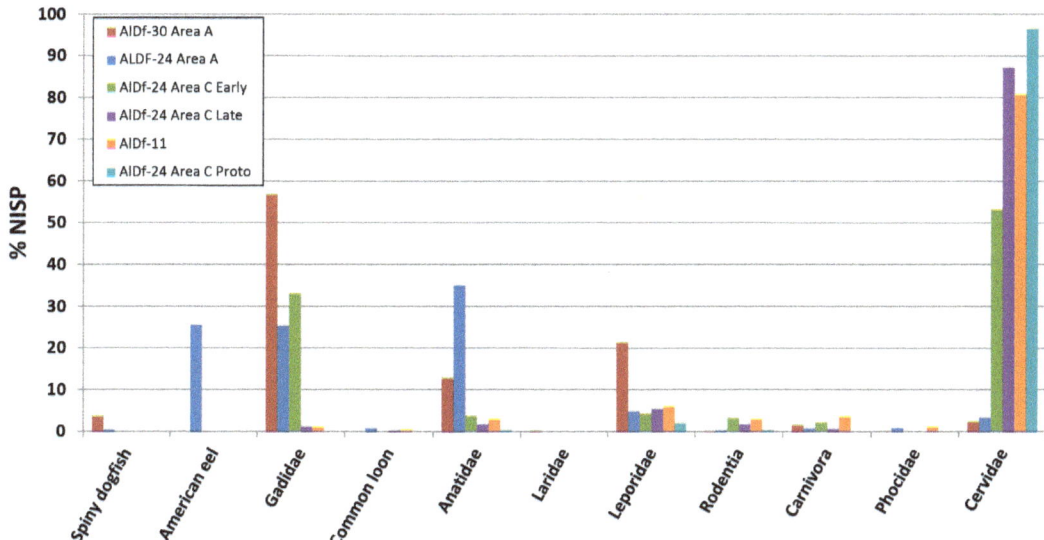

Figure 8.1 Port Joli faunal assemblages: Percentage of number of identified specimens (% NISP) of major taxa. Contexts have been arranged sequentially according to the chronological model developed in Chapter 4.

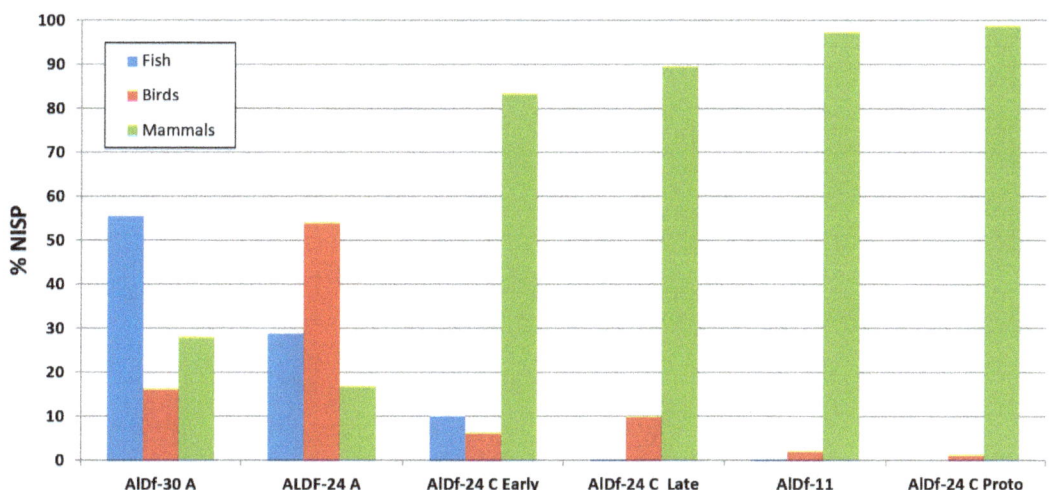

Figure 8.2 Port Joli faunal assemblages: Percentage of number of identified specimens (NISP) by taxonomic class (including "unidentifiable" fraction in each class). Contexts have been arranged sequentially according to the chronological model developed in Chapter 4.

Maritime Woodland shell midden deposits. Spiny dogfish (*Squalus acanthias*) tend to co-occur in assemblages with large numbers of cod remains. They are not present in any Late Maritime Woodland context. These small sharks are migratory and tend to move into bays and inlets between June and November (Leim and Scott 1966).

Bones of Atlantic sturgeon (*Acipenser oxyrhynchus oxyrhynchus*) are very rare in Port Joli shell middens and can only be found in one Late Maritime Woodland deposit, AlDf-08. This site is located very close to Path Lake and its small brook, which may have been attractive to small sturgeon. In general, however, the near total absence of this species in

Table 8.1 Port Joli faunal assemblages by taxa: Number of identified specimens (NISP) per species, percentage of overall NISP, minimum number of individuals (MNI), richness, and unidentified counts.

Taxon	Common Name	AlDf-25, Area A			AlDf-30, Area A			AlDf-30, Black Soil Area			ALDF-24, Area A			AlDf-24, C Levels 3c-3k lower			AlDf-24, C Levels 3-3b upper		
		NISP	%	MNI	NISP	%	MNI	NISP	%	MNI	NISP	%	MNI	NISP	%	MNI	NISP	%	MNI
Squalus acanthias	spiny dogfish	0	0.00	0	78	3.80	1	2	3.33	1	19	0.71	1	0	0.00	0	0	0.00	0
Anguilla rostrata	American eel	0	0.00	0	0	0.00	0	0	0.00	0	692	25.85	6	0	0.00	0	0	0.00	0
Acipenser oxyrhynchus	Atlantic sturgeon	0	0.00	0	0	0.00	0	0	0.00	0	0	0.00	0	0	0.00	0	0	0.00	0
Clupidea	herring	0	0.00	0	0	0.00	0	0	0.00	0	0	0.00	0	0	0.00	0	0	0.00	0
Gadus morhua	Atlantic cod	0	0.00	0	75	3.65	1	14	23.33	1	57	2.13	12	21	11.41	1	2	0.57	1
Migrogadus tomcod	tomcod	0	0.00	0	0	0.00	0	11	18.33	1	37	1.38	2	0	0.00	0	0	0.00	0
	cod/pollock	0	0.00	0	4	0.19	1	0	0.00	0	0	0.00	0	0	0.00	0	0	0.00	0
Gadidae	true cods	2	6.90	1	1089	52.99	8	0	0.00	0	593	22.15	11	40	21.74	1	3	0.85	1
Gavia immer	common loon	0	0.00	0	1	0.05	1	1	1.67	1	28	1.05	2	0	0.00	0	2	0.57	1
Ardea herodia	Great blue heron	0	0.00	0	0	0.00	0	0	0.00	0	0	0.00	0	0	0.00	0	0	0.00	0
Branta canadensis	Canada goose	1	3.45	1	26	1.27	3	2	3.33	1	443	16.55	12	4	2.17	1	4	1.14	1
Anserinae	swan/goose	0	0.00	0	5	0.24	1	0	0.00	0	0	0.00	0	0	0.00	0	0	0.00	0
Anserini	goose	0	0.00	0	2	0.10	1	0	0.00	0	0	0.00	0	0	0.00	0	0	0.00	0
Anas rubripes	black duck	0	0.00	0	49	2.38	7	0	0.00	0	60	2.24	6	0	0.00	0	1	0.28	1
Anatinae	dabbling duck	0	0.00	0	75	3.65	4	1	1.67	1	55	2.05	3	0	0.00	0	0	0.00	0
Aythaya collaris	ring-necked duck	0	0.00	0	4	0.19	1	0	0.00	0	0	0.00	0	0	0.00	0	0	0.00	0
Somateria mollissima	common eider	11	37.93	2	29	1.41	6	0	0.00	0	223	8.33	9	0	0.00	0	0	0.00	0
	black duck/eider	0	0.00	0	57	2.77	5	0	0.00	0	0	0.00	0	0	0.00	0	0	0.00	0
Mergus sp.	Mergus sp.	0	0.00	0	9	0.44	3	1	1.67	1	13	0.49	2	0	0.00	0	0	0.00	0
Anatidae	duck/goose/swan	0	0.00	0	9	0.44	4	4	6.67	1	150	5.60	7	3	1.63	1	2	0.57	1
Larus smithsonianus	herring gull	0	0.00	0	0	0.00	0	0	0.00	0	3	0.11	1	0	0.00	0	0	0.00	0
Laridae	gull	0	0.00	0	6	0.29	1	0	0.00	0	0	0.00	0	0	0.00	0	0	0.00	0
Strix varia	barred owl	0	0.00	0	0	0.00	0	0	0.00	0	0	0.00	0	0	0.00	0	0	0.00	0
Lepus americanus	snowshoe hare	13	44.83	1	442	21.51	17	13	21.67	1	136	5.08	7	8	4.35	1	20	5.68	1
Castor canadensis	North American beaver	0	0.00	0	4	0.19	3	0	0.00	0	6	0.22	1	1	0.54	1	7	1.99	2
Erethizon dorsatum	porcupine	0	0.00	0	0	0.00	0	0	0.00	0	3	0.11	1	2	1.09	1	0	0.00	0
Microtus sp.	vole	0	0.00	0	0	0.00	0	0	0.00	0	0	0.00	0	0	0.00	0	0	0.00	0
Peromyscus sp.	mouse	0	0.00	0	0	0.00	0	0	0.00	0	0	0.00	0	0	0.00	0	0	0.00	0
Muridae	mouse or shrew	0	0.00	0	0	0.00	0	0	0.00	0	4	0.15	1	0	0.00	0	0	0.00	0
Tamias striatus	eastern chipmunk	0	0.00	0	0	0.00	0	0	0.00	0	1	0.04	1	3	1.63	1	0	0.00	0
Rodentia	rodent	0	0.00	0	0	0.00	0	1	1.67	1	1	0.04	1	0	0.00	0	0	0.00	0
Tamiasciurus hudsonicus	American red squirrel	0	0.00	0	1	0.05	1	0	0.00	0	1	0.04	1	0	0.00	0	0	0.00	0
Scurius sp.	squirrel	0	0.00	0	0	0.00	0	0	0.00	0	0	0.00	0	0	0.00	0	0	0.00	0
Vulpes vulpes	red fox	0	0.00	0	0	0.00	0	1	1.67	1	0	0.00	0	0	0.00	0	0	0.00	0
Canis lups	eastern wolf	0	0.00	0	0	0.00	0	1	1.67	1	7	0.26	1	1	0.54	1	0	0.00	0
Canis lupus familiaris	domesic dog	0	0.00	0	18	0.88	1	0	0.00	0	2	0.07	1	1	0.54	1	0	0.00	0
Canis sp.	coyote, wolf, or dog	0	0.00	0	14	0.68	1	1	1.67	1	0	0.00	0	0	0.00	0	0	0.00	0
Ursus americanus	American black bear	0	0.00	0	3	0.15	1	0	0.00	0	2	0.07	1	0	0.00	0	0	0.00	0
Mustelidae	mink or marten	0	0.00	0	0	0.00	0	0	0.00	0	2	0.07	1	0	0.00	0	0	0.00	0
Lontra canadensis	river otter	0	0.00	0	0	0.00	0	0	0.00	0	1	0.04	1	0	0.00	0	0	0.00	0
Lynx canadensis	lynx	0	0.00	0	0	0.00	0	0	0.00	0	6	0.22	1	1	0.54	1	1	0.28	1
Lynx rufus	bobcat	0	0.00	0	0	0.00	0	1	1.67	1	0	0.00	0	0	0.00	0	0	0.00	0
Carnivora	carnivore	0	0.00	0	0	0.00	0	0	0.00	0	7	0.26	1	1	0.54	1	2	0.57	1
Halichoerus grypus	grey seal	1	3.45	1	4	0.19	1	0	0.00	0	6	0.22	1	0	0.00	0	0	0.00	0
Pagophilus groenlandicus	harp seal	0	0.00	0	0	0.00	0	0	0.00	0	3	0.11	1	0	0.00	0	0	0.00	0
Phocidae	small seal	0	0.00	0	0	0.00	0	4	6.67	1	21	0.78	2	0	0.00	0	0	0.00	0
Alces alces	moose	0	0.00	0	15	0.73	1	0	0.00	0	17	0.64	1	4	2.17	1	3	0.85	1
Rangifer tarandus caribou	woodland caribou	0	0.00	0	36	1.75	1	0	0.00	0	52	1.94	2	1	0.54	1	1	0.28	1
Odocoileus virginianus	white-tailed deer	0	0.00	0	0	0.00	0	0	0.00	0	12	0.45	1	22	11.96	2	98	27.84	3
Cervidae	caribou/deer	1	3.45	1	0	0.00	0	2	3.33	1	14	0.52	1	71	38.59	3	206	58.52	4
Totals		29			2055			60			2677			184			352		
Richness		1			16			13			26			11			10		
Spiral Mammal Unident		0			0			2			41			657			1351		
Spiral mammal Ident		0			0			1			0			17			34		
Unidentified Fish		0			850			306			1771			215			25		

Animal and Plant Remains

AIDf-08			AIDf-06			ALDF-24, Area A Feature 2			AIDf-11			AIDf-24 C, Levels 1-2 Proto			AIDf-35			AIDf-31			AIDf-30, Area B		
NISP	%	MNI	NISP	%	MNI	NISP	%	MNI	NISP	%	MNI	NISP	%	MNI	NISP	%	MNI	NISP	%	MNI	NISP	%	MNI
0	0.000	0	0	0.00	0	0	0.00	0	0	0.00	0	0	0.00	0	0	0.00	0	2	1.72	1	13	0.76	1
0	0.000	0	0	0.00	0	0	0.00	0	0	0.00	0	0	0.00	0	0	0.00	0	0	0.00	0	0	0.00	0
2	2.941	1	0	0.00	0	0	0.00	0	0	0.00	0	0	0.00	0	0	0.00	0	0	0.00	0	0	0.00	0
0	0.000	0	0	0.00	0	0	0.00	0	0	0.00	0	0	0.00	0	0	0.00	0	0	0.00	0	7	0.41	1
0	0.000	0	0	0.00	0	1	3.33	0	2	1.23	1	0	0.00	0	0	0.00	0	9	7.76	1	421	24.75	0
0	0.000	0	0	0.00	0	0	0.00	0	0	0.00	0	0	0.00	0	0	0.00	0	1	0.86	1	1112	65.37	9
0	0.000	0	0	0.00	0	0	0.00	0	0	0.00	0	0	0.00	0	0	0.00	0	56	48.28	1	0	0.00	0
2	2.941	1	0	0.00	0	3	10.00	1	0	0.00	0	0	0.00	0	0	0.00	0	0	0.00	0	0	0.00	0
2	2.941	1	0	0.00	0	0	0.00	0	1	0.62	1	0	0.00	0	0	0.00	0	2	1.72	1	1	0.06	0
0	0.000	0	0	0.00	0	0	0.00	0	0	0.00	0	0	0.00	0	0	0.00	0	1	0.86	1	0	0.00	0
0	0.000	0	0	0.00	0	3	10.00	1	0	0.00	0	0	0.00	0	0	0.00	0	0	0.00	0	9	0.53	0
0	0.000	0	0	0.00	0	0	0.00	0	0	0.00	0	0	0.00	0	0	0.00	0	0	0.00	0	0	0.00	0
0	0.000	0	0	0.00	0	0	0.00	0	0	0.00	0	0	0.00	0	0	0.00	0	0	0.00	0	0	0.00	0
2	2.941	1	0	0.00	0	0	0.00	0	0	0.00	0	0	0.00	0	0	0.00	0	13	11.21	1	13	0.76	2
0	0.000	0	0	0.00	0	0	0.00	0	0	0.00	0	0	0.00	0	0	0.00	0	0	0.00	0	0	0.00	0
2	2.941	1	0	0.00	0	0	0.00	0	0	0.00	0	0	0.00	0	0	0.00	0	4	3.45	1	10	0.59	2
0	0.00	0	0	0.00	0	0	0.00	0	0	0.00	0	0	0.00	0	0	0.00	0	0	0.00	0	0	0.00	0
0	0.00	0	0	0.00	0	0	0.00	0	0	0.00	0	0	0.00	0	0	0.00	0	0	0.00	0	0	0.00	0
0	0.00	0	0	0.00	0	2	6.67	1	5	3.09	0	1	0.54	1	0	0.00	0	0	0.00	0	0	0.00	0
0	0.00	0	0	0.00	0	0	0.00	0	0	0.00	0	0	0.00	0	0	0.00	0	0	0.00	0	0	0.00	0
0	0.00	0	0	0.00	0	0	0.00	0	0	0.00	0	0	0.00	0	0	0.00	0	0	0.00	0	1	0.06	1
1	1.47	1	0	0.00	0	0	0.00	0	10	6.17	0	4	2.17	1	0	0.00	0	27	23.28	2	89	5.23	5
0	0.00	0	0	0.00	0	0	0.00	0	4	2.47	1	1	0.54	1	0	0.00	0	0	0.00	0	0	0.00	0
0	0.00	0	0	0.00	0	1	3.33	1	1	0.62	1	0	0.00	0	0	0.00	0	0	0.00	0	0	0.00	0
0	0.00	0	0	0.00	0	0	0.00	0	0	0.00	0	0	0.00	0	0	0.00	0	0	0.00	0	2	0.12	0
0	0.00	0	0	0.00	0	0	0.00	0	0	0.00	0	0	0.00	0	0	0.00	0	0	0.00	0	6	0.35	1
0	0.00	0	0	0.00	0	0	0.00	0	0	0.00	0	0	0.00	0	0	0.00	0	0	0.00	0	0	0.00	0
1	1.47	1	0	0.00	0	0	0.00	0	0	0.00	0	0	0.00	0	0	0.00	0	0	0.00	0	4	0.24	1
0	0.00	0	0	0.00	0	0	0.00	0	0	0.00	0	0	0.00	0	0	0.00	0	0	0.00	0	0	0.00	0
0	0.00	0	0	0.00	0	0	0.00	0	0	0.00	0	0	0.00	0	0	0.00	0	0	0.00	0	0	0.00	0
0	0.00	0	0	0.00	0	0	0.00	0	0	0.00	0	0	0.00	0	0	0.00	0	0	0.00	0	1	0.06	0
0	0.00	0	0	0.00	0	0	0.00	0	0	0.00	0	0	0.00	0	0	0.00	0	0	0.00	0	2	0.12	1
0	0.00	0	0	0.00	0	0	0.00	0	2	1.23	1	0	0.00	0	0	0.00	0	0	0.00	0	0	0.00	0
0	0.00	0	0	0.00	0	0	0.00	0	1	0.62	1	0	0.00	0	0	0.00	0	0	0.00	0	0	0.00	0
0	0.00	0	0	0.00	0	0	0.00	0	2	1.23	1	0	0.00	0	0	0.00	0	0	0.00	0	0	0.00	0
5	7.35	1	0	0.00	0	0	0.00	0	1	0.62	1	0	0.00	0	0	0.00	0	0	0.00	0	0	0.00	0
0	0.00	0	0	0.00	0	0	0.00	0	0	0.00	0	0	0.00	0	0	0.00	0	1	0.86	1	3	0.18	1
0	0.00	0	0	0.00	0	0	0.00	0	0	0.00	0	0	0.00	0	0	0.00	0	0	0.00	0	0	0.00	0
0	0.00	0	0	0.00	0	0	0.00	0	2	1.23	1	0	0.00	0	0	0.00	0	0	0.00	0	0	0.00	0
7	10.29	1	0	0.00	0	1	3.33	1	0	0.00	0	0	0.00	0	0	0.00	0	0	0.00	0	4	0.24	1
0	0.00	0	0	0.00	0	0	0.00	0	9	5.56	1	3	1.63	1	0	0.00	0	0	0.00	0	0	0.00	0
0	0.00	0	0	0.00	0	2	6.67	1	1	0.62	1	0	0.00	0	3	60.00	1	0	0.00	0	0	0.00	0
4	5.88	1	0	0.00	0	0	0.00	0	34	20.99	2	34	18.48	2	2	40.00	1	0	0.00	0	0	0.00	0
40	58.82	2	1	100.00	1	17	56.67	1	87	53.70	2	141	76.63	5	0	0.00	0	0	0.00	0	3	0.18	1
68			1			30			162			184			5			116			1701		
15			1			5			14			5			2			9			15		
114			0			19			25			292			0			0			7		
4			0			1			46			6			0			0			0		
3						193			0			0						34			964		

Taxon	Common Name	AlDf-25, Area A			AlDf-30, Area A			AlDf-30, Black Soil Area			ALDF-24, Area A			AlDf-24, C Levels 3c-3k lower			AlDf-24, C Levels 3-3b upper		
		NISP	%	MNI	NISP	%	MNI	NISP	%	MNI	NISP	%	MNI	NISP	%	MNI	NISP	%	MNI
Unidentified Bird		0			338			54			4922			163			642		
Unidentified Mammal		0			515			361			1539			2128			5475		
Unidentified Indeterminate		0			2281			1475			3138			628			1935		
Cervidae/Anatidae Index		0.077			0.161			0.2			0.091			0.933			0.978		
Phocidae/Anatidae Index		0.077			0.015			0.333			0.031			0			0		
Anatidae/Hare		0.48			0.375			0.381			0.874			0.467			0.259		
Gadidae/Cervidae		0.923			0.839			0.8			0.909			0.067			0.022		

the shell middens is likely related to the lack of large nearby rivers and estuaries of sufficient size to support the spawning of these large fish.

Herring (Clupeidae) remains are also very rare in Port Joli shell-bearing deposits, and have been recovered from only one context, the very rich AlDf-30, Area B Midden. Only seven fragments were found in this very large assemblage, indicating that herring was of relatively minor importance. It is possible that they occur in this context as a bycatch of the similarly sized tomcod that were so important in this deposit. Regardless, the small numbers of herring stand at odds to modern *gaspereau, or kyack,* (alewife, *Alosa pseudoharengus*) populations, which run in the small rivers at the head of Port Joli's harbour. In fact, Erskine (1986: 92) claims to have found massive deposits of herring scales at some sites (e.g., AlDf-03). We will further explore this discrepancy later in this chapter.

Finally, remains of American eel (*Anguilla rostrata*) were recovered from only one context, the large clam-processing midden at AlDf-24, Area A. These were so abundant that they, by NISP, accounted for more than 25 percent of the total faunal assemblage, just slightly less than the total number of Gadidae remains recovered from the deposit. These catadromous fish spawn in the ocean, but return to freshwater systems to mature before returning to the sea to complete their life cycles. Extensive eelgrass (*Zostera marina*) beds at the head of Port Joli's harbour are prime habitat for eels and attract large schools in the summer months (COSEWIC 2006; Weiler 2011: 20). The rarity of eel remains in Port Joli middens is therefore odd, given the prime habitat and extensive ethnohistoric reliance on the species (e.g., Baird 1616; Denys 1968). Given its presence in a very unique deposit, it is possible that the exploitation and consumption of the species occurred only during the season of activity represented by the large processing midden and in the same unique milieu of activities that resulted in the midden's deposition.

Birds

Ten species of birds were recovered from the E'se'get excavations around Port Joli's harbour. Today, Port Joli's harbour contains a migratory bird sanctuary; waterfowl utilize the South Shore both for overwintering and for through-migration to points further north and south. In fact, Port Joli is a noted overwintering location for both Canada goose (*Branta canadensis*) and common eider (*Somateria mollissima*). Not surprisingly, then, both species dominate in assemblages with bird remains. However, in general, bird remains are remarkably limited in most deposits tested during the project. AlDf-24, Area A, had the greatest quantity and diversity of bird remains, followed by the AlDf-30, Area A midden. Both contexts date to

AlDf-08			AlDf-06			ALDF-24, Area A Feature 2			AlDf-11			AlDf-24 C, Levels 1-2 Proto			AlDf-35			AlDf-31			AlDf-30, Area B		
NISP	%	MNI	NISP	%	MNI	NISP	%	MNI	NISP	%	MNI	NISP	%	MNI	NISP	%	MNI	NISP	%	MNI	NISP	%	MNI
34						275			3			24						81			220		
507			22			346			245			1753			5			12			134		
57			1			384			0			123						103			529		
0.917			1			0.792			0.963			0.994			1			0			0.086		
0.636			0			0.167			0.286			0			0			0			0.111		
0.8			0			1			0.333			0.2			0			0.386			0.264		
0.083			0			0.208			0.037			0.006			0			1			0.914		

the Middle Maritime Woodland. Bird remains are distinctly uncommon in Late Maritime Woodland contexts, even those with relatively abundant sample sizes (table 8.1, figure 8.2). In contexts with bird remains, dabbling ducks and sea ducks, as well as other aquatic birds such as common loon (*Gavia immer*), great blue heron (*Ardea herodias*), and gulls (Laridae), occur in small numbers. Surprisingly absent from all contexts are any passerine birds, birds of prey, and shorebirds. The only terrestrial bird identified was a barred owl (*Strix varia*), of which remains were recovered from AlDf-30, Area B.

Mammals

Mammals account for the greatest diversity of species and, in most sites, the greatest quantity of faunal material recovered during the E'se'get Project (table 8.1, figures 8.1 and 8.2). Twenty species of mammal have been identified in the assemblages. Moving taxonomically, snowshoe hare (*Lepus americanus*) is remarkably abundant in many assemblages, and in assemblages with adequate sample sizes they can account for more than 20 percent, based on NISP. Like the birds, they are especially abundant in Middle Maritime Woodland deposits and tend to be less prevalent in Late Maritime Woodland deposits (figure 8.1). There also tends to be an association with near interior sites (see description in Chapter 3), which often contain abundant hare remains.

A variety of other fur-bearers are present in the assemblages, ranging from beavers (*Castor canadensis*), mink/marten (*Mustela vison/Martes americana*), river otter (*Lontra canadensis*), lynx (*Lynx canadensis*), and bobcat (*Lynx rufus*). While present in many Middle Maritime Woodland assemblages, they often occur in trace amounts (less than 1 percent NISP) and are nearly absent in most Late Maritime Woodland assemblages, even those with adequate sample sizes. Of special note is the near complete absence of red fox (*Vulpes vulpes*) bones; only one fox bone was recovered from all of the assemblages tested. Fox was also not identified by Erskine in any of his analyses (see below), suggesting a real bias against a species that is relatively common today. One possible explanation for this is the rather high proportion of domestic dog, wolf, and coyote remains. Foxes are known to avoid areas with high large canid populations (e.g., Fedriani et al. 2000; Gosselink et al. 2003). These large canids may have out-competed foxes (or preyed on them) and extirpated them from areas of higher human population.

Today, grey seals (*Halichoerus grypus*) haul out on the rocky beaches near Scotch Point every fall, and small seals (Phocidae) are frequent visitors to the harbour, attracted by abundant fish populations. It is therefore puzzling that seal remains occur so rarely in Port

Joli shell-bearing deposits. Seals never account for more than 3.5 percent of remains by NISP at any site, and all seal remains are restricted only to Middle Maritime Woodland shell midden deposits. These deposits tend to be located closer to the mouth of the harbour, where seal haulouts are present today and where they are more abundant.

Cervids are by far the most abundant mammalian fauna in Port Joli deposits (table 8.1, figure 8.1). Moose (*Alces alces*) are the least abundant species but are present in low numbers in many Middle Maritime Woodland and Late Maritime Woodland sites. Unexpectedly, at many sites, woodland caribou (*Rangifer tarandus caribou*) and white-tailed deer (*Odocoileus virginianus*) co-occur in the same contexts. This was completely unexpected, as modern ungulate biology in the region indicates that caribou and deer often cannot overlap due to the highly pathogenic effect of meningeal worm on caribou populations (Anderson 1972). We note that *Rangifer tarandus* specimens were very gracile compared to our reference collections, and often it was only possible to identify these remains to family Cervidae (Betts et al. 2017). However, to avoid identifier bias, the assemblages were reviewed by two different zooarchaeologists using different reference collections. Both independently concluded that both species were present, based on morphological characteristics, resulting in high confidence in the speciation of these particular specimens.

How these species were able to overlap in the past is unknown. It is possible that the meningeal parasite was not present in deer populations when the sites were occupied. However, white-tailed deer are often carriers of the disease and are neurologically resistant to its effect, suggesting that the species have co-adapted for a very long time. If the parasite is indigenous to North American deer populations, then the only reasonable explanation is that their habitats were very different in Nova Scotia, and the two species rarely interacted. Indeed, a relict woodland caribou herd still exists in the Gaspé Peninsula (Quebec), which suggests that some form of habitat segregation was possible. However, this seems a less than suitable explanation, given the constrained topography and environment of Port Joli, which would have necessitated overlapping habitats. It is possible that, during the Maritime Woodland Period, the parasite did not infect deer populations on the Maritime Peninsula, which may have been isolated by some mechanism from infected herds further west and south. Much more research is obviously needed to explore the relationships between caribou and deer in prehistoric Nova Scotia.

Shellfish

Shellfish remains were quantified through the sorting and analysis of bulk midden samples recovered from deposits we tested in Port Joli. Bulk samples were collected from each natural or arbitrary level from all contexts tested in the harbour. Samples were recovered from the central portion of the unit, to a depth of 5 cm, with a goal of collecting at least 1000 mL of sediment. Samples were first allowed to slow-dry within bags, and initial sorting took place manually. Fine fraction-sorting occurred under a low-power microscope. Constituent elements, such as faunal remains, identifiable fragments of mollusc shell, artifacts, non-cultural lithics, and charcoal, were separated from the soil fraction. In practice, the soil fraction was often an amalgamation of organic soil and other constituent elements, such as very highly comminuted charcoal and/or shell, which were too small to be sorted without higher magnification (and significantly more labour). Mollusc species were identified via comparison to the faunal reference collection at the Canadian Museum of History. All constituent components were then weighed to the nearest milligram and bagged separately for further analysis and storage.

Only five species of mollusc were identified in Port Joli middens from the bulk-sample analysis, including soft-shell clam (*Mya arenaria*), northern moon snail (*Euspira heros*), green sea urchin (*Strongylocentrotus droebachiensis*), and blue mussel (*Mytilus edulis*). A species of garden snail (Helicidae) was also identified. The low diversity of marine molluscs is partially linked to the actual limited number of species present and to the nature of our sampling procedure, which could not account for every fragment in every level. As a result, we identified two additional species of mollusc as we excavated but which were not found in the bulk samples. These include Atlantic surf clam (*Spisula solidissima*) and Atlantic jackknife (razor) clam (*Ensis directus*). These species occurred in many of the contexts we excavated but in exceedingly rare frequencies, often amounting to only one or two fragments from an entire unit. It is not surprising, then, that they were not captured by our bulk–midden sampling strategy.

Reviewing the results of the bulk-sample analysis indicates that soft-shell clam is the overwhelmingly dominant mollusc species by weight in all contexts (table 8.2, figure 8.3). However, the proportion of clam shell by weight varies drastically between deposits. The lowest proportion, at less than 1 percent clam shell by weight, occurs in the protohistoric context at AlDf-24, Area C, and indeed most black soil midden (i.e., house-floor) contexts exhibit low proportions of clam shell by weight. In other contexts, shell is very abundant, and it accounts for over 50 percent of the bulk fraction by weight in half of the samples.

Blue mussel (*Mytilus edulis*) is the next most abundant species by weight but is in fact uncommon in middens, accounting for less than 0.02 percent of the total weight recovered

Table 8.2 Fort Joli faunal assemblages: Bulk-sample constituents (by percentage of total weight).

Material	AlDf-25 A	AlDf-30	AlDf-24 A	AlDf-31	AlDf-35	AlDf-24C Early	AlDf-24C Late	AlDf-08	AlDf-24C Proto
Faunal remains	0.06	0.42	0.13	0.08	1.40	0.46	0.14	0.28	0.00
Clam (Mya sp.)	56.70	59.56	79.68	53.87	43.38	7.50	5.39	11.54	0.66
Land Snail	0.00	0.00	0.00	0.00	0.00	0.00	0.00	0.00	0.00
Moon Snail	0.00	0.00	0.00	0.00	0.00	0.00	0.00	0.00	0.00
Mussel	0.01	0.01	0.01	0.00	0.00	0.00	0.00	0.00	0.00
Sea Urchin	0.00	0.00	0.03	0.00	0.00	0.00	0.00	0.00	0.00
Non-Cultural Lithic	0.82	1.57	0.50	0.19	5.87	3.07	15.96	6.90	8.66
Charcoal	0.00	0.01	0.03	0.02	0.06	0.07	0.07	0.08	0.18
Soil Fraction	42.40	38.43	19.60	45.65	49.30	88.91	78.44	81.20	90.50
# Artifacts per Kilogram	0.00	1.69	0.43	1.27	4.56	25.11	5.96	4.96	1.06
# Lithic Artifacts per Kilogram	0.00	0.00	0.17	0.00	1.88	25.11	5.96	3.85	1.06
% Charcoal Weight per Kilogram	0.02	0.12	0.33	0.19	0.57	0.65	0.67	0.82	1.78
% Total Shell	56.71	59.57	79.73	53.87	43.38	7.50	5.39	11.54	0.66
% Soil and Non-Cultural Lithics	43.23	40.00	20.10	45.85	55.16	91.98	94.40	88.10	99.16

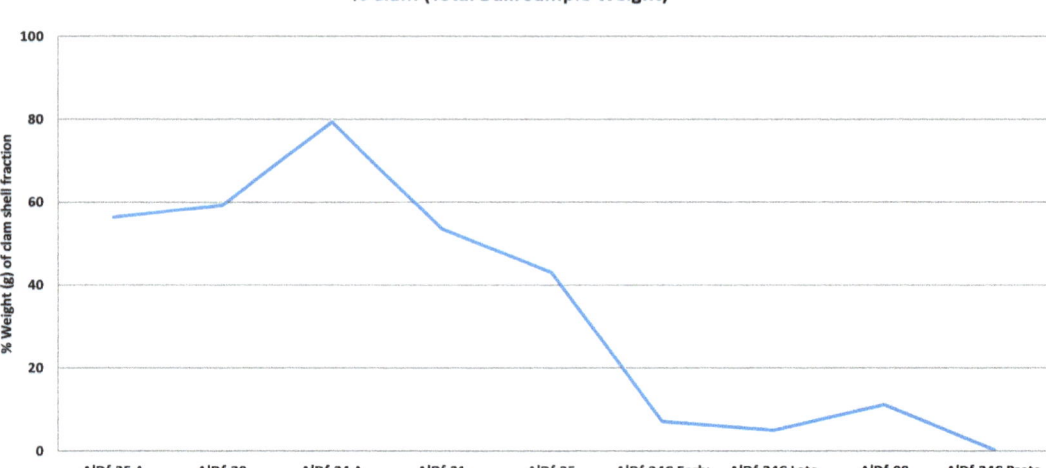

Figure 8.3 Port Joli faunal assemblages: Shell fraction (soft-shell clam). Percentage of weight (in grams) in relation to the total bulk sample. Contexts have been arranged sequentially according to the chronological model developed in Chapter 4.

in all contexts where it is present (figure 8.4). It has not been recovered from black soil midden deposits with any frequency, which may be a consequence of the increased fragmentation and mechanical attrition in these deposits, as it was recovered in both kitchen middens at AlDf-30 and AlDf-24, Area C. Moon snail and sea urchin are exceedingly rare, having only been recovered from AlDf-25 (Erskine 1962) and AlDf-24, both of which are interpreted as shellfish-processing middens. In review, the shellfish exploitation strategy of the inhabitants around Port Joli's harbour during the Maritime Woodland Period was overwhelmingly dominated by soft-shell clam, which accounted for more than 99 percent of all shellfish remains by weight in all contexts. Other species occur in only trace amounts

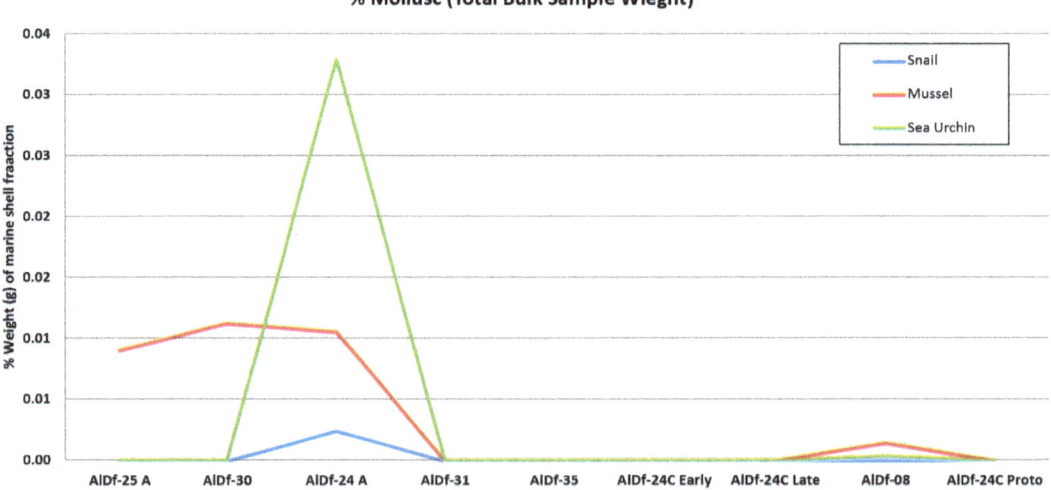

Figure 8.4 Mollusc shell fraction (excluding soft-shell clam): Percentage of weight (in grams) in relation to the total bulk sample. Contexts have been arranged sequentially according to the chronological model developed in Chapter 4.

and must be viewed as opportunistic, bycatch exploitation. Rocky headlands and substrate conducive to mussel as well as urchin habitat do occur in Port Joli today, but it seems clear that the clam flats proved overwhelmingly attractive to the harbour's inhabitants.

Plant Remains

An analysis of pollen samples from several sites was undertaken by Candace Loder, under the supervision of Michael Deal (Loder 2010; see also Deal et al. 2011). Included in the analysis were samples from AlDf-35; AlDf-24, Area A; AlDf-30; and A2009NS27-1. The sampling methodology involved recovering matrix material from sifted backdirt deposits, carefully controlled so as to obtain only material from a specific stratigraphic context, as well as "off-site" material from each site for direct comparison. Overall, the results suggest a relatively low plant diversity recovered in the midden contexts, as compared to similar Maritime Woodland archaeological sites (Deal et al. 2011: 35).

At AlDf-35, ten species plants or fungi were identified from a 1000 mL (580 g) soil sample (Loder 2010: table 1). Among the edible plants were pin cherry (*Prunus pensylvanica*), raspberry or blackberry (*Rubus* spp.), burnet (*Sanguisorba* sp.), and foxtail (*Setaria* sp.). Of these, both pin cherry and raspberry or blackberry were found in the 1000 mL (294 g) off-site control sample.

At AlDf-30, Deal sampled Middle Maritime Woodland house-floor deposits from the black soil area (Test Unit 3, Level 2), resulting in a 3450 mL sample weighing 3130 g. Thirteen species were identified, including edible and/or medicinal plants. Edible plants include buckwheat (*Plygonum* sp.), raspberry or blackberry, thimbleberry (*Rubus parviflorus*), honeysuckle (*Lonicera* sp.), pin cherry (*Prunus pensylvanica*), and elderberry (*Sambucus* sp.). Species known to be used by the Mi'kmaq for medicinal or other purposes include golden dock (*Rumex maritimus*) and staghorn sumac (*Rhus typhina*). This diversity of edible/medicinal plants stands in stark contrast to the control sample, which shared only raspberry/blackberry and elderberry with the archaeological sample. It seems, therefore, that the floor deposits reveal a variety of plant species brought to the home for economic use in the Middle Maritime Woodland Period.

In comparison to the domestic-floor context, the 950 mL (296 g) sample from the AlDf-24, Area A, shellfish processing midden (Test Unit 2) has a very limited diversity of plant species. Only four species were identified, and of those only one raspberry/blackberry was edible. The difference between the Middle Maritime Woodland contexts at AlDf-30 and AlDf-24, Area A, are very striking. The contrast may be accounted for by the contextual difference, indicating that plants were rarely processed or incorporated into the activities that resulted in the formation of the midden. However, at the house contexts, processing and consuming flora was an obviously significant part of the domestic activities in this context. Alternatively, the difference may be accounted for seasonally (e.g., Deal et al. 2011; Loder 2010), with the increased fruit-bearing flora in the domestic contexts the result of a late-summer or fall harvest when the berries are in their prime (Deal et al. 2011: 35).

The sample recovered from A2009NS27-1 contained sixteen distinctly identifiable species from a 1500 mL (880 g) sample, ten of which are considered edible, medicinal, or both. These latter species include alder (*Alnus* sp.), chokecherry (*Prunus virginiana*), buttercup (*Ranunculus* sp.), chokeberry (*Aronia* sp.), serviceberry (*Amelanchier* sp.), raspberry/blackberry, goosefoot (*Chenopodium* sp.), black cherry (*Prunus* sp.), blueberry (*Vaccinium vacillans*), and buckwheat (*Plygonum* sp.). Unfortunately, little is known about this site, due to limited testing, but the significant quantity of edible botanicals in the sample stands in contrast to the other samples described above. If the site is contemporary with the nearby sites of AlDf-05 and AlDf-06, and with other sites at the head of the harbour, which tend to be Late Maritime Woodland in age, then this may indicate an increased reliance on edible botanicals in the Late Maritime Woodland as compared to the Middle Maritime Woodland Period. This hypothesis must remain highly speculative until A2009NS27-1 can be more comprehensively investigated and dated.

Finally, two charred complete halves of butternut fruit (*Juglans cinerea*) were recovered from AlDf-24, Area C, in separate contexts. These specimens were identified by Michael Deal at the Paleoethnobotany Laboratory at Memorial University, in St. John's, Newfoundland (Deal et al. 2011; Loder 2010). The most recent specimen (figure 8.5) was recovered from Feature 4 floor deposits (Level 3), at a depth of 17 cm below unit datum. The second charred butternut fragment (figure 8.6) was recovered from probable floor deposits in Level 3f at a depth of 39 cm. As discussed by Deal et al. (2011), this species was not native to Nova Scotia and could only have been traded from the Saint John River Valley or points further south. Their presence in AlDf-24, Area C, deposits dated between approximately 1260 and 660 cal BP attest to the time depth of this trade.

Data from Legacy Collections

As described above, John Erskine conducted purposive sampling of unique faunal remains, with the goal of highlighting species richness and diversity in the shell middens (Erskine 1986), and often had the remains identified by experts when he was unable to make determinations. In addition to comparing material to a private faunal collection he amassed over the years, as well as early identification aids, he sent specimens to the University of Toronto, Dalhousie University (Halifax), the University of Michigan, the University of Florida, and the Nova Scotia Museum to be identified by experts. Because Erskine did not screen materials or collect all fauna he encountered, it is impossible to quantify the remains from his notes. Table 8.3 describes, on a presence/absence basis, the species recorded by Erskine from his excavations. Where possible, it also records if Erskine described the remains as "common" (abundant). Sources include Erskine's series *Micmac Notes* (Erskine, 1958, 1959, 1961, 1962, 1964), as well as his unpublished notes, compiled by Michael Deal several decades ago (Erskine 1986). Finally, these data are augmented by a review of the faunal remains collected by him, which are currently housed at the Nova Scotia Museum and the Canadian Museum of History.

Table 8.3 reveals that in general, species richness at these sites is consistent with the richness at sites with large faunal samples from the E'se'get Project (table 8.2), ranging between about ten to fifteen non-overlapping taxa (see figure 8.7 for an assessment of richness and sample size for the E'se'get faunal assemblages). Erskine's data reveal that the AlDf-25 midden (his Port Joli No. 3) has significantly higher richness than other deposits (N[umber]=22) and, remarkably, is similar to the richness of AlDf-24 (N=26). It seems clear here that the diversity of bird species identified by Erskine at AlDf-25 (N=13) is at odds with other comparable deposits, namely AlDf-24, Area A (N=6). Specifically, species such

Figure 8.5 Photograph of a charred butternut recovered from AlDf-24, Area C, Feature 4, Level 3 (later Late Maritime Woodland Period).

Figure 8.6 Photograph of a charred butternut recovered from AlDf-24, Area C, Feature 4, Level 3f (early Late Maritime Woodland Period).

Table 8.3 Port Joli faunal assemblages: Presence/absence (and qualitative abundance) in shell middens excavated by John Erskine. Large X means present and common, and small x means present but rare.

Taxon	Common Name	AlDf-03 (PJ8)	AlDf-01/ AlDf-36	AlDf-04 (PJ10)	AlDf-06 (PJ12)	AlDf-08 (PJ7)	AlDf-07 (PJ2)	AlDf-10 (Bill Brook)	AlDf-25 Midden (PJ3)	AlDf-25 Angle Camp (PJ3)	AlDf-2 (PJ11)
Squalus acanthias	spiny dogfish	x							x	x	
Anguilla rostrata	American eel										
Acipenser oxyrhynchus	Atlantic sturgeon	x						x	x	x	
Clupidea	herring	X			X	x					
Gadus morhua	Atlantic cod										
Migrogadus tomcod	tomcod										
	cod/pollock	x						x		X	
	sculpin	x									
Gadidae	true cods								X		
Gavia immer	common loon								x		
Podiceps grisegena	red-necked grebe	x									
Morus bassanus	northern gannet	x									
Phalacrocorax sp.	cormorant								x		
Ardea herodia	great blue heron										
Branta canadensis	Canada goose	x			x	x			x		
Anserinae	swan/goose										
Anserini	goose							x			
Anas rubripes	black duck								x		
Anas crecca	green-winged teal								x		
Anatinae	dabbling duck	x						x			
Aythaya collaris	ring-necked duck										
Somateria mollissima	common eider	x									
	black duck/eider										
Bucephala clangula	common goldeneye	x							x		
Clangula hyemalis	long-tailed duck								x		
Mergus sp.	Mergus sp.	x							x		

		AIDf-03 (PJ8)	AIDf-01/ AIDf-36	AIDf-04 (PJ10)	AIDf-06 (PJ12)	AIDf-08 (PJ7)	AIDf-07 (PJ2)	AIDf-10 (Bill Brook)	AIDf-25 Midden (PJ3)	AIDf-25 Angle Camp (PJ3)	AIDf-2 (PJ11)
Anatidae	duck/goose/swan		x	x	x		x		X	x	X
Bonasa umbellus	ruffed grouse						x		x		
Larus smithsonianus	herring gull										
Laridae	gull										
Pinguinus impennis	great auk					x			x		
Uria lomvia	thick-billed murre	x							x		
Strix varia	barred owl										
Corvus corax	common raven								x		
Lepus americanus	snowshoe hare	x							x	X	
Castor canadensis	North American beaver				x		x	x	x	x	
Erethizon dorsatum	porcupine										
Microtus sp.	vole										
Peromyscus sp.	mouse										
Muridae	mouse or shrew										
Tamias striatus	eastern chipmunk										
Rodentia	rodent										
Tamiasciurus hudsonicus	American red squirrel										
Scurius sp.	squirrel										
Cetacea	whale	x	x				x		x		
Phocoena phocoena	harbour porpoise									x	
Vulpes vulpes	red fox										
Canis lups	eastern wolf	x								x	
Canis lupus familiaris	domesic dog								x		
Canis sp.	coyote, wolf, or dog										
Ursus americanus	American black bear	x							x		
Orocyon lotor	raccoon					x					
Mustelidae	mink or marten					x		x			
Lontra canadensis	river otter	x			x		x	x			
Lynx canadensis	lynx										

		AlDf-03 (PJ8)	AlDf-01/ AlDf-36	AlDf-04 (PJ10)	AlDf-06 (PJ12)	AlDf-08 (PJ7)	AlDf-07 (PJ2)	AlDf-10 (Bill Brook)	AlDf-25 Midden (PJ3)	AlDf-25 Angle Camp (PJ3)	AlDf-2 (PJ11)
Lynx rufus	bobcat										
Furbearers							x		x		
Carnivora	carnivore										
Halichoerus grypus	grey seal					x			x	x	
Pagophilus groenlandicus	harp seal										
Phocidae	small seal	x			x	x			x	x	
Alces alces	moose	X	x	x	x	X	X	X	x	X	X
Rangifer tarandus	woodland caribou	x									
Odocoileus virginianus	white-tailed deer	X			x	X	X	X			X
Cervidae	caribou/deer	x	x		x		X	X	x	X	
Totals											
Spiral Fractrured Mammal Bone		x			x	x	x	x			
Vertebrate Species Richness		14	4		8	9	8	10	22	11	
Softshell Clam	Maya Arenaria	X	X	X	X	X	X	X	X	X	X
Moon snail		x			x		x		x	x	
Surf clam					x	x			x	x	
razor clam											
blue mussel		x							x	x	
Urchin		x					x				

as grebes (Podicipedidae) and cormorants (Phalacrocoracidae), and terrestrial fowl, were never identified in any of the Port Joli middens in the E'se'get analysis, nor at other deposits by Erskine. However, Erskine did dig an enormous amount of material from AlDf-25 (Erskine 1962), excavating nearly the entire midden, which was once described as the largest shell midden in Nova Scotia. It remains possible that these species were present and are just a consequence of the enormous sample Erskine processed.

It is important to note here that whenever herring (Clupeidae) was identified by Erskine, he almost always identified it by large deposits, or "clots" of "scales" which he claims to have found at many sites. A discussion of how this evidence can be harmonized with the new faunal remains analyzed for the E'se'get Project appears below.

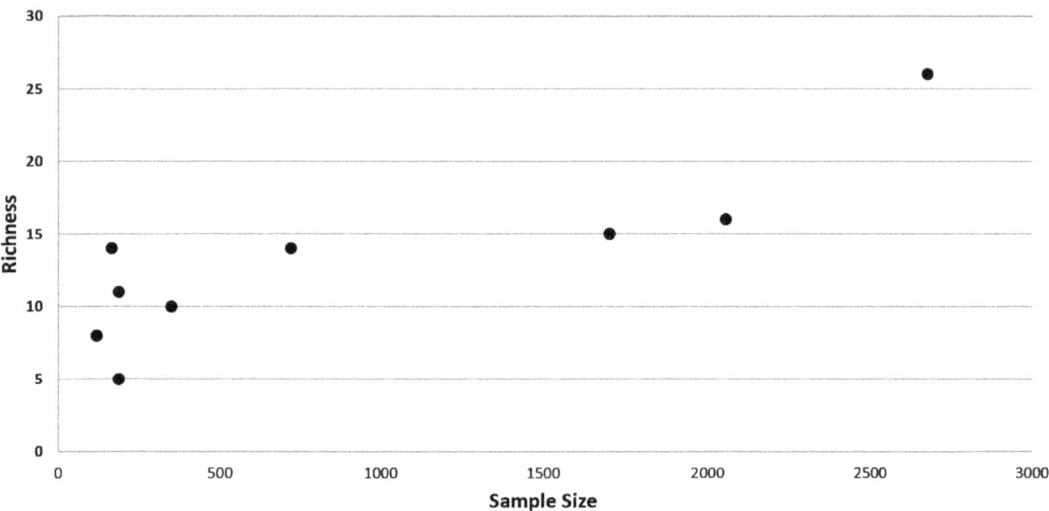

Figure 8.7 E'se'get faunal assemblages: Comparison of species richness to sample size across all sites.

Seasonality Indicators

Inferring seasonality from the animal remains in Port Joli is difficult because many of its migratory species arrive as multiple populations which variously, summer, overwinter, or pass by Port Joli during spring and fall migrations—which means that these migratory species essentially occupy the harbour year-round. Regardless, many of the species are more easily captured or in best condition at certain times of the year, and that information, collated with migratory abundance, can be useful in determining a probable season of occupation for the sites.

Many fish spawn or aggregate in the shallow inlets and harbours of Nova Scotia's South Shore. In September and October, eels begin moving downstream. Spending much of the winter in the mid Atlantic spawning, eels return to streams and rivers in May and June. They are attracted to estuarine eelgrass beds, like the large beds at the head of Port Joli's harbour, and such beds can amass large schools over the summer months (COSEWIC 2006; Weiler 2011: 20). Gaspereau begin to spawn in late April or early May, and runs continue throughout the spring until late June (DFO 2001). Returning from offshore habitat, Atlantic sturgeon spawn in rivers and lakes from May through August (Bradford et al. 2016). Spiny dogfish (*Squalus acanthias*), which are a resident species, tend to move onshore in large numbers between June and November (Leim and Scott 1966).

Atlantic cod (*Gadus morhua*) tend to stay offshore in the winter and move inshore to spawn and feed during the summer months (COSEWIC 2010), though a large resident population is known to stay in the nearshore in southwestern Nova Scotia year-round. Eelgrass, which is plentiful in Port Joli, is attractive to juvenile cod. Pollock, in contrast, spawn in November through February on the Scotian Shelf (DFO 2009). Tomcod (*Microgadus tomcod*) spawn in large schools under the ice from November to February and are most easily captured at that time (along with their predators, cod and pollock).

Waterfowl, such as Canada goose (*Branta canadensis*), frequent the migratory bird sanctuary in Port Joli in large numbers in the winter, but nearly all species, including Canada goose, are common in the area year-round. However, ring-necked duck (*Aythya collaris*) is only present in Port Joli during its migration in December.

Practically all the mammals identified in the middens are year-round residents or visitors to Port Joli. Harp seals, though rare, are known to visit the South Shore during the early spring, in March and April. Grey seals (*Halichoerus grypus*) haul out in large numbers on South Shore headlands and, in particular, at Scotch Point in the summer (Breed et al. 2009: 3217). While caribou (*Rangifer tarandus*), moose (*Alces alces*), and white-tailed deer (*Odocoileus virginianus*) are at their prime in the fall, the latter two are common in the area year-round. It is possible that woodland caribou (*Rangifer tarandus caribou*) migrated in Nova Scotia during the spring and fall, similar to modern woodland caribou herds in the adjacent Gaspé Peninsula. In fact, a Holocene caribou trackway was recently discovered in a dune system in St. Catherine's Bay, on the northern headland of Port Joli's harbour. As described by Ponomarenko and Ponomarenko (2015), the orientation of the numerous tracks imply a consistent travel route up the eastern side of Port Joli's harbour, from the inner to the outer harbour, and back (the tracks are oriented in both directions). A radiocarbon date recovered from the deposit calibrates to 1308 to 1362 AD, consistent with a Late Maritime Woodland migration of ungulates. Ponamarenko and Ponamarenko (2015: 54) suggest that the tracks could only have been preserved if the sand was close to freezing, suggesting late fall or very early spring migration.

The final species with a potential seasonal signature is the eastern chipmunk (*Tamias striatus*), which enters a torpor during the winter months, November to March (Snyder 1982). No evidence of burrowing was present in any deposits encountered in Port Joli, which is likely due to the potential for burrows to collapse in unconsolidated shell-bearing deposits. Therefore, the presence of chipmunk in an assemblage suggests a summer occupation of the site.

A test study of soft-shell clam (*Mya arenaria*) shell stable isotopes provides quantifiable evidence of the season of death of clams (the season in which they were collected and processed) found in Port Joli middens (Betts et al. 2017; Burchell et al. 2014). As described in Betts et al. (2017: 32), chondrophore samples were derived from the Middle Maritime Woodland deposits at AlDf-24, Area A (N56W50 levels 3j and 3m, N=6); AlDf-30, Area A (N52W56, Level 3c, N=6); and the early Late Maritime Woodland deposits at AlDf-24, Area C (N51W51, N52W51, levels 3f and 3j, N=2). Oxygen isotope values were obtained from the ventral growth line of the chondrophore. The lower the value (negative), the warmer the sea temperature was at the time of death, and the higher the value (positive), the colder the sea temperature. As recorded by Betts at al. (2017), AlDf-24, Area A, appeared to have been occupied in the spring and summer months, while AlDf-24, Area C, was only occupied in the spring months. AlDf-30, Area A, in contrast suggests a winter and spring occupation. However, it should be stressed that, with the low sample sizes and limited stratigraphic testing, the whole range of seasonal variability is far from being adequately assessed.

Based on the available isotopic and species information outlined above, it is possible to build up an idea of the seasonal occupation for many of the sites around Port Joli's harbour. AlDf-24, Area A, appears to have been occupied from spring to early fall—essentially a warm-season/summer occupation. The herring scales identified by Erskine at AlDf-03,

AlDf-06, and AlDf-08 also suggest a spring into early-summer occupation at these sites (the presence of grey seal and sturgeon reinforces this interpretation at AlDf-08). AlDf-30, Area A, and its Black Soil Area were likely occupied in the winter, based on isotopic data and the presence of ring-necked duck. The large quantities of tomcod bones at AlDf-30, Area B, surely indicates a cold-season occupation, when they spawn in large numbers. If so, then AlDf-30 is definitively a cold-season site for its entire occupation, an interpretation that accords well with its sheltered location in the near interior coast of the harbour. AlDf-31 provides few specific seasonality indicators, though tomcod may suggest a winter occupation, especially given the small sample size from the site. Its unique location, adjacent to AlDf-30 and its similar structure and faunal profile also argue for it being occupied at a similar time of year as its sister site.

Limited faunal assemblages from E'se'get excavations make the assignment of AlDf-25 to a specific season difficult, but Erskine did identify sturgeon scutes and grey seal from the deposit (and its adjacent "angle camp"), indicating a summer occupation. Furthermore, AlDf-26, another very large shell midden, was interpreted to be a primarily warm-season site based on growth-increment analysis (Quinlan 1996). This suggests that the large processing midden sites in Port Joli are a warm-season phenomenon.

The Late Maritime Woodland and Protohistoric deposits at AlDf-24, Area C, contain so many cervid remains that a fall occupation, when the animals were in their prime, is suggested. However, in conjunction with the isotopic analysis on the clam shell, spring is also indicated. It may be best to interpret the context as a fall-through-spring occupation as cervids are in their poorest condition in the spring. This broader cold-season interpretation accords well with the position of Area C, which is purposefully located in the lee of a large boulder ridge and hill, near the wooded areas at the rear of the site. This would have been an ideal location for protection from winter winds and storms.

Other deposits with significant cervid remains such as AlDf-08, AlDf-10, and AlDf-11 may also have been occupied in the fall, though sturgeon scutes recovered from AlDf-10 suggest a summer component there as well. AlDf-10, like AlDf-11 was likely an ideal interception location for cervids, no matter the season.

Procurement and Consumption Strategies around Port Joli's Harbour

It is now possible to build up an idea of procurement and consumption strategies in Port Joli over the 1,200-year sequence recovered over the approximately sixty years archaeologists have explored the harbour. The earliest evidence for human-animal interactions occur in the later part of the Middle Maritime Woodland Period, represented by AlDf-25; AlDf-30 (Area A and Black Soil Midden); and AlDf-24, Area A. The most striking pattern during this period is the presence of several very large shell middens dominated by soft-shell clam valves, which account for about of 80 percent of the archaeological deposit by weight (table 8.1, figure 8.3). AlDf-24, Area A, is the best-explored example of this type of deposit, and while limited data are available from AlDf-25 and AlDf-26, it seems clear from the detailed descriptions of Erskine (1962, 1986) and Powell (1995), respectively, that these deposits are similar in nature.

The size and depth of AlDf-24, Area A, which was over 30 × 30 m in area and about 1 m deep, is striking when we consider that the lowest layers are chronologically simultaneous with the top layers, according to the current precision of radiocarbon dates (see Chapter 4). The rapid accumulation of such a deposit in the years surrounding approximately 1400 cal BP could only have occurred as the result of intensive shellfish harvesting by a large number of people coming together to share in the labour.

What may have been the reason for the need to share in this activity? Based on the nature of the deposit, which included large amounts of charcoal but few features, a reasonable interpretation is that it accumulated through the intensive processing and, likely, drying or (based on the charcoal) perhaps smoking of clams for later consumption throughout the year. This was almost certainly a summertime activity, based on the isotopic and faunal data. If so, the processing was so intensive that it involved multiple families coming together to pool labour to produce this surplus, likely for use during subsequent seasons.

Sanger (1996: 523) previously hypothesized that such a deposit was possible on the Maritime Peninsula, but prior to the E'se'get Project none had been confidently identified elsewhere in the region. There are hundreds of extremely productive clam flats throughout the Maritime Peninsula, so what made this collective activity possible in Port Joli? The answer potentially lies in the extreme diversity of migratory taxa that phase into the region throughout the year and the abundant resident species that inhabit the South Shore. Fish, especially cod (Gadidae) and American eel (*Anguilla rostrata*), are abundant in the AlDf-24, Area A, assemblage. Both cod and eel dry and smoke readily (e.g., Weiler 2011) and may have been processed and preserved simultaneously with the clams at the midden. Additionally, bird species are very abundant in the AlDf-24, Area A, assemblage, and the large resident and migratory birds attracted to Port Joli would have been a significant draw to the indigenous inhabitants of the South Shore. Caribou (*Rangifer tarandus*), moose (*Alces alces*), white-tailed deer (*Odocoileus virginianus*), and the occasional grey seal (*Halichoerus grypus*) would have rounded out the procurement options during the spring to early fall months that AlDf-24, Area A, was evidently occupied.

Nearly contemporaneous with AlDf-24, Area A, AlDf-30 provides evidence of the cold season (fall to spring) activities of the Middle Maritime Woodland inhabitants of Port Joli. Summertime economic practices evident at AlDf-24, Area A, were simply shifted slightly, with the intensive shellfish-gathering and birding lessened in favour of fishing for cod and hunting hare. A slight increase in the frequency of cervids is evident as well, likely a result of fall hunting when the animals were in their prime. Domestic dog remains were recovered from AlDf-30, Area A, as well, which may provide evidence of cervid hunting using dogs, which was well-described in the Mi'kmaw ethnohistoric literature (Denys 1968: 428; Le Clerq 1910: 275; Lescarbot 1914: 221).

Unfortunately, small sample sizes do not permit significant insights into the evidence for economic practices at the AlDf-30, Black Soil Area (house floors). However, the taxonomic distribution of the sixty total identified specimens is consistent with the proportions of species recovered from the adjacent Area A kitchen midden. Gadids are by far the most abundant taxa, followed closely by snowshoe hare (*Lepus americanus*), with trace amounts of birds, furbearers, and a slightly higher proportion of cervids. It is interesting to note that very few spirally fractured bones were recovered from either AlDf-30 or AlDf-24, Area A, suggesting bone grease or marrow extraction was not a primary processing activity during the Middle Maritime Woodland Period.

The nature of the Port Joli faunal assemblages changes significantly over the course of the Late Maritime Woodland Period (figures 8.1 and 8.8). This is best exemplified in the stratigraphic sequence at AlDf-24, Area C, which spans the early Late Maritime Woodland to Protohistoric Periods. The initial Early Late Maritime Woodland deposit, AlDf-24, Area C (levels 3f–3k), suggests a continuation of the cod-focused economic strategy of the preceding period, but with a significant reduction in the quantity of birds, in favour of cervids. All three species of cervid were exploited—moose, caribou, and white-tailed deer. For the first time, significant quantities of spirally cracked mammal bones (likely cervid) occur in the assemblages. This trend is reinforced in levels 3a and 3b from AlDf-24, Area C, which form the Feature 4 floor deposit and its adjacent midden materials. However, by the time this house was occupied, gadid and bird remains were deposited only in trace amounts, to be replaced almost entirely by cervids and, to a lesser extent, snowshoe hare and other furbearers (the latter occurs in similar frequencies as the Middle Maritime Woodland deposits).

As described above, these repeating series of Late Maritime Woodland house floors were likely occupied from the fall into the spring, and the best comparison is therefore AlDf-30 (Area A and Black Soil Area). The focus on gadids from AlDf-30 is present in the earliest deposits at AlDf-24, Area C, but the similarities end there, as the abundance of cervids and the lack of cod and birds are strikingly different from the Middle Maritime Woodland winter site occupations.

This extreme focus on cervids in the assemblages is expressed in the very small samples from other Late Maritime Woodland contexts, such as AlDf-08; the AlDf-24, Area 2, Feature 2 house; and from the higher sample size assemblage from AlDf-11. Spirally cracked mammal

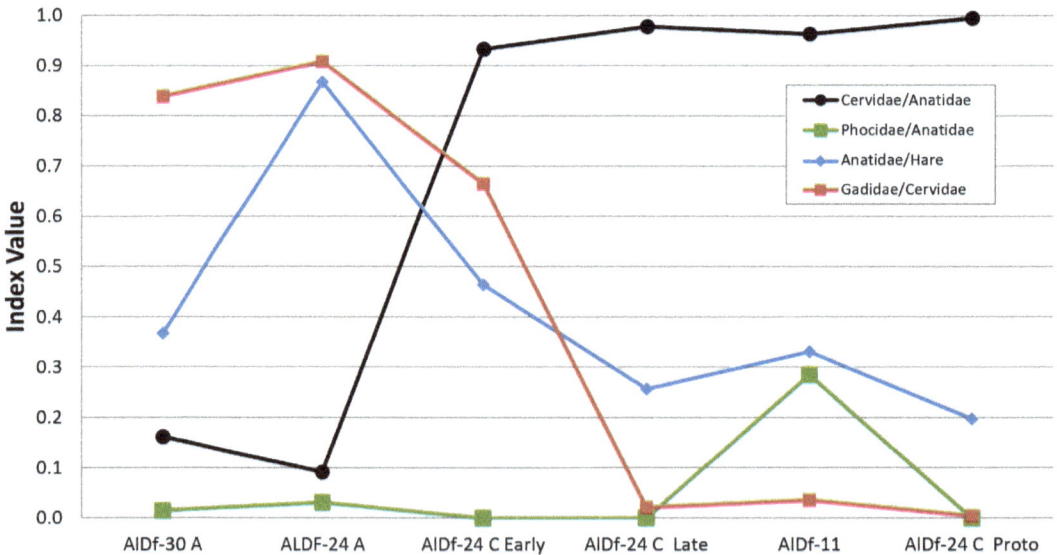

Figure 8.8 Port Joli faunal assemblages: Abundance indices (AI) for select taxa. Contexts have been arranged sequentially according to the chronological model developed in Chapter 4. *Note:* AI measure shifts in the relative abundance of taxa in relation to other taxa. They are, essentially, a normed ratio of taxon A to taxon B, measured as: AI = A ÷ [A + B] (Bayham, 1979; Ugan and Bright, 2001). Values close to 0 reflect low numbers of A taxa (and the complete dominance of the B taxa), and values close to 1 indicate very low numbers of the B taxa (and the complete dominance of the A taxa).

bone is very abundant in AlDf-08 and AlDf-11 despite the extremely small sample sizes, and Erskine described spirally cracked bone present in AlDf-27 as well. As described in Chapter 3, AlDf-11 was not a habitation site, and is likely to have been a hunting site of caribou and white-tailed deer. The similarly dated and similarly structured AlDf-27 was also described by Erskine as exhibiting an abundance of cervid remains, and his description of the fauna indicates limited quantities of fish and birds. Snowshoe hare is only present in quantity in AlDf-11, and birds and fish are present only in significant quantity in AlDf-24, Area A, Feature 2, and in AlDf-08. Thus, the overwhelming pattern for the later Late Maritime Woodland Period appears to be a shift away from bird, fish, and (to a lesser extent) hare exploitation to one significantly focused on cervid hunting. This economic pattern continues in the Protohistoric deposits from AlDf-24, Area C. These deposits exhibit 94 percent cervid remains by NISP, with a significant quantity of spirally cracked mammal bone. Furbearers and waterfowl occur in trace amounts less than 2 percent NISP), and birds are completely non-existent.

If AlDf-11 and AlDf-27 are caribou hunting and processing sites, then it is clear that the Late Maritime Woodland shift brought with it a change in logistical organization and the establishment of specialized task sites. The emphasis on cervids at the habitation sites may have in part been fuelled by this new logistical organization. It was also supported by an apparent change in the nature of cervid processing, as abundant spirally fractured bone in nearly all Late Maritime Woodland deposits in Port Joli suggests that bone-grease and bone-marrow extraction was a fundamental part of the economy during this period.

It is important to recognize that practically all of the Late Maritime Woodland sites are shell-bearing "black soil" deposits, and therefore it is possible that taphonomic issues, which would prioritize dense cervid bones over fish and birds, may be driving this patterning. Indeed, a recent review of the cervid-element distributions indicate significant density-mediated attrition is affecting all the deposits (Betts et al. 2017). However, it is well known that nearly all faunal assemblages are subject to such attrition, and reverse utility curves are the ubiquitous result (e.g., Lyman 1994).

Despite these cautions, we observed that preservation was excellent in all but the most disturbed black soil middens (e.g., AlDf-06, AlDf-07) when even a trace of shell was present (see table 8.3). Indeed, the earliest stratigraphic levels of AlDf-24, Area C, despite highly comminuted shell and an extreme reduction in shell by weight when compared to Middle Maritime Woodland middens, showed similar bird and fish preservation as large shell midden deposits, such as AlDf-24, Area A (table 8.1). Nevertheless, we consciously attempted to mitigate the potential for bone attrition by including the adjacent contiguous associated levels from the Area C kitchen midden in the analysis. Though limited in volume compared to the main excavation, the deposit would have practically guaranteed faunal preservation on par with AlDf-24, Area A, and the AlDf-30, Area A midden, given the nature of the deposit. As a result, bird and fish remains should have been common if they were deposited frequently in the upper two contexts in AlDf-24, Area C, but the faunal assemblages simply do not reflect this.

AlDf-08, which appears to have been occupied in the summer, is the southernmost expression of a new type of site that appeared in the Late Maritime Woodland in Port Joli. These large black soil middens apparently replaced the large shell-processing middens like

AlDf-24, Area A; AlDf-25; and AlDf-26. It is unfortunate that we do not have better data from this site, but the limited assemblage we excavated and Erskine's observations provide a relatively vibrant, if not strictly quantifiable, picture. As described by Erskine, and supported by our limited faunal sample, cervid remains (principally deer and moose) dominate the faunal assemblage from the site, which is similar to the black soil midden from AlDf-24, Area C. Furthermore, spirally fractured mammal bone (likely all cervid) was abundant at AlDf-24. Erskine described finding herring (gaspereau, *Alosa pseudoharengus*) bone here as well (table 8.2); given his excavation techniques and the size of herring bones, they were likely relatively frequent in the deposit. Bird remains were scanty, but included Canada goose (*Branta canadensis*) and great auk (*Pinguinnis impennis*), and several species of furbearers were recovered. Grey seal was also present.

A similar pattern of faunal remains appears to have characterized other large "black soil" sites in the harbour, including AlDf-03 and AlDf-06. These faunal assemblages are described to have large quantities of cervid and herring remains, along with lesser quantities of furbearers and birds. At AlDf-06, Erskine (1986: 87) described the remains of "smelts" (small herring) and at AlDf-03, he described that ". . . great clots of scales, identified as herring or gaspereau scales by Dr. Leim, were found in 29% of yards" (Erskine 1986: 92). AlDf-08, AlDf-06, and AlDf-03 were (or still are) located adjacent to streams that would have attracted spawning herring, likely gaspereau. Additionally, AlDf-03 included abundant leister points (Erskine 1986: 92).

All of these sites appear to be very large but shallow black soil sites, which supported multiple wigwams during the summer months. Their Middle Maritime Woodland counterparts were the similarly large processing middens at AlDf-25; AlDf-24, Area A; and AlDf-26. While the large shell middens do not contain multiple wigwam floors, their very nature suggests the aggregation of multiple families for the purposes of pooling economic labour.

If these large Late Maritime Woodland sites were occupied during the summer months, then the occupations at AlDf-24, Area C, likely represented their cold-season counterpart, just as the cold-season AlDf-30 site represented a cold-season counterpart for the warm-season processing middens. If these interpretations are correct, then year-round occupations occurred in Port Joli, represented by small shifts in occupation from large summer camps to smaller, sheltered, and dispersed cold-season camps. It appears, given the nature of the faunal assemblages, that these cold-season occupations may have been supported by intensive hunting, collecting, and processing activities in the summer months.

In the Middle Maritime Woodland Period, drying or smoking clams, eels, and other fish resulted in preserved stores, while in the Late Maritime Woodland this practice seems to have shifted toward large-scale fishing, and likely intensive processing and drying of gaspereau. In the Late Maritime Woodland, an intensification in cervid hunting in both the warm and cold seasons, and the processing of marrow and/or bone grease for later use, supported this economy. Regardless, it is critical to recognize that the entire economy was underwritten by soft-shell clams, and to a lesser extent the insurance provided by the abundant fish and bird resources available in Port Joli throughout the year. In fact, it is impossible to understate the importance of clams in the development of Port Joli as a focal place.

Chapter 9
An Archaeological History of Port Joli

MATTHEW BETTS

Introduction

The archaeological and contextual data presented in the previous chapters have revealed the complexity of Mi'kmaw life in Emsik, now known as Port Joli, the "Pretty Harbour." This chapter attempts to bring these data together, to build up a culture history of ancient coastal life on the South Shore of Nova Scotia, using Port Joli as a case study. Culture history is an archaeological approach that focuses on description and classification, as well as inductive reasoning, to (a) determine the general nature and sequence of settlement, subsistence, and technological changes, and (b) place those within broader chronological and regional perspective. With the adoption of new paradigms, often borrowed from anthropological and sociological disciplines, many archaeologists moved away from practising culture history to focus on theoretical explorations of meanings and relationships encoded in archaeological sites and assemblages.

With these paradigmatic shifts came a shift in publication effort. Most modern archaeology publications focus on methodological and theoretical explorations of patterning and meaning, and contain only a small subset of the complete data set gathered during excavation. Comprehensive site monographs and reports are rarely published today—part of a declining trend in publishing primary data sets. (For example, this book will be the first comprehensive site monograph published by the Mercury series in twenty-one years.)

As we argued in Chapter 1, we believe that culture-historical publication—that is, describing, cataloguing, classifying, and interpreting the original archaeological material and contexts you excavate and then presenting them in a comprehensive manner—is a critical part of the most responsible archaeological practice. We do not discredit the importance of theory-focused research and publication or the insights it has produced; indeed, we participate in this practice with vigour. But paradigms and theories wax and inevitably wane. Culture-historical data, presented in the form of a site monograph or comprehensive site report, provide a legacy that will outlast the most revelatory theoretical explorations we can make. The site monograph is, therefore, a fundamental responsibility of the conscientious archaeologist.

There is a further, practical, appeal to culture history and site monographs. Archaeology leaves its own, inherently destructive, legacy— we destroy archaeological sites as we excavate them—and so the material removed from these precious sites requires full description and interpretation by those who experienced (and conducted) that destruction first-hand.

This chapter presents an inductive summary interpretation of the discoveries and observations of the E'se'get Archaeology Project and of other archaeological data produced in nearly eighty years of exploration around Port Joli's harbour. It proceeds chronologically, presenting evidence for settlement, economic, and technological change through time around the harbour. Based on the ethos outlined above, this chapter—indeed this book—is not meant to provide highly nuanced and theoretically deep explanations and interpretations of culture change in Port Joli. We have conducted such theoretical explorations previously (e.g., Betts et al. 2012; Betts et al. 2017; Hrynick, 2018; Hrynick and Betts 2014, 2017), and more are planned. Instead, this monograph presents the basic data in as much detail as possible and provides a culture-historical framework for its future interpretation—for archaeologists, Indigenous peoples, and others. It attempts to build up a general history of how people lived around the harbour and how they interacted with each other and the outside world. Ultimately, it explores how the harbour was made into a special place for the Mi'kmaq and how that special place in turn, influenced, reified, and reproduced their unique culture. It ends with a discussion of how it helped to shape Mi'kmaw identity on the South Shore. In short, this is an introduction to what makes Emsik, or Port Joli, a special cultural land- and seascape.

Earliest Times

Archaeological reconnaissance in Port Joli provides very limited evidence of Mi'kmaq occupation before about 1600 years ago. Prior to this time, much of Port Joli was a low valley with a modest river passing through it, fed by myriad streams that now flow directly into the harbour. Evidence, in the form of shell middens, of coastal occupation prior to the Early Maritime Woodland Period (ca. 3200 to 2200 years ago) is very limited on the South Shore of Nova Scotia. The earliest evidence of occupation comes from two Palaeo-Indigenous (e.g., Palaeo-Indian) find spots, where characteristic finely made spear points, dating to about 10,000 to 13,000 years ago, have been recovered, usually from eroding deposits (e.g., Davis and Christianson 1988). One such find spot was recently discovered, in 2017, in the nearby Sable River estuary, southwest of Port Joli (Betts et al. in press), where a fluted projectile point and crude scraper were found eroding at the high-tide mark near a stream. They would have been deposited at a time when the estuary was a low river valley, much like Port Joli would have been about 13,000 years ago. This was a perfect lookout spot for humans to observe migrating herds as they moved along a natural travel route from the inland to the outer coast. It is possible that Port Joli was used similarly, but there is no evidence of such occupation in the harbour.

A handful of inland Archaic sites have been identified near Port Joli, with perhaps the largest and most intensive occupation occurring on the Mersey River and Lake Rossignol (Sanders and Stewart 2007), just northwest of Port Joli's harbour. Here abundant evidence of "Moorehead"-type artifacts have been collected, including large ground-slate lance heads and stone gouges. This material culture likely dates to about 3600 to 4000 years ago, and they were undoubtedly a coastally adapted people, with the gouges representing a developed dugout-canoe technology, and the lances a complex marine hunting toolkit used to dispatch marine mammals and large fish (e.g., Bourque 2012). Archaeologically, there is no evidence of such an Archaic presence (i.e., prior to ca. 3500 years ago) in Port Joli, likely a consequence of the small-river system in the area, which was unsuitable for travel with large, heavy, dugout canoes. Regardless, the Archaic Period occupants of the Mersey River area undoubtedly knew about Port Joli, even if they apparently did not spend a great deal of time there.

The earliest tangible archaeological evidence of occupation in the harbour before the Middle Maritime Woodland Period is a single radiocarbon date from AlDf-25, taken from a charcoal sample at the basal level of the shell midden. This Early Maritime Woodland date (ca. 3450–3330 years ago) is inconsistent with the bulk of the material culture derived from the shell midden and would normally be considered an anomalous date. However, nothing in the sample or assay suggested bias or contamination, and the source of the old charcoal must therefore be considered as possibly anthropogenic.

AlDf-25 sits in advantageous location for intercepting caribou, moose, and deer as they moved from the inner to outer harbour following the beaches and lower terraces, which provided the easiest travel route. (The uplands are quite rocky and boggy in this area, at least today.) Even if Port Joli was not a harbour at this time, this location may have still been advantageous for intercepting caribou, deer, and moose, as the migrating or travelling ungulates were squeezed between the river system and the rocky and boggy uplands of the peninsula. It is therefore possible that this was a site where these animals were intercepted, and the charcoal date may represent the limited use of the river valley as a hunting location. If so, some material culture from AlDf-25 may represent an Early Maritime Woodland occupation of the site. Several very large stemmed rhyolite spear points may be possible candidates, but it is impossible to determine the veracity of this hypothesis without tangible dates and/or contexts. No such technology was encountered in the basal levels of AlDf-24.

Middle Maritime Woodland Period (2200–1300 Years Ago)

As outlined by Neil and Gajewski in chapter 2, as sea levels steadily rose after the last glaciation, what is now the harbour at Port Joli began to inundate. By about 3000 years ago, the sea had transgressed past the outer harbour, but it was not until approximately 1750 years ago that it had progressed past Scotch Point to the inner harbour (figure 2.1), where the water is much shallower. By 1550 years ago, extensive foreshore clam flats had developed in this location, and—given Port Joli's existing flat and shallow bathymetry—they were certainly much more extensive when water levels were lower than they are today (figure 2.1).

Archaeological evidence indicates that the initial settlement of Port Joli occurred right at this critical time in the natural development of the harbour and right in the location where massive clam flats were first established. The original occupation of the harbour can only be described as intensive. The earliest shell-bearing site in the harbour appears to have been AlDf-30, which was first occupied about 1500 years ago. However, this site is essentially contemporary with the large AlDf-24, Area A, shell midden, whose radiocarbon dates suggest developed very rapidly in the decades around 1450 years ago. Both sites are located adjacent to Scotch Point, where the largest clam flats developed in the harbour.

The nearly 1 m depth of pure clam shells at AlDf-24, Area A, indicates that as soon as the clam flats were established in the harbour, ancient Mi'kmaq came here and began to exploit them intensively. As indicated above, the rapidity of the development of the midden, which is essentially contemporaneous, radiometrically, from top to bottom, suggests intensive processing and drying of clams by a substantial group of people. Other animals were also processed and dried in this midden context—notably cod and eels, both of which would have required communal efforts to fish and process. Large numbers of waterfowl were taken as well, providing fresh game for the busy food preservers.

Two other extremely large shell middens, AlDf-25 and AlDf-26, also date to this period and are located adjacent to AlDf-24. While no summer dwellings dating to the Middle Maritime Woodland Period were excavated in the E'se'get Archaeology Project, they were likely present at AlDf-24, Area B, given evidence of black soil deposits in that area, if the "angle camp" from AlDf-25 can be used as an analogue. We are uncertain if these large clam- and fish-processing middens were contemporary with AlDf-24, but given the short span of time they represent (i.e., the end of the Middle Maritime Woodland Period), they almost certainly were. Perhaps families rotated between sites every year, allowing for more pleasant occupations that did not have actively decomposing clam shells next to dwellings. However, given the extensive nature of the clam flats during this period, it is possible that all three of these sites were occupied at the same time. What is clear, however, is that multiple families came together north of Scotch Point every year during this period to share in the collecting and processing of fish and clams, with an emphasis on producing preserved food for later consumption.

The isotope analysis of clam shells from AlDf-24, Area A, indicates that it was occupied from spring into the late summer or early fall; this means that the food surplus was ultimately destined to be used in the cold season. It is difficult to know how this preserved surplus was dispersed among those who created it (see discussion below), but the evidence indicates that not all the surplus, nor all of the families who generated it, stayed around Port Joli's harbour. Some of AlDf-24's occupants appear to have moved just a few hundred metres south, and further into the woods, to live at AlDf-30 during the cold season. The isotopes from clam shells suggest they lived at this sheltered spot during the fall through the early spring. However, in general, the subsistence pattern was very similar to that at AlDf-24, Area A—just with several small shifts in emphasis. The inhabitants of AlDf-30 fished for more cod and took many more hares than they did in the summer months but hunted fewer birds (though the overwintering Canada goose became the dominant bird species). Fishing, shellfish gathering, and goose hunting were likely facilitated by Port Joli's ice-free harbour during the winter months. The inability to add hunted meat to the diet in the harshest days of winter was undoubtedly offset by stored clams and fish, notably eels and cod, from the summer months.

AlDf-30 was repeatedly occupied, with at least one wigwam placed in the same location year after year throughout the Middle Maritime Woodland Period. The adjacent AlDf-31 was likely also occupied at the same time. Both sites are relatively small and only one or two wigwams were likely in use at them in any one season. Unfortunately, these are the only two potential Middle Maritime Woodland winter sites in the harbour that have been discovered to date. The small size and limited number of these sites suggests that not all the families who lived and worked at the big processing middens stayed in Port Joli year-round, and some subset clearly spent the cold season elsewhere, potentially far inland. Regardless, AlDf-24 and AlDf-30 conclusively prove year-round occupation on the coast by Wabanaki. Year-round settlement on the coast is a practice not known in the ethnohistoric literature and has generally been absent from archaeological models of Nova Scotia (e.g., Davis 1987, 1993).

The artifacts and architecture from these two sites (AlDf-24 and AlDf-30), respectively, provide some indication of the social and spiritual lives of the Middle Maritime Woodland peoples of Port Joli, and these subjects will be discussed later in the chapter. However, technologically, the people of this time appear to have used a shared material culture with other Wabanaki peoples throughout the Maritime Peninsula with little modification. Lithic technology included a range of stemmed and corner-notched projectile points highly consistent with other known Middle Maritime Woodland sites in Maine, Nova Scotia, New Brunswick, and Prince Edward Island. Of note was the distinct rarity of chert debitage and the small size of the chert formal tools and bifaces, which potentially suggests that chert was relatively scarce in Port Joli—a likelihood that is supported by the fact that the chert material all seems to be derived from Minas Basin sources many hundreds of kilometers away. However, the abundant local quartz and rhyolite appears to have been used to alleviate this lack of high-quality tool stone, and the abundance of quartz debitage indicates that, though the material was of lower quality, adequate tool stone was really not in limited supply in Port Joli.

There appears to be a general lack of harpooning technology in the Port Joli harbour in comparison to contemporary sites elsewhere in the Maritime Peninsula. This does correspond to a general low frequency of sea mammal remains in assemblages, but perhaps what is more significant is the extreme rarity of sturgeon remains in Middle Maritime Woodland shell middens. With seals available for ambush from the shore at nearby haulouts and few opportunities for sturgeon hunting in lakes and rivers, harpooning technology may not have been critical in the harbour. Ground-stone technology is very rare in Middle Maritime Woodland sites in Port Joli, but small "thumbnail" scrapers are very common in winter house sites. Heavy woodworking appears not to have been a preoccupation of Port Joli inhabitants, while fine birch-bark, textile-, or woodworking obviously were.

Pottery styles during this period are also highly consistent with the ceramic tradition in place on the Maritime Peninsula (e.g., Petersen and Sanger 1993), and the inhabitants in Port Joli clearly participated in broad trends in ceramic manufacture and decoration throughout the Maritime Woodland Period. However, Port Joli potters seemed to have developed some unique attributes as part of a local pottery tradition. The use of interior combing is unique to this area during the Middle Maritime Woodland Period, and, while rocker stamping was common throughout the Maritime Peninsula at this time, it is rare in Port Joli, where simple stamping dominated ceramic decoration. Collared vessels were also very rare during this period at Port Joli. The use of deep punctates to delimit decoration appears to start earlier in Port Joli than elsewhere in the region, and in fact the E'se'get assemblages suggest this unique decorative attribute may have originated on the South Shore and subsequently spread throughout the Maritime Peninsula.

Late Maritime Woodland Period (1300–550 Years Ago)

Black (2002) describes a significant settlement and economic shift in the Quoddy Region of the Bay of Fundy around 1300 years ago, at precisely the same time that settlement and subsistence begin to radically change in Port Joli. In the Quoddy region, large complex Middle Maritime Woodland shell middens were replaced with large black soil middens, often "larger in areal extent" (Black 2002) in the Early Late Maritime Woodland Period. Some Quoddy sites have rock-delineated features, and extensive living surfaces are common in this period. It is remarkable that these traits are consistent with the changes that occur in Port Joli during the Middle to Late Maritime Woodland transition.

Perhaps the most notable change during the Late Maritime Woodland Period is the disappearance of the large deep-processing middens of the preceding period. These large summer aggregation sites appear to be replaced with very large black soil middens, such as AlDf-06, AlDf-03, and AlDf-08. These middens are often much larger (in aerial extent) than the large processing middens, but the clam shell becomes highly comminuted while it decreases in quantity (figure 8.4), to be replaced by "black soil." In fact, bulk-sample analysis indicates that the black soil middens are clearly the result of increased soil fraction (figure 9.1), probably from organic deposition, and an increase in the proportion of charcoal per kilogram of soil over time (figure 9.2). The proportion of clam shell decreases drastically in the middens (figure 8.3). At the same time, the number of all artifacts per kilogram (figure 9.3), and in particular the number of lithic artifacts per kilogram (figure 9.4), all increase substantially from earlier periods, with the highest quantity occurring with the earliest levels of AlDf-24, Area C.

Some shifts evident in the Quoddy region may not be evident in Port Joli. In the Quoddy region, there was a settlement shift, from warm-season sites at insular locations to cold-season sites on the mainland during the Late Maritime Woodland Period. At Port Joli, such settlement shifts were not necessary, and small cold-season sites continue to be occupied in Port Joli during the Late Maritime Woodland, as exemplified by AlDf-24, Area C. However, like the large warm-season sites in Port Joli, they tend to be much more intensively occupied and have deeper stratification, blacker soil, and substantially more artifact deposition.

These Late Maritime Woodland cold-season sites are often located somewhat inland and in sheltered locations, particularly in the lee of large glacial erratics or boulder ridges. They are sometimes located nearby, or even on top of, Middle Maritime Woodland sites of all types, perhaps suggesting a later preference for locations closer to the mouth of the harbour. While no seasonality data are available from AlDf-08, it is possible that this large site, sheltered so deep in the forest, represents a large, multi-family winter campsite—a

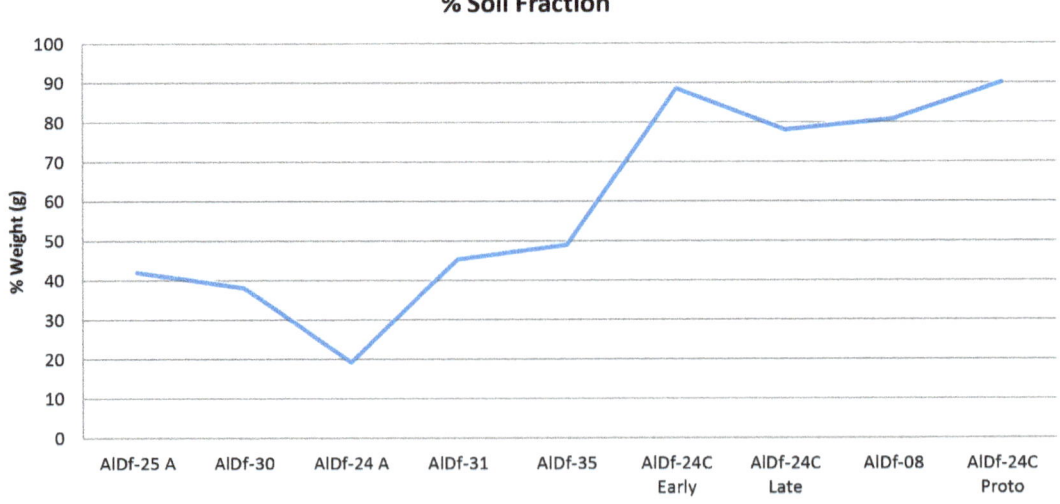

Figure 9.1 E'se'get Project bulk-sample assemblages: Percentage of soil fraction (by weight per gram of bulk sample) by site.

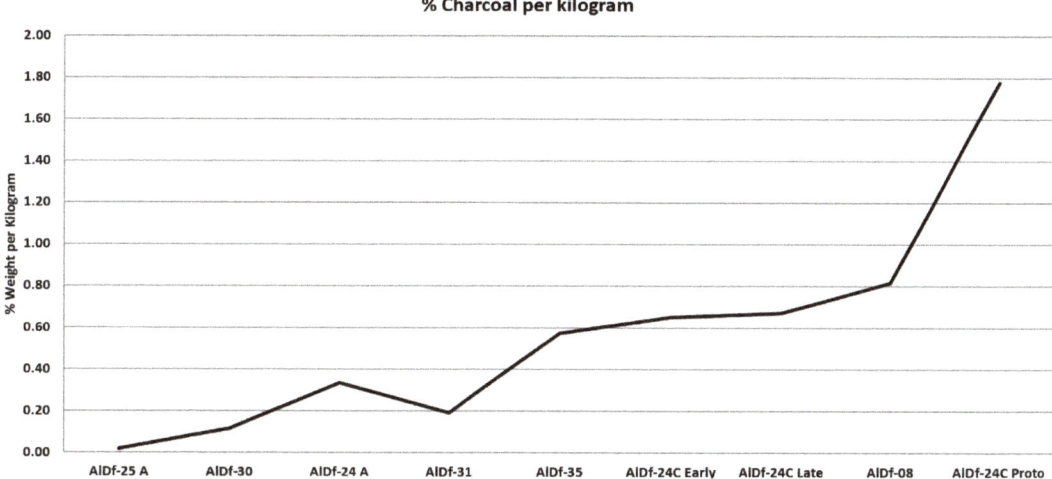

Figure 9.2 E'se'get Project bulk-sample assemblages: Charcoal percentage (by weight per kilogram of soil) by site.

counterpart to the large summer sites like AlDf-06 and AlDf-03. Only more excavation and analysis can confirm this proposition.

While the shift in site location and site structure between the Middle and Late Maritime Woodland Periods are drastic, the shift in economic strategies is even more dramatic. As discussed in Chapter 8, Early Late Maritime Woodland economic practices represent a gradual shift from those in the Middle Maritime Woodland. Cod fishing continued to be an important activity, as was hare hunting in the winter months. Other small furbearers and seals were also important contributors to the diet. However, the bulk sample analysis shows a clear decline in shellfish contribution, while the faunal analysis indicates a significant increase in cervid exploitation in tandem with a radical decrease in waterfowl hunting. This

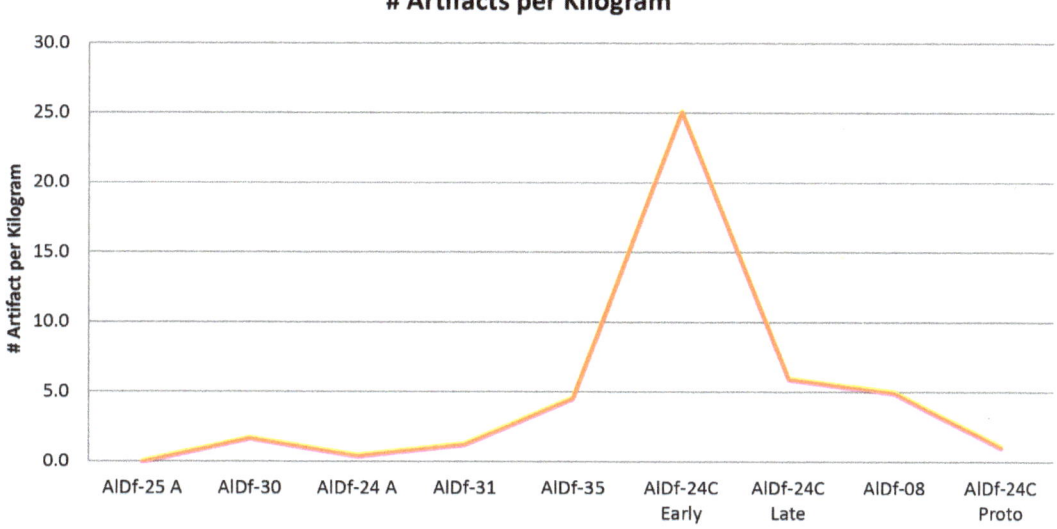

Figure 9.3 E'se'get Project bulk-sample assemblages: Number of artifacts (per kilogram) by site).

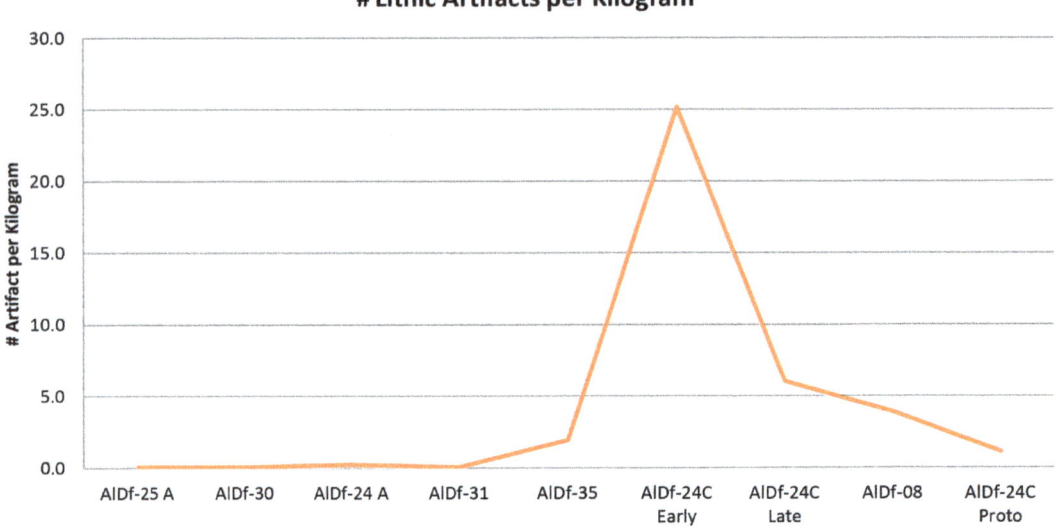

Figure 9.4 E'se'get Project bulk-sample assemblages: Number of lithic artifacts (per kilogram) by site.

shift to cervid exploitation in the Late Maritime Woodland has been noted in Maine by Spiess et al. (2004: 150) at the Indiantown Island site.

In addition to cervid hunting, it appears that greater effort was placed on their processing, with all Late Maritime Woodland sites showing evidence of significant bone-marrow and perhaps bone-grease extraction, in the form of spirally cracked and fragmented cervid bone. This increase in cervid procurement and processing appears to have been facilitated by task-specific hunting camps such as AlDf-11 and AlDf-10, which also have rock-delineated hearth features similar to those found in the Quoddy region during this period (e.g., Black 2002). The increased effort expended in exploiting and processing cervids may be associated with a process of economic intensification (see Betts and Friesen 2004).

Why this intensification may have been necessary is unknown, but it is worth considering why it is associated with a decline in shellfish production, cod fishing, and waterfowl hunting in the later Late Maritime Woodland contexts. As harbour development progressed and the depth of the harbour increased, the size of the clam flats at Scotch Point may have decreased. At the same time the large middens at AlDf-24, AlDf-25, and AlDf-26 indicate that significant harvesting pressure was being placed on these resources, and it is possible that the productivity of the clam flats diminished over time. Intensification of cervid exploitation may have helped to alleviate the strain caused by the decline in shellfish harvesting. Erskine found evidence of herring at some of these later sites (AlDf-03, AlDf-06) and this may have also been part of the solution to the reduction in clams. Regardless, it is important to note that the entire history of Port Joli's harbour is closely linked to soft-shell clams. No sites are located in areas where they were not adjacent to clam flats, and the contribution to diet must have been enormous in all time periods (cf. Spiess 2017).

The inundation of the harbour may also have been responsible for the severe decline in bird exploitation, as eelgrass beds may have been drowned—substantially decreasing the developing harbour's attractiveness to birds—before they could become re-established at the head of the harbour. Climate may also have played a significant factor in the change in food sources. As outlined in Chapter 2, the Middle to Late Maritime Woodland transition, around 1300 years ago, occurred at a time when the dense boreal forest in the harbour transitioned to a wetter pine-dominated forest. This more open type of forest, combined with warmer temperatures, may have proven more attractive to white-tailed deer, whose remains also increased in the middens in the Late Maritime Woodland Period, as moose and caribou declined. The decline in moose and caribou in warmer conditions is consistent with known low-/high-latitude axis adaptations (animals whose adaption and population density changes with latitude) for cervid species in North America (Geist 1998).

Technologically, things changed far less drastically in Port Joli during the Middle to Late Woodland transition. Dwelling construction may have become slightly more informal, with formal axial features that bisected dwellings disappearing at the same time that bilaterally patterned use of space in the dwelling was apparently becoming more rigid (as evidenced by the patterned discard of artifacts, see Chapter 5). It may be possible to see the evolution of this cultural tradition in the Port Joli archaeological record (e.g., Hrynick and Betts 2017). Site structure appears to become less formal as well, with large summer shell middens disappearing completely in favour of mixed-use habitation sites with smaller shell middens but extensive habitation areas. While the processing of clams was probably less intense, it clearly continued, but on a less industrial and segregated scale.

High-quality lithic raw materials appear to become less frequent in shell middens, with larger quantities of lower-quality quartz and rhyolite prevalent both for tools and debitage. Pottery changes subtly, with vessel walls becoming somewhat thinner, and cord-wrapped stick becoming the dominant decorative tool, consistent with the ceramic tradition throughout the Maritime Peninsula. Highly complex designs emerge during this period in Port Joli, and the potential use of knotted cord as a decorative element may be an attribute unique to the South Shore of Nova Scotia.

Finally, the most important transition may have been a demographic one. Was the shift from Middle to Late Maritime Woodland associated with a population increase in Port Joli, as it may have been in the Quoddy region (Black 2001: 313)? In Port Joli, the Late Maritime Woodland Period archaeological record exhibits more sites. This may be a consequence of erosion, with Middle Maritime Woodland sites missing from the exposed eastern side of Port Joli. However, if we consider the western side of the harbour in isolation, there are many more Late Maritime Woodland sites and contexts, with almost all Middle Maritime Woodland deposits overlaid to some extent with Late Maritime Woodland deposits. Furthermore, the isolated Late Maritime Woodland sites closer to the head of the harbour are horizontally much larger than even the largest Middle Maritime Woodland shell middens, and the Late Maritime Woodland deposits seem to provide more evidence of multiple concatenated living floors. Furthermore, the deposits tend to contain much denser concentrations of artifacts per volume of soil, suggesting increased intensity of occupation.

There are also different types of sites, with task-specific sites associated with hunting occurring on the landscape for the first time. Late Maritime Woodland deposits are also extremely artifact-rich, especially in lithics, suggesting significant repeated occupation. Together, these lines of archaeological evidence argue for greater populations around Port Joli's harbour during the Late Maritime Woodland Period. Population increase is often associated with economic and settlement changes, though it is difficult to know if the population increase is related to region-wide trends or the success of the Middle Maritime Woodland lifeway in Port Joli, where clam surpluses being produced every summer contributed to a local population increase.

Protohistoric Period (550–330 Years Ago)

Only one dated context excavated during the E'se'get Archaeology Project dates to the Protohistoric Period (AlDf-24, Area C, Level 2), but the uppermost level of several other sites (including AlDf-03, AlDf-11, AlDf-07, and AlDf-08), appear to have Protohistoric (or very early Historic) components. Protohistoric sites may be archaeologically invisible because of a presumed disruption in seasonal movement and settlement. The desire of Indigenous people to access early European trade may be the reason that Protohistoric sites are placed in locations not currently accounted for by archaeological settlement models (e.g., Bourque and Whitehead 1994, 1985; Hrynick et al. 2017; Whitehead 1993a, 1993b). It could also be responsible for their placement of these sites in headland locations, which are advantageous for intercepting in-shore traders, explorers, and fishermen, but which are also more likely to be impacted by substantial coastal erosion. The implication here is that settlement patterns may have shifted substantially, and the traditional Wabanaki ethnohistoric settlement model—with summers spent on the coast and winters in the interior (presumably to access furbearers)—may have developed as a response to European trade (Hrynick et al. 2017).

What do the Port Joli sites and assemblages contribute to this discussion? From a settlement perspective, both the large warm-season, aggregation sites (AlDf-03, AlDf-08) and the cold-season, sheltered sites (AlDf-24, Area C), as well as task-specific hunting camps (AlDf-11), continued to be occupied during the Protohistoric Period. This evidence indicates no discernable change in settlement around the harbour of Port Joli during the Protohistoric Period, with one caveat. The Protohistoric dwelling surface levels at AlDf-24, Area C, were not as compact nor as easily discernible as the Late Maritime Woodland house floors below it. This may have been the result of taphonomic process; as the uppermost occupation layer of the site, it was not compacted by generations of activity above it and furthermore was exposed to significant root action from the sod above.

Despite evidence of continued site use, Protohistoric contexts do appear to be less frequent around the harbour than Late Maritime Woodland sites. However, there are hints that this may be an illusion, and AlDf-24, Area C, may be instructive in this regard. Only two small fragments of wrought iron were recovered from the Protohistoric deposits at AlDf-24, Area C, and the primary determining factor in identifying the age of the deposit was its associated radiocarbon date. Without that date, and without the two fragments of wrought iron, it is likely that the deposit would have been simply identified as the upper portion of the Late Maritime Woodland deposit. This may be the case for many more Protohistoric contexts in the Maritime Peninsula. It can be expected that most European goods would be highly curated by Mi'kmaq, and until European trade goods became more ubiquitous, these early Protohistoric sites may be artifactually indistinguishable from the Late Maritime Woodland deposits below them. In the absence of radiocarbon dates, such sites would simply appear as typical Late Woodland deposits and occupations.

A brief review of the artifact assemblage from the uppermost levels AlDf-24, Area C, indicates that no appreciable change in technology is evident, the range of shapes and types of artifacts are consistent, and the size and scope of materials are all within the range of variability for the lower levels of the deposit. Debitage is very abundant in this level, though the bulk sample analysis suggests that lithic reduction decreases slightly during the Protohistoric Period. However, the proportion of soil fraction and charcoal fraction all increase to their maximum levels during the Protohistoric Period. The proportion of clam shell in deposits is similar, though a little lower than in Late Maritime Woodland contexts. Cervids are still the dominant taxon, with other species occurring in similar proportions in faunal assemblages as the preceding period. Therefore, the economic pattern established during the Late Maritime Woodland in Port Joli also appears to have been little disrupted during the Protohistoric Period.

Based on the available evidence, the earliest arrival of Europeans appeared to have little discernable impact on the settlement and economic practices of Port Joli's inhabitants, even though there is ample evidence of interaction, in the form of European artifacts. Regardless, this soon changed, and it appears that Port Joli was abandoned by the Mi'kmaq sometime in the later part of the seventeenth century, as evidenced by the lack of archaeological deposits.

Place-making in the Pretty Harbour

Place-making is both a process and effect of human interaction with space (e.g., Creese 2018: 48)—in the case of Port Joli, with a dynamic and changing land- and seascape. It is a process of interaction with ecosystems and species and the development of daily, seasonal, and yearly routines required to make a living within and around these spaces. The actions of ancient Mi'kmaq in Port Joli created it as a special place, but the routines and practices they replicated there, day-in and day-out, year to year, and century to century, also created their identities and histories; in short, Port Joli played a critical role in maintaining and creating their culture (e.g., Betts 2009; Betts et al. 2012; Creese 2018).

If place-making is a process, what was the process at Port Joli? How did the Mi'kmaq create their history? It was marked by a natural event, the establishment of extensive foreshore tidal flats near what is now known as Scotch Point and Forbes Point, around 1500 years ago, following thousands of years of slow sea-level rise and inundation after the last glaciation. The Mi'kmaq had been familiar with collecting and eating clams for centuries prior to this development (e.g., Sanger 1996), but the archaeological record suggests that the extensive clam flats that developed in Port Joli may have been different than those encountered previously. Perhaps because these were larger or more productive than other clam beds on the South Shore, the Mi'kmaq chose to interact with this resource in a way they had not done previously (and, arguably, since). They began to *collectively* exploit the resource, in aggregations of many family groups who came together seasonally to share in the labour.

The labour they dedicated to collecting and processing these clams resulted in the largest shell middens ever known in Nova Scotia. How they organized this cooperative labour, when it may not have been common previously, is difficult to interpret, but the archaeological record provides some clues. A class of artifacts never-before seen archaeologically—the clay-lined clam shell, or spark holder—was found in abundance at AlDf-24, Area A. It is not surprising that such an artifact would be found at a summer aggregation site. Spark holders were used to transport fire from one camp to another, and families travelling from dispersed locations would need to bring sparks to this site to rapidly create fires, for both cooking and smoking the clams.

But for the Mi'kmaq, we know that the creation of fire and the perpetuation of the flame is both a social and spiritual act. A letter by Abbé Pierre Maillard written in the late eighteenth century described an interview with a Mi'kmaw *buoin* (shaman) who described the rituals associated with fire-keeping (Lockerby 2004: 409). Keeping the fire was the domain of Mi'kmaw women, and the activity of preserving and transporting a spark and lighting a fire was a critical spiritual act accompanied by significant group ritual. It is worth noting Maillard's transcription of the shaman's account verbatim (Lockerby 2004: 409–10):

> To preserve fire…we would entrust it to the care of our war-chief's women, who took turns to preserve the spark, using half-rotten pine wood covered with ash. Sometimes this fire lasted up to three moons. When it lasted the span of three moons, the fire became sacred and magical to us.…We would all gather together and, …when our numbers were complete, we would gather round and, without regard to rank or age, light our pipes at the fire. We would suck in the smoke and keep it in our mouths, and one by one would puff it out into the face of the woman who had last preserved the spark, telling her that she was worthy above all to share in the benign influence of the Father of Light, the Sun, because she had so skilfully preserved His emanations.

The account suggests that feasting followed this ritual. It is intriguing that spark holders may be associated with group ritual and feasting, considering that these large Port Joli middens are likely associated with an aggregation of multiple families for the purposes of intensively exploiting local clam beds. Such ritual may have been a critical social activity to reinforce and establish group bonds as the group shifted their economic behaviours from single-family activities in the winter months toward communal goals in the summer months.

This communal action and ritual established these large shell mounds, and the "pretty harbour" where they were located, as important ceremonial and social places, where people came together to share in spiritual and economic acts. From this perspective, it is interesting that the first archaeological deposit at the oldest site in Port Joli, AlDf-30, is a ritual structure. In fact, the sweathouse at AlDf-30 (and the potential sweathouse at AlDf-31) may be associated with the ritual activities at the nearby AlDf-24, Area A. While contemporaneity cannot be conclusively established between the two sites (see Chapter 4), a hypothetical scenario could see AlDf-30 first used as a place for sweats, while domestic activities took place in AlDf-24. It is unknown if these domestic activities were related directly to the sweathouse, but such a possibility is intriguing. For example, ritual preparation in the form of a sweat may have been necessary to ensure the success of fishing, hunting, and shell gathering going on in the summer months (Hrynick and Betts 2017). When AlDf-30 eventually transitioned to a habitation site, the sweathouse may have been moved to AlDf-31. If so, the stratigraphy at AlDf-31 indicates that it too eventually transitioned to a domestic site, and sweats were moved to another location, assuming the practice continued.

Ethnohistoric records often associate sweathouses with male ritual activities (Hrynick and Betts 2014, 2017). If keeping the spark was the domain of women, then it may be possible that a counterpart male ritual domain was necessary at AlDf-30. Sweathouses were important for maintaining proper relationships with the subjects of the natural world (Hrynick and Betts 2017) and might have been a place where men reinforced and enacted the "right" form of action on a group level. Such activity would establish the fen around AlDf-30 as an important ritual space, and it is likely that the rituals that were repeated there helped to cement the social relations of the people who came together to live and cooperate at Port Joli.

The ritual and social practices and the resulting spaces created in Port Joli were a creative response to the economic opportunities the harbour provided—namely the ability to come together to collect clams and to fish, and to preserve the surplus to make the winters easier. The archaeological record indicates that the summer crowds largely left Port Joli in the fall, but some stayed behind, living deep in the woods. At AlDf-30 they re-purposed ritual structures as domestic ones, using the architecture to help them maintain spatial boundaries between men and women, which were also critical to their spiritual relationship with animals (Hrynick and Betts 2017).

The places created around the harbour represented monumental, permanent alterations of the Port Joli landscape. The massive flat-topped mounds of shell transformed the naturally rocky and hummocky terrain of the shoreline in a way that was likely visually striking (Kelley 2018). At least three gleaming white mounds, rising a metre above the shore, would have been clearly visible as one entered the inner harbour. They were (and are) a permanent symbol of the collaborative labour, social relationships, and kinships that created them. They are also a symbol of an identity that was perhaps emerging in the harbour, arising from the bonds created by the recurring and shared social and economic practices of the people who came to this special place year after year.

As the harbour changed, large-scale collaborative clam collecting and cod fishing appeared to wane, and the large communal mounds ceased to grow by 1300 years ago. Yet the Mi'kmaq still congregated in Port Joli, shifting their collective activities to (potentially) exploiting large herring runs and to hunting and processing caribou, deer, and moose. Clams still continued to be collected and were undoubtedly processed for storage, but not in the massive quantities evident in the Middle Maritime Woodland Period. Populations appeared to grow, and sites were larger and more intensively occupied in the Late Maritime Woodland Period. The organizing of the labour needed to collectively exploit clams and herring runs and to ambush and process caribou, moose, and deer must have required group events and ritual to reinforce social ties. Ochre is present in Late Maritime Woodland deposits, but ritual structures and spark holders have not been identified. Ridged social rules were still followed, however, as even in the absence of architectural elements, men and women still maintained a separation of space in their wigwams (e.g., Hrynick et al. 2012).

Even with the loss of the massive clam flats that existed in the Middle Maritime Woodland Period at Port Joli, clam flats were still large and the harbour continued to support major summer aggregations. It is difficult to know if this harbour was more productive than others nearby, but if the modern productivity of clam flats in the region can be used as a proxy, it probably was comparable to other harbours on the South Shore. In fact Port Joli was perhaps deficient in some areas, as, unlike most adjacent harbours, the rivers and streams that feed into its harbour are difficult to navigate by canoe, and do not provide ready access to the resources of large rivers and lakes in the interior. Yet Port Joli continued to attract large numbers of people in the summer, and in densities not evident in adjacent harbours. In fact, Port Joli has the densest concentration of Late Maritime Woodland shell middens and indeed some of the largest sites from this period in the Maritime Provinces.

It was perhaps the history the Mi'kmaq had created at Port Joli—their history with the place they had created—that continued to draw them back, even if other places offered similar resources. Put simply, none of those other places was Port Joli, where for generations families came together every summer to live and work collectively. Here they shared labour and resources, hunting and fishing communally, and reinforcing social and kinship ties through ceremony. It was likely a place of feasting, socializing, ritual, trading, and romance (in the sense of finding partners)—a time to anticipate throughout the year. Some families undoubtedly stayed in Port Joli all year, perhaps on their own (AlDf-24, Area C), or even in larger groups (AlDf-08). But they could always expect the arrival of families and friends after the cold winter and to spend summers at the idyllic spots at the head of the harbour (AlDf-06, AlDf-03, AlDf-04). They transformed these spaces too, creating wide, flat mounds of rich black soil, perfect for even more wigwams to join in every year. They may not have been as visible as the large gleaming shell mounds of a thousand years earlier, but these old mounds led the way to the new special places—places at the precise head of the harbour, a location that could not be missed.

Conclusions: The Future of Archaeological History in Port Joli

This site monograph is not meant to be the definitive statement on Port Joli culture history. Instead, it is a data repository and preliminary framework from which more nuanced explorations can be conducted. Much more can be learned by applying new theoretical and methodological analyses to the data sets, in creative ways that explore different paradigms and theory. Already, the Port Joli data set has been explored thorough the lens of relational ontology (from a perspective of Indigenous spirituality and ways of seeing), resulting in significant insights. Betts et al. (2012), inspired by the discovery of a shark tooth associated with the Middle Maritime Woodland burial site at AlDf-24, Area A, explored the relationship between the Wabanaki, great white sharks, and the sea. The study revealed that ancient Mi'kmaq identified with both sharks and the sea, and that this close relationship existed uninterrupted for at least four thousand years, until it was interrupted by European settlement.

Similarly, Hrynick and Betts (2017) studied the relationship between ontology and the use of domestic space, using the high-resolution stratigraphic information from wigwam house floors in Port Joli. They revealed that a deep connection existed between the activities of men and women in particular spaces and the maintenance of relationships with the natural and spiritual world. Further, they traced how the history of these practices were replicated and changed over time. This was especially evident at sites like AlDf-24, Area C, and AlDf-30, where stratigraphy reveals repeated and recurring uses of the same spaces for house (wigwam) placement, sometimes over thousands of years.

Indeed, much more can be explored about the nature of men and women's work, spaces, and spirituality using the unique artifacts and features documented at Port Joli. Instead of

Figure 9.5 Painting by Mi'kmaw artist Melissa Labrador (Acadia First Nation), 2018. This untitled painting depicts a woman carrying a spark holder; just prior to lighting a fire at a Port Joli shell midden.

a cultural landscape, we may be able to view Port Joli as a palimpsest of male and female spaces and engagements, both between individuals and with the natural world. Such research is poised to add significantly to the ethnographic and oral record about the lives of ancient Mi'kmaw men and women.

New methodologies, specifically with the analyses of soft-shell clams, may provide greater insights into the seasonal occupation of Port Joli and the impact that exploitation had on local soft-shell clam populations (e.g., ; Betts et al. 2017; Burchell et al. 2014). As described in Chapter 8, the study of isotopes from clam shells can precisely reveal the seasonal round of Port Joli's inhabitants and may even provide a means to explore the connection between shellfish exploitation pressure and shifts in site location.

More analyses on the distribution and frequencies of the stone tools, especially the partially studied debitage (Chapter 7), may help to contribute to the understanding of social organization and gender roles. In fact, it may supplant the general local-versus-exotic lithic-source interpretations presented here, in favour of an interpretation of domestic practice by experienced stone-tool makers and users. Similarly, much information about the environment, procurement strategies, and consumption traditions is locked in the animal bones preserved in these middens, and detailed metric and isotopic analyses may reveal much more about how people lived in and exploited ecosystems and animal populations.

In conclusion, perhaps the most important revelation from the data set presented in this book is that Port Joli was a special place, intensively occupied by the Mi'kmaq over thousands of years. Inevitably, the Mi'kmaq created Emsik, or Port Joli, as surely as the place created, and undoubtedly continues to create, them. We hope that this project and monograph will become part of that recursive process, as Acadia First Nation and other Mi'kmaw groups come to terms with the information revealed from our collaboration and weave it into new and existing narratives of their own pasts. We have already witnessed this process in action. The recent archaeology at Port Joli has inspired new Acadia First Nation interpretations of their history, embodied by a new artifact display in the band-operated Sipuke'l Art Gallery in Liverpool, Nova Scotia, and the inclusion of archaeological lectures and experiences in their annual Aboriginal Day celebrations.

Acadia First Nation artists have also been inspired by the information recovered from Port Joli. Artifacts like the spark holders and features like the shell middens, coastal wigwams, and sweathouses have appeared in their artwork and in the narratives they build around it (figure 9.5). These are tangible results of collaborative community-based archaeology and direct information sharing. It is tantalizing to envision how the community will use a reference volume such as this, replete with illustrations, photographs, and primary data, about their own history in Port Joli.

Bibliography

Allen, P. 1980. "*The Oxbow Site: Chronology and Prehistory in Northeastern New Brunswick.*" New Brunswick Manuscripts in Archaeology, no. 1. Fredericton: New Brunswick Archaeological Services.

Allen, P. 1983. *Ceramics from a Stratified Site in Northeastern New Brunswick*. Manuscript on file, Archaeology Branch, Historical Resources Administration. Fredericton.

Allen, P. 2005. *The Oxbow Site 1984. Metepenagiag Mi'kmaq First Nation Miramichi, New Brunswick*. New Brunswick Manuscripts in Archaeology, no. 39. Fredericton: New Brunswick Archaeological Services.

Ambrose, J. 1867. "Observations on the Fishing Grounds and Fish of St. Margaret's Bay, N.S." *Proceedings and Transactions of the Nova Scotian Institute of Natural Science* 2 (1): 67–76.

Anderson, R. C. 1972. "The Ecological Relationships of Meningeal Worm and Native Cervids in North America." *Journal of Wildlife Diseases* 8 (4): 304–10.

Anderson, T. W. 1985. "Late-Quaternary Pollen Records from Eastern Ontario, Quebec, and Atlantic Canada." In *Pollen Records of Late-Quaternary North American Sediments*, edited by V. M. Bryant and R. G. Hollow, 281–326. Dallas: American Association of Stratigraphic Palynologists Foundation.

Anonymous. 1997. *Mi'kmaw Resource Guide*. Truro, NS: Eastern Woodlands Publishing.

Baird, P. 1616. "Relation de la Nouvelle France." In *The Jesuit Relations and Allied Documents: Travels and Explorations of the Jesuit Missionaries in New France 1610–1791*, vol. 3: *Acadia, 1611–1616*, edited by R. Thwaites, translated by J. Covert, 26–301. New York: Pageant Books.

Banning, E. B. *2000. The Archaeologist's Laboratory: The Analysis of Archaeological Data*. Interdisciplinary Contributions to Archaeology. New York: Kluwer Academic/Plenum.

Bayham, F., 1979. "Factors Influencing the Archaic Pattern of Animal Utilization. *KIVA* 44: 219–35.

Beck, C., 1998. "Projectile Point Types as Valid Chronological Units. In *Unit Issues in Archaeology: Measuring Time, Space, and Material*, edited by A. F. Ramenofsky and A. Steffen, 21–40. Salt Lake City: University of Utah Press.

Bekerman, A. 1995. "Relative Chronology of Princess Point Sites." Master's thesis, Department of Anthropology, University of Toronto.

Belcher, William R. 1988. "Archaeological Investigations at the Knox Site (30-21), East Penobscot Bay, Maine." Master's thesis, Quaternary Studies, University of Maine.

Belcher, W. R. 1989. "Prehistoric Fish Exploitation in East Penobscot Bay, Maine: The Knox Site and Sea-level Rise." *Archaeology of Eastern North America* 17: 175–90.

Betts, M. 2011. *The E'se'get Archaeology Project, 2010*. Permit #A2010NS44 Port Joli. Manuscript on file, Nova Scotia Museum, Halifax.

Betts, M. 2010. *The E'se'get Archaeology Project, 2009*. Permit #A2009NS27 Port Joli. Manuscript on file, Nova Scotia Museum, Halifax.

Betts, M. 2009. *The E'se'get Archaeology Project, 2008*. Permit #A2008NS33 Port Joli. Manuscript on file, Nova Scotia Museum, Halifax.

Betts, M., Blair, S., and Black, D. 2012. *Perspectivism, Mortuary Symbolism, and Human-Shark Relationships on the Maritime Peninsula. American Antiquity* 77 (4): 621–45.

Betts, M., Burchell, M., and Schöne, B. 2017. "An Economic History of the Maritime Woodland Period in Port Joli Harbour, Nova Scotia." *Journal of the North Atlantic* 10: 18–41.

Betts, M., and Friesen, T. M., 2004. "Quantifying Hunter-Gatherer Intensification: A Zooarchaeological Case Study from Arctic Canada." *Journal of Anthropological Archaeology* 23 (4): 357–84.

Betts, M., and Hrynick, M. G. 2013. *E'se'get Archaeology Project, 2012 Field Season*. Permit #A2012NS052 Port Joli. Manuscript on file, Nova Scotia Museum, Halifax.

Betts, M., and Hyrnick, M. G. (eds) 2017. "East Coast Shell Midden Research." *Journal of the North Atlantic*. Special volume 10.

Betts, M., Hyrnick, M.G, and Pelletier-Michaud, A. 2018. "The Pierce-Embree Site: A Palaeoindian Findspot from Southwestern Nova Scotia." Canadian Journal of Archaeology 42 (2): 255–262.

Betts, M., Maschner, H., and Clark, D. 2011. "Zooarchaeology of the 'Fish that Stops': Using Archaeofaunas to Construct Long-Term Time Series of Atlantic and Pacific Cod Populations." In *The Archaeology of North Pacific Fisheries*, edited by M. Moss and A. Cannon, 171–95. Anchorage: University of Alaska Press.

Betts, M., Noël, S., Tourigny, E., Burns, M., Pope, P., and Cumbaa, S. 2014. "Zooarchaeology of the Historic Cod Fishery in Newfoundland and Labrador, Canada." *Journal of the North Atlantic* 24: 1–21.

Binford, L. R. 1977. "Forty-Seven Trips: A Case Study in the Character of Archaeological Formation Processes." In Stone Tools as Cultural Markers: Change, Evolution and Complexity, edited by R. V. Wright, 24–38. Atlantic Highlands, NJ: Humanities Press.

Binford, L. R. 1979. "Organization and Formation Processes: Looking at Curated Technologies." *Journal of Anthropological Research* 35 (3): 255–73.

Binford, L. R. 1990. "Mobility, Housing, and Environment: A Comparative Study." *Journal of Anthropological Research* 46 (2): 119–52.

Bishop, J. C., and Black, D. W. 1988. "The Land's Edge Also: Culture History and Seasonality at the Partridge Island Shell Midden." *Canadian Journal of Archaeology* 12: 17–37.

Black, D. W. 2004 (1992). *Living Close to the Ledge: Prehistoric Human Ecology of the Bliss Islands, Quoddy Region, New Brunswick, Canada*. Publications in Northeastern Archaeology, no. 6. St. John's: Copetown Press.

Black, D. W. 1993a. "Stratigraphic Integrity in Northeastern Shell Middens: An Example from the Insular Quoddy Region." In *Prehistoric Archaeology in the Maritime Provinces: Past and Present Research*, edited by M. Deal and S. Blair, 197–211. Fredericton: Council of Maritime Premiers Maritime Committee on Archaeological Cooperation.

Black, D. W. 2000. "That Thing of Shreds and Patches: An Archaeological Narrative of the Bliss Islands Thoroughfare, Quoddy Region, New Brunswick, Canada." In *The Entangled Past: Integrating History and Archaeology: Proceedings of the 30th Annual Chacmool Conference*, edited by M. Boyd, J. C. Erwin, and M. Hendricksen, 146–55. Calgary: The Archaeological Association of the University of Calgary.

Black, D. 2002. Out of the Blue and into the Black: The Middle–Late Maritime Woodland Transition in the Quoddy Region, New Brunswick, Canada." In *Subsistence-Settlement Change, A.D. 700–1300*, edited by J. P. Hart and C. B. Reith, 301–20. Albany: New York State Education Department.

Black, D. W. 2004. "Ponapsqey: Stone Raw Materials." In *Wolastoqiyik Ajemseg Volume 2: Archaeological Results,* edited by S. E. Blair, 91–116). , New Brunswick Manuscripts in Archaeology, no. 36E. Fredericton: New Brunswick Archaeological Services.

Black, D. W. 2017. "Archaeological Sea Mammal Remains from the Maritime Provinces of Canada." *Journal of the North Atlantic* 10: 70–89.

Black, D. W., and Wilson, L. A. 1999. "The Washademoak Lake Chert Source, Queens County, New Brunswick, Canada." *Archaeology of Eastern North America* 27: 81–108.

Blair, S. 1997. *The Jemseg Crossing Archaeological Project: Preliminary Technical Report, Volumes 1–4.* Manuscript on file at New Brunswick Archaeological Services, Culture and Sports Secretariat, Fredericton.

Bock, P. K. 1978. "Micmac." In *Handbook of North American Indians*, vol. 15, edited by B. G. Trigger, 109–22. Washington: Smithsonian Institution.

Bourgeois, V. G. J. 1999. "A Regional Pre-Contact Ceramic Sequence for the Saint John River Valley." Master's thesis, Department of Anthropology, University of New Brunswick.

Bourque, B. J. 1971. "Prehistory of the Central Maine Coast." Doctoral dissertation, Department of Anthropology, Harvard University.

Bourque, B. 1995. *Diversity and Complexity in Prehistoric Maritime Societies, A Gulf of Maine Perspective.* New York" Plenum Press.

Bourque, B. J. 2001. *Twelve Thousand Years: American Indians in Maine.* Lincoln: University of Nebraska Press.

Bourque, B. 2012. *The Swordfish Hunters: The History and Ecology of an Ancient American Sea People.* Piermont: Bunker Hill Publishing.

Bourque, B., and Whitehead, R. H. 1985. *Tarrentines and the Introduction of European Trade Goods in the Gulf of Maine. Ethnohistory* 32 (4): 327–41.

Bourque, B., and Whitehead, R. H. 1994. "Trade and Alliances in the Contact Period." In *American Beginnings: Exploration, Culture, and Cartography in the Land of Norumbega*, edited by E. W. Baker, E. H. Churchill, R. D'Abate, K. L. Jones, V. A. Konrad, and H. E. L. Prins, 132–47. Lincoln: University of Nebraska Press.

Bradford, R. G., Bentzen, P., Ceapa, C., Cook, A. M., Curry, A., LeBlanc, P., and Stokesbury, M. 2016. *Status of Atlantic Sturgeon (Acipenser oxyrinchus oxyrinchus) in the Saint John River, New Brunswick.* DFO Canada Science Advisory Secretariat Research Document 2016/072.

Braun, D. 1980. "Experimental Interpretation of Ceramic Vessel Use on the Basis of Rim and Neck Formal Attributes." In *The Navajo Project: Archaeological Investigations, Page to Phoenix 500 KV Southern Transmission Line*, edited by D. Fiero. Museum of Northern Arizona Research Paper no. 11. Flagstaff.

Breed, G. A., Jonsen, I. D., Myers, R. A., Bowen, W. D., and Leonard, M. L. 2009. "Sex-Specific, Seasonal Foraging Tactics of Adult Grey Seals (*Halichoerus grypus*) Revealed by State-Space Analysis." *Ecology* 90: 3209-21.

Brown T. J. 1922. *Place-Names of the Province of Nova Scotia.* Halifax: N. S. Royal Print & Litho.

Burchell, M., Betts, M., and Patton, K. A. 2014. "Preliminary Analysis of Stable Oxygen Isotopes and Shell Growth in the Softshell Clam, *Mya Arenaria*: Implications for Interpreting Seasonality and Shellfish Harvesting in Port Joli, Nova Scotia." *North Atlantic Archaeology* 3: 93–108.

Burke, A. L. 1993. *The Pelletier Site (CkEe-9), Témiscouata: A Lithic Workshop and Habitation Site.* Mémoire de maîtrise, Département d'Anthropologie, Université de Montréal.

Burke, A. L. 2000. "Lithic Procurement and the Ceramic Period Occupation of the Interior of the Maritime Peninsula." Doctoral thesis, University at Albany, SUNY.

Burke, A. L. 2007. "Quarry Source Areas and the Organization of Stone Tool Technology: A View from Quebec." *Archaeology of Eastern North America* 35: 63–80.

Butler, E. L., and Hadlock, W. S. 1957. *Uses of Birch-Bark in the Northeast.* Bulletin 7, Bar Harbor: Robert Abbe Museum.

de Champlain, S. 1907. *The Voyages of Samuel de Champlain, 1604–1618.* Edited by W. L. Grant. New York: Charles Scribner and Sons.

Carr, C., and Sears, D. W. G. 1985. "Toward an Analysis of the Exchange of Meteoritic Iron in the Middle Woodland." *Southeastern Archaeology* 4 (2): 79–92.

Clarke, D. V. 1978. *Analytical Archaeology.* 2nd ed. London: Methuen and Company.

C.R.C., c. 1036, 10[1].
Connolly, J. 1977. "Archaeology in Nova Scotia and New Brunswick Between 1863 and 1914." *Man in the Northeast* 13: 3–34.
COSEWIC (Committee on the Status of Endangered Wildlife in Canada). 2006. *Assessment and Status Report on the American Eel Anguilla rostrata* in Canada. Ottawa: Committee on the Status of Endangered Wildlife in Canada.
COSEWIC (Committee on the Status of Endangered Wildlife in Canada). 2010. *Assessment and Status Report on the Atlantic Cod Gadus morhua* in Canada. Ottawa: Committee on the Status of Endangered Wildlife in Canada.
Creese, J. 2018. "Place-making in Canadian Archaeology." *Canadian Journal of Archaeology* 42: 46–56.
Curtis, J. E. (2002). "A Revised Temporal Framework for Middle Woodland Ceramics in South-Central Ontario." *Ontario Archaeology* 73: 15–28.
Curtis, J. E. 2004a. "Processes of Cultural Change: Ceramics and Interaction Across the Middle to Late Woodland Transition in South-Central Ontario." Doctoral dissertation, Department of Anthropology, University of Toronto.
Curtis, J. E. 2004b. "A Preliminary Investigation into the Origin and Development of Ceramic Castellations in Ontario." *Ontario Archaeology* 77/78: 45–61.
Davis, M. B. 1981. "Outbreaks of Forest Pathogens." *Quaternary History* 3: 216–28.
Davis, S. 1971. "The Ceramics of the Key Hole Site, New Brunswick." Undergraduate honours essay, Department of Anthropology, University of New Brunswick.
Davis, S. A. 1978. *Teacher's Cove: A Prehistoric Site on Passamaquoddy Bay*. New Brunswick Archaeology series, no. 1. Historical Resources Administration, Fredericton.
Davis, S. A. 1980. "Coastal Erosion, Neglect, Disinterest Threatening Maritime Archaeology and Resources." In *Proceedings of the 1980 Conference on the Future of Archaeology in the Maritimes*, edited by D. Shimabuku, 6–17. Occasional Papers in Anthropology no. 8. Halifax: Saint Mary's University, Department of Anthropology.
Davis, S. A. 1983. "Rising Sea Levels Threaten Archaeological Sites." *Canadian Geographical Journal* 103 (2): 40–46.
Davis, S. A. 1987. *Man, Molluscs and Mammals: A Study of Land Use in the Later Holocene of the Maritime Provinces of Canada*. Doctoral dissertation, University of Oxford.
Davis, S. A. 1993. "The Ceramic Period in Nova Scotia. In *Prehistoric Archaeology in the Maritime Provinces: Past and Present Research*, edited by M. Deal and S. Blair, 85–100. Fredericton: Maritime Committee on Archaeological Cooperation.
Davis, S. A. *1997. Mi'kmaq: Peoples of the Maritimes*. Halifax: Nimbus Publishing.
Davis, S., and Christianson, D. 1981. *Archaeological Resources in the Maritimes: A Coastal Survey—1979*. Reports in Archaeology 4. Fredericton: Council of Maritime Premiers.
Davis, S., and Christianson, D. 1988. "Three Palaeo-Indian Specimens from Nova Scotia." *Canadian Journal of Archaeology* 12: 190–96
Deal, M. 2016. *The Collection of Ages: Precontact Archaeology of the Maritime Provinces*. St. John's: Memorial University.
Deal, M., Halwas, S., Loder, C., and Betts, M. 2011. "Recent Paleoethnobotanical Research at Western Nova Scotia Shell Midden Sites." *Archaeology in Nova Scotia* 2: 30–40.
Denys, N. 1968. *The Description and Natural History of the Coasts of North America*. Translated and edited by W. F. Ganong. Toronto: Champlain Society; New York: Greenwood Press.
DFO (Fisheries and Oceans Canada). 2001. *Gaspereau Maritime Provinces Overview*. DFO Science Stock Status Reports D3–17.
DFO (Fisheries and Oceans Canada). 2009. *Pollock in Div. 4VWX+5*. DFO Canadian Scientific Science Advisory Secretariat Advisory Reports 2009/025.

Domanski, M., and Webb, J. 2007. "A Review of Heat Treatment Research." *Lithic Technology* 32 (2): 153–94.

Dugua de Mons, Pierre, 1939. *Records: Colonial and "Saintongeois,"* edited by W. I. Morse. London: Bernard Quaritch.

Edgecombe, R. B., Scott, D. B., and Fader, G. 1999. "New Data from Halifax Harbour: Paleoenvironment and a New Holocene Sea-Level Curve for the Inner Scotian Shelf." *Canadian Journal of Earth Sciences* 36: 805–17.

Egloff, K. T., and Potter, S. R. 1982. "Indian Ceramics from Coastal Plain Virginia." *Archaeology of Eastern North America* 10: 95–117.

Erskine, J. S. 1958. *Micmac Notes 1958*. Manuscript on file, Nova Scotia Museum, Halifax.

Erskine, J. S. 1959. *Micmac Notes 1959*. Manuscript on file, Nova Scotia Museum, Halifax.

Erskine, J. S. 1960. "Shell-heap Archaeology of Southwestern Nova Scotia." *Proceedings of the Nova Scotia Institute of Science* 24 (4): 339–75

Erskine, J. S. 1961. *Micmac Notes 1960*. Occasional Paper no. 1. Halifax: Nova Scotia Museum, Halifax.

Erskine, J. S. 1962. *Micmac Notes 1962*. Occasional Paper no. 2. Halifax: Nova Scotia Museum.

Erskine, J. S. 1964. *Micmac Notes 1962*. Occasional Paper no. 3. Halifax: Nova Scotia Museum.

Erskine, J. S. 1986. *Unpublished Papers on the Archaeology of the Maritime Provinces*. Compiled by Michael Deal. Halifax: Department of Anthropology, St. Mary's University.

Erskine, J. S. 1998. *Memoirs on the Prehistory of Nova Scotia, 1957–1967*. Edited by M. Deal. Special Report. Halifax: Nova Scotia Museum.

Fedriani, J. M., Fuller, T. K., Sauvajot, R. M. and York, E. C. 2000. "Competition and Intraguild Predation Among Three Sympatric Carnivores." *Oecologia* 125: 258–70.

Fee, S. B., Pettegre, D., and Caraher, W. 2013. "Taking Mobile Computing to the Field." *Near Eastern Archaeology* 76 (1): 50–54

Fenstermacher, R., and Jellison, W. L. 1933. *Diseases Affecting Moose. University of Minnesota Agriculture Exponent State Bulletin 6.*

Forbes, D. L., Manson, G. K., Charles, J., Thompson, K. R., and Taylor, R. B. 2009. "Halifax Harbour Extreme Water Levels in the Context of Climate Change: Scenarios for a 100-Year Planning Horizon." *Geological Survey of Canada*, Open File 6346, iv+22p.

Foulkes, E. V. 1981. "Fulton Island: A Stratified Site in the Saint John River Valley of New Brunswick." Master's thesis, Department of Anthropology, Trent University, Peterborough.

Fox, A. 2015. "A Study of Late Woodland Projectile Point Typology in New York Using Elliptical Fourier Outline Analysis." *Journal of Archaeological Science Reports* 4: 501–9.

Geist, V. 1998. *Deer of the World: Their Evolution, Behaviour, and Ecology*. Mechanicsville, PA: Stackpole Books.

Gero, J. M. 1991. "Genderlithics: Women's Roles in Stone Tool Production." In *Engendering Archaeology: Women and Prehistory*, edited by J. M. Gero and M. W. Conkey, 163–93). Oxford: Blackwell.

Gilpin, J. P. 1874. "On the Stone Age in Nova Scotia." *Proceedings and Transactions of the Nova Scotian Institute of Science* 3: 220–31.

Gilbert, B. M., 1990. *Mammalian Osteology*. Columbia: Missouri Archaeological Society.

Gilbert, B. M., Martin, L., and Savage, H., 1985. *Avian Osteology*. Columbia: Missouri Archaeological Society.

Gilbert, C. D., Gallant, M. J., and Black, D. W. 2005. *Distinguishing Carboniferous- from Mezozoic-associated Chert Toolstones in the Canadian Maritimes*. Online resource, Department of Anthropology, University of New Brunswick:

Godfrey-Smith, D. I., Deal, M., and Kunelius, L. 1997. "Thermoluminescence Dating of St. Croix Ceramics: Chronology Building in Southwestern Nova Scotia." *Geoarchaeology* 12: 251–73.

Goodby, R. G. 2013. "Jack's Reef Points in Northern New England: Exotic Lithics and Long Distance Interaction in the Post-Hopewell Northeast." *Archaeology of Eastern North America* 41: 59–67

Goodwin, T. A. 2008. "Nova Scotia's Involvement in The North American Soil Geochemical Landscape Project." In *Mineral Resources Branch, Report of Activities 2007*, edited by D. R. MacDonald, 29–33. Nova Scotia Department of Natural Resources, Report ME 2008-1.

Gosselink, T. E., Van Deelen, T. R., Joselyn, M. G., and Warner, R. E. 2003. "Temporal Habitat Partitioning and Spatial Use of Coyotes and Red Foxes in East-Central Illinois." *Journal of Wildlife Management* 67: 90–103.

Gramly, R. M. 2000. *Guide to the Palaeo-American Artifacts of North America*. 3rd ed. Buffalo: Persimmon Press.

Greber, N. B. 2010. "Coda: Still Seeking 'Hopewell'." In *Hopewell Settlement Patterns, Subsistence, and Symbolic Landscapes,* edited by A. M. Byers and D. Wymer, 336–48. Gainesville: University of Florida Press.

Green, D. G. 1987. "Pollen Evidence for the Postglacial Origins of Nova Scotia's Forests." *Canadian Journal of Botany* 65: 1163–79.

Haas, J. N., and McAndrews, J. H. 2000. "The Summer Drought Related Hemlock (*Tsuga canadensis*) Decline in Eastern North America 5,700 to 5,100 Years Ago." In *Proceedings: Symposium on Sustainable Management of Hemlock Ecosystems in Eastern North America*, edited by K. McManus, 81–88. USDA Forest Service General Technical Report NE-267. United States Department of Agriculture, Forest Service, Northeastern Research Station, Newtown Square.

Heaton T. J., Blackwell, P. G., and Buck, C. E. 2009. "A Bayesian Approach to the Estimation of Radiocarbon Calibration Curves: The IntCal09 Methodology." *Radiocarbon* 51 (4): 1151–64.

Herbert, J. M. 2009. *Woodland Potters and Archaeological Ceramics of the North Carolina Coast*. Tuscaloosa: University of Alabama Press.

Hoffman, B. G. 1955. "The Historical Ethnography of The Micmac of the Sixteenth and Seventeenth Centuries." Doctoral dissertation, Department of Anthropology, University of California.

Holly, D. H., Jr. 2013. *History in the Making: The Archaeology of the Eastern Subarctic*. , New York: AltaMira Press.

Hornborg, A.-C. 2013. *Mi'kmaq Landscapes: From Animism to Sacred Ecology*. Burlington: Ashgate Publishing.

Holyoke, K. R. 2012. "Late Maritime Woodland Lithic Technology in the Lower Saint John River Valley." Master's thesis, Department of Anthropology, University of New Brunswick.

Hrynick, M. G. 2011. "Woodland Period Domestic Architecture on the Coast of the Maritime Peninsula: A Case Study from Port Joli Harbour, Nova Scotia." Master's thesis, University of New Brunswick.

Hrynick, M. G. 2018. "Maritime Woodland Period Dwelling Surface Construction on the Coast of the Maritime Peninsula: Implications for Site Reuse and Intra-Site Space." *Archaeology of Eastern North America* 46: 1–16.

Hrynick, M. G., and Betts, M. 2014. "Identifying Ritual Structures in the Archaeological Record: A Maritime Woodland Period Sweathouse from Nova Scotia, Canada." *Journal of Anthropological Archaeology* 35: 92–105.

Hrynick, M. G., and Betts, M. 2017. "" *Journal of the North Atlantic Special Volume* 10: 1–17.

Hrynick, M. G., Betts, M. W., and Black, D. W. 2012. "A Late Maritime Woodland Period Dwelling Feature from Nova Scotia's South Shore: Evidence for Patterned Use of Domestic Space." *Archaeology of Eastern North America* 40: 1–25.

Hrynick, M. G., and Black, D. W. 2012. "Bocabec Archaeological Site." In *Canadian Encyclopedia*.

Hrynick, M. G., and Black, D. W. 2016. "Cultural Continuity in Maritime Woodland Period Domestic Architecture in the Quoddy Region." *Canadian Journal of Archaeology* 40 (1): 23–67.

Hrynick, M. G., and Robinson, B. S. 2012. "Quantifying Gravel from a Ceramic Period Living Surface in Downeast Maine." *The Maine Archaeological Society Bulletin* 52 (2): 27–43.

Hrynick, M. G., Webb, W. J., Shaw, C. E., and Testa, T. C. 2017. "Late Maritime Woodland to Protohistoric Culture Change and Continuity at the Devil's Head Site, Calais, Maine." *Archaeology of Eastern North America* 45: 85–108.

Hurley, W. M., and Wagner, N. 1972. *Ceramic Analysis: A Class and Attribute Analysis List for the Northeast.* Research Report 13. Department of Anthropology, University of Toronto.

Jackson, J. B., Kirby, M. X., Berger, W. H., Bjorndal, K. A., Botsford, L. W., Bourque, B., Bradbury, R. H., Cooke, R., Erlandson, J., Estes, J. A., Hughes, T. P., Kidwell, S., Lange, C. B., Lenihan, H. S., Pandolfi, J. M., Peterson, C. H., Steneck, R. S., Tegner, M. J., and Warner, R. R. "Historical Overfishing and the Recent Collapse of Coastal Ecosystems." *Science* 293 (2001): 629–38.

Jirikowic, C. A. 1999. *Final Report on the 1990, 1991, and 1994 Excavations at the Hughes Site (18MO1).* Report prepared by the American University Potomac River Archaeology Survey, Washington, DC.

Jost, A. C. 2009. *Guysborough Sketches and Essays.* Rev. ed. Victoria: Trafford Publishing.

Justice, N. D. 1987. *Stone Age Spear and Arrow Points of the Midcontinental and Eastern United States.* Bloomington: Indiana University Press.

Keenlyside, D. 1983. "Late Prehistoric Populations of Northeastern Prince Edward Island." Paper presented at the 16th Annual Meeting of the Canadian Archaeological Association, Halifax.

Keenlyside, D., and Kristmanson, H. 2016. "The Palaeo-Environment and the Peopling of Prince Edward Island: An Archaeological Perspective." In *Time and Place: An Environmental History of Prince Edward Island,* edited by E. MacDonald, J. MacFadyen, and I. Novaczek, 59–81. Charlottetown: Island Studies Press.

Kelley, A. R. 2018. "Burning Libraries and Drowning Archives: Shell Middens on the Maine Coast." Paper presented at the 83rd Annual Meeting of the Society for American Archaeology, Washington, DC.

Kellogg, D. C. 1994. "Why Did They Choose to Live Here? Ceramic Period Settlement in the Boothbay, Maine, Area." *Northeast Anthropology* 2: 25–60.

[Kinsey. 1972. TK]

Kipfer, B. A. 2007. *The Archaeologist's Fieldwork Companion.* Maiden, MA, and Oxford: Blackwell.

Kristmanson, H. 1992. "The Ceramic Sequence for Southwestern Nova Scotia: A Refinement of The Petersen/Sanger Model." Master's thesis, Department of Anthropology, Memorial University of Newfoundland.

Kristmanson, H. and Deal, M. 1993. "The Identification and Interpretation of Finishing Marks on Prehistoric Nova Scotian Ceramics." *Canadian Journal of Archaeology* 17: 74–84.

Kuhry, P. 1994. "The Role of Fire in the Development of Sphagnum-Dominated Peatlands in Western Boreal Canada." *Journal of Ecology* 82 (4): 899–910.

Latta, M. A. 1980. "A Decorative Paradigm: The Late Ontario Iroquois Ceramic Tradition." In *Proceedings of the 1979 Iroquois Pottery Conference,* edited by C. F. Hayes III, 159–77. Research Records no. 13. Rochester Museum and Science Center, Rochester.

Leim, A. H., and W. B. Scott. 1966. *Fishes of the Atlantic Coast of Canada.* Ottawa: Fisheries Research Board of Canada #155.

Le Clerq, C. 1910. New Relation of Gaspesia: With the Customs and Religion of the Gaspesian Indians. Toronto: Champlain Society.

Lelièvre, M. A. 2017. *Unsettling Mobility: Mediating Mi'kmaw Sovereignty in Post-Contact Nova Scotia. The Archaeology of Indigenous-Colonial Interactions in the Americas.* Tucson: University of Arizona Press.

Lescarbot, M. 1914 [1618]. *The History of New France.* Toronto: Champlain Society.

Leveillee, A., Waller J. N., Jr., and Ingham, D. 2006. "Dispersed Villages in Late Woodland Period South-Coastal Rhode Island." *Archaeology of Eastern North America* 34: 71–89.

Leonard, K. 1995. "Woodland or Ceramic Period: A Theoretical Problem." *Northeast Anthropology* 50: 19–30.

Leonard. K. 1996. "Mi'kmaq Culture During Late Woodland and Early Historic Periods." Doctoral thesis, Department of Anthropology, University of Toronto.

Levac, E. 2001. "High Resolution Holocene Palynological Record from the Scotian Shelf." *Marine Micropaleontology* 43: 179–97.

Levesque et al. 1994. The abrupt change to a cooler and wetter climate in the Younger Dryas caused the vegetation in Nova Scotia to shift from predominantly boreal/woodland forest (*Picea, Pinus, Larix, Abies* and *Betula*) to shrub-tundra and herbaceous tundra

Lockerby, E. 2004. "Ancient Mi'kmaq Customs: A Shaman's Revelations." *The Canadian Journal of Native Studies* 24 (2): 403–23

Loder, Candace (2010). *"A Paleoethnobotanical Analysis of Sediments from Three Woodland Period Shell Midden Sites in Port Joli, Nova Scotia."* Undergraduate honours thesis, Department of Archeology, Memorial University of Newfoundland.

Loucks, O. L. 1962. "A Forest Classification for the Maritime Provinces." Reprinted from the Proceedings of the Nova Scotian Institute of Science 25, part 2, 1959–60

Lennox, B., Spooner, I., Jull, T., and Patterson, W. P. 2010. "Post-Glacial Climate Change and Its Effect on Shallow Dimictic Lake in Nova Scotia, Canada." *Journal of Paleolimnology*– 43 (15): 1527.

Lyman, R. L. 1994. *Vertebrate Taphonomy*. New York: Cambridge University Press.

Lyman, R. L., and O'Brien, M. J. 2004. "A History of Normative Theory in Americanist Archaeology." *Journal of Archaeological Method and Theory* 11 (4): 369–96.

MacDonald, M. A., Horne, R. J., Corey, M. C., and Ham, L. J., 1992. "An Overview of Recent Bedrock Mapping and Follow-Up Petrological Studies of the South Mountain Batholith, Southwestern Nova Scotia, Canada." *Atlantic Geology* 28: 7–28.

MacDonald, S. L. 1994. "Exploring Patterns of Prehistoric Lithic Use in the Insular Quoddy Region, Charlotte County, New Brunswick." Master's thesis, Department of Anthropology, University of New Brunswick.

McBride, K. A. 1984. "Prehistory of the Lower Connecticut River Valley." Doctoral dissertation, Department of Anthropology, University of Connecticut.

Matthew, G. F. 1884. "Discoveries at a Village of the Stone Age at Bocabec." *Bulletin of the Natural History Society of New Brunswick* 3: 6–29.

Martin, Calvin. 1978. *Keepers of the Game: Indian-Animal Relationships and the Fur Trade*. Berkeley: University of California Press.

Martin, B., Spooner, I., and Caverhill, B. 2005. "Environmental Evolution of the Pleasant River Wetland, Nova Scotia." *Program and Abstracts, Atlantic Geoscience Society Colloquium and Annual General Meeting 2005, St. John, New Brunswick*. Paper presented at the Atlantic Geoscience Society Annual General Meeting, St. John.

Mayle, E., and Cwynar, L. C. 1995. "Impact of the Younger Dryas Cooling Event Upon Lowland Vegetation of Maritime Canada." *Ecological Monographs* 65 (2): 129–54.

McCarthy, F. M. G., Collins, E. S., McAndrews, J. H., Kerr, H. A., Scott, D. B., and Medioli, F. S. 1995. "A Comparison of Postglacial Arcellacean ('Thecamoebian') and Pollen Succession in Atlantic Canada, Illustrating the Potential of Arcellaceans for Paleoclimatic Reconstruction." *Journal of Paleontology* 69 (5): 980–93.

Millard, Eric. 1966a. Vogler Shell Heap, August 28th, 1966. Manuscript on file, Nova Scotia Museum, Halifax.

Millard, Eric. 1966b. Indian Camp Site, Port Joli Nova Scotia. McDonald Shell Heap. August 29th, 1966. Manuscript on file, Nova Scotia Museum, Halifax.

Millard, Eric. 1966c. Port Joli, Queens County N.S. Indian Camp Shell Heaps. Manuscript on file, Nova Scotia Museum, Halifax.

Millard, Eric. 1968. Letter dated July 1, 1968. Manuscript on file, Nova Scotia Museum, Halifax.

Miller, C. 2004. *Spatial and Temporal Dynamics of a Rapidly Transgressing Barrier Coast, Sandy Bay, Nova Scotia, Canada*. Waterloo: University of Waterloo.

Moorehead, W. K. 1922. *A Report on the Archaeology of Maine, Being a Narrative of Explorations in the State 1912–1920, Together with Work at Lake Champlain 1917*. Andover: The Andover Press.

Mosseler, A., Lynds, J. A., and Major, J. E. 2003. "Old-Growth Forests of the Acadian Forest Region." *Environmental Reviews* 11: S47–S77.

Mott, R. J. 1974. "Palynological Studies of Lake Sediment Profiles from Southwestern New Brunswick." *Canadian Journal of Earth Sciences* 12: 273–88.

Mott, R. J., and Stea, R. R. 1993. "Late-Glacial (Allerod/Younger Dryas) Buried Organic Deposits, Nova Scotia, Canada." *Quaternary Science Reviews* 12: 645–57.

Mott, R. J., Walker, I. R., Palmer, S. L., and Lavoie, M. 2009. "A Late-Glacial Holocene Palaeoecological Record from Pye Lake on the Eastern Shore of Nova Scotia, Canada." *Canadian Journal of Earth Sciences* 46: 637–50.

Muller, S. D., Richard, P. J. H., and Larouchel, A. C. 2003. "Holocene Development of a Peatland (Southern Québec): A Spatio-Temporal Reconstruction Based on Pachymetry, Sedimentology, Microfossils, and Macrofossils." *The Holocene* 13 (5): 649–64.

Munoz, S. E., and Gajewski, K. 2010. "Distinguishing Prehistoric Human Influence on Late-Holocene Forests in Southern Ontario, Canada." *The Holocene* 20 (6): 967–81.

Murphy, B. M., and Black, D. W. 1996. "Zooarchaeological Research in the Maritimes." *Canadian Zooarchaeology* 9: 2–20.

Myers, H. B. 1972. "Archaeological Survey of Kejimkujik Park, Nova Scotia, 1972." National Historic Parks and Sites Branch Parks Canada. Manuscript 106. Department of Indian and Northern Affairs, Ottawa.

Nash, R. J. and Stewart, F. L. 1990. *Melanson: A Large Micmac Village in Kings County N.S.* Curatorial Report no. 67. Halifax: Nova Scotia Museum.

Neil, K., Gajewski, K., and Betts, M. 2014. Human-Ecosystem Interactions in Relation to Holocene Environmental Change in Port Joli Harbour, Southwestern Nova Scotia, Canada. *Quaternary Research* 81 (2): 203–12.

Nicolar, J. 1883. *Life and Traditions of the Red Man*. Bangor: CH Glass.

Oeschger, H., Siegenthaler, U., Schotterer, U., and Gugelmann, A. 1975. "A Box Diffusion Model to Study the Carbon Dioxide Exchange in Nature." *Tellus* 27 (2): 168–92.

Ogden, J. G. 1986. "Vegetational and Climatic History of Nova Scotia. I. Radiocarbon-Dated Pollen Profiles from Halifax, Nova Scotia." *Canadian Journal of Botany* 65: 1482–90.

Ohlson, M. and Tryterud, E. 2000. "Interpretation of the Charcoal Record in Forest Soils: Forest Fires and their Production and Deposition of Macroscopic Charcoal." *The Holocene* 10: 519–25.

Olsen, S. J., 1964. *Mammal Remains from Archaeological Sites Part 1: Southeastern and Southwestern United States*. Papers of the Peabody Museum of Archaeology and Ethnology 56, no. 1. Cambridge: Peabody Museum at Harvard University.

Olsen, S. J., 1968. *Fish, Amphibian and Reptile Remains from Archaeological Sites: Southeastern and Southwestern United States*. Papers of the Peabody Museum of Archaeology and Ethnology 56, no. 2. Cambridge: Peabody Museum at Harvard University.

Pentz, B. C. 2008. "A River Runs Through It: An Archaeological Survey of the Upper Mersey River and Allains River in Southwest Nova Scotia." Master's thesis, Department of Archaeology, Memorial University of Newfoundland.

Peros, M. C., Munoz, S. E., Gajewski, K., and Viau, A. E. 2010. Prehistoric Demography of North America Inferred from Radiocarbon Data. *Journal of Archaeological Science* 37 (3): 656–64.

Petersen, J. B. and Sanger D. 1991. "An Aboriginal Sequence from Maine and the Maritime Provinces." In *Prehistoric Archaeology in the Maritime Provinces: Past and Present Research,* edited by M. Deal and S. Blair, 113–70. Reports in Archaeology, no. 8. Fredericton: The Council of Maritime Premiers.

Ponomarenko, E. and Ponomarenko, D. 2015. "A Holocene Caribou Trackway in Southwest Nova Scotia, Canada." *Proceedings of Abstracts, Congress of Continental Ichnology*. El Jadida, Morocco: Faculty of Sciences, Chouaib Doukkali University.

Powell, S. 1990. *Archaeological Survey of Sandy Bay Provincial Park, Cole Harbour Day Use Park and Crystal Crescent Beach Provincial Park*. Manuscript on file, Nova Scotia Museum, Halifax.

Powell, S. 1995. *Archaeological Evaluation of AlDf-26, Port Joli*. Manuscript on file, Nova Scotia Museum, Halifax.

Preston, B. 1974. *Excavations at a Complex of Prehistoric Sites along the Upper Reaches of the Shubenacadie River, 1971*. Curatorial Report no. 19. Halifax: Nova Scotia Museum.

Prins, H. E. L., and McBride, B. 2007. *Asticou's Island Domain: Wabanaki Peoples at Mount Desert Island 1500–2000*. Vol. 1. Boston: The Abbe Museum and National Park Service.

Quinlan, T. 1996. "Seasonality Analysis of Mya Arenaria: From AlDf-26, Port Joli." Honours thesis, Department of Anthropology, St. Mary's University, Halifax.

Raddall, T. 1942. *His Majesty's Yankees*. Halifax: Nimbus Publishing.

Raddall, T. n. d. *Indian Kitchen-Midden in Queens County*. Manuscript on file, Dalhousie University Archives, Halifax.

Raddall, T. 1974. *Groundwork and Guesswork*. Manuscript on file, Nova Scotia Museum, Halifax.

Railton, J. B. 1973. "Vegetational and Climatic History of Southwestern Nova Scotia in Relation to a South Mountain Ice Cap." Doctoral thesis, Dalhousie University, Halifax.

Rand, S. T. 1888. *Dictionary of the Language of the Micmac Indians, Who Reside in Nova Scotia, New Brunswick, Prince Edward Island, Cape Breton and Newfoundland*. Halifax: Nova Scotia Printing Company.

[Reimer et al 2009 TK]

Rieth, C. B. 2013. "Space, Time and the Middle Woodland 'Jack's Reef Horizon' in New York." *Archaeology of Eastern North America* 41: 91–112.

Rick, J. W. 1987. "Dates as Data: An Examination of the Peruvian Preceramic Radiocarbon Record." *American Antiquity* 52: 55–73.

Ritchie, W. 1971. *New York Projectile Points: A Typology and Nomenclature*. Bulletin 384. New York: New York State Museum, University of the State of New York.

Robinson, B. S. 1996. "Projectile Points, Other Diagnostic Things and Culture Boundaries in the Gulf of Maine Region." *Maine Archaeological Society Bulletin* 36 (1996): 1–24.

Rojo, A. 1986. "Live Length and Weight of Cod (*Gadus morhua*) Estimated from Various Skeletal Elements. *North American Archaeologist* 7: 329–51.

Rojo, A. 1987. "Excavated Fish Vertebrae as Predictors in Bioarchaeological Research." *North American Archaeologist* 8: 209–26.

Rojo, A. 1990. "Faunal Analysis of Fish Remains from Cellar's Cove, Nova Scotia." *Archaeology of Eastern North America* 18: 89–108.

Rojo, A. 2002. *Morphological and Biometric Study of the Bones of the Buccal Apparatus of Some Nova Scotia Fishes of Archaeological Interest*. Curatorial Report no. 96. Halifax: Nova Scotia Museum.

Rowe, J. S. 1972. *Forest Regions of Canada*. Canadian Forestry Service Publication no. 1300, Ottawa: Department of the Environment.
Sanders, M., and Stewart, W. B. 2007. *Mersey Hydro System Powerhouse Refurbishment Project: 2004 Region of Queens Municipality, Nova Scotia, Archaeological Reconnaissance and Documentation*. Interim Report, Heritage Research Permit A2004NS54. Manuscript on file, Nova Scotia Museum, Halifax.
Sanger, D. 1987. *The Carson Site and the Late Ceramic Period in Passamaquoddy Bay, New Brunswick*. Mercury Series, no. 135. Ottawa: Canadian Museum of Civilization.
Sanger, D. 1996. "Testing the Models: Hunter-Gatherer Use of Space in the Gulf of Maine, USA." *World Archaeology* 27 (3): 512–26.
Sanger, D. 2010. Semi-Subterranean Houses in the Ceramic Period Along the Coast of Maine. *Maine Archaeological Society Bulletin* 50(2):23–46.
Sassaman, K. E. 2010. *The Eastern Arhcaic, Historicized*. New York: Altamira Press.
Scott, D. B., Gayes, P. T., and Collins, E. S. 1995. "Mid-Holocene Precedent for a Future Rise in Sea-Level Along the Atlantic Coast of North America." *Journal of Coastal Research* 11 (3): 615–22.
Serreze, M. C., and Barry, R. G. 2005. *The Arctic Climate System*. Cambridge: Cambridge University Press.
Sheldon, H. L. 1988. *The Late Prehistory of Nova Scotia as Viewed from the Brown Site*. Curatorial Report no. 61. Halifax: Nova Scotia Museum.
Smith, D. G. 1983. *An Analytical Approach to the Seriation of Iroquoian Pottery*. Research Report no. 12. London: Museum of Indian Archaeology.
Smith, D. G. 1987. 1 "Archaeological Systematics and the Analysis of Iroquoian Ceramics: A Case Study from the Crawford Lake Area, Ontario." Doctoral thesis, Department of Anthropology, McGill University, Montreal.
Smith, D. G. 1997. "Radiocarbon Dating the Middle to Late Woodland Transition and Earliest Maize in Southern Ontario." *Northeast Anthropology* 54: 37–73.
Smith, D. G. 2011. *Northeast Woodland Pottery Analytic Code*. Manuscript on file, Department of Anthropology, University of Toronto.
Smith, H. I., and Wintemberg, W. J. 1929. *Some Shell-Heaps in Nova Scotia*. Bulletin no. 47, Ottawa: National Museum of Canada.
Snow, Dean R. 1980. *The Archaeology of New England*. New York: Academic Press.
Snyder, D. P. 1982. "*Tamias striatus*." *Mammalian Species* 168: 1–8.
Speck, F. G. 1917. *Medicine Practices of the Northeastern Algonquians*. Washington, D.C.: International Congress of Americanists.
Speck, F. G. 1997. *Penobscot Man: The Life History of a Forest Tribe in Maine*. 2nd ed. Orono: University of Maine Press.
Spiess, A. E. 2017. "People of the Clam: Shellfish and Diet in Coastal Maine Late Archaic and Ceramic Period Sites." *Journal of the North Atlantic* 10: 105–12
Spiess, A. and Lewis, R. 2001. *The Turner Farm Fauna: 5000 Years of Hunting and Fishing in Penobscot Bay, Maine*. Occasional Publications in Maine Archaeology no. 11, Maine State Museum, Augusta.
Spiess, A., Sobolik, K. Crader, D., Mosher, J., and Wilson, D. 2004. *Cod, Clams and Deer: The Food Remains from Indiantown Island*. Augusta: Maine Historic Preservation Commission.
Spooner, I., Douglas, M. S.V., and Terrusi, L. 2002. "Multiproxy Evidence of an Early Holocene (8.2 kyr) Climate Oscillation in Central Nova Scotia, Canada." *Journal Quaternary Science* 17 (7): 639–45.
Sharon R. S. 2015. *Archaeology of Domestic Architecture and the Human Use of Space*. Walnut Creek, CA: Left Coast Press.

Shepard, A. O. 1965. *Ceramics for the Archaeologist*. Publication no. 609. Washington, D.C.: Carnegie Institution of Washington.

Stapelfeldt. K. 2009. "*A Form and Function Study of Precontact Pottery from Atlantic Canada.*" Master's thesis, Department of Archaeology, Memorial University of Newfoundland.

Stea, R. R., and Mott, R. J. 1989. "Deglaciation Environments and Evidence for Glaciers of Younger Dryas Age in Nova Scotia, Canada." *Boreas* 18: 169–87.

Steponaitis, L. C. 1980. *A Survey of Artifact Collections from the Patuxent River Drainage, Maryland*. Maryland Historical Trust Monograph Series, no. 1. Annapolis: Maryland Historical Trust and Maryland Department of Natural Resources.

[Stuiver et al. 1993 TK]

Tanner, A. 1979. *Bringing Home Animals: Religious Ideology and Mode of Production of the Mistassini Cree Hunters*. St. John's: Institute for Social and Economic Research, Memorial University of Newfoundland.

Thurston, Barrett. 2011. *The Atlantic Coast: A Natural History*. Vancouver: Greystone Books.

Thwaites, R. G., ed. 1898. *The Jesuit Relations and Allied Documents: Travels and Explorations of the Jesuit Missionaries in New France 1610–1791*, vol. 3: *Acadia, 1611–1616*. Cleveland: Burrows Brothers.

Turnbull, C. J., and Allen, P. M. 1988. "Review of Maritime Provinces Prehistory by J. A. Tuck." *Canadian Journal of Archaeology / Journal Canadien d'archéologie* 12: 250–260.

Ugan, A., and J. Bright. 2001. "Measuring Foraging Efficiency with Archaeological Faunas: The Relationship between Relative Abundance Indices and Foraging Returns." *Journal of Archaeological Science* 28: 1309–21.

Wallis, W. D., and Wallis, R. S. 1955. *The Micmac Indians of Eastern Canada*. Minneapolis: University of Minnesota Press.

Wanner, H., Beer, J., Butikofer, J., Crowley, T. J., Cubasch, U., Fluckiger, J., Goosse, H., Grosjean, M., Joos, F., Kaplan, J. O., Kuttel, M., Muller, S. A., Prentice, C., Solomina, O., Stocker, T. F., Tarasov, P., Wagner, M., and Widmann, M. 2008. "Mid- to Late Holocene Climate Change: An Overview." *Quaternary Science Reviews* 27: 1791–1828.

Warner B. G., and Rubec, C. D. A. 1997. *The Canadian Wetland Classification System*. 2nd ed. Waterloo: Canadian National Wetlands Working Group, Wetlands Research Centre, University of Waterloo.

Watts, C. 1997. "A Quantitative Analysis and Chronological Seriation of Riviere au Vase Ceramics from Southwestern Ontario." Master's thesis, Department of Anthropology, University of Toronto.

Watts, C. 2008. "Pot/Potter Entanglements and Networks of Agency in Late Woodland Period (ca. AD 900–1300) Southwestern Ontario, Canada." British Archaeological Reports, International Series, no. 1828. Oxford: Archaeopress.

Weiler, M. H. 2011. *Mi'kmaq and the American Eel: Traditional Knowledge Relating to the American Eel by Mainland Nova Scotia Mi'kmaq*. AFSAR Project no. 1734, Report to Environment Canada & Fisheries & Oceans Canada. Shubenacadie, NS: Mi'kma'ki All Points Services.

Wetzel, R. G. 2001. *Limnology: Lake and River Ecosystems*. 3rd ed., San Diego: Academic Press.

White, C. E. 2012a. *Bedrock Geology Map of the Liverpool Area, NTS sheet 21A/02, Lunenburg and Queens Counties, Nova Scotia*. Open File Map ME 2012-089, scale 1:50 000. Halifax: Nova Scotia Department of Natural Resources, Mineral Resources Branch.

White, C. E. 2012b. *Bedrock Geology Map of the Port Mouton Area, NTS sheet 20P/15, Queens and Shelburne Counties, Nova Scotia*. Open File Map ME 2012-094, scale 1:50 000. Halifax: Nova Scotia Department of Natural Resources, Mineral Resources Branch.

White, C. E. 2012c. *Bedrock Geology Map of the Lockeport Area, NTS sheet 20P/11, Shelburne County, Nova Scotia*. Open File Map ME 2012-097, scale 1:50 000. Halifax: Nova Scotia Department of Natural Resources, Mineral Resources Branch

Whitehead, R. H. 1993a. "The Protohistoric Period in the Maritime Provinces." In *Prehistoric Archaeology in the Maritime Provinces: Past and Present Research*, edited by M. Deal and S. Blair, 227–58. Fredericton: Council of Maritime Premiers Maritime Committee on Archaeological Cooperation.

Whitehead, R. H. 1993b. *Nova Scotia: The Protohistoric Period 1500–1630*. Curatorial Report. Halifax: Nova Scotia Museum.

Whittaker, J. C. 1994. *Flintknapping: Making and Understanding Stone Tools*. Austin: University of Texas Press.

Wilson, W. 2011. "Bryophyte Dynamics Across Wetland and Lakeshore Edges in Southwest Nova Scotia." Undergraduate honours thesis, Department of Environmental Science, Dalhousie University, Halifax.

Young, R. S., Belknap, D. F., and Sanger, D. 1992. "Geoarchaeology of Johns Bay, Maine." *Geoarchaeology* 7 (3): 209–49.

Contributors

Matthew W. Betts has been Curator of Eastern Archaeology since he joined the staff of the Canadian Museum of History in 2007. His research focuses on maritime hunter-gatherers and their complex economic, ideological and social relationships with the animals they exploited. His field projects focus on community archaeology, outreach, and capacity building. He is a fellow of the Royal Canadian Geographical Society, and an adjunct professor in the Department of Anthropology at the University of New Brunswick. He also serves on the advisory board for the Canadian Archaeological Radiocarbon Database.

Jenneth E. Curtis has been an archaeologist with Parks Canada since 2006. For almost ten years she worked from the Atlantic Service Centre in Halifax, Nova Scotia providing archaeological support and advice to National Parks and National Historic Sites in the Atlantic Region. In 2015 she transferred to Parks Canada's National Office in Gatineau and she is currently on assignment with Rouge National Urban Park. Curtis completed her doctorate on the archaeology of southern Ontario at the University of Toronto in 2004.

Konrad Gajewski is a professor at the Department of Geography, Environment and Geomatics at the University of Ottawa, and director of the Laboratory for Paleoclimatology and Climatology. His research involves the quantitative reconstruction and mapping of past climates and environments using proxy- data, especially from lake sediments. He has worked across the Canadian north, including the Yukon, NWT, Nunavut and Nunavik. Gajewski is also working on a project relating archaeological radiocarbon databases to changes in vegetation and climate over the Holocene.

Ken Holyoke is a PhD candidate at the University of Toronto. His dissertation project is exploring place-making at an ancient quarry in the Lower Saint John River Valley of New Brunswick. Ken has over 10 years' experience in academic and consulting archaeology and was formerly a field and discipline lead for Stantec Consulting. He has worked on a variety of academic and CRM projects throughout the Canadian Maritime Provinces, Labrador, British Columbia, and Maine, USA. Holyoke is a co-founder and current Board Member of the of the Association of Professional Archaeologists of New Brunswick (APANB-AAPNB).

M. Gabriel Hrynick is Assistant Professor of Anthropology at the University of New Brunswick, Fredericton. His research has focused on Northeastern North America, coastal hunter-gatherers, and domestic architecture, appearing in such journals as the *Journal of Anthropological Archaeology*, the *Canadian Journal of Archaeology*, and *Archaeology of Eastern North America*. He co-edited the 2017 volume *North American East Coast Shell Midden Research*. He is a founding member of the Association of Professional Archaeologists of New Brunswick and is currently Vice President of that organization.

Erin Ingram is a PhD candidate at the University of Toronto in the Near and Middle Eastern Civilizations Department. She received her BA from Wilfrid Laurier University in Near Eastern and Classical Archaeology, and her MA from the University of Toronto in Egyptology. She worked for six summers at the Canadian Museum of History as an archaeological assistant where she also took part in the Sechelt Archaeological Research Project. Her doctoral research focuses on heart scarabs and the role they played in ancient Egyptian funerary beliefs and practices.

Karen Neil is a PhD candidate at the Department of Geography, University of Ottawa. Her research focuses on high-resolution palaeoecological reconstructions of Holocene environments through the use of multiple biological proxy records from lake sediments. She has worked on the identification and analysis of fossil pollen and micro-charcoal records from sites in Eastern North America, including coastal Nova Scotia and Quebec.

www.ingramcontent.com/pod-product-compliance
Lightning Source LLC
Chambersburg PA
CBHW061126010526
44116CB00023B/2989